The Government and Politics of the European Union

The Government and Politics of the European Union

Fourth Edition

Neill Nugent

Duke University Press
Durham, 1999

First edition 1989
Second edition 1991
Reprinted (twice)
Third edition 1994
Reprinted (six times)
Fourth edition 1999

Published in the United States by
DUKE UNIVERSITY PRESS
Durham, NC 27708-0660
and in the United Kingdom by
MACMILLAN PRESS LTD
Houndmills, Basingstoke, Hampshire, RG21 6XS

Library of Congress Cataloging-in-Publication Data
Nugent, Neill.
Government and politics of the European union / Neill Nugent. —
4th ed.
p.   cm.
Includes bibliographical references and index.
ISBN 0–8223–2207–2 (cloth : alk. paper). — ISBN 0–8223–2223–4
(paper : alk. paper)
1. European Union.   2. Commission of the European Communities.
3. Council of the European Communities.   4. European Parliament.
5. Court of Justice of the European Communities.   I. Title.
JN15.N84   1999
341.242'2—dc21   98–55980
                                                                              CIP

Printed in Great Britain

Summary of Contents

Contents

List of Tables, Figures, Exhibits and Documents

Tables

Figures

Exhibits

Documents

Preface to the Fourth Edition

This edition of *The Government and Politics of the European Union* contains extensive updating, some restructuring, much rewriting and a substantial amount of new material.

The new material is of two main types. First, there are descriptions and analyses of the major developments that have occurred since the third edition. Amongst these developments are the Treaty of Amsterdam, the launch of the single currency and the enlargement of the European Union to fifteen member states and a move towards accommodating over twenty states. Second, there is a new chapter on conceptualising and theorising. This has been added largely in response to comments by colleagues and students who have suggested that it would add considerably to the book's usefulness.

A problem when writing about the European Union is when to use the terms 'European Union' and 'European Community'. The problem derives from the 1992 Maastricht Treaty, which, as is explained in Chapter 5, created a highly confusing situation in this regard. It did so by incorporating what had come to be commonly known as the European Community into a broader European Union, and by renaming the European Economic Community – which was the most important of the *three* Communities that made up the European Community – the European Community! In other words, under the Maastricht Treaty the European Community became one of three European Communities, and these three Communities became component parts of the European Union. In order to keep confusion to a minimum, and to avoid repeated explanations in the text of the usage of terms, I have used the term European Union, and more commonly its acronym EU, wherever possible. Where, however, it would be factually inaccurate to use EU, then EC or EC/EU are used as appropriate.

An explanation is required on how the numbering of treaty articles is dealt with in the book. The Amsterdam Treaty re-numbered the Treaty on European Union (TEU) and the Treaty Establishing the European Community (TEC). As a result, treaty articles that had become extremely well known simply by their number – such as Articles 3b of the TEC (subsidiarity) and 86 of the TEC (abuse of a dominant market position) – were given new numbers. Clearly it will be some time before the new numbers become as familiar as the old, so the approach taken in the book is to use the new numbers but to place the old numbers in brackets on first usage. As a further aid, Tables of Equivalences are included as an Appendix at the back of the book.

Events in the EU are in constant transition. To keep readers of this and related books fully up to date, the publishers are creating a web page where key facts – such as the composition of groups in the European Parliament – will be updated as necessary. It will also provide links to other useful and relevant web sites. The address is http://www.macmillan-press.co.uk/politics/EU

One other matter that ought to be noted here is that, unlike in the earlier editions, references are used in this edition. The reason for not using references previously was to assist ease of reading, but I have been persuaded that in completely eliminating references I perhaps went too far. Accordingly, references are included as appropriate, but on a deliberately limited basis.

Finally, there are people I would like to thank for the assistance they have given me. Charlotte Bretherton and Vincent Wright read individual chapters. My publisher Steven Kennedy was his customary encouraging and helpful self. My daughters Helen and Rachael were, as always, extremely supportive. And my wife, Maureen, working to tight deadlines, produced an excellent typescript.

May 1999   NEILL NUGENT

List of Abbreviations

ACEA	Association of European Automobile Constructors
ACP	African, Caribbean and Pacific Countries
AMCHAM-EU	EU Committee of the American Chamber of Commerce
APPE	Association of Petrochemical Producers in Europe
ASEAN	Association of South-East Asian Nations
BEUC	European Bureau of Consumers' Associations
BRITE	Basic Research in Industrial Technologies for Europe
CAP	Common Agricultural Policy
CCP	Common Commercial Policy
CCT	Common Customs Tariff
CDU/CSU	German Christian Democratic Union/Christian Social Union
CEA	European Insurance Company
CEEC	Central and Eastern European country
CEEP	European Centre of Enterprises with Public Participation
CEFIC	European Chemical Industry Federation
CEN	European Committee for Standardisation
CENELEC	European Committee for Electrotechnical Standardisation
CET	Common External Tariff
CFP	Common Fisheries Policy
CFSP	Common Foreign and Security Policy
COPA	Committee of Agricultural Organisations in the European Union
CoR	Committee of the Regions
COREPER	Committee of Permanent Representatives
CSCE	Conference on Security and Cooperation in Europe
CSF	Community Support Framework
DG	Directorate General
DRIVE	Dedicated Road Infrastructure for Vehicle Safety in Europe
EAGGF	European Agricultural Guidance and Guarantee Fund
EBRD	European Bank for Reconstruction and Development
EC	European Community
ECB	European Central Bank
ECMM	European Community Monitoring Mission
ECOFIN	Council of Economic and Finance Ministers
ECSC	European Coal and Steel Community

ecu	European currency unit
ED	European Democratic Group
EDA	Group of the European Democratic Alliance
EDC	European Defence Community; also European Documentation Centre
EDF	European Defence Fund
EEA	European Economic Area
EEB	European Environmental Bureau
EEC	European Economic Community
EFPIA	European Federation of Pharmaceutical Industry Associations
EFTA	European Free Trade Association
EIB	European Investment Bank
EIF	European Investment Fund
ELDR	Federation of European Liberal, Democratic and Reform Parties
EMI	European Monetary Institute
EMS	European Monetary System
EMU	European Monetary Union
EP	European Parliament
EPC	European Political Cooperation
EPP	European People's Party
ER	Technical Group of the European Right
ERDF	European Regional Development Fund
ERM	Exchange Rate Mechanism
ESC	Economic and Social Committee
ESCB	European System of Central Banks
ESF	European Social Fund
ESPRIT	European Strategic Programme for Research and Development in Information Technology
ETUC	European Trade Union Confederation
EU	European Union
EUCOFIL	European Union of Fruit and Vegetable Wholesalers, Shippers, Importers and Exporters
EUL	European United Left
Euratom	European Atomic Energy Community
EUREKA	European Research Coordinating Agency
EUROBIT	European Association of Manufacturers of Business Machines and Data Processing Equipment
EUROFER	European Confederation of Iron and Steel Industries
FCO	Foreign and Commonwealth Office
FDP	German Free Democratic Party
FEEM	Federation of European Explosives Manufacturers

FN	French National Front
FRG	Federal Republic of Germany
G7	Group of Seven
GATT	General Agreement on Tariffs and Trade
GCECEE	Savings Bank Group of the EEC
GDP	Gross domestic product
GDR	German Democratic Republic
GNP	Gross national product
IEA	International Energy Agency
IGC	Intergovernmental conference
IMF	International Monetary Fund
IMP	Integrated Mediterranean Programme
IUR	International Union of Railways
JET	Joint European Torus
JHA	Justice and Home Affairs
JRC	Joint Research Centre
LDR	Liberal Democratic and Reformist Group
LU	Left Unity
MAGP	Multiannual Guidance Programme
MCA	Monetary compensation amount
MEP	Member of the European Parliament
MSI	Italian Social Movement
NATO	North Atlantic Treaty Organisation
NCB	National Central Bank
NCI	New Community Instrument
NTB	Non-tariff barrier (to trade)
OECD	Organisation for Economic Cooperation and Development
OEEC	Organisation for European Economic Cooperation
OJ	*Official Journal of the European Communities*
OSCE	Organisation for Security and Cooperation in Europe
PASOK	Greek Socialist Party
PDB	Preliminary draft budget
PES	Party of European Socialists
PHARE	Programme of Community Aid for Central and Eastern European Countries
PLO	Palestine Liberation Organisation
qmv	qualified majority voting
RACE	Research and Development in Advanced Communications Technologies for Europe
RBW	Rainbow Group
R & TD	Research and Technological Development
SCA	Special Committee on Agriculture

SEA	Single European Act
SEM	Single European Market
SME	Small and medium-sized enterprise
TAC	Total allowable catch (fish stocks)
TACIS	Programme for Technical Assistance to the Independent States of the Former Soviet Union and Mongolia
TEC	Treaty Establishing the European Community
TEU	Treaty on European Union
UK	United Kingdom
UKREP	United Kingdom Permanent Representation to the European Communities
UN	United Nations
UNCTAD	United Nations Conference on Trade and Development
UNICE	Union of Industrial and Employers' Confederations of Europe
USA	United States of America
VAT	Value added tax
WEU	Western European Union

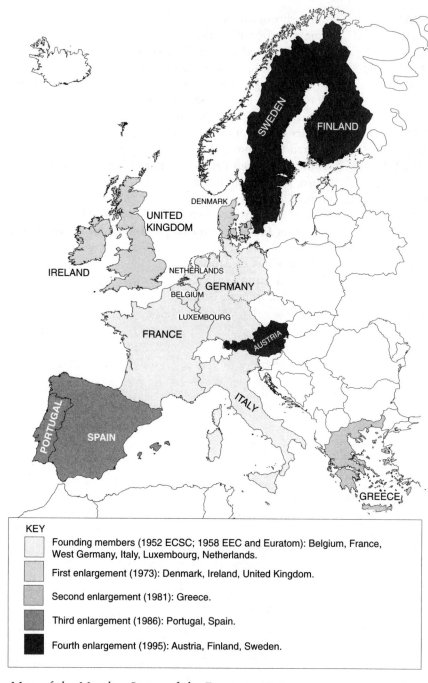

KEY

Founding members (1952 ECSC; 1958 EEC and Euratom): Belgium, France, West Germany, Italy, Luxembourg, Netherlands.

First enlargement (1973): Denmark, Ireland, United Kingdom.

Second enlargement (1981): Greece.

Third enlargement (1986): Portugal, Spain.

Fourth enlargement (1995): Austria, Finland, Sweden.

Map of the Member States of the European Union

Part 1

The Historical Evolution

Introduction

No political system or organisation can properly be understood unless it is set in its historical and operational contexts. The structure and functioning of government institutions, the nature and dynamics of political forces, and the concerns and conduct of those who exercise power do not happen as a matter of chance. They are shaped, and are constantly being remoulded, by evolving forces and events.

Though a relatively new organisation, the European Union is no less subject to these dictates than are long established nation states, and like them its nature cannot be appreciated without reference to its historical sources or to the world in which it functions. (See the Preface for an explanation of the usage of the terms European Union [EU] and European Community [EC] in this book.) Thus, the EU is often criticised for being weak in structure and quarrelsome in nature, with far too much bickering over matters such as the price of butter and not enough visionary thinking and united action to tackle unemployment, regional imbalances and other major problems. Unquestionably there is much in these criticisms, but that the EU should find harmonious collective policy-making difficult is not surprising to anyone with a historical perspective. For before they joined the EC/EU member states made decisions for themselves on most matters. It is not easy, especially for large states or for states that believe themselves to have special interests, to have to cede sovereignty by transferring decision-making responsibilities to a multinational organisation in which other voices may prevail. Any explanation and understanding of what the EU is, and what it has and has not achieved, must recognise this. The EU must, in other words, be seen in the context of the forces that have made it and are still making it. Some of these forces have served to push the states together. Others have resulted in progress towards cooperation and integration sometimes being slow, difficult and contested.

The sovereignty issue may be used to illustrate the importance of both historical background and contemporary operational context in explaining and evaluating the European Union. Many of the EU's opponents and critics subscribe to the view that the nation state, not an international organisation, is the 'natural' supreme political unit. They argue that insofar as transferences of power to Brussels, Luxembourg and Strasbourg

– the three main seats of the EU's institutions – undermine national sovereignty, they should be resisted. But what proponents of this view all too often fail to recognise is that the member states of the EU were seeing their sovereignties being steadily eroded long before the EC/EU was established, and since it was established they have seen their sovereignties further eroded by forces that are not a consequence of EU membership. Whether it has been because of movements in financial markets, transfers of capital within multinational corporations, changing trade patterns, or United States military dominance, virtually all West European states have become increasingly affected by, and at the mercy of, international developments they cannot control. This loss of power may not have involved legal transfers of sovereignty as has been the case within the EU, but it has had a very similar effect. The fact is that in an ever expanding range of policy sectors, states have not been able to act in isolation but have had to adjust and adapt so as to fit in with an array of external influences. The EU should not, therefore, be viewed as constituting a unique threat to the sovereignties of its member states. On the contrary, it is in some ways an attempt to meet this threat by providing a means by which member states, if not able to regain their sovereignty, can at least reassert control over aspects of decision-making by cooperating together at levels and in ways that match post-war internationalism.

The purpose of Part 1 is thus to provide a base for understanding the EU by tracing its evolution and placing it in its historical and operational settings.

In Chapter 1 the sharp divide between pre-war and post-war West European inter-state relations is examined. The factors that explain what amounted to a post-war transformation in those relations are analysed, and the early organisational responses to that transformation are described.

Chapter 2 looks at the main constituent elements of the process of West European integration – the states – and considers their varying positions towards, and inputs into, the process.

Chapter 3 analyses the creation of the three European Communities: the European Coal and Steel Community (ECSC), which was founded by the Treaty of Paris in 1951, and the European Atomic Energy Community (Euratom) and the European Economic Community (EEC), which were both established in March 1957 with the signing of the Treaties of Rome.

Chapter 4 describes the major features of the evolution of the European integration process since the Rome Treaties.

Chapter 5 focuses on the two major EU treaties of recent years: the 1992 Maastricht Treaty and the 1997 Treaty of Amsterdam.

Chapter 1

The Transformation of Western Europe

Historical divisions
The post-war transformation
Explanations of the transformation
Concluding remarks

Historical divisions

It is common today, with Western European integration proceeding apace, with democratic and market-based systems having been established throughout Central and Eastern Europe, and with the two 'halves' of Europe scheduled to be united in the European Union, for commentators on and observers of European affairs to emphasise the increasing unity and identity of the continent.

It is well to remember, however, that such unity and identity as there can be said to exist – and in truth it is limited if all of Europe is lumped together – is of very recent vintage. For the fact is that throughout its history Europe has been characterised much more by divisions, tensions and conflicts than it has by any common purpose or harmony of spirit. Even if attention is restricted to just that part of Europe where unity has been most developed – Western Europe – the peoples and nation states have long differed and been divided from one another in many ways.

Language has been perhaps the obvious divisive force. Linguists may identify structural similarities between European languages, but the fact is that most peoples have not been able to, and still cannot, directly converse with one another. (Today, 24 per cent of the citizens of the European Union speak German as their first language, 17 per cent English, 17 per cent French, and 16 per cent Italian.) Religion has been another source of division, with the northern countries (except Ireland) being mainly Protestant, and the southern countries (including France but excluding Orthodox Greece) being predominantly Catholic. Contrasting cultural traditions and historical experiences have further served to develop distinct identifications – and feelings of 'us' and 'them' – across the map of Europe.

Such differences have helped to bind some peoples together, but they have also served to separate others from one another. Along with the

3

legacies of power struggles and wars they help to explain why Western Europe has been divided into so many states, each with its own identity and loyalties. Some of these states – France, Spain and the United Kingdom for example – have existed in much their present geographical form for centuries. Others – including Germany, Italy and Ireland – were constituted only comparatively recently, mostly in the nineteenth and early twentieth centuries as nationalism flourished and as force was used to bring nation and state into closer alignment.

Until at least the Second World War, and in some cases well beyond, linguistic, religious and cultural divisions between the West European states were exacerbated by political and economic divisions.

Political divisions took the form of varying systems of government and competing ideological orientations. In the nineteenth and early twentieth centuries autocracies existed alongside emerging, and more liberal, parliamentary democracies. Between the two world wars parliamentary democracy found itself under attack and in some cases was overthrown: in Italy in 1922 by Fascism, in Germany in 1933 by Nazism, and in Spain after the 1936–9 civil war by conservative authoritarianism. It was not until the mid 1970s – following the collapse of the dictatorships of the Iberian peninsula and the overthrow of the military regime in Greece – that parliamentary democracy finally became general throughout Western Europe.

Economic divisions were no less marked. From the beginning of the Industrial Revolution until the middle of the nineteenth century Britain was industrially and commercially dominant. Gradually it was challenged – particularly by Germany, but also by Belgium, France and others – so that by the early years of the twentieth century competition between these countries for overseas markets was fierce. At the same time, the economies of the northern countries were increasingly differentiated from those of the south, with the former mostly having substantial industrial bases while the latter remained predominantly agricultural and underdeveloped.

Western Europe was thus long divided and many of its divisions were sources of tension, hostility and war. Finding their expression in economic and ideological competition, in drives for national power and prestige and in territorial disputes, and compounded by dangerous mixtures of assertive/weak/incompetent leaderships, the divisions ensured that until after the Second World War rivalry and distrust governed the relationships between most of the states most of the time.

In the twentieth century alone two devastatingly destructive world wars, both of which began as European wars, were fought. The First (1914–18) saw the countries of the triple entente – Britain, France and Russia – plus Italy from 1915, fighting against Germany and Austria-Hungary. The Second (1939–45) saw Germany, assisted from 1940 by Italy, attempting to impose itself by force on virtually the whole of Europe outside the Iberian peninsula.

The background to the Second World War is worth outlining briefly because it puts in perspective how dramatically different, and how suddenly found, were the more cooperative relationships between the West European states in the post-1945 era. In short, the period between the wars was characterised by particularly sharp and fluid inter-state relations. There was no stable alliance system and no clear balance of power. For the most part, European states, including West European states, regarded one another with, at best, suspicion. Though multilateral and bilateral treaties, agreements and pacts abounded, there was little overall pattern to them and few had any lasting effect. States came together in varying combinations on different issues in a manner that, far from indicating mutual confidence, was increasingly suggestive of fear.

From time to time in the inter-war period proposals for greater cooperation between European states were advanced but little came of them. The international climate – characterised by national rivalries and clashing interests – was not favourable, and most of the leading advocates of closer linkages were seen as having, as indeed they did have, specific national purposes in mind. Aristide Briand, for example, who was French Foreign Minister from 1925 to 1932, supported European cooperation but clearly had as his prime aim a stable European political system that would preserve the peace settlement that had been imposed on Germany by the 1919 Versailles Treaty. Gustav Stresemann, by contrast, who was the German Foreign Minister from 1923 to 1929, saw European cooperation as a way in which Germany could loosen the grip of Versailles and regain its position as a major power.

The lack of any real interest in European cooperation before the Second World War is revealed in the functioning of the League of Nations. Established in 1919 to provide for international collective security, in practice it was dominated by the Europeans and had some potential as a forum for developing understandings and improving relationships between the European states. It failed, and did so for three main reasons. First, its aims were vague and were interpreted in different ways. Second, it was intergovernmental in its structure and therefore dependent on the agreement of all member states before any action could be taken. Third, and crucially, the states wanted different things from it: some – notably France, most of the medium-sized central European countries that had been constituted in 1918–19 out of the collapsed Austria-Hungarian Empire, and to some extent Britain – saw it as a means of preserving the Versailles *status quo*; others – particularly Germany and Italy – wanted to use it to change the 1919 settlement and were prepared to leave or ignore it if it did not serve that purpose.

Inter-war Europe thus experienced rising tensions as national rivalries remained unharnessed and, above all, as German territorial and power ambitions could not be satisfied. When war finally did break out, the Axis Powers (Germany and Italy) gained control for a while over virtually the whole of the continent from the Atlantic to deep inside the Soviet Union. In Western Europe only Britain and those countries which remained neutral (Ireland, Portugal, Spain, Sweden and Switzerland) were not occupied. By May 1945, when German government representatives agreed to unconditional surrender, Nazism and Fascism had been defeated, but economies and political systems throughout Europe had been severely shaken, cities and towns had been destroyed and millions had been killed.

The post-war transformation

Since the Second World War the relations between the states of Western Europe have been transformed. There are three principal aspects of this.

A half-century of peace

The states have lived peacefully with one another since 1945 and armed confrontation between any two does not now appear to be even remotely possible. As Altiero Spinelli, one of the great advocates and architects of European integration, observed in 1985 shortly before his death:

> [a] major transformation . . . has occurred in the political consciousness of Europeans, something which is completely new in their history. For centuries, neighbouring countries were seen as potential enemies against whom it was necessary to be on one's guard and ready to fight. Now, after the end of the most terrible of wars in Europe, these neighbours are perceived as friendly nations sharing a common destiny (Spinelli, 1986, p. xiii).

The belief in a common destiny is perhaps questionable, but the reality and importance of the transformation from hostile to friendly relations is not. Certainly the states have continued to compete against one another in many areas, and this has sometimes led to strains and tensions, but these disagreements have been mostly on issues where military conflict has not been relevant to the resolution of differences.

Indeed, not only has military conflict been irrelevant to the resolution of differences, but such friction as has occurred has been within a context in which West European states have usually shared similar views on who can be seen as friends and who are real or potential enemies. Until the revolutions and upheavals in Eastern Europe and the Soviet Union in the late 1980s/early 1990s, communism was the most obvious common threat and this led most significant Western European states to become full or part members of the same military alliance: the North Atlantic Treaty Organisation (NATO). With the communist danger now removed, Western security arrangements are being revamped to adjust to a situation in which Central and Eastern European countries (CEECs) are seen as potential partners rather than as foes, and in which the main potential security concerns for Western Europe are seen as lying in the Balkans, in bubbling national and ethnic tensions in parts of the former Soviet Empire – not least in Russia – and in the unrest and turbulence of the Middle East. As part of this revamping, new European-wide security arrangements have been developed, three CEECs – Hungary, Poland and the Czech Republic – have become members of NATO, and all ten of the CEECs that have applied to join the EU (see Chapter 4) have become associated in various ways with the linked processes of strengthening the Western European Union (see Chapter 3) and developing within the European Union a Common Foreign and Security Policy (CFSP).

A transformed agenda

Throughout the international system the subject matter of discussions and negotiations between states has become much more varied. Whilst, as regional conflicts show, the case should not be overstated, international agendas have clearly become less focused on traditional 'high policy' issues and more on 'low policy' issues. That is, policies concerned with the existence and preservation of the state (such as territorial issues, defence policy and balance of power manoeuvrings) have been joined by policies that are more concerned with the wealth and welfare of populations (such as policies on trade, monetary stability, environmental protection, and airline safety).

This change in the content of agendas has been particularly marked throughout the Western industrialised world, and above all in Western Europe where a transformation can be said to have occurred. Classic 'power politics' have not of course disappeared, but they are not as dominant or as prominent as they were. When representatives of the fifteen EU states meet it is normally to consider topics that a generation or two ago would not even have been regarded as proper subjects for international negotiations, such as what constitutes 'fair' economic competition, how might research information be pooled to the general advantage, to what extent and by what means should sheep farmers be subsidised, and what should be the maximum weight of lorries permitted on roads?

New channels and processes

Paralleling, and partly occasioned by, the increasingly diverse international agenda, there has been a transformation in the ways in which states interrelate with one another. The traditional diplomatic means of inter-state communications via Ministries of Foreign Affairs and embassies have declined in importance as new channels and processes have become established.

As with changing agendas, changing forms of inter-state communication have been taken further in the Western industrialised world, and particularly in the EU, than anywhere else. There are now few significant parts of any Western state's political and administrative systems that do not have some involvement in the management of external relations. Written communications, telephone conversations, electronically transmitted messages, and bilateral and multilateral meetings between states increase by the year. Contacts range from the *ad hoc* and informal to the regularised and highly structured.

In the EU, representatives of the governments of the member states meet with one another every working day. They may have as their purpose the taking of binding decisions (decisions that in many circumstances may be taken by majority vote), the exploration of possibly advantageous policy coordination, or merely the exchanging of views and information. At the lower end of the seniority scale, junior and middle-ranking officials, often working from tightly drawn negotiating briefs and with their actions subject to later approval from national capitals, convene in committees to try to hammer out detailed agreements on proposed legislation. At the top end of the scale Heads of Government regularly meet, for what are often wide-ranging deliberations, in forums such as: the European Council, which meets at least twice a year and where all fifteen EU states are represented; in bilateral meetings, which in the case of the British Prime Minister, the French President, the German Chancellor and the Italian Prime Minister take place at least once a year; and in the broader setting of the annual Group of Eight summits, which bring together the political leaders of Britain, France, Germany, Italy, Canada, Japan, Russia and the United States, plus the President of the European Commission and the Head of Government of the member state that is currently chairing the EU's Council of Ministers if she or he is not already present.

Explanations of the transformation

In seeking to explain post-war cooperation and integration in Western Europe – which includes locating both the foundations and the reasons for the development of the European Union – different observers have often highlighted different factors, and sometimes indeed have looked in rather different directions. Amongst the questions that have caused difficulties are these: to what extent do the developments have deep historical roots and to what extent have they been a reaction to specifically post-1945 circumstances; what has been the balance between political and economic factors; what has been the role of general international influences as opposed to more narrowly based West European ones; and has there been a constant underlying movement in an integrationist direction or just a series of specific, and not very well coordinated, responses to specific problems?

In looking at the ways in which questions of this sort have been answered, four broad explanatory themes can be found in the literature. For analytical purposes they will be considered here separately, but it should be recognised that, in practice, they are by no means mutually exclusive but rather complement, overlap and reinforce one another. It should be recognised, too, that their usefulness as explanations is not constant, but varies over time. So, for example, whilst political ideals and utopian visions of a united Europe may have had at least some part to play in the early post-war years, more recently they have counted for little and it has been hard-headed national calculations of economic and political advantages and disadvantages that have been the principal determinants of the nature and pace of the integration process.

The deep roots of integration?

Some have found the roots of post-war developments in the distant past. Supporters and advocates of European integration have been especially prominent in this regard. They have suggested that Europe is, and has long been, a unique and identifiable entity. As evidence of this it is often argued that Europe was the cradle of modern civilisation and from this there developed European values and a European culture, art and literature. Walter Hallstein, the first President of the Commission of the EEC, typifies this sort of view:

> Europe is no creation. It is a rediscovery. The main difference between the formation of the United States of Europe and that of the United States of America is not that America did not have to merge a number of

firmly established nation states, but that for more than a thousand years the idea of a unified Europe was never quite forgotten. . .

[The advocates of a European federation] know that Europe shares a sense of values: of what is good and bad; of what a man's rights should be and what are his duties; of how society should be ordered; of what is happiness and what disaster. Europe shares many things: its memories that we call history; achievements it can take pride in and events that are shameful; its joys and its sufferings; and not least its tomorrows (Hallstein, 1972, pp. 15, 16).

Clearly there is much idealism in this. People such as Hallstein are suggesting that transcending the differences, divergences and conflicts between peoples and states there has long been a certain commonality and identity of interest in Europe based on interrelationships between geography and historical, political, economic, social and cultural developments. It is a contentious view and certainly not one to which many historians would attach much importance. Divisions and dissension, they would contend, have been more prominent than identity of interest or shared values and experiences. Such limited commonality as has existed has largely been a consequence of geographical proximity.

But if the 'idealistic' interpretation no longer finds much favour, there are still those who stress the importance of the historical dimension of Western European integration. Inter-state relations in the nineteenth century are sometimes seen as foreshadowing post-1945 developments insofar as peace endured for much of the century and did so, in part at least, as a result of understandings and agreements between the major powers. The problem with this view, is that it rather overstates the extent to which the nineteenth century was a century of peace, and it also exaggerates the extent to which the states did cooperate. Arguably, the so-called Concert of Nations was an embryonic attempt to exercise strategic control through diplomacy and summitry, but that was at a time when conservative autocracies ruled much of Europe and many of today's states did not even exist in their present form. And in any event, the system lasted at best only from 1815 to the Crimean War. It then gave way to the wars of the mid-century and later to the balance of power – which was hardly based on European trust and cooperation – as the means of seeking to preserve the peace.

It is perhaps in the field of economic history that the most fertile ground for identifying long-term influences and explanations is to be found. From about the late eighteenth century *national* economic integration began to occur, as barriers to economic activity *within* states were dismantled. This helped to promote, and in turn was encouraged by, national political integration, which manifested itself in nationalism and in the elevation of the sovereign state to the status of the supreme collective unit. From about the middle of the nineteenth century the achievement and successes of this internal economic and political integration, allied with an increasing interconnectedness in Europe that followed from technological change and economic advance, resulted in increasing inter-state cooperation to promote trade, competition and growth. For some economic historians an embryonic European economy was being established. Pollard, for example, has written of the mid-nineteenth century:

> Europe's industrialisation proceeded relatively smoothly, among other reasons, precisely because it took place within what was in many essentials a single integrated economy, with a fair amount of movement for labour, a greater amount of freedom for the movement of goods, and the greatest freedom of all for the movement of technology, know-how and capital (Pollard, 1981, pp. 38–9).

But unlike the customary pattern within nation states, there was nothing inevitable about European economic integration. Nor was there a clear and developing relationship between it and political integration. On the contrary, from the last quarter of the nineteenth century, states, for a variety of reasons, moved increasingly in the direction of economic protectionism and at the same time developed national identities and consciousness such as had not been seen before. In the first part of the twentieth century, and especially between the wars, the European free trading system virtually disappeared, as states sought to protect themselves at the expense of others and national economies were increasingly reshaped along autarkic lines. Alongside these increasingly closed economic systems developed the ever sharper political tensions and rivalries between the states that were noted earlier.

The European historical experience thus emphasises the extremely important, but often overlooked, fact that although industrialisation and economic liberalisation provide potential bases for the furtherance of interconnections, agreements, and harmonious relations between states, they do not ensure or guarantee them. The powers of Europe went to war with their principal trading partners in 1914. Furthermore, between the wars economic linkages did little to bring the nations together or to act as a restraint on governments when divergences developed in their aims and strategies. This must be borne in mind when, later in this chapter, attention is turned to modernisation and interdependence as explanations for post-war political and economic integration. Doubtless they have both been extremely important, but as pre-1939 European history shows, they do not have an inevitable integrationist logic attached to them. Much depends on their relationship to the circumstances of the time and, as will now be shown, these were very different in the post-1945 world from what they had been before the Second World War.

The impact of the Second World War

The Second World War unquestionably marked a turning point in the West European state system. Just a few years after the end of the war states were cooperating, and in some instances and in some respects were even integrating, in a manner that would have been inconceivable before the war. Fundamental to this transformation were a number of factors resultant upon the war that combined to bring about a radical change in both the climate of opinion and perceptions of requirements. These factors can be grouped under two broad headings:

Political factors

These may be subdivided into four key areas.

(1) The Second World War produced a greater realisation than had existed ever before that unfettered and uninhibited nationalism was a recipe for war, which in the post-1945 world was increasingly seen as meaning mass destruction. At the international level this thinking was reflected in calls for a larger and more powerful body than the pre-war League of Nations, and it played an important part in the establishment of the United Nations in 1944. But the fact that the two world wars had begun as European wars, and that Germany was generally considered responsible for those wars, also brought forth demands and moves for specifically European arrangements. Amongst the strongest advocates of the creation of European arrangements were many of those who had been associated with the Resistance movements of Continental Europe which, from 1943 onwards, had come to be linked via liaising networks and from which ideas and proposals had been generated looking forward to a post-war world that would be based more on cooperation and less on confrontation.

There was thus a widely shared optimism at the end of the Second World War that if the European states could work together in joint schemes and organisations, barriers of mistrust could be broken down. On this basis, over 750 prominent Europeans came together in the Hague in May 1948 and from their Congress issued a call to the nations of Europe to create a political and economic union. This stimulated discussions at governmental levels, and in May 1949 the Statute of the Council of Europe was signed by representatives of ten states. Article 1 of the Statute includes the following:

(a) The aim of the Council of Europe is to achieve a greater unity between its Members for the purpose of safeguarding and realising the ideals and principles which are their common heritage and facilitating their economic and social progress.

(b) This aim shall be pursued through the organs of the Council by discussions of questions of common concern and by agreements and common action in economic, social, cultural, scientific, legal and administrative matters and in the maintenance and further realisation of human rights and fundamental freedoms (Robertson, 1961, Appendix – the Statute).

Despite these grandiose ambitions, however, the Council of Europe proved to be a disappointment to those who had hoped it might serve as the basis for a new West European state system. In part the problem was that its aims were too vague, in part that its decision-making structure was essentially intergovernmental and therefore weak, but the main problem was that some of its members, notably the UK, were not very interested in anything that went beyond limited and voluntary cooperation. (Ernest Bevin, British Foreign Secretary, commented on proposals for a really effective Council of Europe thus: 'Once you open that Pandora's box, you'll find it full of Trojan horses.') All that said, the weaknesses of the Council should not be overstated. It was to perform, and continues to perform, certain useful functions – notably in the sphere of human rights through its European Convention of Human Rights, and as a forum for the discussion of matters of common interest to its member states. (The value of this latter function long lay in the fact that, unlike other Western European regional groups, virtually all Western European states were members of the Council. More recently, as East European countries have become members, an additional value has been as a forum for establishing links and building understanding between Western and Eastern Europe.)

(2) Although it was not immediately apparent when hostilities ceased in 1945, the Second World War was to result in a fundamental redrawing of the political map of Europe. By the late 1940s it was clear that the legacy of war had left the Continent, and with it Germany, divided in two. In Winston Churchill's phrase, an 'Iron Curtain' now divided East from West.

In the West there was no question of the victorious powers – Britain and the United States – seeking or being able to impose anything like a Soviet-style straitjacket on the liberated countries. Nonetheless, if Western Europe did not quite take on the form of a bloc, liberal democratic systems were soon established and not wholly dissimilar political ideas were soon prevailing in most of the states. Inevitably this facilitated intergovernmental relations.

Perhaps the most important idea shared by the governments stemmed directly from the East–West division: a determination to preserve Western Europe from communism. Not only had the Soviet Union extended its influence far into the European heartland, but in France and Italy domestic communist parties were commanding considerable support and from 1947 were engaging in what looked to many like revolutionary activities. The United States shared this anti-communist concern, and the encouragement and assistance which it gave to the West European states after the war to cooperate was partly driven by a belief that such cooperation could play a major part in helping to halt the communist advance. In March 1947 President Truman, concerned with events in Greece – where communists were trying to overthrow the government – outlined what became known as the Truman doctrine, which amounted to a political guarantee of support to 'free peoples who are resisting attempted subjugation by armed minorities or by outside pressures'. This political commitment was quickly followed up in 1948 by economic assistance in the form of Marshall Aid, and in 1949 by military protection with the foundation of NATO and a guarantee to the then ten West European member states (Canada and the United States brought the founding membership to twelve) of US military protection against a Soviet attack.

A role for the United States in Western Europe at this time should not be seen as having been unwelcome, for contrary to the impression that is sometimes given, US aid was not unwillingly or insidiously imposed on the states but was actively sought. At the same time, the extent of US influence should not be exaggerated. By its political, economic, and military interventions and assistance the United States did exert integrationist pressures and did help to make a number of developments possible, but the US government wanted much more West European inter-state integration than was actually achieved.

(3) With the post-war division of Europe, the moving of the international power balance from European state relations to US–Soviet relations, and the onset of the Cold War from 1947–8 producing the possibility of Europe becoming a battleground between East and West, there was a sense from the late 1940s that Western Europe was beginning to look like an identifiable political entity in a way that it had not done before. Not all states or politicians shared this perspective, but amongst many of those who did it produced a desire that the voice of Western Europe should be heard on the world stage and a belief that this could be achieved only through unity and by speaking with one voice. For some of the smaller European states, which had rarely exercised much international influence and whose very existence had periodically been threatened by larger neighbours, the prospects of such cooperation were particularly attractive.

(4) The future of Germany naturally loomed large in the minds of those who had to deal with post-war reconstruction. Three times in seventy years, and twice in the twentieth century, Germany had occupied much of Europe. Rightly or wrongly it had come to be seen as innately aggressive. As a consequence, the initial inclination of most governments after the war was to try to contain Germany in some way. Just how this should be done, however, divided the wartime allies, with the result that matters drifted until what was initially intended as an interim division of Germany into zones gave way, as the Cold War developed, into a *de jure* division: the Federal Republic of Germany (West Germany) and the German Democratic Republic (East Germany) were both formally constituted in 1949.

By this time, the Soviet Union was replacing Germany as the perceived principal threat to democracy and stability in Western Europe. As this occurred, those who were already arguing that a conciliatory approach towards Germany ought to be tried – since a policy of punitive containment had demonstrably failed between the wars – saw their hands strengthened by a growing feeling that attempts must be made to avoid the development of a political vacuum in West Germany that the communists might attempt to exploit. Furthermore, and the US government played an important role in pressing this view from the early 1950s, use of West Germany's power and wealth could help to reduce the contributions that other countries were making to the defence of Europe. The perceived desirability and need to incorporate the Federal Republic into the Western European mainstream thus further stimulated the pressure for inter-state cooperation and integration.

Economic factors

Just as pre-war and wartime experiences helped to produce the United Nations, so they also stimulate an interest in the creation of new international economic and financial arrangements. The first fruits of this were realised at the Bretton Woods Conference in 1944, where the representatives of forty-four countries, with the United Kingdom and the United States playing the leading roles, agreed to the establishment of two new bodies. The first was the International Monetary Fund (IMF), which was to alleviate currency instability by creating facilities for countries with temporary balance of payments difficulties to have access to short-term credit facilities. The second was the International Bank for Reconstruction and Development (the World Bank), which was to provide long-term loans for schemes that required major investment. In 1947, at much the same time as the IMF and the World Bank became operative, international economic cooperation was taken a stage further when twenty-three countries negotiated the General Agreement on Tariffs and Trade (GATT), whose purpose was to facilitate trade through the lowering of international trade barriers.

Although West European governments (or, more usually, national representatives, since governments on the Continent were not properly restored until 1945–6) played their part in creating the new international economic arrangements, it was felt in many quarters that there should also be specifically West European-based economic initiatives and organisations. In 1947–8 this feeling was given a focus, an impetus and an urgency when the rapid post-war economic recovery that most states were able to engineer by the adoption of expansionist policies created massive balance of payments deficits, and dollar shortages in particular. Governments were faced with major currency problems, with not being able to pay for their imports and with the prospect of their economic recovery coming to a sudden and premature end. In these circumstances, and for reasons that were not altogether altruistic – a strong Western Europe was in its political, security and economic interests – the United States stepped in with economic aid in the form of the European Recovery Programme, or Marshall Aid as it came to be known after the US Secretary of State, George Marshall, who championed it. But there was a condition attached to the aid: the recipient states must endeavour to promote greater economic cooperation among themselves. As a result, the first major post-war Western European organisation, the Organisation for European Economic Cooperation (OEEC), was established, with sixteen founding member states in April 1948. Its short-term task was to manage the US aid, encourage joint economic policies and discourage barriers to trade; in the longer term, its stated aim was to build 'a sound European economy through the cooperation of its members'. In the event, although the OEEC did some valuable work – the most notable perhaps being to establish payments schemes which in the 1940s and 1950s did much to further trade between the member countries – it never made much progress towards its grander ambitions. Rather like the Council of Europe, its large and somewhat heterogeneous membership, coupled with the strictly intergovernmental nature of its decision-making structure, meant that ambitious proposals were always successfully opposed. Partly as a result of this, and partly in recognition of growing interdependence among all industrialised countries, in 1961 the OEEC gave way to the Organisation for Economic Cooperation and Development (OECD), whose membership was to be open to non-European countries and which was to have broader objectives reflecting wider and changing interests.

The OEEC thus stemmed from post-war circumstances that mixed the general with the particular. That is to say, attitudes coming out of the war that favoured economic cooperation between West European states were given a direction by particular requirements that were related to the war and its immediate aftermath. Only three years later, as will be described in Chapter 3, a similar mixture of general underlying and specific triggering factors combined to produce the first of the European Communities: the European Coal and Steel Community (ECSC).

The effects of some of the political and economic factors associated with the Second World War that have just been considered, such as the existence of Resistance leaders in governments, were essentially short-term. Furthermore some of the factors, such as the increased need and willingness of the states to cooperate with one another to promote economic growth, were not so much caused by the war as given a push by it. Nonetheless, it can hardly be disputed that the factors taken together produced a set of circumstances that enabled Western European cooperation and integration to get off the ground in the 1940s and 1950s.

States naturally differed in the particulars and perceptions of their post-war situations. As a result, there was no general agreement on precisely what the new spirit of cooperation should attempt to achieve. Many different schemes were advanced and many different organisations were established to tackle particular issues, problems and requirements. Thus the war did not produce anything remotely like a united West European movement between the states. But it did produce new realities and changed attitudes that enabled, or forced, virtually all the states to recognise at least some commonalities and shared interests. As a consequence, it became possible for new inter-state European organisations to be established. Of these organisations, those that were able to offer clear advantages and benefits to members were able to act as a base for further developments. As the ECSC in particular was soon to demonstrate, cooperation and integration can breed more of the same.

Interdependence

It has become customary to suggest that whilst both political and economic factors were crucial to Western European cooperation and integration in the formative post-war years, the former have now declined in relation to the latter. The impact of modernisation is generally agreed to be a key reason for this. It has broadened the international agenda from its traditional power and security concerns to embrace a range of economic and social issues, and at the same time it has produced an interconnected-ness and interrelatedness between states, especially in the economic and monetary spheres, that amounts to an interdependence.

Economic interdependence has arisen particularly from three features of the post-1945 world: the enormously increased volume of world trade; the internationalisation of production, in which multinational corporations have played a prominent part; and – especially since the early 1970s – the fluctuations and uncertainties associated with currency exchange rates and international monetary arrangements. Within Western Europe there have been many regional dimensions to the development of interdependence, two of which have been especially important in promoting the integration process. First, since the Second World War the external trade of all significant Western European countries has become increasingly West European focused. The EC/EU has played an important role in encouraging this trend, and all the EU member states now conduct at least 50 per cent of their trade inside the EU. Second, from the 1960s monetary power within Western Europe increasingly came to be held by those who made the monetary decisions for the strongest economy: Germany. Changes in German interest rates or exchange rates had immense and potentially very destabilising implications elsewhere in Western Europe.

As a result of interdependence a wide variety of economic and financial issues can thus no longer be limited to, and indeed in some respects do not even bear much relationship to, national boundaries. States are increasingly vulnerable to outside events and are increasingly unable to act in isolation. They must consult, cooperate and, some would argue, integrate with one another in the interests of international and national economic stability and growth. In consequence, when a problem has been seen to require a truly international economic effort most West European states have been prepared to try to find solutions at this level: in the IMF, in GATT and its successor the World Trade Organisation (WTO), in the Bank for International Settlements, and elsewhere. When a regional response has seemed more appropriate or more practical, West European-based arrangements have been sought. The most obvious examples of such arrangements are EU-based. For instance: the creation of the Single European Market (SEM) is rooted in the belief that the dismantlement of trade barriers will further economic efficiency and prosperity in the participating states; the creation of Economic and Monetary Union (EMU) is based on the assumption that the coordination and the convergence of national economic and monetary policies and the establishment of a centrally managed single currency is necessary for the completion of the SEM programme and will serve to promote further trade, growth and prosperity; and the development at the EU level of advanced research programmes is a response to the growing belief that European states must pool their scientific and technological resources and knowledge if they are to compete successfully in world markets against the Americans, the Japanese and other competitors.

Economic interdependence is not the only feature of modern interdependence. Advances in communications and travel have necessarily placed on the international and European agendas issues that a generation or two ago either did not exist or were seen as being of purely domestic concern. Now it is commonly accepted that if there is to be any prospect of success they must be dealt with at the inter-state level. Governments thus discuss, and in Western Europe have adopted understandings and made decisions on, matters as diverse as transfrontier television arrangements, data protection, action against drug traffickers and football hooliganism.

But despite all the attention that is now given to interdependence as the motor of West European integration, and despite the associated assertion that economic factors now far outweigh political factors in shaping relations between the West European states, the case should not be overstated. One reason for this is that modern interdependence does not necessarily produce an inescapable and wholly unavoidable set of integrationist processes and developments: there is certainly an integrationist logic attached to modern interdependence, but for much of integration to actually proceed political choices and decisions have to be made. As the history of West European negotiations on integration since the Second World War demonstrate – from the negotiations in the late 1940s to establish the Council of Europe to the negotiations in the mid 1990s on the Treaty of Amsterdam – politicians, and indeed publics, are capable of adopting an array of often sharply conflicting views of what is necessary and what is desirable when they are faced with particular choices and decisions. A second reason for exercising some caution when evaluating the impact on integration of economic interdependence is that political factors continue to be important in shaping the nature and pace of integration processes. This was clearly illustrated in the wake of the 1990 reunification of Germany, when a powerful stimulus to a new round of integrationist negotiations was the growing conviction among decision-making elites, most particularly in France, that if Germany was to be prevented from dominating the Continent it must be tied more tightly to its neighbours. A third reason for not overemphasising the importance of modern interdependence to the neglect of other factors is that interdependence of a quite different kind – different in that it has not arisen from modernisation but rather from the relatively diminished significance of the West European states in the post-1945 period – continues to play a part in encouraging cooperation and integration between states. So, for example, with respect to the external political role of the EU, the fact that the western European states have relatively limited power and weight when acting individually provides a powerful inducement for them to try to speak as one in order to exert a significant influence on world political events. Most of the EU states do wish to exert such an influence and consequently, since the early 1970s, they have gradually strengthened their mechanisms for inter-state foreign policy cooperation so as to enable them to engage in extensive consultations, and increasingly to adopt joint positions, on foreign policy issues. Similar processes have been under way also in respect of security considerations, with the perception, until the collapse of communism, of the Soviet Union as Western Europe's main political enemy, allied with the inability of any single Western Europe state to offer by itself a wholly credible defence capability, encouraging close military cooperation between the states in the context of both the Western alliance and associated Western Europe defence groupings. The Soviet threat has now disappeared, but potential security dangers of many kinds still abound – in the newly independent former Soviet states, in South-East Europe, in the Middle East, and elsewhere – and these have played an important part in ensuring that not only civil security but also military security is now on the EU's agenda, albeit somewhat tentatively.

National considerations

Although most Western European states since 1945 have paid at least lip service to the idea of a united Western Europe, and more recently to a united Europe, there has never been any consensus between them on what this should mean in practice. The rhetoric has often been grand, but discussions on specific proposals have usually revealed considerable variations in ambitions, motives, intentions and perceptions. Most crucially of all, states have differed in their assessments of the consequences for them, in terms of gains and losses, of forging closer relations with their neighbours. As a result, some states have been prepared and able to go further than others, or have been prepared to do so at an earlier time. There has not, therefore, been coherent and ordered progress towards West European unity. In the late 1940s and the 1950s most states were willing to be associated with intergovernmental organisations that made few demands on them – and hence joined the OEEC and the Council of Europe – but they were less enthusiastic when organisations were proposed that went beyond intergovernmental cooperation into supranational integration. Consequently, the more ambitious post-war schemes – for the ECSC, for a European Defence Community (EDC – which in the event was never established), and for the EEC and Euratom – initially involved only a restricted membership. It was not until circumstances and attitudes in other states changed, and until an obstacle that emerged amongst the founding states themselves – in the form of President de Gaulle's opposition to UK membership – was removed, that the EC gradually expanded in the 1970s, 1980s and 1990s to include eventually virtually all of Western Europe's larger and medium-sized states.

So while all West European states have long been touched by at least some of the factors that have been examined on the last few pages, the differences between them have resulted in their interest in, and their capacity and enthusiasm for, cooperation and integration varying in terms of both nature and timing. The nature of these differences is examined in Chapter 2.

Concluding remarks: the ragged nature of the integration process

Since the Second World War the way in which West European governments relate to and communicate with one another has been transformed. A key role in this has been played by new international governmental organisations. Some of these are world-wide in their composition, others are regionally based; some have sweeping but vaguely defined responsibilities, others have specific sectoral briefs; some are purely intergovernmental in structure, others are overlain with supranational powers. At a minimum all provide frameworks in which national representatives meet with one another to discuss matters of mutual interest.

The best known, most developed and most important West European-wide organisation is the EU. But it has never been the only significant West European-wide organisation, and it was not the first such organisation to be established. On the contrary, since the end of the Second World War numerous proposals have been advanced and many arrangements have been set in place for organised cooperation and integration among the states. The more ambitious of these have sought to bring the whole of Western Europe together in some sort of federal union. The more cautious and, it may be thought, the more realistic have limited themselves to the pursuit of restricted aims for just some of the states.

So although the logic of circumstances and of political and economic changes have brought the states much more closely together, there can hardly be said to have been a common and coherent integrationist force at work in Western Europe in the post-war years. Far from the states being bound together in the pursuit of a shared visionary mission, relations between them have frequently been extremely uncomfortable and uneasy, based as they have been on a host of different needs and different perceptions of what is possible and necessary. In consequence, the processes of cooperation and integration have operated in many different forums, at many different levels, in many different ways, and at many different speeds. Even in the EC/EU, which has been at the integrationist core, the course of the integration process has varied considerably, with the mid-1970s until the early 1980s being the years of slowest integrationist advance, and the mid-1980s until the early 1990s being the fastest.

It is, of course, the conflicting nature of many of the factors which affect the integration process that has resulted in the process being so rocky, uncertain and unpredictable. Moreover, the factors themselves have been subject to considerable and unforeseeable change, as has been no more clearly demonstrated than since the late 1980s with the context in which the pressures which affect the furtherance of integration being transformed by the ending of the Cold War and the break-up of the Soviet Union. After four decades of Europe having been politically divided in two, decades in which Western Europe tended to think of itself as *being* Europe, fundamental issues concerning the nature of the Continent as a whole are now on the agenda. In these circumstances, new links, contacts and forms of cooperation are being established between the countries of Western and Eastern Europe. Some of these developments are part of a process that is (as will be shown in Chapter 4) likely to result in at least some former Soviet bloc countries becoming members of the EU in the foreseeable future.

Chapter 2

European Integration and the States of Western Europe

The founding members of the European Community: Belgium, France,
  West Germany, Italy, Luxembourg and the Netherlands
The 1973 enlargement: the United Kingdom, Denmark and Ireland
The 1981 and 1986 enlargements: Greece, Spain and Portugal
The 1995 enlargement: Austria, Finland and Sweden
Non-EU West European countries: Norway, Switzerland and Iceland
The Mediterranean micro states: Cyprus and Malta
Concluding remarks

As was indicated in Chapter 1, much of the explanation for the nature and pace of the development of the European integration process since the Second World War is to be found in factors at the national level. In particular, it is to be found in the different circumstances and needs of the states of Western Europe and in the different attitudes that their governments have taken towards integration. This chapter examines these different circumstances, needs, and attitudes and considers the different types of influence that the states have had on the integration process.

A useful way of grouping the states is according to when, if at all, they assumed EC/EU membership.

The founding members of the European Community: Belgium, France, West Germany, Italy, Luxembourg and the Netherlands

These six states, which in 1951 signed the Treaty of Paris to found the ECSC and in 1957 signed the Treaties of Rome to found the EEC and Euratom, were the first to show a willingness to go beyond the cooperative intergovernmental ventures that were established in Western Europe in the late 1940s. Cautiously, tentatively, and not without reservations, each took the view that the benefits of integration, as opposed to just cooperation, would outweigh what appeared to be the major disadvantage – some loss of sovereignty. Some of the perceived advantages that supranational organisations could offer were shared by all of the six, but there were also more nationally based hopes and ambitions.

For the three Benelux countries, their experience of the Second World War had reemphasised their vulnerability to hostile and more powerful neighbours and the need to be on good terms with West Germany and France. Related to this, their size – Belgium and the Netherlands were only middle-ranking European powers whilst Luxembourg was a micro state – meant that their only real prospect of exercising any sort of influence in Europe, let alone the world, was through a more unified inter-state system. As for economic considerations, they were used to the idea of integration since Benelux economic agreements and arrangements pre-dated the war, and negotiations to re-launch and deepen these had been under way well before the war ended. There was also the simple fact that not one of the Benelux states was in a strong enough position to ignore Franco-German initiatives for economic integration.

Italy too had a number of particular reasons for welcoming close relations with other West European states. First, after more than twenty years of Fascist rule followed by military defeat, European integration offered the prospect of a new start, and from a basis of respectability. Second, in May 1947 (as also occurred in France) the Communist Party left government and for some years thereafter seemed to be intent on fermenting internal revolution. The clear anti-communist tenor of other West European governments looked comforting, and a possible source of assistance, to Italy's nervous Christian Democratic-led governments. Third, Italy faced economic difficulties on all fronts: with unemployment, inflation, balance of payments imbalances, currency instability and – especially in the south – poverty. Almost any scheme that offered the possibility of finding new markets and generating economic growth was to be welcomed.

Integration was seen as helping France to deal with two of its key post-war policy goals: the containment of Germany and economic growth. In the early 1950s the ECSC was especially important in this regard, offering the opportunity to break down age-old barriers and hostilities on the one hand, and giving France access to vital German raw materials and markets on the other. Later in the 1950s, when 'the German problem' was seen as less pressing but German economic competition seemed to be posing an increasing threat, France took steps in the EEC negotiations to ensure that as part of the price of continued integration certain French interests – including economic protection for its farmers – would be given special treatment.

Konrad Adenauer, the West German Chancellor from 1949 to 1963, saw West European unification as the means by which the Federal Republic could establish itself in the international mainstream and German self-respect could be regained. Western Europe would also, along with the Atlantic Alliance, provide a much-needed buttress against the perceived threat from the East. More specifically, the ECSC would enable West Germany to rid itself of Allied restrictions and interference, and the more open markets of the EEC would offer immense opportunities for what, in the 1950s, quickly became the fastest growing economy in Western Europe.

Since helping to create the EC in the 1950s, four of the founding states – Belgium, Luxembourg, the Netherlands and Italy – have remained firm and consistent supporters of the integration process. They have almost invariably backed, and sometimes have been prominent in the initiation of, the many proposals put forward over the years for further integrationist advance. Insofar as they have voiced reservations about the course of integration it has usually been to express concern that it is not proceeding sufficiently quickly.

Germany – or to be strictly accurate West Germany up to 1990 and united Germany since – has also been a fairly dependable member of the integrationist camp. (German unification took the form of the German Democratic Republic – East Germany – integrating into the Federal Republic of Germany, so there was no question of a new state joining the Community and therefore no question of normal enlargement procedures applying.) However, in recent years the enthusiasm for integration has perhaps waned a little, as was demonstrated in 1997 when, for a number of reasons, Chancellor Kohl was unexpectedly cautious about the extension of supranational decision-making in the negotiations that produced the Treaty of Amsterdam (see Chapter 5).

In the early years of the EC France assumed a very wary attitude towards the integration process. This was a consequence of President de Gaulle's hostility to any international organisation that assumed supranational characteristics and, thereby, undermined French national sovereignty. The economic benefits which the Community was bringing to France were recognised and welcomed, but they were not to be paid for with a transfer of national sovereignty to the likes of the Commission, the European Parliament or a Council of Ministers taking its decisions by majority vote. Since de Gaulle's resignation in 1969, France's concerns about loss of sovereignty have been less to the fore and this has enabled it to link up with Germany on many issues and provide much of the impetus for integration. However, concerns about sovereignty have never quite disappeared and this is why even today France, although a strong supporter of monetary integration and defence cooperation (objectives that sit well with the traditional French aim of containing Germany), still tends to take a more intergovernmentalist stance than the other five founding states with respect to the powers of the EU institutions.

The 1973 enlargement: the United Kingdom, Denmark and Ireland

Three factors were especially important in governing the UK's attitude towards European integration in the post-war years. First, the UK saw itself as operating within what Churchill described as three overlapping and interlocking relationships: the Empire and Commonwealth; the Atlantic Alliance and the 'special relationship' with the United States; and Western Europe. Until the early 1960s Western Europe was seen as being the least important of these relationships. Second, successive British governments were not prepared to accept the loss of sovereignty that integration implied. There were several reasons for this, of which the most important were: Britain's long established parliamentary tradition; the record, in which there was considerable pride, of not having been invaded or controlled by foreign powers in modern times; a generally held view that cessation of sovereignty was neither desirable nor necessary, since Britain was still a world power of the first rank; and a certain distaste with the idea of being dependent on the not altogether highly regarded governments and countries of 'the Continent'. Third, Britain's circumstances were such that three of the four main integrationist organisations to be proposed in the 1950s had few attractions in terms of their specific areas of concern: the restrictions on national decision-making powers entailed in the ECSC looked very unappealing to a country whose coal and steel capacity far exceeded that of any of the six; the EDC would have limited governmental manoeuvrability and options at a time when Britain's defences were already stretched by the attempt to maintain a world role; and Euratom looked as though it would involve sharing secrets with less advanced nuclear powers. Only the EEC seemed to have much to offer, but amongst the problems it carried with it was its proposed supranationalism. From 1955 to 1958 attempts were made to persuade the six not to be so ambitious and to direct their attention to the construction of a West European free trade area, but with no success. As a result, and with a view to increasing its bargaining power with the six, Britain looked to other non-signatories of the Treaty of Rome. This led, in January 1960, to the Stockholm Convention, which established the European Free Trade Association (EFTA). The founding members of EFTA were Austria, Denmark, Norway, Portugal, Sweden, Switzerland and the United Kingdom.

Two to three years after the EEC began functioning in 1958 the attitude of the UK government began to change and membership came to be sought. The first enlargement of the Community could, in fact, have occurred much earlier than it did had President de Gaulle not opposed UK applications in 1961 and 1967. There has been much speculation about the reasons for de Gaulle's veto: he feared that the UK would rival and attempt to thwart his desire to place France at the centre of the European stage; he believed UK membership would unsettle the developing Franco-German alliance – an alliance that was given symbolic force with the signing in 1963 of a Friendship Treaty between the two countries; he was suspicious of the UK's close links with the United States and thought they would pave the way for American penetration and domination of Europe if the UK joined the Community. Whatever the reason, the fact is the UK was barred from membership until de Gaulle was replaced as French President by Georges Pompidou in 1969. A different view was then taken in Paris: the UK might serve as a useful counterweight to the increasingly strong and self-confident Germany; UK governments would lend support to France's opposition to pressures from within the Community for increased supra-nationalism; and France would probably gain economically by virtue of having better access to UK markets and as a result of the UK being a net contributor to the Community budget.

The reasons for the UK's changed position on Europe were a mixture of the political and the economic. Politically, it was increasingly clear that the UK was no longer a world power of the first rank. The 1956 Suez debacle underlined the decline, and the increasing tendency from 1960 for key world issues to be discussed between the United States and the USSR on a purely bilateral basis further confirmed it. Paralleling this decline, the nature and status of the 'special relationship' with the United States weakened and became increasingly questionable. Furthermore, the British Empire was giving way to the Commonwealth, a very loose organisation and not one that was capable of providing the UK with much international political support.

On all the usual economic indicators, such as growth in trade, investment, gross national product and income, it was apparent by the early 1960s that the member states of the EC were outperforming the UK. For example, between 1958 and 1969 real earnings in Britain increased by about 38 per cent, whereas in the EC they increased on average by about 75 per cent. Quite simply the figures appeared to show that the Community was a success; all this at a time when the UK's pattern of trade, even when not a Community member, was turning away from the Commonwealth and towards Europe. Moreover, the growing economic strength of the EC seemed to be linked with growing political status.

Thus when Pompidou opened the EC door, the government of Edward Heath entered willingly. However, since joining the Community Britain has been something of an awkward partner. This was especially so during the Conservative Party's term of office between 1979 and 1997, for it took a largely minimalist view of what the EC/EU should be doing and what organisational shape it should take. The strong preference was for it to be concerned primarily with market-related matters, and more particularly for it to direct most of its efforts towards creating an integrated and largely deregulated European market. The proper and efficient operation of this market was not seen to require common economic, financial, and social policies, let alone a single currency. As for the political dimensions of Community/Union membership, the Thatcher and Major governments were willing to support the development of intergovernmental cooperation when that seemed useful – as, for example, in the field of foreign policy and aspects of internal security policy – but they almost invariably sought to resist supranational developments and any loss of national sovereignty. Since the governments of the other member states did not, for the most part, subscribe to these economic and political views of the EC/EU, being, in varying degrees, more integrationist, Britain frequently found itself at odds with its partners during the years of Conservative government.

Since the election of a Labour government in 1997, the British stance in the EU has been much more cooperative, as exemplified by Britain's willingness to incorporate extensions to supranational decision-making in the Amsterdam Treaty and by the much more positive tone of British ministers towards Europe. However, Britain is still clearly in the slow integration stream, as demonstrated by Britain's insistence that it be given an opt-out from Amsterdam Treaty provisions that strengthen the EU's justice and home affairs policies, and also by the decision announced in late 1997 that Britain would not be a first-wave member of the single currency.

Denmark and Ireland were not interested in joining the Communities that were founded in the 1950s. Both of their economies were heavily dependent on agriculture, so the ECSC had lttle to offer them. As for the EEC, there were several reasons to doubt that it would be to their benefit, the most important of which was that both countries had strong economic and historical links elsewhere: in Denmark's case with the other Scandinavian countries and with the UK; in Ireland's case with the UK. These links with the UK resulted in both of them tying their willingness to join the EC with the outcome of the UK's attempts to gain membership, so they both applied and then withdrew their applications on two occasions in the 1960s and then became members in 1973.

Denmark's record since joining the Community has been not wholly dissimilar from that of the UK in that, aware of domestic scepticism about the supposed benefits of EC/EU membership, Danish governments have tended to be cautious in their approach to integration. The most dramatic manifestation of Danish concern with the integration process occurred in 1992, when in a national referendum the Danish people rejected Denmark's ratification of the Maastricht Treaty. This rejection, which was reversed in a second referendum in 1993, upset the schedule for applying the Treaty, took much wind out of the sails of those who wished to press ahead quickly with further integration, and resulted in Denmark distancing itself from certain future integrationist projects. As part of this distancing, Denmark, like the UK, did not join the single currency when it was launched in 1999.

Ireland has created no particular difficulties for the EC/EU since its accession. From time to time Irish governments have intimated that their support for further integration is conditional on Ireland continuing to be afforded generous treatment under the Common Agricultural Policy (CAP) and the Structural Funds, but there has been no significant resistance to developments aimed at deepening the integration process.

The 1981 and 1986 enlargements: Greece, Spain and Portugal

If the 1973 enlargement round resulted in a tilting of the balance of the Community to the north, the two enlargements of the 1980s brought about a counterbalancing to the south and the Mediterranean.

In the 1950s the Greek economy had been unsuitable for ECSC or EEC membership, being predominantly peasant-based. Additionally, Greece's history, culture and geographical position put it outside the West European mainstream. But just as the countries that joined the Community in 1973 would have liked to have become members earlier, so was the accession of Greece delayed longer than Greek governments would have liked. The initial problem, recognised on both sides when Greece made its first approaches to Brussels soon after the EEC came into being, was the underdeveloped nature of the Greek economy. A transitional period prior to membership was deemed to be necessary and this was negotiated in the form of an Association Agreement that came into force in 1962. The object of the Association was the 'continuous and balanced strengthening of trade and economic relations between the contracting parties, having particular regard to the need to secure an accelerated development of the Greek economy'. Full incorporation into the Community would, it was understood, follow when the Greek economy was capable of sustaining the obligations imposed by membership. However, between April 1967, when there was a military coup in Greece, and June 1974, when civilian government was reestablished, the Association Agreement was virtually suspended. It might be thought that this would have further delayed full membership, but in fact it had the opposite effect. After elections in Greece in November 1974 the new government immediately made clear its wish to become a full member of the Community. The Commission issued a formal opinion that Greece was still not economically ready and proposed a pre-accession period of unlimited duration, during which economic reforms could be implemented. In response, the Greek government restated its wish for full membership, and particularly emphasised how membership could help both to underpin Greek democracy and to consolidate Greece's West European and Western Alliance bonds. The Council of Ministers was sympathetic to these arguments and rejected the Commission's proposal. Membership negotiations were opened in July 1976 and Greece entered the Community in 1981.

Since becoming a member, Greece has generally supported the advancement of the integration process. That said, particular Greek policies, concerns, and special needs have sometimes created difficulties: sovereignty reservations have raised their head from time to time; Greece's deep-rooted hostility towards Turkey and its complicated web of friendships and hostilities with parts of the former Yugoslavia have been major obstacles in the way of EU attempts to develop united and effective policies in South-East Europe; Greece's poverty (it is the poorest member state) has contributed to pressures on the EU's redistributive policies and funds; the highly unstable nature of the Greek economy has meant that it has sometimes had to seek special economic assistance from its partners; and although it wished to join the single currency it was the only EU member state that was unable to meet the qualifying convergence criteria for entry into the first wave.

For many years both political and economic circumstances counted against Spanish and Portuguese membership. Politically, both countries were authoritarian dictatorships to which the democratic governments of the founding six did not wish to be too closely attached. Economically, both were predominantly agricultural and underdeveloped, and both pursued essentially autarkic economic policies until the end of the 1950s: factors that hardly made them suitable candidates for the ECSC, and that had the knock-on effect of excluding them from the EEC negotiations, which the founding six opened up only to the UK.

As with Greece, political considerations were extremely important in the relations between the two Iberian states and the Community prior to their accession. Initially the influence was a negative one: if Spain and Portugal had not had dictatorial political systems until the mid 1970s, in all probability they would have been allowed to join much sooner. Not that there was anything in the treaties to specify that members must be liberal democracies: Article 237 of the EEC Treaty simply stated 'Any European State may apply to become a member of the Community'. The assumption was, however – as it explicitly is today – that a democratic political system was a necessary qualification for entry.

So although both Spain and Portugal requested negotiations on association with the Community as early as 1962, and Spain made it quite clear that its request was with a view to full membership at some future date, both countries were treated with caution by the Community. Eventually they were granted preferential trade agreements – that for Spain coming into force in 1970, and that for Portugal in 1973 as part of an agreement between the Community and all EFTA countries – but it was only with the overthrow of the Caetano regime in Portugal in 1974 and the death of General Franco in 1975 that full membership became a real possibility. Portugal applied in March 1977 and Spain in July 1977. The negotiations were protracted and difficult, covering, amongst many problems, the threat posed to other Mediterranean countries by Spanish agriculture, the size of the Spanish fishing fleet, and the implications of cheap Spanish and Portuguese labour moving north. As with the Greek negotiations, political factors helped to overcome these difficulties: the member states wished to encourage political stability in southern Europe; there was the opportunity to widen and strengthen the political and economic base of the Community; and, by helping to link southern Europe to the north, there were seen to be strategic advantages for both Western Europe and NATO.

Since their accession both Spain and Portugal have broadly gone along with integrationist developments, the former perhaps being a little more integrationist than the latter. The fear expressed in some quarters before their accession that they would come to constitute a disruptive Iberian bloc has not been realised. As would be expected, they do frequently adopt similar positions on issues of common concern – issues that in many instances are a consequence of their being southern, comparatively poor, and neighbours – but, as with other member states, their preferences on specific policy matters often diverge.

The 1995 enlargement: Austria, Finland and Sweden

In 1992 the EC formally opened accession negotiations with Austria, Finland and Sweden, and in 1993 it opened negotiations with Norway. These negotiations were concluded successfully in March 1994, with a view to each of the countries becoming members of the EU after the terms of accession had been ratified at national level. However, in Norway the terms were rejected when the people voted against membership in a national referendum. In consequence, there were three rather than four new members of the EU in January 1995.

Two sets of factors stimulated the four countries (and Switzerland too – of which more below) to seek membership of the EU. First, what previously had been regarded as virtually insuperable obstacles to EC membership came in the late 1980s and early 1990s to be seen as less of a problem. For Austria and Sweden (and Switzerland too) the end of the Cold War reduced the importance of their traditional attachment to neutrality. For Finland, the difficulties posed by the country's relative geographical isolation, the close links with other Scandinavian countries, and the special position in relation to the Soviet Union, either withered or disappeared.

The second set of factors stimulating the accession applications stemmed from the relationships of these countries to the EC. Austria, Finland, Sweden and Norway, plus Switzerland, Iceland and the micro state of Liechtenstein, made up the membership of EFTA. When EFTA was constituted in 1960 – with, as noted above, Denmark, Portugal and the UK then also as members, but not, at that stage, Finland, Iceland or Liechtenstein – it had two principal objectives: the establishment of a free trade area in industrial products between the member countries, and the creation of a base for making the whole of Western Europe a free trade area for industrial goods. The first of these objectives was established in 1966 with the removal of virtually all customs duties and quantitative restrictions on trade in industrial products between EFTA countries, and the second was achieved in 1977 with the creation of an industrial free trade area between the EC and EFTA. Over time, however, despite relations between the EC and EFTA being friendly, and being indeed further developed via cooperation in such areas as environmental protection, scientific and technical research and transport policy, the EFTA states increasingly came to view key aspects of the EC–EFTA relationship as unsatisfactory. One reason for their dissatisfaction was that the EC was collectively much stronger than EFTA. A second, and related, reason was that the EC was prone to present EFTA with *de facto* situations to which the EFTA countries had little option but to adjust – as, for example, when the Community laid down product specifications. This latter problem, of having to accept trading rules they had played no part in helping to formulate, became of increasing concern to EFTA countries as the EC's programme to complete the internal market by 1992 – the Single European Market (SEM) programme – gathered pace in the late 1980s and early 1990s. This concern played an important part in encouraging the EFTA countries to reconsider the attractions of EC membership. It also led the EC – concerned that a widening of its membership might threaten its own deepening – to suggest that EC–EFTA relations be strengthened by the creation of a European Economic Area (EEA) which would, in effect, extend the SEM programme to the EFTA states but would stop short of

EC membership. The EEA was duly negotiated, and after a series of delays during the ratification process – which resulted in Switzerland withdrawing from the agreement – came into effect in January 1994. However, by that stage it had come to be accepted by most interested parties – including the governments of the EC, which in the meantime had succeeded in moving Community deepening forward via the Maastricht Treaty – that the ambitions of the governments of Austria, Finland, Sweden and Norway would be satisfied only by full EU membership.

The negotiation of accession terms with the EFTAns (as the applicants were collectively called) was much easier and quicker than in previous negotiating rounds. This was partly because each of the applicants was already well adjusted to EU membership – being prosperous (and hence not posing potential problems for the EU budget), having already incorporated much of the Community's *acquis* into national law, and having a well established democratic political system. It was partly also because many of the matters that normally have to be covered in accession negotiations had already been sorted out in the EEA negotiations and agreement.

Since their accession, none of the 1995 entrants have created any major problems for the EU, although there was disappointment in some quarters with the decision of the Swedish government not to become a founding member of the single currency. Perhaps the most distinctive contribution that the three states have made to the EU has been to oblige the other member states to pay more attention than they might otherwise have done to the issues of openness, transparency and EU democracy.

Non-EU West European countries: Norway, Switzerland and Iceland

There are now only three significant Western European countries that are not members of the EU: Norway, Switzerland and Iceland.

Like Denmark and Ireland, Norway paralleled the UK in applying for EC membership in the 1960s (twice) and early 1970s. On the third occasion terms of entry were agreed by the Norwegian government, but were then rejected by the Norwegian people in a referendum in 1972 following a campaign in which suspicions about the implications for Norwegian agriculture, fishing, and national sovereignty figured prominently. Another application for membership was made in 1992, partly for the reasons set out above in relation to the unsatisfactory nature of EC–EFTA decision-making relations, partly because the government felt that Norway could not afford to ignore the applications of its neighbours and be the only

Scandinavian country not to become an EU member, and partly because there were grounds (although by no means overwhelming grounds) for believing that the long-standing public opposition to membership was no longer as strong as it had been. Accession terms were quickly negotiated, but in the ensuing referendum in 1994 the issues raised echoed those of 1972, though with the additional argument being made by the opponents of membership that Norway had no need to join the EU since it was a prosperous country that, thanks to the EEA, already had the trading ties with the EU that it required. As in 1972, the people rejected membership in the referendum, by 52.2 per cent to 47.8 per cent.

Until December 1992 Switzerland was in much the same position as Austria and Sweden. That is to say, it had long been a member of EFTA, the end of the Cold War had removed the main obstacle to it becoming a member of the EC/EU, an application for accession had been made, and it anticipated entry some time in the mid 1990s. However in December 1992, in a referendum on whether to ratify the EEA, the Swiss people narrowly voted – by 50.3 per cent to 49.7 per cent – against ratification. As a consequence, the timetable for bringing the EEA into effect was delayed, and the Swiss application to join the EU, though left on the table, necessarily had to be put aside.

Iceland considered the possibility of EC membership at the time of the 1973 enlargement but concluded that there were too many policy difficulties in the way, especially with regard to fishing. This continues to be the case and explains why Iceland did not join the other EFTA states in the 1990s when they sought EU accession.

As Switzerland and Norway did not become EU members in the EFTAn enlargement round, EFTA continues to exist, with Iceland and Liechtenstein as its other members. The EEA also continues, although Switzerland, of course, is not a member.

The Mediterranean micro states: Cyprus and Malta

Although they are geographically distant from the West European heartland, the two Mediterranean micro states of Cyprus and Malta are often thought of – and have largely thought of themselves as being – part of the West European tradition. Both countries applied for EC membership in July 1990, but their applications were received with less than enthusiasm – partly because of a reluctance on the EC's part to tackle the institutional questions that would be raised by the accession of very small states and, in the case of Cyprus, partly because it was the view of most EC decision-makers that the problem of Turkey's occupation of Northern Cyprus must be resolved before the accession of Cyprus could be contemplated.

However, the prospects for both countries improved in June 1993 when the Commission issued its official opinion on the two applications: whilst recognising that there were many difficulties ahead, the Commission generally supported the applications and, in a significant break with the past, indicated that it did not favour allowing the partition of Cyprus to be a reason for permanently excluding the accession of Greek Cyprus. The European Council subsequently approved the Commission's opinions and in 1995 the Council of Ministers announced that negotiations with Cyprus and Malta would open six months after the conclusion of the Intergovernmental Conference that was scheduled to begin in 1996. An election in Malta in 1996 then delayed Malta's plans, by bringing to power a government that put the EU application on hold. Nonetheless, the Cyprus application continued to be advanced and accession negotiations opened in March 1998 in parallel with the opening of accession negotiations with five Central and Eastern European countries (see Chapter 4). In September 1998 a further change of government in Malta resulted in the country's membership application being revived.

Concluding remarks

This chapter has sought to show that it is not possible to understand the nature and development of Western European integration without having some understanding of the different political and economic positions in which the states have found themselves and the different attitudes their governments – and sometimes their peoples – have taken towards the advantages and disadvantages of integration. Such differences are central to understanding why, for example, some states in the 1950s were prepared to go beyond inter-state cooperation to inter-state integration, and why some states did not become candidates for EC/EU membership until thirty years or more after the Treaty of Rome. Even today, with many of the sharper edges of inter-state differences having been smoothed, significant differences still exist and these provide much of the explanation for the complexity of Western Europe's institutional architecture and the existence within the EU of conflicting viewpoints on matters ranging from specific policy issues to overall organisational direction.

Given the importance of the states as the main players in the integration process, many of the points made in this chapter will be revisited – either explicitly or implicitly – in later chapters. This revisiting starts in the next chapter, where the manner in which the 'founding six' created the EC is described.

Chapter 3

The Creation of the European Community

The European Coal and Steel Community
From the ECSC to the EEC
The EEC and Euratom Treaties
Concluding remarks

The European Coal and Steel Community

Much of the early impetus behind the first of the European Communities, the ECSC, was provided by two Frenchmen. Jean Monnet, who had pioneered France's successful post-war experiment with indicative economic planning, provided much of the technical and administrative initiative and behind-the-scenes drive. Robert Schuman, the French Foreign Minister from 1948 to early 1953, acted as the political advocate. Both were ardent supporters of European unity; both believed that the OEEC and the Council of Europe – where anyone could be exempted from a decision – could not provide the necessary impetus, and both came to the conclusion that, in Monnet's words, 'A start would have to be made by doing something both more practical and more ambitious. National sovereignty would have to be tackled more boldly and on a narrower front' (Monnet, 1978, p. 274).

Many of those who were attracted to the ECSC saw it in very restrictive terms: as an organisation that might further certain limited and carefully defined purposes. Certainly it would not have been established had it not offered to potential member states – in particular its two main pillars, France and West Germany – the possibility that it might serve to satisfy specific and pressing national interests and needs. But for some, not least Monnet and Schuman, the project was much more ambitious and long term. When announcing the plan in May 1950, Schuman – in what subsequently became known as the Schuman Declaration – was quite explicit that the proposals were intended to be but the first step in the realisation of a vision; a vision of a united Europe that would have Franco-German reconciliation at its heart. But, he warned, 'Europe will not be made all at once, or according to a single plan. It will be built through concrete achievements which first create a *de facto* solidarity' (the Schuman Declaration is reproduced in Salmon and Nicoll, 1997, pp. 44–6). In similar vein, Monnet informed governments during the negotiations:

> The Schuman proposals provide a basis for the building of a new Europe through the concrete achievement of a supranational regime within a limited but controlling area of economic effort. . . . The indispensable first principle of these proposals is the abnegation of sovereignty in a limited but decisive field (Monnet, 1978, p. 316).

Konrad Adenauer agreed with this. Addressing the Bundestag in June 1950 he stated:

> Let me make a point of declaring in so many words and in full agreement, not only with the French Government but also with M. Jean Monnet, that the importance of this project is above all political and not economic (quoted in ibid., pp. 319–20).

Schuman made it clear in his Declaration that whilst he hoped other countries would also participate, France and West Germany would proceed with the plan in any event (West Germany having already agreed privately in principle). Italy, Belgium, Luxembourg and the Netherlands took up the invitation, and in April 1951 the six countries signed the Treaty of Paris, which established the ECSC. It came into operation in July 1952.

The Treaty broke new ground in two principal ways. First, its policy aims were extremely ambitious, entailing not just the creation of a free trade area, but also laying the foundations for a common market in some of the basic materials of any industrialised society: coal, coke, iron ore, steel and scrap. This, it was hoped, would ensure orderly supplies to all member states, produce a rational expansion and modernisation of production, and improve the conditions and lifestyles of those working in the industries in question. Second, it was the first of the European inter-state organisations to possess significant supranational characteristics. These could be found in the new central institutions, which had the power, amongst other things, to: see to the abolition and prohibition of internal tariff barriers, state subsidies and special charges, and restrictive practices; fix prices under certain conditions; harmonise external commercial policy, for example by setting minimum and maximum customs duties on coal and steel imports from third countries; and impose levies on coal and steel production to finance the ECSC's activities. Four main institutions were created.

(1) *The High Authority* was set up 'To ensure that the objectives set out in this Treaty are attained in accordance with the provisions thereof' (Article 8, ECSC Treaty). To enable it to perform its tasks the High

Authority could issue, either on its own initiative or after receiving the assent of the Council of Ministers: decisions (which were to be binding in all respects in the member states); recommendations (which were to be binding in their objectives); and opinions (which were not to have binding force). Matters upon which the High Authority was granted decision-making autonomy included the prohibition of subsidies and aids, decisions on whether or not agreements between undertakings were permissible or not, action against restrictive practices, the promotion of research, and the control of prices under certain conditions. It could impose fines on those who disregarded its decisions.

The High Authority thus had a formidable array of powers at its disposal and this, when taken in conjunction with its membership, gave it a clear supranational character. There were to be nine members, including at least one from each member state, and, crucially, all were to be 'completely independent in the performance of their duties'. In other words, no one would be, or should regard themselves as being, a national delegate or representative.

In a number of respects the High Authority's powers were stronger than those which were to be given to the High Authority's equivalent, the Commission, under the Treaties of Rome. This has meant that since the institutions of the three Communities were merged in 1967, the Commission – which assumed the High Authority's powers – has had rather more room for independent manoeuvre when acting under the Treaty of Paris than it has when acting under the Treaties of Rome. In practice, however, it has not always been possible for these greater powers to be used to the full: from the earliest days of the ECSC, political realities have dictated that the High Authority/Commission must be sensitive to governmental opinions and policies.

(2) *The Council of Ministers* was set up mainly as a result of the Benelux countries' concern that if the High Authority had too much power, and there was no forum through which the states could exercise some control, the ECSC might be too Franco-German dominated. Ministers from the national governments were to constitute the membership of the Council, with each state having one representative.

According to Article 26 of the ECSC Treaty, 'The Council shall exercise its powers in the cases provided for and in the manner set out in this Treaty, in particular in order to harmonise the actions of the High Authority and that of the Governments, which are responsible for the general economic policies of their countries'. More specifically, the Treaty gave the Council formal control over some, but far from all, of the High Authority's actions: the Council had, for instance, to give its assent to the declaration of a manifest crisis which opened the door to production quotas. Decision-making procedures in the Council were to depend on the matter under consideration: sometimes a unanimous vote would be required, sometimes a qualified majority, sometimes a simple majority.

Practice has shown the Council to be not altogether consistent in the manner in which it has exercised its role under the ECSC Treaty. On the one hand, a general reluctance of the states to lose too much power over their domestic industries has normally resulted in the Council seeking to take most major decisions itself. Since decision-making in the Council has customarily proceeded on the basis of consensus, and since the states have often been unable to agree when difficult decisions have been called for, this has frequently led to very weak, or indeed even to an absence of, decision-making. On the other hand, when practicalities and political convenience have combined to suggest a less Council-centred decision-making approach, as they did with steel from the late 1970s, then the Council has been prepared to allow the High Authority/Commission a considerable measure of independence.

(3) *The Common Assembly's* role was to provide a democratic input into ECSC decision-making. In practice it can hardly be said to have done so in the early years: members were not elected but were chosen by national parliaments, and the Assembly's powers – notwithstanding an ability to pass a motion of censure on the High Authority – were essentially only advisory. However, the expansion of the Assembly's remit under the Rome Treaties to cover all three Communities, plus developments since the 1970s such as the introduction of direct elections and more streamlined procedures, have increasingly made for a more effective Assembly (or European Parliament as it is now called).

(4) *The Court of Justice* was created to settle conflicts between the states, between the organs of the Community, and between the states and the organs. Its judgements were to be enforceable within the territory of the member states. In similar fashion to the Assembly, but not the High Authority or Council of Ministers which remained separate until 1967, the Court assumed responsibility for all three Communities when the EEC and Euratom Treaties entered into force in 1958.

In addition to these four main institutions a Consultative Committee, made up of producers, workers and other interested parties, was also created by the ECSC Treaty. The role of the Committee was to be purely advisory.

In its early years the ECSC was judged to be an economic success. Customs tariffs and quotas were abolished, progress was made on the removal of non-tariff barriers to trade, the restructuring of the industries was assisted, politicians and civil servants from the member states became accustomed to working with one another and, above all, output and inter-state trade rapidly increased (although many economists would now query whether the increases were *because* of the ECSC). As a result the ECSC helped to pave the way for further integration.

However, the success of the early years was soon checked. In 1958–9, when cheap oil imports and a fall in energy consumption combined to produce an overcapacity in coal production, the ECSC was faced with its first major crisis – and failed the test. The member states rejected the High Authority's proposals for a Community-wide solution and sought their own, uncoordinated, protective measures. The coal crisis thus revealed that the High Authority was not as powerful as many had believed and was not in a position to impose a general policy on the states if they were determined to resist.

This relative weakness of the High Authority/Commission to press policies right through is one of the principal reasons why truly integrated West European coal and steel industries, in which prices and distributive decisions are a consequence of an open and free market, have not fully emerged. Many barriers to trade still remain. Some of these, such as restrictive practices and national subsidies, the High Authority and then the Commission have tried to remove, but with only limited success. Others, particularly in the steel sector, have been formulated and utilised by the Commission itself as its task has switched from encouraging expansion to managing contraction.

But arguably the major problem with the ECSC has been that as coal and steel have declined in importance in relation to other energy sources, what has increasingly been required is not so much policies for coal and steel in isolation, but a coordinated and effective Community energy policy. National differences have prevented such a policy being developed, although there has been some progress in recent years.

From the ECSC to the EEC

The perceived success of the ECSC in its early years provided an impetus for further integration. Another institutional development of the 1950s also played an important role in paving the way for the creation of the two further European Communities that were to be created in 1957. This was the projected European Defence Community (EDC).

In the early 1950s, against the background of the Cold War and the outbreak of the Korean War, many Western politicians and military strategists saw the need for greater Western European cooperation in defence matters. This would involve the integration of West Germany – which was not a member of NATO – into the Western Alliance. The problem was that some European countries, especially France, were not yet ready for German rearmament, whilst West Germany itself, though willing to re-arm, was not willing to do so on the basis of the tightly controlled and restricted conditions that other countries appeared to have in mind for it. In these circumstances the French Prime Minister, René Pleven, launched proposals in October 1950 which offered a possible way forward. In announcing his plan to the National Assembly he stated that the French government 'proposes the creation, for our common defence, of a European Army under the political institutions of a united Europe' (Pleven's statement is reproduced in Harryvan and van der Harst, 1997, pp. 65–9). By the end of 1951 the six governments involved in the establishment of the ECSC had agreed to establish an EDC. Its institutional structure was to be similar to the ECSC: a Joint Defence Commission, a Council of Ministers, an advisory Assembly and a Court of Justice.

In May 1952 a draft EDC Treaty was signed, but in the event the EDC, and the European Political Community which increasingly came to be associated with it, were not established. Ratification problems arose in France and Italy, and in August 1954 the French National Assembly rejected the EDC by 319 votes to 264 with 43 abstentions. There were a number of reasons for this: continuing unease about German rearmament; concern that the French government would not have sole control of its military forces; doubts about the efficiency of an integrated force; disquiet that the strongest European military power (the United Kingdom) was not participating; and a feeling that, with the end of the Korean War and the death of Stalin, the EDC was not as necessary as it had seemed when it was first proposed.

Following the collapse of the EDC project, an alternative and altogether less demanding approach was taken to the still outstanding question of West Germany's contribution to the defence of the West. This took the form of a revival and extension of the Brussels Treaty 'for collaboration in economic, social and cultural matters and for collective defence' that had been signed in 1948 by the three Benelux countries, France and the United Kingdom. At a conference in London in the autumn of 1954 West Germany and Italy agreed to accede to the Brussels Treaty, and all seven countries agreed that the new arrangements should be incorporated into a Western European Union (WEU). The WEU came into effect in May 1955 as a loosely structured, essentially consultative, primarily defence-orientated organisation that, amongst other things, permitted West German rearmament subject to various constraints. It also enabled West Germany to become a member of NATO.

The failure of the EDC, especially when set alongside the 'success' of the WEU, highlighted the difficulties involved in pressing ahead too quickly with integrationist proposals. In particular, it showed that quasi-federalist approaches in politically sensitive areas would meet with resistance. But, at the same time, the fact that such an ambitious scheme had come so close to adoption demonstrated that alternative initiatives, especially if they were based on the original Schuman view that political union could be best achieved through economic integration, might well be successful. It was partly with this in mind that the Foreign Ministers of the ECSC six met in Messina in June 1955 to discuss proposals by the three Benelux countries for further economic integration. At the Conference the Ministers agreed on a resolution that included the following:

> The governments . . . believe the moment has come to go a step further towards the construction of Europe. In their opinion this step should first of all be taken in the economic field.
>
> They consider that the further progress must be towards the setting up of a united Europe by the development of common institutions, the gradual merging of national economies, the creation of a common market, and the gradual harmonization of their social policies.
>
> Such a policy appears to them to be indispensable if Europe's position in the world is to be maintained, her influence restored, and the standard of living of her population progressively raised (the Resolution is reproduced in Salmon and Nicoll, 1997, pp. 59–61).

To give effect to the Messina Resolution, a committee of governmental representatives and experts was established under the chairmanship of the Belgian Foreign Minister, Paul-Henri Spaak. The United Kingdom was invited to participate and did so until November 1955, but then withdrew when it became apparent that its hopes of limiting developments to the establishment of a loose free trade area were not acceptable to the six. In April 1956 the Foreign Ministers accepted the report of the Spaak Committee and used it as the basis for the negotiations that in 1957 produced the two Treaties of Rome: the more important of these treaties established the European Economic Community (EEC) and the other the European Atomic Energy Community (Euratom).

Both before and after April 1956 the negotiations between the six governments were extensive and intense. At the end of the negotiations it can be said that, in broad terms, clear provisions were made in the treaties for those areas upon which the governments were able to reach agreement, but where there were divisions matters were largely left aside for further negotiations and were either omitted from the treaties altogether or were referred to only in a general way. So the EEC Treaty set out fairly clear rules on trade, but only guiding principles were laid down for social and agricultural policy.

The inclusion in the EEC Treaty of topics such as social and agricultural policy reflected a series of compromises among the six countries, especially between the two strongest ones – France and West Germany. France feared that Germany was likely to become the main beneficiary of the more open markets of the proposed customs union and so looked for compensation elsewhere. This took a number of forms. For instance: insisting on special protection for agriculture – the French farmer had historically been well protected from foreign competition and around one-fifth of the French population still earned their living from the land; pressing the case of an atomic energy Community, which would help guarantee France greater independence in energy; and seeking privileged relations with the six for France's overseas dependencies.

Eventually the negotiations were completed, and on 25 March 1957 the two treaties were signed. Only in France and Italy were there any problems with ratification: the French Chamber of Deputies voted 342 for and 239 against, and the Italian Chamber of Deputies voted 311 for and 144 against. In both countries the largest opposition bloc comprised the communists. The treaties came into effect on 1 January 1958.

The EEC and Euratom Treaties

Of the two Rome Treaties the EEC Treaty was by far the most important. Article 2 of the Treaty laid down the following broad objectives:

> The Community shall have as its task, by establishing a common market and progressively approximating the economic policies of Member States, to promote throughout the Community a harmonious development of economic activities, a continuous and balanced expansion, an increase in stability, an accelerated raising of the standard of living and closer relations between the states belonging to it.

Many of the subsequent Treaty articles were concerned with following up these broad objectives with fuller, though still often rather general, guidelines for policy development. These policy guidelines can be grouped under two broad headings.

Policy guidelines concerned with the establishment of a common market

The common market was to be based on the following:

(1) The removal of all tariffs and quantitative restrictions on internal trade. This would make the Community a free trade area.
(2) The erection of a Common External Tariff (CET). This would mean that goods entering the Community would do so on the same basis no matter what their point of entry. No member state would therefore be in a

position to gain a competitive advantage by, say, reducing the external tariffs on vital raw materials. The CET would take the Community beyond a mere free trade area and make it a customs union. It would also serve as the basis for the development of a Common Commercial Policy (CCP).

(3) The prohibition of a range of practices having as their effect the distortion or prevention of competition between the member states.

(4) Measures to promote not only the free movement of goods between the member states but also the free movement of persons, services and capital.

Policy guidelines concerned with making the Community more than just a common market

Making it exactly what, however, was left unclear, as it had to be, given the uncertainties, disagreements and compromises that formed the background to the signing of the Treaty. There was certainly the implication of a movement towards some sort of general economic integration, and references were made to the 'coordination' of economic and monetary policies, but they were vague and implicitly long term. Such references as there were to specific sectoral policies – as, for example, with the provisions for 'the adoption of a common policy in the sphere of agriculture', and the statement that the objectives of the Treaty 'shall . . . be pursued by Member States within the framework of a common transport policy' – were couched in fairly general terms.

The EEC Treaty was thus very different in character from the constitutions of nation states. Whereas the latter have little, if anything, to say about policy, the EEC Treaty had policy as its main concern. The nature of that concern was such that many have suggested that the policy framework indicated and outlined in the Treaty was guided by a clear philosophy or ideology: that of free-market, liberal, non-interventionist capitalism. Unquestionably there is much in this view: on the one hand the market mechanism and the need to prevent abuses to competition were accorded a high priority; on the other hand there were few references to ways in which joint activities and interventions should be promoted for non-market-based purposes. But the case should not be overstated. First, because competition itself was seen as requiring considerable intervention and management from the centre. Second, because there were some provisions for non-market policies: in the proposed common policy for agriculture, for example, which was given a special place in the Treaty precisely because of (mainly French) fears of what would happen should agriculture be exposed to a totally free market; in the proposed social policy, which was intended to help soften unacceptable market consequences; and in the proposed common transport policy where specific allowance was to be made for aids 'if they meet the needs of coordination of transport or if they represent reimbursement for the discharge of certain obligations inherent in the concept of a public service'. Third, because the Treaty was highly dependent on the future cooperation of the states for successful policy development, there was never any question – given the Christian democratic and social democratic principles of most EC governments – of an immediate abandonment of national economic controls and a remorseless and inevitable drive towards uninhibited free market capitalism.

The policy concerns of the Euratom Treaty were naturally confined to the atomic energy field. Chapters of the Treaty covered such vitally important areas of activity as promotion of research, dissemination of information, health and safety, supplies, and a nuclear common market. However, and probably even more than with the EEC Treaty, differences between the states on key points resulted in the force of many of the provisions of these chapters being watered down by exceptions and loopholes. For example, under Article 52 an agency was established with 'exclusive right to conclude contracts relating to the supply of ores, scarce materials and special fissile materials coming from inside the Community or from outside'. Article 66, however, set out circumstances in which states could buy on the world markets provided Commission approval was obtained. Similarly, Treaty provisions aimed at a pooling and sharing of technical information and knowledge were greatly weakened – largely at French insistence – by provisions allowing for secrecy where national security was involved.

Where the EEC and Euratom Treaties were most similar to national constitutions was in those articles which identified the main institutions of the Communities and those articles which specified the powers and some of the procedures of the institutions. The ECSC served as the institutional model, but with modifications which had as their effect a tilting away from supranationalism towards intergovernmentalism. As with the ECSC, both the EEC and Euratom were to have four principal institutions:

(1) An appointed Commission would assume the role exercised by the High Authority under the ECSC. That is, it would be the principal policy initiator, it would have some decision-making powers of its own, and it

would carry certain responsibilities for policy implementation. But it would have less power than the High Authority to impose decisions on member states.

(2) A Council of Ministers, with greater powers than its equivalent under the ECSC, would be the principal decision-making body. Circumstances in which it must take its decisions unanimously, and circumstances in which majority and qualified majority votes were permissible, were specified.

(3) An Assembly would exercise advisory and (limited) supervisory powers. In the first instance it would be composed of delegates from national parliaments, but after appropriate arrangements were made it was to be elected 'by direct universal suffrage in accordance with a uniform procedure in all Member States'.

(4) A Court of Justice was charged with the duty of ensuring that 'in the interpretation and application of this Treaty the law is observed'.

A Convention, which was also signed on 25 March 1957, specified that the Assembly and the Court of Justice should be common to all three Communities.

These institutional arrangements were rather more intergovernmental in character than those who dreamed of political integration would have liked. In particular, the Council of Ministers was judged to have been given too much power and there was also disappointment that most of the key decisions in the Council would have to be made unanimously. However, there was hope for the future in that there were grounds for believing that the system could, and probably would, serve as a launching pad for a creeping supranationalism. One of these grounds was provision in the EEC Treaty for increased use of majority voting in the Council as the Community became established. Another was the expectation that the Assembly would soon be elected by direct suffrage and that its power would thereby be increased. And a third was the seemingly reasonable assumption that if the Community proved to be a success the member states would become less concerned about their national rights and would increasingly cede greater powers to the central institutions.

Concluding remarks

The Treaty of Paris and the two Treaties of Rome thus constitute the Founding Treaties of the three European Communities. The Treaties are still very much in existence today, as the constituent elements of the first pillar of the European Union. However, as the next two chapters show, the contents of the Treaties – especially the EEC Treaty – have changed considerably over the years as a result of amendments made by subsequent treaties.

Clearly the Treaties marked major steps forward in the development of post-war inter-state relations. They did so most particularly by laying the foundations for signatory states to integrate specific and core areas of their economic activities and by embodying a degree of supranationalism in the decision-making arrangements they established for the new Communities.

Insofar as it was the first treaty, the Treaty of Paris holds a very special place in the history of European integration. In terms of long-term impact, however, the EEC Treaty has been the most important in that it has been on its wide policy base that much of European integration since 1958 has been constructed.

Though they laid down reasonably clear guidelines on and requirements for certain matters, the Founding Treaties were not intended to act as straitjackets with respect to the future shape and development of the Communities. Rather, they provided frameworks within which certain things would be expected to happen and other things could happen if decision-makers so chose.

Attention is, therefore, now turned to the development of European integration since the Rome Treaties came into force in January 1958.

Chapter 4

From European Community to European Union

Supplements and amendments to the Founding Treaties
Enlargement
Development of policy processes
Development of policies
Concluding remarks

Since the European Communities were created, European integration has advanced in many ways. This chapter examines the most important of these ways.

The examination does not take the form of a detailed account of the unfolding of the integration process. For those who want such an account, there are several very useful sources (see for example Arter, 1993; Dinan, 1999; Middlemas, 1995; Urwin, 1995). Nor does the chapter provide a chronological history – a Chronology of Main Events is included at the end of the book. Rather, the chapter provides an overview of the main features of the integration process.

Four main features are considered: supplements and amendments to the Founding Treaties; enlargement; the development of policy processes; and the development of policies.

Supplements and amendments to the Founding Treaties

As discussed in Chapter 3, the Treaty of Paris and the two Treaties of Rome constitute the Founding Treaties of the three European Communities. Over the years, in response to pressure for the treaty framework to be simplified, clarified, extended, made more democratic and generally strengthened, the Founding Treaties have been supplemented and amended by subsequent treaties.

The Treaty Establishing a Single Council and a Single Commission of the European Communities

Signed in 1965, coming into force in 1967, and generally known as the Merger Treaty, this established a single Council of Ministers for all three

Communities (though different individuals would attend different meetings) and merged the High Authority of the ECSC, the Commission of Euratom, and the EEC Commission into one Commission. The powers exercised by these merged bodies were still to be based on the Founding Treaties: in other words, the Treaties and the Communities themselves were not merged. To clarify and simplify the existing texts relating to the single Community institutions, this treaty was repealed by the 1997 Amsterdam Treaty and its relevant parts were incorporated as appropriate into the Community Treaties.

The Treaty Amending Certain Budgetary Provisions of the Treaties and The Treaty Amending Certain Financial Provisions of the Treaties

The first of these treaties was signed in 1970 and the second in 1975. Together, they laid down a budgetary procedure and allocated budgetary powers between the EC institutions. Of particular importance, given its relative weakness in most policy areas, were the powers allocated to the European Parliament. The 1975 Treaty also established a Court of Auditors to examine the accounts of all revenue and expenditure of the Community.

The Act Concerning the Election of the Representatives of the Assembly by Direct Universal Suffrage

Signed in 1976, but not ratified by all the member states until 1978, this Act provided the legal base for direct elections to the European Parliament (EP) and, laid down certain rules for their conduct, but did not in any direct way increase the powers of the EP.

The Single European Act (SEA)

Signed in February 1986, but not coming into force until mid 1987 because of ratification difficulties in Ireland, the SEA was something of a mixed bag, containing tidying-up provisions, provisions designed to give the Community a new impetus, and provisions that altered aspects of the Community's decision-making system. The most important measures of the SEA were as follows:

(1) Completion of the internal market by 1992 was identified as a specific goal and was incorporated into the EEC Treaty via a new Article

8A. A programme for completing the internal market had already been agreed at the Milan European Council meeting in June 1985, but according the goal treaty status enhanced its prospect of success (as did the introduction of qualified majority voting for most internal market decisions – see the third point below).

(2) A number of new policy areas – most of which were already being developed – were formally incorporated into the EEC Treaty, so the capacity for decision-making in these areas was increased. The new policy areas included environment, research and technological development, and 'economic and social cohesion'.

(3) For ten EEC Treaty articles a new legislative procedure was established – the cooperation procedure. The purpose of the new procedure was to improve the efficiency of decision-making in the Council of Ministers, and to increase, though not by too much, the powers of the EP. The key features of the cooperation procedure were as follows: (1) the single reading of legislative proposals by the EP and the Council of Ministers under the traditional consultation procedure was replaced by two readings; (2) the Council could, subject to certain restrictions, take its decisions at both first and second readings by qualified majority vote (qmv) – this amounted to a significant increase in the treaty base for majority voting; (3) the EP's ability to influence the content of EC legislation was increased, though it still did not enjoy full legislative powers; and (4) a strict timetable was established for the later stages of the legislative process. Legislative areas covered by the cooperation procedure included some social policy matters, the implementation of decisions in connection with the regional fund and research and technological development programmes, and, most crucially of all – under a new EEC Article 100A – most of the measures 'which have as their object the establishment and functioning of the internal market'.

(4) The EP's role and potential influence in the Community was further increased by the establishment of a new 'assent procedure'. Under the procedure, the EP's assent, by an absolute majority of members, became necessary both for the accession of new members to the Community (under Article 237, EEC) and for association agreements between the Community and third countries (under Article 238, EEC).

(5) European Political Cooperation (EPC, the then official Community term for foreign policy cooperation), which had increasingly been practised since the early 1970s, but outside the treaty framework, was put on a legal basis (but not by treaty incorporation).

(6) Meetings between the twelve Heads of Government in the framework of the European Council, which had been taking place since 1975, were given legal recognition (but not by treaty incorporation).

(7) The capacity of the Court of Justice, which had been becoming very overstretched, was extended by a provision for the establishment of a new Court of First Instance.

The SEA thus provided a major boost to the European integration process. It did so on the one hand by strengthening the treaty base for policy activity, most particularly in respect of the completion of the internal market where a deadline was set. It did so on the other hand by strengthening the Community's institutional system, especially in respect of the increased capacity of the Council of Ministers to take decisions by qualified majority vote (qmv) and the increased legislative powers given to the EP.

The Maastricht and Amsterdam Treaties

The Treaty on European Union (TEU) – more commonly known as the Maastricht Treaty – was signed in February 1992 and came into effect in November 1993. The Treaty of Amsterdam was signed in October 1997 and came into effect in May 1999. Both Treaties are examined in some detail in Chapter 5. The Maastricht Treaty merits detailed examination because of its enormous importance in furthering the integration process. It did this in two main ways. First, it created the new organisation of the European Union, which was based on three pillars: the European Communities, a Common Foreign and Security Policy (CFSP), and Cooperation in the Fields of Justice and Home Affairs (JHA). Second, like the SEA, it furthered policy and institutional deepening: the former, most notably, by laying down a procedure and a timetable for moving to Economic and Monetary Union (EMU) with a single currency; the latter, most notably, by further extending provision for qmv in the Council and by creating a new legislative procedure – co-decision – which, for the first time, gave the EP the power of veto over some legislative proposals.

The Amsterdam Treaty was neither as far reaching nor as ambitious as the Maastricht Treaty. Indeed, for Euro-enthusiasts it was something of a disappointment. Nonetheless, it was significant for the integration process in that it too carried policy and institutional deepening further forward. In respect of policy deepening, its most important changes were to strengthen the EU's decision-making capacity in certain justice and home affairs spheres. In respect of institutional deepening, its most important changes were to extend the Maastricht-created co-decision procedure to more policy spheres and to virtually abolish the SEA-created cooperation procedure.

Enlargement

From an original EC membership of six, the EU now numbers fifteen member states. As was explained in Chapter 2, this enlargement has taken place in four stages: in 1973 (when Denmark, Ireland and the United Kingdom joined), in 1981 (when Greece joined), in 1986 (when Portugal and Spain joined), and in 1995 (when Austria, Finland and Sweden joined).

All four enlargements have inevitably affected and changed the Union in important ways. First, and most obviously, the Union has, simply by becoming bigger, become a more important international organisation. It now contains a population of about 370 million; its membership includes all the larger, and traditionally more influential, West European states; and it is the world's principal commercial power, accounting for around one fifth of world imports and exports (not counting commerce between the member states themselves).

Second, the EU's institutions have grown in size to accommodate representatives of acceding states, and internal decision-making has become more complex because of the wider range of national and political interests that have to be satisfied. Given the inevitably increased difficulty of obtaining unanimity in the expanded Council, enlargement has been an important driving factor behind the increases in qmv that have been provided for in the rounds of treaty reform since the SEA.

Third, the Franco-German axis, though still doing much to set the pace of the integration process, is not quite as dominant as it was when there were only six member states. More generally, as the number of smaller states has increased, it has not been as easy for the larger states to push through their preferences.

Fourth, policy debates, concerns and priorities have been affected by new members bringing with them their own requirements, preferences and problems – the nature of which were outlined in Chapter 2. For example, the growing influence, as a result of the second and third enlargements, of southern, less industrialised and poorer countries quickly produced pressure both for a reorientation of the Common Agricultural Policy (CAP) away from northern temperate products towards Mediterranean products, and for redistributive policies that directly assist economic development in the south. (The North–South divide does not, of course, coincide completely with industrial–non-industrial or rich–poor divides: much of northern Spain is industrialised, most of Ireland is not; most of the UK outside southern England is relatively poor, much of northern Italy is relatively rich.) In a similar fashion, the 1995 enlargement to the EFTAns has played a part in increasing the attention that is now being given by the EU to such matters as openness and accountability in decision-making and efficiency and sound financial management in decision implementation.

A further enlargement round was virtually under way even before the EFTAn round was completed. This round involves Central and East European countries (CEECs), plus Cyprus (on the Cypriot application see Chapter 2).

On gaining independence following the collapse of communism, most CEECs were soon openly expressing the hope that, as they established liberal democratic and market-based systems and as East–West relations were transformed, the way would be eased for their accession to the EU. The EU was initially reluctant to encourage these hopes and preferred to focus on assisting the CEECs to adjust to their new situation, whilst thinking of accession as very much a long-term prospect. However, in the mid 1990s the EU's position began to shift, not least because between March 1994, when Hungary applied, and January 1996, when the Czech Republic applied, ten CEECs formally applied for EU membership. The European Council requested the Commission to produce opinions on the applications and these were issued in June 1997. The Commission recommended that negotiations should be opened with five of the ten CEECs (Hungary, Poland, the Czech Republic, Estonia and Slovenia), but should be delayed with the other five (Bulgaria, Romania, Slovakia, Latvia and Lithuania) until their economic (and in the case of Slovakia, political) transitions were further advanced. The European Council accepted the Commission's recommendations at its December 1997 Luxembourg meeting and the negotiations duly began in March 1998. It is quite possible that the five applicant countries in these negotiations, plus conceivably one or two other CEECs if they can catch up economically, and Cyprus will join the EU somewhere around 2005.

Development of policy processes

The Founding Treaties indicated a pattern of policy-making and decision-making in which the Commission would propose, the Parliament would advise, the Council would decide, and – when law was made – the Court of Justice would interpret. In important respects this is indeed how relationships and processes have generally worked in practice. But there have also been many additions and amendments to the projected pattern. The nature of these additions and amendments is examined in some detail in later chapters, but four are particularly worth noting at this stage.

First, the relationships between the four institutions themselves have altered in a number of ways. As integration has evolved, all of the institutions have extended their interests and simultaneously become increasingly less compartmentalised and less self-contained within the EU system. This has led not only to a certain blurring of responsibilities as the dividing lines between who does what have become less clear, but also to changes in the power balance and indeed to a more general sharing of powers. So, for example, the Council of Ministers has usurped some of the Commission's proposing responsibilities by becoming progressively more involved in helping to initiate and set the policy agenda; the Court has significantly affected the direction and pace of the integration process by issuing many judgements with considerable policy and institutional implications; and the EP, greatly assisted by treaty changes, has increasingly extended its legislative influence.

Second, an increasing range of participants not associated with the four main institutions have become involved in policy-making and decision-making. The most important of these participants are the Heads of Government who, in regular summits – known as European Council meetings – have come to assume key agenda-setting responsibilities that have had the effect of reducing the power and manoeuvrability of both the Council of Ministers and the Commission. Prominent amongst other actors who have inserted or attempted to insert themselves into decision-making processes are the many national and transnational sectoral interests and pressures that have come to cluster around the main institutions in order to monitor developments and, when possible, to advise or pressurise decision-makers.

Third, policy processes have become more varied and complex over the years as they have come to function in many different ways at many different levels. In addition to what occurs in the structured settings of Council and Commission meetings, Parliamentary plenaries and committees, and Court sittings, there is a mosaic of less formal channels in which representatives of the institutions, the states, and interests, meet and interact to discuss and produce policies and decisions. Which processes and channels operate in particular cases, and what types of interactions occur therein, varies considerably from sector to sector, and can even do so from decision to decision.

Fourth, policy processes have become, in some respects at least, more efficient and democratic. They have become more efficient insofar as treaty reforms have made it possible for an increasing number of Council decisions to be taken by qualified majority vote rather than requiring unanimity. Decision-making has thus been less hampered by having to wait for the slowest. Policy processes have become more democratic insofar as the EP – the only EU institution to be directly elected – has become more influential in decision-making. This is especially the case with legislative decision-making – the Maastricht Treaty having given the EP co-decision-making powers with the Council for some legislative proposals and the Amsterdam Treaty having extended the scope of co-decision to most legislative proposals.

Development of policies

Along with its institutional structure and its policy and decision-making processes, the EU is most distinguished from other international organisations by the range and weight of its policy responsibilities and commitments. These have expanded steadily over the years, stimulated and encouraged by factors such as the provisions laid down in the treaties, the increasing internationalisation and competitiveness of economic forces, a growing recognition of the benefits of working together, integrationist pressures emanating from central institutions (notably the Commission and the EP), and the stimulus that policy development in one sphere often gives to developments in others.

The policies that lie closest to the heart of the EU's policy framework are those related to what used to be called 'the Common Market' and which is now known as 'the internal market' or 'the Single European Market' (SEM). In essence, these policies are designed to promote the free movement of goods, services, capital and people between the member states, and to enable the EU to act jointly and present a common front in its economic and trading relations with third countries. Since the mid 1980s – when the creation of the SEM was given priority via the '1992 programme' and the SEA – there has been considerable development of these market-based policies. This has resulted in a great increase in the range and extent of the EU's regulatory presence, which is somewhat ironic since a key aim of the SEM programme has been to liberalise and deregulate the functioning of the market. It is, however, generally recognised and conceded (by some more readily than by others) that the market can operate on a truly fair and open basis only if key features of it are properly managed and controlled from the centre.

The EU has thus developed many policies with direct implications for the operation of the market. For example EU decision-makers have been, and still are, much concerned with the following regulatory activities: the establishment of essential conditions for product standards and for their testing and certification (the details are usually worked out later by European standards organisations); the opening up of national monopolies and public procurement to competition; the laying down of criteria that companies must satisfy if they wish to trade in the EU market (this has been especially important in the sphere of financial services); and controlling the circumstances in which governments can or cannot subsidise domestic industries.

In addition to these 'pure' market policies, several policy areas in the social sphere that have market implications have also become increasingly subject to EU regulatory control. This has usually been a consequence of some mix of genuine social concern and recognition that divergences of national approaches and standards create – whatever their intended purpose – trade barriers. Examples of policy areas that have become subject to such social regulation are the environment, consumer protection, and working conditions.

The SEM momentum has had other policy consequences too. For example, it has greatly boosted many EU sectoral policies, with transport, telecommunications and energy amongst the policy spheres that have been the subject of considerable attention in recent years. Most importantly of all, the SEM has stimulated the movement towards Economic and Monetary Union (EMU). Having long been identified as a Community goal, real progress towards EMU only began in the late 1980s when most of the member states – strongly encouraged by the President of the Commission, Jacques Delors – came to the view that harmonised macro-economic and financial policies and a single currency were necessary if the SEM was to realise its full potential. Accordingly, a strategy for creating a single currency-based EMU gradually developed. This was put into specific form – with the laying down of procedures and a timetable – in the Maastricht Treaty.

Central to the Maastricht provisions on EMU were conditions – called convergence criteria – that countries would have to meet if they were to become members of the single currency system. The qualifying conditions – low rates of inflation, low interest rates, the avoidance of excessive budgetary and national debt deficits, and currency stability – were designed to ensure that the single currency zone would be based on sound economic and monetary foundations. The conditions were subsequently used as a basis for the development of a Stability Pact, later called the Stability and Growth Pact, which is intended to act as a framework for national economic and monetary policies within the single currency zone, and in so doing to ensure that the stability of the zone is not threatened by national imbalances or 'irresponsible' national policies.

The Maastricht Treaty offered the possibility of the single currency being launched in 1997, but that proved impossible and it eventually came into operation on 1 January 1999, with eleven of the EU fifteen member states participating. Denmark, Sweden and the UK chose not to join. Greece – alone among the member states – could not meet the convergence criteria. The rates of currency exchange between the eleven participating states are thus now irrevocably fixed, and central control – via the European System of Central Banks – has been assumed over interest rate and external exchange rate policies. National banknotes and coins are scheduled to be phased out in the first half of 2002, when they will be replaced by the new European currency – the euro.

A striking feature of the EU's policy portfolio has always been its limited involvement with those policy areas which account for the bulk of public expenditure – such as social welfare, education, health, and defence. The main exception to this lack of involvement with heavy expenditure policy areas has been agriculture, where the Common Agricultural Policy (CAP) has imposed heavy burdens on the EU's annual budget. Since the early 1980s a series of measures have been adopted that have had the effect of bringing at least some aspects of the CAP's problems – including heavy overproduction – under control, but agriculture still accounts for almost half of EU expenditure.

Paralleling the attempts to bring the CAP under control has been increased attention to other policy areas that also impose budgetary demands. Regional and social policies have received particular attention, especially via the development and growth of the EU's two main Structural Funds – the European Regional Development Fund (ERDF) and the European Social Fund (ESF). However, even with the growth of these two areas, and with more funding being channelled to the likes of research policy and energy policy, the EU budget still only accounts for just over one per cent of total EU Gross Domestic Product and less than three per cent of total EU public expenditure.

It might have been thought that the budget would have to increase significantly to accommodate the anticipated accession of the CEECs to the EU in the early 2000s. After all, they are relatively poor countries with large agricultural sectors. However, the Commission, in its 1997 document *Agenda 2000* (Commission, 1997a), indicated that such an increase was not necessary. Rather, it advised the European Council that the CEECs could be accommodated within the existing overall size of the budget – but as a result the CAP and the Structural Funds would have to be reformed. With some modifications, the Commission's *Agenda 2000* budgetary and policy recommendations were accepted by the leaders of the governments of the member states at the March 1999 Berlin summit.

Beyond economic and economic-related policies, over the years the EU has also moved into other policy areas. The most significant examples of this – significant in that they involve highly sensitive policy areas that are far removed from the original EEC policy focus on the construction a common market – are the Common Foreign and Security Policy (CFSP) and the Justice and Home Affairs (JHA) policies. Developments in these areas are still very much in the formative stage, but they have advanced sufficiently to merit explicit treaty recognition: the growing role of foreign policy was acknowledged and given a legal base by the SEA, whilst foreign policy and justice and home affairs policy were important components of, and were strengthened by, the Maastricht and Amsterdam Treaties.

In addition to the development of the CFSP and JHA policies, non-economic ventures that illustrate the extent of the EU's policy net include the involvement – though not usually on mainstream policy matters – in various, educational, health, and cultural programmes.

So extensive and diverse has policy development been since the Community was established that there are now initiatives and developments in virtually every sphere of public policy. No other combination of states has arrangements even remotely like those which apply in the EU, where cooperation and integration are consciously practised across such a wide range of policy sectors, and where so many policy-making and policy-implementation responsibilities have been transferred from individual states to collective institutions.

The nature of the EU's policy interests and responsibilities are examined at length in Part 3.

Concluding remarks

The EU is still recognisably based on the three European Communities that were founded in the 1950s. The most obvious ways in which it is so are in its institutional structure and in the continuance of the common market/internal market as the 'core' of policy activity.

However in many fundamental ways European integration has clearly advanced considerably since it was given its initial organisational expression by the Founding Treaties. This advancement has taken two broad forms. First, there has been a widening, with the EU now embracing virtually the whole of Western Europe and poised to embrace at least some countries in Central and Eastern Europe. Second, there has been a deepening, with the development of institutional and policy integration in numerous and far reaching respects.

As was made clear in the first section of this chapter, an important way in which the integration process has been advanced has been by treaty reform. With this in mind, the next chapter focuses on the most important treaty reforms of recent years.

The internal factors were mostly associated with the stimulus to further integration provided by the 'relaunching' of the Community in the mid 1980s. This relaunching, which was embodied in the Single European Market (SEM) programme and in the SEA, contained its own integrationist logic in that it gave greater urgency to some long-standing but unresolved issues facing the Community and it also served to bring new issues onto the Community's agenda. Four factors were of particular importance in this respect. First, many member states increasingly came to the view that the full benefits of the SEM would only be realised if action was taken to bring about Economic and Monetary Union (EMU). More particularly, a single currency was increasingly seen as being necessary to eliminate the distortions to trade occasioned by changes in the value of currencies. This would provide more stable conditions for business planning and remove the cost of currency conversion. Second, there was growing acceptance of the need for a 'social equity dimension' that would soften and offset some of the liberal market/deregulatory implications of the SEM. In addition to the social equity arguments for a social dimension, member states with high levels of social provision were anxious that there should not be 'social dumping' in the form of businesses being attracted to countries where the level of social provision was low and where, in consequence, business overheads were also likely to be low. Third, the dismantling of border controls in the internal market created pressure for new and greatly improved mechanisms at Community level to deal with such problems as cross-border crime, drug trafficking, international terrorism, and the movement of peoples (the latter including growing concern about the 'threat' of mass migration from Eastern Europe and North Africa to Western Europe). Fourth, the long-standing problem of a 'democratic deficit', which had not been properly addressed in the SEA, was increasingly seen as needing attention as the Community exercised ever more power over a broad range of policy areas but in a political context where its decision-makers were not democratically accountable.

The external factors arose largely from the break-up of the communist bloc and the Soviet Union. There were four main aspects to this. First, the collapse of communism in Central and Eastern Europe from the autumn of 1989, and the emergence in its place of would-be liberal democratic states with market-based economies, produced the likelihood that the Community would increasingly be dealing not just with West European but with Europe-wide issues and problems. In such circumstances – and with the EFTA countries also contributing to the emergence of a wider Europe via the projected EEA and the prospect of EC membership applications – it seemed to many that the Community should consolidate and strengthen itself so as to be better able to meet the challenges of the rapidly transforming Europe. Second, the unification of Germany, which formally took place in October 1990, increased the potential for German domination of the Community and led many to conclude that it was necessary to advance the integration process in order to ensure the consolidation of a European Germany rather than a German Europe. Greater integration would also, it was argued, ensure that the new Germany would not be tempted to start detaching itself from aspects of Community affairs in order to take advantage of the new opportunities to its east. Third, the break-up of the Soviet Union in 1991 added to the sense of uncertainty about the future nature and stability of the European continent. More broadly, it also raised questions about the shape and direction of the international system. In this situation, the existing pressure to strengthen the Community's policy and institutional capacities was inevitably heightened. Fourth, the ending of the Cold War had to be addressed since it heralded the disappearance of the framework that had provided much of the rationale, focus and setting for the foreign and defence policies of most West European countries for over forty years. Questions now inevitably arose about the suitability of existing arrangements in the post-Cold War era. Was it not time for the Community to develop and strengthen its foreign and security policy roles and mechanisms? The belief of many that this was so was reinforced by what was seen as the inadequate Community response to the 1990–1 Gulf crisis and war: during the conflict the twelve member states were able to act in a reasonably united way at the declaratory level, but they could not agree on all aspects of policy action and they adopted very different positions with regard to contributing personnel to the Task Force for Operation Desert Storm.

From the mid 1980s several factors thus combined to build up a head of steam for another round of Community deepening: that is, for further integration between the member states. There were, of course, those who sought to resist the rising pressures – notably the UK government, which had little desire to go much beyond a common market with various forms of intergovernmental cooperation tacked on – but most of the Community's key decision-making elites accepted the need for further integration. Their motives varied considerably: for some, long-held adherences to the federalist cause were a source of inspiration; for many, there was a fear that if deepening was not pursued the Community could be seriously threatened by dilution when the anticipated widening of the Community in the form of accession by EFTA states took place in the mid 1990s; and for virtually all, there was a perceived need to press ahead with, and enhance the Community's competence and authority with regard to, at least some of the issues and matters that had become problematical since the mid 1980s – EMU, the social dimension, foreign and security policy, and the efficiency and accountability of the Community's institutions. As the 1980s gave way to the 1990s there was therefore a widely held belief in most Community circles that further fundamental reforms were necessary.

The making of the Treaty

There were three main stages involved in the making of the Maastricht Treaty: the convening of Intergovernmental Conferences (IGCs), the work of the IGCs and the Maastricht summit, and the ratification of the Treaty.

The convening of Intergovernmental Conferences

At a series of European Council meetings between 1988 and 1990 steps were taken that led to the convening of IGCs on Political Union and on Economic and Monetary Union:

(1) At the June 1988 Hanover summit it was recalled that the SEA had confirmed the objective of progressive realisation of EMU, and it was decided to entrust to a committee chaired by the President of the Commission, Jacques Delors, the task of studying and proposing concrete stages that could lead to EMU.

(2) At the June 1989 Madrid summit it was agreed that the 'Delors Report' (which had been presented in April 1989) represented a basis for further work, that stage one of EMU would begin on 1 July 1990, and that an IGC would be needed to lay down developments beyond stage one.

(3) At the December 1989 Strasbourg summit it was formally agreed – against the wishes of the UK government – to convene an IGC on EMU.

(4) At the special April 1990 Dublin summit (Dublin I), which had initially been called to discuss German unification, the national leaders responded to a Franco-German initiative to broaden the impending IGC on EMU. The European Council 'confirmed its commitment to Political Union' and instructed the Foreign Ministers to carry out a quick and objective study of the possible need for treaty changes with a view to convening an IGC on the matter.

(5) At the June 1990 Dublin summit (Dublin II) it was agreed that IGCs on Political Union and EMU would commence in December at the Rome summit.

(6) At the special October 1990 Rome summit (Rome I) the preparatory work undertaken by officials on EMU was accepted and a framework was set up for the IGC on EMU.

(7) At the December 1990 Rome summit (Rome II) a broad remit was given to the IGC on Political Union and the ceremonial opening of both IGCs was conducted.

At the procedural level the convening of the IGCs was thus very much the result of an incremental process. The need to make specific arrangements for EMU was increasingly accepted, as was the need for a parallel examination of Political Union.

The Intergovernmental Conferences and the Maastricht summit

The IGCs met throughout 1991. They each operated at three levels. At the most senior level were national ministers – Foreign Ministers in the IGC on Political Union and Finance Ministers in the IGC on EMU. Both sets of ministers met once a month for most of the year. At the second level were very senior national officials – in the IGC on Political Union these were usually the Permanent Representatives to the Community (see Chapter 7), whilst in the IGC on EMU they were drawn from Ministries of Finance and Central Banks. The officials in the IGC on Political Union usually met weekly and those in the IGC on EMU met bi-monthly. The third level consisted of working parties of national experts which were established and convened as and when they were deemed to be necessary. Coordination of the work of the two IGCs was the responsibility of the Foreign Ministers.

As their title makes clear, the Conferences were intergovernmental in character, so the two main non-governmental Community institutions – the Commission and the EP – were always likely to have to struggle to exert an influence. The Commission was, in fact, a participant in the discussions at all levels and did its utmost – not least via the submission of numerous position papers – to influence outcomes. However, because it did not enjoy the same negotiating status as the member states, and was certainly in no position to attempt to veto agreements, its negotiating hand was weak. Partly because of this, and partly because it adopted an advanced integrationist position on many issues, the eventual outcome of the IGCs, especially that on Political Union, was a disappointment to the Commission.

The EP was even more disadvantaged than the Commission in that it did not participate in the discussions, though it was given some opportunities to make an input: there were monthly inter-institutional conferences between ministers and a delegation of twelve MEPs (alternating between the two IGCs); the President of the EP was invited to address the opening of ministerial-level meetings; the chairmen of the IGCs attended relevant EP debates and appeared, once during each Council Presidency, before the appropriate EP committee; and the Presidents of the Council, the Commission and the EP met from time to time. On these and other occasions the EP did what it could to promote a significant integrationist advance. The

EP also sought to take advantage of resolutions adopted by the Italian and Belgian parliaments which stated that they would only ratify the Treaty if the EP (which had no formal veto powers) gave its approval. Despite its best efforts, however, the IGC negotiators did not concern themselves too much with the EP's views – not least because it was known that in the last analysis MEPs would be extremely unlikely to reject reforms which advanced the cause of integration, even if they did not advance it as much as the EP wanted. In consequence, the EP – rather like the Commission, and for much the same reasons – was disappointed with the eventual outcome.

As to the positions adopted by the key participants in the IGCs – the representatives of the member states – certain generalisations can be made: the Netherlands, Luxembourg, Belgium and Italy were the most consistent in taking a highly integrationist – federalist, some would call it – outlook; Spain, Ireland, Portugal, Greece and, to a lesser extent, Denmark were willing to support significant integrationist advances but had reservations on a number of specific issues; Spain, Ireland, Portugal and Greece also made it clear that – as the least prosperous member states of the Community – they wished to see a considerable strengthening of policies dealing with economic and social cohesion included in any final agreement; France was very supportive of EMU but tended towards an intergovernmental stance in the Political Union IGC – by arguing, for example, for a stronger European Council and only very limited increases in the powers of the EP; Germany, by contrast with France, was a firm advocate of further political integration, and especially of greater powers for the EP, but was very cautious on EMU; finally, the United Kingdom adopted a minimalist position on virtually all proposals which implied integration with supranational implications.

But generalisations tell only part of the story, for on particular subjects in the IGCs there was often a complex mosaic of views, reflecting different national interests. This can be illustrated by the reactions to a proposal put forward by the Dutch Presidency in early November to apply the proposed co-decision-making procedure (which would greatly enhance the powers of the EP) to a wide span of Community policies: Spain and Portugal opposed the application of the procedure to the research framework programme and to the environment; Luxembourg, with some support from the Commission, opposed its application to internal market harmonisation; France and Spain opposed its application to the objectives of the Community's Structural Funds, and France also opposed its application to development cooperation programmes; and the United Kingdom opposed its application to anything.

Despite all these differences, however, progress was gradually made and, as scheduled, both IGCs presented their reports at the December 1991 meeting of the European Council in Maastricht. The IGC on EMU was able to reach agreement on virtually all issues within its remit and to present clear recommendations on treaty reform to the summit. The IGC on Political Union – which had had to deal with a much wider range of institutional and policy issues – was not so successful, in that a number of particularly contentious matters had to be referred to the summit for final resolution.

At the Maastricht meeting the matters that had proved impossible to resolve during the IGCs were tackled. The most difficult of these were the UK's opposition to any significant extension of the Community's social dimension and its desire not to participate in the projected single currency. After extremely difficult, tense and exhausting negotiations all the outstanding issues were resolved. Concessions were made on all sides and a new treaty – the Treaty on European Union – was agreed.

After careful examination by a working party of legal and linguistic experts, the TEU was formally signed by Foreign and Finance Ministers in Maastricht in February 1992.

Ratification of the Treaty

In accordance with established procedures for Community treaties and treaty amendments, Article R of the TEU stated that ratification by the member states should be 'in accordance with their respective constitutional requirements'. In ten of the member states this meant that ratification would be by parliamentary approval only, whilst in the other two – Ireland and Denmark – it also meant the holding of national referendums.

It was hoped that all ratifications could proceed relatively smoothly and quickly so as to enable the Treaty to enter into force on 1 January 1993. In eight member states – including Ireland – these hopes were realised, but in four they were not:

- In Denmark, in June 1992 the Danish people voted, by 50.7 per cent to 49.3 per cent, against ratification. Naturally this threw the ratification schedule off course, but more importantly it also had considerable implications for the interpretation of the Treaty because it was subsequently decided at European Council meetings that a twin-track approach would be needed to persuade the Danes to give their approval in a second referendum. At the general level, integrationist rhetoric would be toned down and the decentralising subsidiarity principle, which was only briefly referred to in the Treaty, would be given greater precision and a greatly enhanced status. At the level of dealing with specific Danish concerns, Denmark would be given special guarantees, notably in the form of clear opt-outs from the Treaty provisions for a single currency and for a possible future EU defence policy. These 'concessions' to the Danes produced approval of the Treaty, by 56.8 per cent to 43.2 per cent, when the second referendum was held in May 1993.

- Shortly after the Danish vote was announced, President Mitterrand decided that France too would hold a referendum on the Treaty. The main reason for his decision was that he anticipated that the Treaty would be comfortably endorsed and that this would serve to boost his domestic authority. In the event, however, the referendum campaign was bitterly and closely fought, but ratification just squeezed through in September 1992 by 51.05 per cent to 48.95 per cent.
- In the United Kingdom, a combination of several factors – notably the government's narrow majority in the House of Commons, considerable Parliamentary scepticism on the claimed beneficial consequences of the Treaty, and opposition by the Labour Party to the opt-out which had been granted to the UK from the Treaty's Social Chapter – combined to create a protracted ratification process in Parliament which was not completed until July 1993.
- Problems in Germany arose not from the people (there was no referendum) nor from the politicians (both the Bundestag and the Bundesrat ratified the Treaty with huge majorities in December 1992), but rather from claims that ratification would infringe the country's constitution. It was not until October 1993 that the German Constitutional Court ruled that there was no infringement, though it laid down conditions that would have to be met if there were to be significant changes or additions to the Treaty in the future.

German ratification cleared the way for the implementation of the Treaty, which took effect on 1 November 1993 – ten months later than originally planned.

The contents of the Treaty

The Maastricht Treaty created a new organisation, the European Union, which was to be based on three pillars: the European Communities; a Common Foreign and Security Policy (CFSP); and Cooperation in the Fields of Justice and Home Affairs (JHA). The general objectives and overall structure of the EU were set out in Common Provisions (Document 5.1 reproduces these Common Provisions, as amended by the Amsterdam Treaty).

Document 5.1 Common Provisions of the Consolidated Version of the Treaty on European Union

TITLE I

COMMON PROVISIONS

Article 1 (ex Article A)

By this Treaty, the HIGH CONTRACTING PARTIES establish among themselves a EUROPEAN UNION, hereinafter called 'the Union'.

This Treaty marks a new stage in the process of creating an ever closer union among the peoples of Europe, in which decisions are taken as openly as possible and as closely as possible to the citizen.

The Union shall be founded on the European Communities, supplemented by the policies and forms of cooperation established by this Treaty. Its task shall be to organise, in a manner demonstrating consistency and solidarity, relations between the Member States and between their peoples.

Article 2 (ex Article B)

The Union shall set itself the following objectives:

– to promote economic and social progress and a high level of employment and to achieve balanced and sustainable development, in particular through the creation of an area without internal frontiers, through the strengthening of economic and social cohesion and through the establishment of economic and monetary union, ultimately including a single currency in accordance with the provisions of this Treaty;

– to assert its identity on the international scene, in particular through the implementation of a common foreign and security policy including the progressive framing of a common defence policy, which might lead to a common defence, in accordance with the provisions of Article 17;

– to strengthen the protection of the rights and interests of the nationals of its Member States through the introduction of a citizenship of the Union;

– to maintain and develop the Union as an area of freedom, security and justice, in which the free movement of persons is assured in conjunction with appropriate measures with respect to external border controls, asylum, immigration and the prevention and combating of crime;

– to maintain in full the acquis communautaire and build on it with a view to considering to what extent the policies and forms of cooperation introduced by this Treaty may need to be revised with the aim of ensuring the effectiveness of the mechanisms and the institutions of the Community.

→

Document 5.1 continued

The objectives of the Union shall be achieved as provided in this Treaty and in accordance with the conditions and the timetable set out therein while respecting the principle of subsidiarity as defined in Article 5 of the Treaty establishing the European Community.

Article 3 (ex Article C)

The Union shall be served by a single institutional framework which shall ensure the consistency and the continuity of the activities carried out in order to attain its objectives while respecting and building upon the acquis communautaire.

The Union shall in particular ensure the consistency of its external activities as a whole in the context of its external relations, security, economic and development policies. The Council and the Commission shall be responsible for ensuring such consistency and shall cooperate to this end. They shall ensure the implementation of these policies, each in accordance with its respective powers.

Article 4 (ex Article D)

The European Council shall provide the Union with the necessary impetus for its development and shall define the general political guidelines thereof.

The European Council shall bring together the Heads of State or Government of the Member States and the President of the Commission. They shall be assisted by the Ministers for Foreign Affairs of the Member States and by a Member of the Commission. The European Council shall meet at least twice a year, under the chairmanship of the Head of State or Government of the Member State which holds the Presidency of the Council.

The European Council shall submit to the European Parliament a report after each of its meetings and a yearly written report on the progress achieved by the Union.

Article 5 (ex Article E)

The European Parliament, the Council, the Commission, the Court of Justice and the Court of Auditors shall exercise their powers under the conditions and for the purposes provided for, on the one hand, by the provisions of the Treaties establishing the European Communities and of the subsequent Treaties and Acts modifying and supplementing them and, on the other hand, by the other provisions of this Treaty.

Article 6 (ex Article F)

1. The Union is founded on the principles of liberty, democracy, respect for human rights and fundamental freedoms, and the rule of law, principles which are common to the Member States.

→

2. The Union shall respect fundamental rights, as guaranteed by the European Convention for the Protection of Human Rights and Fundamental Freedoms signed in Rome on 4 November 1950 and as they result from the constitutional traditions common to the Member States, as general principles of Community law.

3. The Union shall respect the national identities of its Member States.

4. The Union shall provide itself with the means necessary to attain its objectives and carry through its policies.

Article 7 (ex Article F.1)

1. The Council, meeting in the composition of the Heads of State or Government and acting by unanimity on a proposal by one third of the Member States or by the Commission and after obtaining the assent of the European Parliament, may determine the existence of a serious and persistent breach by a Member State of principles mentioned in Article 6(1), after inviting the government of the Member State in question to submit its observations.

2. Where such a determination has been made, the Council, acting by a qualified majority, may decide to suspend certain of the rights deriving from the application of this Treaty to the Member State in question, including the voting rights of the representative of the government of that Member State in the Council. In doing so, the Council shall take into account the possible consequences of such a suspension on the rights and obligations of natural and legal persons.

The obligations of the Member State in question under this Treaty shall in any case continue to be binding on that State.

3. The Council, acting by a qualified majority, may decide subsequently to vary or revoke measures taken under paragraph 2 in response to changes in the situation which led to their being imposed.

4. For the purposes of this Article, the Council shall act without taking into account the vote of the representative of the government of the Member State in question. Abstentions by members present in person or represented shall not prevent the adoption of decisions referred to in paragraph 1. A qualified majority shall be defined as the same proportion of the weighted votes of the members of the Council concerned as laid down in Article 205(2) of the Treaty establishing the European Community.

This paragraph shall also apply in the event of voting rights being suspended pursuant to paragraph 2.

5. For the purposes of this Article, the European Parliament shall act by a two-thirds majority of the votes cast, representing a majority of its members.

Much time and effort was expended in the IGC on Political Union haggling over how the Treaty should describe the European Union, both in terms of its current character and the stage of its evolutionary progress. Most states wanted the word 'federal' included, and would have settled for a phrase which appeared in drafts where the Treaty was described as marking 'a new stage in the process leading gradually to a Union with a federal goal'. The UK government, however, was unwilling to see 'the F word' appear in any form at all and in the political trading which occurred at the Maastricht summit this point was conceded to the UK and the reference to federalism was replaced by 'This Treaty marks a new stage in the process of creating an ever closer union among the peoples of Europe, in which decisions are taken as closely as possible to the citizen'. To most Continental Europeans the phrase 'ever closer union' sounded more centralist than the word 'federal', but the UK delegation was satisfied.

As can be seen from Document 5.1 (which, apart from Article 7, was little changed by the Amsterdam Treaty), the EU was assigned a range of objectives, would be based on a set of guiding principles (including subsidiarity and respect for democracy and human rights), and would be governed by an institutional structure presided over by the European Council.

Most of the provisions of the Treaty were concerned with the three pillars, which in the case of pillar one meant amending the Treaties of the three European Communities, and in the cases of pillars two and three meant laying down guiding principles and operating rules.

Pillar one: the European Communities

This was by far the most important pillar since it incorporated most of the EU's policy responsibilities. Under the Treaty, the *acquis* of the existing three Communities was preserved and in several important respects was extended and strengthened by revisions of the EEC, ECSC and Euratom Treaties. The revisions of the EEC Treaty were naturally the most significant and it is upon these that attention will focus here.

Article 1 of the revised EEC Treaty stated the following: 'By this Treaty, the High Contracting Parties establish among themselves a European Community'. This meant that the European Economic Community – the EEC – was renamed the European Community. A rather confusing situation was thereby produced, in which the European Community became part of the European Communities, which in turn became part of the European Union.

Two important new principles were introduced into what now became the Treaty Establishing the European Community (TEC). First, the much discussed principle of subsidiarity was formally incorporated by a new Article 3b (Article 5 in the post-Amsterdam Consolidated Treaty):

> The Community shall act within the limits of the powers conferred upon it by this Treaty and of the objectives assigned to it therein.
>
> In areas which do not fall within its exclusive competence, the Community shall take action, in accordance with the principle of subsidiarity, only if and in so far as the objectives of the proposed action cannot be sufficiently achieved by the Member States and can therefore, by reason of the scale or effects of the proposed action, be better achieved by the Community.
>
> Any action by the Community shall not go beyond what is necessary to achieve the objectives of this Treaty.

Clearly Article 3b was very vague and much remained to be worked out in practice. In general, what has happened is that subsidiarity has been taken to mean that policies should be decided at the national level, and perhaps even at regional or local levels, whenever possible. Since the Treaty was negotiated, European Council meetings have developed guidelines designed to assist with the application of the subsidiarity principle.

Second, the TEC established Union citizenship, with every national of a member state becoming a citizen of the Union. Though symbolically significant, the practical effect of this was limited since citizens of the Union would only 'enjoy the rights conferred by this Treaty'. One of these rights was the right to live and work anywhere in the territory of the member states, subject to certain limitations. Union citizens were also given the right to vote and stand as candidates in EP and local elections, again subject to certain limitations.

Because the principles of subsidiarity and Union citizenship were incorporated into the TEC, and not just confined to the Common Provisions of the TEU, they were subject to the jurisdiction of the Court of Justice.

Other revisions made by the Maastricht Treaty to the TEC can be grouped under two broad headings.

(1) Institutional changes. The revisions falling under this heading were mostly designed to improve the efficiency and democratic nature of the Community's institutional structures and decision-making processes. Overall, the greatest impact was on the Council of Ministers, which was empowered to take a greater range of decisions on the basis of qualified majority voting, and on the EP, which was given increased powers and

influence in several areas – notably in terms of legislation. The following list includes the most significant institutional changes.

- A new legislative procedure – the co-decision procedure – was established. In effect the co-decision procedure extended the cooperation procedure established by the SEA, by allowing – if the Council and the EP could not agree at second reading – for the convening of a conciliation committee and for a third reading of legislation by both the Council and the EP. Unlike the cooperation procedure, however, which enabled a determined Council to ignore the EP's expressed views, the co-decision procedure would allow the EP, for the first time, to veto legislative proposals it did not wish to accept.
- The policy areas subject to the cooperation procedure were revised, with some areas previously covered by the procedure being 'transferred out' to the co-decision procedure, and some new policy areas previously subject to the consultation procedure (which only allows for one reading of legislation) being 'transferred in'.
- The scope of the assent procedure, by which EP approval is necessary for certain EC actions, was extended.
- From January 1995 the term of office of Commissioners was extended from four to five years so as to bring the lifespan of a Commission closely into line with the lifespan of a Parliament. The national governments were to nominate by common accord, after consulting the EP, the person they intended to appoint as the President of the Commission. Other members of the Commission were to be nominated by the national governments in the established manner, but now in consultation with the nominee for Commission President. The entire prospective Commission was to be subject to a vote of approval by the EP before being formally appointed by common accord of the national governments.
- A Committee of the Regions was established to provide the Council and the Commission with advice on matters of major importance for the regions. The Committee was to be of the same size and to have the same distribution of national representatives as the Economic and Social Committee, but its members were to be representatives of regional and local authorities.
- The Court of Justice was given the power to impose fines on member states that failed to comply with its judgements or failed to implement Community law.
- The EP was to appoint an Ombudsman to receive complaints from citizens 'covering instances of maladministration in the activities of the Community institutions or bodies, with the exception of the Court of Justice and the Court of First Instance acting in their judicial role'.

(2) Policy changes. The EC's policy competence was extended and strengthened. It was so in four main ways.

- The main features of Economic and Monetary Union (EMU) were defined and a timetable for establishing it was specified. Regarding the features, EMU was to include the irrevocable fixing of exchange rates leading to the introduction of a single currency and to the establishment of a European Central Bank (ECB) which would operate within the framework of a European System of Central Banks (ESCB). The main objective of the ESCB would be to maintain price stability. In so doing it should support the general economic aims and policies of the EC. The basic tasks to be carried out through the ESCB were to be: to define and implement the monetary policy of the Community; to conduct foreign exchange operations; to hold and manage the official foreign reserves of the member states; and to promote the smooth operation of payment systems. Under EMU, member states were to regard their economic policies as a matter of common concern and were to coordinate them within the Council. Regarding the timetable, EMU was to be established in three stages, with stage three beginning no later than 1 January 1999 for those states which could meet the specified convergence criteria. In a protocol attached to the Treaty it was recognised that the United Kingdom 'shall not be obliged or committed to move to the third stage of Economic and Monetary Union without a separate decision to do so by its government and Parliament'. In another protocol the Danish government reserved the right to hold a national referendum before participating in the third stage of EMU.
- Some policy areas in which the Community had not been previously involved, or in which its involvement had not had an explicit Treaty base, were brought into the TEC for the first time. For example, a new chapter of the Treaty confirmed the Community's commitment to help developing countries and to do so by providing multi-annual programmes. Beyond development policy, most of the other policy areas newly introduced into the TEC were brought in only in a rather tentative manner, in the sense that the Community's responsibilities were carefully restricted. Policy areas thus identified included education, public health, consumer protection, trans-European networks, and competitiveness of industry.
- Community responsibilities in some policy areas that were first given treaty recognition in the SEA were further developed. This applied particularly to research and technological development, the environment, and economic and social cohesion. As part of the strengthening of economic and social cohesion, a new fund – the Cohesion Fund – was

established to provide financial assistance for environmental programmes and trans-European transport infrastructures.

- A policy area that created particular difficulties during the negotiations both before and at Maastricht was social policy. Eleven member states wished to build on and give a firm treaty base to the Social Charter, which had been adopted (by eleven votes to one) by the European Council in 1989, whilst the UK government wished to see no extension to the Community's existing responsibilities in this area – either by way of itemising specific social policies that the Community would develop, or by relaxing unanimity requirements and increasing the circumstances in which decisions could be taken by a qualified majority vote. After almost bringing the Maastricht summit to the point of collapse, the impasse was resolved by the eleven contracting a separate protocol and agreement on social policy.

Pillar two: a Common Foreign and Security Policy

The SEA stated that the member states 'shall endeavour jointly to formulate and implement a European foreign policy'. The TEU greatly stiffened this aim by specifying that the EU and its member states 'shall define and implement a common foreign and security policy . . . covering all areas of foreign and security policy', and by further specifying that the common policy 'shall include all questions related to the security of the Union, including the eventual framing of a common defence policy, which might in time lead to a common defence'.

The objectives of the Common Foreign and Security Policy (CFSP) were defined only in general terms: for example, 'to safeguard the common values, fundamental interests and independence of the Union', and 'to develop and consolidate democracy and the rule of law, and respect for human rights and fundamental freedoms'. More specific definition and elaboration of the principles and general guidelines of the CFSP were to be the responsibility of the European Council.

There were to be three principal ways in which the objectives of the CFSP were to be pursued:

- Systematic cooperation was to be established between the member states on any matter of foreign and security policy that was of general interest. Whenever it deemed it necessary the Council should, on the basis of unanimity, define common positions. Member states should ensure that their national policies conformed to such common positions.
- On the basis of general guidelines from the European Council, the Council could decide that a matter was to be the subject of joint action.

In deciding on joint action, or at any stage during the development of a joint action, the Council could determine that implementation decisions should be taken by qualified majority vote.

- The Western European Union (WEU), which 'is an integral part of the development of the Union', was requested 'to elaborate and implement decisions and actions of the Union which had defence implications. The Council shall, in agreement with the institutions of the WEU, adopt the necessary practical arrangements'. There was no provision for qualified majority voting on issues with defence implications. In a Declaration annexed to the Treaty, the Community members of the WEU stated that the WEU 'will be developed as the defence component of the European Union and as the means to strengthen the European pillar of the Atlantic Alliance'.

This second pillar of the TEU thus put European Political Cooperation (EPC), which had been well established for some time, within the broader framework of a Common Foreign and Security Policy. The pillar was also extremely significant in that it introduced two important new elements into the West European integration process. First, although foreign policy remained essentially intergovernmental in character, it nonetheless became potentially subject to some qualified majority voting, if only for 'second-order' decisions. Second, defence made its first formal appearance on the policy agenda, albeit somewhat tentatively.

Pillar three: Cooperation in the Spheres of Justice and Home Affairs

The member states were to regard the following areas as matters of common interest: asylum policy; rules governing, and controls on, the crossing by persons of the external borders of the member states; immigration policy and residence rights of third-country nationals; combating drug addiction; combating international fraud; judicial cooperation in civil matters; judicial cooperation in criminal matters; customs cooperation; and police cooperation to combat terrorism, drug trafficking and other serious crime through an EU-wide police intelligence office (Europol). Any measures taken in regard to these matters was to be in compliance with the European Convention on Human Rights.

In the nine areas of common interest the Council could: adopt joint positions and promote any suitable form of cooperation, with decisions to be taken by unanimity; adopt joint actions, with the possibility of deciding, by unanimity, that measures implementing joint actions could be adopted by a qualified majority; draw up conventions to be recommended to the member states for adoption in accordance with their respective constitutional requirements, with – unless otherwise provided by the conventions – implementing measures to be adopted within the Council by a majority of two-thirds of the member states.

To facilitate cooperation in the areas of common interest the member states were obliged by the Treaty to establish coordinating mechanisms between the relevant departments of their administrations. At the political level these mechanisms were to be headed by the Council of Ministers (Justice and Home Affairs), and at the administrative level by the Article K.4 Coordinating Committee (the Committee being established under Article K.4 of the Treaty).

As with the CFSP pillar of the TEU, the significance of the Justice and Home Affairs (JHA) pillar lay not only in the substantive content of its provisions but also in the broader contribution it would make to the integration process in Europe. There were, as there were with the CFSP pillar, policy and institutional aspects to this. With regard to the policy aspects, a legal base was given to cooperation in areas of activity that in the past had either been dealt with purely on a national basis or had been the subject of only rather loose and informal cooperation between the member states. Regarding the institutional aspects, whilst intergovernmentalism continued to prevail, a small element of supranationalism appeared with the possibility of qualified majority decisions on certain aspects of policy implementation, and a somewhat larger element appeared in this same policy area with provision in the TEC for a common visa policy and for decisions on visas to be determined by qmv from 1996.

The Treaty of Amsterdam

The making of the Treaty

Article N of the TEU specified that another IGC should be convened in 1996 to examine the operation of the Treaty. This specification was included mainly at the behest of those member states which were dissatisfied at what they saw to be the insufficient integrationist progress of the Maastricht Treaty.

The advance notice given in the TEU of the convening of another IGC in 1996 allowed the Amsterdam Treaty to be considered and prepared over a much longer period than any other treaty in the EC/EU's history.

The Reflection Group

In order to smooth the way for what had the potential to be a very divisive IGC (the differences that had troubled the 1991 IGC had not disappeared), the European Council decided at its June 1994 Corfu meeting to establish a preparatory 'Reflection Group'. The task of the Group would be to clear some of the ground for the IGC by examining and elaborating ideas for Treaty revisions. It was not intended that the Group would engage in negotiations or attempt to make final decisions.

The Reflection Group was composed of 18 members: one representative from each member state (mainly junior ministers from Ministries of Foreign/External Affairs, or very senior diplomats); two representatives from the EP (one Socialist and one Christian Democrat); and one representative from the Commission (the Commissioner with responsibility for the IGC, Marcelino Oreja). The chairman of the Group was the Spanish Secretary of State for European Affairs, Carlos Westendorp.

The Group began its work in June 1995 and issued its report in December 1995 (*Reflection Group's Report*, 1995). The report consisted of two parts: a 10-page overview and a 50-page summary of the main deliberations.

The main thrust of the report was to recommend that the IGC should focus on trying to achieve results in three main areas: making Europe more relevant to its citizens; enabling the EU to work better and prepare for enlargement; and giving the EU greater capacity for external action. However, beyond agreement on these questions and on a few broad principles and specific issues, it was clear that there were deep divisions in the Group on the traditionally difficult topics. The positions taken by the national representatives were not identified, but the report was studded with such phrases as 'one of us believes that', 'one of us is opposed to', and 'a broad majority of members of the Group favours'. Given the already well-known position of most governments on most EU issues, and especially the UK's continuing opposition to further integration, most of these phrases could be interpreted without too much difficulty.

The IGC

The experience of the Reflection Group did not thus augur well for the IGC, which was formally launched at a special Heads of Government meeting in Turin in March 1996.

In line with what had become an established pattern after the 1985 and 1991 IGCs, the IGC worked at three levels: Foreign Ministers met once a month; their representatives – a mixture of junior ministers and senior diplomats – met three times a month; and working groups of national officials and experts met as required. As before, the Commission was present at all of the IGC meetings and could join in the discussions, but it was not a party to decision-making. Unlike in previous IGCs, the EP was allowed a formal involvement, though this fell short of the Commission's position: the President of the EP addressed and had an exchange of views with the Foreign Ministers at their monthly meeting; the EP appointed two representatives to engage in monthly detailed exchanges of view with the ministers' representatives (the same two representatives who represented the EP in the Reflection Group); the two representatives were briefed after each IGC meeting; and the EP was sent copies of all working documents and position papers (Corbett, 1997, p. 38).

The 1991 Political Union IGC negotiations had focused mainly on draft treaty texts produced by the Luxembourg and Dutch Presidencies. This had not been altogether successful, so in the 1996–7 IGC a different approach was taken, with the discussions and negotiations in the first few months focusing mainly on position papers that were submitted by the national governments and the EU institutions. However, as had been expected at the start of the Conference, little progress was made in 1996 or early 1997 on the more controversial questions: should there be extensions to qmv in the Council, should the balance of votes in the Council be weighted more towards the larger member states, should the powers of the EP be extended, and should parts of the CFSP and JHA pillars be transferred to the first pillar and/or be placed on a more supranational basis?

The Irish Presidency produced a 140-page draft for the December 1996 Dublin summit, which though useful in that it marked some progress in relatively uncontroversial areas and identified possibilities for agreement after further work, acknowledged that little attempt had been made to tackle the most difficult issues. Few IGC participants, however, were overly concerned about the modest contents of the Irish text. There were two reasons for this. First, EU negotiations on constitutional/institutional issues – and indeed on most major contested issues – customarily begin slowly and then speed up as deadlines approach. Second, there were strong grounds for believing that the main obstacle to achieving progress – the UK government's opposition to further integration – would be at least partly removed by the likely outcome of the impending UK general election, which had to be held before the scheduled conclusion of the IGC at the June 1997 Amsterdam summit.

The UK obstacle was indeed duly removed when, in the May election, the Conservatives were defeated after 18 years in government and replaced by Labour. Tony Blair, the new Prime Minister, declared that his government would pursue a policy of 'constructive engagement' with the EU, and this was immediately reflected in the closing weeks of the IGC when the UK's approach became much more positive than it had been under the Conservatives. There was not a complete policy about-turn, for the UK's position changed little on some issues – notably the need to retain the UK's external borders and the unwillingness to integrate defence further into the EU system. For the most part, however, the UK's previous 'awkwardness' and isolationism largely disappeared.

The UK's changed stance helped to make the Amsterdam summit, which marked the last stage of the IGC, somewhat smoother than the Maastricht summit. But there were still differences to be resolved at Amsterdam, and not a few tensions in the air. Some of these tensions stemmed from positions taken by the French and German governments.

In France, parliamentary elections shortly before the summit brought a new Socialist government, with Lionel Jospin as Prime Minister. On assuming office the government announced that one of its top priorities was to renegotiate the terms of the previously agreed EMU Stability Pact – that is, the economic and monetary policy guidelines that would apply within the European single currency system. Jospin believed that the terms to which President Chirac and Alain Juppé's right-wing government had agreed were too tight and too exclusively concerned with monetary policy. He was especially anxious for some recognition to be given to the need to boost employment in the EU. Accordingly, intensive negotiations with other EU governments, and especially Germany, began almost immediately after the elections, and when these failed to produce a satisfactory outcome the French government insisted on taking its grievances to the summit. Much of the time at Amsterdam was thus taken up discussing EMU rather than the Treaty. The issue was only resolved when, in a typical summit compromise, the Pact was renamed the Stability and Growth Pact and Germany agreed to references to the promotion of employment being included in the Treaty.

The tensions created by Germany arose from Chancellor Kohl adopting an unexpectedly cautious attitude towards some proposed reforms, and in particular his unwillingness to agree to all the extensions of qmv that other states either wanted or were prepared to accept. This stance marked a decided change from Germany's previously strong pro-integrationist position. The change was explained essentially by domestic political difficulties experienced by Chancellor Kohl and it provides a useful illustration of how domestic factors can intrude into EU decision-making, not just in respect of such matters as agricultural support prices and state aids but also in respect of the very nature of the EU as a political system. The domestic factors that intruded in this case, to make Kohl much less integrationist than ideally he would have liked to have been, were: his authority had been weakened by tensions in his three-party coalition government; doubts were increasingly being expressed in German political debate about the cost of EU membership; Kohl's central policy goal was EMU, and he did not wish to see the opposition that already existed to this in Germany grow because of a belief that his government did not stand up in the EU for German interests; and the Länder (states) were strongly opposed to the national veto being given up in policy areas that domestically were their responsibility.

There were, therefore, differences and tensions at Amsterdam, with the positions adopted by France and Germany being major reasons for this. Overall, however, the summit was not marked by the ill-temper, brinkmanship and threat of breakdown that had characterised the Maastricht summit.

Political agreement on the contents of the Treaty was reached at the end of the summit. The necessary legal and translation work was then undertaken and the Treaty was formally signed in October 1997.

Ratification

At the time of the signing of the Treaty it was generally anticipated that there would be no major difficulties with its ratification. The contents of the Treaty were, after all, more modest than those of the TEU, and the Danish government had taken steps to try to ensure that there would be no repeat of the 1992 referendum defeat – notably by securing an opt-out for Denmark from sensitive aspects of the Treaty dealing with the free movement of persons.

But though ratification was never seriously endangered, it was considerably delayed. The problem this time was not a referendum result: only two referendums were held – in Ireland and Denmark – and the Treaty was approved by a comfortable majority in each country. Rather, the problem was that some of the member states were slow to set the ratification process in motion, and some had to deal with domestic political and legal difficulties before ratification could be effected. In France, for example, the ratification process could not even begin until the constitution had been amended to take account of some of the Treaty's justice and home affairs provisions.

France was the last member state to ratify, in March 1999, and the Treaty eventually came into force in May 1999.

The contents of the Treaty

It was always likely that the Amsterdam Treaty would not be as innovative or as important as either the SEA or the TEU. The intention from the outset was that it would essentially be a revising rather than a pioneering treaty. Moreover, even in respect of revisions, the great issue of internal EU debate in the mid to late 1990s – EMU – was not on the IGC's agenda.

Events in the EU do not, of course, always work out as originally intended or anticipated. But there was no great push in the period immediately before or during the IGC to upgrade the Amsterdam Treaty from a modernising and consolidating exercise into a transforming one. Most national leaders had, after all, adopted a somewhat cautious attitude towards integration since the ratification difficulties with the TEU in 1992 had shown the danger of attempting to press ahead too fast. The assertion by Jacques Santer when he became Commission President in 1995 that the aim must be to 'do less, but do it better', captured much of the post-Maastricht mood. Subsidiarity became, and not just rhetorically, an important guiding light.

Another reason why the Amsterdam Treaty was modest in comparison with the SEA and the TEU was that it had no great *projet* to guide and drive it, in the manner that the SEA had the SEM and the TEU had EMU. There was a major new EU *projet* in hand at the time of the negotiations on the Treaty – preparing for the anticipated accession of Central and Eastern European countries (CEECs) – but although this issue certainly featured prominently in the IGC's deliberations it was not placed centre stage in the Treaty itself. This was partly because many of the more important internal EU changes required to accommodate CEECs do not actually require treaty reform. Rather, they require reform of existing policies – notably of the CAP and of the Structural Funds – and such reforms are effected by political agreements and legislation. The Commission initiated the process of bringing about these reforms when, shortly after the Amsterdam summit, it issued proposals for major policy changes as part of its document *Agenda 2000: For a Stronger and Wider Union* (Commission, 1997a).

The lack of a strong focus in the Treaty on preparing for enlargement was also partly accounted for by an insufficient political will amongst the IGC participants to carry through the reforms that require treaty changes – namely, institutional reforms. There are two dimensions to these necessary institutional reforms. First, some of the EU's institutions – most particularly the College of Commissioners and the EP – cannot keep expanding in size. They are already large enough. The size of the College is especially problematical, since there are not sufficient really important jobs for the present 20 Commissioners. However, all existing and future member states inevitably want their 'own' Commissioner. Second, the arrangements for voting in the Council need overhauling. This is partly because the current provisions for unanimous voting will be a recipe for possible deadlock in an EU of over 20 states, and partly because the past practice of accommodating new members by allocating them a number of votes and realigning proportionally the qualified majority threshold will not be possible at the time of the next enlargement. It will not be possible because the EU's existing large member states have become increasingly concerned that they might be frequently outvoted in a much expanded EU, so they will not accept a realignment of Council voting on the basis of the principles that have sufficed hitherto.

These two dimensions of institutional reform were considered at length in the IGC. Some progress was made in that it was agreed to cap the size of the EP at 700, and modest extensions were made to the potential use of qmv in the first (EC) pillar and considerable extensions were made to its potential use in the second (CFSP) pillar. (The prospect of enlargement was not of course the only reason why qmv provisions were extended.) However, no agreement could be reached on the size of the Commission or on Council voting rules after enlargement, though possible bases for agreement were identified and a schedule and format for returning to the issues were laid down in a protocol 'on the institutions with the prospect of enlargement of the European Union'. The key parts of the protocol are as follows:

Article 1

At the date of entry into force of the first enlargement of the Union the Commission shall comprise one national of each of the Member States, provided that, by that date, the weighting of the votes in the Council has been modified, whether by re-weighting of the votes or by dual majority, in a manner acceptable to all Member States, taking into account all relevant elements, notably compensating those Member States which give up the possibility of nominating a second member of the Commission.

Article 2

At least one year before the membership exceeds twenty, a conference of representatives of the governments of the Member States shall be convened in order to carry out a comprehensive review of the provisions of the Treaties on the composition and functioning of the institutions.

Since, as was shown in Chapter 4, the next enlargement round is likely to take EU membership to beyond 20, these two Articles will probably be telescoped together. This will mean that: another IGC will be convened early in the new century; at that IGC the existing five large member states with two Commissioners will agree to have only one; 'in exchange' for this concession by the large member states, voting rules in the Council will be changed so as to give greater voting strength to these member states – which may be achieved either by re-balancing the national votes or by requiring that majorities must consist not only of a specified number of votes but also of votes representing a specified proportion of the EU population.

The Treaty of Amsterdam thus did not contain a central *projet* and was, essentially, a revising treaty. But modest though the Treaty was as compared with the SEA and the TEU, it nonetheless contained changes that were of considerable significance for the governance of the EU. The most significant of these changes – grouped into the six sections of the Treaty – are outlined below.

Section I: Freedom, Security and Justice

This rather mixed section covered some of the principles and values of the Union, strengthened the bases for the establishment of an area in which there could be free movement of persons 'behind' common entry rules, and developed a framework for police and judicial cooperation in criminal matters. The main contents of the section were as follows:

- The common provisions of the TEU (see Document 5.1) were amended to give greater emphasis to the general principles underlying the Union. 'The Union is founded on the principles of liberty, democracy, respect for human rights and fundamental freedoms, and the rule of law' (Article 6). It was specified that applicant states must respect these principles, and for the first time a procedure was laid down for suspending some of the membership rights of any member state that failed to respect the principles.
- The EU became empowered to 'take appropriate action to combat discrimination based on sex, racial or ethnic origin, religion or belief, disability, age or sexual orientation' (Article 12, TEC). However, the consultation legislative procedure would apply (thus giving the EP only a rather weak role) and unanimity would be required in the Council.
- Under a new title of the TEC – Title IV: Visas, Asylum, Immigration and Other Policies Related to Free Movement of Persons – a number of JHA and JHA-related policy areas were transferred to the EC, and the ways in which and the means by which they should be developed were set out in some detail. The main purpose of this was to facilitate, within a period of five years after the entry into force of the Treaty, the adoption of measures that would result in the progressive establishment of 'an area of freedom, security and justice' (Article 61, TEC), in which

there would be free movement of persons behind a common external border. Policy issues to be covered by the TEC included visas, asylum, immigration, refugees and displaced persons, and judicial cooperation in civil matters. Apart from visas, where the consultation procedure with qmv was to apply for five years and the co-decision procedure thereafter, decision-making in all of these policy areas was to be by the consultation procedure and unanimity in the Council. However, provision was made for the Council to be able to decide after five years to change decision-making in any or all of the areas to co-decision with qmv. The UK insisted that its special island status meant that it could not be party to this free movement of persons title, so in a special protocol it and Ireland – which wanted to maintain its Common Travel Area with the UK – were given opt-outs. Denmark also was not to be fully associated with the title because of its 'special position'.

- Underpinning the free movement of persons title, the Schengen *acquis* was integrated into the EU framework through a protocol annexed to the TEU and the TEC. Based on agreements signed by some member states in 1985 and 1990, the *acquis* consisted of rules and supporting measures dealing with the abolition of checks at internal borders. It would be up to the Council, acting unanimously, to determine where each of the provisions and decisions constituting the *acquis* should be located in the EU framework. By the time of the Amsterdam Treaty, all EU member states apart from Ireland and the UK were Schengen members so, as with the free movement of persons title of the TEC, Ireland and the UK were allowed to opt out from the Schengen Protocol.

- The transfer of so many JHA policy issues to the EC inevitably meant that pillar three of the TEU changed in character. Under its new title, 'Provisions on Police and Judicial Cooperation in Criminal Matters', it now focused on providing citizens 'with a high level of safety within an area of freedom, security and justice by developing common action among the Member States in the fields of police and judicial cooperation in criminal matters and by preventing and combating racism and xenophobia' (Article 29, TEU). The common action specified in Article 29 included a number of possible types, most of which were carried over from the JHA pillar but one of which was new – framework decisions, which were to be similar in character to EC directives. A feature of the new pillar three was that the ECJ was given greater jurisdictional power than it had had under the former JHA pillar. However, this was subject to considerable limitations, not least in that it did not extend to reviewing the validity or proportionality of law and order enforcement measures and operations in the member states.

Section II: The Union and its Citizens

This section was also rather mixed, but in broad terms it dealt with policies and issues that directly affect EU citizens. Amongst the provisions of the section were the following:

- A new title on employment was inserted into the TEC. Under Title VIII, the importance that the EU must attach to promoting employment was emphasised and procedures to assist it in achieving this aim were created.
- The Social Chapter of the TEC, which had taken the form of a protocol attached to the Treaty because of the opt-out the UK government had negotiated at Maastricht, was fully incorporated into the TEC.
- The importance of the principles of subsidiarity and proportionality was re-emphasised, and the nature of the principles themselves was given a little more clarification, in a protocol annexed to the TEC.
- The importance attached to environmental, public health and consumer protection policies in the TEC was upgraded and strengthened.
- Provisions for enhancing openness and transparency in EU decision-making were set down in the TEU and the TEC.

Section III: An Effective and Coherent External Policy

The objectives of the CFSP pillar were left largely unchanged, but operational and management mechanisms were strengthened with a view to improving the EU's effectiveness and efficiency:

- The main CFSP policy instruments were left much as before, but they were set out in a clearer and more streamlined manner. There were to be five instruments: definition of the CFSP's principles and general guidelines; common strategies; joint actions; common positions; and strengthened cooperation between the member states.
- The first two policy instruments were to be intergovernmental in character in that decisions would be taken by the European Council acting unanimously. Abstentions would not prevent the taking of a vote. The fifth instrument would also be intergovernmental in that it did not extend beyond inter-state cooperation.
- Qualified majority voting was established as the norm for adopting and implementing joint actions and common positions, thus making these policy instruments essentially supranational. However, if 'for important and stated reasons of national policy' a state declared it proposed to oppose the adoption of a decision by qmv, a vote would not be taken. In such a circumstance the Council, acting by qmv, could decide to refer

the matter to the European Council for decision by unanimity. For the first time – 30 years after the Luxembourg Compromise – a vital national interest veto was thus given formal treaty status in a policy area where qmv could be used.

- A new device, 'constructive abstention', was introduced whereby a state abstaining in a vote could issue a declaration that would result in it not being obliged to apply the decision taken, whilst recognising that the decision did commit the EU.

- A CFSP High Representative was to assist the Council, and especially the Council Presidency, in all CFSP matters, including external representation.

- Under a declaration attached to the Treaty, a policy planning and early warning unit – consisting of personnel drawn from the Council Secretariat, the member states, the Commission, and the WEU – was to be established in the Council Secretariat under the responsibility of the High Representative.

- Attempts by France, Germany and others to develop the defence policy potential of the EU and to integrate the WEU into the EU met with resistance from several countries, with the consequence that there was little advancement on either of these matters other than a slight tightening of the Treaty's language. However, specific security issues were identified for the first time as falling within the remit of the EU, with the incorporation of the so-called Petersberg tasks of 'humanitarian and rescue tasks, peacekeeping tasks and tasks of combat forces in crisis management, including peacekeeping' (TEU, Article 17).

- Though the Treaty did not give the EU explicit legal personality, it came close to doing so by giving it the power to enter into CFSP-related agreements with third countries. A procedure for negotiating and contracting such agreements was specified, based on the Presidency negotiating with the assistance of the Commission, and Council approval requiring unanimity.

- The much disputed issue of CFSP financing was settled, with most expenditure, other than that on operations with military or defence implications, being charged to the EC budget. This has important potential implications for the role of the EP in influencing the CFSP, because although the EP's formal powers in relation to the CFSP were unchanged – it was still restricted to the right to be consulted, to be kept informed and to ask questions – it is, with the Council, the joint budgetary authority. The budgetary process has thus become an arena in which the EP can exert an important policy influence.

In the EU's EC pillar, the powers of the Commission and the Council under Article 113 of the TEC (dealing with external trade) had become disputed in the early 1990s, with the Commission pressing for its sole negotiating power with third countries in respect of goods to be extended to services and intellectual property, and the Council resisting this. A 1994 ECJ ruling on the issue did little to resolve matters. The Amsterdam Treaty contained a supplement to Article 133 (the renumbered Article 113) enabling the Council, 'acting unanimously on a proposal from the Commission and after consulting the European Parliament' to extend the application of the Article to services and intellectual property.

Section IV: The Union's Institutions

This section addressed decision-making and the functioning of the EU institutions. As noted above, some of the more difficult outstanding issues were considered in the IGC, but they could not be fully resolved because of differences between the member states (for a useful summary of different national positions on institutional reform, see Devuyst, 1997). Disappointing, however, though the Treaty was for those who wished to see decision-making and institutional arrangements put in place in preparation for enlargement, the following significant reforms were nonetheless agreed:

- Major revisions were made in the TEC to the application of the EU's four main legislative procedures: assent, consultation, cooperation and co-decision. Details of the new applications are given in Chapter 13, but two important general points ought to be noted here: the cooperation procedure was virtually abandoned, being now restricted to a handful of EMU decisions (it was left for these because the IGC negotiators did not wish to risk opening the highly sensitive EMU 'box'); and the remit of the co-decision procedure was extended to 23 new cases, making this the 'normal' procedure in that it will apply to most EU legislation apart from agriculture and justice and home affairs matters (where the consultation procedure will apply).
- The co-decision procedure was revised in order (1) to streamline the procedure and (2) to strengthen the EP's position under the procedure and virtually establish a bicameral legislative system. Three important changes were made to the procedure. First, it would now be possible for a proposal to be adopted at first reading if the Council and the EP agreed on its contents. Second, the complicated system that had previously applied when the EP wished to reject a proposal – at second reading it had to vote on an intention to reject and then confirm that

intention after a meeting with the Council – was replaced by a much simpler system in which the EP would move straight to a vote on rejection at second reading. Third, any proposal referred to the conciliation committee would now only be able to be adopted if both sides agreed on its contents – the ability of the Council to confirm its version of the proposal, and see it adopted as law unless the EP voted by an absolute majority to reject it, was thus eliminated (see Chapter 13 for a full account of the co-decision procedure).

- There was increased provision for the use of qmv, though not by as much as had been anticipated following Chancellor Kohl's unexpected caution on the matter (see above) and problems that a number of governments had with particular proposed extensions. Within the EC pillar, areas to which qmv was extended included employment guidelines, social exclusion, equal opportunities and treatment for men and women, and various aspects of research decision-making. Within the CFSP pillar, qmv became, as was shown above, the norm for implementing CFSP joint actions and common positions. Within the third pillar there was little change, with unanimity being required except for some implementing decisions.

- A number of changes were made to the TEC in respect of the appointment of the President and other members of the Commission, and the position of the President was strengthened: what had become established in 1994 as a *de facto* right of the EP to approve the European Council's nominee for Commission President was given treaty status; the nominations of the national governments to the College must now be made 'by common accord' with the President-designate; the Commission would now be required to work 'under the political guidance of its President'; and in a Declaration attached to the Treaty it was stated that 'the President of the Commission must enjoy broad discretion in the allocation of the tasks within the College, as well as in any reshuffling of those tasks during a Commission's term of office'.

The institutional changes contained in the Amsterdam Treaty were thus in a similar vein to the changes effected by the SEA and the Maastricht Treaty. The main themes were increasing the efficiency and extending the democratic base of decision-making.

An important consequence of the increased powers given to the EP by the Amsterdam Treaty – most obviously via the extension in scope of the co-decision procedure – is that the institutional base of EU decision-making has shifted further away from its former Commission–Council axis towards a Commission–Council–EP triangle.

Section V: Closer Cooperation – 'Flexibility'

Since the Exchange Rate Mechanism (ERM) of the European Monetary System (EMS) was created in the late 1970s, the European integration process has involved some flexibility in the sense that not all member states have participated in all activities. This type of flexibility was increased in the 1980s, notably with the establishment of the Schengen system on a partial membership basis, and was given treaty status in the Maastricht Treaty with the UK's Social Chapter opt-out and special arrangements for the UK and Denmark on EMU.

Discussions on flexibility intensified after Maastricht, with the more pro-integrationist member states expressing dissatisfaction at being 'held back' by the less integrationist states – especially the UK. This dissatisfaction led to the Amsterdam Treaty incorporating new provisions into the first and third pillars of the TEU to allow a less than full complement of member states – but constituting 'at least a majority' – to establish closer cooperation between themselves, and for this purpose to be able to make use of the EU's institutions, procedures and mechanisms. Flexibility of this kind is to be used only as a last resort and is made subject to various restrictions – it must not, for example, affect the *acquis communautaire* and it must be open to all member states. The authorisation to establish closer cooperation was granted to the Council acting by qualified majority vote, but if 'a member of the Council declares that, for important and stated reasons of national policy, it intends to oppose the granting of an authorisation by a qualified majority, a vote shall not be taken. The Council may, acting by a qualified majority, request that the matter be referred to the Council, meeting in the composition of the Heads of State or Government, for decision by unanimity' (Article 11, TEC; much the same formulation was written into Article 40 of the TEU in reference to pillar three issues).

The rules on closer cooperation thus strike a balance between, as Niels Ersbøll – former Secretary General of the Council and the personal representative of the Danish Foreign Minister in the 1996–7 IGC – has put it, 'an unavoidable need for greater flexibility, as the Union progresses into new and nationally sensitive areas ... and the common interest in maintaining the basic principle of equal rights and obligations, characteristic of European integration from the outset' (Ersbøll, 1997, p. 10). Certainly there seems to be enough protection built into the rules to ensure that a Europe *à la carte* does not develop: it will be very difficult for flexibility to be practised in the EU's core policy areas, and in the areas where it is practiced safeguards are provided for the interests of non-participating states.

Section VI: Simplification and Consolidation of the Treaties

As part of the attempt to make Europe more relevant and accessible to its citizens, a number of redundant articles were repealed from the Treaties establishing the three European Communities, and in a declaration annexed to the Amsterdam Treaty it was stated that there should be 'a consolidation of all the relevant Treaties, including the Treaty on European Union'. Consolidation was deemed necessary because the setting and numbering of the existing treaties was already, and after the Amsterdam Treaty would be even more so, extremely confusing to all but the most informed practitioners and experts. In particular, the repeal of many TEC articles had left numerous gaps in the Treaty's numbering system; the many new articles that had been added to the TEC over the years, notably by the SEA, the TEU, and now the Amsterdam Treaty, had been 'squeezed' in, with the consequence that several articles contained many sub-articles covering significantly different topics – Article 130, for example, extended from Article 130 (industry) to Article 130y (cooperation with third countries and with international organisations); and the TEU articles had not been numbered at all, but had been lettered – so, for example, CFSP articles ran from J to J11 and JHA articles from K to K9.

Renumbering resulted in the TEU articles being numbered from 1–53, rather than from A–S (see Document 5.2). The TEC became numbered from 1–314, rather than from 1–248 (see Document 5.3). (Tables of Equivalences of the previous and new numbering of the TEU and the TEC can be found in the Appendix.) The ECSC and the Euratom Treaties were not renumbered, and a full consolidation of all the EU Treaties into one treaty was not attempted.

The decision not to fully consolidate the Treaties may seem odd. So might the words of the declaration on consolidation which state that the consolidation is 'for illustrative purposes' and 'shall have no legal value'. What these words mean is that only the Amsterdam Treaty itself, read together with the three European Community Treaties, the TEU and the other treaties that over the years have amended and added to the Founding Treaties have the authority of authentic legal texts. The explanation for these two oddities is that there was concern that full consolidation of, and the granting of full legal standing to, the Treaties could necessitate national ratification of their entire contents, not just their new Amsterdam components. Clearly this would have risked disturbing many hornets' nests.

If the partial consolidation of the Treaties did assist simplification (but only marginally), the many protocols and declarations in the Amsterdam Treaty did not. Protocols have the same binding legal effect as treaty articles, but declarations are essentially political statements. The Maas-

---

Document 5.2   Consolidated Version of the Treaty on European Union (contents)

I   TEXT OF THE TREATY
Preamble   *Articles*

II   PROTOCOLS (9)

---

tricht Treaty had been criticised for containing so many protocols (17) and declarations (35), but the Amsterdam Treaty actually exceeded this: one protocol was annexed to the TEU only; four protocols were annexed to the TEU and the TEC; five protocols were annexed to the TEC only; three protocols were annexed to the TEU and to all three Community Treaties; 51 declarations were 'adopted by the Conference'; and there were eight declarations 'of which the Conference took note'. Designed for a variety of purposes – such as providing clarification on treaty articles and laying down bases for extra-treaty policy activity – this large number of protocols and declarations is hardly conducive to the promotion of openness and understanding.

The Treaties and the integration process

Clearly the Maastricht and Amsterdam Treaties have significantly enhanced the deepening of the European integration process. As a result of the Treaties, more policy competences have been passed from the

Document 5.3   Consolidated Version of the Treaty Establishing the European Community (contents)

→

member states to the European level, the powers of the institutions at the European level have been strengthened, and supranationalism has been boosted.

However the EU's political nature is to be described – and this matter is examined in Chapter 18 – the Maastricht and Amsterdam Treaties have contributed significantly to its further development. The Treaties do not, however, in any sense, mark the end of the integration process or even identify where that end may be. The discussions and negotiations which took place before and at Maastricht and Amsterdam were characterised – as have been all such post-war discussions and negotiations – by considerable differences between the participants on the nature and pace of integration. What emerged from the processes that produced the Treaties were compromises: compromises that included aspects of different visions of the future of Europe, and compromises that, while failing to advance integration as much as many governments had hoped, did advance it further than others would have liked (hence the Danish and UK opt-outs from parts of both Treaties).

In terms of understanding the foundations, development and essential nature of the EU, the 'stories' of the Treaties are extremely revealing. They are so because they highlight and confirm the following long-established characteristics and features of the integration process.

Economics before politics

The major advances in integration have taken the form of agreeing to integrate aspects of economic activity and then, at times seemingly as an afterthought, realising that this requires political integration too if there is to be political direction and control. In practice there has naturally been considerable overlap and blurring between the economic and the political, but from 1950–1, when the ECSC was created, the economic has usually preceded the political. So, for example, the strengthening of the EC institutions that was provided for in the SEA was largely a consequence of this being seen to be necessary if the SEM programme was ever to be achieved. Similarly, the decision in 1991 to establish the IGC on Political Union was in considerable measure a follow-on from the earlier decision to establish the IGC on EMU.

Flexibility

When, in the past, the member states, or a sufficient number of them, have wished to act together in a policy area and the established mechanisms have been judged to be not suitable for the purpose, then alternative ways of proceeding have usually been found. This was, for example, the case with the establishment and development of EPC from the early 1970s, the EMS from the late 1970s, and the Schengen System (designed to assist free movement of persons) from the mid 1980s. The Maastricht and Amsterdam Treaties built on and greatly extended this tradition of being adaptable and innovative in respect of policy development. The Maastricht Treaty did so via the construction of two non-Community pillars (some states regarded it as premature to bring the policy areas covered by the pillars into the EC), and via, for the first time, the non-inclusion of member states in policy areas specifically identified in the Treaties (the UK and Danish opt-outs). The Amsterdam Treaty incorporated new opt-outs (for Denmark, Ireland, and the UK), and further 'constitutionalised' flexibility by the general flexibility provisions that were added to the TEC and the third pillar and the constructive abstention provision that was added to the second pillar.

Incrementalism

The integration process has been characterised by an almost constant edging forward, with 'advances' followed by pressure for more advances. The Maastricht and Amsterdam Treaties continued in this tradition with, for example, the Maastricht arrangements for EMU very much a consequence of the unfolding of the SEM programme, and the increased powers given to the EP by both Treaties resulting in large part from the long process of policy transfers to the EC/EU and consequent growing demands for decision-makers to be made more accountable. The Treaties thus reveal, not for the first time, that phases and forms of integration inevitably and logically follow from earlier – and perhaps less significant – phases and forms.

Variable pace

The pace of the integration process has varied considerably since the Community was founded in the 1950s with, in general terms, the period up to the mid 1960s and the mid 1980s to the early 1990s being times of rapid integration, and the late 1960s to the early 1980s and the period since the early 1990s being more sluggish. The Maastricht and Amsterdam Treaties illustrate this variable pace. The Maastricht Treaty was negotiated at a time when the governments of most member states were generally optimistic and ebullient in their attitudes to European integration, with the consequence that they wanted to see, and made sure that they did see, major integrationst advances incorporated into the Treaty. By contrast, when the Amsterdam Treaty was being negotiated the mood was less upbeat – not least because the 1992 Danish referendum had obliged supporters of further integration to become more cautious – and so less was sought from, and less was put into, the Treaty.

Interplay between supranational and national actors

Some analysts of European integration have made much of the role played in the integration process by supranational actors, most particularly the Commission, the EP, and the Court of Justice. Other analysts have played down the role of these actors and have argued that whilst they may have exercised some influence on the course of events, the EU's key actors have been representatives of the governments of the member states meeting in the European Council and the Council of Ministers. (There is a review of these different interpretations of the integration process in Chapter 18.)

At first sight, the decision-making processes associated with the making of the Maastricht and Amsterdam Treaties would appear to provide support only for the second of these analytical interpretations: the membership of the two IGCs consisted of national governmental representatives, with the Commission present but having no vote; decision-making in the IGCs was based on bargaining between the national governmental representatives, with agreements on some particularly difficult issues being reached only after hard direct negotiations between Heads of Government; and the supranational EU institutions – especially the Commission and the EP – were generally disappointed with the outcomes of the IGCs, with both having pressed, for example, for greater extensions to qmv and to their own powers than were incorporated in either Treaty.

However, although the making of the Maastricht and Amsterdam Treaties may appear to provide strong support for an intergovernmental interpretation of the integration process, the case should not be overstated. First, treaty-making processes are not typical EU decision-making processes since they lead to what Peterson (1995) has called 'history-making' decisions, and are therefore the very processes in which the role of national governments is likely to be most prominent. Second, although it did not have voting powers, the Commission was an active participant in both IGCs and, for the first time in the history of IGCs, the EP was allowed to make a direct input into the 1996–7 IGC. Finally, it seems probable, although the case cannot be proved definitively, that pressure from the Commission and the EP was important in helping to bring about at least some of the institutional reforms that were contained in the Treaties – such as the greater powers given to the EP by the creation of the co-decision procedure in the Maastricht Treaty and the simplification and extension of the procedure in the Amsterdam Treaty.

Benefits for everybody

The integrationist advances of 1992 and 1997 were possible because, as with the major treaty advances of 1952 (the Treaty of Paris), 1957 (the EEC and Euratom Treaties) and 1986 (the SEA), the member states judged it to be in their interests to promote integration. Certainly in all of the treaty-making negotiations, not least those that produced the Maastricht and Amsterdam Treaties, there have been disagreements between the states as to just how much, and what kind of, integration they have wanted, but it has nonetheless been recognised that there are benefits for all to be gained from the integration process – with the furtherance of economic growth and the promotion of harmonous relations between the states of Europe being the most obvious benefits.

However, because of their own distinctive needs and preferences, states have sometimes argued that in addition to taking a share of general benefits they should also be awarded special benefits. The award of special benefits in treaties has usually taken the form of providing a base for some sort of policy development that will be especially helpful to a particular state or group of states. The SEA provided such a policy base when, largely at the behest of the poorer member states, it included provisions for the development of redistributive policies. The Maastricht Treaty did much the same thing, with the creation of a Cohesion Fund which would be directed at the four poorest member states (Greece, Ireland, Portugal and Spain).

An elite-driven process

Insofar as political and administrative elites tend to set the policy agenda, and insofar as they usually take decisions without consulting their electorates, political activity in all nation states – in Europe and beyond – may be said to be elite driven. But this is particularly the case in the EU because there are no direct lines of accountability between decision-makers and the citizenry. There is no opportunity to elect a European government or parliament with full decision-making powers. Arguably this would not matter too much if there were grounds for believing that most citizens were strongly supportive of the integration process, or were happy to leave decisions about integration to the appropriate elites. However, public opinion polls have suggested that in some member states considerable reservations and doubts have existed at various times.

The extent to which the integration process is elite driven, and the extent to which elites do not always reflect popular concerns, was clearly demonstrated during the ratification process of the Maastricht Treaty, when not only did the Danes vote 'No' in their first referendum and the French almost vote 'No', but opinion polls indicated that German and UK voters too might have rejected the Treaty if they had been given the opportunity to do so. The increased caution shown by national representatives in the 1996–7 IGC can perhaps be seen as partly reflecting greater sensitivity to the popular concerns that the Maastricht ratification process had highlighted. However, the extent of this sensitivity should not be overstated, as is demonstrated by the fact that despite all the post-Maastricht talk about promoting openness and democracy in the EU, there was no movement towards opening up the treaty-making process to popular participation. On the contrary, only the Danish and Irish governments – which, as with the SEA and the TEU, were virtually compelled to do so – included referendums as part of their national ratification procedures.

The traits and features of the integration process that have just been identified can be expected to recur in the years ahead. For the process has no final goal; there is no point at which integration can be said to have reached its optimum point or to have been completed. Indeed, with the present state of development of the EU contested in some quarters, with the projected accession of CEECs raising major questions about the course of integration, and with another IGC virtually guaranteed before that accession occurs, it can be anticipated that in the years to come there will continue to be intensive discussions and negotiations on the future direction of European integration.

Part 2

The Institutions and Political Actors of the European Union

Introduction

There are five main EU institutions: the Commission, the Council of Ministers, the European Council, the European Parliament, and the Court of Justice. Chapters 6–10 consider each of these institutions and the political actors that are associated with them. Chapter 10 has also been taken as the most appropriate place to examine the nature and status of EU law.

Chapter 11 looks at those institutions and actors which, though not given a chapter in their own right, nonetheless also exercise a significant influence in the EU: the Economic and Social Committee, the Committee of the Regions, the European Investment Bank, the European System of Central Banks, the Court of Auditors, and Interests.

Chapter 6

The Commission

Appointment and composition
Organisation
Responsibilities and powers
Concluding remarks

Frequently portrayed as the civil service of the EU, in reality the Commission is rather more and rather less than that: rather more in the sense that the treaties and political practice have assigned to it much greater policy-initiating and decision-making powers than those enjoyed, in theory at least, by national civil services; rather less in that its role in policy implementation is greatly limited by the fact that agencies in the member states are charged with most of the EU's day-to-day administrative responsibilities.

The Commission is centrally involved in EU decision-making at all levels and on all fronts. With an array of power resources and policy instruments at its disposal – and strengthened by the frequent unwillingness or inability of other EU institutions to provide clear leadership – the Commission is at the very heart of the EU system.

Appointment and composition

The College of Commissioners

Seated at the summit of the Commission are the individual Commissioners who are each in charge of particular policy areas and who meet collectively as the College of Commissioners. Originally they numbered nine, but with enlargements their size has grown: to thirteen, to fourteen, to seventeen, and now to twenty. Each of the five larger countries has two Commissioners (France, Germany, Italy, Spain, and the United Kingdom), and the remaining ten countries each has one.

Appointment procedure

Prior to the College that took office in January 1993, Colleges were appointed every four years by common accord of the governments of the member states. The Maastricht Treaty changed this procedure, primarily in order to strengthen the links between the Commission and the EP. This strengthening was achieved in two ways. The first was by formalising and somewhat stiffening practices that developed in the 1980s regarding the appointment of the Commission and its President: member states now became obliged to consult the EP on who should be President, and the College-designate became obliged to present itself before the EP for a vote of confidence. The second was by bringing the terms of office of the EP and the Commission into close alignment: Colleges would now serve a five-year term and would take up office six months after EP elections, which are held on a fixed basis in the June of years ending in four and nine. (So as to bring about the alignment, a transitional two-year College served from January 1993 to January 1995).

On the occasion of the first application of the new appointments procedure – in respect of the College that assumed office in January 1995 – the EP pressed its new powers to the full. When Jacques Santer, the Luxembourg Prime Minister, was nominated as President-designate in mid 1994 (at short notice and as a compromise candidate following the UK government's refusal to support the Belgian Prime Minister, Jean-Luc Dehaene), the EP was in fact barely consulted. However the EP made it quite clear to the European Council (the forum in which the nominee of the national governments is agreed) that whoever was nominated would be required to appear before Parliament and a vote on confirmation would be held. The assumption would be that if the nominee was not confirmed his candidature would be withdrawn. Chancellor Kohl, acting in his capacity as Council President, confirmed that the EP would indeed have a *de facto* veto over the nomination. In the event Santer was confirmed, but only by a narrow majority: there were 260 votes in favour, 238 against, and 23 abstentions. As for the vote of approval on the whole College, the EP held 'hearings', with each of the Commissioners-designate being required to appear before the appropriate EP committee before the plenary vote was held. There was strong criticism of five of the Commissioners-designate, but given that there was no provision for singling them out in a vote, the EP, after being given certain reassurances by Santer, gave a vote of confidence to the new College by 417 votes to 104.

The Amsterdam Treaty confirmed the *de facto* confirmatory power the EP had assigned to itself on the appointment of the Commission President. The Treaty also gave the President a potential veto over the national nominees for appointment to the College. (Under the Maastricht Treaty he was supposed to be consulted on the national nominees to the College, but in practice this amounted to little in 1994.) Accordingly, the relevant Treaty provisions on the appointment of the President and the College are now as follows:

The governments of the Member States shall nominate by common accord the person they intend to appoint as President of the Commission; the nomination shall be approved by the European Parliament.

The governments of the Member States shall, by common accord with the nominee for President, nominate the other persons whom they intend to appoint as Members of the Commission.

The President and the other Members of the Commission thus nominated shall be subject as a body to a vote of approval by the European Parliament. After approval by the European Parliament, the President and the other Members of the Commission shall be appointed by common accord of the governments of the Member States (Article 214.2, TEC).

The 1999 resignation of the College

At the time the Amsterdam Treaty was negotiated it was assumed that its provisions on the appointment of the College would be given their first use for the College that was due to assume office in January 2000. However, in March 1999 the Santer College was pressurised – most particularly by the EP, which was threatening to dismiss it by passing a motion of censure – into resigning, nine months before the scheduled end of its term of office. (Formally, the EP can only dismiss the Commission by passing a motion of censure by a two-thirds majority of the votes cast that includes a majority of all Parliament's members, but in practice it is likely that a nominal majority vote would so undermine the College's credibility that it would have little option but to resign.) The circumstances that produced deep dissatisfaction with the Santer College and led to its resignation are described on pp. 216–17. Essentially, they centred on confirmation in a report drawn up by independent experts that there was some substance to long-held suspicions that at least one Commissioner (Edith Cresson) had shown favouritism in issuing contracts, that Santer had been insufficiently vigilant in the exercise of some of his responsibilities, that there were problems of financial mismanagement in certain parts of the Commission, and that the College as a whole had displayed a general lack of responsibility for the Commission's actions (Committee of Independent Experts, 1999).

Almost immediately after resigning the Santer College announced that it would stay in office in a caretaker capacity until a replacement College was appointed. This gave the governments of the member states breathing space, both to decide on a collective basis how they should proceed and to consider on an individual basis who they wished to nominate to the replacement College. There were two collective decisions to be made. First, who should replace Jacques Santer as Commission President? Santer initially considered trying to stay on himself, but MEPs quickly made it clear that they would not support him – which forced him to recognise that he could not return. Second, should the replacement College be appointed on an interim basis to see out the remaining months of the Santer College's term or should the process of appointing a new full-term College be brought forward? If the former option was chosen, a consequence would probably be that most of the current Commissioners would seek to stay in office for another few months (although MEPs made it clear that as well as Santer, Cresson would also have to go). If the latter option was chosen, most of the current Commissioners would probably resign or be replaced by their national governments.

A special summit to consider these questions did not have to be called, since one was already timetabled for ten days after the College's resignation. This was the March 1999 Berlin summit, which had been arranged by the German Council Presidency to enable final decisions to be taken on the *Agenda 2000* package of budgetary and policy reforms (see below). At the summit, the national leaders decided to nominate the former Italian Prime Minister, Romano Prodi, to be the new Commission President. They further decided that they did not wish for an interim College, but rather for a full-term one. The relevant passages from the summit's 'Declaration on the Appointment of the President of the Commission' are as follows:

> The Heads of State or Government have noted with respect the resignation of the Commission and expressed their thanks for the work done for Europe.
>
> They decided by common accord to ask Mr Romano Prodi to accept the important task to be the President of the next European Commission.
>
> In accordance with the procedures of the Amsterdam Treaty, this decision shall be communicated to the present European Parliament for approval. After this approval, Mr Prodi should strive to prepare the nomination of a new Commission as soon as possible, in cooperation with the governments of the Member States. The Governments of the Member States shall, by common accord with Mr Prodi, nominate the other persons whom they intend to appoint as members of the Commission. After the June elections, the newly elected European Parliament should give its approval on both the President and the nominees for the Commission. The newly elected European Parliament should start on the procedure for appointing the new Commission as early as July. After approval by the newly elected European Parliament, the President and the other members of the Commission shall be appointed by common accord of the Governments of the Member States.

The European Council wishes to enable the new Commission to start work at the earliest opportunity and to continue that work with a full mandate as from January 2000 for the next five years. (European Council, 1999, Part II).

Mr Prodi's nomination was endorsed by the EP in May by 392 votes to 72, with 41 abstentions.

Impartiality and independence

The emphasis in the appointment procedure that the governments of the member states must act by 'common accord' is designed to emphasise the collective, as opposed to the national, base of the Commission: Commissioners are not supposed to be national representatives but should 'in the general interest of the Community, be completely independent in the performance of their duties'. Much the same sentiments pertain to the requirement that Commissioners should 'neither seek nor take instructions from any government or from any other body' (Article 213, TEC).

In practice, full impartiality is neither achieved nor attempted. Although in theory the Commissioners are collectively appointed, in fact, they are national nominees. It would therefore be quite unrealistic to expect them, upon assuming office, suddenly to detach themselves from previous loyalties and concern themselves solely with 'the wider European interest' – not least since a factor in their appointment is likely to have been the expectation that they would keep an eye on the national interest. (A particularly graphic illustration of this latter point was seen in the way that a UK Commissioner, Lord Cockfield, was not reappointed by Mrs Thatcher to the Commission which took up office in January 1989. She believed he had been over-zealous in his support for aspects of the internal market programme for which he was responsible, and rather than looking to British interests had 'gone native'.)

The Treaty's insistence on the complete independence of Commissioners is therefore interpreted flexibly. Indeed, total neutrality is not even desirable since the work of the Commission is likely to be facilitated by Commissioners maintaining their links with sources of influence through-out the EU, and they can most easily do this in their own member states. But the requirements of the system and the necessities of the EU's institutional make-up are such that real problems arise if Commissioners try to push their own states' interests too hard. It is both legitimate and helpful to bring favoured national interests onto the agenda, to help clear national obstacles from the path, to explain to other Commissioners what is likely to be acceptable in 'my' national capital. But to go further and act consistently and blatantly as a national spokesman is to risk losing credibility with other Commissioners. It also makes it difficult for the Commission to function properly since it clearly cannot fulfil its set tasks if its divisions match those of the Council of Ministers. The Commission appointed to office in January 1985 under the Presidency of Jacques Delors soon ran into difficulties of this kind: the chauvinism of some of its members played an important part in limiting the ability of the Commission to act efficiently as a coherent team. Open criticism by members of the German government of its two Commissioners for allegedly failing to defend their country's interests in Brussels created further problems.

Characteristics of Commissioners

There are no rules or understandings as to what sort of people, with what sort of experience and background, member governments should nominate to be Commisioners. It used to be the case that most Commissioners tended to be former national politicians just short of the top rank. However, as the EU, and the Commission with it, has become increasingly important, so has the political weight of the College's membership increased, and now most Commissioners are former ministers, and some of them very senior ministers: the 1995 Santer College included two former Prime Ministers, three former Foreign Ministers, and one former Finance Minister (Macmullen, 1997:43).

Given the diverse political compositions of the EU's national governments there is naturally a range of political opinion represented in the Commission. The smaller countries tend to put forward somebody from their largest party. The five larger countries vary in what they do, but 'split representations' are common practice. Crucially, all governments have made it their custom to nominate people who are broadly pro-European and have not been associated with any extremist party or any extreme wing of a mainstream party. So whilst Colleges certainly contain party political differences, these are usually within a range that permits at least reasonable working relationships.

The President

The most prestigious and potentially influential College post is that of the Presidency. Although most important Commission decisions must be taken collectively by the twenty Commissioners, the President is very much *primus inter pares*:

- He is the most prominent, and usually the best known, of the Commissioners.
- He is the principal representative of the Commission in its dealings with other EU institutions and with outside bodies.

- He must try to provide forward movement for the EU and to give a sense of direction both to his fellow Commissioners and, more broadly, to the Commission as a whole. This latter role was strengthened by the Amsterdam Treaty, which added the following to the TEC: 'The Commission shall work under the political guidance of its President' (Article 219).
- He is directly responsible for overseeing some of the Commission's most important administrative services – notably the Secretariat General (which, amongst other functions, is responsible for the coordination of Commission activities and for relations with the Council and the EP) and the Legal Service.
- He takes on specific policy portfolios of his own, usually in harness with other Commissioners. For example, Santer chose to take a particular interest in monetary matters, the CFSP, and institutional issues.

Inevitably, given the importance of the office, the European Council is very careful about who is nominated. It has come to be generally accepted that only the most prominent of national politicians will be considered, as is witnessed by the last three nominations: Jacques Delors was a former French Finance Minister, whilst both Jacques Santer and Romano Prodi were former Prime Ministers – the former of Luxembourg and the latter of Italy.

Portfolios

Prior to the implementation of the Amsterdam Treaty, the distribution of the policy portfolios among the Commissioners was largely a matter of negotiation and political balance. The President's will was the most important factor, but he could not allocate posts simply in accordance with his own preferences. He was intensively lobbied – by the incoming Commissioners themselves, and sometimes by governments trying to get 'their' Commissioners into positions that were especially important from the national point of view. Furthermore, the President was made aware that renominated Commissioners – of which there were usually nine or ten – might well be looking for advancement to more important portfolios, and that the five states with two Commissioners expected at least one of 'their' nominees to be allocated a senior post. Bearing in mind all these difficulties, it is not surprising that unless a resignation, death or enlargement enforced it, reshuffles did not usually occur during the lifetime of a Commission.

Clearly this situation meant that the most appropriate people were not necessarily assigned to the most appropriate posts, and also that not much could be done if a Commissioner was not performing satisfactorily. The situation was partly addressed in a declaration attached to the Amsterdam Treaty (Declaration 32), which provided the President with broad discretion in the allocation of tasks within the College and allowed him to effect a reshuffling of the tasks during a College's term of office.

Cabinets

To assist them in the performance of their duties, Commissioners have personal *cabinets*. These consist of small teams of officials, normally numbering six or seven except for the President's *cabinet* which is larger and numbers around twelve. Members of *cabinets* have traditionally been mostly fellow nationals of the Commissioner, but Romano Prodi made it clear shortly after being nominated as Commission President that he wished to see *cabinets* 'acquire a more markedly supranational character' (*European Voice*, 6–11 May 1999). Typically, a *cabinet* member is a dynamic, extremely hard-working, 30–40-year-old, who has been seconded or recruited from some part of the EU administration, from the civil service in the Commissioner's own state, or from a political party or sectional interest with which the Commissioner has links. *Cabinets* undertake a number of tasks: they gather information and seek to keep their Commissioner informed of developments within and outside his or her allocated policy areas; they liaise with other parts of the Commission, including other *cabinets*, for purposes such as clearing up routine matters, building support for their Commissioner's policy priorities, and generally trying to shape policy proposals as they come up the Commission system; and they act as a sort of unofficial advocate/protector in the Commission of the interests of their Commissioner's country. Over and above these tasks, the President's *cabinet* is centrally involved in brokering the many different views and interests that exist amongst Commissioners and in the Commission as a whole to ensure that, as an institution, the Commission is clear, coherent, cohesive and efficient (see below for further discussion of the roles of Commissioners'*cabinets*).

The Commission bureaucracy

Below the Commissioners lies the Commission bureaucracy. This is by far the biggest element of the whole EU administrative framework, though it is tiny compared with the size of administrations in the member states. Of a total permanent EU staff in early 1999 of 28 000, just over 20 000 were employed by the Commission – fewer than in many national ministries, and indeed many large city councils (EU member states average 322 civil servants per 10 000 inhabitants, as against 0.8 per 10 000 for all EU institutions). Of these 20 000, just over 14 000 were employed in administration – including just over 4000 in the policy-making 'A' grades – 3600 were engaged in research and technological development, and 1900 were engaged in the translation and interpretation work neccessitated by the EU's eleven working languages (there are 111 possible language combinations, although most of the Commission's internal business is conducted in French or English). The Commission also makes use of temporary staff of various kinds, including national officials on secondment and experts contracted for specific purposes.

Permanent staff are recruited on the basis of open competitive procedures, which, for the 'A' grades in particular, are highly competitive. (The 'A' grade has an eight-point scale, with A1 at the top for Directors-General and A8 at the bottom for new entrants with little or no working experience.) An internal career structure exists and most of the top jobs are filled via internal promotion. However, pure meritocratic principles are disturbed by a policy that tries to provide for a reasonable national balance amongst staff. All governments have watched this closely and have sought to ensure that their own nationals are well represented throughout the EU administrative framework, especially in the 'A' grades. For the most senior 'A' grade posts something akin to an informal national quota system operates, though this cannot completely disregard meritocratic principles following a ruling in March 1993 by the Court of First Instance (CFI) annulling the appointment of two Directors – at A2 grade – in DGXIV (Fisheries) on the ground that the successful applicants were chosen not because of their qualifications but because the countries from which they came – Italy and Spain – were 'owed' the jobs.

This multinational staffing policy of the Commission, and indeed of the other EU institutions, has both advantages and disadvantages. The main advantages are:

(1) The staff have a wide range of experience and knowledge drawn from across all the member states.
(2) The confidence of national governments and administrations in EU decision-making is helped by the knowledge that compatriots are involved in policy preparation and administration.
(3) Those who have to deal with the EU, be they senior national civil servants or paid lobbyists, can often more easily do so by using their fellow nationals as access points. A two-way flow of information between the EU and the member states is thus facilitated.

The main disadvantages are:

(1) Insofar as some senior personnel decisions are not made on the basis of objective organisational needs but result from national claims to posts and

from the lobbying activities that often become associated with this, staff morale and commitment is damaged. The parachuting of outsiders into key jobs is less easy than it was – partly because staff and staff associations have pressed for a better internal career structure and partly because of the 1993 CFI judgement – but in the Commission's upper reaches promotion is still not based on pure meritocratic principles.

(2) Senior officials can sometimes be less than wholly and completely EU-minded. For however impartial and even-handed they are supposed to be, they cannot, and usually do not wish to, completely divest themselves of their national identifications and loyalties.

(3) There are differing policy styles in the Commission, reflecting different national policy styles. These differences are gradually being flattened out as the Commission matures as a bureaucracy and develops its own norms and procedures, but the differences can still create difficulties, both within DGs – where officials from different nationalities may be used to working in different ways – and between DGs where there are concentrations of officials from one country: French officials, for example, have traditionally been overrepresented in DGVI (Agriculture).

Organisation

The Directorates General

The work of the Commission is divided into separate policy areas in much the same way as national level governmental responsibilities are divided between ministries. Apart from specialised agencies and services – such as the Statistical Office and the Joint Research Centre – the Commission's basic units of organisation are its twenty-four Directorates General. Somewhat confusingly for those who do not know their way around the system, these are customarily referred to by their number rather than by their policy responsibility. So, for example, Competition is DGIV, Agriculture is DGVI, and Energy is DGXVII (Table 6.1).

The size and internal organisation of the DGs varies. Most commonly, DGs have a staff of between 150 and 450, divided into four to six directorates, which in turn are each divided into three or four units. However, policy importance, workloads and specialisations within DGs produce many departures from this norm. Thus in terms of size, DGs range from DGIX (Personnel and Administration), which employs just over 2500 people, to DGVI, which employs around 850, to DGXXII (Education, Training and Youth), DGXXIII (Enterprise Policy) and DGXXIV (Consumer Policy) all of which employ under 100. As for organisational structure, DGVI has nine directorates (three of which are

Table 6.1 *Directorates General and Special Services of the Commission*

Directorates General

DG I	External Relations: Commercial Policy and Relations with North America, the Far East, Australia and New Zealand
DG IA	External Relations: Europe and the New Independent States, Common Foreign and Security Policy and External Missions
DG IB	External Relations: Southern Mediterranean, Middle and Near East, Latin America, South and South-East Asia and North–South Cooperation
DG II	Economic and Financial Affairs
DG III	Industry
DG IV	Competition
DG V	Employment, Industrial Relations and Social Affairs
DG VI	Agriculture
DG VII	Transport
DG VIII	Development
DG IX	Personnel and Administration
DG X	Information, Communication, Culture, Audiovisual
DG XI	Environment, Nuclear Safety and Civil Protection
DG XII	Science, Research and Development
DG XIII	Telecommunications, Information Market and Exploitation of Research
DG XIV	Fisheries
DG XV	Internal Market and Financial Services
DG XVI	Regional Policies and Cohesion
DG XVII	Energy
DG XIX	Budgets
DG XXI	Taxation and Customs Union
DG XXII	Education, Training and Youth
DG XXIII	Enterprise Policy, Distributive Trades, Tourism and Cooperatives
DG XXIV	Consumer Policy and Consumer Health Protection

Main Special Services and Units
Secretariat-General of the Commission
Inspectorate-General
Legal Service
Forward Studies Unit
Joint Research Centre
Spokesman's Service
Translation Service
Joint Interpreting and Conference Service
Statistical Office
Information Directorate
European Community Humanitarian Office
European Supply Agency
Office for Official Publications of the European Communities

themselves subdivided) and 42 units, DGXXIII has four directorates and nine units, and DGXXIV has three directorates and 16 units.

To meet new requirements and improve efficiency, the organisational structure of the DGs is changed relatively frequently. So, for example, to enable the Commission to adapt to the Common Foreign and Security Policy (CFSP) requirements of the Maastricht Treaty, DGI (External Relations) was split in 1993 into two separate entities: DGI (External Economic Relations) and DGIA (External Political Relations). DGI more or less corresponded to the former DGI, but DGIA was quite new. In 1995 there was a further reorganisation of the external relations DGs (commonly known as the RELEX DGs) with responsibilities being organised on a less functional and more geographical basis, and with a new DG (DGIB) being created (further information on the RELEX DGs is provided in Chapter 16).

The hierarchical structure

The hierarchical structure of the Commission is as follows:

- All important matters are channelled through the weekly meetings of the College of Commissioners. At these meetings decisions are taken unanimously if possible, but by majority vote if need be.
- In particular policy areas the Commissioner holding the portfolio in question carries the main leadership responsibility.
- DGs are formally headed by Directors General, who are responsible to the appropriate Commissioner or Commissioners.
- Directorates are headed by Directors, who report to the Director General or, in the case of large DGs, to a Deputy Director General.
- Units are headed by Heads of Unit, who report to the Director responsible.

The structure thus appears to be quite clear, but in practice it is not completely so. At the topmost echelons in particular the lines of authority and accountability are sometimes blurred. One reason for this is that a poor match sometimes exists between Commissioners' portfolios and the policy responsibilities of the DGs. EC/EU enlargements and the consequent increases in the size of the Commission over the years have allowed for greater policy specialisation on the part of individual Commissioners and a better alignment with the responsibilities of individual DGs, but even now some Commissioners carry several portfolios, each of which may touch on the work of a number of DGs. Moreover, the content of portfolio responsibilities is changed from College to College. Some portfolios, such as Budget, Agriculture, or Regional Policy, are more or less fixed, but others, of a broader and less specific kind, can be varied, or even created, depending on how a new President sees the role and tasks of the Commission and what pressures the Commissioners themselves exert.

Another structural problem concerning Commissioners is the curious halfway position in which they are placed. To use the British parallel, they are more than permanent secretaries but less than ministers. For whilst they are the principal Commission spokesmen in their assigned policy areas, they are not members of the Council of Ministers – the body that, often in association with the EP, takes most final policy decisions on important matters.

These structural arrangements mean that any notion of individual responsibility, such as exists in most member states in relation to ministers – albeit usually only weakly and subject to the prevailing political currents – is difficult to apply to Commissioners. It might even be questioned whether it is reasonable that the Commission should be subject to collective responsibility – as it is by virtue of Article 201 of the TEC, which obliges it to resign if a motion of censure on its activities is passed in the EP by a two-thirds majority of the votes cast, representing a majority of all members. Collective responsibility may be thought to be reasonable insofar as all Commission proposals and decisions are made collectively and not in the name of individual Commissioners, but at the same time it may be thought to be unreasonable insofar as the ability of the Commission to undertake its various tasks successfully is highly dependent on other EU actors. In practice no censure motion has been passed, although, as will be shown in Chapter 9, one came close to being so in January 1999.

Decision-making mechanisms

The hierarchical structure that has just been described produces a 'model' route via which proposals for decisions make their way through the Commission machinery:

- An initial draft is drawn up at middle-ranking 'A' grade level in the appropriate DG. Outside assistance – from consultants, academics, national officials and experts, and sectional interests – is sought, and if necessary contracted, as appropriate. The parameters of the draft are likely to be determined by existing EU policy, or by guidelines that have been laid down at senior Commission and/or Council levels.
- The draft is passed upwards – through superiors within the DG, through the *cabinet* of the commissioner responsible, and through the weekly meeting of the *chefs de cabinet* – until the College of

Commissioners is reached. During its passage the draft may be extensively revised.

- The College of Commissioners can do virtually what it likes with the proposal. It may accept it, reject it, refer it back to the DG for redrafting, or defer taking a decision.

From this 'model' route all sorts of variations are possible, and in practice are commonplace. For example, if draft proposals are relatively uncontroversial or there is some urgency involved, procedures and devices can be employed to prevent logjams at the top and expedite the business in hand. One such procedure enables the College of Commissioners to authorise the most appropriate amongst their number to take decisions on their behalf. Another procedure is the so-called 'written procedure', by which proposals that seem to be straightforward are circulated amongst all Commissioners and are officially adopted if no objection is lodged within a specified time, usually a week. Urgent proposals can be adopted even more quickly by 'accelerated written procedure'.

Another set of circumstances producing departures from the 'model' route is when policy issues cut across the Commission's administrative divisions – a very common occurrence given the sectoral specialisations of the DGs. For example, a draft directive aimed at providing a framework in which alternative sources of energy might be researched and developed would probably originate in DGXVII (Energy), but would have direct implications for DGXII (Science, Research and Development), DGXIX (Budgets), and perhaps DGIII (Industry). Sometimes policy and legislative proposals do not just touch on the work of other DGs but give rise to sharp conflicts, the sources of which may be traced back to the conflicting 'missions' of DGs: for example, there have been several disputes between DGIII and DGIV (Competition), with the former tending to be much less concerned than the latter about rigidly applying EU competition rules if European industry is thereby assisted and advantaged. Provision for liaison and coordination is thus essential if the Commission is to be effective and efficient. There are various procedures and mechanisms aimed at providing this necessary coordination. Four of these are particularly worth noting.

First, at the level of the DGs, various management practices and devices have been developed to try to rectify the increasingly recognised problem of horizontal coordination. In many policy areas this results in important coordinating functions being performed by a host of standing and *ad hoc* arrangements: inter-service groups and meetings are the most important of these arrangements, but there are also task forces, project groups, and numerous informal and one-off exchanges from Director General level downwards.

Second, the main institutional agency for promoting coordination is the Secretariat General of the Commission, which is specifically charged with ensuring that proper coordination and communication takes place across the Commission. In exercising this duty the Secretariat satisfies itself that all Commission interests have been consulted before a proposal is submitted to the College of Commissioners.

Third, the President of the Commission has an ill-defined, but generally expected, coordinating responsibility. A forceful personality may be able to achieve a great deal in forging a measure of collective identity out of the varied collection of people from quite different national and political backgrounds who sit around the Commission table. But it can only be done tactfully and with adroit use of social skills. Jacques Delors, who presided over three Commissions between 1985 and 1995, unquestionably had a forceful personality, but he also displayed traits and acted in ways that, according to many observers, had the effect of undermining team spirit amongst his colleagues. For example, he indicated clear policy preferences and interests of his own; he occasionally made important policy pronouncements before fully consulting the other Commissioners; he criticised Commissioners during Commission meetings and sometimes, usually by implication rather than directly, did so in public too; and he frequently appeared to give more weight to the counsel of personal advisers and to people who reported directly to him – drawn principally from his *cabinet* and from the Commission's Forward Studies Unit – than to the views of his fellow Commissioners.

Fourth, the College of Commissioners, in theory at least, is in a strong position to coordinate activity and take a broad view of Commission affairs. Everything of importance is referred to the Commissioners' weekly meeting and at that meeting the whole sweep of Commission interests is represented by the portfolios of those gathered around the table.

Commissioners' meetings are always preceded by other meetings designed to ease the way to decision-making:

- Informal and *ad hoc* consultations may occur between Commissioners who are particularly affected by a proposal.
- The Commissioners' agenda is always considered at a weekly meeting of the heads of the Commissioners' *cabinets*. These *chefs de cabinet* meetings are chaired by the Commission's Secretary General and are usually held two days before the meetings of the Commission itself. Their main purpose is to reduce the agenda for Commission meetings by reaching agreements on as many items as possible and referring only controversial/difficult/major/politically sensitive matters to the Commissioners.

- Feeding into *chefs de cabinet* meetings are the outcomes of the six or seven meetings that are held each week of the *cabinet* members responsible for particular policy areas. These meetings are chaired by the relevant policy specialist in the President's *cabinet* and they have two main purposes: to enable DGs other than the sponsoring DG to make observations on policy and legislative proposals – in other words, they assist in the task of horizontal coordination; and to allow proposals to be evaluated in the context of the Commission's overall policy priorities.
- Officials from the different *cabinets*, who are generally well known to one another, often exchange views on an informal basis if a proposal looks as though it may create difficulties. (Officially *cabinets* do not become involved until a proposal has been formally launched by a DG, but earlier consultation sometimes occurs. If this consultation is seen by DGs to amount to interference, tensions and hostilities can arise – not least because *cabinet* officials are usually junior in career terms to officials in the upper reaches of DGs.)

However, despite these various coordinating arrangements, a feeling persists in many quarters that the Commission continues to function in too compartmentalised a manner, with insufficient attention being paid to overall EU policy coherence. Amongst the problems are the following.

(1) The Commission has a rather rigid organisational framework. Despite the development of horizontal links of the kind that have just been noted, structural relationships, both between and within DGs, remain too vertical. Although encouragement has been given, principally via the President's office, to the creation of agencies and teams that can plan on a broad front, these are not sufficiently developed, and in any event they have found it difficult to assert their authority in relation to the DGs, especially the larger and traditionally more independent ones. As for the President himself, he has, even after the Amsterdam Treaty, only limited powers to direct the actions of DGs, and no formal authority to dismiss or reassign the duties of those in the DGs whom he judges to be incompetent or uncooperative.

(2) Departmental and policy loyalties sometimes tend to discourage new and integrated approaches to problems and the pooling of ideas. Demarcation lines between spheres of responsibility are too tightly drawn, and policy competences are too jealously guarded.

(3) Sheer workload makes it difficult for many Commissioners and senior officials to look much beyond their own immediate tasks. One of the duties of a Commissioner's *cabinet* is to keep him or her abreast of general policy developments, but it remains the case that the Commissioner

holding the portfolio on, say, energy, can hardly be blamed if she or he has little to contribute to a Commission discussion on the milk market regime.

Responsibilities and powers

Some of the Commission's responsibilities and powers are prescribed in the treaties and in EU legislation. Others have not been formally laid down but have developed from practical necessity and the requirements of the EU system.

Whilst recognising that there is some overlap between the categories, the responsibilities and associated powers of the Commission may be grouped under six major headings: proposer and developer of policies and legislation, executive functions, guardian of the legal framework, external representative and negotiator, mediator and conciliator, and the conscience of the Union.

Proposer and developer of policies and legislation

Article 211 of the TEC includes the provision that the Commission 'shall formulate recommendations or deliver opinions on matters dealt with in this Treaty, if it expressly so provides or if the Commission considers it necessary'.

What this means in practice is that under the TEC, and indeed under the ECSC and Euratom Treaties too, the Commission is charged with the responsibility of proposing measures that are likely to advance the development of the EU. Where legislation is envisaged, this power to propose is exclusive to the Commission. The Commission also has proposing and initiating powers under pillars two and three of the EU (in the latter case, only since the Amsterdam Treaty), but these are shared with the member states: there is no exclusive power of proposal since legislation is not made under these pillars.

In addition to its formal treaty powers, political realities arising from the institutional structure of the EU also dictate that the Commission should be centrally involved in formulating and developing policy. The most important of these realities is that there is nothing like an EU Prime Minister, an EU Cabinet, or EU ministers capable of providing the Commission with clear and consistent policy direction, let alone a coherent legislative programme. Senior Commission officials who have transferred from national civil services are often greatly surprised by the lack of political direction from above and the amount of room for policy and legislative initiation that is available to them. Their duties are often only broadly defined and there can be considerable potential, especially for the more senior 'A' grade officials, to stimulate development in specific and, if they wish, new and innovative policy areas. An indication of the scale of this activity is the fact that in an average year the Commission is likely to send the Council or the EP and the Council 500–700 proposals, recommendations and draft instruments, and over 200 communications, memoranda and reports (in 1998 the figures were 576 and 293 respectively [Commission, 1999, p. 416]).

Although in practice they greatly overlap, it will be useful here, for analytical purposes, to look separately at policy initiation and development on the one hand, and legislative initiation and development on the other.

Policy initiation and development takes place at several levels in that it ranges from sweeping 'macro' policies to detailed policies for particular sectors. Whatever the level, however, the Commission – important though it is – does not have a totally free hand in what it does. As is shown at various points elsewhere in this book, all sorts of other actors – including the Council of Ministers, the EP, the member states, sectional groups, regional and local authorities, and private firms – also attempt to play a part in the policy process. They do so by engaging in activities such producing policy papers, issuing exhortations and recommendations, and lobbying. Such activities are frequently designed to exert direct policy pressure on the Commission. From its earliest deliberations on a possible policy initiation the Commission has to take note of many of these outside voices if its proposals are to find broad support and be effective in the sectors to which they are directed. The Commission must concern itself not only with what it believes to be desirable but also with what is possible. The policy preferences of others must be recognised and, where necessary and appropriate, be accommodated.

Of the many pressures and influences to which the Commission is subject in the exercise of its policy initiation functions, the most important are those which emanate from the Council of Ministers. When the Council indicates that it wishes to see certain sorts of proposal laid before it, the Commission is obliged to respond. However, important though the Council has become as a policy-initiating body (see Chapter 7), the extent to which this has produced a decline in the initiating responsibilities and powers of the Commission ought not to be exaggerated. For the Council often finds it difficult to be bold and imaginative, and tends to be better at responding than at originating and proposing. Further to this, there has been an increasing tendency since the early 1980s for major policy initiatives to be sanctioned at European Council rather than Council of

Ministers level, and the Commission has adjusted itself quite well to this shift by not only taking instructions from the European Council but also using it to legitimise its own policy preferences. Four examples, each of which covers issues of great importance, illustrate the mutual interdependence of the Commission and the European Council in terms of policy initiation and development. First, the Commission's 1985 White Paper *Completing the Internal Market*, which spelt out a rationale, a programme, and a timetable for completing the internal market by 1992, was approved at the June 1985 Milan summit. Six months later, at the Luxembourg summit, it was agreed that this policy objective would be incorporated into the EEC Treaty via the SEA and that the institutional reforms that would be necessary if the 1992 objective was to be achieved would also be given treaty status. Commission reports on the internal market – covering both progress made and new measures that are deemed to be required – have subsequently featured regularly on European Council agendas, and have often produced requests from the European Council for follow-up action on the part of both EU institutions and member states. Second, shortly after the SEA came into operation in 1987, the Commission, and more especially Jacques Delors, began pressing the case for Economic and Monetary Union (EMU). The Commission played a major part in helping to set and shape the EMU policy agenda, with the consequence that the EMU provisions of the TEU largely reflected the Commission's preferences. Third, at the Strasbourg European Council in December 1989, the Commission's *Community Charter of the Fundamental Social Rights of Workers* (commonly referred to as 'the Social Charter') was adopted. The Charter did not contain specific legislative proposals for its application – these were left to an accompanying action programme – but the adoption of the Charter has since acted as an important reference point for the development of an EU social dimension. Fourth, much of the policy drive on the enlargement of the EU to the Central and Eastern European countries (CEECs) has been provided by the Commission working within a framework authorised by the European Council. Since the early 1990s there has barely been a European Council meeting that has either not received a report of some kind from the Commission on an aspect of enlargement or has not asked that such a report be prepared. The December 1995 Madrid summit, for example, called upon the Commission 'to take the evaluation of the effects of enlargement on Community policies further, particularly with regard to agriculture and structural policies' and requested the Commission 'to embark upon a preparation of a composite paper on enlargement' (European Council, 1995, p. 23). The composite paper was duly issued as a Commission communication in July 1997 under the title *Agenda 2000: For a Stronger and Wider Union* (Commission, 1997a). The 1300 page communication contained, most notably: (1) opinions on the ten CEEC applications – the recommendation was that accession negotiations should open with five applicants but should be delayed with the other five; (2) analyses of how to strengthen and reform EU policies so they could deal with enlargement and deliver sustainable growth; (3) proposals on how to finance enlargement. *Agenda 2000* has subsequently served to shape policy debate and decision-making within the EU, especially on the reform of the CAP and the Structural Funds, from European Council level downwards.

The Commission's policy-initiating activities are not, of course, restricted to major, cross-sectoral, innovatory policies and policy programmes of the kind just cited. They also, and indeed much more commonly, are directed at specific policy areas. For example: attempting to generate a more integrated approach to a policy area – as with the 1992 White Paper *Communication on the Future Development of the Common Transport Policy* and the more specific 1996 White Paper *A Strategy for Revitalising the Community's Railways;* attempting to strengthen existing policy frameworks – as with the 1997 Communication *Consumer Health and Food Safety* and the associated Green Paper *The General Principles of Food Law in the European Union;* and attempting to promote ideas, discussion and interest as a possible preliminary to getting a new policy area or initiative off the ground – as with the 1993 Green Paper on *The European Dimension of Education* or the 1995 Green Paper *Towards a Fair and Efficient Pricing in Transport – Policy Options for Internalizing the External Costs of Transport in the European Union.* Whatever their particular focus, however, most – though not all – policy initiatives need to be followed up with legislation if they are to have bite and be effective.

If the Commission is well placed with regard to policy initiatives and development, it is even better placed with regard to legislative initiatives and development, for it alone has the power to initiate and draft legislative proposals. The other two main institutions involved in the legislative process, the Council and the EP, can request the Commission to produce proposals (the Council under Article 208 of the TEC and the EP under Article 192), but they cannot do the initiating or drafting themselves. Moreover, after a legislative proposal has been formally tabled the Commission still retains a considerable measure of control, for it is difficult for the Council or the EP to amend it without the Commission's agreement: the Council can only do so by acting unanimously, and the EP can only do so in specified circumstances and then only with the support of an absolute majority of its component members (see Chapter 13 for further details on this).

As with the preparation of policy proposals, the Commission makes considerable use of outside sources, and is often subject to considerable outside pressures, when preparing legislative proposals. The preparation of legislative proposals is thus often accompanied by an extensive sounding and listening process, especially at the pre-proposal stage – that is, before the Commission has formally presented a proposal to the Council and the EP. In this process an important role is played by a vast network of advisory committees that have been established over the years.

The Commission's advisory committee network

The committees are of two main types.

(1) *Expert committees*. These consist of national officials, experts and specialists of various sorts. Although nominated by national governments the committee members are not normally viewed as official governmental spokesmen in the way that members of Council working parties are (see Chapter 7), so it is usually possible for them to conduct their affairs on a very informal basis. Many of these committees are well established, meet on a fairly regular basis, and have a more or less fixed membership; others are *ad hoc* – set up, very frequently, to discuss an early draft of a Commission legislative proposal – and can hardly be even described as committees in that they may only ever meet once or twice. In terms of their interests and concerns, some of the committees are wide-ranging, such as the Advisory Committee on Restrictive Practices and Dominant Positions and the Advisory Committee on Community Actions for the Elderly, while others are more specialised and technical, such as the Advisory Committee on Unfair Pricing Practices in Maritime Transport and the Committee of Experts on International Road Tariffs.

(2) *Consultative committees*. These are composed of representatives of sectional interests and are organised and funded by the Commission without reference to the national governments. Members are normally appointed by the Commission from nominations made by representative EU-level organisations: either umbrella groups such as the Union of Industrial and Employers' Confederations of Europe (UNICE), the European Trade Union Confederation (ETUC), and the Committee of Professional Agricultural Organisations of the European Community (COPA), or more specialised sectoral organisations and liaison groups such as the European Tour Operators' Association (ETOA) or the European Association of Manufacturers of Business Machines and Information Technology (EUROBIT). The effect of this appointments policy is that the consultative committees overwhelmingly comprise full-

time employees of associations and groups. The largest number of consultative committees are to be found in the agriculture sector, where there are over twenty committees for products covered by a market regime, plus half a dozen or so more general committees. Most of the agricultural advisory committees have a membership of thirty to fifty, but there are a few exceptions: the largest are those dealing with cereals, milk and dairy products, and sugar, whilst the smallest are the veterinary committee and the committee on hops.

In addition to these two types of committees there are many hybrids with mixed forms of membership.

Most of the advisory committees are chaired and serviced by the Commission. A few are serviced by the Council and technically are Council committees, but the Commission has observer status on these so the distinction between the two types of committee is of little significance in terms of their ability to advise the Commission.

The extent to which policy sectors are covered by advisory committees varies. One factor making for variation is the degree of importance of the policy within the EU's policy framework – it is hardly surprising, for example, that there should be many more agricultural advisory committees than there are educational advisory committees. Another factor is the dependence of the Commission in particular policy areas on outside expertise and technical knowledge. A third factor is the preferences of DGs – some incline towards the establishment of committees to provide them with advice, while others prefer to do their listening in less structured ways.

The influence exercised by the advisory committees varies enormously. In general, the committees of national experts are better placed than the consultative committees. There are a number of reasons for this. First, Commission consultation with the expert committees is usually compulsory in the procedure for drafting legislation, whereas – despite their name – it is usually optional with the consultative committees. Second, the expert committees can often go beyond offering the Commission technical advice and alert it to probable governmental reactions to a proposal, and therefore to possible problems that may arise at a future decision-making stage if certain views are not incorporated. Third, expert committees also have the advantage over consultative committees of tending to meet more regularly – often convening as necessary when something important is in the offing, whereas consultative committees tend to gather on average no more than two or three times a year. Usually, consultative committees are at their most influential when they have high-ranking figures amongst their membership, when they are given the opportunity to discuss policy at an early stage of development, when the timetable for the enactment of a proposal is flexible, and when the matter under consideration is not too constrained by existing legislation.

Executive functions

The Commission exercises wide executive responsibilities. That is, it is closely involved in the management, supervision and implementation of EU policies. Just how involved varies considerably across the policy spectrum, but as a general rule the Commission's executive functions tend to be more concerned with monitoring and coordinating developments, laying down the ground rules, carrying out investigations and giving rulings on significant matters (such as proposed company mergers, state aids, and applications for derogations from EU law) than they are with detailed 'ground level' policy implementation.

Three aspects of the Commission's executive functions are worth special emphasis.

Rule-making powers

It is not possible for the treaties, or for legislation made in the name of the Council or the European Parliament and the Council, to cover every possible area and eventuality in which a rule may be required. In circumstances and under conditions that are defined by the treaties and/or EU legislation the Commission is therefore delegated rule-making powers. This puts the Commission in a similar position to national executives: because of the frequent need for quick decisions in that grey area where policy overlaps with administration, and because too of the need to relieve the normal legislative process of over-involvement with highly detailed and specialised matters, it is desirable to have truncated and special rule-making arrangements for administrative and technical law.

The Commission used to issue at least 4000 legislative instruments per year in the form of directives, regulations, and decisions (see Chapter 10 for an examination of the different types of EU legislative instrument). In recent years, however, the number of Commission legislative instruments has dropped: in 1998 it issued 773 regulations, 537 decisions and 44 directives (Commission, 1999, p. 428). It remains to be seen whether this drop – which is partly occasioned by pressure on the Commission to simplify the EU legal framework – will prove to be permanent or temporary. The Commission also issues recommendations and opinions, but these do not usually have legislative force.

Most Commission legislation is confined to the filling in of details, or the taking of decisions, that follow automatically from Council, or European Parliament and Council, legislation. So the greatest proportion of Commission legislation is made up of regulations dealing with price adjustments and market support measures under the Common Agricultural Policy. Exhibit 10.1 provides an example of such legislation. But not quite all of the Commission's rule-making powers are confined to the routine and the straightforward. In at least three areas opportunities exist to make not just 'administrative' law but what verges on 'policy' law. First, under the ECSC Treaty the Commission is granted extensive rule-making powers subject, in many instances, only to 'consultations' with the Consultative Committee of the ECSC and the Council of Ministers. Article 60, for example, gives the Commission powers to define what constitutes 'unfair competitive practices' and 'discrimination practices', and under Article 61 it may set maximum prices. If a state of 'manifest crisis' is declared, as it was in October 1980 because of the Community's chronic overproduction of steel, the Commission's powers are increased further: it may then set minimum prices (Article 61) and also, with the 'assent' of the Council of Ministers, establish a system of production quotas (Article 58). Second, the management of the EU's Common External Tariff gives the Commission considerable manoeuvrability. It is, for example, empowered to introduce preventive measures for a limited period in order to protect the EU market from dumping by third countries. Third, in furtherance of the EU's competition policy, the Commission, supported by decisions of the Court of Justice, has taken advantage of the rather generally phrased Article 81 of the TEC (ex Article 85) to clarify and develop the position on restrictive practices through the issuing of regulations and decisions.

Management of EU finances

On the revenue side of the budget, EU income is subject to tight constraints determined by the Council (see Chapter 14 for an explanation of budgetary revenue). In overseeing the collection of this income the Commission has two main duties: to see that the correct rates are applied within certain categories of revenue, and to ensure that the proper payments are made to the EU by those national authorities which act as the EU's collecting agents.

On the expenditure side, the administrative arrangements vary according to the type of expenditure concerned. The Commission must, however, always operate within the approved annual budget (the EU is not legally permitted to run a budget deficit) and on the basis of the guidelines for expenditure headings that are laid down in EU law. Of the various ways in which the EU spends its money two are especially important in that together they account for over 75 per cent of total budgetary expenditure.

First, there is the Guarantee section of the European Agricultural Guidance and Guarantee Fund (EAGGF). This takes up around 45 per cent of the annual budget and is used for agricultural price support purposes. General management decisions concerning the EAGGF – such as whether, and on what conditions, to dispose of product surpluses – are taken by the Commission, usually via an appropriate management committee (see below). The practical application of agricultural policy and management decisions occurs at national levels through appropriate agencies (see Chapter 15).

Second, there are structural operations, the most important of which are conducted via the European Regional Development Fund (ERDF), the European Social Fund (ESF), and the Guidance Section of the EAGGF. Following the inclusion, via the SEA, of a new Title V in the EEC Treaty on 'Economic and Social Cohesion' and, in particular, of a new Article 130A under Title V which stated 'the Community shall aim at reducing disparities between the various regions and the backwardness of the least-favoured regions', it was decided in 1988 to double the size of the Structural Funds over a five-year period so that they would account for 25 per cent of the budget by 1993. It was also decided in 1988 to reform the Funds so that instead of each having its own rules and objectives they would be based on four shared principles: concentration (involving the collective use of the Funds in areas of greatest need); programming (mostly based on medium-term programmes for regional development, rather than 'one-off' projects); partnership (preparation, decision-making, and implementation of programmes and projects to be a shared responsibility between the Commission, national governments, and subnational bodies); and additionality (programmes and projects to be co-financed by the Community and appropriate national bodies). The Funds were to concentrate on shared objectives: developing backward regions, converting or adjusting declining industrial regions, combating long-term unemployment, integrating young people into the job market, and adjusting agricultural structures and developing rural areas.

When the Structural Funds came up for review in 1992–3 it was agreed that the arrangements which had been created in 1988 had worked reasonably well. Accordingly, the size of the Funds was again significantly increased (see Chapter 14) and their principles, objectives, and administrative arrangements were confirmed, subject to some fine tuning. This means that the Structural Funds are managed in the following way:

(1) National governments, in consultation with both the Commission and with the competent regional and local authorities, submit to the

Commission three- to five-year plans. The plans – which can be national, regional or local in scope – identify strategies and priorities for achieving the five objectives and indicate how EU financial assistance is to be used. (2) On the basis of the plans submitted by the member states, in dialogue with the appropriate national and subnational representatives, and after consulting the appropriate advisory committee – either the Advisory Committee on the Development and Conversion of Regions, the Committee of the European Social Fund, or the Committee on Agricultural Structures and Rural Development – the Commission draws up what are known as Community Support Frameworks (CSFs). By setting out a statement of the priorities for action, outlining the forms of assistance that are to be made available, and indicating the financial allocations that are envisaged, CSFs provide a reference framework for the applications for assistance that are made to the Funds.
(3) Procedures for operationalising CSFs vary. The three main forms of implementation are through operational programmes (there may be several types of programme in a particular region), individual applications for large-scale projects, and global grants (whereby the Commission entrusts the administration of a budget to a national or regional intermediary).
(4) Monitoring and assessment of CSFs and individual operations is undertaken by monitoring committees comprising representatives of the Commission and of national, regional and local partners.

Agenda 2000 contained proposals for improving the efficiency and visibility of the Structural Funds. Central to the Commission's proposals were: (1) reducing the number of objectives to three – support for the poorest regions, support for the economic and social conversion of areas with structural difficulties, and support for the development and modernisation of education and training and employment policies; (2) simplifying and decentralising the management of the Funds, essentially by means of a new partnership between the Commission, the member states and the regions. These *Agenda 2000* proposals were subsequently accepted by the member states. As part of the reform of management procedures, it is intended that there should be one programme per region and more room for manoeuvre on the part of the monitoring committees.

Moving beyond the different parts of the Commission's financial management functions to look at the overall financial picture, it is clear that the Commission's ability to manage EU finances effectively is greatly weakened by the fact that the Council and the EP (especially the former) control the upper limits of the revenue base and take framework spending decisions. In the past this sometimes caused considerable difficulties because it meant that if it became obvious during the course of a financial year that expenditure was exceeding income the Commission could not step in at an early stage and take appropriate action by, for example, increasing the Value Added Tax (VAT) ceiling on revenue or reducing agricultural price guarantees. All the Commission could do, and regularly did, was to make out a case as to what should be done. This dependence on the Council and EP remains, but the general situation is not as fraught as it was, because since 1988 there have been planned and clearer controls on the growth of both income and expenditure, and there are provisions for the Commission to act quickly if expenditure expands beyond targets in the main 'problem' area of agriculture.

Another, quite different, factor in weakening the Commission's financial management capability is that it does not itself directly undertake much of the front-line implementation of EU spending programmes and schemes. Rather, it mostly works through and with agencies and companies that act on its behalf. This point is explored in the next section, but it is worth emphasising here too, not least since a major thrust of the criticisms that led to the resignation of the Santer Commission were that the monitoring and control mechanisms in respect of these agencies and companies were too lax. Steps are now being taken to tighten the mechanisms.

Before leaving the Commission's responsibilities for financial management it should also be noted that the Commission has some responsibilities for coordinating and managing finances that are not drawn exclusively from EU sources. These responsibilities mostly cover environmental programmes, scientific and technological research programmes, and educational programmes in which the member states are joined by non-member states.

A particularly important programme area in which the Commission has assumed coordination and management responsibilities is in the provision of Western assistance to states of the former Soviet bloc and Soviet Union. The seven-nation Western Economic Summit of July 1989 called on the Commission to coordinate a programme of assistance from the OECD countries to Poland and Hungary. This resulted in the PHARE programme (Poland and Hungary: Aid for the Restructuring of Economies), which was subsequently extended to other countries of the former Soviet bloc. The PHARE programme (now called Programme of Community Aid for Central and Eastern European Countries) is by no means the only channel via which Western aid is being made available to the fledgling democracies of Central and Eastern Europe, but it is an extremely important one, with billions of euros being made available for purposes such as increasing investment, expanding vocational training and improving environmental standards.

Supervision of 'front-line' policy implementation

The Commission's role with regard to the implementation of EU policies is primarily that of supervisor and overseer. It does undertake a limited amount of direct policy implementation itself – in connection, most notably, with competition policy – but the bulk of the practical/routine/day-by-day/front-line implementation of EU policies is delegated to appropriate agencies within the member states. Examples of such national agencies are: Customs and Excise Authorities (which deal with most matters pertaining to movements across the EU's external and internal borders); veterinary inspection teams (which check quality standards on foodstuffs); and Ministries of Agriculture and Agricultural Intervention Boards (which are responsible for controlling the volume of agricultural produce on domestic markets and which deal directly with farmers and traders about payments and charges). To ensure that policies are applied in a reasonably uniform manner throughout the member states the Commission attempts to supervise, or at least hold a watching brief on, the national agencies and the way they perform their EU duties. It is a task that carries with it many difficulties, four of which are especially important.

First, in general, the Commission is not sufficiently resourced for the job. There just are not enough officials in the DGs, and not enough money to contract the required help from outside agencies, to see that the agriculture, fishing, regional and other policies are properly implemented. The Commission is therefore heavily dependent on the good faith and willing cooperation of the member states. However, even in those policy spheres where it is in almost constant communication with national officials, the Commission cannot be aware of everything that is going on, and with respect to those areas where contacts and flows of communication between Brussels and national agencies are irregular and not well ordered it is almost impossible for Commission officials to have an accurate idea as to what is happening 'at the front'. Even if the Commission comes to suspect that something is amiss with an aspect of policy implementation, lack of resources can mean that it is not possible for the matter to be fully investigated: in respect of fraud, for example, in 1998 there were only 130 officials in the Commission's anti-fraud office, UCLAF. (In early 1999, as the Santer College sought to defend itself against charges that it was not sufficiently robust in tackling fraud, it was announced that UCLAF would be replaced by a larger and independent European Fraud Prevention Office.)

The second difficulty is that even when they are willing to cooperate fully, national agencies are not always capable of implementing policies as the Commission would wish. One reason for this is that some EU policies are, by their very nature, extremely difficult to administer. For example, the Common Fisheries Policy is extremely difficult to police, with the provisions on fishing zones, total allowable catches and conservation requiring surveillance measures such as obligatory and properly kept logbooks, port inspections and aerial patrols. Another reason why national agencies are not always capable of effective policy implementation is that national officials are often poorly trained and/or are overburdened by the complexities of EU rules. The jumble of rules that officials have to apply is illustrated by the import levy on biscuits, which varies according to cereal, milk, fat and sugar content, while the export refund varies also according to egg content. Another example of rule complexity is seen in respect of the export of beef, which is subject to numerous separate regulations, which themselves are subject to an array of permanent and temporary amendments.

The third difficulty is that agencies in the member states do not always wish to see EU law applied. Competition policy, for example, is rich in such examples, but there is often little action the Commission can take against a deliberately recalcitrant state given the range of policy instruments available to governments that wish to assist domestic industries and the secretiveness with which these can often be arranged.

The fourth and final difficulty is that EU law can be genuinely open to different interpretations. Sometimes indeed it is deliberately flexible so as to allow for adjustments to national circumstances.

The role of management and regulatory committees

As is clear from the above discussion, a number of different procedures apply with regard to how the Commission exercises its executive functions. An important dimension of these differences concerns the role of management and regulatory committees. These committees have some role to play with regard to each of the three aspects of the Commission's executive powers outlined above, but particularly the first two. This is because the committees are very important in terms of how the Commission may act when it wishes to adopt appropriate implementing/adaptive measures in respect of Council and European Parliament and Council legislation.

Because the arrangements regarding the Commission's implementing powers were becoming ever more confusing and complex, and because the projected completion of the internal market by 1992 would entail a host of implementing decisions, the Single European Act (SEA) provided for a clarification of the procedures. On the basis of the SEA, and of a Council decision of 13 July 1987, the Commission's management and implementing powers in respect of Council decisions were clarified and streamlined. While no new procedures were introduced, it was established what the possible procedures were, and some guidelines were laid down as to which of these should apply in particular cases.

As can be seen from Table 6.2, there are significant differences between the powers of the different types of committee: advisory committees can only *advise*; management committees can *block* Commission decisions by a qualified majority vote; regulatory committees must give their *approval* for Commission decisions by a qualified majority vote. These differences have led to disputes on 'comitology' between the Council on the one hand and the Commission and the EP on the other regarding which procedure should apply – as is perhaps inevitable given that when the 1987 reforms were being discussed the EP only wanted Procedures I and II and the Commission did not want procedure IIIb or Safeguard Measure b. The main bone of contention is that the Council has made too much use of the regulatory committee procedure and insufficient use of the advisory committee procedure. In 1998 the advisory procedure was selected in less than a dozen cases, the management procedure in about 90 – including over 30 using variant (b) – and the regulatory procedure in over 40, including over ten using variant (b) (Commission, 1999, p. 384).

Concentrating here on just management committees and regulatory committees – advisory committees having been discussed earlier – both types of committee are chaired and serviced by the Commission. The committee members are governmental representatives with, in an average-sized committee, two or three middle-ranking officials from appropriate ministries attending on behalf of each state. There is no hard and fast distinction of either principle or policy responsibility between the two types of committee. In the past management committees were mostly concerned with agriculture – there are currently over thirty of these, most of them having a specific sectoral responsibility for the CAP's product regimes – but there are now an increasing number in other areas too. Regulatory committees tend to be concerned with harmonisation and vary greatly in their sectoral interests. Some, such as the Standing Committee on Foodstuffs, the Steering Committee on Feedingstuffs and the Regulatory Committee on the Improvement of Information in the Field of Safety, Hygiene and Health at the Workplace, have fairly broad briefs. Others, such as the committees 'for the adaptation to technical progress of directives on the removal of technical barriers to trade', are highly specialised: they include committees on dangerous substances and pre-parations, on motor vehicles and on fertilisers.

Both types of committee, management and regulatory, do similar things, with variations occurring not so much between management and regulatory committees as such, but rather between individual committees

Table 6.2 *Procedures to be used in respect of the Commission's implementing powers**

Procedure I (Advisory Committee)	The Commission submits a draft of the measures to be taken to the committee. The committee delivers an opinion on the draft, by a simple majority if necessary. The Commission takes 'the utmost account' of the opinion delivered by the committee.
Procedure II (Management Committee)	The Commission submits a draft of the measures to be taken to the committee. If the Commission's measures are opposed by a qualified majority in the committee then either: Variant (a) The Commission may defer application of its decision for up to one month. Variant (b) The Commission shall defer application of its decision for up to three months. Within the one month and three month deadlines the Council may take a different decision by a qualified majority vote.
Procedure III (Regulatory Committees)	The Commission submits a draft of the measures to be taken by the committee. If the Commission's measures are not supported by a qualified majority in the committee, or if no opinion is delivered, the matter is referred to the Council. The Council may, within a period not exceeding three months, take a decision on the Commission's proposal by a qualified majority. If the Council does not act within the three month period then either: Variant (a) The proposal shall be adopted by the Commission. Variant (b) The proposal shall be adopted by the Commission except where a simple majority in the Council votes against adoption.

$\longrightarrow$

Table 6.2 (*cont.*)

Safeguard Measures (Mainly trade)	No committee is appointed, but the Commission must notify, and in some cases must consult with, the member states in respect of a measure to be taken. If any member state asks for the Commission's measures to be referred to the Council, within a time limit to be determined, then either: Variant (a) The Council may take a different decision by a qualified majority within a time limit to be determined. Variant (b) The Council must confirm, amend, or revoke the Commission's decision. If the Council takes no decision within a time limit to be determined the Commission's decision is revoked.

* Which procedure applies is specified in the enabling legislation.

according to their terms of reference, the nature of the subject matter with which they are concerned, and how they are regarded by the Commission. In addition to considering proposed Commission decisions, agenda items for committee meetings could include analysing the significance of data of various kinds, looking at how existing legislation is working, considering how existing legislation may be modified to take account of technical developments (the particular responsibility of the technical progress committees) and assessing market situations (a prime task for the agricultural committees). Committees meet as appropriate, which means almost weekly in the case of agricultural products that require frequent market adjustments, such as cereals, sugar and wines, and in other cases means hardly at all.

Those who criticise the EU on the ground that it is undermining national sovereignties sometimes cite regulatory and management committees as part of their case. They point to the rarity of adverse opinions, the low number of no opinions, the frequency with which measures go through without unanimous support, and the ability of the Commission – especially under the management procedure – to ignore or circumvent unfavourable votes. There is, however, another side to this; a side which suggests that the power of the Commission to control the committees and impose its will on the states ought not to be exaggerated. Five points in particular ought to be noted. First, although some of the committees do exercise important powers, for the most part they tend to work within fairly narrowly defined limits. Anything very controversial is almost invariably referred to a Council meeting. Second, many negative votes by states are cast tactically rather than as part of a real attempt to stop a proposal. That is, a national delegation might well recognise that a measure is going to be approved but will vote against it or abstain in order to satisfy a political interest at home. Third, as with all aspects of its activity, it is just not in the Commission's long-term interests to abuse its powers by forcing unwelcome or unpopular measures through a committee. It wants and needs cooperation, and if a proposal meets serious opposition in a committee a good chairman will, unless special circumstances apply, suggest revisions rather than press for a vote that may have divisive consequences. Fourth, the Council tends to be jealous of its powers and would move quickly against the Commission if it thought committees of any sort were being used to undermine Council power. Finally, where particularly important policy matters are concerned, or when the member states have been unable to agree on what sort of committee to establish, the Council sometimes reserves implementing powers for itself.

The EP, aggrieved at its inability to exercise much control over decisions taken by the committees, became increasingly critical in the 1990s of comitology and began pressing for a fundamental reform of the system. It had hoped that the issue would be dealt with in the 1996–7 IGC, but no decisions were taken, apart from a request being made to the Commission to look at the matter and make proposals by the end of 1998. When the proposals were delivered they did not meet the Parliament's expectations, being focused primarily on improvements in transparency and communications rather than on structural reform.

The guardian of the legal framework

In association with the Court of Justice, the Commission is charged with ensuring that the treaties and EU legislation are respected. This role links closely with the Commission's supervisory and implementing responsibilities. Indeed the lack of a full EU-wide policy-implementing framework means that its legal watchdog role serves, to some extent, as a substitute for the detailed day-to-day application of policies that at national level involves such routine activities as inspecting premises, checking employee lists and auditing returns. It is a role that is extremely difficult to exercise: transgressors of EU law do not normally wish to advertise their illegal actions, and they are often protected by, or may even be, national governments.

✻   ✻   ✻

The Commission may become aware of possible illegalities in one of a number of ways. In the case of non-incorporation or incorrect incorporation of a directive into national law this is obvious enough, since directives normally specify a time by which the Commission must be supplied with full details of national incorporation measures. A second way is through self-notification. For example, states are obliged to notify the Commission about all national draft regulations and standards concerning technical specifications so that the Commission may satisfy itself that they will not cause barriers to trade. Similarly, under Article 88 of the TEC (ex Article 93), state aid must be referred to the Commission for its inspection. Self-notifications also come forward under Article 81 the TEC (ex Article 85), because although parties are not obliged to notify the Commission of possible restrictive business practices, they frequently do, either because they wish for clarification on whether or not a practice is in legal violation, or because they wish to seek an exemption (if a notification is not made within a specified time limit exemption is not permissible). A third way in which illegalities may come to the Commission's attention is from the many representations that are made by individuals, organisations, firms or member states who believe that their interests are being damaged by the alleged illegal actions of another party. For example, Germany has frequently complained about the amount of subsidies that many national governments give to their steel industries. A fourth way is through the Commission's own efforts. Such efforts may take one of several forms: investigations by one of its small monitoring/investigatory/fraud teams; careful analysis of the information that is supplied by outside agencies; or simply a Commission official reading a newspaper report that suggests a government or a firm is doing, or is not doing, something that looks suspicious under EU law.

Infringement proceedings are initiated against member states for not notifying the Commission of measures taken to incorporate directives into national law, for non-incorporation or incorrect incorporation of directives, and for non-application or incorrect application of EU law – most commonly in connection with internal market and industrial affairs, indirect taxation, agriculture, and environmental and consumer protection. Before any formal action is taken against a state it is informed by the Commission that it is in possible breach of its legal obligations. If, after the Commission has carried out an investigation, the breach is confirmed and continues, a procedure comes into force under Article 226 of the TEC (ex Article 169), whereby the Commission

shall deliver a reasoned opinion on the matter after giving the State concerned the opportunity to submit its observations. If the State concerned does not comply with the opinion within the period laid down by the Commission, the latter may bring the matter before the Court of Justice.

Since most infringements have implications for the functioning of the market, the Commission usually seeks to ensure that these procedures operate according to a tight timetable: normally a state is given about two months to present its observations and a similar period to comply with the reasoned opinion.

Most cases, it must be emphasised, are settled at an early stage. So in an average year the Commission issues over 1000 letters of formal notice, delivers over 300 reasoned opinions and makes 50–100 references to the Court of Justice (see Table 13.2 for a detailed breakdown of recent figures). Italy, France and Greece consistently figure high in these lists. One reason for so many early settlements is that most infringements occur not as a result of wilful avoidance of EU law but rather from genuine differences over interpretation, or from national administrative and legislative procedures that have occasioned delay.

Although there are differences between member states in their enthusiasm for aspects of EU law, most wish to avoid open confrontation with EU institutions. If states do not wish to submit to an EU law it is therefore more customary for them to drag their feet rather than be openly obstructive. Delay can, however, be a form of obstruction, in that states know it could be years before the Commission, and even more the Court of Justice, brings them to heel. Environmental legislation illustrates this, with most states not having fully incorporated and/or implemented only parts of long-standing EU legislation – on matters such as air pollution, bathing water and drinking water.

With regard to what action the Commission can take if it discovers breaches, or prospective breaches, of EU law, that depends very much on the circumstances. Four different sorts of circumstance will be taken as illustrations of this point:

- *Non-compliance by a member state.* Until the entry into force of the Maastricht Treaty in 1993, the Commission was not empowered to impose sanctions against member states that were in breach of their legal obligations. Respect for Commission decisions was dependent on the goodwill and political judgement of the states themselves, backed up by the ability of the Commission to make a referral to the Court of Justice – though the Court too could not impose sanctions. However, the Commission is now permitted, when a member state refuses to comply with a judgement of the Court, to bring the state back before the Court and in so doing to specify a financial penalty that should be imposed. The Court takes the final decision.

- *Firms breaching EU law on restrictive practices.* Treaty provisions (notably Article 81 of the TEC), secondary legislation and Court judgements have established a considerable volume of EU law in the sphere of restrictive practices. If at all possible, however, the Commission avoids using this law to take formal action against firms. This is partly because of the ill-feeling that can be generated by open confrontation, and partly because formal action necessitates the use of cumbersome and protracted bureaucratic procedures within the Commission itself. Offending parties are therefore encouraged to fall into line or to reach an agreement with the Commission during the extensive informal processes that always precede formal action. If this fails, however, fines can result. Thus in 1989 fines totalling 60 million ecu (£42 million) were imposed on 23 plastics groups for price-fixing in the early 1980s (this subsequently led to appeals to the Court of Justice and to the reduction of some of the fines).

- *Firms breaching EU rules on state aid.* Articles 87–9 of the TEC provide the Commission with the power to take action against what is deemed to be unacceptable state subsidisation of business and industry. This power can take the form of requiring that the state aid in question be repaid, as was the case in July 1990 when the Commission instructed the UK government to recover £44.4 million worth of concessions that had been given to British Aerospace at the time of its acquisition of the Rover car group in 1988. (Interestingly, this case then dragged on through appeals and legal technicalities, and when the money was eventually repaid, in May 1993, the total had risen to £57.6 million because of lost interest calculated from August 1990 – this was the first time that aid repayment had involved the reimbursement of interest.)

- *Potential breaches of EU rules on company mergers.* Council Regulation 4064/89 (the so-called Merger Control Regulation), which came into effect in September 1990, specifies the Commission's powers in some detail. Specified information regarding proposed mergers and takeovers above certain limits has to be notified to the Commission. On receipt of the information the Commission must decide within one month whether it proposes either to let the deal go ahead on the ground that competition would not be harmed, or to open proceedings. If it decides on the latter it has four months to carry out an investigation, in the course of which it is entitled to enter the premises of firms and seize documents. Any firm that supplies false information during the course of a Commission inquiry, or conducts a merger or takeover without gaining clearance from the Commission, is liable to be fined up to 10 per cent of its annual sales.

In practice the Commission normally authorises the proposed mergers that are referred to it, though conditions are often laid down requiring, for example, some of the assets of the merging firms to be sold off. The first merger to be blocked was in 1991 when – to the background of a fierce disagreement within the Commission (between those who wished to apply the competition rules strictly and those who wished to be 'flexible' in the interests of building strong, European-based global companies) the College of Commissioners voted by nine votes to eight to block the Aerospatiale (of France)/Alenia (of Italy) bid to buy De Haviland Canada from Boeing.

As with most of its other activities, the Commission's ability to exercise its legal guardianship function is blunted by a number of constraints and restrictions. Three are especially important:

- The problem of limited resources means that choices have to be made about which cases are worth pursuing, and with how much vigour. For example only about sixty officials – in a specially created task force located in DGIV – undertake the detailed and highly complex work that is necessary to give effect to the 1989 Merger Control Regulation.
- Relevant and sufficiently detailed information can be difficult to obtain – either because it is deliberately hidden from prying Commission officials, or because, as is the case with many aspects of market conditions, reliable figures are just not available. An example of an EU law that is difficult to apply because of lack of information is the Council Directive of 2 April 1979 on the Conservation of Wild Birds (79/409/EEC). Amongst other things, the directive provides protection for most species of migrant birds and forbids killing for trade and by indiscriminate methods. Because the shooting of birds is popular in some countries, several governments were slow to transpose the Directive into national law, and have been reluctant to do much about applying the law since it has been transposed. On the first of these implementing problems – transposition – the Commission can acquire the information it needs since states are obliged to inform it of the measures they have taken. On the second of the implementation problems, however – application of the law by national authorities against transgressors – the Commission has been much less able to make judgements about whether states are fulfilling their responsibilities: it is very difficult to know what efforts are really being made by national authorities to catch shooters and hunters.
- Political considerations can inhibit the Commission from acting as vigorously as it might in certain problem areas and in particular cases.

An important reason for this is that the Commission does not normally wish to upset or politically embarrass the governments of member states if it is at all avoidable: the Commission does, after all, have to work closely and continuously with the national governments both on an individual and – in the Council of Ministers – on a collective basis. An example of political pressures inhibiting the Commission in this way is provided by the above-cited Conservation of Wild Birds Directive: in addition to the practical problem of acquiring information on the killing of birds, the Commission's sensitive political antennae serve to hold it in check in that it is well aware of the unpopularity and political difficulties that would be created for some governments if action were taken against the thousands who break this law. Another example of the inhibiting role of political pressures is the cautious line that the Commission has often adopted towards multinational corporations that appear to be in breach of EU competition law: to take action against multinationals is to risk generating political opposition from the member states in which the companies are based, and also risks being self-defeating in that it may cause companies to transfer their activities outside the EU. (There are also, of course, practical problems of the sort noted in the previous point when seeking to act against multinationals: it is very difficult to follow investigations through when dealing with organisations that are located in several countries, some of which may be outside Europe.) In exercising the role of guardian of the legal framework the Commission thus attempts to operate in a flexible and politically sensitive manner. It would not be in its or the EU's interests to use an overly heavy hand.

External representative and negotiator

The different aspects of the Commission's role with respect to the EU's external relations are considered in some detail in Chapter 16, so attention here will be limited to simply identifying those aspects. There are, essentially, six.

First, the Commission is centrally involved in determining and conducting the EU's external trade relations. On the basis of Article 133 of the TEC, and with its actions always subject to Council approval, the Commission represents and acts on behalf of the EU both in formal negotiations, such as those that are conducted under the auspices of the World Trade Organisation (WTO), and in the more informal and exploratory exchanges that are common between, for example, the EU and the United States over world agricultural trade, and between the EU and Japan over access to each other's markets.

Second, the Commission has important negotiating and managing responsibilities in respect of the various special external agreements that the EU has with many countries and groups of countries. These agreements take various forms but the more advanced include not only privileged trading conditions but also such things as European Investment Bank loans, financial aid and political dialogue.

Third, the Commission represents the EU at, and participates in the work of, a number of important international organisations. Three of these are specifically mentioned in the TEC: the United Nations and its specialised agencies (Article 302); the Council of Europe (Article 303); and the Organisation for Economic Cooperation and Development (Article 304).

Fourth, the Commission has responsibilities for acting as a key point of contact between the EU and non-member states. Over 160 countries have diplomatic missions accredited to the EU and the Commission is expected to keep them informed about EU affairs, either through the circulation of documents or by making its officials available for information briefings and lobbying. The EU, for its part, maintains an extensive network of diplomatic missions abroad, numbering over 120 delegations and offices, and these are staffed by Commission employees.

Fifth, the Commission is entrusted with important responsibilities with regard to applications for EU membership. Upon receipt of an application the Council normally asks the Commission to carry out a detailed investigation of the implications and to submit an opinion (an opinion that the Council need not of course accept, which happened in 1976 when it rejected the Commission's proposal that Greece be offered a pre-accession period of unlimited duration and instead authorised negotiations for full membership). If and when negotiations begin, the Commission, operating within Council-approved guidelines, acts as the EU's main negotiator, except on showpiece ministerial occasions or when particularly sensitive or difficult matters call for an inter-ministerial resolution of differences. The whole process – from the lodging of an application to accession – can take years. Portugal, for example, applied in March 1977; the Commission forwarded a favourable opinion to the Council in May 1978; negotiations opened in October 1978 but were not concluded until March 1985; and Portugal eventually joined in January 1986 – eight years and ten months after applying. The ten CEECs that have applied for EU membership lodged their applications between 1994 and 1996, and it is anticipated that none will become members before 2004–5.

Finally, the Commission is 'fully associated' with the work carried out under the CFSP pillar of the TEU. The intergovernmental and non-EC nature of the CFSP pillar naturally means that the Commission's role is essentially supportive and secondary to that of the Council, and not in any way comparable to the role it undertakes with regard to external trade. That said, however, the Commission's CFSP inputs can be important, especially when the Council Presidency is under-resourced or over-stretched and when EC instruments – usually associated with trade – are utilised in support of CFSP activities.

Mediator and conciliator

Much of EU decision-making, especially in the Council of Ministers, is based on searches for agreements between competing interests. The Commission is very much involved in trying to bring about these agreements, and a great deal of its time is taken up looking for common ground, to allow compromises that are somewhat more than the lowest common denominator. As a consequence the Commission is often obliged to be guarded and cautious with its proposals. Radical initiatives, perhaps involving what it really believes needs to be done, are almost certain to meet with fierce opposition. More moderate proposals on the other hand, perhaps taking the form of adjustments and extensions to existing policy, and preferably presented in a technocratic rather than an ideological manner, are more likely to be acceptable. Hence the Commission must often subject itself to a somewhat grudging incrementalism.

The Commission is not the only EU body that consciously seeks to oil the wheels of decision-making. As is shown in Chapter 7, the Council itself has taken steps to improve its own machinery. But the Commission is particularly well placed to act as mediator and conciliator. One reason for this is that it is normally seen as being non-partisan: its proposals may therefore be viewed less suspiciously than any which come from, say, the chairman of a Council working party. Another reason is that in many instances the Commission is simply in the best position to judge which proposals are likely to command support, both inside and outside the Council. This is because of the continuous and extensive discussions which the Commission has with interested parties from the earliest considerations of a policy proposal through to its enactment. Unlike the other institutions, the Commission is represented at virtually every stage and in virtually every forum of the EU's decision-making system.

Although there are naturally limitations on what can be achieved, the effectiveness with which the Commission exercises this mediating role can be considerably influenced by the competence of its officials. While, for example, one Commission official may play a crucial role in driving a proposal through a Council working party, another may be so incompetent as not only to prejudice the Commission's own position but also to threaten the progress of the whole proposal. Many questions must be handled with care and political sensitivity. When should a proposal be brought forward, and in what form? At what point will an adjustment in the Commission's position open the way to progress in the Council? Is there anything to be gained from informal discussions with 'awkward delegations'? These, and questions such as these, call for highly developed political skills.

The conscience of the Union

In performing each of the above tasks the Commission is supposed to stand apart from sectional and national interests. While others might look to the particular, it should look to the general; while others might look to the benefits to be gained from the next deal, it should keep at least one eye on the horizon. As many have described it, the Commission should be the 'conscience' of the Union.

Christopher Tugendhat, a former Commissioner, has commented on this role. Among other things, he states that the Commission exists 'to represent the general interest in the welter of national ones and to point the way ahead, but also drawing the attention of member states to new and more daring possibilities' (Tugendhat, 1986). Ideally this may be so. But in practice it is very difficult to operationalise. One reason for this is that it is highly questionable whether such a thing as the 'general interest' exists: there are few initiatives that do not threaten the interests of at least some – were this not the case there would not be so many disagreements in the Council. Another reason is that many in the Commission doubt whether it is worth pursuing 'daring possibilities' if it is clear that they will be rejected and may even generate anti-Commission feelings.

In practice, therefore, the Commission tends not to be so detached, so far-seeing or so enthusiastic in pressing the *esprit communautaire* as some would like. This is not to say that it does not attempt to map out the future or attempt to press for developments that it believes will be generally beneficial. On the contrary, it is precisely because the Commission does seek to act in the general interest that the smaller EU states tend to see it as something of a protector and hence are normally supportive of the Commission being given greater powers. Nor is it to deny that the Commission is sometimes ambitious in its approach and long-term in its perspective – as demonstrated by the SEM programme, the Social Charter, the championing of the cause of EMU, and the campaign launched in late 1992 that produced a White Paper in late 1993 setting out a medium-term strategy for growth, competitiveness and employment. But the fact is that the Commission does operate in the real EU world, and often that necessitates looking to the short rather than to the long term, and to what is possible rather than what is desirable. It was largely because Jacques Santer recognised that the climate was not ready for new major initiatives that soon after becoming Commission President in 1995 he declared that the aim must be 'to do less, but do it better'.

Concluding remarks

It is frequently stated that there has been a decline in the Commission's powers since the mid 1960s. Commentators have particularly stressed a diminution in the Commission's initiating role and a corresponding weakening of its ability to offer real vision and leadership. It has become, it is claimed, too reactive in exercising its responsibilities: reactive to the pressures of the many interests to which it is subject; reactive to the immediacy of events; and above all reactive to the increasing number of 'instructions' it receives from the Council of Ministers and the European Council.

Unquestionably, there is something in this view. The explanation for why it has happened is to be sought in a combination of factors. The rather rigid vertical lines within the Commission's own organisational structure sometimes make it difficult for a broad vision to emerge. The tensions that are seemingly present between the politically creative elements of the Commission's responsibilities and the bureaucratic roles of administering and implementing have perhaps never been properly resolved. Beyond such internal considerations, factors such as the frequent appearance on the EU agenda of politically sensitive matters, and the desire of politicians not to cede too much power to others if it can be avoided, have resulted in the states being reluctant to grant too much autonomy to the Commission.

But the extent to which there has been a decline should not be exaggerated. Certainly the Commission has had to trim more than it would like, and certainly it has suffered its share of political defeats – not least with regard to its wish for stronger treaty-based powers. But in some respects its powers have actually increased as it has adapted itself to the ever-changing nature of and demands upon the EU. As has been shown, the Commission exercises, either by itself or in association with other bodies, a number of crucially important functions. Moreover, it has been at the heart of pressing the case for, and putting forward specific proposals in relation to, all of the major issues that have been at the heart of the EU agenda in recent years: the SEM, EMU, the social dimension, institutional reform, enlargement, the strategy for promoting growth, and the reform of the CAP and the Structural Funds. Perhaps the Commission is not quite the driving force that some of the Founding Fathers had hoped, but in many ways it is both central and vital to the whole EU system.

Chapter 7

The Council of Ministers

Responsibilities and functions
Composition
The operation of the Council
Concluding comments

The Council of Ministers is the principal meeting place of the national governments and is the EU's main decision-making institution.

When the Community was founded in the 1950s many expected that in time, as joint policies were seen to work and as the states came to trust one another more, the role of the Council would gradually decline, especially in relation to the Commission. This has not happened. On the contrary, by jealously guarding the responsibilities that are accorded to it in the treaties, and by adapting its internal mechanisms to enable it to cope more easily with the increasing volume of business that has come its way, the Council has not only defended, but has in some respects extended, its power and influence. This has naturally produced some frustration in the Commission, and also in the EP. It has also ensured that national governments are centrally placed to influence most aspects of EU business.

There was also a general expectation when the Community was founded that governments would gradually come to be less concerned about national sovereignty considerations and that this would be reflected in an increasing use of majority voting in the Council. Until the 1980s, however, there was little movement in this direction: even when the treaties permitted majority votes, the Council normally preferred to proceed on the basis of consensual agreements. This preference for unanimity naturally bolstered the intergovernmental, as opposed to the supranational, side of the Community's nature and resulted in a tendency for Council decision-making processes to be slow and protracted. As will be shown, this situation has changed considerably in recent years.

Responsibilities and functions

The principal responsibility of the Council is to take policy and legislative decisions. As is shown in Chapters 6, 9 and 13, the Commission and the EP also have such powers, but they are not comparable to those of the Council.

The extent to which the Council must work with, and is dependent upon the cooperation of, the Commission and the EP in respect of policy and decision-making varies between policy areas and according to what type of decisions are being made. In broad terms, the Council has most room for independent manoeuvre when it is acting under pillars two and three of the EU, for then it is not as restricted as it is under pillar one to taking decisions only on the basis of Commission proposals, and the EP is largely limited to, at best, consultative and information-sharing roles.

The Council is less independent under pillar one, especially when legislation is concerned. There are two main reasons for this. First, when making legislation the Council can only act on the basis of proposals that are made to it by the Commission. Second, reforms contained in the SEA, the Maastricht Treaty and the Amsterdam Treaty have resulted in the EP becoming a very important actor in the legislative process. Prior to the TEU the Council was formally the EC's sole legislature, but under the co-decision procedure created by the Maastricht Treaty the EP became co-legislator with the Council in those policy areas where the procedure applies. As shown in Chapters 5 and 13, the procedure has applied to most legislation since the entry into force of the Amsterdam Treaty. In 1998 the Council adopted 27 directives, 202 regulations and 189 decisions in its own name, and under co-decision with the EP adopted 26 directives, no regulations and 7 decisions (Commission, 1999, p. 428). As the Amsterdam Treaty takes effect, the proportion of EU laws adopted in the Council's sole name will fall and those adopted with the EP will increase.

It should not be thought that because the TEC states that the Council can only develop legislation on the basis of Commission proposals, the Council is thereby deprived of all powers of initiation. In practice ways have been found, if not to circumvent the Commission entirely, at least to allow the Council a significant policy-initiating role. Article 208 (ex 152) of the TEC is especially useful: 'The Council may request the Commission to undertake any studies the Council considers desirable for the attainment of the common objectives, and to submit to it any appropriate proposals.' In the view of many observers the use that has been made of this article, and the very specific instructions that have sometimes been issued to the Commission under its aegis, are against its intended spirit. Be that as it may, the political weight of the Council is such that the Commission is bound to pay close attention to the ministers' wishes.

In addition to Article 208, four other factors have enhanced the Council's policy-initiating role.

(1) The increasing adoption by the Council of opinions, resolutions, agreements and recommendations. These are not legal texts but they carry

political weight and it is difficult for the Commission to ignore them. Sometimes they are explicitly designed to pressurise the Commission to come up with proposals for legislation.

(2) The movement of the EU into policy spheres that are not covered, or are not covered clearly, in the treaties. This sometimes produces uncertainty regarding the exact responsibilities of decision-making bodies, and hence grey areas that the Council can exploit.

(3) The increasingly developed Council machinery. There are now many places in the Council's network where ideas can be generated. The emergence of the Council Presidency as a key institutional actor has played a particularly important part in enabling the Council to influence policy directions and priorities.

(4) The increasing willingness of the states to found aspects of their cooperation not on EU law but on non-binding agreements and understandings. This is most obviously seen in the policy areas covered by pillars two and three, but it sometimes also happens in other, more conventional, EU policy spheres where national differences make it very difficult for law to be agreed. Such non-legal arrangements do not have to be initiated by the Commission.

Not only has the Council encroached on the Commission's policy-initiating function but it has also joined it in exercising important responsibilities in the key activities of mediation and consensus building. Of course, as the forum in which the national representatives meet, the Council has always served the function of developing mutual understanding between the member states. Moreover, a necessary prerequisite for successful policy development has always been that Council participants display an ability to compromise in negotiations. But as the EC/EU has grown in size, as more difficult policy areas have come onto the agenda, and as political and economic change has broken down some of the pioneering spirit of the early days, so has positive and active mediation come to be ever more necessary: mediation primarily between the different national and ideological interests represented in the Council, but also between the Council and the Commission, the Council and the EP, and the Council and non-institutional interests. The Commission has taken on much of this task, but so too have agencies of the Council itself – most notably the Presidency and the Secretariat.

The Council has both gained and lost responsibilities over the years. The most obvious gain has been the extended scope of its policy interests. As is noted at several points in this book, the EU's policy remit is now such that there are very few spheres of public policy in which the EU is not involved to at least some extent. This in turn means that there are few policy spheres in which the Council is not seeking to launch or shape initiatives and to take decisions of some sort.

There are two principal respects in which the Council may be said to have lost responsibilities, or at least have been obliged to come to share them. First, the European Council – the body that brings together the Heads of Government two or three times a year – has assumed increasingly greater responsibility for taking the final political decisions on such 'history-making' issues as new accessions, institutional reform, and the launching of broad policy initiatives (see Chapter 8). Second, as is noted above and in Chapter 5, the legislative powers of the EP have been increased, to such an extent that most Commission proposals for legislation now need its approval as well as that of the Council.

Composition

The ministers

Ministerial meetings are at the apex of the Council machinery. Since the 1965 Merger Treaty entered into force in 1967 there has legally been only one Council of Ministers, but in practice there are many in the sense that the Council meets in different formations to deal with different policy areas. The General Affairs Council, which is composed of Foreign Ministers, has the widest brief: it deals with general issues relating to policy initiation and coordination, with external political relations, and often with matters that, for whatever reason, are particularly politically sensitive. More sectoral matters are dealt with in twenty or so sectoral or technical Councils, which are made up of Ministers of Agriculture, of Energy, the Environment and so on (Table 7.1).

Often, the national representatives who attend ministerial meetings differ in terms of their status and/or policy responsibilities. This can inhibit efficient decision-making. The problem arises because the states themselves decide by whom they wish to be represented, and their decisions may vary in one of two ways:

(1) *Level of seniority*. Normally, by prior arrangement, Council meetings are attended by ministers of a similar standing, but circumstances do arise when the various delegations are headed by people at different levels of seniority. This may be because a relevant minister has pressing domestic business or because it is judged that an agenda does not warrant his or her attendance. Occasionally she or he may be 'unavoidably delayed' to avoid attending an unwanted or politically awkward meeting. Whatever the

Table 7.1   *Formations and meetings of the Council of Ministers*

	1997	1996
General Affairs	15	13
Agriculture	11	13
Economic and Finance (Ecofin)	10	8
Labour and Social Affairs	5	4
Environment	4	4
Transport	4	4
Telecommunications	3	5
Fisheries	3	5
Energy	3	3
Internal Market	3	3
Justice and Home Affairs	3	3
Industry	2	4
Development	2	3
Research	2	3
Education	2	2
Budget	2	2
Consumers	2	2
Culture/Audiovisual	2	2
Health	2	2
Tourism	1	1
Youth	1	0
Ecofin and Labour Social Affairs Jointly	1	0
Civil Protection	0	1
Total 1997 Council sessions	83	87

Source: Corbett (1998a, pp. 46–7).

reason, a reduction in the status and political weight of a delegation may make it difficult for binding decisions to be agreed.

(2) *Sectoral responsibility.* Usually it is obvious which government departments should be represented at Council meetings, but not always. Doubts may arise because agenda items straddle policy divisions, or because member states organise their central government departments in different ways. As a result, it is possible for ministers from rather different national ministries, with different responsibilities and interests, to be present. The difficulties this creates are sometimes compounded, especially in broad policy areas, by the minister attending not feeling able to speak on behalf of other ministers with a direct interest and therefore insisting on the matter being referred back to national capitals.

*   *   *

States are not, therefore, always comparably represented at ministerial meetings. But whether a country's principal spokesman is a senior minister, a junior minister or, as occasionally is the case, the Permanent Representative or even a senior diplomat, care is always taken to ensure that national interests are defended. The main way this is done is by the attendance at all meetings of not only the national spokesmen but also small national delegations. These delegations comprise national officials and experts plus, at important meetings or meetings where there is a wide-ranging agenda, junior ministers to assist the senior minister. (Trade Ministers, for example, usually accompany Foreign Ministers to meetings of the General Affairs Council when trade issues are to be considered.) Normally five or six officials and experts support the 'inner table team' (that is, the most senior national representatives who actually sit at the negotiating table), but this number can vary according to the policy area concerned (Foreign Ministers may be accompanied by teams of as many as eight or nine), the importance of the items on the agenda, and the size of the meeting room. The task of the supporting teams is to ensure that the head of the delegation is properly briefed, fully understands the implications of what is being discussed, and does not make negotiating mistakes. Sometimes, when very confidential matters are being discussed or when a meeting is deadlocked, the size of delegations may, on a proposal from the President, be reduced to 'Ministers plus two', 'Ministers plus one' or, exceptionally, 'Ministers and Commission'.

Altogether there are usually about 80 Council meetings in an average year (83, for example, in 1997) with a certain bunching occurring in relation to key features of the EU timetable: the budgetary cycle, the annual agricultural price-fixing exercise, and the ending of a country's six-month Presidency. Meetings are normally held in Brussels, but the April, June, and October meetings are held in Luxembourg.

The regularity of meetings of individual Councils reflects their importance in the Council system and the extent to which there is an EU interest and activity in their policy area. So, as can be seen from Table 7.1, Foreign Ministers, Agriculture Ministers, and Economic and Finance Ministers (in what is customarily referred to as the Ecofin Council) meet most regularly: usually about once a month, but more frequently if events require it. Internal Market Ministers, Environment Ministers, Fisheries Ministers, and Transport Ministers have about four or five meetings per year. Other Councils – such as Research, Social, Energy, and Industry usually meet only two or three times a year, or even just once or twice a year in fringe areas such as Health and Cultural Affairs.

Unless there are particularly difficult matters to be resolved, meetings do not normally last more than a day. A typical meeting begins about

10.00 a.m. and finishes around 6.00 p.m. or 7.00 p.m. Foreign Ministers, Agriculture Ministers and Budget Ministers are the most likely to meet over two days, and when they do it is common to start with lunch on day 1 and finish around lunchtime on day 2.

Outside the formal Council framework some groups of ministers, particularly Foreign Ministers and Ecofin Ministers, have periodic weekend gatherings, usually in the country of the Presidency, to discuss matters on an informal basis without the pressure of having to take decisions.

The Committee of Permanent Representatives

Each of the member states has a national delegation – or Permanent Representation as they are more usually known – in Brussels, which acts as a kind of embassy to the EU. The Permanent Representations are headed by a Permanent Representative, who is normally a diplomat of very senior rank, and are staffed, in the case of the larger states, by thirty to forty officials, plus back-up support. About half of the officials are drawn from the diplomatic services of the member states, the others being seconded from appropriate national ministries such as Agriculture, Trade or Finance.

Of the many forums in which governments meet 'in Council' below ministerial level, the most important is the Committee of Permanent Representatives (COREPER). Although no provision was made for such a body under the Treaty of Paris, ministers established a coordinating committee of senior officials as early as 1953, and under the Treaties of Rome the Council was permitted to create a similar committee under its Rules of Procedure. Under Article 4 of the Merger Treaty these committees were merged and were formally incorporated into the Community system: 'A committee consisting of the Permanent Representatives of the Member States shall be responsible for preparing the work of the Council and for carrying out the tasks assigned to it by the Council.'

There are in fact two COREPERs. Each normally meets once a week. COREPER 2 is the more important and is made up of the Permanent Representatives plus support staff. Because of its seniority it is the more 'political' of the two COREPERs and works mainly for the Foreign Ministers (and through them for the European Council) and Ecofin. It also usually deals with issues for other Council meetings that are particularly sensitive or controversial. COREPER 2 is assisted in its tasks by the Antici Group, which is made up of senior officials from the Permanent Representations and which, in addition to assisting COREPER 2, acts as a key information-gathering and mediating forum between the member states. COREPER 1 consists of the Deputy Permanent

Representatives and support staff. Amongst the policy areas it normally deals with are the environment, social affairs, transport and the internal market. Agriculture, because of the complexity and volume of its business, is not normally dealt with by COREPER except in regard to certain aspects, of which the most important are finance, harmonisation of legislation, and commercial questions that relate to non-EU countries. Most agricultural matters are dealt with by the Special Committee on Agriculture (SCA), which is staffed by senior officials from the Permanent Representations and from national Ministries of Agriculture. Like the two COREPERs, the SCA normally meets at least once a week.

Committees and working parties

A complicated network of committees and working parties assists and prepares the work of the Council of Ministers, COREPER and the SCA.

The *committees* are of different types. They include the following:

- Council committees in the strict sense of the term are those standing committees which are serviced by Council administrators. There are only a handful of these, of which the Energy Committee, the Committee on Education, and the Employment and Labour Market Committee are examples. Council committees are composed of national officials and their role is essentially to advise the Council and the Commission as appropriate and, in some instances, as directed.
- A particularly important and rather special Council committee is the Article 133 (formerly 113) Committee, which deals with commercial policy. Any significant action undertaken by the EU in international trade negotiations is preceded by internal coordination via this Committee. It normally meets once a week: the full members – who are very senior officials in national Ministries of Trade or the equivalent – meet monthly, and the deputies – who are middle-ranking officials from the Ministries, or sometimes from the Permanent Representations – meet three times a month. The Committee performs two main functions: it drafts the briefs that the Commission negotiates on behalf of the EU with third countries (the Committee's draft is referred, via COREPER, to the Ministers for their approval); and it acts as a consultative committee to the Council and the Commission – by, for example, indicating to the Commission what it should do when problems arise during the course of a set of trade negotiations.

- The main Council committees under pillars two and three of the EU are, respectively, the Political Committee and the Police and Judicial Cooperation Coordinating Committee. Both committees are explicitly provided for in the TEU: the former in Article 25 and the latter (which before the Amsterdam Treaty was known as the K.4 Committee) in Article 36. The Political Committee is composed of the political directors of the Foreign Ministries of the member states, and the Coordinating Committee is composed of senior officials from Ministries of Justice and Home Affairs. Both committees make use of sub-committees and working parties.

- A committee that is likely to become extremely important is the Economic and Financial Committee, which was established at the start of the third stage of EMU in January 1999. The Committee is given a broad brief in very important policy areas, the main focus of its work being economic and financial policy, capital movements, and international monetary relations. The members of the Committee – of which there are two from each member state (one from the administration and one from the national Central Bank), plus two from the Commission, and two from the European Central Bank – are senior and influential economic and financial experts: they are, in other words, people who can normally communicate directly with whomso-ever they wish, and who are customarily listened to.

- The Standing Committee on Employment is also a Council-serviced committee, but its membership is unusual in two respects. First, it is composed not only of governmental representatives but also of sectional interest representatives – the latter being drawn from both sides of industry. Second, the governmental representations are headed by the ministers themselves, or, if they are unable to attend, their personal representatives. The Committee meets twice a year to discuss matters of interest and, where possible, to make recommendations to the Labour and Social Affairs Council. The nature of the membership of the Committee, with ministerial representation, means that when general agreement can be reached, the matter is likely to be taken up by the Council.

- In addition to the formally constituted committees that have just been described – formally constituted in the sense that they have been established by the treaties or by EU legislation – many other committees also assist the work of the Council. Not always referred to as committees, but sometimes as groups or simply meetings, these are most often found in emerging policy areas. There has been an increasing tendency in recent years for *ad hoc* committees of senior national officials – usually referred to as '*High-Level Groups*' – to be established for the purpose of developing initiatives and policies (though not of course for the purpose of drafting legislation) in new and sometimes sensitive areas – the control of drugs, for example.

The role of *working parties* (or working groups) is more specific than that of most of the committees in that they are responsible for carrying out detailed analyses of formally tabled Commission proposals for legislation. The number of working parties in existence at any one time varies according to the overall nature of the EU's workload and the preferences of the Presidency in office, but in recent years there have usually been somewhere in the region of 150. (It is impossible to give a precise figure because over half of the working parties are *ad hoc* in nature.) Members of the working parties, of whom there may be up to three or four per member state, are almost invariably national officials and experts based either in the Permanent Representations or in appropriate national ministries. Occasionally governments appoint non-civil servants to a working party delegation when highly technical or complex issues are under consideration.

Working parties meet as and when required, usually with an interval of at least three weeks between meetings so as to allow the Council's Secretariat time to circulate minutes and agendas – in all of the languages of the member states. For permanent working parties with a heavy workload meetings may be regular, whilst for others, where nothing much comes up within their terms of reference, there may be very few meetings. Up to fifteen or so different working parties can be in session in Brussels on some days. On completion of their analyses of the Commission proposals, working parties report to COREPER or to the SCA.

The General Secretariat

The main administrative support for the work of the Council is provided by the General Secretariat. This has a staff of around 2500, of whom 250 or so are at the 'A' grade diplomatic level. The Secretariat's base, which also houses Council meetings, is near the main Commission and EP buildings in Brussels.

The Secretariat's main responsibility is to service the Council machinery – from ministerial to working party levels. This involves activities such as preparing draft agendas, keeping records, providing legal advice, processing and circulating decisions and documentation, translating, and generally monitoring policy developments so as to provide an element of continuity and coordination in Council proceedings. This last task includes seeking to ensure a smooth transition between Presidencies by performing a liaising role with officials from the preceding, the incumbent and the incoming Presidential states.

In exercising many of its responsibilities, the Secretariat works closely with representatives from the member state of the President-in-office (see below). This is essential because key decisions about such matters as priorities, meetings and agendas are primarily in the hands of the Presidency. Before all Council meetings at all levels Secretariat officials give the Presidency a full briefing about subject content, the current state of play on the agenda items and possible tactics – 'the Danes can be isolated', 'there is strong resistance to this in Spain and Portugal so caution is advised', 'a possible vote has been signalled in the agenda papers and, if taken, will find the necessary majority', and so on.

The extent to which Presidencies rely on the Secretariat varies considerably, with smaller countries, because of their more limited administrative resources, tending to be most reliant. Even the larger countries, however, have much to gain by making use of the Secretariat's resources and knowledge of what approaches are most likely to be effective in particular situations.

The main reason why Presidencies are sometimes a little reluctant to make too much use of the Secretariat is that there is a natural tendency for them to rely heavily on their own national officials as they seek to achieve a successful six-month period of office by getting measures through. It is largely for this reason that the staff of a state's Permanent Representation increases in size during a Presidential tenureship. Something approaching a dual servicing of the Presidency is apparent in the way at Council meetings, at all levels, the President sits with officials from the General Secretariat on one side and national advisers on the other.

The operation of the Council

The Council Presidency

Council of Ministers meetings are normally convened by the country holding the Presidency, but it is possible for the Commission or any member state to take the initiative. The Presidency rotates between the states on a six-monthly basis: January until June, July until December (see Figure 7.1 for the order of rotation). The main tasks of the Presidency are as follows.

(1) Arranging (in close association with the General Secretariat) and chairing all Council meetings from ministerial level downwards (apart from the few committees and working parties that have a permanent

Figure 7.1   *Rotation of Council Presidency between the states and seating arrangements in Council meetings*

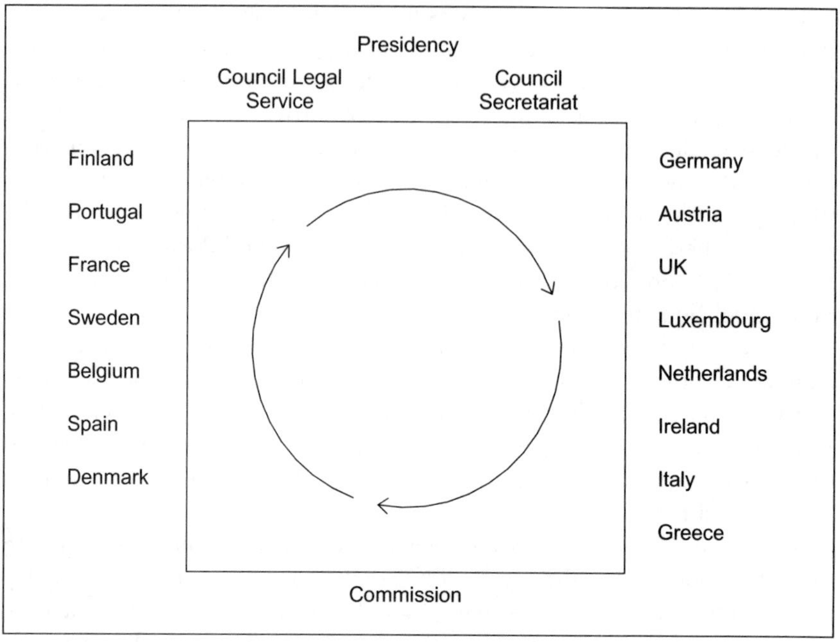

Notes:
1. Figure 7.1 shows the position under the July–December 1999 Finnish Presidency. National delegations sit according to the order in which they will next assume the Presidency, which rotates in a clockwise direction.
2. The arrangements apply in all Council meetings at all levels.

chairman). These responsibilities give the Presidency considerable control over how often Councils and Council bodies meet, over agendas and over what happens during the course of meetings.

(2) Launching and building a consensus for initiatives. A successful Presidency is normally regarded as one that gets things done. This can usually only be achieved by extensive negotiating, persuading, manoeuvring, cajoling, mediating and bargaining with and between the member states, and with the Commission and the EP.

(3) Ensuring some continuity and consistency of policy development. An important way in which this is achieved is via the so-called 'troika' arrangements, which provide for cooperation between the preceding, the incumbent and the succeeding Presidencies.

(4) Representing the Council in dealings with outside bodies. This task is exercised most frequently with regard to other EU institutions (such as

regular appearances before the EP), and with non-member countries in connection with certain external EU policies, especially the CFSP.

Holding the Presidency has advantages and disadvantages. One advantage is the prestige and status that is associated with the office: during the six-month term of office the Presidential state is at the very heart of EU affairs; its ministers – especially its Head of Government and its Foreign Minister – meet with prominent international statesmen and dignitaries on behalf of the EU; and media focus and interest is considerable. Another advantage is that during its term of office a Presidency can do more than it can as an ordinary member state to help shape and set the pace of EU policy priorities. The extent of the potential of the Presidency in terms of policy development should not, however, be exaggerated: though Presidencies set out their priorities when they enter office, they do not start with a clean sheet but have to deal with uncompleted business from previous Presidencies; related to this last point, an important part of the 'troika' arrangement is 'rolling work programmes', in which measures to be taken by the Council are coordinated between the three participating states rather then being left solely to the preferences of the incumbent state; and, finally, six months is just not long enough for the full working through of policy initiatives – especially if legislation is required.

As for the disadvantages of holding the Presidency, one is the blow to esteem and standing that is incurred when a state is judged to have had a poor Presidency. Another is the heavy administrative burdens that are attached to the job – burdens that some of the smaller states find difficult to carry.

The hierarchical structure

As indicated above, a hierarchy exists in the Council. It consists of: ministers – with the General Affairs Council and increasingly now also the Ecofin Council informally recognised as being the most senior Councils; COREPER and the SCA; and the committees and working parties. The European Council is also sometimes thought of as being part of this hierarchy, but in fact it is not properly part of the Council system, even though it does have the political capability of issuing what amount to instructions to the ministers.

The Council's hierarchical structure is neither tight nor rigidly applied. The General Affairs Council's seniority over the sectoral Councils is, for example, very ill-defined and only very partially developed, whilst important committees and working parties can sometimes communicate directly with ministers. Nonetheless, the hierarchy does, for the most part, work. This is best illustrated by looking at the Council's procedures for dealing with a Commission proposal for Council, or EP and Council, legislation.

The *first stage* is initial examination of the Commission's text. This is normally undertaken by a working party or, if it is of very broad application, several working parties. If no appropriate permanent working party exists, an *ad hoc* one is established.

As can be seen from Table 7.2, several factors can affect the progress of the proposal. A factor that has greatly increased in importance in recent years is whether the proposal will be subject to qualified majority voting rules (see below) when it appears before the ministers (votes are not taken below ministerial level). If it is not, and unanimity is required, then working party deliberations may take as long as is necessary to reach an agreement – which can mean months or even years. If it is, then delegations that find themselves isolated in the working party are obliged to anticipate the possibility of their country being outvoted when the ministers consider the proposal, and therefore engage in damage limitation. This usually involves adopting some combination of three strategies. First, if the proposal is judged to be important to national interests, then this is stressed during the working party's deliberations, in the hope that other delegations will take a sympathetic view and will either make concessions or not seek to press ahead too fast. Second, if the proposal is judged to be not too damaging or unacceptable, then attempts will be made to amend it, but it is unlikely that too much of a fuss will be made.

Table 7.2   *Principal factors determining the progress of a proposal through the Council machinery*

- The urgency of the proposal
- The controversiality of the proposal and support/opposition amongst the states
- The extent to which the Commission has tailored its text to accommodate national objections/reservations voiced at the pre-proposal stage
- The complexity of the proposal's provisions
- The ability of the Commission to allay doubts by the way it gives clarifications and answers questions
- The judgements made by the Commission on whether, or when, it should accept modifications to its proposals
- The competence of the Presidency
- The agility and flexibility of the participants to devise (usually through the Presidency and the Commission) and accept compromise formulae
- The availability of, and willingness of the states to use, majority voting

Third, an attempt may be made to 'do a deal' or 'come to an understanding' with other delegations so that a blocking minority of states is created.

The General Secretariat of the Council is always pressing for progress and tries to ensure that a working party does not need to meet more than three times to discuss any one proposal. The first working party meeting normally consists of a general discussion of key points. Subsequent meetings are then taken up with line-by-line examination of the Commission's text. If all goes well, a document is eventually produced indicating points of agreement and disagreement, and quite possibly having attached to it reservations that states have entered to indicate that they are not yet in a position formally to commit themselves to the text or a part of it. (States may enter reservations at any stage of the Council process. These can vary from an indication that a particular clause of a draft text is not yet in an acceptable form, to a general withholding of approval until the text has been cleared by the appropriate national authorities.)

The *second stage* is the reference of the working party's document to COREPER or, in the case of agriculture, to the SCA. Placed between the working parties and the Council of Ministers, COREPER acts as a sort of filtering agency for ministerial meetings. It attempts to clear as much of the ground as possible to ensure that only the most difficult and sensitive of matters detain the ministers in discussion. So when the conditions for the adoption of a measure have been met in a working party, COREPER is likely to confirm the working party's opinion and advance it to the ministers for formal enactment. If, however, agreement has not been reached by a working party, COREPER can do one of three things: try itself to resolve the issue (which its greater political status might permit); refer it back to the working party, perhaps with accompanying indications of where an agreement might be found; or pass it upwards to the ministers.

Whatever progress proposals have made at working party and COREPER levels – and Hayes-Renshaw and Wallace (1995) estimate that about 70 per cent of Council business is agreed at working party level and a further 15–20 per cent at COREPER level – formal adoption is only possible at ministerial level. Ministerial meetings thus constitute *the third and final stage* of the Council's procedure.

Items on ministerial meeting agendas are grouped under two headings: 'A points' and 'B points'. Matters that have been agreed at COREPER level, and on which it is thought Council approval will be given without discussion, are listed as 'A points'. These can cover a range of matters – from routine 'administrative' decisions to controversial new legislation that was agreed in principle at a previous ministerial meeting but upon which a formal decision was delayed pending final clarification or tidying up. 'A points' do not necessarily fall within the policy competence of the particular Council that is meeting, but may have been placed on the agenda because the appropriate formation of the Council is not due to meet for some time. Ministers retain the right to raise objections to 'A points', and if any do so the proposal may have to be withdrawn and referred back to COREPER. Normally, however, 'A points' are quickly approved without debate. Such is the thoroughness of the Council system that ministers can assume they have been thoroughly checked in both Brussels and national capitals to ensure they are politically acceptable, legally sound, and not subject to scrutiny reservations. Ministers then proceed to consider 'B points', which may include items left over from previous meetings, matters that have not been possible to resolve at COREPER or working party levels, or proposals that COREPER judges to be politically sensitive and hence requiring political decisions. All 'B points' will have been extensively discussed by national officials at lower Council levels, and on most of them a formula for an agreement will have been prepared for the ministers to consider. (There is a detailed analysis of the nature of 'A' and 'B' points and how they are managed by the Council in Van Schendelen, 1996).

As can be seen from Exhibit 7.1, ministerial meetings – in this case a meeting of Agriculture Ministers – can have very wide and mixed agendas. Four observations are particularly worth making about the sorts of agenda items that arise.

- There are variations regarding what ministers are expected to do. The range of possibilities includes the taking of final decisions, the adoption of common positions (see below and Chapter 13), the approval of negotiating mandates for the Commission, the resolution of problems that have caused difficulties at lower levels of the Council hierarchy, and – simply – the noting of progress reports.
- Some items concern very general policy matters, whilst others are highly specialised and technical in nature.
- Most items fall within the sectoral competence of the ministers who have been convened, but a few do not. 'Extra sectoral' items are usually placed on agendas when everything has been agreed, a decision needs to be taken, and the relevant sectoral Council is not scheduled to meet in the immediate future.
- As well as policy issues, agenda items can also include administrative matters, such as appointments to advisory committees.

The position of the General Affairs Council rather suggests that there would, in certain circumstances – such as when a policy matter cuts across sectoral divisions, or when sectoral councils cannot resolve key issues – be a fourth decision-making stage in the Council involving the Foreign Ministers. In practice, recourse to such a stage is not common. A principal reason for this is that the theoretical seniority enjoyed by the General Affairs Council over other Councils has no legal basis. Rather it stems only from an ill-formulated understanding that the General Affairs Council has special responsibility for dealing with disputes that cannot be resolved by the sectoral Councils, for tackling politically sensitive matters, and for acting as a general coordinating body at ministerial level. Another factor limiting the role of the General Affairs Council is that often the Foreign Ministers are not able, or willing, to act any more decisively in breaking a deadlock than is a divided sectoral Council. Members of the General Council may, indeed, have no greater seniority in rank, and may even be junior, to their national colleagues in, say, the Ecofin, Budget or Agriculture Councils. In any case, sectoral Councils are often not willing to refer their disputes 'upwards': Ministers of Agriculture, Trade, Environment and so on have as much authority to make EU law as do Foreign Ministers, and as Van Schendelen has noted with regard to the Agriculture Council, ministers want to find their own solutions rather than refer dossiers to the 'cross-sectoral' General Affairs Council 'where agricultural interests might be traded off against quite different ones' (Van Schendelen, 1996, p. 54). All formations of the Council thus normally prefer to take their own decisions – unless something that is likely to be very unpopular can be passed on elsewhere. The General Affairs Council is thus of only limited effectiveness in resolving issues that have created blockages in the sectoral Councils and in counteracting the fragmentation and sectoralism to which the Council of Ministers is unquestionably prone. The same is true of joined or 'jumbo' Councils, which bring together, but only on an occasional basis, different groups of ministers.

This absence of clear Council leadership and of an authoritative coordinating mechanism has had the consequence of encouraging the European Council to assume responsibilities in relation to the Council of Ministers, even though it is not formally part of the Council hierarchy. Increasingly the Heads of Government at their meetings have gone beyond issuing general guidelines to the Council of Ministers, which was intended to be the normal limit of European Council/Council of Ministers relationships when the former was established in 1974. Summits have sometimes been obliged to try to resolve thorny issues that have been referred to them by the Council of Ministers, and have also had to seek to ensure that there is some overall policy direction and coherence in the work of the Council of Ministers. The European Council can only go so far, however, in performing such problem-solving, leadership, and coordinating roles: partly because of the infrequency of its meetings; partly because some national leaders prefer to avoid getting too involved in detailed policy discussions; but, above all, because the Heads of Government are subject to the same national and political divisions as the ministers.

Exhibit 7.1   A Council of Ministers meeting: items considered and decisions taken

2118th Council Meeting – AGRICULTURE – Brussels, 28 September 1998

COMMON ORGANISATION OF THE MARKET IN WINE

The Council held a policy discussion on the basis of a Presidency questionnaire on the Commission proposal for the reform of the wine sector. The discussion gave Ministers an opportunity to make an initial assessment and to comment on general aspects and on the thrust of the proposal, in particular as regards the analysis of market prospects, the maintenance of certain management instruments and the need to promote the conversion of vineyards.

The Council also noted that the initial aim of the technical analysis of the proposal was to consider all the implications of the proposal. It underlined the importance of this whole matter and confirmed that it intended to take a decision on the proposal as soon as possible in the framework of Agenda 2000 once the European Parliament had delivered its Opinion.

The Special Committee on Agriculture was instructed to continue discussing the proposal in the light of the outcome of the technical analysis and to submit a progress report to the Council at its next meeting.

PROTECTION OF LAYING HENS KEPT IN VARIOUS SYSTEMS OF REARING

The Council held a policy discussion on the Commission communication on the protection of laying hens, on the basis of a report from the Permanent Representatives Committee on the veterinary aspects and of a report from the Special Committee on Agriculture on the economic, social and financial implications of the Commission proposal. It took note of the progress made and of delegations' comments and instructed COREPER and the SCA, each within its own remit, to expedite discussion of the Commission proposal and to report to it at a forthcoming meeting.

The Presidency announced that, in the light of the discussions held, it would establish the key political issues which would make it possible to speed up the decision-making process. It also called upon delegations to collaborate in this exercise in order to arrive at a rapid result on this politically sensitive matter.

→

IMPLICATIONS FOR THE AGRICULTURAL MARKETS OF THE SITUATION IN RUSSIA

The Council:

- undertook, inter alia, on the basis of an analysis by Commissioner FISCHLER's departments, an assessment of the implications of the current situation in Russia on Community agricultural markets, notably in the beef and veal, pigmeat, poultry and milk products sectors covered by the analysis and other sectors mentioned by one or other Member State;
- expressed its concern at the negative effects already resulting from the slow-down in exports to Russia and which might become more acute if the present situation were to continue or worsen;
- therefore thought that everything should be done to keep the impact that the crisis in Russia was having on Community agriculture as low as possible and to restore the positive trend in exports of Community agricultural produce to that country as rapidly as possible;
- while taking note of the initial measures already adopted by the Commission, accordingly asked it to take all other appropriate and feasible measures to alleviate the difficulties encountered by certain sectors of production.

The Agriculture Council:

- took note of the fact that the General Affairs Council was developing a longer-term global approach for future cooperation with Russia. Priority should be given to efforts to restore normal commercial exports. In this connection, however, the matter of food aid should also be considered, however, provided that:

  - an official request was submitted which identifies the recipients and shows which channels of distribution may be used so that the aid reaches those recipients;
  - the budgetary authorities provided the corresponding financial resources;
  - this aid was designed to be compatible with the food aid provisions in Article 10 of the WTO Agriculture Agreement and could thus be recognised in the international fora concerned;

- instructed the President to inform the Presidency of the General Affairs Council of the discussions and of the questions raised.

PLANT-HEALTH PROBLEMS: ACTION TAKEN BY THE COMMISSION IN RESPONSE TO REQUESTS FROM MEMBER STATES

The Council heard a statement by the Portuguese Minister, Mr. F. GOMES DA SILVA, concerning the failure of the Commission to take a decision on Member States' requests for a financial contribution in connection with plant-health problems under Directive 97/3/EC.

→

Exhibit 7.1 continued

Following a brief exchange of views, the Council took note of the concern expressed by the Portuguese delegation, backed by the French delegation, and of the Commission's intention to adopt a decision on these matters as quickly as possible.

OTHER DECISIONS

Adopted without discussion. In the case of legislative acts, votes against or abstentions are indicated. Decisions containing statements which the Council has decided to release to the public are indicated by asterisks; the statements in question may be obtained from the Press Office.

AGRICULTURE

Beef and veal*

The Council adopted a Regulation on publicity measures on the labelling on beef and veal in response to the conclusions of the Agriculture Council on 22 to 26 June 1998.

The Regulation provides for the Community financing of publicity measures designed to inform the consumer of the guarantees provided by the labelling arrangements introduced by Regulation (EC) No 820/97 of 21 April 1997 establishing a system for the identification and registration of bovine animals and regarding the labelling of beef and veal.

Rice

The Council adopted an amendment to Regulation (EC) No 3072/95 on the common organisation of the market in rice with regard to the scheme for compensatory payment.

This amendment follows on from the conclusions of the Agriculture Council in June 1988 and from the wish of certain Member States to introduce regional sub-divisions of the maximum guaranteed area so as to maintain the areas given over to rice in certain regions where there was no real possibility of growing alternative crops.

Honey

The Council adopted a Regulation amending Regulation (EC) No 1221/97 laying down general rules for the application of measures to improve the production and marketing of honey.

→

FISHERIES

Spain/South Africa and Portugal/South Africa Agreements

The Council adopted two Decisions authorising

- Spain to extend until 7 March 1999 the Agreement on mutual fishery relations with South Africa;
- Portugal to extend until 7 March 1999 the Agreement on mutual fishery relations with South Africa.

EXTERNAL RELATIONS

Relations with the Gulf States

The Council authorised the Commission to conduct negotiations on the accession of the EC to the Middle East Desalination Research Centre established at Muscat (Sultanate of Oman).

This Centre was created with the approval of the countries participating in the multilateral working group on water resources set up in the framework of the Middle East peace process and the countries of the region directly involved (Jordan, Palestine, Israel), considering that the problem of water has to be dealt with in a regional context.

The Community is the largest contributor to the Centre, with a grant of ECU 3 million awarded under the MEDA programme.

TRANSPARENCY

Public access to documents

The Council agreed on the replies to the sixth and seventh confirmatory applications for access to Council documents from Mr Tony BUNYAN in 1998. The Danish, Swedish and United Kingdom delegations voted against the reply to the sixth confirmatory application while the Danish and Finnish delegations voted against the reply to the seventh confirmatory application.

INTERNAL MARKET

Food additives other than colours and sweeteners*

Following European Parliament approval of the text resulting from the Council's first reading ("Common Position"), the latter adopted, without amendment in accordance with the Treaty, the new Directive on food additives other than colours or sweeteners, amending Directive 95/2/EC. The Belgian and German delegations abstained while the Austrian and Danish

→

Exhibit 7.1 continued

delegations voted against. Five delegations gave the explanations of vote set out below.

The aim of the new Directive is to adjust Directive 95/2/EC to recent scientific and technical developments. It also extends the list of authorised additives given in the Annex to that Directive to include additives used for traditional foodstuffs in the three new Member States. The Directive follows the guiding principles for food legislation in the Community: observance of the opinion of the Scientific Committee for Food concerning the risk to human health; justification of use on the basis of technological requirements; respect for Member States' traditions.

Explanations of vote:

1. *Explanation of the Belgian delegation's vote*

    The text of the Directive amending Directive 95/2/EC on food additives other than colours and sweeteners is unsatisfactory in the view of the Belgian delegation on three counts. For that reason the Belgian delegation abstained from the vote on the Directive. . .

2. *Explanation of the Danish delegation's vote*

    It is the aim of the Danish Government to restrict the use of additives as far as possible. It takes the view that additives should be authorised only if they pose no danger to health, are unlikely to mislead consumers or are necessitated by technological requirements.

    The Danish Government cannot record agreement on the final adoption of the Directive by the Council since it is reluctant to extend the use of sulphite and nisin in foodstuffs. . .

3. *Explanation of the German delegation's vote*

    The German delegation regrets that additives E500 (sodium carbonates), E338 (phosphoric acid), E339 (sodium phosphates), E340 (potassium phosphates), E341 (calcium phosphates), E343 (magnesium phosphates), E450 (diphosphates), E451 (triphosphates) and E452 (polyphosphates) have been generally authorised for soured-cream butter although there was no technological requirement which justified it. The German delegation believes that the additive E500 (sodium carbonates) and the phosphates actually used should be authorised only for specific products in the manufacture of which such substances are traditionally used in Sweden and Finland. . .

→

4. *Explanation of the Swedish delegation's vote*

The Directive also provides for the authorisation to use a number of food additives in foodstuffs for healthy infants and young children. Sweden considers that additives should as far as possible be restricted in foodstuffs for babies, in particular babies between birth and three months of age, in respect of whom scientific opinions on food additives are not applicable from every point of view. The additives currently referred to are not, however, such as to endanger children's health and can therefore be accepted.

5. *Explanation of the Austrian delegation's vote*

- Regarding the general authorisation of the addition to soured-cream butter of the sodium carbonates and the phosphates listed in Annex IV

As already stated in the recitals to Directive 95/2/EC, it is generally accepted that certain foodstuffs should be free of additives. Butter in particular is indisputably a product that one is entitled to expect to meet such a purity requirement, particularly as in Austria – just as in other Member States, evidently – there is no technological requirement that would justify the use of such additives. Austria would have no objection to the addition of phosphates and carbonates to Swedish and Finnish butter only (which is obviously necessitated by technological considerations).

- Regarding the extension of the authorisation of thaumatin for water-based flavoured non-alcoholic drinks and desserts, dairy and non-dairy

The assessment of thaumatin carried out by the Scientific Committee for Food (SCF) in 1988, in the course of which, *inter alia*, the possibilities for its use, limited from a technological point of view, were insisted on, was based on a totally different assumption concerning exposure to this product.

The conclusions of that study are no longer relevant to the extension of the authorisation of thaumatin.

In the absence of a further, prior assessment by the SCF the use of thaumatin in the foodstuffs in question, which are also, furthermore, consumed in large quantities by children, should be ruled out.

Source: Council of the European Union, General Secretariat, Press Release, 11391/98.

Decision-making procedures

The treaties provide for three basic ways in which the Council can take a decision: unanimously, by a qualified majority vote, or by a simple majority vote.

- *Unanimity* used to be the normal requirement when a new policy was being initiated or an existing policy framework was being modified or further developed. However, the SEA, the Maastricht Treaty, and the Amsterdam Treaty have greatly reduced the circumstances in which a unanimity requirement applies and it is now largely confined to policy direction decisions under the CFSP and Police and Judicial Cooperation pillars of the EU (though implementing decisions may – especially under the CFSP pillar – usually be taken by qualified majority vote), and to various sensitive and particularly important matters that fall under the TEC, such as 'constitutional' and financial issues. (See Chapters 5 and 19 for details.) Unanimity is also required when the Council wishes to amend a Commission proposal against the Commission's wishes.

  Abstentions do not constitute an impediment to the adoption of Council decisions that require unanimity. Furthermore, as noted in Chapter 5, the Amsterdam Treaty provided for 'constructive abstentionism' under the CFSP pillar, whereby an abstaining state 'shall not be obliged to apply the decision, but shall accept that the decision commits the Union' (Article 23, TEU). If constructive abstentions represent more than one-third of the weighted votes, decisions cannot be adopted.

- *Qualified majority voting* now applies to most types of decision under the EC pillar, to some types of decision under the CFSP pillar, and to a few types of decision under the Police and Judicial Cooperation pillar (see Chapters 5 and 13 for details).

  Under the qualified majority voting rules, France, Germany, Italy and the UK have ten votes each; Spain has eight; Belgium, Greece, the Netherlands and Portugal have five; Austria and Sweden have four; Denmark, Finland and Ireland have three; and Luxembourg has two. Of this total of 87 votes, 62 votes (that is 71.3 per cent of the total) constitute a qualified majority and 26 a blocking minority. This means that the five larger states cannot outvote the smaller seven, and also that two large states cannot by themselves constitute a blocking minority. An abstention has the same effect as a negative vote, since the total vote required to achieve a majority is not reduced as a result of an abstention.

In 1994, at the time of the EFTAn enlargement round, the UK and Spain argued that the blocking minority should be retained at its then figure of 23 rather than be increased. The effect of so doing would have been to raise the qualified majority threshold from 71 per cent to 78 per cent. Other governments did not wish to depart from the qualified majority and blocking minority proportions that had long been established, but in a concession to the UK and Spain the so-called Ionnina Compromise was agreed, whereby the blocking minority was increased but if 'members of the Council representing a total of 23 to 25 votes indicated their intention to oppose the adoption by the Council of a decision by a qualified majority', then 'a reasonable time' would be allowed to elapse to see if an agreement could be found before the new blocking minority figure was used. (The Ionnina Compromise can be located in the *Official Journal*, C105/1, 13 April 1994, and in Hayes-Renshaw and Wallace, 1997, p. 313). It had been intended that the Ionnina Compromise would be phased out at the time of the 1996–7 IGC, but because of the IGC's inability to agree on revised Council voting figures it was decided, largely at Spanish insistence, that the Compromise would stay in force until the next EU enlargement.

- *Simple majority voting*, in which all states have one vote each, is used mainly for procedural purposes and, since February 1994, for anti-dumping and anti-subsidy tariffs within the context of the Common Commercial Policy (CCP).

Until relatively recently, proposals were not usually pushed to a vote in the Council when disagreements between the states existed, even when majority voting was perfectly constitutional under the treaties. To appreciate the reasons for this it is necessary to go back to the institutional crisis of 1965.

In brief, events unfolded in the following way. The Commission, in an attempt to force progress in areas that had almost ground to a halt, put forward a package deal that had important policy and institutional implications. The most important aspects of its proposals were completion of the CAP, changing the basis of Community income from national contributions to own resources, and the granting of greater powers of control to the EP over the use of those resources. The French President, Charles de Gaulle, objected to the supranational implications of these proposals and used the occasion to register his opposition to what he saw as the increasing political role of the Commission and to the imminent prospect of the Community moving into a stage of its development in which there was to be more majority voting in the Council. When no agreement could be reached on these matters in the Council, France withdrew its representatives from the Community's decision-making institutions in July 1965, though it continued to apply Community law. This so-called 'policy of the empty chair' continued for six months and ended only when the French government, under strong domestic pressure, accepted a fudged deal at a special Council meeting in Luxembourg in January 1966. The outcome of that meeting is usually referred to as the *Accords de Luxembourg* or the Luxembourg Compromise. In fact, there was little agreement or genuine compromise but rather a registering of differences. This is apparent from the official communiqué:

I　Where, in the case of decisions which may be taken by majority vote on a proposal of the Commission, very important interests of one or more partners are at stake, the Members of the Council will endeavour, within a reasonable time, to reach solutions which can be adopted by all the Members of the Council while respecting their mutual interests and those of the Community, in accordance with Article 2 of the Treaty.

II　With regard to the preceding paragraph, the French delegation considers that where very important interests are at stake the discussion must be continued until unanimous agreement is reached.

III　The six delegations note that there is a divergence of views on what should be done in the event of a failure to reach complete agreement.

IV　The six delegations nevertheless consider that this divergence does not prevent the Community's work being resumed in accordance with the normal procedure (*Bulletin of the European Community*, 1966, no. 3, pp. 8–9).

Although it had no constitutional status, the Luxembourg Compromise came to profoundly affect decision-making in the Council at all levels. It did so because point II of the communiqué came to be interpreted as meaning that any state had the right to exercise a veto on questions that affected its vital national interests – and the states themselves determined when such interests were at stake.

The Luxembourg Compromise did not, it should be emphasised, replace a system of majority voting by one of unanimous voting. On the contrary, before 1966 majority voting was rare, and indeed it was its proposed phasing in that most concerned de Gaulle. After 1966 the norm became not one of unanimous voting but of no voting at all, except in a few areas where decisions could not be indefinitely delayed or postponed, such as during the annual budgetary cycle and on internal staffing matters. Most decisions, even on routine issues, came to be made by letting deliberations and negotiations run until an agreement finally emerged. As a result, there was rarely a need for the veto to be formally invoked, and it was so only very occasionally – no more than a dozen times between 1966 and 1985.

Because it produced a norm of consensual, and therefore very slow, decision-making, in which decisions were all too often of the lowest common denominator type, the Luxembourg Compromise was naturally never liked by those who wished for an efficient and dynamic Community. By the mid 1980s the damaging effects of the Compromise were coming to be generally acknowledged and the practice of majority voting began to develop where it was so permitted by the treaties. The 1986 SEA, which greatly increased the circumstances in which majority votes were permitted by the treaties, seemed to signal the final demise of the Compromise. In the event it did not quite do so in that Greece attempted – with only marginal success – to invoke the Compromise in 1988 in connection with a realignment of the 'green drachma', and in 1992–3 France threatened to invoke it in connection with the GATT Uruguay Round trade settlement that was proposed by the Commission. These are, however, isolated incidents and on many occasions when it might have been expected that the Compromise would have been invoked had it still had bite – such as by the United Kingdom in connection with unwanted social legislation – it has not been so. Everything thus indicates that whilst the Compromise may not be quite completely dead, it is in the deepest of sleeps and is subject only to very occasional and largely ineffective awakenings. (For further discussion on the Luxembourg Compromise, see Teasdale, 1995. See also Chapter 5 for an account of what some observers see as a partial revival of the spirit of the Compromise by the Amsterdam Treaty.)

Clearly, the most visible aspect of the Luxembourg Compromise was the right to exercise a national veto in most decision-making contexts. A less visible, but in practice much more significant, effect was that it stimulated the Council to take virtually all of its decisions unanimously. But the preference for unanimity, which still exists today despite the greatly increased use of majority voting, was not and is not just a consequence of an unofficial agreement made in the mid 1960s. There are strong positive reasons for acting only on the basis of unanimity. In many ways the functioning and development of the EU is likely to be enhanced if policy-making processes are consensual rather than conflictual. Thus, national authorities (which may be governments or parliaments) are unlikely to undertake with much enthusiasm the necessary task of transposing EU directives into national law if the directives are perceived as domestically damaging, or if they are imposed on a dissatisfied state following a majority vote in the Council. Nor is it likely that national bureaucracies will be helpful about implementing unwanted legislation. More generally, the overuse of majority voting on important and sensitive

matters could well create grievances that could have disruptive implications right across the EU's policy spectrum.

For good reasons, as well as perhaps some bad, decision-making in the
Council thus usually proceeds on the understanding that difficult and
controversial decisions are not imposed on dissenting states without full
consideration being given to the reasons for their opposition. When it is
clear that a state or states have serious difficulties with a proposal, they are
normally allowed time. They may well be put on the defensive, asked fully
to explain their position, pressed to give way or at least to compromise,
but the possibility of resolving an impasse by a vote is not the port of first
call. Usually the item is held over for a further meeting, with the hope that
in the meantime informal meetings or perhaps COREPER will find the
basis for a solution. All states, and not just the foremost advocates of
retention of the veto (initially France, more latterly Denmark, the United
Kingdom and, to a more limited extent, Greece, Ireland and Sweden)
accept that this is the only way Council business can be done without
risking major divisions.

But though there are good reasons for preferring unanimity, it is now
generally accepted that the principle cannot be applied too universally or
too rigidly. Were it to be so decision-making would, as in the 1970s, be
determined by the slowest, and much needed decisions may never be made
at all. Qualified majority voting has thus become common when the
treaties so allow.

Several closely interrelated factors explain this increased use of majority
voting.

- The 'legitimacy' and 'mystique' of the Luxembourg Compromise were
  dealt a severe blow in May 1982 when, for the first time, an attempt to
  invoke the Compromise was overridden. The occasion was an attempt
  by the British government to veto the annual agricultural prices
  settlement by proclaiming a vital national interest. The other states did
  not believe that such an interest was at stake (and with some reason
  given that the UK had already approved the constituent parts of the
  package). The view was taken (correctly) that the British were trying to
  use agricultural prices to force a more favourable outcome in concurrent
  negotiations over UK budgetary contributions. Agriculture ministers
  regarded this attempted linkage as quite invalid. They also thought it
  was over-demanding, since the dispute was being played out against the
  background of the Falklands crisis, in which the UK government was
  being supported by its Community partners even though some were
  unenthusiastic. Prompted by the Commission, the Belgian Presidency
  proceeded to a vote on the regulations for increasing agricultural prices
  and they were approved by seven (of the then ten) states. Denmark and

Greece abstained, not because of any sympathy for Britain but because they had reservations about the possible supranational implications of the majority vote.

- Attitudes have changed. There has been increasing recognition, even amongst the most rigid defenders of national rights and interests, that decision-making by unanimity is a recipe not only for procrastination and delay, but often for unsatisfactory, or even no, decision-making. The situation whereby consensus remains the rule even on issues where countries would not object too strongly to being voted down, has increasingly been seen as unsatisfactory in the face of the manifest need for the EU to become efficient and dynamic in order, for example, to assist its industries compete successfully on world markets.
- The enlargements of the EC/EU – from an EC6 to an EU15 – have clearly made unanimity on policy issues all the more difficult to achieve and hence have increased the necessity for majority voting.
- The SEA, the Maastricht Treaty and the Amsterdam Treaty have all extended the number of policy areas in which majority voting is constitutionally permissible (see Chapter 5 for details). Moreover, the discussions that accompanied the three treaties were based on the assumption that the new voting provisions would be used.
- In July 1987, the General Affairs Council, in accordance with an agreement it had reached in December 1986, formally amended the Council's Rules of Procedure. Among the changes was a relaxation of the circumstances by which votes could be initiated: whereas previously only the President could call for a vote, since the amended Rules came into effect it has been the case that any national representative and the Commission also have the right, and a vote must be taken if a simple majority agrees.

Hayes-Renshaw and Wallace (1997, pp. 53–4) have estimated that in the year after the TEU came into effect (from December 1993 to December 1994), one in four legislative decisions – 64 in number – were contested where qmv was possible. Of the 64, 28 were abstentions only, and of these 26 were by just one member state. Of the other 36 decisions, 11 were with one member state opposing, nine with one opposing and one abstaining, one with one opposing and two abstaining, nine with two opposing, and six with three or four opposing. Hayes-Renshaw and Wallace's figures thus indicate contested votes being held in about one quarter of the cases when they are possible, and resistance usually limited. The extent of the resistance to the directive on food additives contained in Exhibit 7.1 is thus not common on the basis of their figures: figures that in general have remained fairly consistent – in 1997, for example, the Council adopted 48 internal legislative acts by a qualified majority (Commission, 1998, pp. 399).

Table 7.3, which is based on a later and longer time frame than that of Hayes-Renshaw and Wallace, gives an indication of the frequency of member states' negative votes and abstentions when votes are held in the Council. The most striking feature is that Germany – one of the most pro-integration states – is the leading dissenter. The main explanation for this is that German representatives in the Council tend not to be so subject to central government control as are most other national representatives, so tend to have a freer hand and be more able to respond to domestic opposition on sensitive issues. The UK's position in second place is explained in quite another way: the presence in government up to May 1997 of the Conservative Party, which opposed many EU legislative proposals on ideological/Eurosceptical grounds.

It should be emphasised that the figures provided by Hayes-Renshaw and Wallace and those in Table 7.3 are indicative rather than definitive. Neither set provides a full picture of the impact of qmv on voting behaviour in the Council. This is partly because not all information on voting is publicly available, but mainly because what really amounts to majority voting sometimes occurs without a formal vote being taken. This can take the form of a state that is opposed to a proposal that otherwise commands general support preferring to try to extract concessions through negotiation – perhaps at working party or COREPER stage – rather than run the risk of pressing for a vote and then finding itself outvoted. Or it

Table 7.3   *Voting patterns in the Council: January 1995–January 1998*

	'No' votes	Abstentions	Total
Germany	40	12	52
UK	27	14	41
Italy	22	8	30
Sweden	20	2	22
Netherlands	16	3	19
Denmark	15	3	18
Spain	9	7	16
Greece	9	1	10
Portugal	8	7	15
Austria	8	2	10
France	6	6	12
Belgium	7	4	11
Ireland	7	2	9
Finland	7	0	7
Luxembourg	2	5	7

Source: European Voice, 15–21 October 1998, p. 4

can take the form of the Presidency announcing that 'we appear to have the necessary majority here', and this being left unchallenged by a dissenting state and therefore not formally voted on: unless an important point of principle or a damaging political consequence is at stake, a country in a minority may prefer not to create too much of a fuss.

Majority voting is thus significant and has certainly increased in importance over the years, but its impact should not be overstated. Consensual decision-making remains and can be expected to remain a key feature of Council processes. Quite apart from the fact that unanimity is still required by the treaties in some important areas, there is still a strong preference for trying to reach general agreements where 'important', 'sensitive', and 'political' matters, as opposed to 'technical' matters, are being considered. This may involve delay, but the duty of the national representatives at all Council levels is not only to reach decisions but also to defend national interests.

The formal processes by which Council meetings are conducted and business is transacted are broadly similar at ministerial, COREPER, and working party levels.

Meetings are held in large rooms, with national delegations sitting together. At one end or one side of the meeting table sits the Presidency – whose delegation is led by the most senior figure present from the country currently holding the Presidency; at the other end or side sit the Commission representatives; and ranged between the Presidency and the Commission are the representatives of the member states – with the delegation from the country holding the Presidency sitting to the right of, but separate from, the President (see Figure 7.1).

As indicated earlier, the Presidency plays a key role in fixing the agenda of Council meetings, both in terms of content and the order in which items are considered. The room for manoeuvre available to the Presidency should not, however, be exaggerated, for quite apart from time constraints there are several other factors that serve to limit options and actions. For example, it is difficult to exclude from the agenda of Council meetings items that are clearly of central interest or need resolution; the development of rolling programmes means that much of the agenda of many meetings is largely fixed; and anyone in a COREPER or a ministerial meeting can insist that a matter is discussed provided the required notice is given. Therefore, a Presidency cannot afford to be too ambitious or the six-month tenureship will probably come to be seen as a failure. With this in mind, the normal pattern for an incoming President of a reasonably important sectoral Council is to take the view that of, say, eight proposed directives in his or her policy area, she or he will try to get four particular ones through. This is then reflected in the organisation of Council business, so that by the end of the Presidency two may have been adopted by the Council, while another two may be at an advanced stage.

At ministerial level Council meetings can often appear to be chaotic affairs: not counting interpreters there can be around 100 people in the room – with each national delegation putting out a team of perhaps six or seven, the Commission a similar number, and the Presidency being made up of both General Secretariat and national officials; participants frequently change – with ministers often arriving late or leaving early, and some of the officials coming and going in relation to items on the agenda; ministers are constantly being briefed by officials as new points are raised; there are huddles of delegations during breaks; requests for adjournments and postponements are made to enable further information to be sought and more consideration to be given; and telephone calls may be made to national capitals for clarifications or even, occasionally, for authorisation to adopt revised negotiating positions. Not surprisingly, delegations that are headed by ministers with domestic political weight, are well versed in EU ways, have mastered the intricacies of the issues under consideration, and can think quickly on their feet, are particularly well placed to exercise influence.

A device that is sometimes employed at Council meetings, especially when negotiations are making little progress, is the *tour de table* procedure, whereby the President invites each delegation to give a summary of its thinking on the matter under consideration. This ensures that the discussion is not totally dominated by a few, and more importantly it allows the position of each member state to be established. It can thus help to reveal possible grounds for agreement and provide useful guidance to the President as to whether a compromise is possible or whether an attempt should be made to proceed to a decision. However, there are also drawbacks with the procedure. In particular, states may find it difficult to alter their position once they have 'gone public', and it is very time consuming – even if each state restricts itself to just five minutes a *tour* takes over an hour. Presidencies do then tend, and are normally advised by the General Secretariat, to be cautious about using the procedure unless there seems to be no other way forward. It is usually better to use another approach, such as inviting the Commission to amend its proposal, or seeking to isolate the most 'hard line' state in the hope that it will back down.

This last point highlights how important the Presidency can be, not only at the agenda-setting stage but also during meetings themselves. An astute and sensitive chairman is often able to judge when a delegation that is causing difficulties is not terribly serious: when, perhaps, it is being awkward for domestic political reasons and will not ultimately stand in the way of a decision being made. A poor chairman, on the other hand, may allow a proposal to drag on, or may rush it to such an extent that a state which, given time, would have agreed to a compromise may feel obliged to dig in its heels.

A final feature of Council decision-making procedures that must be noted is the extremely important role of informal processes and relationships. Three examples demonstrate this. First, many understandings and agreements are reached at the lunches that are very much a part of ministerial meetings. These lunches are attended only by ministers and a minimal number of translators (many ministers can converse directly with one another, usually in French or English).

Second, when difficulties arise in ministerial negotiations a good chairman will make advantageous use of scheduled or requested breaks in proceedings to explore possibilities for a settlement. This may involve holding off-the-record discussions with a delegation that is holding up an agreement, or it may take the form of a *tour* of all delegations – perhaps in the company of the relevant Commissioner and a couple of officials – to ascertain 'real' views and fall-back positions.

Third, many of the national officials based in Brussels come to know their counterparts in other Permanent Representations extremely well: better, sometimes, than their colleagues in their own national capitals or Permanent Representations. This enables them to judge when a country is posturing and when it is serious, and when and how a deal may be possible. A sort of code language may even be used between officials to signal their position on proposals. So if, for example, a national representative states that 'this is very important for my minister', or 'my minister is very strongly pressurised on this', the other participants recognise that a signal is being given that further deliberations are necessary at their level if more serious difficulties are to be avoided when the ministers gather.

Concluding comments

The structure and functioning of the Council are generally recognised as being unsatisfactory in a number of important respects. In particular, power is too dispersed, there is insufficient cohesion between and sometimes within the sectoral Councils, and decision-making processes are still often rather cumbersome and slow.

Many have argued that what is most needed to deal with these weaknesses is some sort of 'super' Council with the authority to impose an overall policy pattern on subsidiary sectoral Councils. Such a Council may indeed be useful for identifying priorities and knocking a few heads together, but it would be unwise to hold out too many hopes for it, even if the practical obstacles to its establishment it could be overcome. As the experience of the European Council demonstrates (see Chapter 8), the dream of authoritative national leaders rationally formulating policy frameworks in the 'EU interest' just does not accord with political realities.

But if fundamental structural reforms are unlikely, it should be recognised that the Council has undergone, and is still undergoing, quite radical changes in an attempt to deal with the increasing demands on it. The most important of these changes are the greatly increased use of majority voting, the enhancement of the role of the Presidency and the increased cooperation that occurs between Presidencies − of which the development of rolling policy programmes is especially important. Further changes can be expected in the future, not least because the membership and functioning of the Council will be much affected when Central and Eastern European countries join the EU.

The European Council

Origins and development

Although no provision was made in the Founding Treaties for summit meetings of Heads of Government, a few such gatherings did occur in the 1960s and early 1970s. At the Paris summit in 1974 it was decided to institutionalise these meetings with the establishment of what soon became known as the European Council.

The main reason for the creation of the European Council was a growing feeling that the Community was failing to respond adequately or quickly enough to new and increasingly difficult challenges. Neither the Commission, whose position had been weakened by the intergovernmental emphasis on decision-making that was signalled by the Luxembourg Compromise, nor the Council of Ministers, which was handicapped both by sectoralism and by its practice of proceeding only on the basis of unanimous agreement, were providing the necessary leadership. A new focus of authority was seen as necessary in order to make the Community more effective, both domestically and internationally. What was needed, argued France's President Giscard d'Estaing, who with West Germany's Chancellor Schmidt was instrumental in establishing the European Council, was a body that would bring the Heads of Government together on a relatively informal basis to exchange ideas, further mutual understanding at the highest political level, give direction to policy development, and perhaps sometimes break deadlocks and clear logjams. It was not anticipated that the leaders would concern themselves with the details of policy.

The formal creation of the European Council was very simple: a few paragraphs were issued as part of the Paris communiqué. The key paragraphs were as follows:

Recognising the need for an overall approach to the internal problems involved in achieving European unity and the external problems facing

Europe, the Heads of Government consider it essential to ensure progress and overall consistency in the activities of the Communities and in the work on political cooperation.

The Heads of Government have therefore decided to meet, accompanied by the Ministers of Foreign Affairs, three times a year and, whenever necessary, in the Council of the Communities and in the context of political cooperation.

The administrative secretariat will be provided for in an appropriate manner with due regard for existing practices and procedures. (The full communiqué is reproduced in Harryvan and van der Harst, 1997, pp. 181–3.)

Two points about this communiqué are particularly worth emphasising. First, it was vague and left a number of questions largely unanswered, especially with regard to the precise role and functioning of the European Council.

Second, the communiqué had no constitutional or legal standing. It announced a political agreement between the national leaders but it did not formally or legally integrate the European Council into the Community framework.

In a somewhat similar fashion to the Luxembourg Compromise and European Political Cooperation (EPC), the European Council was thus to be part of the 'unofficial' approach to integration rather than the 'official' treaty-based approach. Over the years, however, there has been something of a formalisation of the position and role of the European Council, albeit on a tentative and cautious basis. This has occurred in four steps. First, declarations by the European Council itself in the late 1970s and early 1980s – notably London (1977) and Stuttgart (1983) – did something, though not a great deal, to clarify its role. Second, in 1986 the European Council was given legal recognition for the first time via the SEA, even if only in two short paragraphs that were confined to clarifying membership and reducing the minimum number of meetings per year from three to two. The paragraphs were not incorporated into the Community Treaties. Third, the Maastricht Treaty, expanding on the SEA, contained three 'sets of references' to the European Council: it was assigned responsibility for identifying the general direction of the EU's development; it was given certain duties and decision-making powers in respect of EMU; and it was provided with important powers in the CFSP pillar. Fourth, the Amsterdam Treaty confirmed the Maastricht provisions in respect of its general directional role and with regard to EMU, and greatly strengthened the European Council's position in respect of the CFSP. The European Council's treaty powers are thus now as follows:

- The Common Provisions of the TEU specify the following under Article 4 (ex Article D):

The European Council shall provide the Union with the necessary impetus for its development and shall define the general political guidelines thereof.

The European Council shall bring together the Heads of State or of Government of the Member States and the President of the Commission. They shall be assisted by the Ministers for Foreign Affairs of the Member States and by a Member of the Commission. The European Council shall meet at least twice a year, under the chairmanship of the Head of State or of Government of the Member State which holds the Presidency of the Council.

The European Council shall submit to the European Parliament a report after each of its meetings and a yearly written report on the progress achieved by the Union.

The general role of the European Council in the EU is thus laid down in a legal document. It is so, however, in only vague terms and – because the Common Provisions are not incorporated into the Community Treaties – on such a legal basis that whatever interpretation the European Council gives to its role, or indeed to any of the other provisions of Article 4, it cannot be challenged in the Court of Justice.

- In Title VII (ex Title VI) of the TEC, which deals with Economic and Monetary Policy, the Heads of Government were brought into the framework of the Communities for the first time. There are two references to the European Council under Title VII: under Article 99 (ex 103) it is given an important role in determining 'the broad guidelines of the economic policies of the Member States and of the Community'; and under Article 113 (ex 109b) it is required to be presented with the annual report of the European Central Bank. Under Title VII the Heads of Government are also mentioned in a capacity separate from their membership of the European Council. In one formulation, under Articles 112 (ex 109a), members of the European Central Bank are to be appointed 'by common accord of the Governments of the Member States at the levels of Heads of State or of Government'. In the other formulation, which is used in Articles 121 (ex 109j) and 122 (ex 109k), certain key decisions in the transition to EMU – including the suitability of countries to join the third stage – are to be taken by qualified majority vote in the Council of Ministers 'meeting in the composition of Heads of State or of Government'.

- Article 13 of the TEU, as amended by the Amsterdam Treaty, places the European Council in a potentially very important position in respect of the CFSP:

1. The European Council shall define the principles of and general guidelines for the common foreign and security policy, including the matters with defence implications.
2. The European Council shall decide on common strategies to be implemented by the Union in areas where the Member States have important interests in common.
   Common strategies shall set out their objectives, duration and the means to be made available by the Union and the Member States.
3. The Council shall take the decisions necessary for defining and implementing the common foreign and security policy on the basis of the general guidelines defined by the European Council.
   The Council shall recommend common strategies to the European Council and shall implement them, in particular by adopting joint actions and common positions.
   The Council shall ensure the unity, consistency and effectiveness of action by the Union.

It might have been thought that the limited treaty base of the European Council – not recognised until the SEA, largely outside the Founding Treaties, and a lack of legal clarity even today on its precise roles (especially in pillars one and three) – would have hindered the ability of the European Council to exercise influence and establish itself as an important decision-making institution. In practice it has not been a hindrance at all because the status of those who attend meetings – particularly the national leaders – is such that they can more or less decide amongst themselves what the European Council will and will not do. As a result, the evolution, operation and influence of the European Council have owed much more to the preferences of the participants and to political and practical necessities than they have to agreed rules and requirements. Indeed, in order to give itself maximum flexibility and manoeuvrability, the European Council has been careful to avoid being based on or subject to rules and requirements – especially those which might arise, not least from Court of Justice jurisdiction, if the European Council were to be placed firmly within the context of the Community Treaties.

The opportunity to decide for itself what it does has resulted in the European Council exercising a number of roles and performing a number of functions. The precise nature of these roles and functions are explained in some detail below, so suffice it to note here that they add up to an extremely important and impressive portfolio. Indeed, they put the European Council at the very heart of EU decision-making – not on a day-to-day basis in the manner of the other four main EU institutions, but rather from a more distanced position where it is centrally involved in setting the overall parameters of the EU system. Final and legally binding EU decisions may be made by other EU institutions, but major political decisions concerning the institutional and policy development of the EU are now generally taken by, or at least are given clearance by, the European Council.

Membership

As Article 4 of the Common Provisions of the TEU (see above) makes clear, there are two 'levels' of membership of the European Council: the Heads of State or Government of the member states and the President of the Commission; and the Foreign Ministers of the member states and one other member of the Commission, who attend to provide assistance. In practice the only Heads of State to take part in the European Council are the French and Finnish Presidents, whose political powers are much greater than the largely nominal and/or occasional powers of other Heads of State. Sometimes Foreign Ministers are replaced by other ministers, most notably when French politics are in a period of 'cohabitation', when the Prime Minister attends.

Apart from the 32 participants just identified, only a very restricted number of other people are permitted to be present at the formal sessions of the European Council: interpreters; six officials – two from the country holding the Presidency, one from the Council Secretariat (a major job of these three officials is to make an accurate record of proceedings), and three from the Commission – including the Secretary General of the Commission; and national civil servants, but only on the basis of one adviser per country being allowed entrance at any one time.

In recent years, in response to the increasing importance of EMU, the practice has developed of Ecofin Council ministers also travelling to European summits, though not necessarily staying for the whole meeting. The Ecofin ministers usually hold parallel meetings to discuss matters that fall within their sphere of competence, and usually join with the other European Council participants for a session to discuss and/or take decisions on economic and financial issues.

Each member state has a suite in the vicinity of the summit meeting room, which is available to its official delegation and from which officials may be summoned as required. Official delegations are normally restricted in number, but states always supplement their official delegations with numerous other officials who make up what are customarily described as the non-official or technical delegations.

The European Council membership is thus based on the Council of Ministers model in the sense that it is made up of national delegations, plus the Commission. Unlike in the Council of Ministers, however, the participants in formal European Council sessions are not accompanied by teams of national officials. The original thinking behind this restriction on access to the summit meeting room was that it would encourage relaxed informality, and in any event was not strictly necessary as the European Council was not a law maker. However, in practice it has proved difficult to achieve the desired mood, not least because of the increased number of participants following enlargements and the increased importance of decisions taken at European Council meetings.

Organisation

Preparing European Council meetings

Much of the responsibility for preparing European Council meetings rests with the Presidency – a post that is held concurrently with the Presidency of the Council of Ministers. How closely the Head of Government of the incumbent Presidency becomes involved in these preparations depends very much on circumstances, style and personal preference. A (declining) few act in a low-key manner and do little more than circulate to the other summit participants a letter indicating the topics to be discussed and the ways in which it is proposed to try to deal with them. Most, however, and especially those who are faced with a difficult meeting or who are looking for media attention, may well play a very active and public role – including making a tour of some or all of the national capitals.

Whatever the preparatory work that Heads of Government themselves choose to do, national officials and Foreign Ministers are invariably extensively engaged in pre-European Council preparations. The 'standard' procedure is for senior officials from the Presidency, working in liaison with the Secretariat of the Council of Ministers (the European Council does not have its own Secretariat), the Antici Group (see Chapter 7), and the Commission, to identify topics that can be, ought to be, or need to be discussed. These are then channelled through COREPER and, in the case of CFSP matters, through the Political Committee (which is made up of Political Directors from Foreign Offices). Finally, about ten days before the European Council meeting, Foreign Ministers, and often also Ecofin Ministers, meet to finalise the general shape of the agenda and, usually, to engage in exploratory pre-summit negotiations. To this 'standard' procedure may well be added – especially when it looks as though a European Council meeting will be difficult – numerous preparatory meetings of officials and the convening of extra ministerial meetings.

Setting the agenda

European Council agendas are almost invariably crowded.

- Some issues are almost always on the agenda because of their intrinsic importance. So time is usually allowed for a discussion of the general economic situation in the EU, and in recent years time has usually also been set aside for some consideration of developments relating to the SEM, to EMU, to the promotion of employment, and to enlargement.
- The Commission may be pressing an initiative towards which the Presidency and at least some of the states are sympathetic. This was, for example, the background to the establishment of a plan of action at the December 1992 Edinburgh summit to promote growth and combat unemployment.
- The Presidency, perhaps supported or even pressed by the Commission and all or some of the other member states, may wish to use a European Council meeting to make or to formalise an important policy or institutional breakthrough. The events leading up to the Maastricht Treaty illustrate this: the decision to call an IGC on EMU was taken at the 1989 Strasbourg summit; the decision to call a parallel IGC on Political Union was taken at the special April 1990 Dublin summit; the setting of dates for the opening of the two IGCs was taken at the June 1990 Dublin summit; the IGCs were formally opened at the December 1990 Rome summit; and the IGCs reported to, and the final decisions on the contents of the TEU were taken at, the December 1991 Maastricht summit. The events leading up to the Amsterdam Treaty were not dissimilar.
- Decisions may be needed on matters that have come to be accepted as needing European Council resolution, or at least approval. For example, the decision to open EU accession negotiations in the spring of 1998 with five CEECs and Cyprus was taken at the December 1997 Luxembourg summit.
- Business may be left over from, or have been referred from, a previous summit. For example the June 1998 Cardiff summit invited the Commission 'to report to future European Councils' on progress made in integrating environmental protection into EU policies so as to achieve sustainable development (European Council, 1998, p. 12).

- Reports may have to be considered, or at least noted. For instance, reports on the following were submitted to the December 1997 Luxembourg summit: by the Council on enlargement and *Agenda 2000*; by the Council on preparations for Stage 3 of EMU; by the Council on achievements in the field of justice and home affairs in 1997; by the Council on drugs; by the Commission on regional cooperation in Europe; by the Commission on 'better lawmaking'; by the Commission on the implementation of the action plan on the internal market; by the Commission on trans-European networks (annual report); by the Commission on the implementation of the recommendations of the Personal Representatives Group on Sound and Effective Management (SEM 2000), and the Council's conclusions on that report (European Council, 1997b, Appendix 4).
- International circumstances may require discussions, declarations or decisions. For instance, the June 1998 Cardiff summit considered, amongst other matters, international trade, EU–US relations, South Africa, Russia, the Middle East Peace Process, and India/Pakistan nuclear tests (European Council, 1998: Annex III).

The normal twice yearly European Council meetings have on their agendas a mixture of most of the sort of items just listed. When special summits are held, however – and there is usually at least one a year – the situation is rather different for they are mostly convened for a specific purpose, last no more than one day, and inevitably have a much narrower agenda. For example, the special Birmingham summit of October 1992 was nominally convened to discuss the recent crisis in the Exchange Rate Mechanism (ERM). However, by the time the summit was held the immediacy of the crisis had passed, the other states had intimated their unwillingness to examine what the UK government was referring to as 'the fault lines in the ERM', so the agenda was broadened to include a discussion on subsidiarity and transparency. The special Luxembourg summit of November 1997 was arranged to strengthen employment policies in the EU, and focused on guidelines drawn up by the Commission and discussed by the Ecofin and Employment and Social Affairs Councils separately and in a joint Council in preparation for the summit.

Location and timing of meetings

The six-monthly meetings of the European Council that are specifically provided for in the TEU are held in the country of the Presidency. When the provision for twice-yearly meetings was first established in the SEA it had been anticipated that any extra meetings would be held in Brussels, but in practice they too are often held in the country of the Presidency.

The regular meetings of the European Council take place towards the end of a Presidency – in June and December. They are held over a two-day period and normally, though by no means always, begin in the morning of day one and end in the late afternoon of day two. The timing and length of special summits depends largely on the reasons for which they have been called, but they rarely last longer than one day – the March 1999 Berlin summit, which was convened to take final decisions on the *Agenda 2000* proposals, was extremely unusual in that it spread over three days.

The conduct of business

The customary, though by no means rigid, format for the regular European Council meetings is as follows.

- The participants gather for dinner on the eve of the summit, or sometimes after breakfast on the first day. On the basis of the (normally loose) agenda that has been agreed in advance, a full plenary session is held. Since 1987 this opening session has included an address from the President of the European Parliament. Ecofin Ministers may hold a separate meeting at this time (see above).
- Lunch is a drawn-out affair, which allows time for informal discussions and bilateral meetings. During lunch, and indeed during most breaks, there are meetings between the summit participants and their national delegations.
- Another full plenary is usually held in the afternoon, although sometimes the Heads of Government and the Foreign Ministers have separate meetings.
- In the evening, dinner provides another opportunity for further informal discussions. The Heads of Government and the President of the Commission on the one hand, and the Foreign Ministers and the other representative of the Commission on the other, used to take dinner separately, but this practice has been dropped and a large ceremonial dinner is usually held, often with the host Head of State presiding.
- What happens after dinner rather depends on what progress has been made during the day. The customary format used to be that the Heads would hold informal 'fireside chats' while the Foreign Ministers discussed EPC (now CFSP) business. At recent summits, however, informal sessions have not been so common. Occasionally there have been reconvened plenaries in an attempt to make progress with uncompleted business, and often bilateral late-night meetings are held.
- During the night, Presidency and Council Secretariat officials prepare a draft of conclusions on the first day's business and/or work on a

form of words that can serve as a basis for further negotiations the next day.

- Another plenary session is held in the morning and sometimes the afternoon of day two. This usually picks up from the previous day's discussions, but with the draft that has been worked on during the night now tabled. With the leaders now trying to move towards conclusions, breaks in the proceedings may be called for, usually by the Presidency, to permit delegations to study the implications of proposals or to allow informal discussions to take place.

- The summit normally ends some time in the afternoon or early evening with the publication of a statement in the form of 'Presidency Conclusions'. Everything in the statement is customarily agreed to by all summit participants, though there have been four occasions when particular European Council decisions have been taken by majority vote. On each occasion the vote was held largely because of exasperation with what was seen as unreasonable UK opposition to integrationist developments: at Milan in 1985, Denmark, Greece and the UK were outvoted on the establishment of the IGC that led to the SEA (Denmark and Greece did not oppose the principle of establishing the SEA, but did oppose the principle of using majority votes in the European Council); at Strasbourg in 1989 the UK was in a minority of one in opposing the adoption of the Social Charter and the holding of an IGC on EMU; and at the special Rome summit in 1990 the UK was again alone with regard to the setting of a date for Stage 2 of EMU.

  Exhibit 8.1 provides extracts from the Presidency Conclusions of a fairly typical European Council meeting. (It is not possible to reproduce the full document since it runs to 50 pages, which is about the average length of Presidency Conclusions.) As can be seen, a wide range of issues are considered at summits, a variety of types of decisions are taken, a number of initiatives are launched, and various instructions and guidance are issued to the member states and other EU institutions.

- Press conferences are held for the hundreds of journalists who attend European Councils and do so much to turn the summits into major media events. The President of the European Council and the President of the Commission normally hold a joint press conference, and each delegation holds one of its own. Different versions of what has happened are often given on these occasions.

The negotiating, bargaining and compromising that can be such a major part of European Council meetings, and the variable forms that meetings can take, is worth illustrating with an example. The December 1992 Edinburgh summit – one of the most important meetings in the history of

Exhibit 8.1   A European Council meeting: Presidency Conclusions (extracts)

Vienna European Council, 11 and 12 December 1998

The European Council met in Vienna on 11 and 12 December 1998 to discuss the main issues and challenges facing the European Union. It began its proceedings with an exchange of views with Mr José María GIL-ROBLES, President of the European Parliament, on the main subjects for discussion.

Its discussions on employment, growth and stability also benefited from the exchange of views between the Troïka and the social partners which had taken place the day before.

A meeting was held with the Heads of State or Government and the Ministers of Foreign Affairs of the Central and Eastern European countries and Cyprus participating in the accession process.

The European Council expressed its gratitude to the former Federal Chancellor of Germany, Helmut Kohl, for his outstanding contribution to the development of the European Union and decided to award him the title 'Honorary Citizen of Europe'.

I.   VIENNA STRATEGY FOR EUROPE

1. European integration has gained new momentum. The single currency is about to be launched. Coordinated efforts to promote employment have produced encouraging results. The enlargement process is well under way. As the millennium draws to a close, the Union will have to strengthen its ability to serve its citizens.

2. At Cardiff, the European Council initiated a broad debate on the future development of the European Union. The Pörtschach meeting emphasised the need for a strong and effective Union. In this spirit, the Vienna European Council has identified four issues of primary concern to European citizens where rapid and effective action is necessary. It has therefore agreed on the following 'Vienna Strategy for Europe':

Promoting employment, economic growth and stability

- Report to the Cologne European Council on the development of a European Employment Pact in the framework of the Luxembourg process.
- Reinforcement of mechanisms for economic policy coordination; review of instruments and experience at the Helsinki European Council.
- Political agreement on the key elements of the tax policy package; report to the Helsinki European Council.
- Improvement of the international financial architecture; report to the Cologne Europe Council.
- Promotion of investment in European infrastructure and in human capital; report to the Cologne European Council.

Exhibit 8.1 continued

Improving security and the quality of life

- Implementation of the Action Plan on establishing an area of freedom, security and justice; review at the special meeting of the European Council in Tampere.
- Improvement of the citizens' access to justice; review at the Tampere meeting.
- Reinforcement of European Union action in the field of human rights; report to the Cologne European Council.
- Integration of environment and sustainable development in European Union policies; review at the Helsinki European Council.

Reforming the Union's policies and institutions

- Political agreement on the Agenda 2000 package in March 1999 in order to achieve its final adoption before the European Parliament elections in June 1999.
- Decision at the Cologne European Council on how and when to tackle the institutional issues not resolved at Amsterdam.
- Improvement of the functioning of the Council; review at the Helsinki European Council.
- Internal reform of the Commission; report by the President of the Commission to the Cologne European Council.
- Effective fight against fraud; review of progress at the Helsinki European Council.

Promoting stability and prosperity throughout Europe and in the world

- Dynamic continuation of accession negotiations and preparations, and the submission of progress reports by the Commission on candidate countries in view of the Helsinki European Council.
- Effective application of the new Common Foreign and Security Policy (CFSP) instruments following the entry into force of the Amsterdam Treaty (High Representative, CFSP planning and early warning unit, improved decision-making mechanisms); review at the Helsinki European Council.
- Preparation of the first Common Strategies on Russia, Ukraine, the Mediterranean Region and the Western Balkans; first adoption at the Cologne European Council.
- Continuation of reflection on the development of a European security and defence policy; examination at the Cologne European Council.

Building on these elements, the European Council will, at its meeting in Helsinki, adopt a 'Millennium Declaration' on the Union's priorities for future years.

II.   HUMAN RIGHTS

   3.   On the occasion of the 50th anniversary of the adoption of the Universal Declaration of Human Rights, the European Council

→

reaffirms the primary importance which it attaches to this declaration. The Universal Declaration is a cornerstone in the edifice built after World War II for the protection and promotion of human rights at the national, regional and global level and is the foundation for advancing and ensuring human dignity worldwide . . .

III.   EMPLOYMENT, GROWTH, STABILITY AND ECONOMIC REFORM

A.   Economic and monetary union: a major step ahead

(i)   Birth of the euro

12.   The European Council notes with great satisfaction that the transition to the third stage of Economic and Monetary Union on 1 January 1999 will be achieved smoothly in spite of turbulence on the world financial markets. This is the result of prudent economic policies in the context of EMU which must be continued . . .

(ii)   Europe as a global player

Speaking with one voice

14.   The introduction of the euro will be a major event for the international monetary system. It is imperative that the Community should play its full role in international monetary and economic policy cooperation within fora like the G7 and the International Monetary Fund. The European Council endorses the report of the Council on the external representation of the Community, which foresees that the President of the ECOFIN Council, or if the President is from a non-euro area Member State, the President of the Euro 11, assisted by the Commission, shall participate in meetings of the G7 (Finance) (see Annex II). The ECB, as the Community body competent for monetary policy, should be granted an observer status at the IMF board. The views of the European Community/EMU on other issues of particular relevance to the EMU would be presented at the IMF board by the relevant member of the Executive Director's office of the Member State holding the euro Presidency, assisted by a representative of the Commission. The European Council invites the Council to act on the basis of a Commission proposal incorporating this agreement. . .

(iii)   Strengthening internal economic coordination

Tax policy

21.   The European Council welcomes the report of the Council on reinforced tax policy cooperation and emphasises the need to combat harmful tax competition. Cooperation in the tax policy area is not aiming at uniform tax rates and is not inconsistent with fair tax competition but is called for to reduce the continuing distortions in the single market, to prevent excessive losses of tax revenue or to get tax structures to develop in a more employment-friendly way.

→

Exhibit 8.1 continued

22. In particular, the European Council
     – welcomes the fact that the work of the Code of Conduct Group has proceeded satisfactorily and encourages the Group to conclude its work at the latest by the Helsinki European Council;
     – asks the Commission to submit a study on company taxation to the Council in accordance with the ECOFIN Council conclusions;
     – invites the Council to pursue work on the proposals for a Directive on the taxation of savings and for a Directive on interest and royalties with a view to reaching agreement before the Helsinki European Council;
     – welcomes the intention of the Commission and the Council to begin talks with third countries on problems concerning the taxation of interest income; and
     – encourages the Council to pursue its own work on a framework for energy taxation on the basis of the ECOFIN Council report, also taking into account its implications for the environment.

23. The European Council invites the Council to submit to it a second progress report on tax policy cooperation in time for the European Council in June 1999. . .

B.   Sustainable employment for Europe

1.   *Towards a European employment pact*

26. Employment is the top priority of the European Union. It is the best way of providing real opportunity for people and combating poverty and exclusion effectively, thereby serving as the basis for the European social model.

27. The European Council notes with satisfaction the substantial progress that has been achieved in creating jobs and reducing unemployment. It applauds the efforts made by Member States in implementing the 1998 Guidelines. . .

31. When revising their National Plans, Member States should pay particular attention to the following:
     – achieving tangible progress in promoting equal opportunities between women and men, in particular using benchmarks and a gender mainstreaming approach;
     – making a reality of the concept of lifelong learning, in particular setting a national target for participants benefiting from such measures;
     – fully exploiting the potential of the service sector and industry-related services, in particular information technology and the environmental sector;
     – creating a climate in which business, especially small businesses, can flourish;

→

- examining tax-benefit systems in order to provide incentives for the unemployed and inactive to take up work or training opportunities and for employers to create new jobs;
- supporting older workers to increase their participation in the labour force;
- promoting social inclusion and equality of opportunity for disadvantaged groups. . .

2. *A favourable environment for employment*

(i) *Investing for jobs. . .*

41. The European Investment Bank has maintained the momentum of its lending operations in favour of sound investment projects, including those in priority sectors under its Amsterdam Special Action Programme, such as investments in education, health and urban environment projects.

42. In this context, the European Council invites the Bank to consider an accelerated release of funds for risk capital operations, within the ceiling of ECU 1 billion expected initially to be reached by 2000, the objective being that these operations will take place in all Member States. This could include in particular an early doubling of the resources allocated to the European Technology Facility.

43. The European Council invites the Bank to review existing financing arrangements for environmental projects in the Union and in applicant countries, taking due account of the employment effects of such projects . . .

V. *ENLARGEMENT*

58. The European Council had a thorough discussion on all aspects of the enlargement process. It welcomes the fact that the overall enlargement process launched in Luxembourg is now well under way. The European Council welcomes the Commission's first Regular Progress Reports on the basis of its conclusions in Luxembourg and Cardiff and endorses the annexed Council conclusions of 7 December 1998 on European Union enlargement. The European Council stresses that each country will continue to be judged on its own merits. The European Council invites the Commission to present its further progress reports with a view to the Helsinki European Council.

59. The European Council notes with satisfaction that the six Accession Conferences with Cyprus, Hungary, Poland, Estonia, the Czech Republic and Slovenia have entered into substantive negotiations and reached the first concrete results. It urges the Council, the Commission and the candidate countries to maintain the momentum in order to permit intensive negotiations in the first half of 1999.

60. The European Council also welcomes progress in preparation for accession negotiations with Romania, Slovakia, Latvia, Lithuania and

→

Exhibit 8.1 continued

Bulgaria as described in the Commission's reports. It notes that the transition from the multilateral to the bilateral phase of the analytical examination of the acquis as from the beginning of the next year will confer new dynamism to the process and thus foster preparation for negotiations. . .

VIII. SUBSIDIARITY

79. The European Council reaffirms its determination to ensure full application of the principle of subsidiarity. Decisions should be taken as closely as possible to the citizens of the Union. Subsidiarity and proportionality are legally binding principles, enshrined in Article 3b of the EC Treaty, which the Institutions must respect fully.

Recalling the discussions held at the informal meeting in Pörtschach, it agrees that:

- the institutions shall be guided as from now by the criteria and practices contained in the 'subsidiarity and proportionality Protocol' which will be annexed to the EC Treaty when the Amsterdam Treaty comes into force;
- the Commission's annual 'Better law-making' report should be the basis for reporting on and examining developments over the past year; future reports should be presented in good time to allow for thorough discussion in the various institutions and bodies concerned (European Parliament, Council, Committee of the Regions, COSAC, Economic and Social Committee) and, therefore, for optimum preparation of the European Council;
- the Council should conduct an orientation debate on future Green and White Papers from the Commission in the light of the principle of subsidiarity, not undermining in any way the Commission's right of initiative;
- before the Commission proposes a significant new piece of legislation, it should examine whether other Community legislation already existing on the same issue needs to be modified or consolidated, or repealed if no longer justified . . .

X. JUSTICE AND HOME AFFAIRS

83. The European Council endorses the Action Plan drawn up by the Council and the Commission on establishing an area of freedom, security and justice, which opens a new dimension for action in the field of Justice and Home Affairs after the entry into force of the Amsterdam Treaty and which sets a concrete framework for the development of activities in these fields. It urges the Council to start immediately with the implementation of the 2-year priorities defined in this Action Plan. . .

86. The European Council stresses the importance of rapidly integrating Schengen into the European Union. It calls especially for solutions on

→

the allocation of legal bases to the Schengen acquis and on the integration of the Schengen Information System and of the Schengen Secretariat into the framework of the EU. The European Council welcomes the fact that the negotiations with Iceland and Norway are close to conclusion . . .

XII. EXTERNAL ISSUES

International trade/WTO

98. The European Council reiterates its commitment to the WTO as the basis for the EU's commercial policy and the main framework for further trade liberalisation. It reaffirms its support for comprehensive, wide-ranging WTO negotiations starting from 2000, and invites the Council and Commission to intensify work in order to secure agreement to this objective at the Third WTO Ministerial Conference to take place towards the end of 1999. . .

Northern dimension

109. The European Council welcomed the Interim Report on a Northern Dimension for the Policies of the European Union submitted by the Commission. It underlined the importance of this subject for the internal policies of the Union as well as its external relations, in particular towards Russia and the Baltic Sea region. It emphasised the need for further exchange with all countries concerned on the development of a concept on the Northern Dimension and invited the Council to identify, on the basis of the Commission's interim report, guidelines for actions in the relevant fields. It welcomes the Finnish initiative to arrange, in cooperation with the European Commission, a conference on the topic during the second half of 1999 . . .

Newly independent states

113. The European Council also expressed its concern at the deteriorating economic situation in the Newly Independent States, particularly those with close financial or trade links with Russia. It therefore invites the European Commission to provide a report to the Council on these developments, including proposals on ways and means of addressing these economic issues, not only within the framework of the existing assistance programmes at its disposal, but also through the Partnership and Cooperation Agreements as they come into force. . .

Euro-Mediterranean partnership

116. The European Council reaffirmed the importance it attaches to the Euro-Mediterranean Partnership and stressed its satisfaction with the on-going multifaceted dialogue in this forum. The third Euro-Mediterranean Ministerial meeting in Stuttgart in April 1999 will permit the Union and its Mediterranean Partners to continue the successful work and give new impetus to the Partnership. . .

Source: General Secretariat of the Council.

the European Council because of the many decisions it produced – will be used for the purpose.

Several key issues were on the agenda and needed resolution. Likened to a Rubik cube by the summit's chairman, UK Prime Minister John Major, these issues included: a strategy to assist the Danish government to 'overturn' the referendum of June in which the Maastricht Treaty had not been approved (the Danish government hoped to be able to hold a second referendum in which it could say, amongst other things, that it had firm guarantees that Denmark would not be obliged to participate in EMU or in a common defence policy); clarification of how the concepts of subsidiarity and transparency – which were emerging, post-Maastricht, almost as guiding principles for the future – were to be operationalised; agreement on the size and composition of the budget for the period 1993–7 (it was ten months since the Commission had put forward proposals – in the so-called 'Delors II' budgetary package); what action was to be taken on the Commission's plans for the adoption of measures designed to promote growth and employment; whether to authorise the opening of enlargement negotiations with EFTA applicants (it had been decided at the June 1992 Lisbon summit that negotiations could begin once the budgetary issue was settled and the TEU was ratified); and the siting of several new EU institutions.

Much of the plenary session on the morning of day one was taken up with the problem of the Danish ratification. The focus of the debate was a paper by the Presidency that had been circulated two days before the meeting. This paper was based on an earlier Presidential draft that had been amended at a Foreign Ministers meeting five days before the summit. By the lunchtime of day one the Danes were largely satisfied with the text that was emerging. The Director-General of the Council's Legal Service was called into the plenary to give assurance that the decision (not declaration) would be legally binding and would not require re-ratification of the Treaty by these ten member states that had already done so. The morning plenary also made progress with subsidiarity and transparency.

Over lunch, taken at Edinburgh Castle, the Commission's plans for an economic growth initiative were the main focus of discussion.

The afternoon plenary was mainly taken up with the budgetary issue. Sharp differences existed over both the overall size of the budget (with the UK taking the most restrictive line) and the shape of the budget (with the four poorer countries – Greece, Ireland, Portugal and Spain – pressing for large increases in the redistributive Structural Funds).

Running parallel with the summit meeting there was an all-day Ecofin meeting. In the morning the participants reviewed the general economic situation in the Community and in the afternoon considered the Commission's proposals for an investment package to promote growth.

The evening dinner was ceremonial rather than working, with the summit participants joining the Royal Family on the Royal Yacht Britannia. The seating arrangements went through a reported twenty-four drafts!

Before breakfast on day two all delegations were presented with Presidential drafts covering day one business.

The morning plenary was delayed for nearly three hours whilst the Presidency consulted individual delegations on issues that were proving difficult. During this period, Foreign Ministers (who focused mainly on former Yugoslavia) and Ecofin Ministers (who wrestled with the budgetary issue) met separately. President Mitterrand went shopping!

By early afternoon it was clear that most issues had been settled, either in the previous day's plenary sessions, in the meetings of Ecofin and of Foreign Ministers, or in bilateral meetings. However, Spain led the poorer countries in pressing for a more favourable settlement on the budgetary issue and made it clear that final agreement on all issues was conditional on this particular issue being settled. This led to protracted negotiations in which the hand of the main player – Spanish Prime Minister Felipe González – was extremely strong for he knew that all the other participants, especially the UK Presidency, wanted a deal and the summit to be a success.

As negotiations dragged on into the evening and 'technical' points were referred to officials, the question was raised of the siting of EU institutions, which it had been thought might be postponed until the next summit. This produced two hours of discussions, but only limited progress was made because of the many competing claims that were being pressed: the site of existing institutions was confirmed (to the satisfaction of France, Belgium and Luxembourg), but no decision was taken on the location of new institutions.

Eventually at 10.30 p.m. – instead of at lunchtime as had been planned – the summit ended and the press conferences began.

Three aspects of the final summit agreement merit particular comment in regard to the light they throw on the functioning of the European Council. First, compromise was a central feature. This was most obvious in the budgetary deal, in which the finally agreed size and distribution of planned future expenditure was higher and more generous than the UK would have liked but not quite as high or as generous as the Commission and the poorer countries had advocated. Second, whilst all the participants played a part in influencing the shape of the final agreement, the hand of Chancellor Kohl of Germany was especially apparent, for example in giving clear support to the poorer countries on the budgetary issue on day two of the summit and thereby obliging the UK to give more ground than it had anticipated, and in not pressing the case for a final agreement on the siting of the new institutions – in the (as it turned out correct) belief that a future summit would agree to the European Monetary Institute (and therefore, in time, the European Central Bank) being located in Germany. Third, further evidence was provided of how much the European Council is completely its own master when it decided not to apply the two conditions that it had laid down itself only six months earlier at the Lisbon summit in respect of the opening of accession negotiations with the EFTA applicants: although the TEU was still some months away from being ratified and one of the conditions had not yet been met, it was agreed that the negotiations could open in early 1993.

Roles and activities

As was noted above, the European Council is relatively free to decide what it may and may not do. The few treaty and other legal provisions that relate to its responsibilities are, for the most part, vague, whilst the political status of its members is such as to put it generally beyond much challenge.

As a result, the activities undertaken by the European Council have tended to vary, according both to the preferences of the personalities involved and changing circumstances and requirements. So, in the second half of the 1970s, when President Giscard d'Estaing and Chancellor Schmidt determined much of the direction and pace, considerable time was given over to general discussions of major economic and monetary problems. For much of the 1980s, by contrast, when some participants – notably Margaret Thatcher and the representatives of the Commission – began to press particular distributional questions, and when policy issues were increasingly referred 'upwards' from the Council of Ministers for resolution, the summits came to be much concerned with quite detailed decision-making. Towards the end of the 1980s another shift began to occur as summits devoted increasing time and attention to the general direction and development of the Community. This shift has continued and has resulted in the European Council increasingly assuming the role of a sort of board of directors: setting the overall framework and taking decisions about the major initiatives to be pursued, but tending to leave the operationalisation of its pronouncements and decisions to management (which in this case is essentially the Commission and the Council of Ministers).

Extrapolating from the items appearing on European Council agendas (see Exhibit 8.1 and the outline of agenda items earlier in the chapter), the main topics and areas with which the European Council concerns itself can be grouped under five headings.

The evolution of the European Union

Although this item appears only occasionally on European Council agendas as a topic in its own right, reviewing and guiding the general evolution of the EU is what several specific items are, in effect, concerned with. The most important of these items – constitutional and institutional reform, EMU, and enlargement – are dealt with separately below, but others that are worth noting include: the monitoring of progress in the creation of the Single European Market; 'troubleshooting' when progress in building the European Union is threatened – as with the measures agreed at the Edinburgh summit to deal with 'the Danish problem'; setting out framework principles when this is deemed necessary – as with periodic statements since 1992 emphasising the importance of subsidiarity; and framing the parameters of EU income and expenditure by determining the size and shape of the EU's multi-annual financial perspectives – as with the agreement at the special March 1999 Berlin summit on the 2000–6 financial perspective (see Chapter 14 on financial perspectives).

Constitutional and institutional matters

These come up in the European Council in four main forms. First, all key decisions relating to new accessions are taken at the summits. For example, in the current enlargement round – dealing with the applications from CEECs and Cyprus – amongst many key decisions have been: the agreement at the June 1993 Copenhagen summit that CEECs could become members of the EU; the setting out at the December 1994 Essen summit of a pre-accession strategy; and the confirmation at the Luxembourg 1997 summit of the Commission's recommendation that negotiations should open with five CEECs and Cyprus in 1998. Second, summits are also the venue to consider, and sometimes take action on, a range of specific institutional matters. For example, at the December 1992 Edinburgh summit the final decision (which confirmed a proposal made by the EP) was taken on the size of the EP following German unification and the prospect of enlargement, whilst the location of EU institutions was settled partially at Edinburgh (for established institutions) and partially at the special October 1993 Brussels summit (for new institutions). Third, the European Council takes some important personnel decisions, notably on the nominee for Commission President and on the appointment of the President of the European Central Bank (ECB). These decisions can become extremely politicised and very difficult: the UK government vetoed the nomination of the Belgian Prime Minister, Jean-Luc Dehaene, as Commission President at the June 1994 Corfu summit, with the consequence that a special summit had to be held in Brussels a fortnight later; France objected at the special Brussels summit in May 1998 to the appointment of Wim Duisenberg of the Netherlands Central Bank as first President of the ECB rather than Claude Trichet of the French Central Bank, and it was only after a deal was negotiated that involved Duisenberg agreeing to step down before his term of office had expired that the matter was resolved. Fourth, the European Council takes important decisions in the context of the movement towards the 'constitutionalisation' of European integration. It has been a key player in all three major revisions of the Founding Treaties: (1) the June 1985 Milan summit established the IGC that paved the way for the SEA, which was agreed at the December 1985 Luxembourg summit; (2) the IGCs that worked on what became the Maastricht Treaty were established over a series of four summits in 1989 and 1990 (two regular and two special), and the final negotiations on the Treaty were conducted at the December 1991 Maastricht summit; (3) preparations and arrangements for the 1996–7 IGC were decided at summits between 1994 and 1996 – notably Corfu in June 1994, Cannes in June 1995, and Madrid in December 1995 and the Amsterdam Treaty itself was finalised at the June 1997 Amsterdam summit.

The economic and monetary policies of the European Union

Summits have long reviewed the overall economic and social situation within the EU and looked in a general way at questions relating to economic growth, trade patterns, inflation, exchange rates, and unemployment. Until the early 1990s, however, differences between the member states about what should be done, coupled with a widely shared determination to ensure that national hands remained firmly placed on key economic controls, meant that these discussions usually produced little beyond general exhortations on topics such as controlling inflation, tackling unemployment and encouraging investment. However, as EMU has developed three factors have given these economic deliberations much more bite. First, the European Council is the place where the major features and timetable of the EMU programme are finalised. Second, since EMU requires convergence between key national economic policies, proposals for concerted economic action are now considered in the European Council. Third, and this has been stimulated by economic recession as well as the impulsion of EMU, it is now widely accepted that the EU should itself be directly tackling economic problems with programmes of its own.

The June 1993 Copenhagen summit illustrates just how important this issue now is at European Council meetings. Building on principles that had been set out six months earlier at the Edinburgh summit, the Copenhagen summit sought to promote growth and combat unemployment through a series of recommendations to the member states and a range of EU-sponsored measures. The recommendations to the member states included giving priority to investment in national budget planning and making fiscal adjustments to lower the cost of labour and reduce consumption of scarce energy resources. The measures at EU level included authorising the European Investment Bank and the Commission to increase by three billion ecu the temporary facility of five billion ecu that had been agreed at Edinburgh to promote European infrastructure and competitiveness, and inviting the Commission to present a White Paper on a medium-term strategy for growth, competitiveness and employment for consideration at the December 1993 Brussels summit.

The May 1998 Brussels meeting of the 'Council of the European Union, meeting in the composition of the Heads of State or Government' provides an example of a different kind of summit activity in respect of economic and financial matters. Technically it was not, of course, a European Council meeting but rather a Council of Ministers meeting held under the auspices of Article 121(4) of the TEC (see above). In terms of level of participation, however, it was a European Council meeting in all but name: all Heads of Government or of State attended, as did most Foreign Ministers and/or Finance Ministers. At the meeting, decisions were formally taken on which countries would participate in the third stage of EMU and who would be President, Vice-President and members of the Executive Board of the ECB (Council Press Release, 2–3 May 1998, 8170/1/98, Presse 124).

External relations

The European Council is involved in the EU's external relations in three principal ways.

First, many economic issues are not purely internal EU matters. They have vitally important global dimensions and summits often look at these either with a view to considering the EU's relations with other economic powers (especially the United States and Japan), or with a view to coordinating the EU's position in international negotiations (such as G8 summits or in the World Trade Organisation).

Second, the European Council has long issued declarations on important aspects of international political affairs. Sometimes the declarations have had policy instruments attached to them, but because these have been 'soft' instruments – usually in the form of mild economic sanctions or modest economic aid – there is little evidence of summits having had much effect on world political events. They may, however, do so in the future under the CFSP pillar with the realisation of the stated intention to develop a more coherent EU foreign policy, and linking that in time to a common defence policy and possible common defence. The guidance role specifically allocated to the European Council under Article 13 of the CFSP pillar (see above) should ensure that all major policies, initiatives and actions are at its behest, or at least have its general approval.

Third, the European Council has played an extremely important role since the break-up of the former Soviet bloc in setting the guidelines for the EU's relations with the CEECs. Initially this took the form of authorising aid programmes, encouraging economic liberalisation and political democratisation, and promoting cooperation and association agreements. However, as noted above, EU–CEEC relations have increasingly been based on the presumption of future CEEC accessions, and this has been reflected in the way the European Council has not only constantly addressed the issue of CEEC accessions but also encouraged and authorised ever closer EU–CEEC relations. The December 1997 Luxembourg summit confirmed the Commission's recommendations in *Agenda 2000* (see Chapter 6) that from 1998 there would be an 'enhanced pre-accession strategy', in which Accession Partnerships with each of the CEECs would 'mobilise all forms of assistance to the countries of Central and Eastern Europe within a single framework' (European Council, 1997b, p. 6).

Specific internal policy issues

Despite the original intention that the European Council should operate at a fairly general level, in practice it often concerns itself with quite specific internal policy issues. There are three main reasons for this: (1) some issues are so sensitive and/or so intractable that it requires the authority of national leaders to deal with them; (2) the European Council is, because of its non-sectoral nature, often the best placed institution to put together broad-ranging policies or broker deals that cut across policy sectors; and (3) the status of the European Council in the EU system is now such that the general expectation and assumption is that most policy matters of significance ought at least to be given clearance, if not determined, at European Council level.

These differing reasons have resulted in three broad types of policy involvement by the European Council. First, the European Council sometimes plays a significant role in policy initiation. Since the late 1980s several initiatives have been taken in such areas as immigration, drugs and terrorism. Second, policy involvement can take the form of tackling issues that the Council of Ministers has been unable to resolve or which it is deemed necessary that the European Council should resolve. Such an instance occurred in connection with the institutional crisis that developed in the EU in 1996 following the export ban placed on British beef because of the high incidence of Bovine Spongiform Encephalopathy (BSE) in British cattle: the Commission drew up a plan for resolving the crisis, and it was referred to the June Florence summit for approval. Third, and this has been of increasing importance in recent years as the number of policy issues that are 'referred up' from the Council of Ministers for final resolution has declined (largely as a consequence of qualified majority voting resulting in fewer blockages at Council of Ministers level), the European Council has become less concerned with arbitrating and acting as a final court of appeal on internal policy issues and more concerned with encouraging and guiding. This is illustrated by the frequent messages it sends to other EU institutions via Presidency Conclusions: almost invariably these conclusions are studded with phrases such as the European Council 'invites a report on', 'calls for action to be taken in regard to', 'confirms its full support for', 'welcomes the progress made by', 'endorses the steps taken in connection with' and so on.

The European Council thus concerns itself with various matters, the relative importance of which can vary from summit to summit. Six functions, which can be analytically separated but which in practice greatly overlap, are associated with these matters. First, the European Council is a forum, at the highest political level, for building mutual understanding and confidence between the governments of the EU member states. Second, it identifies medium- and long-term EU goals. Third, it is a policy initiator and dispenser of policy guidelines. Fourth, it makes an important contribution to the coordination of EU policy goals and activities. Fifth, it is a decision-maker – both on matters that have come to be accepted are its ultimate responsibility (most notably constitutional and major institutional issues), and on matters that, because of their importance or their political complexity and sensitivity, are not resolved by the Council of Ministers. Sixth, it exercises responsibilities in the sphere of external relations.

One function, it must be emphasised, that the European Council does not exercise is that of legislator. It does have the potential to make EU law – by transforming itself into a special Council of Ministers – but it has never done so. Its decisions are thus political decisions. When it is intended that its decisions should be given legal effect, the customary EU legislative procedures have to be applied. (There is, it should be said, no guarantee that an agreement in the European Council will automatically produce ease of passage through these procedures. One reason for this is that the guidelines laid down by the European Council are sometimes insufficiently precise to clear all political obstacles. Another reason is that governments occasionally decide after a summit that their delegations have given too much away and that ground must be recovered by taking a tough line in the Council of Ministers.)

The European Council and the EU system

Institutionalised summitry in the form of the European Council has inevitably strengthened the position of national governments in the EU system. It has also added an extra intergovernmental element to the nature of the EU by virtue of the fact that the leaders usually act on the basis of unanimous agreement – either because they prefer to or, when subsequent legislation is required to give their decisions effect, because they may in effect be required to.

However, although the European Council has unquestionably become an important EU institution, its role, or more accurately roles, are still shifting. Certainly it has, since the mid to late 1980s, come to approximate more to the original idea that it would provide overall strategic direction and not become too involved in policy detail, but this position is by no means fixed, or indeed applied with complete consistency. What happens at individual summits is not part of any regularised or consistent pattern. Thus some summits are relatively low-key affairs and do little more than pronounce on some aspects of current international developments, indicate one or two policy initiatives in fringe policy areas, and cobble together a concluding statement exuding general goodwill. Other summits, in contrast, are surrounded by an atmosphere of crisis and prophecies of catastrophe should they fail to produce firm decisions on key and pressing issues. Occasionally they do fail, but the catastrophes never quite happen, and the next summit, or next but one, is usually able to find an agreement via the customary EU method of compromise.

The creation and development of the European Council has inevitably had implications for the role and functioning of the other principal EU institutions.

- The Commission has experienced further undermining of its special position regarding policy initiation. ('Further' because, as was shown in Chapters 6 and 7, the Council of Ministers has increasingly exercised policy-initiating and mediating responsibilities.) However, the Commission has to some extent been compensated for this by being permitted to enter into political discussions with national leaders at the summits, and also by being able – and sometimes required – to submit reports and documents to the summits (see Chapter 6 for examples of influential Commission submissions to summits).

- The Council of Ministers has lost power to the European Council by virtue of the increasing tendency of most major issues to go through the summits in some form. However, the extent of this loss should not be exaggerated. One reason why it should not be so is that there is no rigid hierarchical relationship between the two bodies in the sense that the Council of Ministers always feels obliged to refer all significant matters 'upwards' for final decisions. It is true that most broad-based or very significant initiatives are referred to the European Council, but often that is for little more than political approval or for noting. Certainly it would be quite erroneous to suppose that the European Council takes all 'first-order' decisions and the Council of Ministers is confined to 'second-order' decisions. A second reason why the extent of the loss should not be overstated is that there is no consistent line of division between the two regarding who does what, other than the Council of Ministers being responsible for making legislation. A third reason is that most issues considered by the European Council have already been prepared, channelled and filtered by the appropriate formation of the Council of Ministers. And a fourth reason is that since the European Council normally only meets for four to six days a year, it cannot normally hope to do anything more than sketch outlines in a restricted number of areas.

- The EP has been largely by-passed by the European Council and so could be regarded as having experienced some net loss of power. It is true that the President of the European Council gives a verbal report on each summit meeting to the next EP plenary session, and it is also the case that the EP President addresses the opening sessions of summits in order to inform the national leaders of the EP's thinking on key issues. However, there is no evidence that either of these procedures produce much in the way of influence. Far more important is the almost complete lack of input by the EP into European Council agendas or deliberations, and the tendency of the Council of Ministers to take the view that proposals that stem from European Council decisions do not permit it much manoeuvrability when dealing with the EP.

- Since the European Council operates largely outside the framework of the TEC, and since its decisions are political rather than legal in character, its existence has had few implications for the Court of Justice. Or rather it has had few direct implications. It can, however, be argued that any increase in a non-treaty approach to integration necessarily constitutes a corresponding decrease in the influence of the Court of Justice, given its attachment to, indeed its restriction to, questions that have a legal base.

Chapter 9

The European Parliament

Powers and influence
Elections
Political parties and the European Parliament
Composition
Organisation and operation
Concluding remarks

Powers and influence

Since it was first constituted as the Assembly of the European Coal and Steel Community, the European Parliament – the title it adopted for itself in 1962 – has generally been regarded as a somewhat ineffectual institution. This reputation is no longer justified, for whilst it is true that the EP's formal powers are not as strong as those of national legislatures, developments over the years have come to give it a considerable influence in the EU system. As with national parliaments this influence is exercised in three main ways: through the legislative process, through the budgetary process, and through control and supervision of the executive.

Parliament and EU legislation

The EP has a number of opportunities to influence EU legislation.

First, it sometimes participates in policy discussions with the Commission at the pre-proposal legislative stage. The Commission may, for example, float a policy idea before an EP committee, or committee members themselves may suggest policy initiatives to the Commission.

Second, the EP can formally adopt its own ideas for suggested legislation. There are two main ways in which it can do this. First, it can adopt own initiative reports – reports that the Parliament itself initiates. There is however a major weakness with these reports, which is that whilst the Commission may feel pressurised by them it is not obliged to act upon them. Partly because of this weakness, the number of such reports has declined sharply in recent years: from, for example, 120 in 1993 to 36 in 1997. Second, the Maastricht Treaty created a new TEC article – now Article 193, formerly Article 138b – which states that 'The European Parliament may, acting by a majority of its members, request the

Commission to submit any appropriate proposal on matters which it considers that a Community act is required for the purpose of implementing this Treaty.' Clearly Article 193 considerably strengthens the EP's initiating powers, for political realities make it difficult for the Commission not to act if there is the necessary majority in Parliament. Only a handful of Article 193/138b requests have, however, been passed to date, in no small part because poor attendance at EP plenaries often makes absolute majorities difficult to obtain. An example of a Commission legislative proposal stemming from this article is its 1998 proposal for a directive on settling the insurance claims of victims of accidents occurring outside the victim's country of origin, the first EP reading of which was held – under the co-decision procedure – in July 1998.

Third, the annual budgetary cycle provides opportunities to exercise legislative influence. In large measure this dates back to the *Joint Declaration of 30 June 1982 by the European Parliament, the Council and the Commission on various measures to improve the budgetary procedure.* Amongst the 'various measures', it was agreed that if the EP put appropriations into the budget for items for which there was no legal base – in other words if the EP opened new budget lines – the Commission and the Council would seek to provide the necessary base. It was further agreed that expenditure limits in respect of legislation should not be set in the legislative process, but in the budgetary process – where the EP has more power. For the most part this understanding between the institutions has worked well and has enabled the EP to promote favoured policies, for example in 1998 it promoted a policy on employment generation in the area of small and medium-sized enterprises. It is an understanding, however, that requires the three institutions to work closely together, as was demonstrated in 1998 when the Court of Justice ruled in favour of four member states that claimed that a number of EU programmes approved under the budgetary procedure were illegal because they did not have an authorised legal base.

Fourth, the EP can influence, albeit perhaps rather indirectly, the Commission's annual legislative programme – which is essentially a planning tool of an indicative nature. The procedure is as follows: (1) The Commission adopts its annual work programme, which includes all proposals of a legislative nature, in October. Several factors determine the contents of the programme, most notably: commitments that are pending; initiatives that are deemed to be necessary to give effect to existing policy developments; preferences that have been indicated by the Council and the EP, perhaps in inter-institutional meetings; and the priorities of the incoming Council Presidencies – which are likely to be known for the first half of the year, but not always for the second. (2) The programme is considered by appropriate EP committees, with a dialogue often taking place between MEPs and Commission representatives. (3) A resolution on the programme is voted on in plenary session, usually in December.

Fifth, and most important of all, the EP's views must be sought – though its approval is only required in certain circumstances – in connection with most of the EU's important/significant/sensitive legislation. If the Council of Ministers acts prematurely and does not wait for Parliament to make its views known, the 'law' will be ruled invalid by the Court of Justice. Any uncertainty on this point was removed by the isoglucose case ruling in 1980, when the Court annulled a Council regulation on the ground that it had been issued before Parliament's opinion was known. The isoglucose case ruling does not give the EP an indefinite veto over Council legislation, for it is obliged by treaty to issue opinions and in some of its judgements the Court has referred to the duty of loyal cooperation among EC/EU institutions, but it does give it a very useful delaying power.

Until July 1987 and the entry into force of the Single European Act (SEA), all legislation referred to the EP was subject to what is known as the consultation procedure. However, the SEA created two new procedures – the cooperation procedure and the assent procedure – and the Maastricht Treaty introduced a further one – the co-decision procedure. There are thus now four possible procedures to which legislation may be subject (plus some variations within these procedures). The nature of these procedures and the policy areas to which they apply are described in some detail in Chapter 13, so the discussion here will be restricted to how they affect the EP.

- *The consultation procedure.* Under this procedure the EP is asked for an opinion on Commission proposals for Council legislation on only one occasion. Once that opinion is given the Council may take a decision. What use the EP is able to make of this single referral depends, in part at least, on its own subject competence and its tactical skills. The standard way of proceeding is to take advantage of Article 250 (ex 189a) of the TEC, which states: 'As long as the Council has not acted, the Commission may alter its proposals during the procedures leading to the adoption of a Community act.' If the Commission can be persuaded to alter a proposal so as to incorporate the EP's views, the prospect of those views becoming part of the text that is finally approved by the Council is greatly enhanced. With this in mind, the EP attempts to convince or to pressurise the Commission. Normally pressurising takes the form of voting on amendments to proposals, but delaying voting on the resolution that formally constitutes the opinion until after the Commission has stated – as it is obliged to do – whether or not it accepts the amendments. If the Commission does accept the amendments the EP votes for the legislative resolution and the amendments are incorporated into the Commission's proposal. If the Commission does not accept the amendments, or at least not all of them, the EP may judge the Commission's position to be unsatisfactory, and as a result may seek to delay the progress of the proposal by referring it back to the appropriate Parliamentary committee for further consideration.

- *The cooperation procedure.* Whereas under the consultation, or single reading, procedure the Council can take a final decision after the EP has issued its opinion, under the cooperation procedure there is a second reading process. On first reading the Council is confined to adopting a 'common position', which must then be referred back to the EP. When doing so, the Council is obliged to provide the EP with an explanation of its common position – including reasons for any EP amendments that have been rejected – and if the EP is dissatisfied it can exert further pressure at its second reading by amending or rejecting the common position by absolute majority vote. Such votes do not amount to vetoes, but because they carry considerable political weight, and because they can only be overcome in the Council by unanimous vote, they put considerable pressure on the Commission and the Council to take the EP's views seriously and to engage in inter-institutional bargaining.

- *The co-decision procedure.* This procedure is similar to the cooperation procedure up to the point when the EP issues its second reading, except that – under a change to the procedure made by the Amsterdam Treaty – if the Council and the EP reach agreement on the proposal at first reading, the proposal can be adopted at that stage. Assuming the Council and the EP are still at odds after the second reading, the proposal falls if the Parliament has rejected it by an absolute majority of its members and it is referred to a conciliation committee if the EP has amended it by an absolute majority. The conciliation committee is composed of an equal number of representatives from the Council and the Parliament. If agreement is reached in the conciliation committee, the text must be approved by the EP by a majority of the votes cast and by the Council acting by qualified majority. If no agreement is reached the proposal falls. (Under the Maastricht Treaty it was possible for the Council to attempt to press ahead with the proposal in the event of a conciliation committee failure, but the Amsterdam Treaty removed this possibility.) The key feature of the co-decision procedure is thus that it provides the EP with the potential to veto legislative proposals. The significance of the Parliament's powers under the procedure is symbolised by the fact that legislation that is subject to the procedure is made in the name of the EP and the Council, whereas legislation that is made under the consultation and cooperation procedures is made in the name of the Council only.

- *The assent procedure.* Under this procedure the EP must consider proposals at a single reading and with no provision for amendments. In some circumstances the assent requires an absolute majority of Parliament's members. Again, the EP thus has veto powers under this procedure.

Which procedure applies to a particular legislative proposal depends on which treaty article(s) the proposal is based. It is in the EP's interest that as much as possible is based on the co-decision procedure, where its powers are strongest, and as little as possible is based on the consultation procedure, where its powers are weakest. The Amsterdam Treaty benefited the EP in this regard, with some policy areas 'upgraded' from consultation to co-decision, and with the cooperation procedure virtually eliminated and the policy areas which had fallen within its remit moved to the co-decision procedure.

Details of the applicability of the four procedures are set out in Chapter 13, but in broad terms the situation post-Amsterdam is that most EU legislation – apart from agricultural, justice and home affairs, trade, fiscal harmonisation and EMU issues – is subject to the co-decision procedure. The consultation procedure is largely confined to agriculture and those justice and home affairs issues that are located in the TEC, the cooperation procedure is restricted to four areas of EMU, and the assent procedure is not – and never has been – used for 'normal' legislation but is reserved for special measures such as international agreements of certain kinds, EU enlargements, and the framework of the Structural Funds.

Table 9.1 shows the number of times the four procedures were used in 1998 for legislative proposals that were considered by the EP. As the Amsterdam Treaty takes effect, these proportions will, of course, change.

It is very difficult to estimate the precise effect of EP deliberations on the final form of legislative acts. One reason for this is that a great deal of EP persuading and lobbying is impossible to monitor because it is carried out via informal contacts with Commission and Council representatives. Another reason is that the Commission and the Council often go halfway in agreeing to the sense of EP amendments, but object to the way in which they are phrased or to specific parts of them. But though it is impossible to be precise, two things are quite clear. First, the EP is centrally involved in a process of legislative bargaining with the Commission and the Council, both on an informal basis and in formal inter-institutional meetings. Second, figures show that a very significant percentage of EP amendments are accepted by the Commission and the Council, with the former being generally more sympathetic than the latter. For example, under co-decision: of the amendments requested by the EP at first reading, on

Table 9.1   Parliamentary proceedings from January to December 1998
Resolutions and decisions adopted

Consultations (single reading)	Cooperation procedure		Co-decision procedure			Assent	Other opinions[1]	Budget questions	Own-initiative reports and resolutions			Miscellaneous decisions, declarations and resolutions[4]
	First reading	Second reading	First reading	Second reading	Third reading				Reports	Resolutions[2]	Urgent subjects[3]	
215[5]	38[6]	24[7]	41[8]	43[9]	11	4	135	16	55	51	107	10

Notes:

1. Mainly opinions on Commission reports or communications.
2. Resolutions in response to statements by other institutions or following oral questions.
3. Resolutions on topical and urgent subjects of major importance.
4. Decisions concerning waiver of immunity, amendments to the Rules of Procedure and interinstitutional agreements.
5. Including 138 cases in which Parliament proposed amendments to the Commission proposal.
6. Including 37 cases in which Parliament proposed amendments to the Commission proposal.
7. Including 18 cases in which Parliament amended the Council's common position.
8. Including 32 cases in which Parliament proposed amendments to the Commission proposal.
9. Including 22 cases in which Parliament amended the Council's common position.

Questions asked:

Of the Commission	4650
of which:	
written	3737
oral with debate	125
during question time	788
Of the Council	923
of which:	
written	377
oral with debate	79
during question time	467

Source: Adapted from Commission (1999), pp. 411–13.

average over 50 per cent are accepted by the Commission and over 40 per cent by the Council; at second reading – where many EP amendments are in effect rejected first-reading amendments – over 40 per cent are accepted by the Commission and over 30 per cent by the Council; and in conciliation committees a joint text is virtually always agreed, usually after accommodation by both sides. To present the situation in another way, of the 130 co-decision procedures completed between the entry into force of the Maastricht Treaty in November 1993 and July 1998: agreement between the Council and the EP was reached in 127 cases – 78 without convening the conciliation committee (56 without amendments to the common position, 22 with amendments accepted by the Council), and 49 following agreement on a joint text by the conciliation committee; in only three cases did the two institutions fail to agree on a joint text – in 1994 on a directive concerning the applicability of open network provision (the Council subsequently confirmed its common position but this was rejected by the EP), in 1995 when the EP rejected an agreement reached in the conciliation committee on a biotechnology directive, and in 1998 when the conciliation committee failed to reach agreement on a directive on investment levies (European Parliament, 1998a, p. 21).

Having established that the EP does have a genuine legislative influence – an influence that many national parliaments cannot match – the weaknesses to which it is subject will now be outlined.

The first and most obvious weakness is that the EP does not have full legislative powers. Unlike national parliaments, it does not have the final say over what is and what is not to become law. On the one hand it does not have the capacity to exercise a fully 'positive' legislative role by initiating, developing and passing into law its own proposals. On the other hand its 'negative' legislative role is also considerably circumscribed, for whilst the co-decision and assent procedures do give it a veto over most legislative proposals, under both the consultation and cooperation procedures the Council has the power to overturn EP amendments that have or have not been accepted by the Commission, and to ignore the EP's rejection of legislative proposals. The Council can also choose not to act at all on legislative proposals it does not like – at any one time there are usually around 200–300 proposals upon which the Parliament has given an opinion that still await a Council decision. (Proposals subject to the cooperation and co-decision procedures are not exempt from such Council inaction, since the restricted timetable that is attached to the procedures only comes into play once the Council has adopted its common position.)

The second weakness is that although the EP usually attempts to deliver opinions as soon as possible to ensure they are available to the Council at an early stage of its deliberations, it is by no means unusual for the Council, before the opinion of the EP has been delivered, to take decisions or to adopt common positions 'in principle' or 'pending the opinion of the European Parliament'. This is especially common when the initial referral to the EP is delayed, when there is some urgency about the matter, or when a Council Presidency is anxious to push the proposal through. Whatever the reason, in such circumstances the EP's opinion, especially under the consultation procedure, is likely to have only a very limited effect.

The third weakness is that the EP is not consulted on all Council legislation. The greatest gaps in this regard are its lack of any right to be consulted on most of the external agreements the Council concludes with third countries on behalf of the EU. Most importantly, trade agreements concluded under Article 133 of the TEC (ex Article 113) do not require EP approval. In practice the Council, and more particularly the Commission (which conducts the actual trade negotiations), usually do discuss forth-coming and ongoing trade matters with the EP on an informal basis, but they are not obliged to do so and there is not much evidence of Parliament bringing influence to bear on the EU's negotiating stance. In only two sets of circumstances where EU law is being made with regard to external agreements is EP approval necessary, in both cases by the assent of an absolute majority of MEPs: under Title VII Article 49 of the TEC (ex Article O) for new accessions to the EU, and under Article 300 of the TEC (ex Article 228) for specific types of agreement, including association agreements, cooperation agreements, and agreements with important budgetary implications. The first of these circumstances is obviously only for very occasional use. The second, however, has a more recurring application and has been used to some effect, notably in putting pressure on countries to improve their human rights records if they wish to receive the financial assistance that is usually an important component of association and cooperation agreements. (It should perhaps be added here that the EP also has the right to be informed and consulted about various other forms of EU external relations – notably under the CFSP pillar of the EU – but these do not involve legislation, and the EP's powers are purely advisory.)

The fourth and final weakness is that the EP does not have to be consulted on – although in practice it is notified of – Commission legislation. This is despite the fact that, numerically, Commission legisla-tion makes up most of EU legislation. There are different views on the significance of this. Pointing to the political and expenditure implications of some Commission legislation, MEPs have long argued that this is another example of executive power and legislative and democratic weakness. The Council and Commission, however, have emphasised that Commission legislation is usually highly technical and of a kind that needs quick decisions; as such, it is similar to the decrees, ordinances and other minor legislative acts that national administrations issue and which are commonly accepted as an inevitable aspect of decision-making in the modern world.

Parliament and the EU budget

Thanks mainly to the 1970 *Treaty Amending Certain Budgetary Provisions of the Treaties* and the 1975 *Treaty Amending Certain Financial Provisions of the Treaties* the EP enjoys considerable treaty powers in relation to the EU budget. These powers include:

(1) The right to propose 'modifications' to compulsory expenditure (this principally means agriculture , which comprises over two-fifths of the total budget). Modifications that entail increases in total expenditure require qualified majority support in the Council to be accepted. Where increases are not involved, owing perhaps to a proposed increase being offset by a proposed decrease, a qualified majority vote is required for rejection – a negative majority as it is called.

(2) The right to propose 'amendments' to non-compulsory expenditure (which means most things apart from agriculture) subject to the ceilings set by the financial perspective (see below). Acting by a qualified majority the Council may modify these amendments, but Parliament can reinsert and insist on them at its second reading of the budget.

(3) Under Article 272(8) of the TEC (ex Article 203(8)), Parliament, 'acting by a majority of its members and two-thirds of the votes cast, may, if there are important reasons, reject the draft budget and ask for a new draft to be submitted to it'. In other words the EP may reject the whole budget if it does not like the Council's final draft.

Following the introduction of direct elections for MEPs in 1979, in the 1980s extensive use was made of the powers just listed. Virtually every aspect of the rules, including the power of rejection, were tested to see how far they could be taken. Major confrontations with the Council, far from being avoided, seemed at times almost to be sought as the EP attempted to assert itself. For most of the 1980s, however, this assertion was limited in its effect, because although the EP formally enjoyed joint decision-making powers with the Council on the budget, the powers of the two bodies were not equally balanced. Parliament was still very much restricted in what it could do: restricted by the Treaty, which gave it very little room for manoeuvre in the major budgetary sector – compulsory expenditure; restricted by the Council's attitude, which tended to be one of wishing to limit Parliament's influence as much as possible; and restricted by its own inability – because of conflicting loyalties and pressures – to be wholly consistent and resolved in its approach.

For the most part these restrictions still apply. However, developments occurred in 1988 that increased the EP's influence. Following decisions taken by the European Council in February 1988 on budgetary matters, the EP, together with the Commission and the Council of Ministers, put its name, in June 1988, to *The Interinstitutional Agreement on Budgetary Discipline and Improvement of the Budgetary Procedure*. This committed all three institutions to a financial perspective for the years 1988 to 1992. Key features of the perspective were provisions for a significant increase in non-compulsory expenditure and a significant decrease in compulsory expenditure (thus realising aims the EP had been pressing for years), and the setting of clear ceilings for both types of expenditure. The main benefits of the Interinstitutional Agreement, in power terms, for the EP were twofold. First, its influence over compulsory expenditure, which in the past had been very limited, was potentially increased because Parliament's approval was now required for any upward movement of the ceiling. Second, the very act of the Council agreeing to sign a financial perspective with the EP gave to the latter an extra element of leverage in budgetary discussions.

When the 1988–92 financial perspective was revised in 1992–3, the EP's influence was not, it must be said, as great as MEPs had hoped or anticipated. Whilst it was accepted by the Commission and the Council that a precedent had been set in 1988 and that the next financial perspective would require the EP's endorsement, the key institutions in determining the size and shape of what became a seven-year financial perspective covering the years 1992–9 were the Commission, the Council of Ministers and the European Council. As it turned out there was much in the new financial perspective of which the EP approved – most notably further cuts in agricultural expenditure and further increases in non-agricultural expenditure – but these were largely the outcome of battles fought in the Council of Ministers and at the decision-making European Council meeting at Edinburgh rather than EP influence. Dissatisfied with the negotiating role it had been allowed, the EP delayed ratifying the agreement until November 1993 – though this did enable it to wring concessions from the Council with regard to its future influence over compulsory expenditure.

As with the 1988–92 and 1992–3 financial perspectives, the key actors in shaping the 2000–6 perspective were the Commission – which set the contours of the debate and the negotiations in its *Agenda 2000* document (Commission, 1997a) – and the member states. The EP exerted as much influence as it could – by producing reports and recommendations, questioning the Council and Commission, and holding debates and votes – but the key decisions were taken in the Council of Ministers and by the Heads of Government at the March 1999 Berlin summit. The EP subsequently managed to persuade the Council to make some modest adjustments to the perspective, the endorsement that it gave to the perspective in May 1999 was essentially an endorsement of a Commission-sponsored and member state-negotiated deal.

Control and supervision of the executive

Virtually all parliaments have difficulty exercising controlling and supervisory powers over executives. On the one hand, they are usually hampered by the executives themselves, which do not welcome the prospect of being investigated and therefore seek to protect themselves behind whatever constitutional, institutional or party political defences are available. On the other hand, parliamentarians themselves tend not to have the requisite information, the specialist knowledge, or the necessary resources that are required to properly monitor, and if necessary challenge, executive activity.

The EP shares these problems but also has two additional ones of its own. First, a key aspect of control and supervision of executives concerns policy implementation: is policy being implemented efficiently and for the purposes intended by the relevant law? The Commission is the most obvious body to be called to account on this question. But in many policy spheres the Commission's executive role is very limited and consists essentially of attempting to coordinate the work of outside agencies operating at different administrative levels. Such agencies, of which national governments are the most important, are often reluctant to open the books or cooperate with EP investigators. Certainly there is little question of government ministers allowing themselves to be grilled by the EP on the competency and honesty of their national bureaucracies.

The second problem specific to the EP is that on broad controlling and supervisory issues – such as whether the EU executive is acting responsibly in the execution of its duties, and whether it is fulfilling its treaty obligations – problems arise from the blurring of roles between the Commission, the Council of Ministers and the European Council. Insofar as the Council of Ministers and the European Council undertake what are in effect executive powers, the EP's supervisory powers are weakened. This is because Parliament's treaty powers are not so strong in relation to the Council of Ministers as they are to the Commission, nor does it have the same access to the former as it does to the latter. As for the European Council, the EP has virtually no treaty powers in relation to it, and only very limited access.

The EP's ability to control and supervise the Commission, the Council of Ministers and the European Council will now be considered separately.

The Commission

In relation to the Commission, the EP has eight main powers and channels at its disposal.

First, as was shown in Chapter 6, the nominee for Commission President must be approved by the EP. The narrow vote of approval given to Jacques Santer in 1994 showed that confirmation of the European Council's nominee cannot be assumed.

Second, again as was shown in Chapter 6, the 'President and the other members of the Commission thus nominated shall be subject as a body to a vote of approval by the European Parliament (Article 214, TEC, ex Article 158). This was a daunting exercise for most Commissioners in 1995, with each subject to a grilling by the appropriate EP committee before the confirmation vote – which cannot be on individual Commissioners but must be on the College as a whole – was taken. (For further consideration of the significance of the EP's powers of confirmation of the Commission President and College, and indeed for the wider powers of appointment that it is acquiring, see Westlake, 1998.)

Third, the EP can dismiss the College – but not individual Commissioners – by carrying a motion of censure by a two-thirds majority of the votes cast, including a majority of all MEPs. This power of dismissal is obviously too blunt a controlling instrument for most purposes and it has never been carried through. However, it came close to being so in January 1999 when a number of factors came together to produce a groundswell of dissatisfaction amongst MEPs with the Santer College. Amongst the factors were: a Court of Auditors report that revealed (yet again!) evidence of 'missing' EU funds and was strongly critical of aspects of Commission management practices; the suggestion that some Commissioners were favouring relatives and friends for appointments and the awarding of contracts; and a rather dismissive response by Jacques Santer to the criticisms that were being made about himself and some of his colleagues. It was only after Santer agreed to the creation of a special committee of independent experts to investigate the allegations of fraud, nepotism and mismanagement that the threat of censure receded, though even then the motion of censure was supported by 232 MEPs, with 293 voting against.

The special committee's report was issued two months later, in March, and was highly critical of aspects of the College's work and behaviour (Committee of Independent Experts, 1999). Particular criticisms were made of: Santer in his capacity as the official responsible for the Commission's Security Office, for taking 'no meaningful interest in its functioning' and allowing it to develop as 'a state within a state' (point 6.5.7); Edith Cresson, the Commissioner responsible for Research, for showing favouritism to someone known to her when issuing contracts (points 8.1.1–8.1.38); and Commissioners as a whole for being reluctant to assume responsibility for their actions - 'The studies carried out by the Committee have too often revealed a growing reluctance among the members of the hierarchy to acknowledge their responsibility. It is becoming difficult to find anyone who has even the slightest sense of responsibility' (point 9.4.25). Meeting almost immediately after the report was published, faced with a refusal by Santer and Cresson to resign, and aware that MEPs might well carry a motion of censure on it by the necessary two-thirds majority, the Santer College collectively resigned. The resignation was widely interpreted as a triumph for the EP and as a highly significant step forward in its long campaign to exercise greater control over Commission activities.

Fourth, under Article 220 of the TEC (ex Article 143), the EP 'shall discuss in open session the annual general report submitted to it by the Commission'. This debate used to be one of the highlights of the Parliamentary year, but there is little evidence of it ever having produced concrete results. It has come to be superseded in importance by debates on the Commission's annual work programme.

Fifth, under Article 275 of the TEC (ex Article 205a) 'The Commission shall submit annually to the Council and to the European Parliament the accounts of the preceding financial year relating to the implementation of the budget. The Commission shall also forward to them a financial statement of the assets and liabilities of the Community.' On the basis of an examination of the accounts and the financial statement, and having examined also the annual report of the Court of Auditors, Parliament 'acting on a recommendation from the Council which shall act by a qualified majority, shall give a discharge to the Commission in respect of the implementation of the budget' (Article 276, TEC, ex Article 206). Under its discharge powers the EP can require the Commission and other institutions to take appropriate steps to ensure action on the comments appearing in the decision on discharge. Occasionally the EP's discharge powers lead to confrontation with the Commission, as in 1998 when the Parliament initially postponed the discharge in order to give the Commission time to respond to charges of mismanagement and fraud in the running of some programmes, and then positively voted not to give discharge because of dissatisfaction with the way the Commission was dealing with these problems. This negative vote was an important factor in bringing about the January 1999 censure motion (see above). (The 1998 discharge dispute is considered further in Chapter 11.)

Sixth, the remits of EP standing committees are broad enough to allow them to attempt to exercise supervisory functions if they so choose. However, the Commission is not anxious to encourage investigations of itself, and the committees are not sufficiently well resourced to be able to probe very deeply. The Committee on Budgetary Control, which is specifically charged with monitoring policy implementation, is in a typically weak position: with only a handful of 'A' grade officers employed to assist it, it cannot hope to do anything other than cover a small fraction of the Commission's work.

Seventh, the Maastricht Treaty empowered the EP to establish temporary committees of inquiry 'to investigate . . . alleged contraventions or maladministration in the implementation of Community law, except where the alleged facts are being examined before a court and while the case is still subject to legal proceedings' (Article 193, TEC, ex Article 138c). The rules governing the rights of EP committees of inquiry were subsequently set out in an EP–Council–Commission inter-institutional agreement signed in 1995. Clearly the work of committees of inquiry are not just concerned with Commission activities, but they certainly can focus on them, as demonstrated in 1996 when many of the recommendations that were made by the committee established to investigate the BSE crisis were directed at the Commission. According to one well-placed Commission insider, 'Parliament's debates with the Commission on 16 July 1996 and 18 February 1997 [on the BSE crisis, and framed by the work of the committee] can be seen as classic examples of a legislature holding the executive to account' (Westlake, 1997, p. 23). Following publication of the committee's report there was a move to censure the Commission, but – aware that blame for the crisis was widely shared – the EP opted to employ what it called a 'conditional censure', which involved imposing a deadline on the Commission to carry out the EP's recommendations. (The application of this concept of conditional censure – which has no legal base – is typical of the way the EP has long been extremely innovative in interpreting and using its formal powers to the full.)

Finally, questions can be asked of the Commission. These take different forms: written questions, oral questions in question time, and oral questions with debate (see Table 9.1).

The Council

The EP is less able to control and supervise the Council of Ministers than it is the Commission. There are three main reasons for this.

The first reason arises from the role of the Council as the meeting place of the member states. To make it, or any of its members, directly responsible to the EP would be to introduce a measure of supranationalism into the EU that is unacceptable to most governments. The view has been taken that Council members should be principally responsible to their national parliaments. In other words the Council as a collective body should not be responsible to anyone, whilst individual members should not be responsible to another EU institution. (It might be added that this does not always stop ministers, if they find themselves being pressed too hard in their national legislatures, from hiding behind Council meetings and 'immovable' EU partners.)

Second, in respect of certain key policy sectors – most notably the CFSP, Police and Judicial Cooperation, and aspects of EMU – the EP's powers are relatively weak. This is partly because decisions in these spheres sometimes need to be made quickly and in secret and partly because some member states favour intergovernmentalism as the prevailing decision-making mode in these sensitive areas. The EP is thus left to make the best it can of its powers to be consulted, to be kept informed, to ask questions, and to make recommendations.

Third, the very nature of the Council – with its ever-changing composition, its specialist Councils, and its rotating Presidency – means that continuity of relations between it and the EP is difficult to establish.

The amount of access the EP gets to the Council depends in large part on the attitude of the country holding the Presidency. There are, however, certain set points of contact which, if they do not enable the EP to exercise control over the Council, at least provide it with opportunities to challenge the Council on its general conduct of affairs. First, the Presidency of the Council, usually represented by the Foreign Minister, appears before EP plenaries at the beginning and end of each six-month term of office. On the first occasion the Presidency's priorities are explained and on the second an assessment of the Presidency is given. On both occasions MEPs are given the opportunity to ask questions. Second, ministers from the Presidency usually attend the EP committees that deal with their spheres of responsibility at least twice during their country's Presidency. MEPs can use these occasions for informal discussions with the Council, or to have wide-ranging question and answer sessions on the Council's priorities and performance. Third, ministers from the Presidency also regularly attend EP plenary sessions and participate in important debates. Fourth, the EP can, through the Presidency, ask questions of the Council (see Table 9.1).

The European Council

If the EP is not able to call the Commission fully to account and is greatly restricted in its ability to exercise control over the Council of Ministers, it is almost wholly bereft of any supervisory power over the European Council. This is largely because of the nature of the European Council: it is an intergovernmental institution that is largely outside the framework of the TEC; it meets for only between four and six days a year; and most of its more important members, the Heads of Government, not only have no great wish to be accountable to MEPs but can also ensure that they do not become so, since it is at European Council meetings that final decisions on the contents of the treaties – which set out the main operating principles of the EU – are taken.

The TEU and the TEC make provision in a few instances – such as in regard to EMU under the TEC – for the European Council, or the Heads of Government meeting in the composition of the Council of Ministers, to inform or consult the EP, but these are anticipated as being for only occasional use. In only two sets of circumstances does the European Council come into regular contact with the EP, and one of these is a consequence of political practice rather than legal requirement. The non required contact is at the opening session of European Council meetings, when the EP President is permitted to address the summit to inform it of the views of MEPs on current issues. The second contact is after European Council meetings, when the President of the European Council delivers a report and answers questions on the outcome of the summit before an EP plenary session.

What this all adds up to is that the EP can exert very little influence indeed on the European Council, let alone control over what it does. The fact is that there are very limited linkages between the two institutions, and there is no reason to suppose that the participants at summits make a habit of looking over their shoulders in anticipation of how the EP will view the outcome of their deliberations and negotiations.

Elections

Until 1979 MEPs were nominated by the national parliaments from amongst their members. Various consequences followed from this: parties not represented in their national legislature could not be represented in the EP; virtually all MEPs were pro-integrationist, since sceptics and opponents in national parliaments were generally unwilling to allow their names to be considered for nomination; and MEPs had limited time to devote to their European responsibilities.

However, Article 138 of the EEC Treaty included the following provision: 'The Assembly shall draw up proposals for elections by direct universal suffrage in accordance with a uniform procedure in all Member States.' The Assembly approved such proposals as early as 1960, but found itself frustrated by another Article 138 requirement which stated: 'The Council shall, acting unanimously, lay down the appropriate provisions, which it shall recommend to Member States for adoption in accordance with their respective constitutional requirements.' That the first set of direct elections were not held until 1979 is witness to the feeling of some member governments – initially mainly the French, later the Danes and the British – that direct elections were rather unwelcome, both because they had supranational overtones and because they might be followed by pressure for institutional reform in the EP's favour. Even after the principle of direct elections was eventually won and it was agreed they would be held on a fixed five-year basis, no uniform electoral system could be agreed, nor has been agreed since. Consequently, the five sets of direct elections held to date – in 1979, 1984, 1989, 1994 and 1999 – have all been contested on the basis of different national electoral arrangements (Table 9.2). The 1999 elections did, however, bring a significant movement in the direction of standardisation in that the UK did not use its tradititonal single member constituency first past the post system but rather proportional representation on a regional basis, which meant that for the first time a form of proportional representation was used in all member states.

As well as the differences between their electoral systems, two other differences between the states' EP electoral arrangements merit note. The first is that voting does not take place on the same day. In 1999, for example, most countries voted on Sunday 13 June but a few voted on other days: the UK, for instance, traditionally holds all its elections on Thursdays, so the European election was held on Thursday 10 June. The second difference, and one that is important in terms of the democratic base of the EP, is that there is a considerable variation in the size of the electorate per MEP. The range is from one per 820 000 voters in Germany, through one per 450 000 in the Netherlands, Belgium and Greece, to one per 65 000 in Luxembourg. The reason for this imbalance is that EP seats are distributed not just on grounds of national equitability but also with an eye to ensuring that the representations of small states are not totally swamped in EP decision-making processes. In most states the ratio is between one per 350 000 and one per 650 000.

A subject that has been much discussed in the context of EP elections is voter turnout. Many have argued that a high turnout would serve to enhance the EP's legitimacy and democratic base, and as a consequence would also place the EP in a strong position to press for increased powers.

In the event, turnout has been relatively low. In 1979 only 62 per cent of those eligible to vote did so, in 1984 the figure was 61 per cent, in 1989 it was 58 per cent and in 1994 it was 56.5 per cent. Belgium and Luxembourg – where voting is obligatory – have had the highest national turnouts, with around 90 per cent voting, whilst the United Kingdom has displayed the lowest: 33 per cent in 1979, 33 per cent in 1984, and 36 per cent in 1989 and 1994.

Table 9.2 *National electoral arrangements for the 1999 elections to the European Parliament*

	Number of MEPs	Electoral system	Number of constituencies
Austria	21	PR with PV	1
Belgium	25	PR with PV	4
Denmark	16	PR with PV	1
Finland	16	PR with PV	4
Germany	99	PR without PV	16
Greece	25	PR without PV	1
Spain	64	PR without PV	1
France	87	PR without PV	1
Ireland	15	PR with STV	4
Italy	87	PR with PV	5
Luxembourg	6	PR with vote splitting	1
Netherlands	31	PR with PV	1
Portugal	25	PR without PV	1
Sweden	22	PR with PV	1
United Kingdom	87	PR without PV (except Northern Ireland, which has 3 seats based on STV)	12
Total	626		

Notes:
PR with PV: proportional representation with preferential vote.
PR without PV: proportional representation without preferential vote.
PR with STV: proportional representation with single transferable vote.
PR with vote splitting: proportional representation, with voters being able to choose candidates from different lists.

There are also some variations within these system: for example, in Germany and Finland voters can choose between a national list and a regional list, and in Sweden candidates are placed on a hierarchical list but voters have the option of one individual choice – which can result in the list order being changed.

Three main factors combine to explain the low turnouts. First, because EP elections do not offer any prospect of a change of government, switches in policy or the making or unmaking of political reputations, they stimulate little popular interest or political excitement. Second, the election campaigns have little overall coherence or coordination. They are essentially national contests, but of a secondary sort. 'European' issues have never made much of an impact. In 1989, for example, there was little sense of the 1984–9 Centre-Right EP majority defending its record, or of the Left seeking to gain control. Third, those actors who do much to focus attention on and generate interest in national electoral campaigns approach the EP elections in, at best, a half-hearted manner: few 'big names' have been candidates in recent elections; national political parties have been generally reluctant to commit resources to their Euro campaigns; party activists have tended to be uninterested; a conscious attempt has been made by some governments to play down the importance of the elections because they are frequently interpreted as being, in part at least, 'mid-term' national elections, or unofficial referendums on the government's performance in office; and media interest has been limited.

Political parties and the European Parliament

Party political activity takes place at three main levels in relation to the EP: the transnational, the political groups in the EP, and the national.

The transnational federations

Very loosely organised transnational federations, grouped around general principles, exist for coordinating, propaganda, and electioneering purposes. They are based on affiliation by national parties, from both within and outside the EU.

The three main federations were created in similar circumstances in the mid 1970s out of existing, but extremely weakly based, liaising and information-exchanging bodies, and as a specific response to the continuing development of the EC and the anticipated future use of direct elections to the EP. These three federations are: the European People's Party (EPP), which is composed of Christian Democratic parties and their allies; the European Liberal, Democrat and Reform Party (ELDR); and the Party of European Socialists (PES).

Some supporters of European integration have hoped that the federations might develop into organisations providing leadership, vision and coordination at the European level, and perhaps might even serve as agents of unification to their heterogeneous memberships. They have failed to do so. Their principal weakness is that, unlike national parties or the EP political groups, they are not involved in day-to-day political activity in an institutional setting. Hence they have no clear focus and cannot develop attachments and loyalties. From this, other weaknesses flow: low status; limited resources – they are heavily dependent on the EP political groups for administrative and financial support; and loose organisational structures based on periodic congresses and bureaux meetings.

The federations, therefore, have not been able to do very much, even though there certainly are tasks that EU-wide transnational parties could usefully perform, such as long-term policy planning, the harmonisation of national party differences, and educating the electorate about Europe. Such influence as they have exercised has been largely confined to very loose policy coordination (effected partly through periodic meetings of national leaders, often before European Council meetings), and to EP elections when manifestos have been produced and a few joint activities have been arranged. Even the manifestos, however, have reinforced the general picture of weakness for they have usually been somewhat vague in content (necessarily so given the need to reconcile differences), and have been utilised by only a few of the constituent member parties (because EP elections are contested, for the most part, along national lines).

Beyond the three main federations, other groupings of an even looser nature have surfaced from time to time, usually in order to coordinate election activities. They have included Green, Regional, Communist and Extreme Right alliances. All have been internally divided and have been hard pressed to put together even minimal common statements. (For more detailed information on Europe's transnational party federations see Hix and Lord, 1997, especially ch. 7.)

The political groups in the European Parliament

Partisan political activity in the EP is mainly channelled via the political groups. Under the Rules of Procedure the minimum number of MEPs required to form a political group is 29 if they come from one member state, 23 if they come from two member states, 18 if they come from three member states, and 14 if they come from four or more member states.

Groups have been formed and developed for a number of reasons. The principal basis and unifying element of most of the groups is ideological identification. Despite the many differences that exist between them, MEPs from similar political backgrounds and traditions are naturally drawn to one another. All the more so when cooperation serves to maximise their influence, as it does in the EP in all sorts of ways – from electing the President to voting on amendments.

Organisational benefits provide another inducement to political group formation. For example, funds for administrative and research purposes are distributed to groups on the basis of a fixed amount per group (the non-attached being regarded as a group for these purposes), plus an additional sum per member. No one, therefore, is unsupported, but clearly the larger the group the more easily it can afford good back-up services.

There are also advantages in the conduct of Parliamentary business that stem from group status, since the EP arranges much of what it does around the groups. Although non-attached members are not formally excluded from anything by this – indeed they are guaranteed many rights under the Rules of Procedure – in practice they can be disadvantaged: in the distribution of committee chairmanships for example, or in the preparation of the agendas for plenary sessions.

In recent years there have usually been between eight and ten political groups in the EP. The main reason for there being so many is that, with proportional representation being used for EP elections in all EU states except, until 1999, the UK, MEPs reflect the wide range of political opinion that exists across the EU with regard to ideological and national orientation. Since direct elections were introduced in 1979 there have never been fewer than sixty national political parties represented in the EP. At the beginning of the 1994–9 Parliament 101 political parties were represented (Hix and Lord, 1997, p. 1).

The main characteristics of the political groups in the EP, as of May 1999, will now be outlined. The sizes of the groups are shown in Table 9.3. (The information presented below and in Table 9.3 will be updated periodically on the Macmillan EU web page.)

- *Group of the Party of European Socialists (PES).* The Socialists are the largest single group in the EP and include at least one MEP from each member state. Reflecting the breadth of European Socialism and Social Democracy, the members of the group have sometimes found cooperation difficult. In part this has been because of ideological diversity within the group, with opinions ranging from 'far left' state interventionists to 'moderate' social democrats. In part it has been caused by national party groups being reluctant to concede national interests to wider European interests. And in part it has stemmed from differences within the group on the very bases and direction of European integration.
- *Group of the European People's Party (EPP).* The EPP used to be based on European Christian Democracy, and in particular the large Christian Democratic parties of Germany and Italy. Over the years, however, other Centre-Right parties, mostly from a conservative tradition, have been absorbed into the group. Like the PES, the group has members from all member states, and also like the PES it has had some difficulty maintaining internal ideological cohesion – not least on the nature of the integration process, with MEPs located in the Christian Democratic

Table 9.3 Political groups in the European Parliament[1]

	Belgium	Denmark	Germany	Greece	Spain	France	Ireland	Italy	Luxem-bourg	N'lands	Austria	Portugal	Finland	Sweden	UK	Total
PES[2]	6	4	40	10	21	16	1	19	2	7	6	10	4	7	61	214
EPP	7	3	47	9	29	13	4	36	2	9	7	9	4	5	17	201
ELDR	6	5			2	1	1	4	1	10	1		5	3	3	42
UFE				2		18	7	3		2		3				34
EUL/NGL				4	9	7		5				3	2			34
Greens	2		12				2	3	1	1	1		1	3	1	27
ERA	1				3	12		2						4	1	21
I-EN		4				9				2					2	16
IND	3					12		15			6				1	37
Total	25	16	99	25	64	87	15	87	6	31	21	25	16	22	87	626

Source: Session News: Strasbourg Briefing, 3–7 May 1999 (Brussels: European Parliament Directorate for Press and Audiovisual Services), p. 38.

Notes:

1. Situation as of May 1999.
2. The full names of the political groups are given in the text.
3. The informtion presented here will be updated periodically on the Macmillan EU web page, which can be reached at: http://www.macmillan-press.co.uk/politics/EU

family tending to be stronger supporters of integration than other members of the group.

- *Group of the European Liberal, Democratic and Reform Party (ELDR)*. A centrist group, but one that is diffficult to pinpoint in terms of its core ideas. Basically it consists of a combination of parties of the Centre and the Right, but there are also certain Leftist elements. It has members from twelve member states.

- *Union for Europe Group (UFE)*. This is a Centre-Right group that grew out of the *Group of the European Democratic Alliance (EDA)* in the pre-1994 Parliament. Its main component parties before and after 1994 have been French Gaullists and Irish Fianna Fail, which are not large enough to constitute a group of their own but, for different reasons, have been reluctant to link up with one of the more established Centre-Right groups. The UFE, and the EDA before it, has thus served as a useful marriage of convenience for its two main components, and also for a scattering of MEPs from other groups. For a time after the 1994 elections the Italian Forza party was also a member of this group, but in 1996 it left to join the EPP.

- *Confederal Group of the European United Left/Nordic Green Left (EUL/NGL)*. This group is made up mainly of 'hard-left' elements from Communist or former Communist parties, plus a small number of Nordic Leftist Greens.

- *The Green Group in the European Parliament*. Beyond a common concern with green issues, the Greens are not a very homogeneous group, with some of their MEPs coming from a clear Left background and others seeing themselves as neither Left nor Right.

- *Group of the European Radical Alliance (ERA)*. This small group is based on the Énergie Radicale list of candidates put together for the 1994 EP elections in France by the businessman Bernard Tapie, supplemented by a scattering of MEPs from other countries representing mainly regional parties. The group considers itself as 'progressive left' in orientation. It strongly supports the goal of a federal Europe.

- *Group of Independents for a Europe of Nations (I-EN)*. Dominated by French members who led the opposition in France to the ratification of the Maastricht Treaty, this group is committed to the defence of the nation state and is strongly opposed to further integration.

- Most of the MEPs who are not attached to political groups are from far Right parties, the largest number being French National Front members. There was an Extreme Right group in the 1984–9 and 1989–94 Parliaments, but internal differences have since prevented them from coming together. It is quite possible that another such group will be constituted in the future.

*   *   *

As suggested in the above outlines, group formation and composition is highly fluid. The extent of this is demonstrated, for example, by the fact that although there were eight political groups in the EP in the periods immediately before the 1989 and 1999 EP elections, only three groups survived those ten years – the PES, the EPP and the ELDR (compare Table 5.3 on p. 126 of the first edition of this book with Table 9.3 above). However, the nature of the membership of these three groups changed significantly over that period, partly because of election results, partly because of the 1995 enlargement, and partly – especially in the EPP's case – because of defections from smaller groups.

As the above outlines also suggest, all the political groups have significant internal divisions, usually of both an ideological and a national character. This is especially so of the PES and the EPP, which over the years have grown in size in relation to other groups as some smaller groups, recognising the advantages of large group membership, have joined them. Internal divisions do of course undermine coherence, which has a weakening effect. So, for example, it is difficult, whatever their ideological principles might suggest to them, for French MEPs to vote for a cut in agricultural prices or for Portuguese MEPs not to support increases in the Regional Fund.

Three other factors also make for looseness and a limited ability on the part of the groups to control and direct their members. The first of these factors arises from the political powers of the EP and the institutional setting in which it is placed. With no government to sustain or attack and no government-sponsored legislation to pass or reject, MEPs do not have the semi-automatic 'for' or 'against' reaction that is so typical of much national parliamentary behaviour. The second factor is structural. Unlike parties in national legislatures, the political groups are not part of a wider organisational framework from which emanate expectations of cooperative and united behaviour, and generally recognised notions of responsibility and accountability. Rather, most of them are weak, quasi-federal bodies functioning in a multicultural environment. This is evidenced in a number of ways: the constituent member parties of the larger groups hold their own separate meetings and have their own leaderships; in seeking to encourage group unity, group leaders can invoke no effective sanctions against, and can withhold few rewards from, MEPs who do not fall into line; and in looking to their political futures, it is not only their political group or its leadership that MEPs must cultivate but also their national parties at home. The third factor is that MEPs may have claims on their loyalties and votes that compete with the claims of the political groups. One source of such claims are the numerous interest groups with which many MEPs are closely associated. Other sources are the EP intergroups, which bring together, usually on a relatively informal basis, MEPs from different political groups who have similar views on particular issues. About 50 intergroups exist, of which 25 or so meet on a regular basis. The intergroups come in many different forms and vary considerably in the nature and range of their policy focus. Amongst their number are the Federalist Intergroup for European Union, the Friends of Israel Intergroup, the Central American Intergroup, the Media Intergroup, the Rural Areas Intergroup, the Animal Welfare Intergroup, and the Elderly People Intergroup.

However, despite the many weaknesses of the groups, it is important to emphasise that they are of considerable importance in determining how the EP works.

Some of their functions and tasks and the privileges they enjoy are specifically allocated to them under the Rules of Procedure or by parliamentary decisions. These include guaranteed representation on key EP bodies and committees, and speaking rights in plenary sessions.

Other functions have not been formally laid down but have developed out of political necessity, advantage, or convenience. This is most obviously illustrated by the way the groups are the prime determiners of tactics and voting patterns in the EP, the decisions on which are normally taken in the week prior to plenary sessions, which is set aside for political group meetings. At these meetings efforts are made to agree a common group position on matters of current importance. For example, should a deal be attempted with another political group on the election of the President?; what is the group's attitude towards a Commission proposal for a Council directive?; what tactics can the group employ to prevent an unwelcome own initiative report being approved by a committee? In dealing with such questions internal group differences may have to be tackled, and sometimes they may not be resolved. But of the many influences bearing down on MEPs, political group membership is normally the single most important factor correlating with how they vote.

Before leaving the political groups a few comments on the overall political balance of the EP are required.

From 1979–89 a nominal Centre-Right majority existed, from 1989–94 there was a nominal Left-Green majority, and in the 1994–99 Parliament there was no nominal majority either to the Right or to the Left. The nature of the political balance existing at any one time unquestionably affects the interests and priorities of the EP, with groups from the Left tending, for example, to be more sympathetic to social and environmental issues than groups from the Right. However, the significance of the nature of the overall balance is not as great as it normally is in national parliaments. There are three main reasons for this. First, important issues, sometimes of an organisational or domestic political nature rather than an ideological nature, can divide groups that otherwise appear to be obvious voting partners. The various liaising channels and mechanisms that exist in the EP via which groups attempt to reach agreements and strike deals cannot always bridge these divisions. On many issues it is by no means unusual for the views of political groups on the Centre-Left and Centre-Right, or at least of many MEPs within these groups, to be closer to each other than to the views of other Left and Right groups. The second reason is that many matters that come before the EP cut across traditional Left–Right divisions. Such is the case with much of the essentially technical legislation with which Parliament deals. Such too is the case with issues like action to combat racism in Europe, the provision of assistance to the countries of the developing world, and the further development of economic and political European integration. The third reason is that the EP frequently and consciously attempts to avoid being divided along Left-Right lines when it votes because it is in its institutional interests to do so. For example, under the co-decision procedure an absolute majority of MEPs must support EP amendments and rejections for votes to be effective. This can be difficult to achieve, especially since only about three-quarters of MEPs vote regularly (*European Voice*, 4–10 June 1998). In consequence, it is necessary for groups from both Left and Right, and especially from the PES and the EPP, to work together if the EP is to make effective use of its powers.

Given these circumstances it is not surprising that the most dominant voting pattern in the EP is not along Left–Right lines but is grouped around an alliance of Centre-Left and Centre-Right. The PES, the EPP, and the ELDR vote together on average about 75–80 per cent of the time (Hix and Lord, 1997, p. 137).

National parties

National political parties are involved in EP-related activities in three main ways. First, most candidates in the EP elections, and virtually all of those who are elected, are chosen by their national parties. This means that MEPs inevitably reflect national party concerns and are normally obliged, if they wish to be reselected, to continue to display an awareness of these concerns.

Second, EP election campaigns are essentially national election campaigns conducted by national parties. Use may be made of transnational manifestos, but voters are directed by the parties primarily to national issues and the results are mainly assessed in terms of their domestic implications. That the European dimension is limited is no more evident than in the lack of any consistent Left–Right movement in voting patterns across the member states in European elections.

Finally, in the EP itself national party groups exist within the political groups. This is an obvious potential source of political group disharmony and sometimes creates strains. Problems do not arise so much from the national groups having to act on specific domestic instructions. This does sometimes occur, but in general the organisational links between the national groups and national party leaderships are weak and the former have a reasonably free hand within general party guidelines. The problem is simply that each national party group inevitably tends to have its own priorities and loyalties.

Composition

In addition to party political attachments, three other aspects of the composition of the EP are particularly worthy of comment.

The dual mandate

After the 1979 elections some 30 per cent of MEPs were also members of their national legislature. This figure was inflated, however, because many MEPs had contested the election primarily for domestic political reasons and had no firm commitment to completing their terms of office. By the end of the Parliamentary term the number of dual mandates had been more than halved. What therefore seemed to be a big drop after the 1984 elections, to around 12 per cent of MEPs holding a dual mandate, in fact reflected a trend that was already well under way; a trend that has been assisted since 1984 by some parties actively trying to discourage dual mandates and by Belgium and Spain forbidding them altogether under national law.

Among the consequences of this decline in the dual mandate has been a weakening of links between the EP and national parliaments. Most parties have procedures of some kind for maintaining contact between the two levels but they tend to be weak, and frequently the EP group is seen as something of a poor relation. A more positive outcome of the decline of dual mandates has been that MEPs with just one mandate have more time and energy to devote to their EP duties. This is reflected in more days spent in plenaries and committees, more Parliamentary questions, and more reports.

Continuity

Change and turnover in personnel affects the way most organisations work. The EP is no exception to this: the more effective MEPs tend to be those who have developed policy interests and expertise in European affairs over time and have come to know their way around the EU system.

Lack of continuity in membership was a problem after the first EP elections in 1979, with nearly one-quarter of MEPs being replaced before the 1984 elections. However, as noted above, that was always likely as many of the prominent politicians who stood in 1979 had no intention of making a political career in the EP. Things have since settled down and now only a relatively small proportion of MEPs resign before the end of their term of office. The turnover of MEPs between parliaments is certainly higher than is common in national parliaments, but not alarmingly so: just over half of those who were elected in 1989 were returnees, whilst in 1994 the figure was just over 40 per cent.

Competence and experience

It is sometimes suggested that MEPs are not of the same calibre and do not carry the same political weight as their counterparts in national legislatures. Because the EP is not high-profile, the argument runs, it mostly attracts second-rate parliamentarians, or those who regard it merely as a stepping stone to a national career or advancement.

There is some truth in this view. Major national figures have tended either not to contest EP elections or not to complete their terms of office. (The provision in the 1976 'Direct Elections Act' making national governmental office incompatible with EP membership has not helped in this regard.) Additionally, a few MEPs have transferred from the EP to national legislatures.

But the situation should not be exaggerated. The competition to become an MEP is normally fierce and requires all the customary political skills. Most MEPs have considerable public experience, either in national or regional politics, or in an executive capacity with a major sectional interest.

Perhaps the key point to be emphasised is that it should not be assumed that those who choose to stand for and work in the EP are necessarily settling for second best. Many are firmly committed to their responsibilities and have developed competencies and experience that may be different from, but are not necessarily inferior to, those of national parliamentarians.

Organisation and operation

The multi-site problem

The work of the EP is carried out on three sites in three different countries. Full plenary sessions are held in Strasbourg whilst mini-plenary sessions are held in Brussels. Committees usually meet in Brussels. Around 3000 of the 4000 staff who work in the EP Secretariat (600 of whom are in temporary posts) are based in Luxembourg, with the rest mainly in Brussels. (These figures do not include the 700 who work in the Secretariats of the political groups.)

This situation is clearly unsatisfactory and is a source of grievance and annoyance for most MEPs. Reasonably conscientious MEPs may well have to change their working location half a dozen times in an average month. An average work diary is likely to look something like this: one week attending the monthly plenary in Strasbourg; from two to five days in committee(s), probably in Brussels but sometimes elsewhere; two to four days in political group meetings and group working parties, probably in Brussels; whatever time remains is spent in the constituency (if the MEP has one), visiting somewhere as part of an EP delegation, in Luxembourg consulting with officials on a report, or at home.

If the EP had just one base, and especially if that was Brussels, it is likely that the EP's efficiency, influence and visibility would all be increased. However, the Council has the power of decision on the matter, and hard lobbying from the Luxembourg and French governments has ensured that arguments for 'sense to prevail' and a single site to be agreed have not been acted upon.

Arranging parliamentary business

Compared with most national parliaments the EP enjoys considerable independence in the arrangement of its affairs. This is not to say it can do whatever it likes. The treaties oblige it to do some things – such as deliver opinions on Commission proposals for Council and EP and Council legislation – and prevent it from doing others – such as censuring the Council. But on many agenda, timetable and other organisational matters it remains, to a considerable degree, its own master.

A major reason for this independence is, once again, the special institutional setting in which the EP operates. The EU executive does not have to be as concerned to control what the EP does as do national governments with their legislatures. This is because although EP pronouncements and activities can be unwelcome to the Council and the Commission, they do not normally have politically damaging or unmanageable consequences.

A second, and closely related, reason is the lack of any clear and consistent identification, of either a positive or a negative kind, between the EP and the EU executive. In national parliaments business is shaped to a considerable degree by political attachments. But the Commission is made up of officials who are nominally non-partisan, whilst the Council is multi-party, multi-ideological, and multi-national in its membership. As for the 'persuasive devices' that national executives have at their disposal to encourage loyalty, neither the Commission nor the Council has patronage to dispense.

A third reason is that the EP is entitled to adopt its own Rules of Procedure. This it has done, amending and streamlining the Rules in order to make itself more efficient and more influential.

Most decisions about the operation and functioning of the EP are not taken in plenary session but are delegated to the President, the Bureau, or the Conference of Presidents.

The President of the EP is elected to office for a two and a half year term. According to Rule 19 of the Rules of Procedure, the President 'shall direct all the activities of Parliament and of its bodies under the conditions laid down in these Rules' (European Parliament, 1998b). In practice this means that the President has many functions, such as presiding over debates in the chamber, referring matters to committees as appropriate, and representing the EP in dealings with other EU institutions and outside bodies. An effective President must be an administrator and a politician, skilled in organising and also in liaising and bargaining.

The Bureau consists of the President and the EP's fourteen Vice-Presidents. Like the President, the Vice-Presidents are elected for a two and a half year term of office, though by tradition the posts are distributed amongst the member states. Various financial and administrative organisational matters are dealt with by the Bureau, such as drawing up the EP's draft estimates and deciding on the composition and structure of the Secretariat. To assist it in the performance of its duties, and in particular to take responsibility for financial and administrative matters concerning members, five Quaestors, who are also elected, sit in the Bureau in an advisory capacity.

Organisational matters, other than matters of routine which are dealt with by the Bureau, are the responsibility of the Conference of Presidents. This is composed of the EP President and the chairmen of the political groups. MEPs who are not attached to any political group can delegate two of their number to attend meetings. Matters that fall within the remit of the Conference of Presidents include the following: deciding on the seating arrangements in the Chamber – a potentially sensitive and highly symbolic issue when groups do not wish to be seated too far to the left or too far to the right of the hemicycle; arranging the EP's work programme, including assigning the drafting of reports to committees and drawing up the draft agendas for plenary sessions; and authorising the drawing up of own initiative reports. By and large the Conference responds to matters coming before it from EP committees and groups rather than imposing itself on Parliament. Decisions are made by consensus whenever possible, but if none exists matters are put to the vote, with group chairmen (though not the non-attached delegates who do not have voting rights) having as many votes as there are members of the group.

Two other Conferences also have an organisational role: the Conference of Committee Chairmen and the Conference of Delegation Chairmen. (The latter brings together the chairmen of the EP delegations to the interparliamentary delegations and joint parliamentary committees that have been established with the parliaments of over thirty non-EU states.) These Conferences are essentially advisory in character, though they can also have certain tasks assigned to them by the Conference of Presidents.

The committees of the EP

Much of the EP's work is carried out by committees. These are of two main types. The first and by far the most important are standing or permanent committees, of which there are twenty (Table 9.4). The second are *ad hoc* committees, which are established to investigate specific problems and topics.

MEPs are assigned to the standing committees at the beginning and half way through each five-year term. Assignment to the *ad hoc* committees is as required. According to the Rules of Procedure, all committee members are elected to their positions on the basis of proposals made by the Conference of Presidents to Parliament which are 'designed to ensure fair representation of Member States and of political views'. What this means in practice is that the political groups negotiate the share-out of committee memberships on a basis proportionate to their size. Most MEPs become a member of one standing committee – though a few are on as many as three – and a substitute member of another.

The standing committees, which in most cases have 50–60 members, perform various duties, such as exploring ideas with the Commission, fostering own initiative reports, and discussing developments with the President-in-Office of the Council. Their most important task, however, is

Table 9.4   *Standing committees of the European Parliament*

Title
1   Foreign Affairs, Security and Defence Policy
2   Agriculture and Rural Development
3   Budgets
4   Economic and Monetary Affairs and Industrial Policy
5   Research, Technological Development and Energy
6   External Economic Relations
7   Legal Affairs and Citizen's Rights
8   Employment and Social Affairs
9   Regional Policy
10   Transport and Tourism
11   Environment, Public Health and Consumer Protection
12   Culture, Youth, Education and the Media
13   Development and Cooperation
14   Civil Liberties and Internal Affairs
15   Institutional Affairs
16   Budgetary Control
17   Fisheries
18   Rules of Procedure, the Verification of Credentials and Immunities
19   Women's Rights
20   Petitions

to examine legislative proposals upon which an EP opinion is required. The customary way of proceeding (other than when a proposal is completely straightforward and uncontroversial, which may result in it being dealt with by special procedures allowing for rapid approval) is as follows.

(1) Each proposal is referred to an appropriate committee. Should a proposal overlap the competency and interest of several committees, up to three may be asked for their views, but one is named as the committee responsible and only it reports to the plenary session.

(2) The responsibility for drawing up the committee's report is entrusted to a *rapporteur*. Though formally chosen by their fellow committee members, in practice *rapporteurs* are, as are committee chairman and many others in the EP who hold nominally elected positions, appointed as a result of negotiations between the political groups: negotiations that in this case are carried out by group 'coordinators' from the different committees. When drawing up the report the *rapporteur* can call on various sources of assistance: from the EP Secretariat, from her or his own research services

(the EP provides funds to enable each MEP to have at least one research assistant), from the Secretariat of his or her political group, from research institutes, and even from the Commission. Some *rapporteurs* hardly use these facilities and do most of the work themselves; others do little more than present what has been done on their behalf.

(3) A first draft is produced for consideration by the committee according to an agreed timetable. Drafts are normally presented in four main parts: Amendments to the Commission Proposal (if there are any); a Draft Legislative Resolution; an Explanatory Statement; and Annexes (if there are any), including the opinions of other committees. How much discussion the draft provokes, and how many committee meetings are required before a text is adopted that can be recommended to the plenary, depends on the complexity and controversiality of the subject matter. Factors that are likely to shape the reactions of committee members include national and ideological perspectives, lobbying by outside interests, and views expressed by the Commission.

(4) The *rapporteur* acts as the committee's principal spokesman when the report is considered in the plenary. In this capacity he or she may have to explain the committee's view on amendments put forward by non-committee members, or be called upon to use his or her judgement in making recommendations to Parliament on what it should do when the Commission goes some, but not all, of the way towards accepting committee-approved amendments. Occasionally – when, for example, the Commission offers a mixed package – committee meetings may be hurriedly convened during plenary sessions.

(5) Where the cooperation and co-decision procedures apply, the role and activity of committees at the second reading stage is similar to that at the first reading. That is, they examine the proposal (which is now in the form of the Council's common position) and make recommendations to the plenary. The responsibility for drawing up reports is conferred automatically on the committees involved in the first reading and the *rapporteur* remains the same. The reports normally have two main sections: Recommendations for the Second Reading (which may include approval of, rejection of, or amendments to, the common position – amendments are often aimed at re-establishing the EP's position as defined at the first reading, or producing a compromise with the Council); and Justifications or Explanatory Statements.

(6) The committee that has dealt with a proposal at the first and second readings is not directly concerned with the proceedings if a conciliation committee is convened under the co-decision procedure. However, the EP delegation to a conciliation committee always includes some members of the committee concerned, including the chairman and the *rapporteur*.

*　　*　　*

A number of factors help determine how the EP committees work and how much influence they exercise, the most important of which are as follows.

- *The significance of the policy area within the EU system.* The Committee on Agriculture, for example, deals with matters that loom larger in the EU scale of things than the Committee on Women's Rights.
- *The extent of EU policy development.* There can be more opportunities to exercise influence when EU policy is in the process of formation than when it is well established. So, for example, the Committee on Environment, Public Health and Consumer Protection is advantaged in this regard, whereas the Committee on Agriculture is disadvantaged.
- *The power of the EP within the policy area.* The influence of the Committee on Budgets is enormously enhanced by the real budgetary decision-making powers that the treaties give to the EP. Similarly, the Committee on Budgetary Control would be much weaker if the EP did not have the statutory responsibility to grant, postpone, or refuse a discharge to the Commission in respect of the implementation of the EU budget. The Committee on Foreign Affairs, Security and Defence Policy, in contrast, though dealing with extremely important subject material, is greatly limited in what it can do because of the essentially intergovernmental and non-EC character of the policies with which it deals.
- *Committee expertise.* Many committee members just do not have the requisite specialised skills to be able to explore relevant issues in depth or to question the Commission on the basis of a fully informed understanding of policy. For example, few members of the Committee on Research, Technological Development and Energy have an appropriate technical background (though they may of course have, or may develop as a result of their committee membership, a great knowledge of relevant subject material). The Committee on Legal Affairs and Citizen's Rights, on the other hand, is composed mainly of lawyers or legal experts.
- *Secretariat support.* In terms of numbers, all committees have restricted administrative back-up. On average, each has only about five or six senior officials and these, because of the EP recruitment policy, usually have a generalist rather than a specialist background. However, amongst these small teams there appears to be, in varying amounts perhaps, a high degree of competence and enthusiasm.
- *Committee chairmanship.* Committee chairmen can be vital in guiding the work of committees. They can help to push business through; they can assist *rapporteurs* in rallying support for reports that are to be debated in plenaries; they can help to create committee harmony and a constructive working atmosphere; and they can do much to ensure that

a committee broadens its horizons beyond simply reacting to initiatives presented to it by others.

- *Committee cohesiveness.* One of the reasons why, for example, the Committee on Development and Cooperation is rather more influential than a number of other committees is that it tends to display a high degree of cohesiveness. With members of the committee being united on the desirability of improving conditions in the developing countries, discussions tend to revolve around questions of feasibility rather than ideological desirability. The Agriculture Committee, on the other hand, attracts MEPs who are both supportive and critical of the CAP and hence it often tends to be sharply divided.

Plenary meetings

There are twelve plenary meetings, or part-sessions as they are officially known, each year: one each month apart from August, plus an extra one in October when the EP holds its first reading of the budget. The plenaries are held in Strasbourg and last from Monday afternoon to Friday midday.

Most MEPs do not believe the extra plenary in October is necessary, but they are obliged to convene it following a 1998 ruling by the Court of Justice that the EP is bound by a decision taken at the December 1992 Edinburgh summit that there should be twelve full plenaries, including the budget session, each year. The Edinburgh decision has subsequently been reinforced by a protocol to the same effect attached to the Amsterdam Treaty. The French government – concerned at the slow drift of many of the EP's activities to Brussels – was the main force behind both the Court case and the Amsterdam Treaty protocol.

In addition to full plenaries, four to six mini-plenaries are held each year. They normally take up two half days (from lunchtime on day one to lunchtime on day two) and are held in Brussels.

The agenda for plenaries is drafted by the President and the Conference of Presidents in consultation with the Conference of Committee Chairmen and the EP Secretariat. Their recommendations have to be approved by the plenary itself. With time so tight, items that many MEPs consider important inevitably do not get onto the agenda, and those that do make it normally have to be covered at pace. Strict rules govern who can speak, when, and for how long: the effect of the rules is often to restrict speakers to committee and political group spokesmen.

Full plenaries have three standard elements. First, the bread and butter business is the consideration of reports from committees. As indicated earlier, these reports usually lead either to resolutions embodying opinions or to resolutions embodying own initiatives. Second, time is set aside for debates on topical and urgent matters. As with the reports, these debates frequently result in the adoption of resolutions. Finally, there is a one and a half hour Commission Question Time and a one and a half hour Council Question Time. Who answers on behalf of the Commission and the Council depends on the policy content of the questions (which are known in advance), preferences expressed by the EP, and who is available. (Table 9.1 provides a statistical breakdown of the 'outputs' of these three elements of EP activity.)

In addition to the three standard activities, there are a number of other possible agenda items. For example: statements by the Commission and the Council; addresses by distinguished foreign guests; and – at least twice a year – a report on European Council meetings by the Head of Government of the incumbent Presidency.

The EP in plenary does not, it should be said, give the impression of being the most dynamic of places. Attendance in the chamber is poor, the translation problem limits spontaneity, and much immediacy is lost by the practice of taking most votes in clusters at allocated voting times rather than at the end of debates. (These times are often not even on the same day as the debate.) Nonetheless, working procedures have been gradually improved over the years, most notably by the removal of much minor business from the floor of the chamber.

Concluding remarks: is the EP becoming a 'proper' parliament?

The EP has clearly assumed an increased role in the EU over the years. Several factors account for this, not least the Parliament's own efforts to increase its powers.

In attempting to enhance its role and influence, the EP has pursued a dual strategy. On the one hand there has been a *maximalist* approach, which has been directed at achieving fundamental reform of inter-institutional relations, and especially increasing the powers of the Parliament *vis-à-vis* the Council of Ministers. In 1984 this approach led to the EP approving the *Draft Treaty Establishing the European Union*, which played a part – though perhaps not as important a part as its supporters have claimed – in helping to bring about the SEA. In the 1990s, in the context of the growing debate about the 'democratic deficit', and as part of its submissions to the Maastricht and Amsterdam IGCs, the approach led to the EP approving reports that called, amongst other things, for co-decision-making legislative powers with the Council across the policy spectrum (significant progress was achieved via both treaties), and for the right to elect the President of the Commission on a proposal from the European Council (granted in the Amsterdam Treaty). On the other hand there has been a *minimalist* approach, in which the EP has used its existing powers to the full and done whatever it can to determine how far these powers can be pressed. As part of this approach the EP has, for example, interpreted its Maastricht-granted confirmation power on an incoming College of Commissioners as giving it the power to 'interview' Commissioners-designate, and it has contracted a number of inter-institutional agreements with the Commission and the Council (on such matters as the budgetary procedure and conciliation meetings) that have enhanced its institutional position.

But notwithstanding all its efforts and the increased influence it has secured for itself, the EP is still commonly regarded as not being quite a proper parliament. The main reason for this is that its formal powers remain weaker than those of national parliaments: in several important spheres of EU policy activity – including Economic and Monetary Union, the Common Foreign and Security Policy, external trade policy, and police and judicial cooperation – it is largely confined, at best, to information-receiving and consultative roles; it does not have full legislative powers; its budgetary powers are circumscribed; and it cannot overthrow a government.

However, when assessing the importance of the EP, attention should not be restricted to its formal capabilities. For when the comparison with national parliaments is extended to encompass what actually happens in practice, the powers exercised by the EP are, in several key respects, comparable to the powers exercised by many national parliaments. Indeed, it is not difficult to make out a case that in exercising some of its functions – scrutinising legislative proposals, for example, and contributing to debates on future developments – the EP exerts a greater influence over affairs than do the more executive-dominated parliaments of some member states.

Chapter 10

European Union Law and the Courts

The need for EU law

An enforceable legal framework is the essential basis of decision-making and decision application in all democratic states. Although not itself a state, this also applies to the EU, because the EU is more than merely another international organisation in which countries cooperate with one another on a voluntary basis for reasons of mutual benefit. Rather it is an organisation in which states have voluntarily surrendered their right, across a broad range of important sectors, to be independent in the determination and application of public policy.

If there was no body of law setting out the powers and responsibilities of the institutions and the member states of the EU, and if there was no authority to give independent rulings on what that law is and how it should be interpreted, effective EU decision-making would not be possible. Of course law is not the only factor shaping the EU's decision-making processes. As in any organisation, practice evolves in the light of experience of what is possible and what works best. The tendency not to press for a vote in the Council even when it is legally permissible is an obvious example of this. But the law does provide the basic setting in which decisions are made. It lays down that some things must be done, some cannot, and some may be. So, for example, it is by virtue of EU law that agricultural prices can no longer be fixed in national capitals but must be agreed at EU level, that the Commission is entitled to take decisions on proposed large company mergers, and that the EP is permitted to increase the annual budget within specified limits.

The existence of EU law is also crucial with regard to policy implementation. For if decisions only took the form of vague intergovernmental agreements, and if those agreements could be interpreted by member states in whatever way was most beneficial to and convenient for them, common policies would not in practice exist and the whole rationale of the EU would be undermined. The likes of the *common* agricultural policy, the *common* competition policy, the *common* commercial policy, and the harmonisation of matters as diverse as maximum axle weights for lorries and minimum safety standards at work, can be fully effective only if they are based on *common laws* that are capable of *uniform* interpretation in *all* member states.

The sources of EU law

An EU legal order is thus an essential condition of the EU's existence. The sources of that order are to be found in a number of places: the treaties, EU legislation, judicial interpretation, international law, and the general principles of law.

The treaties

The EU's treaty structure is, as was shown in Chapter 5, made up of several component parts. Some of these parts are subject to the jurisdiction of the European Court of Justice (ECJ) whilst others are not. Article 46 (ex Article L) of the TEU makes it clear that the parts of the treaties that are subject to the jurisdiction of the Court are: the three Founding Treaties, as amended over the years, notably by the SEA, the Maastricht Treaty, and the Amsterdam Treaty; certain aspects of the Police and Judicial Cooperation in Criminal Matters pillar, though quite explicitly not 'the exercise of the responsibilities encumbent upon Member States with regard to the maintenance of law and order and the safeguarding of internal security' (Article 35.5); the provisions for closer cooperation between (a less than full complement of) member states that are set out in both the TEU and the TEC; actions of the institutions in relation to respecting fundamental human rights; and the Final Provisions of the TEU, which include matters relating to treaty amendments and accession to the EU. The parts of the treaties that are not subject to the Court are: most of the Common Provisions of the TEU, which include the general objectives of the Union, the membership and role of the European Council, and actions against member states that are deemed to be in breach of their fundamental human rights objectives; the Common Foreign and Security Policy (CFSP) pillar; and declarations attached to the treaties.

Clearly this all makes for a rather messy and untidy legal framework. It also makes for a rather confusing and potentially contentious one since in some circumstances there is considerable legal ambiguity and uncertainty. For example, the principle of subsidiarity, which has been widely hailed since the early 1990s as one of the key guiding principles of the EU, is established as a principle in the Common Provisions, but the only definition of it is in Article 5 (ex Article 3b) of the TEC – and that definition is so vague as to provide no real guidance on how the principle should be applied in practice.

One of the consequences of the complicated legal nature of the treaties is that commentators on the EU have adopted different positions on whether to use the term 'EU law' or 'Community law'. Since there is not much that falls outside the three Community Treaties that is subject to the jurisdiction of the Court, and since legislation can only be made in a Community context, many commentators – especially lawyers – prefer 'Community law'. Others, however, prefer 'EU law': partly because the Communities are part of the EU; partly because some, albeit very limited, legal activity is not based on the Communities; and partly because to keep moving between 'EU' and 'Community' is a recipe for confusion. In this chapter, as elsewhere in the book, the term 'EU law' is used, except when this would be clearly inaccurate or potentially misleading.

Those parts of the treaties that are subject to the jurisdiction of the Court constitute the so-called primary law of the EU. They may also be regarded as making up the EU's written and legal constitution. It could be argued that the treaties as a whole make up the EU's political constitution.

National constitutions in liberal democracies normally do two main things: they establish an institutional structure for decision-making, and they set out – often in a bill of rights – the freedoms of the individual and restrictions on the power of decision-makers over the citizenry. The relevant component parts of the treaties cover the first of these tasks, and up to a point the second too. The establishment of the institutional structure can be seen, most obviously, in the identification of the Commission, the European Council, the Council of Ministers, the Court of Justice, and the European Parliament as the key decision-making institutions, and by the laying down of rules governing relations between them and between them and the member states. As for the establishment of individual rights, the treaties (mainly through the TEC) are most specific about economic freedoms, but there is also the general provision of Article 6 of the TEU that '(t)he Union shall respect fundamental rights, as guaranteed by the (1950) European Convention for the Protection of Human Rights and Fundamental Freedoms . . . and as they result from the constitutional traditions common to the Member States, as general principles of Community Law.'

As well as covering 'traditional' constitutional matters, the treaties are also much concerned with something that is not normally considered to be appropriate subject matter for constitutions: policy. This takes the form of general principles on the one hand and the identification of policy sectors that are to be developed on the other. The main general principles are those that are designed to promote competition and the free movement of goods, persons, services and capital, all behind a common external tariff (CET) and a common commercial policy (CCP). The policy issues and sectors that are identified, with varying degrees of precision on how they are to be developed, include: coal and steel (ECSC Treaty); atomic energy (Euratom Treaty); and agriculture, social affairs, transport, regional affairs, the environment, research and technological development, and economic and monetary union (TEC).

EU legislation

Laws adopted by the EU institutions constitute secondary legislation. They are concerned with translating the general principles of the treaties into specific rules and are adopted by the Council, by the European Parliament and the Council, or by the Commission according to the procedures described in other chapters of this book. While there is no hard and fast distinction between Council, EP and Council, and Commission legislation, the first two tend to be broader in scope, to be concerned with more important matters, and to be aimed at laying down a legal framework in a policy sphere. Commission legislation of which in terms of volume there is much more than Council and European Parliament and Council legislation – is largely administrative/technical in nature and is usually subject to tight guidelines laid down in enabling Council, or EP and Council, legislation.

The treaties distinguish between different types of legislation (Article 14, ECSC; 249 [ex 189], TEC; 161 Euratom): regulations, directives, decisions, and recommendations and opinions.

Regulations

A Regulation (called a general decision under the ECSC) is:

(1) Of 'general application'; that is, it contains general and abstract provisions that may be applied to particular persons and circumstances.

(2) 'Binding in its entirety'; that is, it bestows rights and obligations upon those to whom it is addressed, and member states must observe it in full and as written.

(3) 'Directly applicable in all member states'; that is, without the need for national implementing measures it takes immediate legal effect right across the EU on the date specified in the regulation. Normally this is the same day as, or very shortly after, the regulation is published in the *Official Journal of the European Communities*. This in turn is usually only a day or two after the regulation has been adopted.

Most regulations are adopted by the Commission and concern highly specific and technical adjustments to existing EU law. The majority relate to the CAP. Exhibit 10.1 is a typical regulation.

Directives

A directive (called a recommendation under the ECSC) 'shall be binding, as to the result to be achieved, upon each Member State to which it is addressed, but shall leave to the national authorities the choice of form and methods' (Article 249, TEC).

In theory, a directive is thus very different from a regulation: it is not binding in its entirety but only in 'the result to be achieved'; it is addressed to member states and does not claim general applicability; it is not necessarily addressed to all member states; and appropriate national measures need to be taken to give the directive effect. As a consequence directives tend to be rather more general in nature than regulations. They are less concerned with the detailed and uniform application of policy than with the laying down of policy principles that member states must seek to achieve but can pursue by the appropriate means under their respective national constitutional and legal systems. (Such appropriate means can vary from administrative circulars to new laws approved by national legislatures.)

The distinction between regulations and directives should not, however, be exaggerated because in practice a number of factors often result in a blurring. First, directives are almost invariably addressed to all states. An important reason for this is that directives are frequently concerned with the harmonisation or approximation of laws and practices in fields of EU activity. Exhibit 10.2 is a typical approximating directive. Second, some directives are drafted so tightly that there is very little room for national authorities to incorporate adjustments. Third, directives contain a date by which the national procedures to give the directive effect must have been completed. The Commission has to be notified of national implementing measures, and states that fail to comply by the due date are liable to have proceedings initiated against them, which can ultimately result in a case before the Court of Justice. Fourth, the Court has ruled that in some instances directives are directly applicable: for example when national implementing legislation has been unduly delayed or it has departed from the intent of the original directive.

Decisions

A decision (called an individual decision under the ECSC) 'shall be binding in its entirety upon those to whom it is addressed' (Article 249, TEC). It may be addressed to any or all member states, to undertakings, or to individuals. Many decisions are highly specific and, in effect, are administrative rather than legislative acts. Others are of a more general character and can be akin to regulations or even, occasionally, directives.

Decisions are adopted in a whole range of circumstances. For example: to enforce competition policy; to institute a pilot action programme; to authorise grants from one of the EU's funds; to allow an exemption from an existing measure; or to counter dumping from a third country. Exhibit 10.3 is a typical decision.

Recommendations and opinions

Recommendations and opinions (opinions only under the ECSC) have no binding force and so, strictly speaking, do not formally constitute part of EU law. However, on occasions the Court of Justice has referred to them, so their legal status is not always completely clear. The same applies to some of the other non-binding devices used by the EU institutions for such purposes as floating ideas, starting a legislative process, promoting coordination, and encouraging harmonisation. These include memoranda, communications, conventions, programmes, guidelines, agreements, declarations, resolutions, and decisions not made under Article 249 of the TEC.

In order to accommodate the mosaic of different national circumstances and interests that exist on many policy issues the EU legislative framework needs to be creative, flexible, and capable of permitting differentiation.

Exhibit 10.1   Commission Regulation (EC) No 1539/98 of 16 July 1998 fixing the export refunds on cereal-based compound feedingstuffs

THE COMMISSION OF THE EUROPEAN COMMUNITIES,

Having regard to the Treaty establishing the European Community,

Having regard to Council Regulation (EEC) No 1766/92 of 30 June 1992 on the common organization of the market in cereals([1]), as last amended by Commission Regulation (EC) No 923/96([2]), and in particular Article 13 (3) thereof,

Whereas Article 13 of Regulation (EEC) No 1766/92 provides that the difference between quotations or prices on the world market for the products listed in Article 1 of that Regulation and prices for those products within the Community may be covered by an export refund;

Whereas Regulation (EC) No 1517/95 of 29 June 1995 laying down detailed rules for the application of Regulation (EEC) No 1766/92 as regards the arrangements for the export and import of compound feedingstuffs based on cereals and amending Regulation (EC) No 1162/95 laying down special detailed rules for the application of the system of import and export licences for cereals and rice([3]) in Article 2 lays down general rules for fixing the amount of such refunds;

Whereas that calculation must also take account of the cereal products content; whereas in the interest of simplification, the refund should be paid in respect of two categories of 'cereal products', namely for maize, the most commonly used cereal in exported compound feeds and maize products, and for 'other cereals', these being eligible cereal products excluding maize and maize products; whereas a refund should be granted in respect of the quantity of cereal products present in the compound feedingstuff;

Whereas furthermore, the amount of the refund must also take into account the possibilities and conditions for the sale of those products on the world market, the need to avoid disturbances on the Community market and the economic aspect of the export;

Whereas, however, in fixing the rate of refund it would seem advisable to base it at this time on the difference in the cost of raw inputs widely used in compound feedingstuffs as the Community and world markets, allowing more accurate account to be taken of the commercial conditions under which such products are exported;

Whereas the refund must be fixed once a month; whereas it may be altered in the intervening period;

Whereas the measures provided for in this Regulation are in accordance with the opinion of the Management Committee for Cereals,

HAS ADOPTED THIS REGULATION:

Article 1

The export refunds on the compound feedingstuffs covered by Regulation (EEC) No 1766/92 and subject to Regulation (EC) No 1517/95 are hereby fixed as shown in the Annex to this Regulation.

Article 2

This Regulation shall enter into force on 17 July 1998.

→

This Regulation shall be binding in its entirety and directly applicable in all Member States.

Done at Brussels, 16 July 1998.

For the Commission
Franz FISCHLER
Member of the Commission

(¹) OJ L 181, 1. 7. 1992, p. 21.
(²) OJ L 126, 24. 5. 1996, p. 37.
(³) OJ L 147, 30. 6. 1995, p. 51.

ANNEX

to the Commission Regulation of 16 July 1998 fixing the export refunds on cereal-based compound feedingstuffs

Product code benefitting from export refund (¹):

2309 10 11 9000, 2309 10 13 9000, 2309 10 31 9000,
2309 10 33 9000, 2309 10 51 9000, 2309 10 53 9000,
2309 90 31 9000, 2309 90 33 9000, 2309 90 41 9000,
2309 90 43 9000, 2309 90 51 9000, 2309 90 53 9000.

(ECU/tonne)

Cereal products (²)	Amount of refund (²)
Maize and maize products:	
CN codes 0709 90 60, 0712 90 19, 1005, 1102 20, 1103 13, 1103 29 40, 1104 19 50, 1104 23, 1904 10 10	34,40
Cereal products (²) excluding maize and maize products	33,95

(¹) The product codes are defined in Sector 5 of the Annex to Commission Regulation (EEC) No 3846/87 (OJ L 366, 24. 12. 1987, p. 1), amended.
(²) For the purposes of the refund only the starch coming from cereal products is taken into account.

Cereal products means the products falling within subheadings 0709 90 60 and 0712 90 19, Chapter 10, and headings Nos 1101, 1102, 1103 and 1104 (excluding subheading 1104 30) and the cereals content of the products falling within subheadings 1904 10 10 and 1904 10 90 of the combined nomenclature. The cereals content in products under subheadings 1904 10 10 and 1904 10 90 of the combined nomenclature is considered to be equal to the weight of this final product.

No refund is paid for cereals where the origin of the starch cannot be clearly established by analysis.

Source: *Official Journal of the European Communities*, L201: 86 (17 July 1998).

Exhibit 10.2 Directive 98/71/EC of the European Parliament and of the Council of 13 October 1998 on the legal protection of designs

THE EUROPEAN PARLIAMENT AND THE COUNCIL OF THE EUROPEAN UNION,

Having regard to the Treaty establishing the European Community and in particular Article 100a thereof,

Having regard to the proposal by the Commission ([1]),

Having regard to the opinion of the Economic and Social Committee ([2]),

Acting in accordance with the procedure laid down in Article 189b of the Treaty([3]), in the light of the joint text approved by the Conciliation Committee on 29 July 1998,

(1) Whereas the objectives of the Community, as laid down in the Treaty, include laying the foundations of an ever closer union among the peoples of Europe, fostering closer relations between Member States of the Community, and ensuring the economic and social progress of the Community countries by common action to eliminate the barriers which divide Europe; whereas to that end the Treaty provides for the establishment of an internal market characterised by the abolition of obstacles to the free movement of goods and also for the institution of a system ensuring that competition in the internal market is not distorted; whereas an approximation of the laws of the Member States on the legal protection of designs would further those objectives;

(2) Whereas the differences in the legal protection of designs offered by the legislation of the Member States directly affect the establishment and functioning of the internal market as regards goods embodying designs; whereas such differences can distort competition within the internal market;

(3) Whereas it is therefore necessary for the smooth functioning of the internal market to approximate the design protection laws of the Member States;

(4) Whereas, in doing so, it is important to take into consideration the solutions and the advantages with which the Community design system will provide undertakings wishing to acquire design rights;

(5) Whereas it is unnecessary to undertake a full-scale approximation of the design laws of the Member States, and it will be sufficient if approximation is limited to those national provisions of law which most directly affect the functioning of the internal market; whereas provisions on sanctions, remedies and enforcement should be left to national law; whereas the objectives of this limited approximation cannot be sufficiently achieved by the Member States acting alone;

(6) Whereas Member States should accordingly remain free to fix the procedural provisions concerning registration, renewal and invalidation

of design rights and provisions concerning the effects of such invalidity . . .

HAVE ADOPTED THIS DIRECTIVE:

Article 1

Definitions

For the purpose of this Directive:

(a) 'design' means the appearance of the whole or a part of a product resulting from the features of, in particular, the lines, contours, colours, shape, texture and/or materials of the product itself and/or its ornamentation;

(b) 'product' means any industrial or handicraft item, including *inter alia* parts intended to be assembled into a complex product, packaging, get-up, graphic symbols and typographic typefaces, but excluding computer programs;

(c) 'complex product' means a product which is composed of multiple components which can be replaced permitting disassembly and reassembly of the product.

Article 2

Scope of application

1. This Directive shall apply to:

(a) design rights registered with the central industrial property offices of the Member States;

(b) design rights registered at the Benelux Design Office;

(c) design rights registered under international arrangements which have effect in a Member State;

(d) applications for design rights referred to under (a), (b) and (c).

2. For the purpose of this Directive, design registration shall also comprise the publication following filing of the design with the industrial property office of a Member State in which such publication has the effect of bringing a design right into existence.

Article 3

Protection requirements

1. Member States shall protect designs by registration and shall confer exclusive rights upon their holders in accordance with the provisions of this Directive.

2. A design shall be protected by a design right to the extent that it is new and has individual character.

3. A design applied to or incorporated in a product which constitutes a component part of a complex product shall only be considered to be new and to have individual character:

(a) if the component part, once it has been incorporated into the complex product, remains visible during normal use of the latter, and

(b) to the extent that those visible features of the component part fulfil in themselves the requirements as to novelty and individual character.

4. 'Normal use' within the meaning of paragraph (3)(a) shall mean use by the end user, excluding maintenance, servicing or repair work.

Article 4

Novelty

A design shall be considered new if no identical design has been made

Exhibit 10.2 continued

available to the public before the date of filing of the application for registration or, if priority is claimed, the date of priority. Designs shall be deemed to be identical if their features differ only in immaterial details.

Article 5

Individual character

1. A design shall be considered to have individual character if the overall impression it produces on the informed user differs from the overall impression produced on such a user by any design which has been made available to the public before the date of filing of the application for registration or, if priority is claimed, the date of priority.

2. In assessing individual character, the degree of freedom of the designer in developing the design shall be taken into consideration.

Article 6

Disclosure

1. For the purpose of applying Articles 4 and 5, a design shall be deemed to have been made available to the public if it has been published following registration or otherwise, or exhibited, used in trade or otherwise disclosed, except where these events could not reasonably have become known in the normal course of business to the circles specialised in the sector concerned, operating within the Community, before the date of filing of the application for registration or, if priority is claimed, the date of priority. The design shall not, however, be deemed to have been made available to the public for

the sole reason that it has been disclosed to a third person under explicit or implicit conditions of confidentiality.

2. A disclosure shall not be taken into consideration for the purpose of applying Articles 4 and 5 if a design for which protection is claimed under a registered design right of a Member State has been made available to the public:

(a) by the designer, his successor in title, or a third person as a result of information provided or action taken by the designer, or his successor in title; and

(b) during the 12-month period preceding the date of filing of the application or, if priority is claimed, the date of priority.

3. Paragraph 2 shall also apply if the design has been made available to the public as a consequence of an abuse in relation to the designer or his successor in title.

Article 7

Designs dictated by their technical function and designs of interconnections

1. A design right shall not subsist in features of appearance of a product which are solely dictated by its technical function.

2. A design right shall not subsist in features of appearance of a product which must necessarily be reproduced in their exact form and dimensions in order to permit the product in which the design is incorporated or to which it is applied to be mechanically connected to or placed in, around or against another product so that either product may perform its function.

→

3. Notwithstanding paragraph 2, a design right shall, under the conditions set out in Articles 4 and 5, subsist in a design serving the purpose of allowing multiple assembly or connection of mutually interchangeable products within a modular system. . .

Article 12

Rights conferred by the design right

1. The registration of a design shall confer on its holder the exclusive right to use it and to prevent any third party not having his consent from using it. The aforementioned use shall cover, in particular, the making, offering, putting on the market, importing, exporting or using of a product in which the design is incorporated or to which it is applied, or stocking such a product for those purposes.

2. Where, under the law of a Member State, acts referred to in paragraph 1 could not be prevented before the date on which the provisions necessary to comply with this Directive entered into force, the rights conferred by the design right may not be invoked to prevent continuation of such acts by any person who had begun such acts prior to that date.

Article 13

Limitation of the rights conferred by the design right

1. The rights conferred by a design right upon registration shall not be exercised in respect of:
(a) acts done privately and for non-commercial purposes;
(b) acts done for experimental purposes;
(c) acts of reproduction for the purposes of making citations or of teaching, provided that such acts are compatible with fair trade practice and do not unduly prejudice the normal exploitation of the design, and that mention is made of the source.

2. In addition, the rights conferred by a design right upon registration shall not be exercised in respect of:
(a) the equipment on ships and aircraft registered in another country when these temporarily enter the territory of the Member State concerned;
(b) the importation in the Member State concerned of spare parts and accessories for the purpose of repairing such craft;
(c) the execution of repairs on such craft. . .

Article 18

Revision

Three years after the implementation date specified in Article 19, the Commission shall submit an analysis of the consequences of the provisions of this Directive for Community industry, in particular the industrial sectors which are most affected, particularly manufacturers of complex products and component parts, for consumers, for competition and for the functioning of the internal market. At the latest one year later the Commission shall propose to the European Parliament and the Council any changes to this Directive needed to complete the internal market in respect of component parts

→

Exhibit 10.2 continued

of complex products and any other changes which it considers necessary in light of its consultations with the parties most affected.

Article 19

Implementation

1. Member States shall bring into force the laws, regulations or administrative provisions necessary to comply with this Directive not later than 28 October 2001.

When Member States adopt these provisions, they shall contain a reference to this Directive or shall be accompanied by such reference on the occasion of their official publication. The methods of making such reference shall be laid down by Member States.

2. Member States shall communicate to the Commission the provisions of national law which they adopt in the field governed by this Directive.

Article 20

Entry into force

This Directive shall enter into force on the 20th day following its publication in the *Official Journal of the European Communities*.

Article 21

Addressees

This Directive is addressed to the Member States.

Done at Luxembourg, 13 October 1998.

For the European Parliament
The President
J. M. GIL-ROBLES

For the Council
The President
C. EINEM

———————

(^{1}) OJ C 345, 23. 12. 1993, p. 14 and OJ C 142, 14. 5. 1996, p. 7.
(^{2}) OJ C 388, 31. 12. 1994, p. 9 and OJ C 110, 2. 5. 1995, p. 12.
(^{3}) Opinion of the European Parliament of 12 October 1995 (OJ C 287, 30. 10. 1995, p. 157), common position of the Council of 17 June 1997 (OJ C 237, 4. 8. 1997, p. 1), Decision of the European Parliament of 22 October 1997 (OJ C 339, 10. 11. 1997, p. 52). Decision of the European Parliament of 15 September 1998. Decision of the Council of 24 September 1998.

Source: Official Journal of the European Communities, L389/23–33 (28 October 1998).

Exhibit 10.3 Commission Decision of 13 May 1998

derogating, for the 1997/98 marketing year, from certain provisions of Commission Regulation (EEC) No 1202/89 as regards aid applications and applications for supervised storage of unginned cotton originating in certain Greek prefectures

(Only the Greek text is authentic)

(98/341/EC)

THE COMMISSION OF THE EUROPEAN COMMUNITIES,

Having regard to the Treaty establishing the European Community,

Having regard to protocol 4 on cotton annexed to the Act of Accession of Greece, as last amended by Regulation (EC) No 1553/95 (^{1}),

Having regard to Council Regulation (EC) No 1554/95 of 29 June 1995 laying down the general rules for the system of aid for cotton and repealing Regulation (EEC) No 2169/81 (^{2}), as amended by Regulation (EC) No 1584/96 (^{3}), and in particular Article 11(1) thereof,

Whereas Commission Regulation (EEC) No 1201/89 of 3 May 1989 laying down rules implementing the system of aid for cotton (^{4}), as last amended by Regulation (EC) No 1740/97 (^{5}), lays down 31 March as the time limit for placing unginned cotton in supervised storage but allows the possibility for the Member States to set a later time limit under certain conditions; whereas for the 1997/98 marketing year Greece used that provision by setting the time limit for supervised storage at 31 January 1998; whereas, as a result of exceptional weather conditions, it proved impossible to harvest the unginned cotton until the beginning of March 1998 in certain Greek prefectures; whereas, therefore, the start of supervised storage and the lodging of the corresponding aid applications should be accepted without penalty for the unginned cotton originating in those prefectures up to a date allowing for the other time limits in the rules to be complied with;

Whereas the measures provided for in this Decision are in accordance with the opinion of the Management Committee for Flax and Hemp,

HAS ADOPTED THIS DECISION:

Article 1

1. By derogation from the first indent of Article 5(3), from Article 7(1) and from the first and second subparagraphs of Article 9(2), the following conditions shall apply for the 1997/98 marketing year to unginned cotton harvested in the Greek prefectures indicated in paragraph 2:
(a) aid applications lodged by 15 April at the latest may be accepted;
(b) if the aid applications are lodged between 1 April and 15 April, the aid to be granted shall be that valid on the previous 31 March;

$\longrightarrow$

Exhibit 10.3 continued

(c) applications for supervised storage lodged by 15 April at the latest may be accepted.
2. The Greek prefectures referred to in paragraph 1 are: Kavala, Xanthi, Rodopi and Evros.

Article 2

This Decision is addressed to the Hellenic Republic.
Done at Brussels, 13 May 1998.

For the Commission
Franz FISCHLER
Member of the Commission

(^{1}) OJ L 148, 30. 6. 1995, p. 45.
(^{2}) OJ L 148, 30. 6. 1995, p. 45.
(^{3}) OJ L 206, 16. 8. 1996, p. 16.
(^{4}) OJ L 123, 4. 5. 1989, p. 23.
(^{5}) OJ L 244, 6. 9. 1997, p. 1.

Source: Official Journal of the European Communities, L151: 34 (21 May 1998).

There are four main ways in which it is so:

- As has just been shown, the EU makes use of a variety of formal and quasi-formal legislative instruments.
- There are considerable variations between directives regarding the time periods permitted for incorporation into national law. For example, amending directives may have to be incorporated almost immediately, whereas innovative or controversial directives, or directives that require substantial capital expenditure in order to be properly applied – as is common with environmental directives – may not be required to be incorporated for some years.
- Devices that allow for adaptation to local conditions and needs are often either attached to legal texts or are authorised by the Commission after an act has come into force. Examples of such devices include exemptions, derogations, and safety clauses.
- Provided the Commission is satisfied that the relevant provisions 'are not a means of arbitrary discrimination or a disguised restriction on trade between Member States' (Article 95, TEC, ex Article 100A), states are permitted to apply national legislation that is 'tougher' than EU legislation in respect of certain matters – notably protection of the environment and of the working environment.

There used to be several thousand legislative instruments issued each year, comprised of around 4000 regulations, 2000 decisions, and 120 directives.

However, the number has dropped considerably in recent years, partly because of the virtual completion of the Single European Market (SEM) legislative programme, but mainly because of a drive by all decision-making institutions to simplify the EU legislative framework. Table 10.1 shows the number of legislative instruments enacted in 1998. The vast majority of these instruments consist of administrative measures of a routine, non-political, recurring kind. Many are replacements for instruments that have either been repealed (usually because, as with most CAP-related legislation, they have become outdated as a result of changing market conditions) or because they have expired.

Judicial interpretation

Although case law has not traditionally been a major source of law in most of the EU member states (the United Kingdom and Ireland are the main exceptions), the rulings of the European Court of Justice have played an important part in shaping and making EU law. This stems partly from the Court's duty to ensure that EU law is interpreted and applied correctly. It

Table 10.1   *Legislative instruments enacted, repealed or expiring in 1998*

Enacting institution	Number of instruments	Regulations	Directives	Decisions	Recommend-ations
European Parliament and Council (co-decision)	Enacted in 1998	0	26	7	0
	Repealed or expiring in 1998	0	2	5	0
Council alone	Enacted in 1998	202	27	189	10
	Repealed or expiring in 1998	146	44	187	1
Commission	Enacted in 1998	773	44	537	13
	Repealed or expiring in 1998	551	13	260	1
Total enacted		975	97	733	23

Source: Commission (1999), p. 428.

stems also from the fact that much of EU statute law is far from clear or complete.

The lack of precision in much of the EU's statute law is due to a number of factors: the relative newness of the EU and its constituent Communities; problems with the decision-making processes often lead to weak compromises and the avoidance of necessary secondary legislation; and the speed of change in some spheres of EU activity makes it very difficult for the written law to keep abreast of developments. In many fields of apparent EU competence the Court thus has to issue judgements from a less than detailed statutory base. In the different types of case that come before it – cases of first and only instance, cases of appeal, cases involving rulings on points of EU law that have been referred by national courts – the Court therefore inevitably often goes well beyond merely giving a technical and grammatical interpretation of the written rules. It fills in the gaps in the law and, in so doing, it not only clarifies the law but it also extends it.

International law

International law is notoriously vague and weak, but the Court of Justice has had occasional recourse to it when developing principles embodied in EU law. Judgements have also established that insofar as the EU is increasingly developing an international personality of its own and taking over powers from the states, the same rules of international law apply to it as apply to them, for example with regard to treaty law and the privileges and immunities of international organisations.

The many international agreements to which the EU is a party are sometimes viewed as another dimension of international law. However, since they are implemented by legislative acts they are probably better viewed as constituting part of EU legislation.

The general principles of law

All three Community Treaties charge the Court of Justice with the task of ensuring 'that in the interpretation and application of this Treaty the law is observed' (Article 220, TEC, ex Article 164; Article 136, Euratom; Article 31, ECSC). The implication of this, and of certain other Treaty articles (notably 230 and 288 of the TEC), is that the Court need not regard written EU law as the only source of law to which it may refer.

In practice this has meant that the Court, when making its judgements, has had regard to general principles of law when these have been deemed relevant and applicable. Exactly what these general principles of law are is a matter of controversy. Suffice to note here that the principles that have been cited by the Court include proportionality (the means used to achieve a given end should be no more than is appropriate and necessary to achieve that end), non-discrimination (whether between nations, product sectors, firms or individuals), adherence to legality, and respect for procedural rights.

The content of EU law

The content of EU law is described at some length in Chapter 12, in the context of the examination that is presented there of EU policies. Attention here will, therefore, be confined to a few points of general significance.

The first point is that EU law is not as wide-ranging as national law. It is not, for instance, directly concerned with criminal law or family law. Nor does it have much to do with policy areas such as education or health. What EU law is primarily concerned with – and in this it reflects the aims and provisions of the treaties – is economic activity. More particularly, EU law is strongly focused in the direction of the activities of the EC which, as set out in Article 3 of the TEC, include

> a common commercial policy . . . an internal market characterised by the abolition, as between Member States, of obstacles to the free movement of goods, persons, services and capital . . . a common policy in the spheres of agriculture and fisheries . . . a system ensuring that competition in the internal market is not distorted . . . the approxima- tion of the laws of Member States to the extent required for the functioning of the common market . . . a policy in the sphere of the environment.

The second point is that no policy area, with the exception of the common commercial policy, contains a comprehensive code of EU law. Even in areas where there is a high degree of EU regulation, such as with the functioning of agricultural markets, national laws covering various matters still exist. As Tables 12.1 and 12.2 show, EU law thus sits side by side with national law, constituting an important part of the overall legal framework of member states in some policy spheres, whilst being of only marginal significance in others.

The third point is that the range of EU law has broadened considerably over the years. As already noted, EU law is primarily economic in character, but less dominantly so than it was. A good illustration of this is seen in the considerable volume of EU environmental law that now exists: there are over 200 EU environmental laws in force, dealing with matters as diverse as air and water pollution, the disposal of toxic waste, and the protection of endangered bird species. This expansion of EU law into an increasing number of policy areas has occurred, and is still occurring, for several reasons, prominent among which are: sectional interest pressures; increasing recognition of the benefits that joint action can bring to many fields of activity; and increasing acceptance that the SEM can function smoothly, efficiently and equitably only if there are common rules not just on directly related market activities but also on matters such as health and safety at work, entitlement to social welfare benefits, and mutual recognition of educational and professional qualifications.

The status of EU law

In Case 6/64, *Costa v. ENEL*, the ECJ stated:

> By creating a Community of unlimited duration, having its own institutions, its own personality, its own legal capacity of representation on the international plane and, more particularly, real powers stemming from limitation of sovereignty or a transfer of powers from the states to the Community, the Member States have limited their sovereign rights, albeit within limited fields, and have thus created a body of law which binds both their individuals and themselves.

EU law thus constitutes an autonomous legal system, imposing obligations and rights on both individuals and member states, and limiting the sovereignty of member states. There are three main pillars to this legal system: direct applicability, direct effect, and primacy.

Direct applicability

EU law is directly applicable when there is no need for national measures to be taken in order for the law to have binding force within the member states. Of the different statutory sources of EU law, only regulations are always directly applicable. However, it has been established, principally via ECJ judgements, that other legal acts may also be directly applicable when their structure and content so allow and certain conditions are satisfied.

Direct effect

This term refers to the principle whereby certain provisions of EU law may confer rights or impose obligations on individuals that national courts are bound to recognise and enforce. Having initially established the principle in 1963 in the case of *Van Gend en Loos* (Case 26/62), the Court, in a series of judgements, has gradually strengthened and extended the scope of direct effect so that it now applies to most secondary legislation except when discretion is explicitly granted to the addressee. Many of the provisions of the treaties have also been established as having direct effect, although the Court has ruled that it does not apply in some important spheres, such as the free movement of capital.

Although the details of what is an extremely complicated legal debate cannot be rehearsed here, it should be noted that the distinction that has just been drawn between direct applicability and direct effect is not one that all lawyers accept. A consequence of this is that the terms have given rise to considerable confusion and much debate. Even official EU sources, including the Court itself, have not always used the terms consistently or with precision.

Primacy

Somewhat surprisingly, there is no explicit reference in the treaties to the primacy or supremacy of EU law over national law. Clearly the principle is vital if the EU is to function properly, since if member states had the power to annul EU law by adopting or giving precedence to national law, then there could be no uniform or consistent EU legal order: states could apply national law when EU law was distasteful or inconvenient to them. From an early stage, therefore, the Court took an active part in establishing the primacy of EU law. National courts, it has consistently asserted, must apply EU law in the event of any conflict, even if the domestic law is part of the national constitution. An example of Court statements on primacy may be taken from *Simmenthal v. Commission* (Case 92/78) where the Court concluded that:

> Every national court must, in a case within its jurisdiction, apply Community law in its entirety and protect rights which the latter confers on individuals and must accordingly set aside any provision of national law which may conflict with it, whether prior or subsequent to the Community rule.

In general, national courts have accepted this view and given precedence to EU law. A few problems remain – notably in relation to fundamental rights guaranteed by national constitutions – but for the most part the authority and binding nature of EU law is fully established.

Powers and responsibilities of the Court of Justice

The European Court of Justice – which is based in Luxembourg and must not be, though often is, confused with the Strasbourg-based European Court of Human Rights – has two main functions. First, it is responsible for directly applying the law in certain types of case. Second, it has general responsibility for interpreting the provisions of EU law and ensuring that the application of the law, which on a day-to-day basis is primarily the responsibility of national courts and agencies, is consistent and uniform.

Inevitably, for the reasons explained earlier, these duties result in the Court making what, in effect, is judicial law. This is most clearly seen in four respects.

First, as noted above, the Court has clarified and strengthened the status of EU law. Landmark decisions of the 1960s and 1970s, such as *Van Gend en Loos*, were crucial in paving the way to the establishment of a strong legal system, but later decisions have also been important. For example, in its 1992 judgement in *Francovich and Bonifaci v. Italy* (Joined Cases 6/90 and 9/90) the Court ruled that individuals are entitled to financial compensation if they are adversely affected by the failure of a member state to transpose a directive within the prescribed period.

Second, EU policy competence has been strengthened and extended by Court judgements. Social security entitlements illustrate this. Most governments have not wished to do much more about entitlements than coordinate certain aspects of their social security systems. The Court, however, through a number of judgements, often based on the TEC rather than on legislation, has played an important part in pushing the states towards the harmonisation of some of their practices, for example with regard to the rights of migrant workers. It has also extended the provisions of certain laws in ways the states did not envisage when they gave them their approval in the Council.

Another example of the Court strengthening and extending policy competence is a judgement it gave in May 1990 in a preliminary ruling case. The case – *Barber v. Guardian Royal Exchange Assurance Group* (Case 262/88) – had been referred by the UK Court of Appeal. The Court of Justice ruled that occupational pensions are part of an employee's pay and must therefore comply with Article 119 of the EEC Treaty dealing with equal pay for men and women. Regarding the particular issue that gave rise to the case, the Court stated that it was contrary to Article 119 to impose different age requirements for men and women as conditions for obtaining pensions on compulsory redundancy under a private pension scheme.

The area where the Court has exercised the greatest influence in strengthening and extending EU policy competence is in regard to the SEM. In some instances this has been a result of practices being ruled illegal by the Court, and in others it has been a consequence of Court judgements pressurising, enabling or forcing the Commission and the Council to act – as, for example, in de-regulating air transport following the 1986 *Nouvelles Frontières* case, in which the Court held that the treaty rules governing competition applied to air transport.

Third, and of crucial importance in respect of the SEM, Court judgements have saved the EU the need to make law in existing areas of competence. A particularly influential judgement was issued in February 1979 in the *Cassis de Dijon* case (Case 120/78), which concerned the free circulation of the French blackcurrant liqueur of that name. The Court ruled that national food standards legislation cannot be invoked to prevent trade between member states unless it is related to 'public health, fiscal supervision and the defence of the consumer'. The principle of 'mutual recognition' – whereby a product lawfully produced and marketed in one member state must be accepted in another member state – was thus established, with the result that the need for legislation to harmonise standards in order to facilitate trade was much reduced. Of course the *Cassis de Dijon* judgement does not rule out challenges to the principle of 'mutual recognition', or to its application. For example, in the much publicised case *Commission v. Germany* (Case 178/84), the German government attempted to protect its brewers by arguing that whereas their product was pure, most so-called foreign beers contained additives and should be excluded from the German market on health grounds. In March 1987 the Court upheld the 'mutual recognition' principle and ruled that a blanket ban on additives to beer was quite disproportionate to the health risk involved; the German insistence on its own definition of beer amounted to a barrier to trade. In a similar ruling in July 1988 (Case 407/85) the Court ruled against an Italian prohibition on the sale in Italy of pasta products that are not made (as all Italian pasta is) from durum (hard) wheat; the Court stated that German pasta – which is made from a mixture of hard and soft wheat – presented no threat to Italian consumers' health, nor did the product mislead consumers.

Fourth, the powers and functioning of the institutions have been clarified and in important respects significantly affected by the Court. Four important judgements will be cited to illustrate this. First, in October 1980, in the isoglucose case (Case 138/79), the Court ruled that the Council could not adopt legislation until it had received the EP's opinion (see Chapter 9 for further consideration of this case). Second, in October 1988, in the 'Wood Pulp' cases (Joined Cases 89, 104, 114–117, 125–129/85), the Court upheld and strengthened the power of Community institutions to take legal action against non-EC companies. (In this case the Commission had imposed fines on a number of American, Canadian and Finnish producers of wood pulp in respect of concerted practices that had affected selling prices in the Community. The Court ruled that the key factor in determining the Community's jurisdiction was not where companies were based, nor where any illegal agreements or practices were devised, but where illegalities were implemented.) Third, in 1992, in *Spain, Belgium and Italy v. Commission* (Joined Cases 271, 281 and 289/90) – which involved the liberalisation of the monopolistic telecommunications services market – the Court ruled that the Commission's powers in relation to competition policy were not limited to the surveillance of rules already in existence, but extended to taking a proactive role to break monopolies. The fact that the Council could have taken appropriate measures did not affect the Commission's competence to act. Fourth, in May 1998, in *United Kingdom v. Commission (Case 106/96)*, the Court ruled that the Commission was funding pilot projects to combat poverty and social exclusion without having a legal base to do so. The Court stated that only 'non-significant' activities could be funded without there being an act to authorise the expenditure.

The Court has thus had a very considerable impact on the content of EU law. It has done so for a number of reasons, not least because, as Alter (1996, p. 479) has pointed out, those EU politicians who have been dissatisfied with judicial activism (representing a minority on most issues) have found it difficult to constrain, let alone reduce, the powers of the Court.

The independent influence of the Court should not however be overstated. As Wincott (1999) has argued, the Court is not normally in a position to create a fully fledged policy by itself. There are two main reasons for this. First, the Court must usually have a treaty or legislative base upon which to act. This means that its judgements are normally constrained to at least some extent by an existing, albeit sometimes very sketchy, policy framework. Second, judgements can only be issued on cases that are referred to the Court. It cannot initiate cases itself. Consequently, as Wincott says, 'where the Court has made a striking contribution to the character of a particular policy, usually its contribution has been to unsettle an established policy regime or to break up a gridlock . . . rather than to create a policy itself'. Court judgements have certainly impacted on EU policy, but the most important impact has often been not so much direct as rather 'the provocation of further legislation' (Wincott, 1999).

*   *   *

As has just been noted, in fulfilling its responsibilities the Court cannot itself initiate actions. It must wait for cases to be referred to it. This can happen in one of a number of ways, the most important of which are:

Failure to fulfil an obligation

Under Articles 226 and 227 of the TEC (ex 169 and 170), the Court rules on whether member states have failed to fulfil obligations under the Treaty. Actions may be brought either by the Commission or by other member states. In either eventuality, the Commission must first give the state(s) in question an opportunity to submit observations and then deliver a reasoned opinion. Only if this fails to produce proper compliance with EU law can the matter be referred to the Court of Justice.

In practice, failures to fulfil obligations are usually settled well before they are brought before the Court. When an action is brought the Commission is almost invariably the initiator. It is so partly because if a member state is behind the action it is obliged to refer the matter to the Commission in the first instance, and partly because member states are extremely reluctant to engage in direct public confrontation with one another (though they do sometimes try to encourage the Commission to, in effect, act on their behalf). Such cases have led to rulings against Italy (that its duties on imported gin and sparkling wine were discriminatory), against the United Kingdom (that it had introduced insufficient national measures to give full effect to the 1976 directive on sexual discrimination), and Belgium (for failing to implement directives to harmonise certain stock exchange rules).

The Maastricht Treaty gave to the Court, for the first time, the power to impose penalties on member states. Under Article 228 of the TEC (ex 171) the Commission can initiate action against a state that it believes has not complied with a judgement of the Court in a case involving failure to fulfil an obligation under the Treaty. The first stages of the action involve giving the state in question the opportunity to submit its observations and issuing a reasoned opinion that specifies the points on which the state has not complied with the judgement of the Court and which also specifies a time limit for compliance. If the state does not comply with the reasoned opinion within a specified time limit, the Commission may bring it back before the Court. In so doing the Commission must specify the amount of the lump sum or penalty payment to be paid by the member state concerned, 'which it considers to be appropriate in the circumstances'. If the Court finds that the member state has not complied with its judgement, it may impose a lump sum or penalty payment – with unlimited jurisdiction applying with regard to penalties.

As can be seen from Table 10.2, actions involving failure to fulfil an obligation constitute the second highest number of cases referred to the Court.

Application for annulment

Under Article 230 of the TEC (ex 173), the Court of Justice 'shall review the legality of acts adopted jointly by the European Parliament and the Council, of acts of the Council, of the Commission and of the ECB, other than recommendations and opinions, and of acts of the European Parliament intended to produce legal effects *vis-à-vis* third parties'. The Court cannot conduct reviews on its own initiative, but only in response to actions brought by a member state, the Council, the Commission or – where their prerogatives are concerned – the EP and the European Central Bank. Reviews may be based on the following grounds: 'lack of competence, infringement of an essential procedural requirement, infringement of this Treaty or of any rule relating to its application, or misuse of powers'. If an action is well founded, the Court is empowered under Article 231 of the TEC (ex 174) to declare the act concerned to be void.

An increasingly important aspect of Court activity under this heading arises in connection with the Treaty base(s) upon which EU legislation is proposed and adopted. There are several procedures by which EU law can be made (see Chapter 13 for details), each of which is different in terms of such key matters as whether qualified majority voting rules apply in the Council and what are the powers of the EP. Which procedure applies in a particular case depends on the article(s) of the Treaty upon which legislative proposals are based. So, for example, if a proposal concerned with the competitiveness of industry in the internal market is based on Article 95 of the TEC (ex 100a, approximation of laws – internal market), the co-decision procedure applies with qualified majority voting in the Council. This means that Council approval does not depend on all member states supporting the proposal, but the EP has a potential veto over the proposal. If, however, the proposal is brought forward on the basis of Article 157 of the TEC (ex Article 130, industry), the consultation procedure applies, with unanimity in the Council. This means that a single member state can veto the proposal in the Council, whilst the EP's powers are weak. It thus naturally follows that if a legislative proposal is brought forward by the Commission on a legal base that the Council or the EP believe to be both damaging to their interests and legally questionable, and if political processes cannot bring about a satisfactory resolution to the matter, they may be tempted to appeal to the Court.

Table 10.2 Activities of the Court of Justice in 1997: analysed by type (EC Treaty)

| | | | 173 | | | | | | | | | | Article 220 | | |
	93(2)	169	By govern-ments	By Community institutions	By individuals	Total	175	177	178 and 215	181	185 and 186	228(6)	Conven-tions	Appeals	Total
Actions brought	1	121	25	6	4	35	–	234	–	6	1	–	6	35	439
Cases not resulting in a judgement	–	37	6	–	–	6	–	60	–	1	–	–	1	–	105
Cases decided	–	46	15	2	3	20	–	231	–	2	1	–	6	32	338
in favour of applicant	–	41	3	1	–	4	–	–	–	–	–	–	–	6	51
dismissed on the merits	–	5	11	1	1	13	–	–	–	1	1	–	–	24	44
rejected as inadmissible	–	–	1	–	2	3	–	–	–	1	–	–	–	1	5
other[2]	–	–	–	–	–	–	–	–	–	–	–	–	–	1	1

Proceedings brought under the following articles of the Treaty[1]

1. ECSC: four actions brought (one Article 33, one Article 42, two appeals), four cases dismissed on the merits (appeals), one case declared inadmissible (Article 33); Euratom: four actions brought (two Article 141, one Article 151, one appeal), one case decided in favour of applicant (Article 141), one declared inadmissible (Article 141) and two not resulting in a judgement (Article 151).
2. These are cases of which the outcome does not fit into any of the above categories (e.g. declared inadmissible or well-founded only in part).

Note: The types of proceeding covered by the Treaty articles are explained in the text of this book. Use also the Tables of Equivalences (at the back of the book) as appropriate.

Source: Commission (1998), p. 418.

Similarly, institutions sometimes appeal to the Court when they believe their prerogatives have been infringed during a legislative procedure. The EP has been very active in this regard, taking a number of cases to the Court, usually on the grounds that either it should have been consulted but was not, or that the Council changed the content of legislation after it left the EP and the EP was not reconsulted. In general, the Court has supported the EP in such cases.

Article 230 also allows any 'natural or legal person' (that is private individuals or companies) to institute proceedings for annulment. Rulings under this provision have tended to strengthen the hand of EU institutions and to serve as useful underpinnings to some EU policies, notably competition policy and commercial policy.

In certain policy spheres, notably competition, the Commission is empowered to impose financial penalties to ensure compliance with EU regulations. Under Article 229 of the TEC (ex 172), the regulations governing such policy spheres may allow unlimited jurisdiction to the Court with regard to the penalties. This means that aggrieved parties may appeal to the Court against Commission decisions and the penalties it has imposed. As such, this is another form of action for annulment. The Court may annul or confirm the decision and increase or decrease the penalties. In the great majority of judgements the Commission's decisions are upheld.

Failure to act

Under the three Community Treaties there are provisions for institutions to be taken before the Court for failure to act. These provisions vary in nature between the Treaties. Under the TEC, should the EP, the Council or the Commission fail to act on a matter provided for by the Treaty, the member states, the institutions of the Community and, in restricted circumstances, 'natural or legal persons', may initiate an action before the Court under Article 232 (ex 175) to have the infringement established. Such actions are not common, but one that attracted much attention was initiated by the EP, with the support of the Commission, against the Council in 1983. The case concerned the alleged failure of the Council to take action to establish a Common Transport Policy, despite the provision for such a policy in the EEC Treaty. The judgement, which was delivered in May 1985, was not what the EP or the Commission had hoped for. The Court ruled that whilst there was a duty for legislation to be produced, it had no power of enforcement because the Treaty did not set out a detailed timetable or an inventory for completion; it was incumbent upon the national governments to decide how best to proceed.

Failure to act cases are now usually dealt with by the Court of First Instance (see below).

Action to establish liability

'In the case of non-contractual liability, the Community shall, in accordance with the general principles common to the laws of the Member States, make good any damage caused by its institutions or by its servants in the performance of their duties' (Article 228, TEC, ex 215). Under Article 235 (ex 178) the Court has exclusive jurisdiction to decide whether the Community is liable and, if so, whether it is bound to provide compensation.

This means that the Community may have actions brought against it on the ground of it having committed an illegal act. The complex mechanisms of the CAP have produced by far the greatest number of such cases, threatening indeed to overwhelm the Court in the early 1970s. As a consequence the Court became increasingly unwilling to accept non-contractual liability cases, at least on the basis of first instance, and made it clear that they should be brought before national courts.

In the 1970s the Court also ruled that the circumstances in which the Community could incur non-contractual liability and be liable for damages were strictly limited. Of particular importance in this context were judgements in 1978 on two joined cases concerning skimmed milk (Cases 83 and 94/76, and 4, 15 and 40/77). Community legislation obliged the food industry to add skimmed milk to animal feed as part of an effort to reduce the surplus of powdered milk. A number of users challenged the legality of this on the ground that the Community's solution to the problem was discriminatory. In its first judgement the Court ruled that the powdered milk regulations were, indeed, invalid because they did not spread the burden fairly across the agricultural sector. In its second judgement, however, it ruled that only in exceptional and special circumstances, notably when a relevant body had manifestly and seriously exceeded its powers, should the Community be liable to pay damages when a legislative measure of a political and economic character was found to be invalid.

Like failure to act cases, action to establish liability cases are now usually referred to the Court of First Instance.

Reference for a preliminary ruling

The types of case referred to in the sections above are known as direct actions. That is, the Court is called upon to give a judgement in a dispute between two or more parties who bring their case directly before the Court. References for preliminary rulings are quite different, in that they do not involve the Court itself giving judgements in cases, but rather require it to give interpretations on points of EU law to enable national courts to make a ruling.

References are made under Article 234 of the TEC (ex 177), which states that national courts may, and in some circumstances must, ask the Court to give a preliminary ruling where questions arise on the interpretation of the Treaty or the validity and interpretation of acts of the institutions of the Community. The Court cannot make a pronouncement on a case that happens to have come to its attention unless a reference has been made to it by the appropriate national court, and parties to a dispute have no power to insist on a reference or to object to one being made. It is the exclusive prerogative of the national court to apply for a preliminary ruling. Once a reference has been made, the Court is obliged to respond, but it can only do so on questions that have been put to it and it may not pronounce on, or even directly attempt to influence the outcome of, the principal action. Interpretations made by the Court during the course of preliminary rulings must be accepted and applied by the national court that has made the referral.

Preliminary rulings constitute the largest category of cases that come before the Court. With only occasional dips, references have progressively increased: from one in 1961, to 32 in 1970, 106 in 1979, 194 in 1993, and 234 in 1997. Preliminary rulings serve three principal functions. First, they help to ensure that national courts make legally 'correct' judgements. Second, because they are generally accepted by all national courts as setting a precedent, they promote the uniform interpretation and application of EU law in the member states. Third, they provide a valuable source of access to the Court for private individuals and undertakings who cannot directly appeal to it, either because there is no legal provision or because of insufficient of funds. Exhibit 10.4 provides a summary outline of a preliminary ruling case.

Appeals

Under Article 225 of the TEC (ex 168a) all decisions of the Court of First Instance (see below) are subject to appeal to the ECJ.

Appeals cannot be made on the substance of a case, but only on points of law. There are three broad grounds for appeal: the CFI lacked jurisdiction, it breached procedural rules, or it infringed Community law. There are, on average, around 30 appeals each year, most of which fail.

Exhibit 10.4   A preliminary ruling case

Judgement of the Court of 14 May 1998 in Case C-364/96
Verin für Konsumenteninformation v Österreichische Kreditsversicherungs AG

The Court of Justice rules on the application of the Directive on package travel, package holidays and package tours to the case of two Austrian tourists forced to pay for their holiday twice over

Mr and Mrs Hofbauer had booked a holiday in Crete with an Austrian travel agency. They had paid the full cost of the package including the air tickets and their half-board accommodation before departure.

At the end of their holiday, the owner of the hotel demanded payment in full for their accommodation and even prevented them from leaving the premises until they had paid. The travel agency was insolvent and was no longer able to pay the hotelier.

Mr and Mrs Hofbauer were thus forced to pay for their accommodation a second time. When they returned and the travel agency's insurers refused to reimburse the money they had paid to the hotel, the consumer association brought an action on their behalf before the competent national court (the Bezirksgericht für Handelssachen Wien).

The association argued that Mr and Mrs Hofbauer were entitled to cover for 'the refund of money paid over' or for the expenditure necessary for 'the repatriation of the consumer' within the meaning of Council Directive 90/314/EEC of 13 June 1990 on package travel, package holidays and package tours and that the insurers were therefore liable to refund those sums of money if the travel organiser became insolvent.

The national court therefore requested the Court of Justice to rule on the question whether the Directive could be interpreted in that way.

The Court observed that the purpose of the Directive was to protect consumers against the risks stemming from the payment in advance of the price of a package holiday and from the spread of liability between the travel organiser and the various providers of the services which in combination make up the package.

Accordingly, it considered that the Directive was intended to cover the situation in which a hotelier forces a holidaymaker to pay for the accommodation provided, claiming that he will not be paid that sum by the insolvent travel organiser. The risk involved for the consumer who has purchased the package holiday derives from the travel organiser's insolvency.

The Court concluded that, since the consumer had actually paid the cost of the accommodation twice over, first to the travel organiser and then again to the hotelier, the insurer's obligation was to refund . . . money paid over. The holidaymaker having been accommodated at his own expense, the sums he paid to the travel organiser would have to be refunded to him since, following the organiser's insolvency, the services agreed upon were not supplied to him by the organiser.

Source: European Court of Justice, Press and Information Division, Press Release 34/98.

The seeking of an opinion

Under Article 300 of the TEC (ex 228) the Council, the Commission, or a member state may obtain the opinion of the Court on whether a prospective international agreement is compatible with the provisions of the Treaty. Where the opinion of the Court is adverse, the agreement cannot enter into force without being suitably amended or without the Treaty being amended.

An opinion that created considerable publicity and difficulties was issued in December 1991 when the Court, after considering – at the Commission's request – the Agreement between the Community and the EFTA countries to establish the European Economic Area, issued opinion 1/91 declaring that the judicial review arrangements envisaged by the Agreement were incompatible with the EEC Treaty. This necessitated further Community–EFTA negotiations and a further reference to the Court when revisions had been agreed. The revisions were subsequently approved by the Court and the Agreement was finally signed, several months later than had been anticipated, in May 1992.

An extremely important opinion was issued in 1994 in respect of external powers. The Commission took the case before the Court, arguing that Article 113 (now 133), which gives the Commission sole negotiating powers in respect of certain international commercial agreements, should extend to trade in services and trade-related aspects of intellectual property rights. The Court ruled (Opinion 1/94) that the Community and the member states shared competence to conclude such agreements and therefore the Commission did not have sole negotiating powers.

Membership and organisation of the Court

The Court consists of 15 judges – one from each member state. Each judge is appointed for a six-year term of office that may be, and frequently is, renewed. To ensure continuity, turnover is staggered in three-yearly cycles.

According to the Community Treaties, judges are to be appointed 'by common accord of the Governments of the Member States' from amongst persons 'whose independence is beyond doubt and who possess the qualifications required for appointment to the highest judicial offices in their respective countries or who are juriconsults of recognised competence'. In practice there is something of a gap, in spirit at least, between these treaty provisions and reality. First, because each state is permitted one nomination and this is automatically accepted. Second, because when making their choices governments have tended not to be overly worried about the judicial qualifications or experience of their nominations and have instead looked for a good background in professional activities and public service. There is no evidence of 'political' appointments being made, in the way that they are to the United States Supreme Court, but the fact is that soundness and safeness seem to be as important as judicial ability. At the time of initial appointment the typical judge is a legally qualified 'man of affairs' who has been involved with government in his native country in some way, but who has, at best, served in a judicial capacity for only a limited period.

The judges elect one of their number to be President of the Court for a term of three years. The President's principal function is to see to the overall direction of the work of the Court by, for example, assigning cases to the Court's chambers, appointing judge-*rapporteurs* to cases, and setting schedules for cases. The President is also empowered, upon application from a party, to order the suspension of Community measures and to order such interim measures as he deems appropriate.

Assisting the judges in the exercise of their tasks are nine advocates-general. The duty of advocates-general is 'acting with complete impartiality and independence, to make, in open court, reasoned submissions on cases brought before the Court of Justice' (Article 222, TEC, ex 166). This means that an advocate-general, on being assigned to a case, must make a thorough examination of all the issues involved in the case, take account of all relevant law, and then present his conclusions to the Court. The conclusions are likely to include observations on the key points in the case, an assessment of EU law touching on the case, and a proposed legal solution.

In principle, advocates-general are appointed on the same treaty terms and according to the same treaty criteria as the judges. In practice, since not all states can claim an advocate-general, appointments are more genuinely collective than is the case with judges – but only up to a point, since the larger states have usually been able to ensure that they have one post each. At the same time, the judicial experience of advocates-general tends to be even less than that of the judges; certainly few have ever served in a judicial capacity in their own states.

In addition to the judges and the advocates-general, each of whom is assisted by two legal secretaries, the Court employs a staff of around 750. Most of these are engaged either in administrative duties – such as registering and transmitting case documents – or in providing language services.

The increasing number of cases coming before the Court – in the 1960s there were around 50 in an average year, today there are between 400 and 500 – has made it impossible for everything to be dealt with in plenary session. There has therefore been an increasing tendency for cases to be assigned to one of the Court's six chambers. In general, a matter is referred to a chamber of three judges if it is based upon relatively straightforward facts, raises no substantial points of principle, or where the circumstances are covered by existing case law. Cases that involve complex findings of fact, or novel or important points of law, and do not require to be heard by the full Court, are assigned to a chamber of five judges.

Following amendments made by the Maastricht Treaty, the only circumstances in which the Court is required to sit in plenary session is 'when a Member State or a Community institution that is a party to the proceedings so requests' (Article 221, TEC, ex 165). In practice the Court sometimes also chooses to sit in plenary session when cases are deemed especially important. A quorum for the plenary Court is seven judges.

The procedure of the Court

The procedure of the Court of Justice involves both written and oral stages. The former are more important, with cases being conducted largely away from the public eye via the communication of documents between interested parties and Court officials. Not much happens in open court.

Without going into all the details and possible variations, direct action cases proceed broadly along the following lines.

- Relevant documentation and evidence is assembled. In complicated cases, involving for example the alleged existence of cartels, hundreds or even thousands of separate items of evidence may be collected. The Court, under the direction of a duly appointed judge-*rapporteur,* may have to take a very proactive role in gathering the information that it needs and in soliciting the views of interested parties. This may involve holding a preparatory inquiry at which oral and documentary evidence is presented. (In preliminary ruling cases the procedure is very different: the national court making the reference should have provided with its submission a summary of the case and of all relevant facts, a statement of the legal problem, and the – abstract – question it wishes the Court to answer.)
- A public hearing is held at which the essentials of the case are outlined, the various parties are permitted to present their views orally, and the judges and advocates-general may question the parties' lawyers.
- Following the public hearing, the advocate-general appointed to the case examines it in detail. He and his staff look at all relevant EU law and then come to a decision that they consider to be correct in legal

terms. A few weeks after the public hearing the advocate-general presents his submission to an open session of the Court.

- Acting on the advocate-general's submission, and on the basis of a draft drawn up by the judge-*rapporteur*, the Court prepares its decision. Deliberations are in secret and if there is disagreement the decision is made by majority vote. Judgements must be signed by all the judges who have taken part in the proceedings and no dissenting opinions may be published. (In their oath of office members swear to preserve the secrecy of the deliberation of the Court.)

Three problems associated with the Court's proceedings ought to be mentioned. First, there is a lengthy gap between cases being lodged at the Court and final decisions: on average, about eighteen months for preliminary rulings and over two years for direct actions. In special cases, however, interim judgements are issued and accelerated procedures are used. Second, lawyers' fees usually mean that going before the Court can be an expensive business, even though there is no charge for the actual proceedings in the Court itself. This does not, of course, place much of a restriction on the ability of member states or EU institutions to use the Court, but it can be a problem for individuals and small firms. There is a small legal aid fund, but it cannot remotely finance all potential applicants. Third, the use of majority voting, coupled with the lack of opportunity for dissenting opinions, has encouraged a tendency, which is perhaps inevitable given the different legal backgrounds of the judges, for judgements sometimes to be less than concise, and occasionally even to be fudged.

The Court of First Instance

Under the SEA the ECJ was given a means of dealing more expeditiously and more effectively with its constantly expanding workload: the Council was empowered to establish, at the request of the Court, a Court of First Instance. Such a request was quickly made and in 1988 the Court of First Instance (CFI) was established by Council Decision 88/591. The CFI began to function in November 1989.

The CFI is made up of one judge from each member state. The conditions of appointment and terms of office of the CFI judges are similar to those of the ECJ judges. Most of the work of the CFI is undertaken in one of five chambers, each with a membership of three to five judges.

Unlike in the ECJ, no advocates-general are appointed to the CFI. When the exercise of the function of advocate-general is seen as being necessary – which it is not in all cases – the task is undertaken by one of the judges; the judge so designated cannot take part in the judgement of the case.

The jurisdiction of the CFI was initially limited to three areas: disputes between the Community and its staff, actions brought against the Commission under the ECSC Treaty, and certain aspects of the competition rules. However, in 1993 the Council of Ministers (General Affairs) agreed to give the CFI jurisdiction to hear and determine at first instance all actions brought by natural or legal persons other than anti-dumping cases, upon which a decision was deferred; jurisdiction in anti-dumping cases was eventually agreed in February 1994. The 1993 extension of the CFI's jurisdiction did not extend to preliminary rulings.

The CFI does not deal with particularly sensitive cases or those directly involving national governments. It does, however, deal with most direct action cases involving private applicants. The work of the CFI is primarily taken up with two types of case: staff disputes (under Article 236 of the TEC, ex 179) and applications for annulment by private applicants (Article 230, TEC). Cases under the second of these include appeals by companies against Commission decisions to refuse to authorise subsidies and challenges to Commission decisions on abuse of dominant trading positions, restrictive practices, and company mergers. The very large number of 'action to establish liability' cases appearing in Table 10.3 is artificial since it is mainly composed of linked cases of an identical nature: the usual number of action to establish liability cases is between 15 and 20.

As noted above in the account of the work of the ECJ, all decisions of the CFI are subject to appeal to the Court of Justice on points of law.

Concluding comments

The legal framework described in the previous pages constitutes the single most important feature distinguishing the EU from other international organisations. The member states do not just cooperate with one another on an intergovernmental basis but have developed common laws designed to promote uniformity. The claim to legal supremacy in the interpretation, application and adjudication of these laws constitutes a central element of the supranational character of the EU.

This has necessarily involved the member states in surrendering some of their sovereignty, since they are obliged to submit to a legal system over which they have only partial control, and as a corollary their governments are sometimes prevented from introducing national laws they themselves desire.

Table 10.3 *Activities of the Court of First Instance in 1997: analysed by type (EC Treaty)*

	Proceedings brought under the following articles of the Treaty[1]						
	173 individuals	175 individuals	178 and 215	179	181	185 and 186	Total
Actions brought	125	9	327	152	2	15	630
Cases not resulting in a judgement	12	5	4	20	–	5	46
Cases decided	52	6	9	61	–	12	140
in favour of applicant	6	–	3	16	–	–	25
dismissed on the merits	18	1	4	33	–	11	67
rejected as inadmissible	25	5	2	12	–	1	45
other	3	–	–	–	–	–	3

1. ECSC: six actions brought (Article 33), one case decided in favour of applicant (Article 33), three dismissed on the merits (two Article 33 and one Article 39), three cases declared inadmissible (Article 33), one not resulting in a judgment (Article 33); Euratom: two actions dismissed on the merits (Article 146).
2. These are cases of which the outcome does not fit into any of the above categories (e.g. declared inadmissible or well-founded only in part).

Note: Types of proceeding covered by the Treaty articles are explained in the text of this book. Use also the Tables of Equivalences (at the back of the book) as appropriate.

Source: Commission (1998), p. 420.

The EU's Courts – primarily through ECJ judgements, but increasingly through CFI judgements too – have played, and continue to play, an extremely important part in establishing the EU's legal order. This is because between them they exercise three key legal roles (Lenaerts, 1991). First, there is the role of constitutional court – adjudicating, for example, inter-institutional disputes and disputes about the division of powers between EU institutions and member states. Second, there is the role of supreme court, as most obviously with preliminary rulings that have as their purpose the uniform interpretation and application of EU law. And third, there is the role of administrative court, as when the ECJ and the CFI are called upon by private parties to offer protection against illegal executive acts by EU institutions.

In exercising their responsibilities the Courts, and especially the ECJ, sometimes not only interpret law but also make it. Of course judges everywhere help to shape the law, but this is especially so in the EU where the Courts have much more manoeuvrability available to them than is customary within states. They have used this to considerable effect: to help clarify relations between the institutions and between the institutions and the member states; to help clarify and extend policy content in many different spheres; and to help develop and foster the *esprit communautaire*.

Chapter 11

Other Institutions and Actors

The Economic and Social Committee
The Committee of the Regions
The European Investment Bank
The European System of Central Banks
The Court of Auditors
Interests

The Economic and Social Committee

Origins

In the negotiations that led to the Rome Treaties it was decided to establish a consultative body composed of representatives of socio-economic interests.

There were four principal reasons for this decision. First, five of the six founding states – West Germany was the exception – had such bodies in their own national systems. The main role of these bodies was to provide a forum in which sectional interests could express their views, and in so doing could supplement the popular will as expressed via parliaments. Second, the essentially economic nature of the Community meant that sectional interests would be directly affected by policy developments and would be key participants in, and determiners of, the development of integration. Third, it was not thought that the Assembly (as the EP was then called) would be an effective forum for the expression of sectional views. Fourth, the institutional framework of the Rome Treaties was based on the Treaty of Paris model, and that had provided for a socio-economic advisory body in the ECSC Consultative Committee.

Accordingly, the EEC and Euratom Treaties provided for a common Economic and Social Committee (ESC). It was to have an advisory role and it was to be made up of representatives of various types of economic and social activity.

Membership

The ESC has 222 members. These are drawn from the member states as follows:

Austria	12	Italy	24
Belgium	12	Luxembourg	6
Denmark	9	Netherlands	12
Finland	9	Portugal	12
France	24	Spain	21
Germany	24	Sweden	12
Greece	12	United Kingdom	24
Ireland	9		

The members of the ESC are proposed by national governments and are formally appointed by the Council of Ministers. The term of office is four years, which may be renewed.

To ensure that a broad spectrum of interests and views is represented, the membership is divided into three groups that are more or less equal in size. Each national complement of members is supposed to reflect this tripartite division. The three groups are as follows:

- *Group I: Employers.* Just less than half of this group are drawn from industry. The rest are mostly from public enterprises, commercial organisations, banks, insurance etc.
- *Group II: Workers.* The great majority in this group are members of national trade unions.
- *Group III: Various interests.* About half of this group are associated with either agriculture, small and medium-sized businesses, or the professions. The rest are mostly involved with public agencies and local authorities, consumer groups, environmental protection organisations and so on.

All members are appointed in a personal capacity and not as delegates of organisations. However, since most members are closely associated with or are employees of national interest organisations (organisations that in many cases are affiliated to Euro-organisations) it is inevitable that they do tend to act as representatives of, and be spokesmen for, a cause.

The administrative support for the ESC is organised by its Secretariat General. Just over 130 staff work exclusively for the ESC and around 520 work in departments that are shared with the Committee of the Regions (see below).

Organisation

Every two years the ESC elects a President, two Vice Presidents, and a Bureau from amongst its members. The Presidency rotates amongst the three groups, with the two groups that do not occupy the Presidency each assuming a Vice Presidency. There are 27 members of the Bureau: the President, the two Vice Presidents, and 24 members drawn from the three groups in equal proportion.

The main role of the President is to see to the orderly conduct of the ESC's business and to represent the ESC in its relations with other EU institutions, member states, and outside bodies. The Vice Presidents assist him or her in these tasks. The main tasks of the Bureau are to provide guidelines for the ESC's work, to coordinate that work, and to assist with external representation.

The groups operate in a somewhat similar fashion to the political groups in the EP. That is to say, they meet on a regular basis – there are about 90 group meetings per year – to review matters of common concern, to discuss ongoing ESC work, and (particularly in the more cohesive groups I and II) to attempt to agree voting positions on proposals and issues that are due to be considered in plenary sessions. Group representatives in sections and study groups (see below) also sometimes meet together to coordinate their activities.

Most of the work of the ESC consists of giving opinions on EU-related matters. In a manner similar to the way in which the detailed work on opinions in the EP is undertaken by committees, so in the ESC it is undertaken by sections, each of which draws its membership from the groups. There are six sections:

- Agriculture, Rural Development and the Regions
- Economic and Monetary Union and Economic and Social Cohesion
- Employment, Social Affairs and Citizenship
- External Relations
- The Single Market, Production and Consumption
- Transport, Energy, Infrastructure and the Information Society

The sections appoint *rapporteurs* to prepare draft opinions on their behalf. How *rapporteurs* go about this depends on circumstances and preferences. Usually use is made of a sub-committee or study group; assistance may be called for from the ESC Secretariat, though resources for this purpose are thin; and – a common occurrence – help may be sought from, or be offered by, Euro or national sectional interests. In the sections attempts are usually made to develop common positions on opinions, though on controversial issues this is not always possible to achieve. In an average year there are usually around 70–80 section meetings and some 300 meetings of sub-committees and study groups. (In addition, there are 300–400 miscellaneous meetings and meetings sponsored by the three groups. Many of these are concerned in some way with the preparation of opinions.)

Plenary meetings are held in Brussels, over a two-day period, about nine or ten times a year. Agendas are dominated by consideration of reports from the sections. The standard procedure for dealing with reports is for each to be introduced by its *rapporteur*, for a debate to be held, and for a vote to be taken. On uncontroversial items the vote may be taken without discussion or debate.

Functions

The ESC engages in a number of activities:

(1) It issues information reports on matters of contemporary interest and concern.
(2) It liaises, via delegations, with a host of other international bodies and groupings.
(3) It seeks to promote understanding between sectional interests by, for example, organising conferences, convening meetings, and being represented at congresses and symposia.
(4) It seeks to take advantage of various contacts it has with other EU institutions to press its views. The most regularised of these contacts is with the Commission: Commission officials, and sometimes Commissioners themselves, attend plenaries and meetings of sections. Occasionally ministers address plenaries.
(5) Above all, as noted above, it issues opinions on a range of EU matters. Opinions are issued in one of three sets of circumstances:

- *Mandatory referral.* Under Article 262 of the TEC (ex 198) and Article 170 of the Euratom Treaty 'The Committee must be consulted by the Council or by the Commission where this Treaty so provides.' Compared with the EP there are fewer policy areas where the Treaties do so provide, but extensions made by the SEA, the Maastricht Treaty and the Amsterdam Treaty have resulted in most important policy areas now being subject to ESC mandatory referral. So, under the TEC, amongst the policy spheres upon which the ESC must be consulted are agriculture, freedom of movement of workers, internal market issues, economic and social cohesion, social policy and the European Social Fund (ESF), regional policy and the European Regional Development

Fund (ERDF), the environment, and research and technological development. Under the Euratom Treaty the ESC has to be consulted on such matters as research and training programmes, health and safety, and investment.

- *Optional consultation.* The ESC may be consulted by the Council or the Commission 'in all cases in which they consider it appropriate' (Article 262, TEC; Article 170, Euratom Treaty). Until the entry into force of the SEA some 80 per cent of ESC opinions were based on optional consultation. With the widening of the scope of mandatory referral this figure has fallen to around 60 per cent.

- *Own initiatives.* The ESC has the right to issue opinions on its own initiative. Thus, in theory it can pronounce on almost any matter it wishes, other than those which fall under the ECSC.

The reason for the exclusion of the ESC from ECSC matters is because, as noted above, the ECSC has a separate Consultative Committee. With 96 members – divided into three equal groups of producers, workers, consumers and dealers – the Consultative Committee performs similar functions for the ECSC as does the ESC for the EC and Euratom. The Consultative Committee meets about six times a year.

The ESC normally issues 150–200 consultative documents per year, of which the vast majority are opinions on Commission proposals and communications, 20–30 are own initiative opinions, and 3–4 are information reports. So, for example, in 1997 the ESC adopted 179 opinions and 3 information reports. Of the 179 opinions, 63 were on mandatory referral, 89 were optional consultations, and 27 were own initiatives (Commission, 1998, p. 436).

The sorts of opinions issued by the ESC may be illustrated by citing a few of those approved in just one plenary session, that held on 9–10 September 1998: noise emission by equipment used outdoors; the harmonisation of certain aspects of copyright and related rights; interior fittings of motor vehicles; reform of the Structural Funds; resistance to antibiotics as a threat to public health (own initiative); and the impact of the introduction of the euro on the single market (produced by the Single Market Observatory, which is part of the ESC, as an own initiative).

A point of contrast worth noting between ESC and EP opinions is that the ESC is not as concerned as the EP to reach a single position that excludes all minority views. It is quite possible for minority positions to be attached as annexes to ESC opinions that have received majority support in the plenary.

Influence

The influence exercised by the ESC on EU policy and decision-making is limited. Evidence of this is provided, for example, by the Commission's follow-up reports to ESC opinions: these rarely constitute unambiguous acceptance of ESC recommendations and include many evasive comments along the lines of 'The Commission has taken note of the ESC opinion' or 'The opinion will be useful to the Commission staff in their exchanges of views with the Council'. Such ESC recommendations as are taken up usually cover relatively minor points, and are often as much a consequence of pressure exerted by other institutions and interests as by ESC pronouncements (this point is discussed further in Chapter 13).

There are a number of reasons why the ESC has only limited power. First, the Council and the Commission are not obliged to act upon its views. Of course, this also applies to the EP outside the co-decision procedure, but in its case even when co-decision does not apply it *has* to be consulted on *most* important proposals, its opinion *must* be delivered before proposals can be given legislative effect, and delaying powers are available to strengthen its bargaining position. The ESC is not so well placed: the range of issues upon which consultation is mandatory is more restricted; the deliverance of its opinion is often therefore not necessary for further progress; and even when its opinion is required it can be made subject to a timetable that is so tight as not to allow sufficient time for a considered response – the Council and the Commission can, if they consider it necessary, set a time limit as short as one month for the submission of an ESC opinion.

The second weakness follows on from this last point: it is by no means uncommon for proposals to be referred to the ESC at a stage of policy advancement when agreements between the key decision-makers have already been made in principle and are difficult to unscramble.

Third, the ESC is not the only, and in many circumstances is not even the most important, channel available to sectional interests wishing to exert pressure on EU decision-makers. Direct access to Council representatives and Commission officials, and representation in advisory committees, is seen by many as being more useful than activity in the ESC – not least because these other channels often offer greater opportunities than does the ESC for influencing policy proposals at the pre-proposal stage.

Finally, the members of the ESC serve only on a part-time basis and are therefore very limited in what they can do. In addition, the fact that they serve – in theory at least – in a personal rather than a representational capacity means that there are rarely strong reasons for the Commission or the Council to listen to them if they do not wish to do so.

*   *   *

The ESC is perhaps best thought of as a functional complement to the EP. It should not, however, be thought of as in any way comparable to the EP, for it simply does not have anything like the same capacity, status, influence or power.

The ESC basically does two things. First, it provides a useful forum in which representatives of sectional interests can come together on a largely cooperative basis to exchange views and ideas. Second, it is a consultative organ that provides some limited – though in most cases very limited – opportunities for interests to influence EU policy and decision-making.

The Committee of the Regions

Origins

Regionalism, regional issues and regional politics have come to assume a not insignificant role and importance in the EU. The main factors accounting for this are as follows:

- There are considerable variations in wealth and income between member states and between regions in the member states. In the late 1990s the ten most prosperous regions, headed by Groningen in the Netherlands and Hamburg in Germany, were three times richer and invested three times more in their basic economic fabric than the ten poorest regions in Greece and Portugal. Such disparities have long produced calls for compensatory and rectifying measures to be taken at EU level, and these calls have increased since the SEM programme was launched in the mid 1980s.
- Since the ERDF was established in 1975, regional and local groupings have had a clear focus for their attention at EU level: the attraction of funds. The Commission has encouraged subnational levels of government to play a full part in ERDF management, especially since the launching of its partnership programme under the 1988 reform of the Structural Funds.
- Partly as a consequence of the financial opportunities offered by the ERDF and other funds, but partly too because they do not wish to be wholly controlled by their national governments, many subnational levels of government have established direct lines of communication with decision-makers in Brussels. In those states where subnational governments have strong constitutional positions – most obviously Germany because of its quasi-federal system – it is customary for the regional governments to have their own offices in Brussels.

- Over the years several transnational organisations that bring together the subnational governments of different member states have been established to promote common interests and, where appropriate, to make representations and exert pressure at the EU level. These organisations include the Association of European Border Regions, the Assembly of European Regions, the Association of Regions of Traditional Industry and the Association of Frontier Regions.

In response to this developing regional dimension of Community affairs, in 1988 the Commission established the Consultative Council of Regional and Local Authorities. For some governments, notably the German and Belgian, the Consultative Council did not go far enough and they took advantage of the 1990–1 IGC on Political Union to press the case for a stronger body to be established. Differing views were expressed in the IGC – with France, Spain and the UK putting up some resistance to the creation of a new body – but it was eventually agreed to establish, as part of the EU, a Committee of the Regions (CoR).

Membership, organisation, functions and powers

The size and national composition of the *membership* of the CoR is the same as that of the ESC: a total of 222 members, with the 'big four' states each having 24 members, Spain 21, Austria, Belgium, Greece, the Netherlands, Portugal and Sweden 12 each, Denmark, Finland and Ireland 9 each, and Luxembourg 6. The members are appointed for a renewable four-year term of office by the Council of Ministers on the basis of proposals from the member states.

As to the qualities and characteristics of the CoR's members, the TEC simply states the Committee shall consist of 'representatives of regional and local bodies' (Article 263, ex 198a). The implications of the lack of insistence in the Treaty that members should be *elected* representatives of regional and local bodies led to considerable debate in some member states when theCoR was founded, but in the event virtually all of those nominated to the CoR have been elected representatives of subnational levels of government of some kind. Those countries with clear regional structures – Belgium, France, Germany, Italy, the Netherlands and Spain – have allocated at least half of their places to regional representatives. The more centralised countries have mostly sent representatives from local councils and authorities.

*   *   *

The *organisational structure* of the CoR is similar to that of the ESC. The planning and overseeing of the work of the Committee is undertaken by its Bureau, which consists of a President, a first Vice President, and 34 other members. The members of the Bureau are elected for a two-year term, on the basis of three members from each of the larger states and two from each of the smaller states.

Most of the work of the CoR is channelled through eight specialised commissions and four sub-commissions:

- Commission 1: Regional Development, Economic Development, Local and Regional Finance.
  Sub-Commission 1: Local and Regional Finance.
- Commission 2: Spatial Planning, Agriculture, Hunting, Fisheries, Forestry, Marine Environment and Upland Areas.
  Sub-Commission 2: Tourism and Rural Areas.
- Commission 3: Transport and Communications Networks.
  Sub-Commission 3: Telecommunications.
- Commission 4: Urban Policies.
- Commission 5: Land-use Planning, Environment and Energy.
- Commission 6: Education and Training.
- Commission 7: Citizens' Europe, Research, Culture, Youth and Consumers.
  Sub-Commission 7: Youth and Sport.
- Commission 8: Economic and Social Cohesion, Social Policy and Public Health.

The commissions report to CoR plenary sessions, of which there are normally five each year.

The CoR's administrative support is organised by its Secretariat General. Much of the routine work (translation, informational technology, printing) is undertaken by services shared with the ESC.

The *functions and powers* of the CoR are, like those of the ESC, of an advisory nature. The key Treaty references to what the CoR can do are set out in Article 265 of the TEC (ex 198c):

The Committee of the Regions shall be consulted by the Council or by the Commission where this Treaty so provides and in all other cases, in particular those which concern cross-border cooperation, in which one of these two institutions considers it appropriate. . .

> Where the Economic and Social Committee is consulted . . . the Committee of the Regions shall be informed by the Council or the Commission of the request for an opinion. Where it considers that specific regional interests are involved, the Committee of the Regions may issue an opinion on the matter.
>
> The Committee of the Regions may be consulted by the European Parliament.
>
> It may issue an opinion on its own initiative in cases in which it considers such action appropriate.

The Maastricht Treaty provided for the CoR to be consulted about education, training and youth; economic and social cohesion, including the Structural Funds; trans-European transport networks and energy infra-structure networks; public health; and culture. The Amsterdam Treaty provided for some extensions to this list, most notably to transport policy, EU enlargement, combating social exclusion, the environment, and, in Article 265 itself (see above), cross-border cooperation.

As they can with the ESC, the Council or the Commission can set a time limit on the CoR for the delivery of its opinion, which can be as little as one month. Upon expiry of the time limit, the absence of an opinion cannot prevent the Council or the Commission from proceeding.

An indication of the volume of work undertaken by the CoR is its adoption in 1997 of 66 opinions. Amongst the opinions it gave in response to requests from the Council and/or the Commission were ones on maritime strategy, progress made in economic and social cohesion, structural policy after 1999, and renewable energy sources. Issues covered in own-initiative opinions included the Euro-Mediterranean partnership, rural development, and spatial planning. Not surprisingly, a common theme running through many CoR opinions is that subnational levels of government should play an important role in the identification, manage-ment, and evaluation of EU policies that affect them.

Within the spheres of its competence, and especially where mandatory consultation applies, the influence of the CoR appears to be at least comparable to that of the ESC. Like the ESC it is weakened by the fact that its 'clients' – subnational authorities in its case – also have other channels of political influence to utilise, including the Council of Ministers itself in those cases where the national governments of countries with strong regional governmental structures allow regional representatives to partici-pate in their 'delegations' on some issues. The CoR is strengthened, however, in that many of it's members are experienced politicians at regional and local levels and press hard to ensure that the Committee is not confined to the role of a marginal sounding board, which is what some governments would like.

The European Investment Bank

The European Investment Bank (EIB) was created in 1958 under the EEC Treaty. Its members are the member states of the EU. The Bank is located in Luxembourg.

Responsibilities and functions

The responsibilities and functions of the EIB are referred to in several articles of the TEC. Article 267 (ex 198e) is especially important: it sets out the task of the EIB as being to contribute, on a non-profit making basis, via the granting of loans and the giving of guarantees, to the 'balanced and steady development of the common market in the interests of the Community'. What this means in practice is that the Bank's main job is to act as a source of investment finance for projects that further certain EU goals. In so doing, it is by far the largest provider of EU loan finance. In 1998 EIB lending totalled 29.5 billion ecu. Around 90 per cent of EIB loans are for projects within the member states and the remainder for projects outside. The latter mainly involves the Bank in operations in Central and Eastern Europe, the Mediterranean countries, and the ACP states which are linked to the EU via the Lomé Convention.

With regard to the loans made within the EU, two main conditions have to be satisfied for the EIB to consider providing finance. First, projects must comply with the policy objectives laid down in Article 267 and with credit directives from the Bank's Board of Governors. These objectives are interpreted fairly broadly but at least one of the following criteria normally has to be met:

(1) Projects must further economic and social cohesion by contributing to the economic development of the EU's less prosperous regions. Around two-thirds of loans are used for regional development purposes and to help the EU's poorest areas. This finance is used primarily to assist with communications and other infrastructure, the productive sector, and capital spending on energy installations.

(2) Projects must involve modernisation and must contribute to the competitiveness of EU industry. Under this heading, particular support is given to the introduction and development of advanced technology, and to the integration of industry at the European level.

(3) Projects must be of common interest to several member states or to the EU as a whole. In this connection, major transport and telecommunications developments and the EU's energy objectives are given a high priority. The EU's environmental policies also receive considerable support, with around half of the 'environmental loans' being made to

the water sector (catchment, treatment and supply) and the rest going to projects dealing with such problems as atmospheric pollution, waste management, land conservation, and urban improvement.

Second, projects must be financially and technically viable, and loans must be guaranteed by adequate security. This is because although the EIB is not a profit-making body it is not a loss-making one either: apart from in certain specified and strictly limited circumstances, the Bank's loans are not subsidised from the EU budget but must be financed from its own capital. This capital comes from two sources: paid in or due to be paid in capital by the member states, and borrowing – in the EIB's own name and on its own credit – on capital markets inside and outside the EU. Of these two sources, borrowing is by far the largest element, and since the sums raised must be repaid from the Bank's own financial operations it must take appropriate steps to protect itself.

A major attraction for potential EIB borrowers is that loans are offered at very competitive rates. They are so because the Bank enjoys a first class international credit rating and is thus itself able to borrow at favourable rates, and also because the Bank is not profit-making and is thus able to pass on its favourable rates. Other advantages of EIB loans are that they are generally made available at fixed interest rates, repayments can often be deferred for the first two or three years, and the repayment periods are usually medium to long term (between five and twelve years for industrial projects and up to twenty years or more for infrastructure projects).

Two other features of EIB loans are also worth noting. First, the Bank does not usually lend more than 50 per cent of the investment cost of a project unless it is part of a special programme. Borrowers need to find additional sources of loan finance, with the consequence that the Bank very frequently operates on a co-financing basis with other banks. Second, the Bank generally only deals directly with large loans – of more than about 10 million euro. This does not however mean that only large-scale investment is supported because, mainly via its global loan facility, the Bank opens lines of credit to intermediary institutions – such as regional development agencies and, more commonly, national financial institutions – which lend on the money in smaller amounts. Global loans account for around 25 per cent of total EIB lending and are directed principally towards small and medium-sized enterprises (SMEs). An administrative problem with global loans is that the intermediary agencies that act on the EIB's behalf and are delegated responsibility for appraising applications and negotiating with potential borrowers on the basis of the EIB's lending criteria, tend sometimes to make their decisions according to traditional banking criteria and with little eye to EU objectives.

*   *   *

In addition to the activities just described – which may be thought of as the Bank's 'standard' activities – certain other activities are undertaken, including the following:

- The Commission also borrows funds on capital markets in connection with certain ECSC and Euratom activities. The Commission decides on the granting of loans, and the EIB is responsible for financial appraisal and management.
- Some projects are eligible for both EIB loan finance and EU grant aid. When this is the case – and it applies mainly in connection with the European Regional Development Fund (ERDF) and the Cohesion Fund – the Bank works closely with other interested parties, especially the Commission, to work out appropriate financial arrangements.
- The December 1992 Edinburgh European Council laid the foundations for a European Investment Fund (EIF), whose purpose was to be the provision of guarantees for loans to finance projects of common European interest and projects promoted by SMEs. By the end of 1998 the EIF's signed guarantee operations totalled 2.6 billion ecu, of which nearly 67 per cent was for infrastructure projects (mainly trans-European networks) and 33 per cent for operations involving SMEs. The Fund's subscribed capital is drawn from three sources: 40 per cent is provided by the EIB, 30 per cent by other EU sources (channelled through the Commission), and 30 per cent by public and private banks. The EIF has its own administrative and decision-making structure within the EIB.
- As part of a resolution it adopted on growth and employment at its June 1997 Amsterdam meeting, the European Council urged the EIB 'to step up its activities' in 'creating employment through investment opportunities in Europe' (European Council, 1997a, p. 12). The European Council particularly wished to see the promotion of investment projects in three areas: high-technology projects by SMEs; education, health, the urban environment, and environmental protection; and large infrastructure projects. To give effect to the resolution, the EIB quickly established a special action programme, with new financing and new financial instruments in the three specified areas.

Organisation

The EIB's main decision-making bodies are as follows:

The *Board of Governors* decides on the Bank's subscribed capital and lays down general directives on the Bank's activities. It is also responsible for formally appointing the members of the Board of Directors and the Management Committee. The Board of Governors is composed of one minister per member state – usually the Minister of Finance – and normally meets once a year. Certain major Board decisions have to be made unanimously, whilst others can be made by a majority of members representing at least 45 per cent of subscribed capital.

The *Board of Directors* has general responsibility for ensuring that the Bank is managed according to the provisions of the TEC, the Bank's Statute, and directives issued by the Governors. More specifically, the Board has sole responsibility for deciding on loans and guarantees, raising funds, and fixing interest rates. There are 25 Directors: 24 are nominated by the member states and are senior figures in national financial institutions or national Ministries of Finance/Economics/Industry; one is nominated by the Commission. The Board of Directors normally meets every four to six weeks.

The *Management Committee* controls current operations, makes recommendations to the Board of Directors and is responsible for implementing decisions made by the Directors. The Committee is a full-time body consisting of the Bank's President and seven Vice-Presidents. It meets at least weekly.

Supporting, and operating under, these decision-making bodies is the EIB's administration. This is divided into seven Directorates: General Administration; Operations in the Community 1; Operations in the Community 2; Operations Outside the Community; Finance and Treasury; Research; and Legal. There is also a Technical Advisory Service. In all, the EIB employs around 850 staff.

Concluding comments

The EIB is a bank, not a grant-dispensing body. This means that it must observe certain basic banking principles. At the same time, however, it is an EU institution charged with furthering a number of policy objectives. These two roles – banker and EU institution – do not always sit easily together.

The scale of EIB borrowing and lending is small when compared with the total operations of commercial banks across the member states. The role of the Bank should not, however, be underestimated. Indeed, it is the largest international financial institution on capital markets, and within the EU it is an important source of finance for capital investment. Between

1994 and 1998 it signed contracts to lend 105 billion ecu for projects in member states. In 1998 alone, EIB financing within the EU helped to support, on the basis of an average 30 per cent coverage of total costs, overall investment estimated at 83 billion ecu, which corresponds to about 5 per cent of aggregate gross fixed capital formation. This percentage was naturally much higher in those lower-income countries and regions where EIB loans are concentrated – Portugal, Greece, Spain, Ireland, and southern Italy.

The EIB thus acts as a useful source of medium- and long-term finance for EU-oriented projects. It complements other public and private funding resources for the promotion of capital investment projects that, in general terms, promote economic development and further integration within the EU.

The European System of Central Banks

The operating context

As the EU moved forward during the 1990s with the construction of Economic and Monetary Union (EMU), an institutional structure was created to manage it. The nature of what the structure should be was extensively debated, with two issues particularly strongly contested. First, given that the single currency – which the December 1995 Madrid European Council meeting decided would be called the euro – would require common monetary policies, what should the balance be between politicians and bankers in the determination of those policies? Second, given that the single currency would require some harmonisation of macroeconomic policies – though the extent of this was disputed – should harmonisation and other EMU-related policy issues be considered and determined by the representatives of all EU governments or only by the representatives of single currency members?

The first of these questions was agreed by all national governments from an early stage: it was specified in the Maastricht Treaty that bankers should be responsible for the day-to-day management of common monetary policies. However, it was also agreed – much more enthusiastically by some than by others – that in exercising their management role the bankers should not have a completely free hand: they should be subject, albeit at a general level, to some political direction and accountability.

On the second question, agreement was difficult to reach. Those countries that were not to be part of the first wave of the single currency – Denmark, Greece, Sweden, and the UK – were concerned that they might be excluded from important decision-making forums. The UK in particular pressed the view that single currency members should not create forums from which non members were excluded. The impasse was only resolved by a fudged deal in which it was agreed that the single currency ministers would sometimes meet as a group, but their gatherings would be for the purpose of consultation and cooperation rather than decision-making.

As a result of these debates and agreements, the principal components of the EMU institutional structure are as follows.

- *The Ecofin Council of Ministers*. Composed of national Ministers of Finance from all EU member states, the Ecofin Council (whose position in the Council structure was explained in Chapter 7) is responsible for the broad outlines of EU macroeconomic policy. The Ecofin Council also has a number of specific EMU-related responsibilities, including deciding upon whether to take action against euro zone states with excessive government deficits and deciding on a range of issues in connection with external monetary and foreign exchange matters.
- *The Euro 11 'Council'*. Composed of Ministers of Finance from single currency member states only, the role of the Euro II 'Council' is not clearly defined. The UK government – which as a non euro state is not a Euro 11 member – has been concerned that it might develop into a sort of pre-Ecofin Council, whilst the French government has sometimes indicated that it would like Euro 11 to be a political counterweight to the European Central Bank. In all probability it will develop into a forum in which euro zone issues – including most particularly the external representation of the zone – are considered and, in some circumstances, decided.
- *The European Central Bank* (ECB). The ECB, whose tasks and structure are examined in detail below, operates within the framework of the *European System of Central Banks* (ESCB). The ESCB is composed of the ECB and the EU national central banks (NCBs). NCBs of the member states that are not part of the euro area have a separate status within the ESCB: because they continue to have their own national monetary policies, they do not take part in decision-making on the single monetary policy of the euro area.
- Other EU institutions and actors with significant EMU-related responsibilities are:
  - The *European Council*, which is obliged to discuss, under Article 99 of the TEC, 'a conclusion of the broad guidelines of the economic policies of the Member States and of the Community', and in practice can consider anything else that it wishes.
  - The *Commission*, which is responsible for monitoring and producing reports on national economic, and especially budgetary perfor- mances, and for making recommendations to the Council when states

are deemed to be in breach of their Treaty and Stability and Growth Pact requirements (see Chapter 4).
- The *Economic and Financial Committee*, whose remit includes financial policy, capital movements, and international monetary relations (see Chapter 7 for the membership of the Committee).
- The *European Parliament*, which has few powers in relation to EMU, but does have a range of consultation and information-receiving rights.

Objectives and tasks

Article 105 (TEC) states that

> The primary objective of the ESCB shall be to maintain price stability. Without prejudice to the objective of price stability, the ESCB shall support the general economic policies in the Community with a view to contributing to the achievement of the objectives of the Community as laid down in Article 2 [of the TEC].

These two sentences of Article 105 contain the seeds of possible future disputes over ESCB policies, since Article 2 identifies Community tasks as including 'a high level of employment and of social protection' and 'economic and social cohesion and solidarity among Member States': tasks that in some circumstances might be seen as not sitting easily alongside policies aimed at ensuring low inflation. It is not difficult to imagine politicians seeking to exert pressure on ESCB decision-makers to give greater priority to employment promotion and cohesion objectives than to the maintenance of low inflation. However, ESCB decision-makers are given a certain amount of protection in that the Treaty emphasises that the ESCB must be independent. When performing ESCB-related tasks 'neither the ECB, nor a central bank, nor any member of their decision-making bodies shall seek or take instructions from Community institutions or bankers, from any government of a Member State or from any other body' (Article 108, TEC, ex 107).

Article 105 also states that the basic tasks to be carried out through the ESCB are 'to define and implement the monetary policy of the Community', 'to conduct foreign exchange operations', 'to hold and manage the official foreign reserves of the member states' and 'to promote the smooth operation of payment systems'. In addition, the ESCB is charged with providing advice to the Community and national authorities on matters that fall within its competence, especially where legislation is envisaged, and contributing to the smooth conduct of policies pursued by the competent authorities relating to the prudent supervision of financial institutions.

The ECB's capital (5 billion euro) and foreign reserve assets (50 billion euro) are drawn from the NCBs of euro zone states, according to criteria based on the size of GDP and population.

Organisational structure

'The ESCB shall be governed by the decision-making bodies of the ECB which shall be the Governing Council and the Executive Board' (Article 107, TEC, ex Article 106).

The Governing Council

The main responsibilities of the ECB Governing Council are:

- To adopt guidelines and make the necessary decisions to ensure the performance of the tasks entrusted to the ESCB.
- To formulate the Community's monetary policy, including, as appropriate, decisions relating to intermediate monetary objectives, key interest rates and the supply of ESCB reserves, and to establish the necessary guidelines for their implementation (European Central Bank, 1999).

The Governing Council is made up of the members of the Executive Board and the governors of euro member NCBs. The President of the Council and a member of the Commission may attend Governing Council meetings, but do not have the right to vote.

The Executive Board

The main responsibilities of the ECB Executive Board are:

- To implement monetary policy in accordance with the guidelines and decisions laid down by the Governing Council, and in so doing to give the necessary instructions to the national central banks.
- To execute such policies as have been delegated to it by the Governing Council (European Central Bank, 1999).

The Executive Board consists of the ECB President, Vice-President, and four other members. They are appointed 'from among persons of recognised standing and professional experience in monetary or banking matters by common accord of the governments of the Member States at the level of Heads of State or Government, on a recommendation from the Council, after it has consulted the European Parliament and the Governing Council of the ECB' (Article 112, TEC, ex 109a). The term of office is a non-renewable eight years.

As was shown in Chapter 8, the appointment of the first Executive Board, and more especially of the first President, became highly politicised, with France pressing for the appointment of its candidate, Claude Trichet, as President, rather than the Dutchman, Wim Duisenberg, who was favoured by other states. The impasse was only resolved by what most participants regarded as a very unsatisfactory informal understanding in which Duisenberg agreed to step down well before his eight-year term expires, at which point he will be replaced by Trichet.

In addition to its Governing Council and Executive Board, the ECB also has a General Council. Its membership comprises the ECB President and Vice-President and the governors of all the NCBs (that is, from both euro and non euro zone states). The four other members of the ECB Executive Board may participate in Governing Council meetings, but do not have the right to vote.

The Governing Council has a number of tasks to perform, including supervision of the functioning of the post single currency Exchange Rate Mechanism, considering the monetary and exchange rate policies of the member states that are not in the euro zone, and undertaking various advisory, administrative, and technical duties.

The governing bodies of the ECB are supported by an ECB staff complement of around 550 employees.

Concluding comments

The ESCB is an extremely important component of the EMU enterprise. Its decisions and performance will do much to determine whether or not EMU is a success. The ESCB will thus be closely watched in the years to come, by EU participants and observers alike.

But there is also another reason why the ESCB will be closely watched, and doubtless much discussed too: some important EU actors are not happy about aspects of the powers and structures of the ESCB. Matters about which there is unease include: should bankers have so much power?; given that the bankers have been given considerable power, should they not be made to be more accountable?; and are decision-making arrangements sufficiently clear in respect of when an issue is or is not a euro zone only issue?

The Court of Auditors

The 1975 *Treaty Amending Certain Financial Provisions of the Treaties . . .,* which entered into force in 1977, replaced the then two existing Community audit bodies – the Audit Board of the EEC and Euratom and the ECSC Auditor – with a single Court of Auditors. The Maastricht Treaty enhanced the Court of Auditors' standing by raising it to the rank of a fully fledged Community institution. The Court is based in Luxembourg.

Membership and organisation

There are as many members of the Court of Auditors as there are EU states. Each member is appointed by a unanimous vote by the Council of Ministers on the basis of one nomination per member state after consultations with the EP. As with Commissioners-designate, the EP uses its right of consultation to hold hearings with nominees: before the Budgetary Control Committee.

At its November 1989 part-session, the EP voted, for the first time, to reject nominations – one made by France and one by Greece. The EP vote was not binding on the Council, but France nonetheless submitted a new name. Greece claimed difficulty in finding a suitable alternative candidate, so at the following December part-session the EP decided to accept both appointments so that the two posts could be filled by the new year. The EP hoped that this episode established its right to veto any nominee whom it considered to be unsuitable, but this proved not to be the case for in 1993 the Council confirmed the appointment of two candidates about whom the EP had expressed reservations. As Westlake (1998, p. 433) notes, the Council might have been more prepared to be influenced by the EP's views if the media had taken any interest in the matter.

At the time of their appointment, members of the Court of Auditors must belong to, or have belonged to, an external audit body in their own country, or be appropriately qualified in some other capacity. The appointment is for a renewable six-year period. As with other 'non-political' EU bodies, a condition of appointment is that the members will act in the general interest and will be completely independent in the performance of their duties.

The members elect one of their number to be the President of the Court. The term of office is three years and is renewable. The President sees to the general efficient running of the Court and also represents it in its external relations.

The members are assigned a specific sector of activity for which they hold a particular responsibility regarding the preparation and implementation of the decisions of the Court. Each sector falls under one of three audit groups which act primarily as coordinating agencies and filters for plenary sessions of the whole Court. All important decisions are taken in plenaries, by majority vote if need be.

As with several other EU institutions, the administration supporting the Court of Auditors is rather small in size given the potential importance of the work to be done. In 1998 just over 500 people were employed by the Court, of whom around 330 were directly engaged in audit duties, 80 were in the language service, and 90 were in administrative departments. Inevitably such modest staffing resources greatly restricts the number of things the Court can attempt to do.

Activities of the Court

The task of the Court of Auditors is to examine all EU revenue and expenditure accounts, and those of bodies set up by it unless the relevant legal instruments preclude such examination. In exercising this responsibility the Court engages in two main types of activity.

The first is to carry out audits to see whether revenue has been received and expenditure has been incurred in a lawful and regular manner, and also to examine whether the financial management of EU authorities has been sound. The auditing powers of the Court cover the general budget of the EU, plus certain financial operations that are not included in the budget such as the borrowing and lending facilities of the ECSC and aid to developing countries that is financed by national contributions.

The auditing of the general budget, which is the Court's most important single task, and the related process of granting a discharge to the Commission on its implementation of the budget, proceed as follows.

- The Commission is required to draw up, for each financial year, accounts relating to the implementation of the budget, a financial statement of the assets and liabilities of the EU, and an analysis of the financial year. The main responsibility for collecting and presenting this information (the internal audit) lies with DGXX (Financial Control). The documentation must be forwarded to the Council, the EP, and the

Court of Auditors by no later than 1 June of the following financial year.

- The Court undertakes its audit (the external audit) partly on the basis of an examination of Commission documentation and partly on the basis of its own independent investigations. The latter is an ongoing process and involves the examination of records supplied by and requested from EU institutions and member states (which in the case of member states means liaising closely with national audit bodies and appropriate national agencies), and when necessary carrying out on-the-spot investigations. The purpose of this Court audit is not to replicate what has already been covered by the internal audit, but rather to add an extra dimension to the EU's overall auditory control by examining the adequacy of internal procedures – particularly with regard to their ability to identify significant irregular and unlawful transactions – and to evaluate the extent to which correct financial management (in terms of economy, efficiency and effectiveness) is being practised. The Court transmits to all relevant institutions any comments that it proposes to include in its annual report to which it believes there should be a reply, or to which an institution may wish to reply. After receipt of the replies, the Court completes the final version of its annual report. This has to be communicated to the other EU institutions by 30 November.

  The format of the annual report changed with the report on the 1997 financial year so as to allow the Court's work to be more manageable and measured. Whereas the report used to contain the detailed results of enquiries, it now consists largely of general observations grouped into chapters – on, for example, the CAP, structural measures and external aid – and a summary of the audit conclusions of special reports issued throughout the year. Amongst the special reports in 1997 were ones on EU humanitarian aid, management of the Community's cereals trade, and TACIS subsidies allocated to Ukraine.

- The EP, acting on a recommendation of the Council, is supposed to give discharge to the Commission in respect of the implementation of the budget by 30 April of the following year. To this end, the EP's Budgetary Control Committee examines all relevant documentation, particularly that produced by the Court of Auditors, and makes a recommendation to the EP. Normally discharge is given by the due date, but not always and there have been occasions when discharge has been deferred until after the Commission has taken remedying measures to deal with the problem. Most dramatically in this context, in March 1998 the EP deferred discharge on the 1996 budget after a series of cases involving alleged Commission mismanagement and fraud came to light, particularly in respect of the PHARE and TACIS programmes, aid for

Eastern Europe, and the MEDA aid programme. When the discharge vote was eventually held, in December 1998, the EP – angered by what it saw as an insufficiently robust Commission response to its concerns and aware that in November the Court had again strongly criticised the Commission in its report on the 1997 financial year – voted against giving discharge, even though the Budgetary Control Committee had voted narrowly (by 14 votes to 13) to recommend that discharge be given. The President of the Commission, Jacques Santer, responded by calling on the EP either to back or to sack the College of Commissioners. As was shown in Chapters 6 and 9, the sacking option came fairly close to being taken when other causes of dissatisfaction with the Commission became caught up in the vote of censure on the College in January 1999. Though the vote was not passed, the circumstances that led to it being held were important factors in paving the way to the events that resulted in the resignation of the College two months later, in March.

The second main activity of the Court of Auditors is to submit observations and deliver opinions on a range of subjects. This it does in two main sets of circumstances. First, an EU institution may ask the Court to submit an opinion on a matter, usually concerning financial aspects of draft legislation. Amongst the opinions issued in 1997 were ones on the condition governing the implementation of CFSP expenditure and the draft financial regulation applicable to specified development finance cooperation. Second, when the Council enacts a financial regulation it is obliged to seek an opinion from the Court on the draft text.

The effectiveness of financial controls

There is no doubt that control over EU revenue and expenditure could be improved if the political will to do so existed. For example, procedures could be tightened so as to prevent member states from imposing the limitations they occasionally apply to the audit enquiries considered necessary by the Court of Auditors. The Court's own attempts to extend its influence beyond questions of financial rectitude into considerations of policy efficiency could be encouraged, and even formalised. And the particular problem of fraud – which is generally thought to account for at least 10 per cent of the EU budget, most of it in connection with agriculture payments and foreign aid contracts (10 000 such contracts were awarded in 1997 alone) – could be tackled more effectively if resources at both EU and member state levels were increased and if proposals that have long been advocated by the Court for streamlining administrative practices were adopted.

A few extracts from Chapter 5 (External Aid) of the Court's *Annual Report Concerning the Financial Year 1997* may be cited to illustrate the sort of financial weaknesses the Court regularly identifies and seeks to remedy:

> The Commission is increasingly committed to ambitious external actions, involving substantial budgetary funding, without sufficient regard to its administrative, financial and logistical capacity to manage them. . .
>
> Greater account needs to be taken of the wider context, generally beyond the Commission's control, in which a programme and/or project will be implemented. . .
>
> The Commission's monitoring of the financial and material progress of projects is in many cases weak, largely because of excessive project numbers combined with complex reporting requirements, poor communication with implementing partners, poor accountancy mechanisms and the low priority accorded to this activity (*Official Journal*, C 349, 17 November 1998, pp. 94–9).

Observations of this kind make it clear that the EU's financial control mechanisms need to be improved. Periodic scandals, such as that which arose in 1998 in connection with 'missing' humanitarian aid funds, bear further testimony to this need. However, the extent of the shortcomings should not be overstated. One reason why they should not be is that the internal and external audits have contributed to an improvement of many procedures and administrative practices in recent years. There has, for example, been a tightening of the rules governing the way contracts are awarded to outside agencies. Another reason is that total EU expenditure is still relatively modest (see Chapter 14 for details), which means that EU decision-makers, far from being able to be financially profligate with surplus funds are, for the most part, obliged to work to tight budgets and within limited resources.

Interests

Different types

A vast range of non-governmental interests concern themselves with EU processes. These are of four main types.

Subnational levels of government

As noted above in the discussion on the Committee of the Regions, many subnational governmental bodies from the member states seek to influence, or even play a direct role in, EU decision-making processes. The degree of their involvement and activity depends largely on the degree of autonomy and manoeuvrability they enjoy at the national level. Where regional government with real powers exists, then direct lines of communication have usually been opened up with EU institutions, notably the Commission, and offices have been established in Brussels. More commonly, however, regional and local authorities work with the EU mainly through their national governments and, where appropriate, through liaison organisations and the locally based 'European office' that many have created.

Private and public companies

Many large business firms, especially multinational corporations, are very active in lobbying EU institutions. Over 200 such firms have established offices in Brussels (*European Voice*, 16–22 November 1995). Adopting, usually, multiple strategies, business lobbying is channelled through both national and Euro interest groups (see below), and is also conducted on a direct basis. Direct lobbying has the advantage of not requiring a collective view to be sought with other firms, and also enables sensitive issues to be pursued when there is no desire to 'go public', for example when competition and trading matters are involved. The car industry is an example of a sector where direct lobbying by firms, and not just European firms, is common – as is indicated by the fact that most large car firms in Europe have lobbying/information offices in Brussels.

National interest groups

Many circumstances result in national interest groups attempting to involve themselves in EU processes. For example, several national environmental interest groups have pressed for more effective implementation of existing EU legislation on the disposal of sewage into the sea. In some policy areas, especially those concerned with business and trade matters, many national interest groups are from non-EU countries: one of the most influential of all is the EU Committee of the American Chamber of Commerce (AMCHAM-EU). In seeking to play a part in EU processes, most national interest groups are confined to working from their national offices or via a European interest group, but a few of the larger industrial and agricultural groups have, in addition to a domestic and a European group base, their own representatives and agents permanently based in Brussels.

Eurogroups

There are somewhere in the region of 700 Eurogroups (Greenwood, 1999). These are groups that draw their membership from several countries and operate at – and in so doing seek to represent the interests of their sector or cause at – the EU level. Given their particular EU orientation it is worth looking at Eurogroups in detail.

Their *policy interests* naturally reflect the policy priorities and concerns of the EU. Of the 700 or so Eurogroups, approaching 70 per cent represent business, about 20 per cent are public interest groups, about 10 per cent represent the professions, and about 3 per cent represent trade unions, consumers, environmentalists, and other interests (ibid.). Within these broad categories a multiplicity of specific interests and groups are to be found. For example, within the business category, agricultural interests are a major and diverse component, ranging in nature from the broadly based Committee of Agricultural Organisations in the European Union (COPA), which seeks to represent most types of farmer on most issues, to highly specialised groups representing the likes of yeast producers and pasta manufacturers.

The reason why such an array of Eurogroups have been constituted and are active at the EU level is quite simple: pressure groups go where power goes. As policy responsibilities – in agriculture, in the regulation of the market, in the protection of the environment and so on – have been transferred from national capitals to the EU, so has a Euro-lobby developed to supplement – not to replace – the domestic lobbies.

The *membership* of Eurogroups also varies considerably. It does so in four main respects. First, there are variations in the breadth of the membership base. Some groups – the so-called umbrella groups – have a broad membership base and are usually trans-sector or sectoral-wide in character. Examples of umbrella groups are the Union of Industrial and Employers Confederation of Europe (UNICE), the European Trade Union Confederation (ETUC), the European Environmental Bureau (EEB), the European Bureau of Consumers' Associations (BEUC), and COPA. Because of the breadth of their membership some of these umbrella groups have considerable difficulty in maintaining internal cohesion and present-ing a common front: ETUC, for example, has traditionally had to try to reconcile differences between socialist, communist, and christian trade unions, whilst COPA has had problems with managing the varying agricultural sectoral implications of reforms to the CAP. Most groups, however, are more narrowly focused than the umbrella groups and seek to speak on behalf of a specific industry, process, service, or product. Examples of such groups are the European Union of Fruit and Vegetable Wholesalers, Shippers, Importers and Exporters (EUCOFIL), the European Association of Manufacturers of Business Machines and Information Technology (EUROBIT), and the Federation of European Explosive Manufacturers (FEEM).

Second, there are variations in terms of whether membership is direct or via affiliation. In most cases membership is based on affiliation by national sectoral or, in the case of a few of the larger Eurogroups, national peak (cross-sectoral) organisations. Since the mid 1980s, however, there has been a growth in direct membership groupings and organisations. The most important development in this regard has been the coming together of major industrial, often multinational, companies, frequently as a supplement to their involvement in affiliation-based sectoral groups. Examples of Eurogroups that are dominated by large companies are the Association of European Automobile Constructors (ACEA), which represents most of the EU's major non-Japanese car manufacturers, and the Association of Petrochemical Producers and Exporters (APPE). A few lobbying-related linkages between major companies are relatively informally based and in some respects are perhaps more like think tanks and forums for the generation of ideas than Eurogroups. The best known example of such a 'think tank' is the European Round Table of Industrialists which brings together, on an invitation only basis, fifty or so heads of major European industries. The Round Table produces reports that are intended to identify how the right conditions can be created for business to flourish.

Third, there are variations in the representativeness of groups. Since most Eurogroups are based on national affiliates, the number of people they can claim to represent naturally reflects the factors determining group membership at the national level. Hence sectional interests are usually better placed than promotional interests. Similarly, amongst sectional interests, Eurogroups representing interests that are well mobilised at the national level, such as dairy farmers and textile manufacturers, naturally tend to be much more genuinely representative than groups acting on behalf of poorly mobilised sections of the population such as consumers or agricultural labourers.

Fourth, there are variations in the width of the EU base of groups. At one end of the spectrum, many Eurogroups draw their members from only a few states, which in the case of activities that are carried on throughout the EU can weaken a group's representational claims. At the other end of the spectrum, some groups are not EU-specific and draw members from many other European states: both ETUC and UNICE for example, have thirty or so affiliates from over twenty countries. Membership of this latter sort, which goes beyond the geographical borders of the EU, has advantages and disadvantages: on the one hand it can help to promote international cooperation and increase group resources; on the other hand, and this is a charge that has frequently been laid against ETUC, it can serve to dilute group concentration on, and therefore influence within, the EU.

In terms of *resources*, over half of all Eurogroups have a turnover exceeding 100 000 euro. As regards staffing, over half have at least three employees, over one-third have five or more, and over 10 per cent have eleven or more (Greenwood, 1999). The best resourced groups are mostly either large business groups – such as the European Chemical Industry Council (CEFIC), COPA, UNICE, the European Insurance Committee (CEA), and the European Federation of Pharmaceutical Industry Associations (EFPIA) – or global public interest groups such as Friends of the Earth and the World Wide Fund for Nature. The most poorly resourced groups, which are not of a particular type but exist amongst business, public interest, and other groups, usually do not have strong corporate backing and/or have a narrow membership base.

There are thus wide variations in group resources. On the one hand there are very well resourced groups with twenty or more staff (CEFIC is the largest with around 100 and COPA the second largest with around 50) and ample and well-appointed accommodation. On the other hand some groups do not even stretch to one employee and work through affiliates, consultants, and part-time and temporary representatives whose services are called upon as and when they are needed. (It is not difficult to find people prepared to act as contract agents: there are around 140 professional public consultancies and 160 law firms based in Brussels that are willing to take on 'EU business'.)

The *organisational structure* of most Eurogroups is extremely loose. The central group organs usually enjoy only a very limited independence from the national affiliates, whilst the affiliates themselves are autonomous in most respects and are not subject to central discipline. In addition, key decisions made at the centre are frequently taken only on the basis of unanimous votes, though some groups do have provisions for weighted majorities on some issues. These loose structures can weaken the effectiveness of Eurogroups by making them slow to react and making it difficult for them to put forward collective views that are anything more than rather vague lowest common denominators. At the same time, however, moves to create stronger structures risks groups not affiliating, or national affiliates concentrating almost exclusively on their national activities.

The extent and complexity of groups' organisational structures varies. The more specialised and poorly resourced groups usually operate on a fairly rudimentary basis, often merely via an annual meeting and an executive committee that meets as required. The large umbrella groups, in contrast, usually have an extensive structure that typically includes a general meeting at least once a year, an executive committee that meets once every four to six weeks, specialist policy committees whose frequency of meeting depends on the business in hand, a President, and a full-time Secretariat headed by a Secretary General. COPA has the most developed structure (Figure 11.1).

Finally, with regard to their *functions*, Eurogroups normally attempt to do two main things. First, they seek to gather and exchange information, both in a two-way process with EU organs and with and between national affiliates. Second, they seek to have their interests and views incorporated into EU policy, by persuading and pressurising those who make and implement policy. Not all Eurogroups, of course, attempt or are able to exercise these functions in equal measure: for example, in those sectors where EU policy is little developed, Eurogroups often choose to give a higher priority to the first function than they do to the second.

Access to decision-makers

The long, complex and multi-layered nature of EU processes provides many points of access for interests, and hence many opportunities for them to keep themselves informed about developments and press their cases with those who influence, make, and implement decisions. The main points of access are national governments, the Commission, and the European Parliament.

National governments

A major problem for interests is that they cannot normally directly approach either the European Council or the Council of Ministers. This is partly because there are practical problems with lobbying what are in effect international negotiations, it is partly because the meetings are held behind closed doors, but it is mainly because neither body wishes to make itself available, as a collective entity, for regularised or intensive interest targeting. Only a few direct linkages therefore exist, and these are largely restricted to the most powerful interests. So, the President-in-Office of a sectoral Council may occasionally meet the president of a powerful Euro-group, or a written submission from an influential interest may be

Figure 11.1   *Organisational structure of COPA*

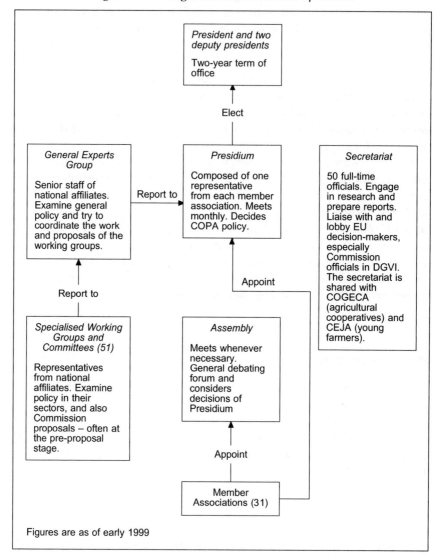

officially received and circulated prior to a European Council or Council of Ministers meeting. More usually, however, the only way an interest can hope to establish contact with, and perhaps exert pressure on, the European Council or the Council of Ministers is indirectly: through a government or governments looking favourably on its cause or feeling obliged to act on its behalf.

Much time and effort is therefore spent by interests, especially national interests, attempting to influence the positions adopted by governments in EU negotiations. In the case of the European Council, this task usually has to be undertaken at least at one stage removed because national leaders do not normally allow themselves to be directly lobbied. With the Council of Ministers, however, one of a number of factors may result in doors being opened. Amongst such factors are: some interests, such as most of the major national agricultural groups, enjoy – for a mixture of political, economic, technical and other reasons – insider status with the relevant government departments, which means they are consulted as a matter of course on proposals and developments within their sphere of interest; when a technically complicated matter is under consideration, governments usually seek the advice of relevant interests at an early stage of the Council process – with perhaps Council working party or management committee members communicating directly with interest representatives; and when the cooperation of an interest is important for the effective implementation of an EU proposal, its views may well be actively sought, or received and listened to if an approach is made.

This last point touches on another reason (in addition to trying to influence Council decision-making), why interests may approach national governments: they may wish to influence the way EU decisions are implemented. One way in which they can attempt to do this is by making their views known to governments when measures are being devised to incorporate EU directives into national law. And if relevant ministries can be persuaded to delay, or not to monitor too closely, the implementation of directives on, say, the disposal of pollutants or safety standards in the workplace, some interests may well have much to gain financially.

The Commission

The Commission is the main target for most interests. It is so, primarily, because of its central importance in so many respects: in policy initiation and formulation; in taking many final decisions; in following proposals through their legislative cycle; in managing the EU's spending programmes; and in policy implementation. An important contributory reason why the Commission attracts so much attention is simply that it is known to be approachable.

The Commission makes itself available to interests because several advantages can accrue to it from so doing. First, interests often have access to specialised information and to knowledge of how things are 'at the front' which the Commission needs if it is to be able to exercise its own responsibilities efficiently. Second, the Commission's negotiating hand with the Council of Ministers is strengthened if it can demonstrate that its proposals are supported by influential interests – as, for example, many of its attempts to approximate European standards are supported by multinational corporations, and indeed in some cases may have originated from them. Third, and this is in some ways the other side of the coin of the previous point, if the Commission does not consult with and try to satisfy interests, and comes forward with proposals to which influential interests are strongly opposed, the proposals are likely to meet with strong resistance at Council of Ministers level. Fourth, with specific regard to Eurogroups, when groups come forward with broadly united and coherent positions they can greatly assist the Commission by allowing it to deal with already aggregated views and enabling it to avoid entanglement in national and ideological differences between sectional interests. For this reason, Commission DGs generally keep 'recognised' Eurogroups informed about matters that are of interest to them and are usually prepared to consult them too. (There are no explicit Commission rules on recognition, in the sense that there is no proper system of accreditation or registration, but informal consultation lists do exist. The main reasons for non-recognition are either that the Commission does not regard the group as a proper Eurogroup – perhaps because it consists of just two or three large companies – or that it is not seen as being very effective in 'delivering' aggregated and coordinated views.)

Until about the mid 1970s the Commission displayed a strong preference for talking to Eurogroups rather than national groups, and to national governments rather than subnational levels of government. This attitude, however, has since been relaxed and most interests of significance, and most interests which can provide useful information that is presented in a clear manner, have been able to have their views at least considered by the Commission. The procedures by which the contacts and communications occur are many and are of both a formal and an informal nature. They include the following:

- The extensive advisory committee system that is clustered around the Commission primarily exists for the precise purpose of allowing interests to make their views known to EU authorities, and in particular to the Commission (see Chapter 6).
- The Social Dialogue provides for an exchange of views between the Commission and the two sides of industry. Since 1985 it has regularly brought together, at the most senior and at working group levels, representatives from the Commission, trade union representatives from ETUC and representatives from the two main employers' and industrial organisations – UNICE and the European Centre of Enterprises with

Public Participation (CEEP). The Maastricht Treaty's Social Charter greatly extended the scope of the Commission's consultations with management and labour and it is even possible for legislative proposals to be developed within its framework.

- Commissioners and DG officials receive numerous delegations from interests of all sorts.
- Representatives of the Commission travel to member states to meet interests and to attend conferences and seminars where various interests are represented.
- A few of the larger Eurogroups invite Commission representatives to attend some of their working parties and committee meetings.
- Informal meetings and telephone conversations between Commission and interest representatives occur constantly.
- Interests present the Commission with a mass of written communications in the form of information, briefing, and policy documents.

Naturally, the extent and nature of the communications between interests and the Commission vary considerably according to a number of factors. A small national interest in a specialised area may only require occasional contact at middle-ranking official level with one particular DG. In contrast, an active umbrella group may wish to be permanently plugged into the Commission at many different points. As an indication of how extensive the links can be, some of the access channels available to COPA are worth noting: about every three months the Presidium of COPA meets the Commissioner for Agriculture; the Secretary General of COPA and the Director General of DGVI (Agriculture) meet regularly and often speak to each other on the telephone; at all levels the staff of COPA are in almost constant touch with staff in DGVI and, less frequently, are also in close contact with staff in other DGs – notably DGXIX (Budgets); and COPA is strongly represented, both in its own right and via affiliates, on all the agricultural advisory committees and also on certain other leading advisory committees such as the Standing Committee on Employment and the Harmonisation of Legislation Committee.

The European Parliament

It has been very noticeable, not least in the swelling ranks of lobbyists who attend the Strasbourg plenaries, that as the role and influence of the EP in the EU system has grown it has increasingly attracted the attention of interests. Among the lobbying possibilities available to interests in respect of the EP are the following:

- The EP considers most important legislative proposals and is in a position, especially when the co-decision procedure applies, to exercise considerable influence over the content of legislation (see Chapters 9 and 13). It can thus be very fruitful for interests to lobby MEPs, especially *rapporteurs* and members of committees dealing with relevant legislation. The relative lack of political group discipline in the EP (relative, that is, to the party discipline that applies in the legislatures of most member states) enhances the possibility of individual MEPs being 'persuadable'.

- The power conferred on the EP by the Maastricht Treaty to request the Commission to submit legislative acts created the possibility of interests using MEPs to get legislative initiatives off the ground.

- MEPs and officials engaged in preparing reports for EP committees often approach appropriate interests for their views, or allow themselves to be approached. This can be for a number of reasons but is usually because they wish to make use of the knowledge and expertise of interests and/or because the future progress of reports is likely to be eased if they do not come up against stiff oppositional lobbying from interests.

- Interests have some opportunities for direct contact with EP committees and political groups. Committees, for example, sometimes hold 'hearings' and occasionally travel to member states for the precise purpose of meeting interest representatives, whilst political groups sometimes allow themselves to be addressed when they judge it to be appropriate.

- Attempts can be made to encourage MEPs to draw up own initiative reports. If progress is made – and the prospects are usually much better than under the request to the Commission procedure, noted above, which requires majority support of the EP's members – then this could prompt the Commission and/or the Council into action of a desired sort.

- Intergroups, which (as was explained in Chapter 9) are loosely organised and voluntary groupings of MEPs with shared concerns about particular issues or areas of activity, are natural targets for interests. For example, interests acting on behalf of disabled people will clearly wish to be in contact with the Handicapped Intergroup, while those acting on behalf of citrus fruit producers will wish to be in touch with, amongst others, the Israel and the Mediterranean Intergroups.

- A general circulation of literature amongst MEPs may have the effect of improving the image of an interest or changing the climate of opinion in the interest's area of concern.

- Attempts can be made to persuade individual MEPs to take matters up with governments and the Commission.

All of these avenues are used by interests, with the bigger and better researched ones – which, for the most part, are business interests – making use of most of them to at least some extent.

Many possible avenues are thus available to interests to enable them to promote their causes. Which are the most suitable, the most available, and the most effective, naturally varies according to circumstances. For example, a local authority that wishes to attract ERDF funds would be well advised to establish contact with DGXVI (Regional Policy), but it should also court good relations with regional and national civil servants since the ERDF functions on an EU–national–regional partnership basis. In contrast, an environmental group in a country where the government is not noted for its sympathy to green issues might be most effective working as part of a Eurogroup in order to: launch public information and relations campaigns that help persuade the EP to pass a resolution; pressurise the Commission to produce legislative proposals and increase its efforts to ensure that existing legislation is properly implemented; and find a route to the Council of Ministers via some of the national affiliates that are leaning on their governments.

Influence

The factors that determine the influence exercised by interests in the EU are similar to those which apply at the national level. The more powerful and more effective interests tend to have at least some of the following characteristics:

Control of key information and expertise

Effective policy-making and implementation requires a knowledge and understanding that often can only be provided to EU authorities by interests. This obviously puts some interests in a potentially advantageous position – as evidenced, to some extent, by the fact that the influence that interests exercise via official forums is often much greater in specialised advisory committees than it is in more general settings such as the ESC or the CoR.

Adequate resources

The better resourced an interest is, the more likely it is to be able to make use of a variety of tactics and devices at a number of different access points. So, with regard to proposed legislation, a well-resourced interest is likely to be in a position to feed its views through to the Commission, the EP, and perhaps the Council from the initiating stage to the taking of the final decision. Similarly, a regional or local authority hoping for EU funds is more likely to be successful if it employs people who know what is available, how to apply, and with whom it is worth having an informal word.

Economic weight

Important economic interests – be they major companies or cross-sectoral representational organisations – usually have to be listened to by EU decision-makers, not least because their cooperation is often necessary in connection with policies designed, for instance, to encourage EU-wide investment, expand employment in the less prosperous regions, stimulate cross-border rationalisations, or improve industrial efficiency. Examples of economic weight being an important factor in political influence include: the way in which the chemical industry – via its Eurogroup CEFIC – has managed to persuade the Commission to investigate numerous cases of alleged dumping; the way in which EUROFER (the steel manufacturers' association) has worked closely with the Commission and governments to limit the damage caused to its members by steel rationalisation programmes; and the way in which the pharmaceutical industry – acting through EFPIA – has persuaded the Commission to allow it to regulate itself rather than be regulated. Writing about EFPIA's achievement, Greenwood (1997, pp. 21–2) comments that 'EFPIA's performance of a public protection function on behalf of a self-regulatory code makes the organisation a full mechanism of governance'.

Political weight

Many interests have political assets that can be used to advantage, usually via governments. For example, a national pressure group that is closely linked to a party in government may be able to get that government to virtually act on its behalf in the Council of Ministers. At a broader level, electoral factors can be important, with ministers in the Council not usually anxious to support anything that might upset key voters, especially if an important national or local election is looming. Farmers' organisations in France, Italy, Germany and elsewhere are the best examples of interests that have benefited from the possession of electoral significance.

Genuine representational claims

National pressure groups and Eurogroups that genuinely represent a sizeable proportion of the interests in a given sector are naturally in a stronger position than those which do not. The representativeness of CEFIC, for example, is one important reason why the chemical industry has been permitted to exercise a certain degree of self-regulation.

Cohesion

Some interests find it difficult to put forward clear and consistent views and are thereby weakened. As was noted earlier, this often applies to Eurogroups, especially umbrella Eurogroups, because of their varied membership and loose confederal structures. Increasing difficulty in maintaining internal coherence and consensus has contributed to a decline in COPA's lobbying influence over the years (Clark and Jones, 1993).

Access to decision-makers

Most of the characteristics just described play some part in determining which interests enjoy good access to decision-makers and which do not. Clearly, those which do have good access – especially if it is at both national and EU levels – are more likely than those which do not to be fully aware of thinking and developments in decision-making circles, and to be able to present their case to those who matter. At the EU level, COPA is, notwithstanding its declining influence, an obvious example of such an 'insider' interest, whilst at the national level COPA affiliates usually also enjoy an advantageous position (see Chapter 15 for an examination of the access enjoyed by – and indeed for an examination of the general influence of – agricultural interests).

Concluding comments

There are both positive and negative aspects to the involvement of interests in EU processes. Of the positive aspects, two are especially worth emphasising. First, interest activity broadens the participatory base of the EU and ensures that policy and decision-making is not completely controlled by politicians and officials. Second, interests can provide EU authorities with information and viewpoints that improve the quality and effectiveness of their policies and decisions. Of the negative aspects, the most important is that some interests are much more powerful and influential than others. This lack of balance raises questions about whether interests unduly, perhaps even undemocratically, tilt EU policy and decision-making in certain directions – towards, for example, a legislative framework that tends to favour producers more than such 'natural' opponents as consumers and environmentalists.

But irrespective of whether interest activity is judged to be, on the whole, beneficial or not, its importance is clear. Interests are central to many key information flows to and from EU authorities, and they bring considerable influence to bear on policy and decision-making processes from initiation through to implementation. There are few, if any, EU policy sectors where interests of at least some significance are not to be found.

Policies and Policy Processes of the European Union

Introduction

Part 3 examines what the EU does and how it does it.

Chapter 12 looks at EU policies. The origins, the range, and the context of the policies are all considered. Particular themes of Chapter 12 are the breadth and diversity of EU policy interests, and the less than complete nature of many of the policies.

Chapter 13 focuses on patterns, practices and features of the EU policy-making and decision-making machinery. Having examined the EU institutions and political actors in Part 2, Chapter 13 considers how the various pieces fit together. What sort of policy-making and decision-making system are they part of and have they helped to create? A central concern of Chapter 13 is to emphasise that even the most general statements about how the EU operates normally have to be qualified. For one of the few things that can be said with certainty about EU processes is that they are many, complex and varied. A truly accurate account of how the EU functions therefore requires something that just cannot be attempted here: an analysis of the procedures and practices that apply in every policy area with which the EU is involved.

In Chapter 14 the EU budget is examined. From where does the EU get its money, and on what does it spend it? The budgetary decision-making process, which in several important respects is distinctly different from the processes that apply in policy areas, is also examined. Chapter 15 considers one particular policy area in depth. As such, the chapter offers something of a contrast to the necessarily rather general approach of Chapters 12 and 13. Agriculture has been selected for this special examination, not because of any suggestion that it is typical – the variability of the EU policy processes precludes any policy area being described as such – but simply because of its significance in the EU context.

The external relations of the EU are increasingly important and these constitute the subject matter of Chapter 16. The examination is undertaken on the basis of the four main component parts of the EU's external policies: trade policy, foreign and security policy, development cooperation policy and the external dimension of internal policies.

Finally, Chapter 17 focuses on one of the most important and certainly one of the most distinctive features of EU processes: the mechanisms and arrangements used by the member states to control their relations with the EU and, insofar as it is possible, to control the EU itself.

Chapter 12

Policies

The origins of EU policies
The EU's policy interests and responsibilities
Characteristics of EU policies
Concluding comments

The origins of EU policies

The origins of EU policies lie in a number of places. At a general level, the changed post-war mood in Western Europe has played a part. So has the increasingly interdependent nature of the international system, which has resulted in national borders becoming ever more ill-matched with political and economic forces and realities. This interdependence has helped to persuade West European states to transfer policy responsibilities to a 'higher' level in an attempt to shape, manage, control, take advantage of, and keep pace with the modern world.

At a more specific level, the treaties are generally seen as key determinants of EU policy. However, their influence is not as great as is commonly supposed. Certainly they are important stimuli to policy development and they also provide the legal base upon which much policy activity occurs. For example, such 'core' EU policies as the Common Commercial Policy (CCP), the Common Agricultural Policy (CAP), and the Competition Policy have their roots – though by no means all their principles – in the EEC (now EC) Treaty. Similarly, EU involvement with coal and steel cannot possibly be fully understood without reference to the Treaty of Paris. But treaty provision for policy development does not guarantee that it will occur. The very limited progress made towards the establishment of a Common Transport Policy, despite it being provided for in the EEC/EC Treaty, illustrates this. So too does the non-fulfilment of most of the hopes that were held for Euratom. A third, and crucially important in its implications for the nature of the EU, example of limited development of treaty provisions is the only very partial implementation, until the late 1980s, of Part 3 Title 2 of the EEC Treaty, under which member states were supposed to treat their macroeconomic policies 'as a matter of common concern' and were to coordinate, cooperate and consult with one another on key economic and financial questions. In practice it is quite clear that although there was cooperation and consultation in these areas –

319

carried out mainly under the Ecofin Council of Ministers by committees of very senior national officials – the states did not work or act as closely together as the Treaty envisaged. Furthermore, one of the key steps towards financial cooperation – the creation in 1979 of the European Monetary System (EMS) which, amongst other things, was designed to fix maximum and minimum rates of exchange for currencies in the system – was created outside the treaty system because of concern in some quarters about the rigidities that a treaty-based approach might entail, and also because not all member states (notably the United Kingdom) wished to be full participants. It was only in 1987–8, thirty years after the EEC Treaty was signed, that clear, significant, formal, and Community-based moves towards economic and monetary integration between the member states began to be initiated and implemented.

If treaty provision is no guarantee of policy development, lack of provision is no guarantee of lack of development. Environmental policy illustrates this. Until it was given constitutional status by the Single European Act (SEA), the environment was given no specific mention in the treaties. Yet from the early 1970s Community environmental policy programmes were formulated and legislation was approved. Legal authority for this was held to lie in the (almost) catch-all Articles 100 and 235 of the EEC/EC Treaty (Articles 94 and 308 post-Amsterdam). The former allowed the Community to issue directives for the approximation of laws 'as directly affect the establishment or functioning of the common market' and the latter enabled it to take 'appropriate measures' to 'attain, in the course of the operation of the common market, one of the objectives of the Community'. Environmental policy was therefore able to find a tentative constitutional base. However, even the most liberal readings of these two articles cannot stretch to some policy areas, but this has not prevented policy development from occurring. Foreign policy cooperation prior to the SEA illustrates this. Aware that there were no treaty provisions for such cooperation, and unenthusiastic about subjecting such a sensitive area to the formalities and restrictions of treaty processes, the EC member states in the early 1970s simply created a new machinery – which they entitled European Political Cooperation (EPC) – alongside, rather than inside, the formal framework of the treaties.

EPC was first given legal (but not EEC Treaty) status by the SEA, and it subsequently provided much of the basis for the Common Foreign and Security Policy (CFSP) pillar of the Maastricht Treaty. This 'constitutional evolution' of foreign policy highlights a key feature of the nature of EU policy development: the treaties are facilitators and enablers of policy development, but they are not always the main causes. Indeed, many of the amendments made to the Founding Treaties by the SEA and the Maastricht and Amsterdam Treaties have taken the form of acknowledging and giving recognition to changes that have been occurring outside their frameworks.

If the treaties thus provide only a partial explanation for policy development, what other factors have been influential? Three have been especially important: the leadership offered by the Commission; the perceptions of the member states of what is desirable; and the individual and collective capacities of the member states to translate their perceptions into practice.

To begin with Commission leadership, it is generally recognised that the Commissions led by Walter Hallstein (1958–66), Roy Jenkins (1977–80), and Jacques Delors (1985–94) were more dynamic and forceful than other Commissions. This is not to suggest that all their ideas and proposals were translated into practice – given the reliance of the Commission on other institutions that would be an unfair criterion upon which to judge Commission success – but it is to say that they were particularly innovative in helping to bring issues onto the policy agenda and in pointing to what could, and perhaps should, be done. The ability of the Commission, in favourable circumstances, to have a real effect on policy development is no more clearly illustrated than in the way the Delors-led Commissions helped to force the pace on such key issues as the Single European Market (SEM) programme, EMU, and the social dimension.

Regarding the perceptions of the states – or, to be more precise, of national governments – a fundamental precondition of successful policy development is that the advantages of acting together are judged to outweigh the disadvantages. The advantages are mainly, though not entirely, economic in kind: those that stem from having, in an increasingly interdependent and competitive world, a single and protected market, a common external trading position, and some collective action and some pooling of resources in particular functional and sectoral areas. The principal disadvantage is the loss of national decision-making powers and sovereignty that transfers of power and responsibilities to the EU inevitably entail. Some states are more concerned about this than others, but even the strongest supporters of integration are hesitant about ceding powers that may, at a later stage, result in their national room for manoeuvre being limited in areas that are important to them.

As for the capacity of the states to operationalise their perceptions of what is desirable, there are many problems. At the individual state level, a government may be favourably disposed towards an EU initiative but inhibited from supporting it in the Council of Ministers because of opposition from a powerful domestic interest or because it could be electorally damaging. Following this through to the EU level, opposition from just one state, whether it is principled or pragmatic, can make policy development difficult to achieve given the continuing treaty requirement of unanimity in the Council of Ministers on several issues and the preference in the Council for progress through consensus – especially on major issues – even when majority decisions are legally permissible.

The EU's policy interests and responsibilities

The EU's main policy interests and responsibilities can be grouped under five headings: establishing the Single European Market, economic and financial policies, functional policies, sectoral policies, and external policies.

Establishing the Single European Market

The single most important reason why the dynamism and profile of the EC was raised so high in the 1980s was that the Community embarked on a programme to complete the internal market by 1992.

This programme was really a development of the Community's long-established goal of creating a common market. After years in which only modest progress had been made in this direction, a number of factors combined in the 1980s to convince the governments of the member states that a greater thrust was needed: the sluggish economic growth of the second half of the 1970s was continuing; the Community was clearly falling behind its competitors (notably Japan and the United States) in the new technologies; there was an increasing appreciation that the continuation of still essentially fragmented national markets was having a damaging effect on the economic performance of the member states; and the accession of three new countries (Greece in 1981 and Spain and Portugal in 1986) made it clear to all that to continue on the same path and in the same way would mean that the common market would never be properly established.

Against this background, in April 1985 the Commission produced the White Paper *Completing the Internal Market* (Commission, 1985; see also Chapters 6, 8 and 13). The White Paper identified some 300 measures that would have to be taken to enable the internal market to be completed, and suggested that 31 December 1992 should be set as the deadline for the adoption of the measures. The European Council, at its June 1985 Milan meeting, accepted the White Paper, and at its December 1985 Luxembourg meeting agreed that both the internal market objective and the 1992 deadline be included in the Single European Act. Crucially, their inclusion in the SEA involved additions and amendments to the EEC Treaty. Article 13 of the SEA, incorporating a new Article 8A of the EEC Treaty, was especially important:

> The Community shall adopt measures with the aim of progressively establishing the internal market over a period expiring on 31 December 1992. . . . The internal market shall comprise an area without internal frontiers in which the free movement of goods, persons, services and capital is ensured in accordance with the provisions of this [the EEC] Treaty.

The White Paper sought, in essence, to establish the conditions in which market activities – buying and selling, lending and borrowing, producing and consuming – could be done as easily on a Community basis as they could on a national basis. The hope was that by removing the obstacles and barriers that sectionalised and fragmented the Community market, efficiency, growth, trade, employment, and prosperity could all be promoted. In the context of a general deregulatory approach, three sorts of obstacle and barrier were identified as needing to be removed: physical, technical, and fiscal.

The Commission was not of course starting from scratch with its internal market programme. A free and open market had been provided for in the EEC Treaty and much progress had been made. What the White Paper was intended to do was to inject a new focus, impetus and dynamism into a fundamental Treaty objective that was proceeding far too slowly, and in some respects had gone rather off the rails. Much of what was proposed in the White Paper, therefore, was not new, but had been around for some time – awaiting decisions by the Council of Ministers.

The White Paper thus needs to be placed in the context of the Community's long-standing aim to create a common market – or, as it has come to be known in recent years, an internal market or a Single European Market (SEM). That aim was being pursued, but with only limited success, before the White Paper appeared, and it has been vigorously pursued since, not only via the implementation of the White Paper but also via new measures that did not appear in the White Paper.

These new measures have largely been a response to, on the one hand, an increasing recognition by EU elites and decision-makers of the importance of the SEM project and, on the other hand, an increasingly expansive view of what the SEM should encompass – either to make the market function as effectively as possible or to compensate for some of the market's costs.

The SEM rests on four main pillars.

The first pillar is the guarantee of *free movement of goods, persons, services and capital* between the member states. Of these, the free movement of goods was the first to be tackled. It is a freedom that, it might be thought, would be fairly easy to realise: all barriers to trade must be dismantled according to the guiding principles of the TEC, which states that customs duties, quantitative restrictions, and measures having equivalent effect are not permitted. Great steps were quickly made in the 1960s with the first two of these and by 1968 customs duties and quantitative restrictions had been removed. Measures having equivalent effect, however, have been more difficult to deal with and have frequently acted, and been used, as obstacles to trade. Attempts to eliminate such measures have generated a considerable amount of secondary legislation, much activity in the Court of Justice, and constituted a central part of the White Paper programme.

In seeking to establish the conditions for the free movement of persons, the Treaty provides for both the employed and the self-employed. The free movement of the former is to be attained by 'the abolition of any discrimination based on nationality between workers of the Member States as regards employment, remuneration and other conditions of work and employment' (Article 39, TEC, ex Article 48). The free movement of the latter is concerned principally with rights of establishment, that is with the right of individuals and undertakings to establish businesses in the territory of other member states. As with the free movement of goods, secondary legislation and Court rulings have done much to clarify and extend the free movement of persons. They have done so in two main ways. First, by providing for mutual recognition of many educational, professional, and trade qualifications. Second, by providing key facilitators, notably in the form of the establishment of various legal entitlements, irrespective of nationality and place of domicile, to education and job training, health care, and social welfare payments.

Some of the legislation and Court judgements that have promoted the free movement of persons, and more particularly rights of establishment, have also helped to give effect to the Treaty declaration that restrictions on the provision of services should be abolished. Until recently financial services were a particular problem, but legislation has now been passed – on, for example, banking, insurance and insider trading – that is having the effect of opening up this hitherto highly protected and fragmented sector.

Until the late 1980s only limited progress was made in establishing the free movement of capital. Treaty provisions partly explain this, since the elimination of restrictions on the movement of capital under Article 67 of the EEC Treaty (now abolished) was required only 'to the extent necessary

to ensure the proper functioning of the common market'. More importantly, however, and notwithstanding the creation of the European
Monetary System (EMS) in the late 1970s, the necessary political will
did not exist in the first three decades of the Community's life. For many
states, control of capital movements was an important economic and
monetary instrument and they preferred it to remain largely in their own
hands. However, as part of the SEM programme, much of this former
resistance was withdrawn or overcome, and all the major capital markets
have – subject to a few derogations and some national protective measures
– been more or less open since 1990. (This does not, however, mean that in
practice there is complete free movement of capital, since taxation rates
have not been made common and banking rules have not all been
standardised.)

The second pillar of the SEM involves *the approximation of such laws,
regulations or administrative provisions of the Member States as directly
affect the establishment or functioning of the common market* (Article 94,
TEC; ex Article 100). Prior to the Maastricht Treaty, Article 100 referred
to 'the approximation, *or harmonisation* of such legal provisions in the
Member States' (emphasis added), but the word harmonisation was
dropped from the amended EC Treaty to reflect the more flexible and less
rigid approach that had developed towards differences in national
standards and requirements.

The need for approximation arises because, as noted above, the
dismantling of barriers is not in itself sufficient to guarantee free movement. This is most clearly seen with regard to the movement of goods,
where prior to the 1992 programme many non-tariff and non-quantitative
barriers existed that inhibited, even prevented, free movement across the
Community's internal borders. These barriers had, in the words of the
Treaty, the 'equivalent effect' of tariffs and quantitative restrictions, and as
such were obstacles to the creation of a market based on free and open
competition. Moreover, they tended to be barriers of a kind that could not
be removed simply by issuing general prohibitions. Many took the form of
different national standards, national requirements, and national provisions and practices that had been adopted over the years. Sometimes they
had been adopted for perfectly good reasons, but sometimes they had been
adopted as a deliberate attempt to protect a domestic market from
unwanted competition without actually infringing Community law. Whatever the intent, the effect was often the same: because of the need to adapt
products to meet the different national standards of different states, and
because of the need for products to be subject to re-testing and re-
certification procedures, efficiency was not maximised and producers in
one member state often could not compete on an equal basis with

producers in another. Examples of non-tariff barriers (NTBs) included different national technical specifications for products, different health and safety standards, charges for the inspection of certain categories of imported goods, and taxes that, though nominally general in their scope, were discriminatory against imported goods in their effect.

Approximation, and before it harmonisation, is concerned with the removal of barriers of this type and is vital if free movement across national boundaries is to be achieved. Council directives and EP and Council directives are the main instruments for achieving approximation (see Exhibit 10.2), although Court of Justice rulings have also been supportive and helpful. Most approximation law is naturally to be found in relation to the free movement of goods, and consists largely of matters such as the setting of common standards on technical requirements, design specifications, product content, and necessary documentation. Critics of the EU often present such measures as harmonisation for harmonisation's sake, and from time to time proposals do indeed appear to smack of insensitivity to national customs and preferences. Sight should not be lost, however, of what approximation – or harmonisation as some still insist on calling it – is all about: creating conditions that allow, encourage and increase the uniform treatment of persons, goods, services and capital throughout the EU.

As was briefly explained in Chapter 10, and as is further explained in Chapter 13, the Community's approach to harmonisation changed in the 1980s. Following the 'breakthrough' *Cassis de Dijon* case in 1979 – when the Court of Justice ruled that products that conform with the standards of one member state cannot be excluded from the markets of other member states unless they can be shown to be damaging to health, safety, the environment, or other aspects of the public interest – the Community became less concerned with the harmonisation of technical details. A 'new approach' was taken, under which a simpler and speedier process applies. There are three main aspects to this process: (1) whenever possible, legislation does not seek to harmonise but rather to approximate in that it is restricted to laying down the essential requirements that national standards and specifications must meet – on health and safety requirements for example; (2) as long as the essential conditions are met, member states must mutually recognise each other's specifications and standards; and (3) national specifications and standards are gradually being replaced by European specifications and standards drawn up by European standards organisations.

Competition policy is the third pillar of the SEM. The basic rules on competition are outlined in Articles 81–9 of the TEC (ex 85–94). They have three principal aspects to them. First, under Article 81 (ex 85) there is a prohibition on 'all agreements between undertakings, decisions by associations of undertakings and concerted practices which may affect trade between Member States and which have as their object or effect the prevention, restriction or distortion of competition within the common market'. Second, under Article 82 (ex 86), 'Any abuse by one or more undertakings of a dominant position within the common market or in a substantial part of it shall be prohibited or incompatible with the common market insofar as it may affect trade between Member States'. Third, under Article 87 (ex 92), state aid 'which distorts or threatens to distort competition by favouring certain undertakings or the production of certain goods shall, insofar as it affects trade between Member States, be incompatible with the common market'.

All of these Treaty prohibitions – on restrictive practices, dominant trading positions, and state aids – have been clarified by subsequent EC/EU law, both in the form of legislation and Court judgements. It has been established, for example, that a 'dominant position' cannot be held to apply on the basis of an overall percentage market share, but only in relation to factors such as the particular product, the structure of its market, and substitutability. Similarly, exemptions to state aid prohibitions, which are only generally referred to in the Treaty, have been confirmed as legally permissible if they are for purposes such as regional development, retraining, and job creation in potential growth industries.

Much of the work and time of the Commission's Directorate General for Competition (DGIV) is taken up examining allegations of breaches in competition law and considering applications for exemptions. Under the SEM momentum it has been much more vigorous than it used to be and has, for example, as Peterson and Bomberg (1999) note, boldly wielded competition powers in relation to 'revenue-producing monopolies' to open up hitherto protected telecommunications markets.

An effective competition policy is of course necessary for an open and integrated market. To try to improve the policy and ensure that it is sufficiently effective the EU has adopted a twin-track approach in recent years. First, the Commission has become much more active in examining cases of apparent malpractice. For example, using its powers as investigator, prosecutor, judge and jury (though with its decisions subject to appeal to the Court of Justice) it has been more willing to take action against member states in connection with state aids. Second, legislation designed to broaden the competition policy base has been approved. An important instance of such legislation is the 1989 Company Merger Regulation, which gives considerable powers to the Commission to disallow or set conditions on mergers that it judges will have an adverse effect on competition. Other examples of legislation, in a very different area of competition policy, are the directives that are designed to open up public procurement – an area of activity that accounts for around 15 per cent of EU GDP.

The fourth pillar of the SEM is the *Common External Tariff* (CET) or, as it is also known, the *Common Customs Tariff* (CCT). The purpose of the CET is to further the course of fair and equal trading by surrounding all the member states with common trade barriers so that goods entering the EU via, say, Liverpool or Rotterdam do so on exactly the same terms as they do via Athens or Marseilles. No member state can therefore gain a competitive advantage by having access to cheaper raw materials and none can make a profit from exporting imported goods to an EU partner. The CET takes the EU beyond being just a free trade area – where, at best, external tariffs are only approximated – and makes it a customs union.

Establishing the CET was relatively easy and maintaining it has not been too difficult. The external tariffs were in place by 1968, to coincide with the removal of the internal tariffs, and since then governments have had no independent legal authority over the tariff rate on goods entering their country. The terms of trade of the member states are established and negotiated on a EU-wide basis via the Common Commercial Policy (CCP). If a member state wishes to seek exemptions from, or changes to, these terms of trade it must go through the appropriate EU decision-making processes. Naturally there have been frequent disagreements between the states over different aspects of external trade and the CCP – tariff rates, trade protection measures and alleged dumping are amongst the issues that have created difficulties – but the existence of a clear and binding legal framework has ensured that, for the most part, the common external protection and front system has worked.

Clearly much has been and still is being achieved in the move towards a single market. Some of the most intractable problems – such as the removal of internal border controls and setting limitations on the rates of indirect taxation – have witnessed progress. However, it is clear that it will be some years before the SEM is as open or as integrated as national markets. This is because not all of the barriers to free movement are being removed, and not all of the national policies that serve to fragment the market are being made common. The obstacles to a completely open and integrated market are of three main types.

First, there are the somewhat intangible, but nonetheless very important, obstacles arising from different historical experiences, cultures, traditions and languages. These obstacles are unquestionably being broken down, but only slowly. EU laws may, for example, oblige public authorities to receive tenders for contracts from throughout the EU, but laws cannot control the many informal processes that often incline decision-makers to award contracts whenever possible to fellow national, or even locally-based, companies.

Second, there is still some member state resistance – almost invariably based on reasons of national interest – to developing and applying fully specific aspects of the SEM project. Whilst virtually all of the original legislative programme has now been processed, some of the legislation is rather loose (because this was seen as necessary to overcome opposition in the Council) whilst some of it is only being weakly applied. Spheres of market activity so affected include financial services, veterinary and phytosanitary controls, and the recognition of some diplomas and professional qualifications.

Third, there are economic factors that were not included in the 1985 White Paper and which have never formally been part of the SEM project that act as obstacles to complete market integration. Economists and politicians dispute exactly what economic factors do constitute such obstacles, and what their relative importance is, but prominent amongst the factors that are generally recognised are the following: the non-participation of four member states from the single currency system and hence also their non-involvement in the single monetary and exchange rate policies of 'Euroland'; the only partial development of common regional, social, environmental, and consumer policies; and the diversity of corporate direct taxation systems.

Macroeconomic and financial policies

Notwithstanding certain EEC Treaty provisions, and despite declarations by the Heads of Government in 1969 and 1972 that their intention was to establish an economic and monetary union by 1980, only limited practical progress was made until the late 1980s in moving towards Economic and Monetary Union (EMU).

Ministers and senior national officials did regularly convene to consult and to exchange ideas on macroeconomic policy, and at their meetings they periodically considered Commission submissions for the adoption of common guidelines and for short-term and medium-term strategies. But ultimately it was up to the states themselves as to what they did. For example, when the Commission in its quarterly economic report published in February 1987 stated that Germany had the greatest margin for manoeuvre to stimulate domestic demand, and France and the UK could do more to boost their productive capacity, there was no guarantee that national policies would thereby be adjusted. A state may have been unwise to fall too much out of step with its partners – as the French government was in 1981–2 when it attempted to stimulate its economy against the general trend – but it was perfectly entitled and able to embark on such a course of action.

Financial policy (which in practice, of course, is inextricably linked to economic policy) was also the subject of frequent contacts between the states – at ministerial, official and central bank levels – but, like economic policy, most of what came out of such exchanges was of an exhortive rather than a directionist nature. That said, however, the creation in 1979 of the European Monetary System (EMS) did provide Community financial policy with some central structure and some powers, since amongst its features were: a common reserve fund to provide for market intervention, the European Currency Unit (ecu) to act as a reserve asset and a means of settlement, and, in the Exchange Rate Mechanism (ERM) of the EMS, fixed – though adjustable when necessary – bands of exchange for participating currencies.

Until the late 1980s the Community's macroeconomic and financial policies thus had only relatively weak policy instruments attached to them. Attempts to strengthen these instruments, in order to build up a more effective policy framework, traditionally met with at least four obstacles. First, there were differences over which – the economic or the financial – naturally came first and should be accorded priority. Second, the Community's rather sectionalised policy-making mechanisms inhibited an overall and coordinated approach. Third, different aspects of economic and monetary integration had different implications for the states, which resulted in them being viewed with different degrees of enthusiasm. Fourth, for some states the possibility of ceding key macroeconomic and financial powers to the Community raised fundamental sovereignty questions.

But notwithstanding the many obstacles in the way of policy development, real progress towards EMU began to be made in the late 1980s. As a result of a number of factors – notably an increasing appreciation by governments of the benefits for the SEM of economic and financial integration, the enthusiasm of the Commission for progress, and the amendment of the EEC Treaty by the SEA to include a new chapter on 'Co-operation in Economic and Monetary Policy' – the Community formally embarked on the road to EMU. Differences remained between the states over what precisely EMU should consist of and what should be the timetable for its full implementation, but all (apart from the UK) subscribed to the broad outlines of the scheme that was put forward in April 1989 by the Delors Committee in its *Report on Economic and*

Monetary Union (see Chapter 8 for the circumstances in which the Committee was established). The Committee proved to be the forerunner of the 1990–1 IGC on EMU, in that not only did it clear much of the ground for the establishment of the IGC, but many of its proposals – including the principle of a three-stage transition to EMU – were accepted by the IGC and incorporated in the Maastricht Treaty.

The Maastricht provisions on EMU and their subsequent application were described in Chapters 4 and 5, so will not be repeated here. Suffice it to say that the Treaty established a scheme and a timetable for progression to EMU. The main feature of the scheme was increasing coordination and convergence of the economic and monetary policies of all member states, leading to a single currency in which monetary policy would be made within the framework of a European System of Central Banks (ESCB). The main feature of the timetable was a three-stage transitional process leading to the adoption of a single currency by January 1999 at the latest.

The single currency duly came into operation in January 1999, with eleven of the EU's fifteen member states as members – Denmark, Sweden and the UK chose not to participate, and Greece did not meet the qualifying convergence criteria. Amongst the principal features of the single currency system are the following:

- The exchange rates between single currency members are irrevocably fixed. In the first half of 2002 the banknotes and coinage of members will be replaced by single currency – that is, euro – banknotes and coinage.
- Euro zone countries can no longer take individual decisions on what monetary policies – including interest rate policies – they should pursue. The euro zone has common monetary policies, which are determined through the zone's own institutional structures. At the heart of these monetary policies is a strong anti-inflationary ethos. (See the section on the ESCB in Chapter 11 for an account of the nature of the euro zone's institutional structure and the policy remit within which it must act.)
- The macroeconomic policies of euro zone countries, though not common like monetary policies, must be closely aligned. The framework for this alignment is known as the Stability and Growth Pact, which obliges members to practice prudent fiscal policies and, more particularly, to maintain broadly balanced national budgets over the economic cycle. Non-compliance with the terms of the Stability and Growth Pact can lead to sanctions being applied to offenders.
- The four non euro member countries are not tied to the terms of euro zone monetary and fiscal policy, but they are expected broadly to coordinate their economic policies with the others. Furthermore, they are obliged to continue to comply with the 'multilateral surveillance'

system of national economies that was established as part of the preparation for the single currency. If at some point they decide to join the euro system, they will be required to meet qualifying criteria similar to those applying to the founding members.

Clearly the establishment of the single currency marks a major step forward in the European integration process. On the one hand, the single currency has considerable symbolic significance, with the replacement of the French franc, the German deutschmark, the Italian lira, the Spanish peseta and so on with the euro. It may well be that this will provide much impetus to the development of a common European identity. On the other hand, single currency states have given up sovereign control of two key policy instruments – exchange rate and interest rate levels – and have accepted stiff limitations on what they can do in respect of budgetary and fiscal policy. The powers of Euro-level bodies have been further extended.

But though the single currency system advances European integration, it remains to be seen whether it will be judged a success. The rationale is that, by creating a more stable economic and monetary environment and thus providing greater predictability for investments and markets, the single currency will promote growth and prosperity. But problems may well arise. There may well, for example, be conflicts between 'expansionist' politicians and 'cautious' bankers over the contents of policies. There may be differences between national governments over policies: will, for instance, the governments of countries with high levels of unemployment accept – given that they no longer have interest rate or exchange rate adjustments available to them – tight fiscal policies that are judged to be in the general interest of Euroland? And there may be sharp disputes if any member states are seen to be endangering the euro system by not abiding by the terms of the Stability and Growth Pact.

Functional policies

The EU has interests and responsibilities in many functional policies: that is, policies with a clear functional purpose and a more specific nature than the policies considered under the previous heading.

Probably the best known of the EU functional policies are the justice and home affairs, cohesion, and research and technological development policies. Less prominent functional policies include education policy, cultural policy, and consumer protection policy. Since it is not possible to examine all of the EU's functional policies here, attention will be directed to six of the more important ones. The examinations that follow will, in addition to explaining the features of the six policy spheres in question, also illustrate the range and varying depth of EU involvement in different functional areas.

Justice and home affairs policies

In the mid 1970s the EC member states began to exchange information and cooperate with one another on matters relating to the monitoring and control of terrorism, drugs, and organised crime. A series of mechanisms, which were quite outside the framework of the Community Treaties and came to be known as the Trevi process, were developed and brought together, often on a semi-secret basis, officials from Interior and Justice ministries, senior police and intelligence officers, and ministers. Over the years the issues covered by Trevi developed – due in no small part to the need to dismantle internal border controls as part of the SEM programme – and by the late 1980s the original 'threats' of terrorism, drugs and organised crime had been joined by a variety of matters relating to immigration, visas, public order, and customs controls.

This array of policy interests, and the plethora of *ad hoc* arrangements developed to deal with them, were brought together and strengthened by the Maastricht Treaty. They were so mainly under the third pillar of the Treaty – dealing with Provisions on Cooperation in the Fields of Justice and Home Affairs (JHA). The contents of the Maastricht third pillar were set out in Chapter 5, so they will be only summarised here. First, the member states were to regard nine policy areas – including asylum policy, immigration policy, and the combating of drug addition – as 'matters of common interest'. Visa policy was incorporated into the TEC, with the requirement that a common visa policy should be adopted, by qualified majority voting rules in the Council, by 1 January 1996. Second, the Council was empowered to adopt joint positions and joint actions (through, for example, the issuing of resolutions and recommendations), and to draw up conventions. Third, new institutional arrangements to promote cooperation and coordination, and to enable the EU to fulfil its obligations under the Treaty, were to be established.

For the most part, the JHA policy sphere has been something of a disappointment to those who have wished to see it become the focus of robust EU-level policy activity. Certainly there has been no shortage of activity, and there have been developments of significance. For example: resolutions have been adopted on, amongst other matters, common rules for the admission of third-country nationals for employment and study purposes (1994) and asylum procedures (1995); conventions have been adopted, including ones on the use of information technology for customs purposes (1995) and extradition between member states (1997); and the

European Police Office (Europol), whose creation had been agreed in a 1995 convention, has been established. (For a fuller account of JHA developments, see Monar, 1998; Ucarer, 1999.)

However, despite these achievements, progress in most JHA policy areas has been slow. Moreover, where there has been progress there have often been implementation problems. The early history of Europol is illustrative: the Europol Convention – establishing a criminal investigation office to facilitate the exchange of intelligence between the police forces of member states in order to prevent and combat serious cross-border crime – was signed in July 1995; national ratifications of the Convention were not completed until June 1998; the Convention did not fully enter into force until October 1998; even when it did enter into force its work was largely confined to anti drugs activities and it will be some time before Europol becomes fully operational, not least because there have been major policy and technical difficulties in establishing its vast computer database.

There are a number of reasons why JHA policy has been difficult to develop. The most important is that many JHA policies are of a highly sensitive kind, raising deep cultural issues – on, for example, the exchange of sensitive information and individual rights – and touching directly on national sovereignty concerns. Because it is a sensitive policy area, decision-making is largely intergovernmental in character with unanimity normally required in the Council, which makes decision-making very difficult. Another problem is that many JHA policies are extremely complex, with, for example, numerous – often non congruent – national agencies involved and very different national civil laws applying.

Dissatisfaction with the operation of the third pillar resulted in it being much discussed in the 1996–7 IGC and in it being the policy area most strengthened by the Amsterdam Treaty. The ways in which this strengthening was undertaken were set out in some detail in Chapter 5 so, as with the contents of the JHA elements of the Maastricht Treaty, only the major points of the Amsterdam Treaty will be summarised here. First, several JHA policy areas – including immigration, asylum, and refugees and displaced persons – were transferred from the intergovernmental pillar three to the much more supranational pillar one. Within the EC pillar, most decisions were to be taken by unanimous vote in the Council (apart from visa policy), but provision was made for the possible introduction of qualified majority voting after five years. Second, policy objectives were clarified. Third, the Schengen Agreement – of which most member states were signatories and which had been used, on an extra-treaty basis, to remove most internal border controls – was to be incorporated into the EU framework. Fourth, pillar three, which was to continue to be intergovernmental in character, was refocused and retitled 'Provisions on Police and Judicial Cooperation in Criminal Matters'.

The Amsterdam Treaty quite explicitly makes the point that the aim of JHA and JHA-related policy at EU level is to create 'an area of freedom, security and justice' in which there is free movement of persons behind common external borders. This policy area is thus very much part of the broad policy goal to create a border-free Europe, with as many as possible of the internal barriers to free movement removed. Because, however, it is a policy area that contains many complexities and sensitivities, it is moving forward only hesitantly. One aspect of this hesitancy is the cautious attitude taken towards the use of qmv. Another aspect is the various flexibility provisions associated with the policy area – as seen, for example, in the Amsterdam Treaty provision permitting Denmark, Ireland and the UK to refrain from participating in parts of the policy, and in Ireland and the UK's non membership of the Schengen system.

Cohesion policy

There are a number of policies, grouped under the general name of cohesion policy, that are designed to provide a partial counterbalance to the 'natural' effects of the internal market by promoting a more balanced distribution of resources and economic development across the EU.

The main policy instruments of cohesion policy are the Structural Funds, of which the European Regional Development Fund (ERDF) and the European Social Fund (ESF) are the most important. The nature and operation of these Funds is considered in Chapters 6 and 14, so let it just be noted here that they account for over one-third of the EU budget (the largest proportion after the Common Agricultural Policy), and they are used for the general purposes of regional economic generation and combating unemployment. For example, the ESF has made an important contribution to employment training and retraining in the member states, especially in respect of young people and the long-term unemployed, to whom it is mainly directed.

Another policy instrument is the Cohesion Fund. Created at the 1992 Edinburgh summit this is a much smaller-scale operation than the Structural Funds – accounting for only 3 per cent of the EU budget. It is available, for infrastructure and environmental projects, in only four member states: Greece, Ireland, Portugal, and Spain.

Increased importance has been attached to cohesion policy since the mid 1980s. This partly reflects feelings that a vigorous cohesion policy is necessary for reasons of social justice; it partly reflects beliefs that weaker parts of the EU economy can become stronger if they are given focused and directed assistance; and it partly reflects hard political bargaining by the governments of those member states that are the main beneficiaries of cohesion policy – Spain, in particular, has threatened on more than one occasion to cause problems in other policy areas if cohesion policy is not prioritised/protected/structured in a manner that is to Spain's advantage.

Social policy

The EEC Treaty provided for the development of a Community social policy. It did so in two ways: Articles 117–22 stated that there should be closer cooperation between the member states in the social field, and particularly specified (in Article 119) that member states should apply the principle that men and women should receive equal pay for equal work; Articles 123–8 laid the foundation for the ESF (see above and Chapters 6 and 14).

Although the ESF was quickly established, little was done for many years to give effect to Articles 117–22, apart from some developments – via legislation and Court of Justice judgements – in areas such as working conditions, entitlement to benefits, and equal opportunities. However, in 1989 a major boost was given to Community social policy when the Commission – believing that the SEM programme should have a 'social dimension' – produced *The Community Charter of Fundamental Social Rights for Workers*. The Charter was inevitably somewhat general in character and terminology, but it contained the fundamental principles that should apply to twelve main themes. Amongst these themes were: free movement of workers on the basis of equal treatment in access to employment and social protection; employment on the basis of fair remuneration; improvement of living and working conditions; freedom of association and collective bargaining; and protection of children and adolescents. The Charter was adopted by eleven member states (the UK was the exception) at the December 1989 Strasbourg European Council meeting. The Strasbourg summit also took 'note of the fact that the Commission has drawn up an action programme on the application of the Charter and calls upon the Council to deliberate upon the Commission's proposals in the light of the social dimension of the internal market and having regard to the national and Community responsibilities' (European Council, 1989, p. 7).

By the end of 1993 the Commission had presented detailed proposals on all 47 measures listed in its action programme, including 29 that required legislative action. Included amongst the latter were several very controversial proposals, such as the Directive on the Organisation of Working Time, to which the UK government was strongly opposed. The Working Time Directive, which had first been presented in 1990, was eventually approved by the Council in December 1993, with the UK, after winning several concessions and derogations, abstaining. The Directive lays down provisions on such matters as maximum weekly working time, daily rest breaks, weekly rest, annual paid leave, and night-time working hours.

The opposition of the UK government to much of the Social Charter and the action programme was carried into the negotiations leading up to the Maastricht Treaty. As was noted in Chapter 5, the UK was unwilling to sanction Treaty extensions of the remit and the decision-making powers of the EU in the social field, with the consequence that the other eleven member states contracted a separate Protocol and Agreement on Social Policy. Important features of the Agreement between the eleven included: a recalling and strengthening of 'traditional' social policy interests; a broadening of the scope of social policy to embrace new matters relating to human resources, social protection, social exclusion, and employment (with 'employment' being extended to include the protection of workers when their employment contract was terminated, and the representation and collective defence of the interests of workers and employers); and management and labour were offered greater consultation, and also the opportunity to negotiate agreements at EU level that could be implemented either on the basis of established national procedures or – at the joint request of the signatory parties – by a Council decision on a proposal from the Commission.

The Amsterdam Treaty further strengthened the treaty base of social policy. It did so in two main ways. First, the UK, now with a Labour government, removed its objections to the Maastricht Agreement on Social Policy, with the consequence that the Agreement was incorporated into the TEC. Second, a new Employment Title was created in the TEC, with a focus on encouraging and exhorting member states to regard the promotion of employment as a matter of high priority and common concern.

What effects the Amsterdam Treaty's strengthening of social policy will have remains to be seen, but it is clear that with most EU governments greatly concerned with increasing market competitiveness, there is not much prospect of strong employee protectionist measures that could threaten labour market flexibility. The focus is likely to be, as it has been for some years, more on market-related measures that boost employment. These measures are taking a number of (essentially voluntary) forms, including the attempted coordination of member state activities through employment guidelines, and the monitoring of national employment plans.

That all said, however, the extent of EU involvement in protective social policy measures should not be underestimated. By way of illustration of this, just a few of the directives that have been passed in recent years may be cited: health and safety of temporary workers (1991); safety signs at work (1992); protection of pregnant women at work and women who have recently given birth (1992); organisation of working time (1993); protection of young people at work (1994); and parental leave from work (1996). In addition, the EU runs social policy programmes of various kinds, including public health programmes and programmes to assist the elderly and the disabled.

Energy policy

Given the existence of the ECSC and Euratom Treaties, the centrality of energy to any modern economy, the disruption and damage that was caused by oil price increases in the 1970s, and the immense savings that the Commission has for years identified as accruing from an integrated energy market, it is perhaps surprising that until the late 1980s very little progress was made towards a common energy policy (as opposed to having some policies for particular energy sectors). The main obstacle to progress was that the member states – with their differing domestic energy resources, differing energy requirements, and large, state-owned, monopolistic energy industries – preferred essentially national solutions.

Since the late 1980s, however, there has been greater receptivity to the idea of a common energy policy. This has been stimulated in no small part by the realisation that energy cannot be isolated from the increasingly integrated SEM, and also by increased appreciation of the over-reliance of the EU on external suppliers – the EU depends on non-member countries for almost half of its energy requirements, with this dependence being as high as 70 per cent in the case of oil. Attitudes have thus been changing, and this is bringing about a rapid evolution in energy policy. The process is focused on three basic objectives:

- *Developing an internal market in energy.* Progress has been made in a number of areas, including opening up public procurement in the energy equipment sector, standardisation of energy equipment and products, and liberalisation of the electricity and gas markets.
- *Developing external energy relations and ensuring security of supply.* Initiatives in this sphere have largely focused on establishing binding rules at the international level for the sale and transportation of energy. A major breakthrough was achieved in 1991 when 47 countries signed the Commission-promoted European Energy Charter. The principles and objectives set out in the Charter were then used as a base for the negotiation of the Energy Charter Treaty and Energy Charter Protocol on energy efficiency and related environmental aspects, which were agreed by 50 countries in 1994. Central to the Treaty are requirements that energy trade should be conducted on the basis of World Trade Organisation (WTO) rules, and associated energy policies – on

exploration, production, and transportation – should be non-discrimi-natory. (For further information on the Treaty and Protocol, and on EU energy policy more generally, see Matlary, 1997.)

- *Minimising the negative impact on the environment of energy use and production.* Measures here include a variety of programmes with such purposes as developing alternative sources of non-polluting energy and reinforcing domestic and industrial efficiency. However, several proposals to give the environmental dimension of energy policy real teeth by establishing fiscal incentives (for energy saving and the reduction of environmental pollution) and disincentives (for polluting) have met with resistance in the Council of Ministers.

Clearly there has been significant progress in the energy policy field, though much still remains to be done. According to a senior official in DG XVII (Energy) six elements have been identified by the Commission 'to get the structure right': there must be complete liberalisation of energy generation; adequate liberalisation must take place at the customer base; an effective network must be established to allow access to the grid; 'unbundling' is required for markets to work fully; effective and independent regulation is needed to prevent discrimination; and facilitating mechanisms must be put in place to make trade work in practice (*The Parliament Magazine,* 5 October 1998, p. 10).

Research and technological development policy

There was no mention of research and technological development (R & TD) policy in the original EEC Treaty, but it nonetheless began to be developed from the late 1970s in response to a growing concern that the EC's member states were not sufficiently promoting innovation or adapting to innovation, especially in high-tech and other advanced sectors. Recognising, and wishing to promote further, the importance of this policy area, the member states added a new title on 'Research and Technological Development' to the EEC Treaty via the SEA. The title was then developed a little by the Maastricht Treaty, whilst preserving the same broad objective of 'strengthening the scientific and technological bases of Community industry and encouraging it to become more competitive at international level' (Article 163, TEC, ex 130f).

The EU's R & TD policy is pursued, on the one hand, by directly managing and financing research activities, and on the other hand by attempting to create a framework and environment in which research that falls within the EU's priorities is encouraged and facilitated. More specifically, research activity takes four main forms:

(1) Research is undertaken directly by the EU itself at its Joint Research Centre (JRC). The JRC consists of seven establishments and employs over 2000 people. Most of the work of the JRC is concerned with nuclear energy (especially safety issues), materials, remote sensing and, increasingly, industrial research related to the SEM.

(2) The largest part of EU R&TD consists of shared-cost or contract research. This research is not undertaken by Commission employees but by tens of thousands of researchers in universities, research institutes, and public and private companies. The EU's role is to develop and agree the principles, aims, and conditions of the programmes under which the research is conducted, to coordinate activities, and to provide some of the finance (usually around 50 per cent of the total cost of the research). The better known programmes in this approach to research activity include ESPRIT (information technology), BRITE (industrial technology) and RACE (advanced telecommunications).

(3) There are concerted action-research projects where the EU does not finance the actual research, but facilitates and finances the coordination of work being done at the national level. The EU's medical research programme takes this form.

(4) Some of the research activity takes none of the above three 'conventional' forms, but consists of arrangements in which, for example, only some member states participate, or in which the EU cooperates with non member states and international organisations. Work undertaken within the framework of the European Research Coordinating Agency (EUREKA) is of this type, with EUREKA's membership including not only EU states but also Norway, Switzerland, Central and Eastern European countries, and Russia.

The EU uses multi-annual framework programmes to coordinate and give strategic direction to its R&TD policies and activities. The First Framework Programme covered 1984–7, the Second 1987–91, the Third (which overlapped with the Second) 1990–4, the Fourth 1994–8, and the Fifth 1999–2002. The themes of, and the funding allocated to, the Fifth Programme are as follows: improving the quality of life and management of living resources – 2.4 billion euro (£1.7 billion); creating a user-friendly information society – 3.6 billion euro (£2.5 billion); promoting competitive and sustainable growth – 2.7 billion euro (£1.9 billion); energy, environment and sustainable development – 2.1 billion euro (£1.5 billion); international cooperation – 475 million euro (£333 million); promotion of innovation and participation of small and medium-sized enterprises – 363 million euro (£225 million); and improving human research potential and the socioeconomic knowledge base – 1.28 billion euro (£898 million). In addition, 1 billion euro (£715 million) is allocated to the Joint Research

Centre and 1.26 billion (£884 million) to the Euratom nuclear research programme. The grand total of 14.96 billion euro (£10.5 billion) represents an increase of 4.6 per cent in real terms over the Fourth Framework programme.

Environmental policy

As with R & TD policy, there was no mention of environmental policy in the original EEC Treaty, but it was incorporated by the SEA through a new title – 'Environment'. The Maastricht Treaty and (to a lesser extent) the Amsterdam Treaty built on the SEA provisions, though less in terms of objectives – which remain so vague as to be virtually meaningless – than in terms of operating principles. There are two key TEC articles in this respect:

> Environmental protection requirements must be integrated into the definition and implementation of the Community policies and activities referred to in Article 3 (which lists the other main areas of EC policy activity), in particular with a view to promoting sustainable development. (Article 6)

> Community policy on the environment shall aim at a high level of protection taking into account the diversity of situations in the various regions of the Community. It shall be based on the precautionary principle and on the principles that preventive action should be taken, that environmental damage should as a priority be rectified at source and that the polluter should pay. (Article 174 (2), ex 130(2))

Since Community legislation began to appear in the early 1970s, over 200 legal instruments have been adopted, most of them in the form of directives. They cover matters as important and as diverse as water and air pollution, disposal of chemicals, waste treatment, and protection of species and natural resources. Alongside, and supporting, the legislation are several other policy instruments, ranging from information campaigns to arrangements for the collection of environmental data – the latter being the particular responsibility of the European Environment Agency, which after long delays caused by disagreements in the Council over its siting, was eventually established in Copenhagen in 1994.

Many of the environmental policy instruments, both legislative and non-legislative, have been designed to give effect to the series of Environmental Action Programmes that have been adopted since 1973. The Fifth Programme, entitled *Towards Sustainability* and running from 1993 to 2000, seeks to give effect to the principles identified above (sustainability, preventative action, the polluter pays and so on) and to bring about major innovations in EU environmental policy. These innovations include:

- A greater focus on the sources rather than the receptors of pollution.
- An identification of five 'main target sectors' where an EU-level approach is seen as being particularly necessary: industry, energy, transport, agriculture, and tourism.
- A more holistic approach based on addressing the behavioural patterns of producers, consumers, governments and citizens, and on ensuring that all EU policies are assessed in terms of their environmental impact.
- An increased emphasis on the shared responsibilities of different levels of government (European, national, regional and local) towards the environment.

This last innovation – shared responsibilities – touches on a very important and unsatisfactory aspect of environmental policy: implementation. Because of the way in which the EU is structured, and because of the Commission's limited resources, implementation of policies and laws is a problem in several EU policy spheres and sectors. It is so, however, particularly in respect of the environment. There are a number of reasons for this, of which expense is frequently the most crucial. It is, for example, very costly to implement the measures required to meet the standards set out in the 1975 bathing water directive – a directive that is notorious for poor implementation.

Sectoral policies

Some EU policies are directed towards specific economic sectors. A few such policies – covering coal and steel, atomic energy, agriculture and transport – were explicitly provided for in the Founding Treaties. Others have their origins in a combination of factors: difficulties in adjusting to changed market conditions; rapid sectoral decline; and effective political lobbying by interested parties.

The most obvious example of a sectoral policy is the Common Agricultural Policy (CAP), which consumes by far the largest proportion of EU expenditure and where most policy-making responsibilities have been transferred from the member states to the EU (the CAP is examined in some detail in Chapter 15). Other, though more modest and less comprehensive, examples of sectoral policies include atomic energy, where important work is undertaken in areas such as research and safety standards, and shipbuilding, where a code of practice includes specified limitations on governmental subsidies and aid and where support is available to bolster competitiveness and increase industrial cooperation. (Most EU measures on shipbuilding are scheduled to be eventually replaced by the OECD Shipbuilding Agreement, which is intended to create a framework for controlling subsidies, enforcing fair competition and preventing unfair trading priorities at a world level.)

Two important sectoral policies will be taken to illustrate EU sectoral activity: fishing and steel.

Fishing

After years of discussion and the periodic issuing of laws regulating aspects of the industry, a legally enforceable Common Fisheries Policy (CFP) was agreed in 1983. The essential rationale of the CFP is to ensure that, with resources diminishing, existing fish stocks are exploited responsibly, with due care for the marine ecosystem and with the interests of fishermen and consumers protected as far as possible. The main pillars of the CFP are as follows:

- *Access.* All waters within the EU's exclusive fishing zone, which extends to 200 nautical miles from its coastlines, are open to all EU fishermen. However, within a 12-mile limit of their own shores member states may reserve fishing for their own fishermen and those with traditional rights.
- *Conservation.* Atlantic and North Sea fish stocks are controlled by the annual setting of total allowance catches (TACs), which are divided into national quotas. The size of TACs and quotas has been reduced over the years in an attempt to protect endangered stocks. These reductions are agreed within the framework of Multiannual Guidance Programmes (MAGPs). In MAGP IV (covering the years 1997–2001) the aim is to reduce fishing by up to 30 per cent for stocks in danger, with national governments being allowed some choice as to how to meet targets: either by laying up vessels, reducing time at sea, or a combination of these two options.

    TACs and quotas are notoriously difficult to enforce and there is known to be widespread abuse, with the landing of fish that are over quota or undersized. The EU has tried to tackle the problem by strengthening policy implementation mechanisms. Amongst the mechanisms in place are the following: all EU fishing vessels are required to have a fishing licence on board; Commission inspectors (of which there are only a few) have the right of unannounced arrival in ports and on vessels; and use is made of satellite technology to monitor fishing activities.

- *Market management*. There is a market organisation for fish that covers a price system, marketing arrangements, and an external trade policy.
- *Structural measures*. Funding is made available from the EU budget for matters such as processing and market development projects, conversion and modernisation schemes, and redeployment.
- *External negotiations*. Negotiations with non EU countries on fishing – which mostly concern access to waters and the conservation of fish stocks – are conducted by EU representatives on behalf of all member states.

Steel

The ECSC Treaty is essentially based on a liberal economic philosophy in the sense that it is principally concerned with the removal of barriers to trade. So, for the products falling within its jurisdiction – of which, of course, steel is one – it provides for the removal of internal tariffs, quantitative restrictions and most state aids. It also forbids, subject to certain exemptions, price discrimination and cartels. However, some direct intervention is also permitted and the ECSC authorities have the power to grant loans for capital investment, to finance research and development and, above all, to set mandatory minimum prices and production quotas when a 'manifest crisis' is deemed to exist. These policy instruments, developed and clarified by secondary legislation, do not add up to a comprehensive legal framework for steel – key decisions on individual enterprises, for example, are still taken primarily at the national level – but they do constitute a very important part of the sectoral law. Indeed, the EU authorities have a potentially greater power of intervention in steel than in any other sector apart from agriculture and fisheries, and they have used these powers to try to deal with the problem of falling demand that gave rise to crises in the steel industry in the late 1970s/early 1980s and again in the 1990s. The way in which these powers have been used are described in Chapter 13.

External policies

The nature of the EU's external policies are examined at length in Chapter 16, so just two key points will be made here. First, there are many aspects to the external policies but they can be grouped broadly under four headings: external trade policies, foreign and security policy, development cooperation policy, and the external dimension of internal policies. Second, external policies constitute an extremely important part of the overall EU policy agenda, and they are likely to loom even larger in the future, not least as foreign policy is more fully developed and defence policy is tackled.

Characteristics of EU policies

Three features of EU policies are particularly striking.

The range and diversity of EU policies

The EU is still sometimes referred to as 'the Common Market'. It is so because many of its policies and laws centre on the promotion and defence of an internally free and externally protected market. Hence, there are policies that are designed to encourage the free movement of goods, persons, services, and capital; there is the competition policy, which seeks to facilitate fair and open competition within and across the borders of the member states; there is the common external tariff (CET); and there is the common commercial policy (CCP). In practice, however, not all of these policies are complete or wholly successful. There are still, for example, barriers related to company law and company taxation that can make it difficult for firms in different member states to engage in joint commercial activities, and despite strenuous activity on harmonisation and approximation many non-tariff barriers to internal trade still exist. In consequence, the EU is, in some respects, less than the common market it is commonly supposed to be.

But in other respects it is more than a common market, in that many of its policy concerns range far beyond matters that are part and parcel of a common market's requirements. The policy concerns of the EU are not, in other words, just concerned with dismantling internal barriers and providing conditions for fair trade on the one hand, and presenting a common external front on the other. There are two main aspects to this.

First, with regard to the EU's economic policies, many of these are not based solely on the non-interventionist/*laissez faire* principles that are often thought of as providing the ethos, or even the ideology, of the EU. In some spheres the EU tends very much towards interventionism/managerialism/regulation, and in so doing it does not always restrict itself to 'market efficiency' policies. This is most obviously seen in the way in which the regional, social, and consumer protection policies, plus much of the CAP, have as their precise purpose the counteracting and softening of nationally unacceptable or socially inequitable market consequences. On a broader front, there are the euro-related policies which clearly take the EU – and especially Euroland – far beyond being 'just' a common market and give it many, though not yet all, of the characteristics of an economic and monetary union.

Second, the EU has developed policies that are not only non-market focused but also non-economic focused. Of these the most obvious are those that fall within the CFSP framework, where the states consult and attempt to coordinate their positions on key foreign policy questions. In addition to the CFSP, there are many other policy areas – such as the environment, broadcasting, and combating crime – which were long thought of as not being the EU's concern, but where important developments have occurred.

The differing degrees of EU policy involvement

The EU's responsibility for policy-making and policy management varies enormously across its range of policy interests. In those spheres where significant responsibilities are exercised, arrangements are usually well established, and effective policy instruments – legal and financial – are usually available. Where, however, EU involvement is marginal, policy processes may be confined to little more than occasional exchanges of ideas and information between interested parties, whilst policy instruments may merely be of the exhortive and persuasive kind such as are common in many international organisations. Table 12.1 provides an indication of the varying extent of EU involvement in different policy areas, and Table 12.2 gives an indication of the varying nature of EU policy involvement.

Examples of extensive EU involvement are the CCP, the CAP, and the CFP. Here, most major policy decisions, such as those on external tariffs, agricultural prices, and fishing quotas, are taken at the EU level, whilst their detailed and supposedly uniform implementation is left to the states, acting as agents of the EU. In areas where these so-called common policies are not in reality totally common – and both the CAP and the CFP allow room for governments to provide national aids and assistance – decisions of any significance normally require at least clearance from Brussels.

Moving along the spectrum of EU policy involvement, there are many spheres in which the EU's interests and competence, though less comprehensive than in the examples just given, are still very significant, and complement and supplement the activities of the states in important ways. Competition policy is one example. This seeks to encourage free and open competition throughout the EU by, for instance, setting out conditions under which firms can make and sell their products, laying down conditions under which national authorities may assist firms, and imposing restrictions on certain types of company merger. Social policy is another example, with much of the focus in this sphere being on job

Table 12.1 *The extent of EU policy involvement*

Extensive EU policy involvement	*Policy responsibility shared between the EU and the member states*	*Limited EU policy involvement*	*Virtually no EU policy involvement*
Trade	Regional	Health	Housing
Agriculture	Competition	Education	Civil liberties
Fishing	Industrial	Defence	Domestic crime
Market regulation	Foreign	Social welfare	
Monetary (for euro members)	Environmental		
	Equal opportunities		
	Working conditions		
	Consumer protection		
	Movement across external borders		
	Macroeconomic (especially for euro members)		
	Energy		
	Transport		
	Cross-border crime		

Table 12.2 *The nature of EU policy involvement*

Heavy reliance on legal regulation	*A mixture of legal regulation and inter-state cooperation*	*Largely based on inter-state cooperation*
Trade	Industrial	Health
Agriculture	Environmental	Education
Fishing	Transport	Foreign
Regional	Movement across external borders	Defence
Competition	Macroeconomic	Energy
Consumer protection	Energy	Law and order
Working conditions	Social welfare	
Equal opportunities		
Market regulation		

training and retraining, labour mobility, working conditions, and the general promotion of employment.

Turning finally to policy spheres where the EU's involvement is at best limited, examples include education, health, housing, pensions, and social welfare payments. As these examples make clear, many of the policies that fall into this category of low EU involvement are 'merit goods' (as opposed to 'public goods') and also have major budgetary implications.

Interestingly, if one looks back to, say, 1970, many issues that would have been listed then as being in the category of limited policy involvement – such as environment and foreign policy – are now no longer so marginal. Environment has spawned policy programmes and legislation, foreign policy has evolved its own machinery and has seen increasingly coordinated policy development, and both have been awarded treaty recognition. At the same time, some policy spheres which in 1970 the Community would not have been thought of as having any competence in at all, have crept onto the agenda. Examples include defence policy and the various JHA policies.

The patchy and somewhat uncoordinated nature of EU policies

The overall EU policy framework can hardly be said to display a clear pattern or coherence. Some effort is now being made to pull it together and give it a rationale, notably via the so-called subsidiarity principle which implies that only those policies which it is agreed are best dealt with at EU level rather than national level do become the EU's concern. The problem with this principle, however, both as a description of the present reality and as a prescription for future action, is that it is vague and question-begging. Descriptions of the present and evolving policy framework as being centred on 'managed and tempered capitalism' or 'a controlled open market' are perhaps of more use in capturing the essence of the EU's policy interests, but they too are still far from wholly satisfactory in that they do not embrace the full flavour of the array and varying depths of EU policy interests, nor do they draw attention to the conflicting principles that underlie different parts of the policy network.

The fact is that the considerable national and political differences that exist in the EU make it difficult to develop coordinated and coherent policies based on shared principles and agreed objectives very difficult. This is so because any policy development is usually only possible if searching questions are answered to the satisfaction of a large number of EU actors. From the viewpoint of the member states these questions include: is the national (or at least government) interest being served?; is the cooperation and integration that the policy development involves politically acceptable?; and, if the policy sphere does require closer relations with other states, is the EU the most desirable arena in which it should occur? As the EU's extensive range of policies demonstrates, these questions have often been answered in the affirmative, though normally only after being subject to caveats and reservations which sit uneasily beside, and sometimes clash with, one another. But often, too, the responses have been in the negative, or at least have been so on the part of a sufficient number to prevent progress.

Policy development has consequently been as much about what is possible as what is desirable. In the absence of a centre of power with the authority and internal coherence to take an overall view of EU requirements and impose an ordered pattern, policies have tended to be the outcome of complex and laboured interactions, where different, and often contrasting, requirements, preferences, reservations, and fears have all played a part. As a result, the EU's overall policy picture is inevitably patchy and rather ragged. A few spheres – such as the CAP and, increasingly, the operation of the SEM – are well developed. Other spheres, however, which it might have been expected would be developed, are either developed only in uncoordinated and partial ways, or are barely developed at all.

Industrial policy is a prime example of just such an uncoordinated and underdeveloped policy. With industry employing 35 per cent of the EU's active population and accounting for 40 per cent of the gross value added of the EU's economy, and with industrial growth in the EU lagging behind competitors, it might be expected that an industrial policy would be at the very centre of EU policy concerns. In practice, a fully developed, comprehensive, and coherent industrial policy does not exist. What do exist are a large number of policies, themselves usually only partially developed, which affect industry, but which do not in any sense constitute an integrated industrial framework with clear and consistent goals. The most obvious of these policies are those that are designed to promote the free movement of goods, persons, services and capital throughout the EU. Others include the competition policy, the research policy, aspects of the regional and social policies, and specific policies for some expanding and some contracting sectors.

Concluding comments

A central theme of this chapter has been the range and diversity of the EU's policy responsibilities and interests. There are now few policy areas with which the EU does not have at least some sort of involvement.

But another theme has been that there are many deficiencies in EU policies. Industrial policy, energy policy, and regional policy are but three examples of key policy areas where there are not, if EU effectiveness is to be maximised, sufficiently strong or integrated policy frameworks with clear and consistent goals. They are too partial and too fragmented. They are also, in general, underfunded.

Of course, similar critical comments about underdevelopment and lack of cohesion can also be levelled against most national policy frameworks. But not to the same extent. For, at the individual state level, there is, even when the political system is weak and decentralised, usually more opportunity than there is in the EU for direction from the centre. This is partly because national decision-makers have access to more policy instruments than do EU decision-makers. It is mainly, however, because at state level there is normally some focus of political authority capable of offering leadership and imposing a degree of order: a Head of Government perhaps, a Cabinet or Council of Ministers, a Ministry of Economics or Finance, or a dominant party group. In the EU, the Commission, the Council of Ministers and the European Council are the main foci of political authority and leadership, but none is constituted or organised in such a way as to enable it to establish an overall policy coherence or to enforce a clear and consistent policy direction.

However, as Chapter 13 will attempt to show, the situation is changing.

Chapter 13

Policy Processes

Variations in EU processes
Factors determining EU policy processes
The making of EU legislation
EU legislation after adoption
Characteristic features of EU policy processes
The efficiency of EU policy processes

Variations in EU processes

There cannot be said to be a 'standard' or 'typical' EU policy-making or decision-making process. A multiplicity of actors interact with one another via a myriad of channels.

The actors

There are three main sets of actors: those associated with the EU institutions, with the governments of the member states, and with Euro and national interests. As has been shown in previous chapters, each of these has responsibilities to fulfil and roles to perform. But so variable and fluid are EU policy processes that the nature of the responsibilities and roles may differ considerably according to circumstances. For instance, in one set of circumstances an actor may be anxious to play an active role and may have the power – legal and/or political – to do so. In a second set of circumstances it may not wish to be actively involved, perhaps because it has no particular interests at stake or because prominence may be politically damaging. And in a third set of circumstances it may wish for a leading part but not be able to attain it because of a lack of appropriate power resources.

The channels

The channels vary in four principal respects:

(1) *In their complexity and exhaustiveness.* Some types of decision are made fairly quickly by a relatively small number of people using procedures that are easy to operate. In contrast, others are subject to

complex and exhaustive processes in which many different sorts of actor attempt to determine and shape outcomes.

(2) *In the relative importance of EU-level processes and member state-level processes and in the links between the two levels.* One of the EU's major structural difficulties is that it is multi-layered and there are often no clear lines of authority or hierarchy between the different layers or levels.

(3) *In their levels of seniority.* EU policy processes are conducted at many different levels of seniority, as illustrated by the numerous forums in which the member states meet: Heads of Government in the European Council; Ministers in the Council of Ministers; Permanent Representatives and their deputies in COREPER; and senior officials and national experts in working parties, management and regulatory committees, and expert groups.

(4) *In their degree of formality and structure.* By their very nature the fixed and set-piece occasions of EU policy processes – such as meetings of the Council of Ministers, plenary sessions of the EP, and Council of Ministers/ EP delegation meetings called to resolve legislative and budgetary differences – tend to be formal and structured. Partly because of this, they are often not very well equipped to produce the horse trading, concessions, and compromises that are so often necessary to build majorities, create agreements and further progress. As a result they have come to be supported by a vast network of informal and unstructured channels between EU actors, ranging from the after dinner discussions that are sometimes held at European Council meetings to the continuous rounds of soundings, telephone calls, lunches, lobbying opportunities, and pre-meetings that are such a part of EU life in Brussels, Strasbourg, Luxembourg and national capitals.

Factors determining EU policy processes

The central point made in the previous section – that EU policy-making and decision-making processes are multi-faceted in nature – is illustrated in some detail in Chapters 14, 15 and 16 on the budget, agricultural policy, and external relations. Taken together, these chapters demonstrate how difficult it is to generalise about how the EU functions.

It would of course be expected that, as in individual states, there would be some differences between EU processes in different policy arenas. What is distinctive about the EU, however, is the sheer range and complexity of its processes: a host of actors, operating within the context of numerous EU and national-level institutions, interact with one another on the basis of an array of different decision-making rules and procedures.

In trying to bring an overall perspective to the complexity of EU processes a number of factors can be identified as being especially important in determining the particular mix of actors and channels that are to be found in any particular context.

The treaty base

As was explained in Part 1, the EU is based on four treaties: the Treaty on European Union (TEU), the Treaty Establishing the European Community (TEC), the Treaty Establishing the European Coal and Steel Community, and the Treaty Establishing the European Atomic Energy Community.

One of the most important things these treaties do is to lay down many different decision-making procedures and to specify the circumstances in which they are to be used. As a result the treaties – and especially the TEU and the TEC – are of fundamental importance in shaping the nature of the EU's policy processes and determining the powers exercised by institutions and actors within these processes. This may be illustrated by giving a few examples of the variety of policy-making and decision-making procedures provided for in the TEU and the TEC post-Amsterdam (these procedures are all explained at length elsewhere in the book, either below or in other chapters).

- There are four 'standard' procedures for 'non-administrative' legislation: the consultation, cooperation, co-decision and assent procedures. Key points of difference between these procedures include: (1) the EP can exercise veto powers under the co-decision and assent procedures but cannot do so under the consultation and cooperation procedures; and (2) there are single readings in the Council and the EP under the consultation and assent procedures, two readings under the cooperation procedure, and potentially three readings – or, perhaps more accurately, two readings and a third voting stage – under the co-decision procedure.
- External trade agreements negotiated under Article 133 of the TEC have their own special procedure, under which the Commission and the Council decide and the EP, at best, is only able to offer advice.
- The annual budget also has its own arrangements, under which the Council and the EP are joint budgetary authorities.
- Under the 'flexibility' provisions added to the TEU and the TEC by the Amsterdam Treaty, it is possible for a group of EU member states – constituting less than the full membership but at least a majority – to establish 'closer cooperation' between themselves and to make use of EU institutions, procedures and mechanisms. A decision to so act can be taken by qualified majority, but no such vote may be taken if any

member state objects on the grounds of 'important and stated reasons of national policy'.

- Pillars two and three of the EU (dealing respectively with foreign and security policy and police and judicial cooperation in criminal matters) set out largely, though not wholly, intergovernmental decision-making frameworks that enable non-legislative decisions of various sorts to be taken. In broad terms, most major policy decisions under both pillars require unanimity in the Council and consultation with the EP, whilst operational and procedural decisions can usually be taken by qualified majority vote (qmv) if the Council so decides and without consulting with the EP. Whether or not the EP is consulted, the Council must keep it regularly informed of developments under the two pillars.

The proposed status of the matter under consideration

As a general rule, procedures tend to be more fixed when EU law is envisaged than when it is not. They are fixed most obviously by the treaties, but also by Court of Justice interpretations (for example, the obligation that the Council must wait upon EP opinions before giving Commission proposals legislative status) and by conventions (for example, the understanding in the Council that when a member state has genuine difficulties the matter will not normally be rushed and an effort will be made to reach a compromise even when qmv is permissible).

When law is being made, Commission legislation is usually subject to much less review and discussion than Council or EP and Council legislation. The reason for this is that Commission legislation is normally of an administrative kind – more technical than political. Indeed, much of it consists of updates, applications or amendments to already existing legislation, usually in the sphere of external trade or the CAP. As a result, Commission legislation, prior to being introduced, is often only fully discussed by appropriate officials in the Commission, and perhaps by national officials in a management or regulatory committee. Some Council legislation, on the other hand, and all EP and Council legislation, is broader in scope and is subject to a full legislative procedure. As such it becomes the subject of representations and pressures from many interests, is assessed by the EP and often also by the ESC and the CoR, and is scrutinised in detail in national capitals and in Council forums in Brussels.

Where policy activity does not involve law making, considerable discretion is available to key decision-makers, especially governments, as to which policy processes will be used and who will be permitted to participate. A common procedure when states wish the EU to do something, but do not necessarily wish a new law to be made (which may be because there is no agreement on what the law should be or because, as with foreign policy pronouncements, law is inappropriate), is to issue Council resolutions, declarations, or agreements. These can be as vague or as precise as the Council wishes them to be. Often, resolutions and the like can have a very useful policy impact, even if it is just to keep dialogue going, but because they are not legal instruments they are not normally as subject as most Council or EP and Council legislation to examination and challenge by other EU institutions and actors.

The degree of generality or specificity of the policy issue

At the generality end of the scale, EU policy-making may consist of little more than exchanges of ideas between interested parties to see whether there is common ground for policy coordination, the setting of priorities or possible legislation. Such exchanges and discussions take place at many different levels on an almost continuous basis, but the most important, in the sense that their initiatives are the ones most likely to be followed up, are those which involve *les grands messieurs* of the Commission and the member states.

Far removed from *grands tours d'horizon* by *les grands messieurs* is the daily grind of preparing and drafting the mass of highly detailed and technical regulations that make up the great bulk of the EU's legislative output. Senior EU figures, especially ministers, are not normally directly involved in the processes that lead to such legislation. There may be a requirement that they give the legislation their formal approval, but it is Commission officials, aided in appropriate cases by national officials, who do the basic work.

The newness, importance, controversiality or political sensitivity of the issue in question

The more these characteristics apply, and the perception of the extent to which they do may vary – what may be a technical question for one may be politically charged for another – the more complex policy processes are likely to be. If, for example, it seems likely that a proposal for an EP and Council directive on some aspect of animal welfare will cause significant difficulties for farmers, it is probable that the accompanying decision-making process will display all or most of the following features: particularly intensive pre-proposal consultations by the Commission; the raising of voices from many sectional and promotional interest groups; very careful examination of the proposal by the EP and the ESC; long and exhaustive negotiations in the Council; considerable activity and manoeuvring on the fringes of formal meetings, and in between the meetings; and, overall, much delay and many alterations en route to the (possible) eventual adoption of the proposal.

The balance of policy responsibilities between EU and national levels

Where there has been a significant transfer of responsibilities to the EU – as, for example, with agricultural, commercial, and competition policies – EU-level processes are naturally very important. In such policy spheres, EU institutions, particularly the Commission, have many tasks to perform: monitoring developments, making adjustments, ensuring existing policies and programmes are replaced when necessary, and so on. On the other hand, where the EU's policy role is at best supplementary to that of the member states – education policy and health policy are examples – most significant policy and decision-making activity continues to be channelled through the customary national procedures, and policy activity at EU level may be very limited in scope.

Circumstances and the perceptions of circumstances

This is seemingly rather vague, but it refers to the crucially important fact that policy development and decision-making processes in the EU are closely related to prevailing political and economic circumstances, to the perceptions by key actors – especially states – of their needs in the circumstances, and to perceptions of the potential of the EU to act as a problem-solving organisation in regard to the circumstances. Do the advantages of acting at EU level, as opposed to national level, and of acting in the EU in a particular way as opposed to another way, outweigh the disadvantages?

It is best to explain this point about circumstances with a specific example. Steel will be taken because it shows in a particularly clear manner how changing circumstances may bring about related changes in EU processes.

As was explained in Chapter 3, the Treaty of Paris gave considerable powers to the High Authority (later Commission). Until the mid 1970s these powers were used primarily to liberalise the market, with the High Authority/Commission expending much of its time and energy on ensuring that internal barriers would be removed and cartels eliminated. From 1974, however, market conditions began to deteriorate as a result of falling internal and external demand, reduced profit margins, and increased costs. This led the Commission to look more towards its hitherto largely neglected interventionist powers. Initially an essentially voluntarist path was preferred, but when this proved to be ineffective a stronger approach was taken. By the end of 1980 an assortment of highly *dirigiste* policy instruments, some of which were mandatory, had been put in place. These included common external positions in the form of price agreements and export restraint agreements, strict controls on national subsidies, restrictions on the investment decisions of individual firms, and compulsory quotas (which became possible following the declaration by the Council of a 'manifest crisis' in October 1980).

Thus between 1974 and 1980 the emphasis of steel policy switched from promoting the freedom and efficiency of the market to managing the market. This switch had very important implications for decision-making processes. Four of these implications are particularly worth noting. First, there was now more policy responsibility and activity at the ECSC level than previously. As a result of this, the overall policy picture as regards steel became a complicated mixture of Community and national processes, with not all of them pulling in the same direction. Second, the assumption by the Community of new and important policy powers, many of which had direct distributional consequences, inevitably created tensions in the Council. At the same time, it also resulted in the Council, as a collective body, taking greater care to ensure that, on key decisions, the Commission acted under its direction. (Although this did not stop governments from using the Commission as a useful device for deflecting the blame for necessary but unpopular decisions away from themselves.) Third, the Commission, notwithstanding its obligation to work within a Council-approved framework, extended its roles and functions in several important respects: as an initiator and proposer of policy; as a mediator amongst national and corporate interests (by, for example, putting together complicated production quota packages for the different types of steel product); as the Community's external negotiator (the Treaty of Paris did not establish a customs union and it was not until the late 1970s that the states began to adopt a common external position); and as a decision-maker (the Commission assumed more powers to act directly, for example on investment aid subsidies). Fourth, non-institutional and non-governmental interests inevitably sought to become much more involved in decision-making as the Community developed policies with a very obvious and very direct impact on output, prices, profits, and employment. A striking illustration of this was the way in which EUROFER (the European Confederation of Iron and Steel Industries, representing about 60 per cent of Community steel capacity) negotiated with the Commission on production quotas.

The steel crisis of the late 1970s/early 1980s thus significantly altered the nature of the Community's decision-making processes as regards steel. A consequence of this was that when, in the 1990s, the European steel industry faced another major crisis – characterised by falling demand, depressed prices, and many plants working below capacity – these processes again came into play. The Commission brought forth a package of restructuring measures that the Council, after long drawn-out negotiations – in which the Italian, Spanish and German governments were especially prominent in seeking to build in protection for their steel industries – eventually agreed to in December 1993. An important aspect of the 1993 restructuring package was that it was not imposed in the manner of the 'manifest crisis' measures of the late 1970s/early 1980s, but was based more on a dialogue between the Commission and steel producers: a dialogue in which the steel industry played a central part in identifying capacity reductions (though not as many as the Commission wanted) and in which the Commission offered 'compensation' in the form of financial aid, temporary subsidies, and increased tariffs and tight quotas on steel imports from Eastern and Central Europe. In an attempt to ensure that the scheme was effective, which was problematical given its semi-voluntaristic nature, the Council increased the monitoring and implementing powers of the Commission.

The making of EU legislation

Having established that there are considerable variations in EU policy-making and decision-making processes, it is necessary to emphasise that there are some common, shared, and recurring features. This is no more clearly seen than in relation to EU legislation, most of which is made via one of three 'set routes':

(1) Administrative/management/regulatory/implementing legislation is issued mainly in the form of Commission regulations and decisions. The basic work on this type of legislation is undertaken by officials in the relevant Directorate General. Commissioners themselves are only involved in the making of such legislation when it is not straightforward or someone asks them to take a look.

National officials usually have the opportunity to voice their comments in a committee, but whether they have the power to stop legislation to which they object depends on which committee procedure applies. As was explained in Chapter 6, the Commission is in a much stronger position when it works through advisory committees than it is when it works through management and, in particular, regulatory, committees.

When this type of legislation is issued as Council legislation, it naturally results in national officials playing a more active role, and formal ministerial approval is required.

(2) Much of the legislation that is enacted in connection with EU external trade policies is based on agreements with third countries, and is therefore subject to special decision-making procedures. These procedures are described in Chapter 16. Amongst their distinctive features are the following: the Commission usually acts as the EU's main negotiator in economic negotiations with third countries; the Council seeks to control and monitor what the Commission does during negotiations; the EP does not normally exercise much influence – except when cooperation and association agreements are proposed; and most legislation produced as a result of negotiations, including virtually all legislation that is intended to establish the principles of a legal framework, is enacted in the form of Council regulations and decisions and therefore requires formal ministerial approval.

(3) Most of what remains consists of legislation that is deemed to require examination via one of the EU's full legislative procedures. There are no hard and fast rules for deciding which proposals fall into this category, but in general they are those that are thought to be significant or concerned with establishing principles. The broader in scope they are, the more likely they are to be in the form of directives.

Because of their obvious importance, these full legislative procedures need to be examined here. However, since much of the detail of how the EU institutions exercise their particular legislative responsibilities has already been set out in Part 2, a comprehensive account is not attempted in what follows. Attention is restricted to highlighting the principal features of the legislative procedures.

Since the Maastricht Treaty entered into force there have been four different legislative procedures: the consultation, cooperation, co-decision, and assent procedures. There are also internal variations to these procedures, the most important of which is that under the consultation, co-decision, and assent procedures, qualified majority voting rules apply in the Council when legislation is being made under certain Treaty articles, whereas unanimity is required under other articles. Descriptions of the consultation, co-decision, and assent procedures now follow. The cooperation procedure is not described since, although it used to be very important, it was virtually abolished by the Amsterdam Treaty. Indeed, it would have been completely abolished had the member states not been reluctant to tamper with its application to four aspects of EMU for fear of opening up the whole EMU issue in the Amsterdam IGC. Should any reader wish to know about the procedural nature of the cooperation procedure, it is outlined on p. 50 and described fully in the third edition of this book.

The consultation procedure

Prior to the SEA, the consultation procedure was the only procedure for non-administrative legislation. However, the creation of the cooperation procedure by the SEA and of the co-decision procedure by the Maastricht Treaty, coupled with the 'elevation' by the SEA and the Maastricht and Amsterdam Treaties of policy areas from the consultation procedure to these other procedures, has meant that the number of policy areas to which the consultation procedure applies has been reduced over the years. It is now largely confined to agriculture and to those justice and home affairs issues that are located within the TEC.

The consultation procedure is a single reading procedure in which the Council is the sole final decision-maker. However, it cannot take a final decision until it has received the opinion of the EP. On some proposals it must also await the opinions of the Economic and Social Committee (ESC) and the Committee of the Regions (CoR).

Initiation

The starting point of any legislative proposal is when somebody suggests that the EU should act on a matter. Most likely this will be the Commission, the Council, or the EP: the Commission because it is the only body with the authority formally to table a legislative proposal, and because of its special expertise in, and responsibility for, EU affairs; the Council because of its political weight, its position as the natural conduit for national claims and interests, and its power under Article 208 of the TEC to request the Commission 'to undertake any studies the Council considers desirable for the attainment of the common objectives, and to submit to it any appropriate proposals'; and the EP because of the desire of MEPs to be active and because under Article 192 of the TEC 'The European Parliament may, acting by a majority of its members, request the Commission to submit any appropriate proposals on matters on which it considers that a Community act is required for the purpose of implementing this Treaty'. (In practice only a handful of such EP requests have been made since the EP was given this power under the Maastricht Treaty.)

Beyond the Commission, the Council, and the EP there are many other possible sources of EU legislation, but little progress can be made unless the Commission decides to take up an issue and draft proposals. Many factors may result in it deciding to do so, the most frequent being that such legislation is required as part of an ongoing policy commitment or programme. Sometimes, however, it is very difficult, when looking at specific proposals, to determine why the Commission decided to act and to identify precisely who originated the initiative. For example, a Commission proposal that seems to have been a response to a Council request may, on inspection, be traced beyond the Council to a national pressure group influencing a minister, who then gradually and informally introduced the issue into the Council as an option to be considered. Similarly, a Commission proposal may seem to have been a response to an EP request or to representations from European-wide interests, but in fact the Commission may itself have dropped hints to the EP or to interests that they should look at the matter (thus reinforcing the Commission's own position *vis-à-vis* the Council).

Preparation of a text

In preparing a text, a number of matters must be carefully considered by the Commission in addition to the direct policy considerations at issue.

- The proposal must have the correct legal base – that is, it must be based on the correct treaty article(s). Normally this is a straightforward matter and there is no room for argument, but sometimes disputes arise when a proposal cuts across policy areas and the Commission chooses a legal base that is deemed by a policy actor to be unsatisfactory. For example, a member state that is concerned about the possible implications of a policy proposal is likely to prefer a procedure where unanimity applies in the Council, whilst the EP always prefers the co-decision procedure to be used because this gives it a potential veto. The question of legal base can therefore be controversial, and has resulted in references to the Court of Justice.
- Justification of the proposal must be given in terms of the application of the subsidiarity principle. This takes the form of answers to a series of questions on subsidiarity in the explanatory memorandum that is attached to each proposal.
- Where appropriate, justification must be given in terms of the environmental impact of the proposal. This usually applies, for example, to transport and agriculture proposals.
- The probable financial implications for the EU budget of the proposal must be assessed.

*   *   *

The standard way in which proposals are prepared is as follows. The process begins with a middle-ranking official in the 'lead' DG assuming the main responsibility for preparing an initial draft. In the course of preparation the draft is discussed with all other DGs and specialised Commission services which have an interest, both in informal exchanges and in the more formal setting of inter-service meetings. The draft is then passed upwards through superiors, and when all directly involved Commission interests have given their approval the draft is sent to the *cabinet* of the Commissioner responsible for the subject. The *cabinet*, which may or may not have been involved in informal discussions with Commission officials as the proposal was being drafted, may or may not attempt to persuade Commission officials to re-work the draft before submitting it to the Commissioner for approval. When the Commissioner is satisfied, she or he asks the Secretariat General to submit the draft to the College of Commissioners. The draft is then scrutinised, and possibly amended, by the *chefs de cabinet* at their weekly meeting. If the draft is judged to be uncontroversial the Commissioners may adopt it by written procedure; if it is controversial the Commissioners may, after debate, accept it, reject it, amend it, or refer it back to the relevant DG for further consideration.

In preparing a text officials usually find themselves the focus of attention from many directions. Knowing that the Commission's thinking is probably at its most flexible at this preliminary stage, and knowing too that once a proposal is formalised it is more difficult to change, interested parties use whatever means they can to press their views. Four factors most affect the extent to which the Commission is prepared to listen to outside interests at this pre-proposal stage. First, what contacts and channels have already been regularised in the sector and which ways of proceeding have proved to be effective in the past? Second, what political considerations arise and how important is it to incorporate different sectional and national views from the outset? Third, what degree of technical knowledge and outside expertise is called for? Fourth, how do the relevant Commission officials prefer to work?

Assuming, as it is normally reasonable to do, Commission receptivity, there are several ways in which external views may be brought to the attention of those drafting a proposal. The Commission itself may request a report, perhaps from a university or a research institute. Interest groups may submit briefing documents. Professional lobbyists, politicians, and officials from the Permanent Representations may press preferences in informal meetings. EP committees and ESC sections may be sounded out. And use may be made of the extensive advisory committee system that clusters around the Commission (see Chapter 6).

Hence there is no standard consultative pattern or procedure. An important consequence of this is that governmental involvement in the preparation of Commission texts varies considerably. Indeed, not only is there a variation in involvement, there is also variation in knowledge of the Commission's intentions. Sometimes governments are fully aware of Commission thinking, because national officials have been formally consulted in committees of experts. Sometimes sectional interests represented on consultative committees will let their governments know what is going on. Sometimes governments will be abreast of developments as a result of having tapped sources within the Commission, most probably through officials in their Permanent Representations. But occasionally governments are not aware of proposals until they are published.

The time that elapses between the decision to initiate a proposal and the publication by the Commission of its text naturally depends on a number of factors. Is there any urgency? How keen is the Commission to press ahead? How widespread are the consultations? Is there consensus amongst key external actors and does the Commission want their prior support? Is there consensus within the Commission itself? Not surprisingly, elapses of well over a year are common. Moreover, in some policy spheres these elapses appear to have become longer: in the environmental area, for example, McCormick (1999b) cites DGXI (Environment) officials as complaining that the development of proposals can now take six to seven years, as opposed to the former two to three.

The opinions of the European Parliament, the Economic and Social Committee, and the Committee of the Regions

On publication, the Commission's text is submitted to the Council of Ministers for a decision and to the EP and, if appropriate, the ESC and the CoR, for their opinions.

The EP is by far the most influential of the consultative bodies. Though it does not have full legislative powers under the consultation procedure, it has enough weapons in its arsenal to ensure that its views are at least taken into consideration, particularly by the Commission. Its representational claims are one source of its influence. The quality of its arguments and its suggestions are another. And it has the power of delay, by virtue of the requirement that the EP's opinion must be known before the proposal can be formally adopted by the Council.

As was shown in Chapter 9, most of the detailed work undertaken by the EP on proposed legislation is handled by its specialised committees and, to a lesser extent, its political groups. Both the committees and the groups advise MEPs on how to vote in plenary.

The usual way in which plenaries act to bring influence to bear is to vote on amendments to the Commission's proposal, but not to vote on the draft legislative resolution – which constitutes the EP's opinion – until the Commission states, as it is obliged to do, whether or not it will change its text to incorporate the amendments that have been approved by the EP. (Under all legislative processes the Commission can amend, or even withdraw, its text up to the point of adoption.) If the amendments are accepted by the Commission a favourable opinion is issued, and the amended text becomes the text that the Council considers. If all or some of the amendments are not accepted, the EP can exert pressure by not issuing an opinion and referring the proposal back to the committee responsible. A reference back can also be made if the whole proposal is judged to be unacceptable. Withholding an opinion does not, it should be emphasised, mean that the EP has power of veto, because it is legally obliged to issue opinions and the Court of Justice has referred to the duty of loyal cooperation between EU institutions. What the withholding of opinions does do, however, is to give the EP the often useful bargaining and pressurising tool of the power of delay.

For the reasons outlined in Chapter 9, and which are considered further below, it is difficult to estimate the precise impact the EP has on EU legislation. In general terms, however, it can be said that the record in the context of the consultation procedure is mixed.

On the positive side, the Commission is normally sympathetic to the EP's views and accepts about three-quarters of its amendments. The Council is less sympathetic and accepts well under half of the amendments, but that still means that many EP amendments, on many different policy matters, find their way into the final legislative texts.

On the negative side, there are three main points to be made. First, there is not much the EP can do if the Council rejects its opinion. The best it can normally hope for is a conciliation meeting with the Council (not to be confused with a conciliation committee meeting under the co-decision procedure), but such meetings usually achieve little – mainly because the Council has no wish to reopen questions that may put at risk its own, often exhaustively negotiated, agreements. Second, the Council occasionally – though much less than it used to – takes a decision 'in principle' or 'subject to Parliament's opinion', before the opinion has even been delivered. In such circumstances the EP's views, once known, are unlikely to result in the Council having second thoughts. Third, it is possible for the text of proposals to be changed after the EP has issued its opinion. There is some safeguard against the potential implications of this insofar as the Court of Justice has indicated that the Council should refer a legislative proposal back to the EP if the Council substantially amends the proposal after the EP has issued its opinion. Moreover, there is a Council–EP understanding that the former will not make substantial changes without referring back to the EP. In practice, however, the question of what constitutes a substantial amendment is open to interpretation, and references back do not always occur.

In general the ESC and the CoR are not so well placed as the EP to examine legislative proposals. As was explained in Chapter 11, a major reason for this is that their formal powers are not as great: while they must be consulted on draft legislation in many policy spheres, consultation is only optional in some. Furthermore, when they are consulted the Council or the Commission may lay down a very tight timetable, can go ahead if no opinion is issued by a specified date, and cannot be frustrated by delays if either the ESC or the CoR wants changes to a text. Other sources of weakness include the part-time capacity of their members, the personal rather than representational nature of much of their memberships, and the perception by many interests and regional bodies that advisory committees and direct forms of lobbying are more effective channels of influence.

Decision-making in the Council

The Council does not wait for the views of the EP, the ESC and the CoR before it begins to examine a proposal. Indeed, governments may begin preparing their positions for the Council, and informal discussions and deliberations may even take place within the Council itself, before the formal referral from the Commission.

The standard procedure in the Council is for the proposal to be referred initially to a working party of national representatives for detailed examination. The representatives have two principal tasks: to ensure that the interests of their country are safeguarded; and to try to reach an agreement on a text. Inevitably these two responsibilities do not always coincide, with the consequence that working party deliberations can be protracted. Progress depends on many factors: the controversiality of the proposal; the extent to which it benefits or damages states differentially; the number of countries, especially large countries, pressing for progress; the enthusiasm and competence of the Presidency; the tactical skills of the national representatives and their capacity to trade disputed points (both of which are dependent on personal ability and the sort of briefs laid down for representatives by their governments); and the flexibility of the Commission in agreeing to change its text.

Once a working party has gone as far as it can with a proposal – which can mean reaching a general agreement, agreeing on most points but with reservations entered by some countries on particular points, or very little agreement at all on the main issues – reference is made upwards to COREPER or, in the case of agriculture, the Special Committee on Agriculture (SCA). At this level, the Permanent Representatives (in COREPER II), their deputies (in COREPER I), or senior agriculture officials (in the SCA) concern themselves not so much with the technical details of a proposal as with its policy and, to some extent, political implications. So far as is possible differences left over from the working party are sorted out. When this cannot be done, bases for possible agreement may be identified, and the proposal is then either referred back to the working party for further detailed consideration or forwarded to the ministers for political resolution.

All proposals must be formally approved by the ministers. Those that have been agreed at a lower level of the Council machinery are placed on the ministers' agenda as 'A' points and are normally quickly ratified. Where, however, outstanding problems and differences have to be considered a number of things can happen. One is that the political authority that ministers carry, and the preparatory work undertaken by officials prior to ministerial meetings, may clear the way for an agreed settlement: perhaps reached quickly over lunch, perhaps hammered out in long and frequently adjourned Council sessions. A second and increasingly utilised possibility is that a vote is taken when the treaty article(s) upon which the proposal is based so allows. This does not mean that the traditional preference for proceeding by consensus no longer applies, but it does mean that it is not quite the obstacle it formerly was. A third possibility is that no agreement is reached and a vote is either not possible under the treaties or is not judged to be appropriate.

If no agreement can be reached in the Council – either by consensus or by the use of qmv – the legislative process does not necessarily end in failure. On the contrary, the proposal may well be referred back down the Council machinery, referred back to the Commission with a request for changes to the existing text, or referred to a future meeting in the hope that shifts in position will take place in the meantime and the basis of a solution will be found. If agreement is reached, the decision-making process at EU level ends with the Council's adoption of a text.

The co-decision procedure

The co-decision procedure was created by the Maastricht Treaty. However, it was not named as such in the Treaty, but rather was referred to by reference to the article that set out its provisions – Article 189b. The Amsterdam Treaty similarly did not provide for a formal naming of the procedure, so under the renumbered TEC it is the Article 251 procedure.

The procedure grew out of and extended the cooperation procedure, which had been created by the SEA. The cooperation procedure was established for two main reasons. First, it was seen as being necessary, especially with the SEM programme in mind, to increase the efficiency, and more especially the speed, of decision-making processes. This was achieved by enabling qmv to be used in the Council when decisions were made under the procedure and by laying down time limitations for the institutions to act during the later stages of the procedure. Second, it was a response to concerns about 'the democratic deficit', and more particularly pressures for more powers to be given to the EP. This was achieved by introducing a two reading stage for legislation, and increasing the EP's leverage – though not to the point of giving it a veto – over the Council at second reading.

Democratic deficit concerns and pressures from the EP were also very much behind the creation of the co-decision procedure in the Maastricht Treaty. While the cooperation procedure had certainly increased the EP's influence, it still did not have the power of veto under the procedure if the Council was resolved to press ahead with a legislative proposal. The co-decision procedure gives the EP this power of veto.

This power was restricted to 15 treaty articles under the Maastricht Treaty, but has been extended to 37 by the Amsterdam Treaty. Eleven of the new 22 articles made subject to the procedure by the Amsterdam Treaty were previously subject to cooperation, two to consultation, one to assent and eight were additional articles. As a result of the extensions to the remit of the procedure under the Amsterdam Treaty, most EU legislation apart from agriculture, justice and home affairs, trade, fiscal harmonisation, and EMU issues are now subject to co-decision (Table 13.1).

The nature of the co-decision procedure will now be described. It will be seen that it is a one, two, or three stage procedure. Proposals only advance to the third stage if the EP and the Council cannot reach agreement at the first or second stage. It will also be seen that it is a procedure that strongly encourages the EP, the Council, and the Commission to engage in intensive and extensive inter-institutional bargaining. Such bargaining was already developing before the co-decision procedure was established as a result of the creation of the cooperation procedure (see Neunreither, 1999), and under co-decision it has become an absolutely central part of the legislative process. The nature of the procedure is such that if the three institutions do not liaise and work closely with one another, protracted delays may occur in the early legislative stages and impasses may occur in the later stages. Since, though they may disagree on points of detail, each of the institutions

Table 13.1   *The application of, and Council voting rules under, the co-decision procedure post-Amsterdam*

- *Article 12* (ex Article 6), rules to prohibit discrimination on grounds of nationality (qmv)
- *Article 18* (ex Article 8a(2)), provisions to facilitate the exercise of the right of citizens to move and reside freely within the territory of the member states (unanimity)
- *Article 40* (ex Article 49 (1)), free movement of workers, internal market (qmv)
- *Article 42* (ex Article 51), internal market, social security rules for Community migrant workers (unanimity)
- *Article 45* (ex Article 54(2)), freedom of establishment, internal market (qmv)
- *Article 46* (ex Article 56(2)), freedom of establishment, internal market, coordination of provisions laid down by law, regulation or administrative action on the treatment of foreign nationals (qmv)
- *Article 47* (ex Article 57(1)), mutual recognition of diplomas, certificates and other evidence of formal qualifications in relation to access to self-employed activities (qmv)
- *Article 47* (ex Article 57(2) (in fine)), coordination of provisions laid down by law, regulation or administrative action in the member states with respect to access to and the exercise of self-employed activities (qmv)
- *Article 47* (ex Article 57(2)), amendment of the existing principles laid down by law governing the professions with respect to training and conditions of access for natural persons (unanimity)
- *Article 55* (ex Article 66), free movement of services, internal market (qmv)
- *Article 71* (ex Article 75 (1)), transport policy, common rules applicable to international transport to or from a member state or passing across the territory of one or more member states; conditions under which non-resident carriers may operate transport services within a member state and measures to improve transport safety (qmv)
- *Article 80* (ex Article 84), transport policy, sea and air transport (qmv)
- *Article 95* (ex Article 100a(1)), internal market, approximation of legislation that has as its object the establishment and functioning of the internal market (qmv)
- *Article 95* (ex Article 100b(1), second subparagraph), internal market, list of non-harmonised provisions and equivalences (qmv)
- *Article 116* (ex Article 135), customs cooperation (new treaty provision) (qmv)

- *Article 129* (ex Article 109r), incentive measures to boost employment (qmv)
- *Article 137* (ex Article 118), aspects of social policy – health and safety at work, working conditions, the information and consultation of workers, the integration of persons excluded from the labour market, equality between men and women with regard to labour market opportunities and treatment at work (qmv)
- *Article 141* (ex Article 119), equal opportunities and treatment in matters of employment and occupation (qmv)
- *Article 148* (ex Article 125), implementing decisions relating to the European Social Fund (qmv)
- *Article 149* (ex Article 126(4)), education, incentive measures excluding any harmonisation (qmv)
- *Article 150* (ex Article 127(4)), vocational training, measures to achieve the objectives of vocational training (qmv)
- *Article 151* (ex Article 128(5)), culture, incentive measures excluding any harmonisation (unanimity)
- *Article 152* (ex Article 129), public health, previous basis Article 43, minimum requirements regarding the quality and safety of organs and veterinary and phytosanitary measures which have as their direct objective the protection of public health (qmv)
- *Article 152* (ex Article 129(4)), public health, incentive measures excluding any harmonisation (qmv)
- *Article 153* (ex Article 129a(2)), consumer protection (qmv)
- *Article 156* (ex Article 129d), trans-European transport networks, guidelines on general objectives, priorities and projects of common interest (qmv)
- *Article 162* (ex Article 130e), implementation of ERDF decisions (qmv)
- *Article 172* (ex Article 130o(2)), adoption of provisions for implementing the R & TD framework programme (qmv)
- *Article 175* (ex Article 130s), Community action to achieve the environmental objectives referred to in Article 174 (qmv)
- *Article 175* (ex Article 130s(3)), environment general action programmes setting out priority objectives (unanimity)
- *Article 179* (ex Article 130w), development cooperation (qmv)
- *Article 181* (ex Article 130y(1)), cooperation with third countries and competent international organisations (unanimity)
- *Article 255* (ex Article 191a), principles on transparency (qmv)
- *Article 280* (ex Article 209a), fight against fraud affecting the financial interests of the Community
- *Article 285* (ex Article 213a), statistics (qmv)
- *Article 286* (ex Article 213b), establishment of an independent advisory body on data protection (qmv)

Source: Adapted from European Parliament (1997), pp. 34–5.

normally want legislative proposals to become legislative texts, the inevitable requirement is that they spend a lot of time communicating with one another – in forums ranging from a mushrooming number of formal inter-institutional meetings to casual off-the-record conversations between key institutional policy actors. Figure 13.1 provides a diagrammatic representation of the procedure.

First stage

The pre-proposal processes are much as they are under the consultation procedure, though with the Commission taking rather more care as to the EP's likely reactions given its greater powers under co-decision.

After the Commission has published its proposal it is examined by the EP and the Council through their normal mechanisms: that is, with most of the detailed work being undertaken by the relevant committee in the EP and by working parties and COREPER in the Council.

Prior to the Amsterdam Treaty it was not possible for a text to be adopted at this first legislative stage under co-decision. However, as part of a general attempt to streamline what was widely agreed to be a somewhat cumbersome procedure, the Treaty made provision for a text to be adopted at first reading providing the Council and the EP agree on its contents and that other 'standard' legislative requirements are met – notably the ESC and the CoR are consulted as appropriate, and amendments with which the Commission does not agree receive unanimous support in the Council. (This latter requirement applies to all stages of all legislative procedures, apart from the final – conciliation – stage of the co-decision procedure.)

If the Council and the EP do not reach agreement at the first reading, the Council, on receipt of the EP's opinion, adopts a common position – with qmv usually, but not quite always, being available for this purpose (see Table 13.1 for Council voting rules under the procedure).

Second stage

At its second reading, the EP can approve, amend, reject, or take no action on a common position. To assist it in its deliberations, the Council must provide the EP with an explanation of the common position and the Commission must also explain its position, including in respect of whether or not it will accept EP amendments.

If the EP approves or takes no action on a common position the Council can, within three months, adopt it as a legislative act (using the same voting rules as applied at the first reading). If the EP rejects the common position by an absolute majority of its members the proposal falls. And if the EP amends the common position by an absolute majority of its members and the Council at its second reading is unable to accept the text approved by the EP, a third legislative stage occurs.

Third stage

This stage opens, within six weeks of the Council failing to approve the text supported by the EP, with the contested proposal being referred to a conciliation committee composed of an equal number of representatives of the Council and the EP. About 40 per cent of legislative proposals subject to the co-decision procedure require the convening of a conciliation committee. In the committee, the Council is normally represented by senior officials from the national Permanent Representations to the EU and the EP is represented by a mixture of semi-permanent conciliation committee members and members of relevant Parliamentary committees. If the conciliation committee agrees on a joint text – and it normally has six weeks to do so – the proposal is referred back to the Council and the EP for final adoption within a period of six weeks. In this final vote the Council acts by qmv and the EP by a majority of the votes cast. (When the co-decision procedure was created in the Maastricht Treaty, the Council could attempt to impose the common position in the event of non-agreement in the conciliation committee, but this possibility was removed by the Amsterdam Treaty, with the consequence that failure by the Council and the EP to agree on a text means the proposal cannot be adopted.)

Up to the end of 1998 there had been only three outright failures under the co-decision procedure: in 1994 the EP rejected the Council's confirmed common position on a directive concerning the application of open network provision to voice telephony; in 1995 the EP rejected an agreement reached in the conciliation committee on a biotechnology directive; and in 1998 the conciliation committee failed to reach agreement on a directive on investment services and the Council decided not to confirm its common position. Significantly, both the voice telephony and biotechnology directives were subsequently re-presented by the Commission in a form that enabled them to be approved by the Council and EP.

The assent procedure

The assent procedure, which was established by the SEA, is simple in form. It is a single stage procedure in which proposed measures that are subject to it have to be approved by both the Council and the EP. Unanimity is

Figure 13.1 *The co-decision (Article 251) procedure post-Amsterdam*

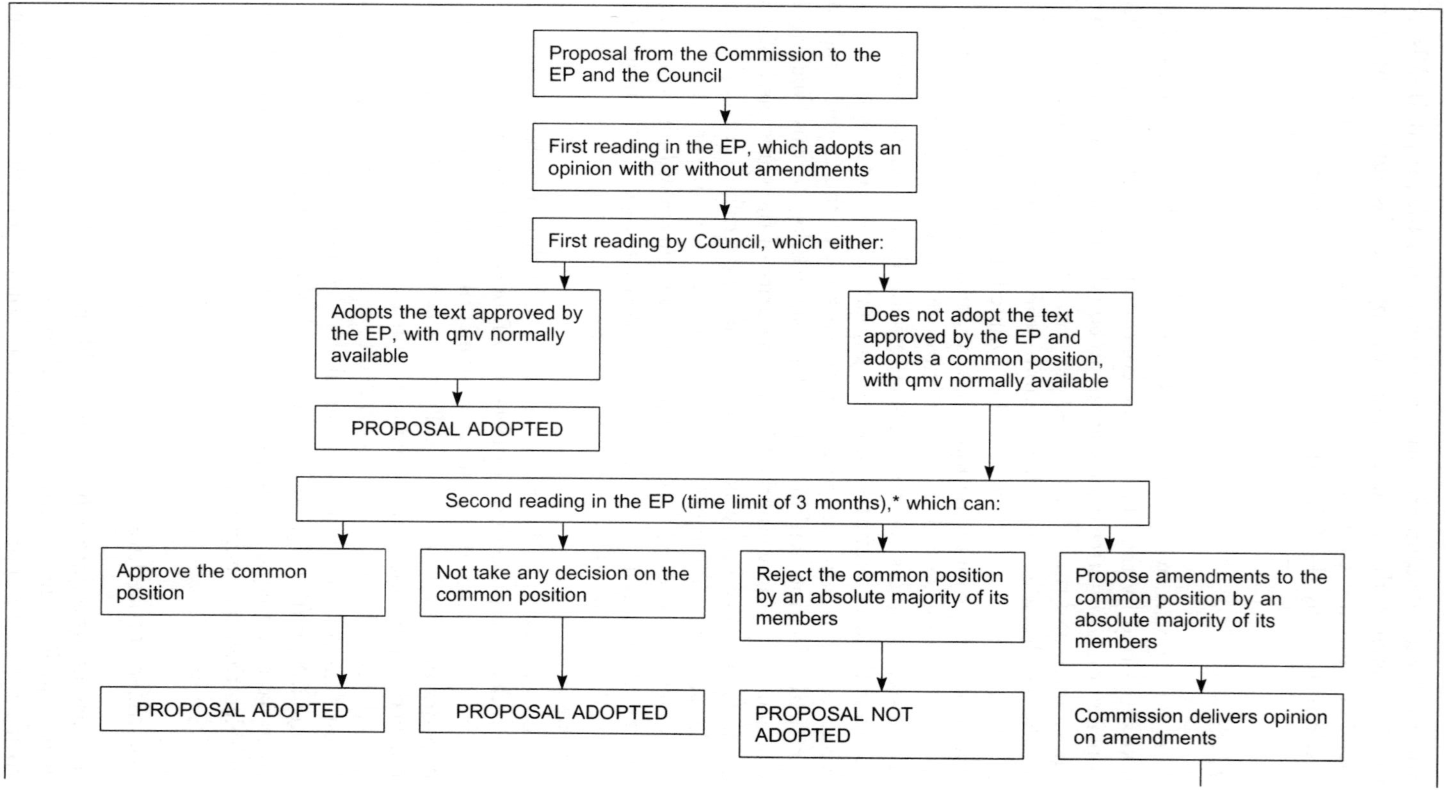

Proposal from the Commission to the EP and the Council

↓

First reading in the EP, which adopts an opinion with or without amendments

↓

First reading by Council, which either:

Adopts the text approved by the EP, with qmv normally available
→ PROPOSAL ADOPTED

Does not adopt the text approved by the EP and adopts a common position, with qmv normally available
↓

Second reading in the EP (time limit of 3 months),* which can:

Approve the common position → PROPOSAL ADOPTED

Not take any decision on the common position → PROPOSAL ADOPTED

Reject the common position by an absolute majority of its members → PROPOSAL NOT ADOPTED

Propose amendments to the common position by an absolute majority of its members → Commission delivers opinion on amendments

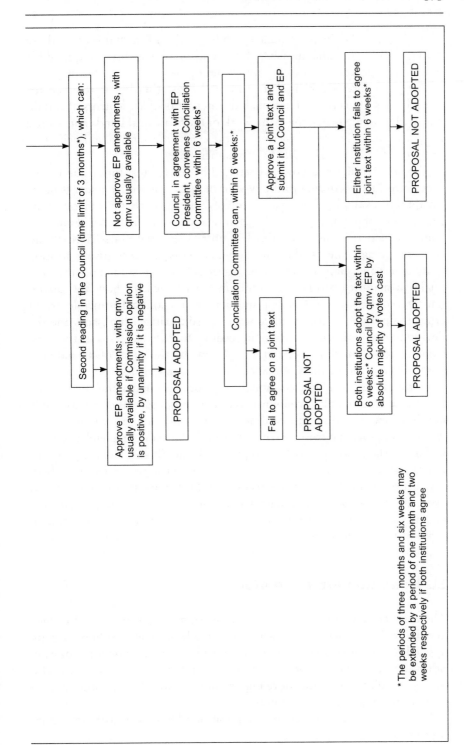

Second reading in the Council (time limit of 3 months*), which can:

Approve EP amendments: with qmv usually available if Commission opinion is positive, by unanimity if it is negative

PROPOSAL ADOPTED

Not approve EP amendments, with qmv usually available

Council, in agreement with EP President, convenes Conciliation Committee within 6 weeks*

Conciliation Committee can, within 6 weeks:*

Fail to agree on a joint text

PROPOSAL NOT ADOPTED

Approve a joint text and submit it to Council and EP

Both institutions adopt the text within 6 weeks:* Council by qmv, EP by absolute majority of votes cast

PROPOSAL ADOPTED

Either institution fails to agree joint text within 6 weeks*

PROPOSAL NOT ADOPTED

* The periods of three months and six weeks may be extended by a period of one month and two weeks respectively if both institutions agree

normally required in the Council, whilst in the EP a majority of those voting suffices for some measures but an absolute majority is required for others. The procedure does not allow the EP to make amendments.

The procedure is not used for 'normal' legislation but is reserved for special types of decision. These include international agreements of certain kinds, EU enlargements, the framework of the Structural Funds and – since the Amsterdam Treaty – sanctions in the event of a serious and persistent breach of fundamental rights by a member state.

The precise rules and powers exercised by the EU institutions under the procedure vary according to the type of decision for which assent is being sought. For example, if the decision involves a matter that has involved the preparation of detailed proposals (as in relation to the Structural Funds) or complex negotiations with third countries (as with association and cooperation agreements) then the Commission is in a very strong position to influence and shape the outcomes, especially if, as is sometimes the case, qualified majority voting rules apply in the Council. If, however, unanimity is required in the Council and matters of political principle are of crucial importance – for example with regard to citizenship issues and the devising of a uniform electoral procedure for EP elections – then the Commission is much less favourably placed and the views of the national governments, and of the Council collectively, are crucial.

As for the EP, it might be thought that because under the rules of the procedure it can only pronounce on final proposals and cannot table amendments, it would be confined to a rather limited confirmatory/withholding role. To some extent it indeed is, but not completely, because by having the power to say 'no' to proposals the EP also has the power to indicate to what it would say 'yes'. It has used this power most notably to take action on the human rights records of third countries that have signed association and cooperation agreements with the EU, and to put pressure on the Commission and the Council to amend and change the terms of some of these agreements.

EU legislation after adoption

There are considerable variations in what happens to proposals after they are adopted as EU legislation, what use is made of them, and how they are applied. Many of these variations are considered on an individual basis in other chapters – notably in Chapters 6, 10 and 17 – but it will be useful briefly to pull together the more important variations here in order to give an indication of the overall picture.

Much legislation requires the adoption of additional legislative/regulatory measures:

- Whereas regulations and most decisions do not require any measures to be taken at national level before they apply, directives do not assume legislative force until they have been incorporated into national law by the appropriate national authorities. The member states themselves determine which are the appropriate national authorities in their case, and by what process the incorporation is to be made. As a result, the mechanisms by which directives are incorporated at the national level varies between member states according to differing national legislative procedures and differing perceptions of the importance of particular directives. The general pattern, however, is for incorporation to be achieved by attaching appropriate administrative measures to existing primary or secondary legislation, introducing new secondary legislation, or adding new clauses to already planned primary legislation. States are given anything from a few weeks to a few years to effect the incorporation – the final date being specified in the directives – and are obliged to notify the Commission of the national legislation, regulations, or administrative provisions they have adopted to give formal effect to each directive.

- Much Council and European Parliament and Council legislation needs to be supplemented by implementing legislation so as to fit it to particular circumstances and keep it up to date. Indeed, on a quantitative basis the vast bulk of EU legislation is implementing legislation, usually issued in the form of Commission regulations.

- Some Council and European Parliament and Council legislation needs to be followed up not just with implementing legislation but with further 'policy' legislation. This is most obviously the case in respect of 'framework' legislation, which is legislation that lays down general principles for an area of activity and basic rules that states have to follow, but which needs usually to be complemented by more narrowly focused legislation that covers in a reasonably detailed manner policies/issues/initiatives that fall within the remit of the framework. An example of framework legislation is the *Council Directive of 12 June 1989 on the introduction of measures to encourage improvements in the safety and health of workers at work* (89/391/EEC). That this legislation was intended to be a base and a focus for further legislation is seen in Article 16 of the Directive, which states: 'The Council acting on a proposal from the Commission, based on 118a of the Treaty, shall adopt individual Directives, inter alia, in the areas listed in the Annex.'

- Legislation that also requires further measures, but measures that are very different in character from those just outlined, is the 'new approach' legislation that constitutes an important part of the internal market legal framework. Under the approach, the EU does not try to harmonise all the specifications and technical standards of marketed goods, but confines itself to producing relatively short texts that lay down 'essential requirements', in particular requirements relating to health and safety matters and consumer and environmental protection. As long as member states abide by the 'essential requirements' they can have their own national standards which are subject to mutual recognition by other states. However, national standards are generally supposed to be replaced as quickly as possible by European standards which are agreed by European standards bodies. The main such bodies are the European Committee for Standardisation (CEN) and the European Committee for Electrotechnical Standardisation (CENELEC). Both CEN and CENELEC include non EU countries amongst their membership, and both use weighted voting procedures for the taking of final decisions on standards. Once European standards are agreed, EU states must adopt them within a fixed time limit, and within the same time limit must remove all conflicting national standards.

Issues arising in connection with the implementation of EU legislation were well aired in Chapter 6 in the examination of the Commission's executive and legal guardianship functions. Attention here will therefore be restricted to just a few key points.

Regarding the incorporation of directives into national law, the Commission must – as noted above – be informed of the measures taken by member states. It therefore has a reasonably good picture of what is happening. Notwithstanding this, however, some states – including Denmark, Germany, and the UK – have a considerably better record of incorporating directives than do others. In consequence, there are variations between the states in terms of the speed at which, and extent to which, directives are applied, and variations too in terms of the frequency with which states are subject to Commission and Court action for non/incomplete/incorrect incorporation of EU law (Table 13.2).

Regarding the application of EU legislation, responsibilities are shared between EU authorities and national authorities. The main EU authorities are the various DGs that are responsible for particular policies, DGXX (Financial Control), the European Fraud Prevention Office, the Court of Auditors, and the EP's Budgetary Control Committee. The national authorities are the numerous agencies and officials whose responsibility it is to collect excise duties, read tachographs, monitor fishing catches, check that beef for which payments are made is of the quality that is claimed, and so on. In very broad terms the division of responsibilities between the two levels in terms of day-to-day policy implementation is thus that the Commission oversees and the national authorities do most of the 'front line' work. This means that the Commission needs to move carefully and, assuming it does not wish to stoke up national resentments, must negotiate and discuss implementing problems with national authorities rather than rush them to the Court.

However, despite – or in some respects because of – the range of agencies that have some responsibility for policy implementation and implementation control, it is evident that all is not well with the application of some EU policies. This is seen most obviously in respect of those policies involving budgetary expenditure, in particular the CAP and the Structural Funds. The problem is partly one of fraud, which according to some estimates might account for 5–10 per cent of the EU budget. The main problem, however, appears to be administrative irregularities: that is, not deliberate deception but incorrect understanding and application of EU law. Doubtless the control mechanisms and administrative procedures could be improved, not least in respect of flows of information between the Commission and the national agencies. But the fact is that with the Commission being unable to conduct very much direct surveillance of its own because of limited powers and resources, and with much EU legislation being so complicated that it is barely comprehensible even to the expert, it will probably never be possible to ensure that all laws are fully, properly and uniformly implemented.

Characteristic features of EU policy processes

A number of general features are characteristic of EU policy processes. They include compromises and linkages, inter-institutional cooperation, difficulties in effecting radical change, tactical manoeuvring, and variable speeds.

Compromises and linkages

The diversity of competing interests across the member states, coupled with the nature of the EU's decision-making system, means that successful policy development is frequently heavily dependent on key actors, especially governments, being prepared to compromise. If they are not so prepared, effective decision-making can be very difficult.

As part of the process wherein compromises provide the basis for agreements, deals are frequently formulated in which different and some-times seemingly unrelated policy issues are linked. Linking issues together in 'package deals' can open the door to agreements by ensuring that there are prizes for everybody and not, as might be the case when only a specific issue is taken, for just a few.

Table 13.2 Infringement proceedings classified by member state, stage reached and legal basis

Member state	State of the infringement proceeding	1995 Total	Directives No notif.	Impl. prob.	Appl. prob.	Treaties Regulations Decisions	1996 Total	Directives No notif.	Impl. prob.	Appl. prob.	Treaties Regulations Decisions	1997 Total	Directives No notif.	Impl. prob.	Appl. prob.	Treaties Regulations Decisions
Belgium	FN	80	59	3	8	10	72	31	8	16	17	90	65	8	7	10
	RO	19	15	0	1	3	62	48	4	7	3	35	15	2	5	13
	REF	6	4	1	1	0	20	19	0	1	0	18	11	2	3	2
Denmark	FN	42	36	0	6	0	22	18	0	2	2	63	52	6	2	3
	RO	1	1	0	0	0	0	0	0	0	0	1	0	0	1	0
	REF	0	0	0	0	0	0	0	0	0	0	0	0	0	0	0
Germany	FN	92	63	5	14	10	62	31	6	17	8	121	70	12	27	12
	RO	25	15	4	5	1	37	23	6	5	3	35	23	4	5	3
	REF	10	7	2	1	0	8	7	0	1	0	19	12	2	4	1
Greece	FN	113	90	1	13	9	58	34	0	16	8	108	86	3	7	12
	RO	26	14	0	8	4	51	43	2	6	0	23	14	0	5	4
	REF	12	8	0	2	2	17	13	0	1	3	10	8	1	1	0
Spain	FN	81	61	1	12	7	59	22	7	9	21	107	67	11	13	16
	RO	15	9	0	4	2	30	13	3	10	4	25	10	3	8	4
	REF	6	5	0	1	0	9	3	1	4	1	7	2	0	3	2
France	FN	97	70	3	11	13	88	33	6	29	20	154	72	7	44	31
	RO	17	8	0	5	4	46	31	4	7	4	52	15	5	18	14
	REF	6	4	0	0	2	11	6	0	3	2	15	9	1	4	1
Ireland	FN	67	59	1	3	4	43	28	5	9	1	83	67	4	11	1
	RO	3	3	0	0	0	36	34	0	1	1	15	9	3	3	0
	REF	6	6	0	0	0	4	1	1	1	1	6	5	0	1	0

Italy	FN	114	85	3	10	16	75	30	9	18	18	122	64	11	24	23
	RO	36	16	1	10	9	71	50	3	7	11	35	18	3	5	9
	REF	17	13	0	2	2	9	5	0	3	1	20	14	1	5	0
Luxembourg	FN	71	66	0	3	2	39	32	2	3	2	75	64	5	5	1
	RO	9	6	1	1	1	28	26	2	0	0	16	10	3	2	1
	REF	3	3	0	0	0	4	1	0	3	0	8	7	0	0	1
Netherlands	FN	59	47	1	8	3	32	14	0	9	9	55	34	5	9	7
	RO	4	1	1	2	0	9	4	1	3	1	11	3	1	5	2
	REF	0	0	0	0	0	2	0	0	2	0	3	1	0	2	0
Austria	FN	4	0	0	2	2	132	123	0	9	0	93	68	5	11	9
	RO	0	0	0	0	0	2	0	1	1	0	38	33	0	4	1
	REF	0	0	0	0	0	1	0	0	1	0	0	0	0	0	0
Portugal	FN	115	98	4	9	4	54	34	5	12	3	117	83	8	19	7
	RO	22	15	1	4	2	49	37	8	4	0	35	18	6	5	6
	REF	4	4	0	0	0	6	5	1	0	0	14	7	5	2	0
Finland	FN	2	0	0	1	1	290	284	0	5	1	72	63	2	4	3
	RO	0	0	0	0	0	0	0	0	0	0	8	8	0	0	0
	REF	0	0	0	0	0	0	0	0	0	0	0	0	0	0	0
Sweden	FN	2	0	0	1	1	69	61	1	4	3	80	57	8	10	5
	RO	0	0	0	0	0	0	0	0	0	0	6	6	0	0	0
	REF	0	0	0	0	0	0	0	0	0	0	0	0	0	0	0
United Kingdom	FN	77	65	1	4	7	47	26	3	16	2	96	64	9	18	5
	RO	15	11	0	2	2	14	11	1	1	1	8	1	2	5	0
	REF	2	2	0	0	0	1	0	1	0	0	1	0	0	1	0
Total	FN	1016	799	23	105	89	1142	801	52	174	115	1436	976	104	211	145
	RO	192	114	8	42	28	435	320	35	52	28	343	183	32	71	57
	REF	72	56	3	7	6	92	60	4	20	8	121	76	12	26	7

Notes: FN = Letter of Formal Notice; RO = Reasoned Opinion; REF = Reference to the Court. These different stages are explained in Chapter 6. No notif. = No notification; Impl. prob. = Implementation (transposition) problem; Appl. prob. = Application problem.
Source: Adapted from the *Fifteenth Annual Report on Monitoring the Application of Community Law – 1997*, in *Official Journal of the European Communities*, C250 (10 August 1998).

The European Council has been instrumental in formulating some of the EU's grander compromises and linked deals. For example, the 1992 Edinburgh summit pulled together an agreement on a range of matters that had been causing considerable difficulties, including budgetary proposals, financial aid to the poorer EU countries, the opening of enlargement negotiations, and the application of the subsidiarity principle.

One of the reasons the European Council has become involved in the construction of overarching deals of the kind just described is that other EU institutions and actors, and EU processes as a whole, are ill-adapted to the linking of different policy areas and the construction of complex package deals. The General Affairs Council and the Ecofin Council have some potential in this regard, but in practice they are only occasionally able to 'impose' global solutions on sectoral Councils. As for the sectoral Councils, they do not normally become involved in discussions beyond their immediate policy concern, and they certainly do not have the means – except occasionally in joint Councils – of linking difficulties in their own areas with difficulties being experienced by ministers elsewhere.

Much EU policy-making and decision-making thus tends to be rather compartmentalised, and it is within rather than across policy compartments that the trading, bargaining, linkaging and compromising that are so characteristic of EU processes are mainly to be found. At Council working party level, trading may consist of little more than an official conceding a point on line eight of a proposed legal instrument in exchange for support received on line three. At ministerial level, it may result in a wide-ranging and interconnected package, such as is agreed annually between Agriculture Ministers to make up the farm price settlement.

Inter-institutional cooperation

As this and other chapters show, policy processes are frequently marked by disagreements and disputes between the EU institutions. These disagreements and disputes mostly concern policy matters, but they can also concern institutional matters – especially if an institution is seen to abuse its powers in some way.

But the extent of inter-institutional disagreements and disputes should not be exaggerated, for EU policy processes are also characterised by close inter-institutional cooperation of many different kinds. Indeed, not only are the processes characterised by such cooperation but they are highly dependent on it. If cooperation was not to be generally forthcoming, policy processes would be much more difficult, protracted and halting than they are. For example, at the 'macro' level, policy processes would always be highly conflictual if the Commission was seen by MEPs to be over-dismissive of EP amendments to legislative proposals, whilst at the 'micro' level processes would be extremely inefficient if the Commission, the Council, and the EP did not cooperate with each other on legislative planning and timetabling.

Inter-institutional cooperation has grown over the years as the range of policy activities in which the EU is involved has spread, and more especially as policy processes have become more numerous and more complex. The growth has taken many different forms. So, for example, there has been a mushrooming of informal contacts between officials of the Commission, the Council, and the EP, and it is now commonplace for these officials to liaise closely with their counterparts on policy dossiers. At a rather more formal level, there are trialogue meetings – that is, meetings between representatives of the three institutions – of various kinds. For instance, there is a monthly meeting to monitor the progress of proposals identified in the Commission's annual work programme. There is also a monthly meeting of the Presidents of the three institutions during the EP Strasbourg plenary week to consider relevant issues. At an even more formal level, several inter-institutional agreements have been signed to regularise, clarify and generally facilitate inter-institutional relations. An example of such an inter-institutional agreement is the 1995 Code of Conduct between the Commission and the EP, which strengthens, and in some cases provides for new, practices that are designed to improve relations between the two institutions (*Official Journal*, C89, 10 April 1995). Amongst the practices specified in the Code of Conduct are: 'Parliament and the Commission agree to maintain any appropriate contacts, in particular between their legal services, to facilitate discussion of the choice of legal basis' (p. 69); 'The Commission undertakes to give Parliament and the Council prior notification before withdrawing its proposals' (p. 70); and 'In order to improve legislative planning, the European Parliament undertakes . . . to take account of the priorities considered by the Commission and the Council in planning its activities' (p. 72).

The Maastricht-created co-decision procedure illustrates in a specific way the growth in inter-institutional cooperation. Amongst its consequences it has: (1) encouraged the institutions to devise/accept a compromise text at an early legislative stage (an encouragement that is even stronger since the Amsterdam Treaty, which allows a text to be agreed at first reading); (2) increased the need for the Council to be sensitive to the EP's views; (3) made trialogue meetings between representatives of the Commission, the Council and the EP a vital feature of conciliation meetings; and (4) promoted (the already extensive) informal exchanges between representatives of institutions to sound out positions, discover what may be possible, and identify areas where progress may be made. In short, the co-decision procedure has given a powerful stimulus to a 'cultural' change in the relations between the Commission, the Council and the EP that has been underway since the creation of the cooperation procedure by the SEA. At the heart of this cultural change is the notion that the three institutions must work closely with one another, and when legislation is being made they must operate on the basis of a genuinely triangular relationship.

Difficulties in effecting radical change

Partly as a consequence of the prevalence of compromise, much EU policy-making and decision-making displays a deep gradualism and incrementalism. It is just not possible for the Commission, the Council Presidency, a national government, or anyone else, to initiate a clear and comprehensive policy proposal, incorporating bold new plans and significant departures from the *status quo*, and expect it to be accepted without being modified significantly – which usually means being watered down. Ambitious proposals customarily find themselves being smothered with modifications, escape clauses, and long transitional periods before full implementation.

The obstacles to innovation and radical change are powerful, and stem from a range of different national and ideological positions and perspectives. Moreover, some of the obstacles have increased in force over the years. One reason for this is that the way forward is not as clear as it was in the 1960s, when specific treaty obligations were being honoured and 'negative integration' (that is, the dismantling of barriers and the encouragement of trade liberalisation) was generally accepted as the main policy priority. Another reason is that the EU has become more politically and ideologically heterogeneous. This is partly because of enlargement and partly because the broad Keynesian consensus on social and economic policy that existed in most Western European countries until the mid 1970s no longer exists. Although there has been a measure of consensus on the benefits of moving towards a more liberal model of integration, there have been significant differences between the governments of the member states on the extent to which and the ways in which economic life should be directed and managed. A third reason why some obstacles to change have increased in force is that policy development has inevitably created and attracted interests that have a stake in the *status quo*. This is most obviously the case in agriculture, where Commission proposals for reform invariably produce protests from powerful sectional groups and electorally sensitive governments.

All this is not to suggest that change and reform are not possible. On the contrary, since the mid 1980s there clearly have been major integrationist advances, of both an institutional and a policy kind. These changes have been driven by a range of external and internal factors, and have been guided and shaped by complex interactions between EU and national political forces. The existence of obstacles to change does not, therefore, preclude it occurring, but what it does do is to suggest that since just about any policy innovation is likely to meet with at least some resistance from some quarter(s), bold initiatives are always likely to be weakened/checked/ delayed.

Tactical manoeuvring

Tactical manoeuvring and jockeying for position are universal characteristics of policy processes. However they are especially apparent in the EU as a result of its multiplicity of actors and channels and the diversity of its interests.

It is not possible to present a comprehensive catalogue of tactical options here, but a sample of the questions that often have to be considered by just one category of key EU actors – national representatives in the Council – will give a flavour of the intricacies and potential importance of tactical considerations:

- Can a coalition be built to create a positive majority or a negative minority? If so, should it be done via bilateral meetings or in an EU forum?
- Is it necessary to make an intervention for domestic political purposes? (Although Council meetings are not open to the public or the media, most of what goes on, especially in ministerial meetings, is reported back, either through unofficial channels or through formally minuted national objections to Council decisions.)
- Is it possible for a state to disguise its opposition to a proposal by 'hiding' behind another state?
- Should concessions be made in a working party or in COREPER to ensure progress, or should they be held back until the ministers meet in the hope that this will be seen as conciliatory and helpful, with the consequence that it might reap dividends on another occasion?
- Where is the balance to be struck between being seen to be tough in defence of the national interest and being seen to be European minded and ready to compromise? (Often, on a particular issue, some states have a vested interest in an agreement being reached, whilst the interests of others are best served by the absence of any agreement and, as a result, the absence of EU obligations.)

Variable speeds

EU processes are often criticised for being cumbersome and slow. Unquestionably they can be, but it should be recognised that they are not always so. Procedures exist that allow certain types of decision to be made as and when necessary. So, for example, farm price and budgetary decisions are made (more or less) according to a predetermined annual timetable, Commission legislation can be issued almost immediately, and Council regulations and decisions can be pushed through via urgent procedures if the circumstances require it.

As for 'standard' EU legislation, treaty changes starting with the SEA have greatly speeded up decision-making once a proposal has been formally made by the Commission. Whereas the average time between transmission and adoption of a directive was around 36 months in the mid 1980s, it is now around 18 months. There are three main factors determining the speed at which particular proposals are adopted. First, whether or not they command general support in the Council and the EP. Second, the legislative procedures that apply and the use that is made of them. When, for example, proposals are referred for conciliation under the co-decision procedure a few months are usually added to the length of the decision-making process. Third, whether qmv rules apply in the Council. If they do, ministers are not normally prepared to wait – as they must if unanimity is required – for everyone to agree to all aspects of a proposal. Rather it is customary to give a state that objects strongly to a proposal time to adjust to the majority view – perhaps with encouragement via compromises and derogations – and then proceed to a vote.

Decision-making is thus likely to be at its slowest when a proposal creates difficulties of principle in the Council and/or the EP, and this is combined with a decision-making process that is not subject to the dictates of a timetable and in which qmv cannot be used in the Council. In such circumstances the Council's decision-making capacity is weak and it can be very difficult for progress to be made. There may not even be much of a concerted effort to force progress if it is felt that one or more minority states genuinely have considerable difficulties with the proposal, for governments tend to be very sensitive to the needs of one another – not least because they are aware that they themselves may be in a minority one day.

The efficiency of EU policy processes

The EU lacks a fixed, central, authoritative point where general priorities can be set out and choices between competing options can be made. In other words, there is no adequate framework or mechanism for determining and implementing an overall policy view in which the requirements of agriculture, industry, the environment and so on are weighed and evaluated in relation to one another and in relation to resources. The Commission, it is true, attempts to set general priorities but it does not have the decision-making power to carry them through. In the Council of Ministers, the sectoral Councils do not link up with one another in a wholly satisfactory manner, and although incoming Presidencies do set priorities, these are essentially short term in nature and in most policy sectors are not part of a properly integrated long term programme. As for the European Council, it has had some limited success in coordinating policies, but it has never attempted to set out anything like a comprehensive EU policy programme.

Within individual policy sectors there are, as has been shown, many obstacles to coherent and properly ordered policy development. For example, resistance by states to what they regard as an excessive transfer of powers to the EU has undoubtedly resulted in many policy spheres being less integrated and comprehensive in their approach than is, from a policy efficiency perspective, ideally desirable. Regional policy, industrial policy, and environmental policy are examples of policy areas where policy responsibilities are shared between the EU and the states, where frequently the activities of the two levels are not properly coordinated, and sometimes where they are not even mutually complementary.

EU policy thus tends not to be the outcome of a rational model of decision-making. That is to say, policy is not normally made via a procedure in which problems are identified, objectives are set, all possible alternatives for achieving the objectives are carefully evaluated, and the best alternatives are then adopted and proceeded with. Rather, policy tends to evolve in a somewhat messy way, which means that models of decision-making other than the rational model are often more useful for highlighting key features of EU processes. For example:

- The *political interests* model of decision-making draws attention to the interaction of competing interests in the EU, to the variable power exercised by these interests in different decision-making situations, and to the ways in which decisional outcomes are frequently a consequence of bargaining and compromise between interests.
- *Political elite* models highlight the considerable concentrations of power, at official and political levels, that exist across the EU's decision-making processes. Concentration is especially marked in areas such as monetary policy and foreign policy, where processes are more secret and more closed than they are in steel or agriculture for example. Political elite models also draw attention to the paucity of mechanisms available

to EU citizens to ensure direct accountability on the part of EU decision-makers.

- The *organisational process* model of decision-making emphasises how the rules and understandings via which EU decisions are made do much to shape the nature of the decisions themselves. That is, the organisational processes are not neutral. So when a wide range of national, regional and sectional interests are entitled to be consulted before policy can be developed and decisions can only be made by unanimity in the Council, progress is frequently slow and the outcome is often little more than the lowest common denominator. When, on the other hand, the process is more streamlined – and permits, for example, qmv in the Council of Ministers, or the Commission to disburse funds directly – then decision-making is likely to be more decisive and, perhaps, more coherent. (On models and conceptualisations of EU policy processes, see also Chapter 18.)

Having identified weaknesses in the quality of EU policy processes, some re-balancing is now in order lest the impression be given of a system that is wholly and uniquely disordered and undemocratic. There are three main points to be made.

The first point is that, in many respects, EU policy processes are not so different from national processes. This is not, of course, to say that important differences do not exist. The international nature of the EU, for example, makes for more diverse and more powerful opposition to its policy initiatives than customarily exists within states. It is also the case that EU decision-makers are less directly accountable than national decision-makers to those who are subject to their decisions. Another difference is that the EU's policy structures are more complex, and in some respects collectively weaker, than their national counterparts.

But recognition of these and other differences should not obscure similarities of type – if not perhaps intensity – between EU and national processes: political interest, political elite, organisational process and other models of decision-making can, after all, throw light on features of the latter, as well as the former. For example, in all member states, especially those with coalition governments (which is the norm in most EU states), political accommodation is an everyday occurrence and policy trimming is common. Furthermore, in countries with a considerable geographical decentralisation of power, for example Germany, tensions between levels of government over who does what and who pays for what are by no means unusual. In short, many of the EU's policy-making 'problems' – such as the prevalance of incrementalism and of policy slippages – are by no means absent in national political systems.

The second point is that not all EU policy processes consist of cobbling together deals that can satisfy the current complexion of political forces. This certainly is a crucially important feature, but it does not amount to the complete picture. In recent years greater efforts have been made, especially by the Commission, to initiate rather than just react, to look to the medium term rather than just the short term, and to pull at least some of the pieces together into coordinated programmes.

At the level of overarching policy coordination, progress towards more forward-looking and coordinated policy planning has, it must be said, been only modest, but it is developing. For example, the Commission's 1987 document *The Single Act: A New Frontier* made recommendations for dealing with what it saw as the central priorities for the period up to 1992. The programme outlined in the document became the subject of exhaustive Council and European Council negotiations. These negotiations led, at the 1988 Brussels summit, to a package deal which, though the outcome of the usual political trading, did at least address, in an interlinking five-year financial programme, some, though by no means all, of the Community's most pressing problems. Similar proceedings occurred in 1992 when the 1988 package needed to be renewed. On this occasion the Commission's proposals were presented in its document *From the Single Act to Maastricht and Beyond: The Means to Match Our Ambitions* (Commission, 1992), and the final deal – on a financial programme for 1993–9 – was concluded at the December 1992 Edinburgh summit. With the conclusion of the 1993–9 financial programme looming, and with the prospect of accession by Central and Eastern European countries raising many important policy questions, the Commission produced another major and overarching policy planning document in 1997: *Agenda 2000: For a Stronger and Wider Union* (Commission, 1997a). As is shown in Chapters 12 and 14, *Agenda 2000* drew together proposals for a new financial perspective covering the period 2000–6, with recommendations both on how the enlargement process should proceed and on major policy reforms – especially in respect of the CAP and the Structural Funds. After almost two years of negotiations between the member states on the *Agenda 2000* proposals, agreement was reached at the March 1999 Berlin summit on a new financial perspective and a package of policy reform measures.

At the operational level, evidence of movement towards greater coordination and forward policy planning is provided by the increased importance that has been attached over the years to the Commission's annual work programme. This sets out priorities and proposed actions for the year ahead and is discussed with the Council and the EP with a view to ensuring that the three institutions work in the same policy direction.

Further evidence is provided by the increasing practice of Council Presidencies developing their priorities and goals in association with preceding and succeeding Presidencies.

Coordinated forward planning is also to be found in particular policy sectors, with the existence of medium to long term policy objectives and rounded programmes. These are drawn up by the Commission, usually in consultation with appropriate consultative committees and committees of experts, and have to be approved by the Council to be given effect. They appear in various forms. For example: White Papers (such as the 1995 White Paper on energy policy [Commission, 1995]); communications (such as the 1997 communication on a new shipbuilding policy [Commission, 1997b]); framework and legislation programmes (such as the multi-annual programmes for the environment and for research and technological development [see Chapter 12]); and action programmes.

It is worth saying a little about action programmes to illustrate how, within specified fields of activity, a measure of coordinated development over a planned medium term period is possible. Action programmes vary in nature, from the broad and general to the highly specific. Broad and general programmes typically include measures to improve the monitoring and supervision of existing legislation, ideas for new legislation, running a pilot scheme, and spending programmes. Amongst the fields of activity where such action programmes exist are equal opportunities, public health, and access to educational training programmes. In contrast, specific action programmes are more specialised in their areas of concern and tighter in their provisions. Examples are the ECSC social research programmes on such matters as safety in mines and industrial hygiene, which are given appropriations for a given period and provide up to about 60 per cent of the cost of approved research projects.

The third and final 're-balancing' point to be made about EU policy processes is that critical judgements of them ought to be placed in the context of the very considerable degree of policy cooperation and integration that has been achieved at the EU level. There is no comparable international development where states have voluntarily transferred so many policy responsibilities to a collective organisation of states, and in so doing have surrendered so much of their national sovereignty. It is hardly surprising, given the enormity of the exercise, that pressures and desires for cooperation and integration should so often be challenged, and held in check, by caution, uncertainty, conflict, and competition.

The Budget

The EU raises and spends money in many different ways. Mostly it does so within the framework of the annual budget and it is with the budget that this chapter is primarily concerned.

However, in order to give a full picture of the EU's financial activities and instruments, an outline of the main non-budgetary financial operations will be presented first.

Non-budgetary operations

The main non-budgetary operations are as follows:

- The EU borrows sums on capital markets that are then made available, in the form of loans, to both public and private undertakings for investment. The European Investment Bank (EIB), which is the principal source of EU investment finance, has already been discussed in this connection (see Chapter 11).
- The December 1992 Edinburgh summit established a European Investment Fund (EIF), the main objective of which is to stimulate investment and economic growth by providing guarantees for both publicly and privately funded projects.
- Borrowing and lending activities are occasionally undertaken to enable member states to cope with balance of payments difficulties. The last such loan made to a member state for balance of payments purposes was 8 billion ecu to Italy in January 1993.
- The ECSC is resourced from its own funds, the principal component of which is a levy on coal and steel production.
- The EU provides loans and loan guarantees to certain non-member states. Particular beneficiaries in recent years have been countries of the former Soviet bloc and former Soviet Union.

- The European Development Fund, which provides aid to African, Caribbean and Pacific countries under the Lomé Convention (see Chapter 16), is not resourced from the budget but from direct contributions by the member states.

The budget in context

Turning now to the EU budget, one point needs to be emphasised at the outset: despite the considerable attention it has received over the years, and despite the political tensions it has sometimes generated, the size of the budget is relatively small. In 1999 it totalled 96.93 billion euro in commitment appropriations: about £66.85 billion or $108.6 billion at February 1999 exchange rates. This represented only 1.11 per cent of the Gross National Product (GNP) of the member states and about 2.5 per cent of their total public expenditure.

The reason why the budget is so small is that most of the policy sectors that make up the bulk of public expenditure – defence, education, health, social welfare and so on – remain primarily the responsibility of the member states. Many of the EU's policy activities, such as those concerned with the regulation of the market, involve little in the way of operational costs. When EU policies do involve significant operational costs, for example where they impose an obligation to introduce measures to conform with EU environmental legislation, the financial impact usually falls not on the EU budget but on private firms and public authorities in the member states.

The modesty of the EU budget should therefore be borne in mind when assessing the budget's financial and policy impact. Clearly the budget cannot, and does not, serve to effect a major transfer of financial resources from national exchequers to the EU, or *vice versa*.

The financial perspectives

In the early 1980s the EC was plagued by budgetary crises. There were three main reasons for this. First, there were increasing financial obligations, particularly in respect of the Common Agricultural Policy (CAP) which at that time accounted for over 70 per cent of total budgetary expenditure. Second, budgetary resources – which consisted of customs duties, agricultural levies, and a proportion of Value Added Tax (VAT) up to a 1 per cent ceiling – could not generate enough income to meet the financial obligations. The member states could have resolved this problem by altering the resources base, but some states – the UK in particular –

were reluctant to do this. Third, the UK government under Mrs Thatcher was campaigning vigorously to reduce what it saw to be excessive UK net budgetary contributions.

The crises of the early 1980s eventually led to the conclusion of a complicated deal at the 1984 Fontainebleau European Council. Key elements of the deal included new rules on budgetary discipline, a formula for reducing UK budgetary contributions, and an expansion of resources through the setting of a new 1.4 per cent ceiling for VAT from 1986. The Fontainebleau agreement was, however, too little too late, in that no sooner had the 1.4 per cent ceiling been introduced in 1986 than it was exhausted and the Commission was forced to open a new campaign for a further expansion of the revenue base.

That campaign culminated in the 1988 Brussels summit which brought a further, and compared with Fontainebleau much more radical, reform designed to deal with the EC's recurring budgetary difficulties. The Brussels reform was given added force in June 1988 when its key elements were incorporated in the *Interinstitutional Agreement on Budgetary Discipline and Improvement of the Budgetary Procedure*, which was signed by the Presidents of the Council of Ministers, the Commission, and the European Parliament (European Communities, 1987). The importance of the *Interinstitutional Agreement* was that it contained a formal commitment by all three institutions to the framework of a financial perspective for the years 1988–92. Included in the perspective were: a phased reduction in CAP expenditure, with annual budgets having to conform to the principles of what was called the agricultural guideline – by which the rate of increase in agriculture guarantee expenditure in any one year must not exceed 74 per cent of the annual rate of increase in EU GNP; a phased increase in expenditure on structural operations, with spending ceilings set for each of the five years of the perspective; a continuation of special abatement arrangements for the UK; a much tighter framework for ensuring budgetary discipline; and a significant expansion of resources through the creation of a new budgetary resource based on the GNP of each state. An increase in resources was thus linked to an expanding spending programme, subject to the limitation that the total amount of resources for any one year could not exceed the following percentages of the total GNP of the Community for the year in question – 1988: 1.15; 1989: 1.17; 1990: 1.18; 1991: 1.19; 1992: 1.20.

In 1992 the Commission put forward proposals for a new financial perspective under the title *From the Single Act to Maastricht and Beyond: the Means to Match Our Ambitions* (Commission, 1992). After negotiations between the member states in the Council of Ministers and the European Council, which took up much of 1992, a financial perspective for the years 1993–9 was agreed at the December 1992 Edinburgh summit. The core elements of this new financial perspective, which were incorporated in 1993 into another inter-institutional agreement, were based on the principles of the 1988 financial perspective: further stabilisation of agricultural expenditure and a further increase in funding for structural operations; a specified annual ceiling for categories of expenditure; an increase in resources, up to a ceiling of 1.27 per cent of GNP in 1999; continuation of the existing four revenue resources, though with some modifications to make them weigh less heavily on the poorer states; continuing tight budgetary discipline; and no changes in the abatement arrangements for the UK. (The appropriations and resource ceilings of the 1993–99 financial perspective are set out on p. 346 of the third edition of this book.)

In 1997–8, as part of its *Agenda 2000* package of reforms, the Commission put forward proposals for a third financial perspective covering the period 2000–6. (Commission, 1997a). As with the Commission's proposals for the 1988–92 and 1993–9 financial perspectives, the *Agenda 2000* proposals were scrutinised thoroughly by the member states and prompted extensive political debate and controversy. That there should be controversy in such circumstances is almost inevitable since not only is the EU budget – like all budgets – an expression of political priorities, but it also has significant implications for national exchequers. Amongst the concerns of national governments were the following: the governments of net contributor states, especially Germany, wanted the size of their contributions reduced; the UK government wanted to retain the UK abatement; and the governments of states benefiting from spending programmes – such as France from the CAP and Spain from the Structural Funds – were resistant to these programmes being reduced, even if the released funds were to be directed to the 'good cause' of assisting Central and Eastern European countries (CEECs) to prepare for EU membership.

After numerous rounds of negotiations between the member states – channelled through many formations of the Council, but primarily Foreign, Ecofin, and Agriculture Ministers – the Heads of Government agreed on a seven year financial perspective for the years 2000–6 at the special Berlin summit in March 1999. The EP endorsed the perspective in May following Council agreement to make modest increases to internal policy expenditure. A new inter-institutional agreement was then concluded between the Council, Commission and EP (see Table 14.1). The main features of this third financial perspective are as follows:

- The overall expenditure total is to be stabilised. It is not possible to predict future EU expenditure with precision – not least because of uncertainties concerning the date(s) of CEEC accessions and the financial consequences of CAP reforms agreed at Berlin – but it is likely that over the period of the financial perspective total expenditure will increase approximately in proportion to economic growth. If CEEC accessions are delayed, as they may well be, EU expenditure will fall as a proportion of GNP.

- The 1.27 per cent ceiling on own resources is to be maintained, even if enlargement occurs during the lifetime of the financial perspective. (The working assumption was made that new member states will start acceding from 2002.)
- The revenue base is to be modified, with the VAT element being reduced and the GNP element being increased. The main aim of this modification is to make national funding of the budget less regressive.
- CAP expenditure is to increase marginally over the six year period.
- Structural Fund expenditure is to decrease. This is to be achieved primarily by a greater concentration of structural spending on the areas of greatest need. As part of this greater concentration, the number of Structural Fund objectives are to be reduced from seven to three.
- Over 3 billion euro is to be made available annually for pre-accession aid to CEECs, and much more is to be available when CEECs become EU members.
- The UK abatement is to be virtually unchanged.

The composition of the budget

Revenue

Following a decision by the member states in 1970, the funding of the budget was changed between 1970 and 1975 from a system based on national contributions to one based on 'own resources'. A major reason for introducing this change was that it would provide the Community with greater financial independence. The member states would determine the upper limit of the own resources, but the resources themselves would belong to the Community and not the states.

Since the creation of the GNP-based resource in 1988, the own resources have consisted of the following.

- *Common Customs Tariff duties and other duties*, which are collected in respect of trade with non-member countries.
- *Agricultural levies, premiums and other duties,* which are collected in respect of trade with non-member countries within the framework of the CAP. These differ from customs duties in that they are not fixed import taxes, but are fluctuating charges designed to have the effect of raising import prices to EU levels. There are also certain internal agricultural levies and duties, notably connected with the framework of the common organisation of the market in sugar to limit surplus production.
- *The application of a uniform percentage rate to the VAT assessment base,* which is determined in a standardised manner for member states.

Table 14.1   The financial perspective 2000–6

EUR million – 1999 prices – Appropriations for commitments	2000	2001	2002	2003	2004	2005	2006
1. AGRICULTURE	40920	42800	43900	43770	42760	41930	41660
CAP expenditure (excluding rural development)	36620	38480	39570	39430	38410	37570	37290
Rural development and accompanying measures	4300	4320	4330	4340	4350	4360	4370
2. STRUCTURAL OPERATIONS	32045	31455	30865	30285	29595	29595	29170
Structural Funds	29430	28840	28250	27670	27080	27080	26660
Cohesion Fund	2615	2615	2615	2615	2515	2515	2510
3. INTERNAL POLICIES	5930	6040	6150	6260	6370	6480	6600
4. EXTERNAL ACTION	4550	4560	4570	4580	4590	4600	4610
5. ADMINISTRATION	4560	4600	4700	4800	4900	5000	5100
6. RESERVES	900	900	650	400	400	400	400
Monetary reserve	500	500	250	0	0	0	0
Emergency aid reserve	200	200	200	200	200	200	200
Guarantee reserve	200	200	200	200	200	200	200

7. PRE-ACCESSION AID	3120	3120	3120	3120	3120	3120	3120
Agriculture	520	520	520	520	520	520	520
Pre-accession structural instrument	1040	1040	1040	1040	1040	1040	1040
PHARE (applicant countries)	1560	1560	1560	1560	1560	1560	1560
TOTAL APPROPRIATIONS FOR COMMITMENTS	91995	93385	93805	93005	91465	90795	90260
TOTAL APPROPRIATIONS FOR PAYMENTS	89590	91070	94130	94740	91720	89910	89310
APPROPRIATIONS FOR PAYMENTS AS % OF GNP	1.13%	1.12%	1.13%	1.11%	1.05%	1.00%	0.97%
AVAILABLE FOR ACCESSION (appropriations for payments)			4140	6710	8890	11440	14220
Agriculture			1600	2030	2450	2930	3400
Other expenditure			2540	4680	6640	8510	10820
CEILING ON APPROPRIATIONS FOR PAYMENTS	89590	91070	98270	101450	100610	101350	103530
CEILING ON APPROPRIATIONS FOR PAYMENTS AS % OF GNP	1.13%	1.12%	1.18%	1.19%	1.15%	1.13%	1.13%
MARGIN	0.14%	0.15%	0.09%	0.08%	0.12%	0.14%	0.14%
OWN RESOURCES CEILING (%GNP)	1.27%	1.27%	1.27%	1.27%	1.27%	1.27%	1.27%

Source: European Council (1999) and European Parliament *Daily Notebook* (6 May 1999)

In order to protect countries whose VAT base was high, under the 1988–92 financial perspective the assessment base for VAT could not exceed 55 per cent of the Gross National Product at market prices. To reduce further the regressive aspect of this element of budgetary resources, it was decided at the 1992 Edinburgh summit to lower the uniform rate of VAT from 1.4 per cent to 1 per cent between 1995 and 1999, and to cut the assessment base for the VAT resource from 55 per cent to 50 per cent of GNP. At the 1999 Berlin summit it was decided to cut the 1 per cent rate to 0.75 per cent from 2002 and to 0.5 per cent from 2004. (It should be emphasised that these VAT rules still allow countries to vary their national VAT rates, subject to EU limitations on minimum rates on exemptions.)

- *The application of a rate to a base representing the sum of member states' Gross National Product at market prices.* The rate is determined under the budgetary procedure in the light of the total of all other revenue and the total expenditure agreed. Since this resource is very much like a national contribution, it has been suggested by some observers that it does not have quite the own resource character of the other resources. Key features of this resource are that it introduces into the EU's revenue system a link with ability to pay, and it can be easily adjusted to bring budgetary revenue into balance with budgetary expenditure. The agreements at the Edinburgh and Berlin summits to reduce the VAT component of budgetary resources means this GNP component has become, and will continue to become, progressively more important.

Precisely what proportion of total budgetary revenue comes from each resource is naturally determined primarily by the rules governing the resources. As has just been shown, these rules change periodically. However, the proportions also vary a little from year to year according to such factors as trade flows, world agricultural prices, and national growth rates. In 1999 the projected proportions from the four resources were as follows: VAT – 35.5 per cent; GNP resource – 45.9 per cent; customs duties – 15.5 per cent; agricultural and sugar levies – 2.5 per cent.

As regards the member states and budgetary resources, the larger states – Germany, France, Italy, and the UK – are naturally the largest gross contributors to the revenue pool. However, France, Italy and the UK are not so large net contributors: France because it is a major beneficiary of the CAP; Italy because it benefits significantly from the CAP and the Structural Funds; and the UK because of the abatement on its contributions. Germany is by far the largest net contributor, followed by, in relative terms (as a percentage of GNP), the Netherlands, the UK, Sweden, and Austria.

Expenditure

The EU makes a distinction between expenditure that is a direct result of treaty application or acts adopted on the basis of the treaties – called compulsory (or obligatory) expenditure – and that which is not – called non-compulsory (or non-obligatory) expenditure. Each accounts for around 50 per cent of the total budget for payments.

The most striking feature of EU expenditure is that virtually all compulsory expenditure is used for the CAP. Two main factors account for the very strong position of agriculture in the budget. First, agriculture has seen a greater transfer of financial responsibility from national budgets to the EU budget than any other major policy area. Second, as will be explained in Chapter 15, an agricultural price guarantee policy has been pursued that has kept EU prices above world prices, and in a number of product sectors this has resulted in production levels well in excess of the capacity of the market. In consequence, the EU has had to pay for agricultural produce it does not require: by buying up surplus production, by storing it, by selling it at subsidised rates on domestic and world markets, and by converting it into animal feed.

On a rational and commonsense basis this can hardly be justified. Agriculture appears to be proportionately overfunded, whilst policy areas drawing on non-compulsory expenditure – such as regional policy, research policy and energy policy – appear to be underfunded. Certainly the relatively modest sums available in all categories other than the CAP means that the EU's financial ability to act as an agent for such pressing problems as under-investment, technological change, unemployment, and resource imbalances is limited. However, budgetary expenditure, like budgetary income, is not determined by 'objective' criteria but by political interplay. And in that interplay there are many powerful forces that wish to maintain high levels of spending on agriculture: governments anxious to receive farmers' votes do not normally wish to upset this often volatile section of the electorate; net beneficiaries of the CAP (both states and sectional interests) are not inclined voluntarily to surrender their gains; and, as will be shown in Chapter 15, agriculture is regarded by many decision-makers as 'special'.

However, notwithstanding these obstacles to reform, the pressures for radical change became intense by the mid to late 1980s: previous schemes for reducing agricultural expenditure were having only a marginal effect; ever-larger surpluses for some products were being predicted; and some states were becoming increasingly anxious to increase non-agricultural spending. As a result, measures designed to bring about at least a partial shift in the EU's pattern of expenditure were important features of the 1988–92 and 1993–9 financial perspectives with, in particular, phased reductions in agricultural expenditure and increases in expenditure on structural operations.

As can be seen from Table 14.2, which provides an outline of the main categories and volumes of expenditure in the 1999 budget, EU budgetary expenditure falls under six main headings:

- *Agriculture*. In the 1999 budget this accounted for around 47 per cent in payments and 42 per cent in commitments. Most of the funding is used for price guarantee purposes, though under the *Agenda 2000* reforms it is scheduled to move more towards providing direct income support to farmers (see Chapter 15).
- *Structural operations*. Accounting for 35 per cent of the 1999 budget in payments and 40 per cent in commitments, the two main component parts of structural operations are the European Regional Development Fund (ERDF) and the European Social Fund (ESF) (see Chapter 12). The poorer member states, and more particularly poorer regions within the poorer member states, are the main beneficiaries of structural operations, and this will be even more the case when the *Agenda 2000* provisions for narrower targeting of structural expenditure come into effect.
- *Internal policies*. This heading is allocated around 6 per cent of total budgetary expenditure. Research and technological development accounts for over half of internal policy expenditure. Other significant funding areas include education and training, industry, trans-European networks and the environment.
- *External policies*. Also accounting for around 6 per cent of total budgetary expenditure, the largest components under this heading in recent years have been assistance to Central and Eastern European countries and to Mediterranean and Middle East countries.
- *Administration*. This accounts for around 5 per cent of total budgetary expenditure.
- *Reserves*. Accounting for just over 1 per cent of total budgetary expenditure, these are used for a variety of purposes, including emergency aid.

Budgetary decision-making

The budgetary process

A timetable and set of procedures for drawing up and approving the annual budget is laid down in Article 272 (ex 203) of the TEC. However, in practice, Article 272 gives only an approximate and rather formal guide to what actually happens. It provides a framework that has been fleshed out and adapted over time in response to pressures, necessities, and convenience.

In broad terms, and assuming no major problems exist or arise to disrupt the process severely, the pattern of budgetary decision-making is as follows.

Preparation of the Preliminary Draft Budget

The budgetary process is constantly ongoing. The preparation of each annual budget may, however, be said to begin during the winter of the year before it is due to come into effect, for it is then that the Commission prepares spending plans. In attempting to look this far ahead – almost twelve months to the beginning of the financial year (in January) and twenty-four months to its close – the Commission is necessarily faced with many uncertainties on both the revenue and expenditure sides. Agriculture causes particular difficulties. For example, crop yields cannot be foreseen: a small change in weather conditions might raise production in a particular product from 101 per cent of consumer demand to 102 per cent, thus resulting in a considerable underestimate of the amount of budget support required for that product. Another problem is that agriculture expenditure is highly dependent on world agricultural prices and currency movements, which cannot be controlled: a falling dollar can have a drastic effect on EU finances because export subsidies for farm products are linked to dollar-denominated international market prices.

The Commission, therefore, has to make many assumptions, some of which may not be realised. If changed situations become apparent during the course of the budgetary cycle corrections can be made fairly easily by sending rectifying or amending letters to the Council and the EP. If, however, the financial situation changes for the worse during the budgetary year itself the position is more serious. It used to be the case that 'temporary' solutions, such as the postponement of payments, delays in the introduction of new programmes, and supplementary budgets were used. Since the 1988 Brussels agreement, however, the Commission has had available, and has used, a range of stronger management powers to enable it to take appropriate action at an early stage if agricultural expenditure – the main problem – gets out of hand. It can, for example, impose levies and price support cuts on certain products if designated production ceilings are exceeded.

The prime responsibility within the Commission for drawing up what is known as the Preliminary Draft Budget (PDB) falls to the Directorate General for Budgets (DGXIX). Inevitably it is subject to pressures from many sides: from other DGs, which forward their own estimates and bids; from national representatives, both through the Council and on a direct

Table 14.2   The EU budget 1999: different stages

	Budget 1998	Financial perspective 1999	Preliminary draft budget	Council first reading	EP first reading	Council second reading	Budget 1999
Common Agricultural Policy	39.9	45.2	41.0	40.4	40.5	40.4	40.4
Structural operations, including:	33.5	39.0	39.0	39.0	39.0	39.0	39.0
ERDF	14.0		15.6	15.6	14.9	15.6	15.6
ESF	8.6		9.6	9.6	9.1	9.6	9.6
EAGGF – Guidance	4.2		5.2	5.2	4.9	5.2	5.2
Internal policies, including: research (and technological development)	5.8	6.4	5.9	5.4	6.4	5.8	5.9
trans-European networks	3.5		3.6	3.4	3.6	3.5	3.5
education (vocational training and youth)	0.6		0.6	0.6	0.6	0.6	0.6
	0.4		0.4	0.3	0.4	0.4	0.4
External action, including: Mediterranean countries and Middle East	5.7	6.9	5.9	6.0	6.9	5.8	6.0
	1.1		1.1	1.1	1.1	1.1	1.1
Central and Eastern Europe	1.1		1.5	1.6	1.4	1.4	1.4
food aid	0.5		0.5	0.5	0.5	0.5	0.5
New Independent States and Mongolia	0.5		0.4	0.4	0.4	0.4	0.4

Administration	4.5	4.7	4.5	4.4	4.7	4.5	4.5
Reserves	1.2	1.2	1.2	1.2	1.2	1.2	1.2
Total appropriations for commitments	90.7	103.4	97.5	96.5	98.6	97.0	96.9
of which:							
compulsory expenditure	41.9		42.8	42.3	42.3	42.3	42.3
non-compulsory expenditure	48.7		54.7	54.2	56.9	54.6	54.6
Total appropriations for payments	83.5	96.7	86.9	85.9	89.6	85.5	85.6
of which:							
compulsory expenditure	42.0		42.9	42.4	42.4	42.4	42.4
non-compulsory expenditure	41.5		44.0	43.5	47.1	43.1	43.1

Notes:

1. Figures in billion euro
2. All figures are appropriations for commitments, apart from those in the bottom horizontal column
3. Figures have been rounded up where appropriate, hence some seemingly minor discrepancies

Source: Adapted from Commission (1999), p. 365.

lobbying basis; from the EP, especially leading figures on its Committee on Budgets; and from sectional interests. The Budget Commissioner and officials from DGXIX have many meetings, both formal and informal, to enable many of these interested parties to have their say. Naturally, those with the best chance of achieving some satisfaction are those that carry political weight and/or are already in tune with the Commission's thinking.

Under the terms of the 1993 Interinstitutional Agreement it was decided, as part of an attempt to improve relations and understandings between the Commission, the Council, and the EP during the budgetary procedure, that at some point before the Commission takes a final decision on the PDB there should be a trialogue meeting (delegations from the three institutions). The purpose of the meeting is 'to discuss the possible priorities for the budget of that year, with due account being taken of the institutions' powers'.

Once DGXIX has its proposals ready, they must be presented by the Commissioner to the other Commissioners and all must agree on the package. When they do, the proposals officially become the Preliminary Draft Budget.

Prior to the 1988 reform, the PDB usually disappointed those who wanted to see the budget used as the motor for change in EC priorities. The Commission did make several attempts to use the PDB to effect at least modest shifts in policy emphasis – notably by proposing the containment of agricultural expenditure and expansion of the Structural Funds – but its manoeuvrability was always severely restricted by existing expenditure commitments, and also by the knowledge that any significant proposed change from the *status quo* would be fiercely resisted in the Council. The existence since 1988 of financial perspectives has changed this situation by setting out a framework and a programme for using the budget to effect change.

The budget must be set within the framework of the financial perspective, which, as was noted above, is essentially a multi-annual financial programme laying down revenue and expenditure parameters. The Commission, the Council, and the EP are bound to respect the principles and ceilings set out in the financial perspective.

The financial perspective does not, it should be emphasised, totally constrain the Commission when it draws up the PDB. It does have manoeuvrability below the expenditure ceilings and it does have options within expenditure headings. Indeed, by the last year of the 1993–9 perspective the Commission, in theory at least, had considerable manoeuvrability thanks to lower than expected CAP expenditure and tight budgets: there was room below the overall financial perspective ceiling for a growth of 7 per cent in commitments and 10.5 per cent in payments. To have proposed such an increase was, of course, seen by the Commission as being neither desirable nor politically feasible, and in the event it proposed a 2.4 per cent increase in commitments and a 2.9 per cent increase in payments. The 1999 situation does, however, illustrate, if perhaps in a somewhat exaggerated manner, that whilst the financial perspective places clear limits on what the Commission can do, it is not a straitjacket.

The Commission presents the PDB in two forms: payment appropriations, which cover actual expenditure during the financial year; and commitment or engagement appropriations, which cover expenditure during the financial year plus liabilities extending beyond the year. Commitment appropriations are naturally higher than payment appropriations. The spending plans of the PDB are grouped under the headings of the EU budget that were outlined earlier in the chapter: agriculture, structural operations, internal policies, external policies, administration, and reserves. Within these headings, hundreds of budget lines identify specific policies, programmes, and projects. (Table 14.2 outlines the PDB for 1999, which was issued in April 1998.)

Council first reading

Assuming there are no major or special problems, the PDB is referred to the Council in late April or some time in May.

Most of the Council's detailed examination of the budget is undertaken by the Budget Committee, a working group of national officials who, in what are frequently long and exhaustive sessions, examine the PDB chapter by chapter, line by line. As the date of the Ministers' meeting in the Budget Council approaches, the Committee is likely to meet with increasing frequency in order to resolve as many issues as possible. The negotiators are in almost constant contact with their national capitals about what transpires in the meetings, and hence they mostly have a prepared view when items come up for discussion. When this produces a rigidity in negotiating positions, much of the responsibility to find a solution is thrown on the chairman – the Council's President-in-Office. The Commission can provide assistance with this task.

From the Budget Committee the draft proceeds to COREPER. The number of unresolved items put before the Permanent Representatives naturally depends on what has happened in the Committee. Normally, much remains to be done, and COREPER attempts, like the Committee, to clear as many items as possible before the Ministers meet. It is usually most successful with those issues that do not have a potentially conflictual political aspect.

If it becomes apparent at some point prior to the meeting of the Ministers that a disagreement may arise with the EP over the categorisation of expenditure between compulsory and non-compulsory, then there is provision for a conciliation procedure. (Because, as was explained in Chapter 9, the EP's powers are stronger over non-compulsory expenditure than they are over compulsory expenditure, it always wants as much expenditure as possible to be classified as non-compulsory.) The conciliation procedure begins with a trialogue meeting, which is convened in sufficient time to enable the institutions to reach an agreement by no later than the date set by the Council for establishing its first draft. At this trialogue meeting the institutions' delegations are led by the President of the Council (Budgets), the Chairman of the EP's Committee on Budgets, and the Commissioner with responsibility for the budget. Following the trialogue meeting, further conciliation meetings may be held as necessary.

The Ministers customarily meet in mid July, although on occasion they have not gathered until September. Their examination of the PDB is preceded by a meeting with a delegation from the EP, made up mainly of members of the Budget Committee. At this meeting the EP delegation sets out the priorities the EP wishes to pursue during the budgetary procedure. Matters of mutual concern may also be discussed, as in July 1998 when much of the meeting was taken up with the issue of implementing appropriations entered in the budget when there was no legal base. This issue arose from a May 1998 ruling by the Court of Justice that such a legal base is required (Case 106/96, see Chapter 10). The ruling resulted in the Council, the Commission and the EP delegation agreeing at the July meeting to a draft inter-institutional agreement on legal bases and implementation of the budget (for the text of the agreement, see *Council Press Release*, 10394/98, 17 July 1998).

Prior to the establishment of financial perspectives, the July Budget Council normally lasted for a couple days and involved 15 to 20 hours of negotiations in formal sessions, plus extensive informal discussions and manoeuvrings in the wings. Qualified majority voting usually allowed a draft to be eventually agreed, but on controversial proposals a blocking minority sometimes existed. On two occasions the divisions between the member states were such that the July meeting was unable to approve a draft, which meant there had to be a reference back to officials. The officials then produced a new package for the Ministers to consider when they returned in September, by which time the timetable was pressing and an agreement had to be reached.

The reason why the July meeting was often so difficult was that the states differed, both in their views about the balance to be struck between restraint and expansion and in their perceptions of problems and priorities. What emerged, therefore, was a draft reflecting accommodations and compromises. Almost invariably, however, the general thrust of the draft was, on the one hand, to propose a tighter overall budget than that envisaged in the PDB and, on the other hand, to propose some shift from non-compulsory expenditure to compulsory expenditure – that is, from items such as regional, social and research expenditure (which were relatively 'soft' because of their non-compulsory character) to agriculture (which was difficult to touch given the existing commitments).

Financial perspectives have constrained the Council, as they have the Commission, in what it can do. This has had two effects on the Council's first reading stage. First, the decision-making process is now less divisive and troublesome than it was in the past. Second, though the Council still customarily cuts the PDB, its hands are largely tied and it is obliged to produce a draft that is very similar to the PDB (see Table 14.2).

Parliament first reading

On being approved, the Council's first draft is referred to the EP. If the timing is suitable the President of the Budget Council may formally present the draft himself: to the Budget Committee and/or in an address to the plenary.

Although this presentation of the Council's draft marks the first public point at which the EP becomes formally involved in the budgetary process, in practice it will have been attempting to exert its influence for some time: before the PDB is agreed the EP, normally at its March plenary meeting, approves guidelines that it hopes will be followed by the Commission; a trialogue meeting will have been held with the Commission and the Council to discuss budgetary plans for the year (see above); the PDB is sent by the Commission to the EP at the same time as it is referred to the Council, and the Committee on Budgets begins its considerations almost immediately; and, as indicated above, conciliation procedures may have been held to try to resolve differences over whether appropriations should have been categorised as compulsory or non-compulsory expenditure.

Now, with the Council's draft available, the pace is stepped up. There is a brief debate in plenary session, but the detailed work is given over to committees. The Committee on Budgets naturally has most responsibility. It examines the budget in detail and also acts as a coordinating agency for reports submitted to it by other EP committees that look at the budget to see how their sectors will be affected. The Committee on Budgets does not, however, have the power completely to control what goes forward to the plenary: it cannot, for example, stop an amendment that has support elsewhere, especially if it is backed by any of the larger political groups. Partly in consequence of this, hundreds of proposed changes are usually put forward, many of which conflict with one another or are even mutually exclusive. Much, therefore, rests on the liaising, organising, and leadership skills of the chairman of the Committee on Budgets and the appointed *rapporteur*.

The intention is normally to hold the plenary session dealing with the budget in mid to late October, although on occasion it has been delayed until November. At the plenary, MEPs can do three things with the contents of the Council's draft: accept them; propose amendments to non-compulsory expenditure (which requires the majority support of MEPs); or propose modifications to compulsory expenditure (which requires a majority of the votes cast).

As with both the drafting of the PDB and the Council's first reading, the EP's first reading has been affected by the establishment of financial perspectives. There is not now such a gap as there normally used to be between the positions of the Council and the EP. This has been because of the obligations and constraints of the financial perspectives which, in addition to partly satisfying some of the EP's policy ambitions – through changes in expenditure patterns – have also reduced, though by no means eliminated, the significance of the distinction between compulsory and non-compulsory expenditure.

Since 1988 disagreements between the Council and the EP in the budgetary process have focused primarily on two sorts of issues. First, the EP has cusomarily pressed for higher levels of non-compulsory expenditure than the Council. Second, the EP has urged that expenditure be classified in ways that increase its institutional powers, and to this end it has long campaigned for the abolition of the distinction between compulsory and non-compulsory expenditure.

After the EP has debated the draft budget in plenary session, and after all amendments and modifications have been voted upon, a resolution on the budget is adopted (see Table 14.2 for the main contents of the resolution on the 1999 budget).

Council second reading

From the EP the draft goes back to the Council, where officials prepare it for the ministerial second reading, which is usually held in mid to late November. If any issues remain to be settled the activity can be feverish, and many meetings – including trialogue meetings – may be held to try and achieve progress.

Before the November meeting formally gives a second reading to the draft budget, ministers normally meet again with an EP delegation, which invariably has much the same composition as the delegation that met with the Council at the first reading. The purpose of the meeting is to try to iron out differences and identify grounds for compromise. So, in respect of the 1999 budget, a number of compromises were indeed reached at this meeting, and grounds for a possible agreement were considered on what had been a thorny issue concerning flexibility in the use of reserves (*Council Press Release*, 13299/98, 24 November 1998).

On matters where there is still disagreement with the EP, the options available to the Budget Council depend on the type of expenditure concerned and whether the EP has proposed expenditure increases. In broad terms, the situation is that the Council has the last word on compulsory expenditure so can reject EP amendments if it wishes, whilst the EP has the last word on non-compulsory expenditure so the Council can only modify EP amendments.

The usual approach of the Council at the second reading is to strike a balance between accommodating the EP on the one hand whilst reaffirming its first reading position on the other (see Table 14.2).

Parliament second reading

The EP holds its second reading on the budget in mid December. What happens before, at, and after the plenary depends very much on the extent to which contentious issues remain unresolved.

If the situation is relatively straightforward and most problems have been sorted out, then the normal procedure is for the Committee on Budgets to meet, to reinsert such non-compulsory expenditure as it legally can and, on this basis, to recommend adoption. The plenary then votes, and if the budget is approved the President formally signs it and declares it to be adopted (see Table 14.2 for an outline of the budget that was adopted for 1999).

But when, as was frequently the case prior to the Brussels summit, major differences between the Council and the EP remain, the two sides are obliged to get down to negotiations. Various procedures can come into play: the President of the Budget Council, accompanied by the Budget Commissioner, may meet with the Committee on Budgets; the President of the Budget Council may make an appeal to the plenary; a trialogue meeting may be held; or a special Budget Council may be hurriedly called – perhaps to meet again with an EP delegation, perhaps to give the budget what is, in effect, a third reading. If all efforts to reach a Council–EP agreement fail, the latter can reject the budget by a majority of its members, including two-thirds of the votes cast.

Non-approval of the budget

In five of the first nine years after the introduction of direct elections in 1979, budgets were not approved in time to be implemented at the beginning of the financial year on 1 January. These were the budgets of 1980 and 1984–8.

If a legal budget is not approved by the EP before 1 January a fall back position applies. This allows for funding to continue, but only on the basis of what are known as 'provisional twelfths', which means that spending is limited to the monthly average expenditure of the previous year. Therefore policies do not collapse, but some payments may have to be suspended, and programmes, especially new ones, may have to be delayed. A speedy agreement on the budget of what by this stage is the current financial year is thus desirable.

There is no formal procedure or set pattern of action in the event of non-adoption. The expectation and assumption is that the process will be resumed at the point at which it broke down, but practice has shown that matters are not so simple. Developments following non-adoption have varied considerably, depending principally on the reasons for the non-adoption. For example, the 1986 budget was, like those for 1985 and 1988, not approved until halfway through the financial year. The problem with the 1986 budget was not that a budget was not approved by the EP in December 1985, but rather that the Council judged that the budget adopted by the EP was illegal on the ground that it included more non-compulsory expenditure than was legally permissible. The Council therefore asked the Court of Justice for a ruling. On 3 July 1986 the Court eventually delivered its judgement, and in essence upheld the Council's claim that the budget was illegal. The next week saw hectic activity, a truncated budgetary procedure and, on 10 July, the adoption of a budget in which creative accountancy and financial ingenuity played prominent parts.

The adoption of medium-term financial perspectives and inter-institutional agreements has removed, or at least blunted the sharpness of, many of the problems that occasioned the non-adoption of budgets in the 1980s. In particular, agricultural expenditure has been made subject to stronger budgetary discipline, the Structural Funds have been increased, mechanisms have been established to improve the match between income and expenditure, and decision-making procedures have been made less confrontational. Of course, not all differences or potential problems have been totally erased. But the prospect of budgets being adopted at December plenaries has been considerably enhanced, and all budgets since 1988 have indeed been so adopted.

Implementation of the budget

The implementation of, and the monitoring of the implementation of, the budget may also be considered as part of the budgetary process. Only a couple of general points will be made here about these activities, however, since both receive attention elsewhere in the book, notably in Chapters 6, 11 (in the section on the Court of Auditors), and 13.

The first point is that, as with other aspects of EU policy implementation, much of the 'front-line' budgetary implementation is undertaken by national agencies in the member states. The Commission makes transfer payments to the agencies – which are mainly, although by no means exclusively, national and regional governmental bodies – and they manage them on the Commission's behalf. This delegation to agencies does not, however, absolve the Commission from overall responsibility for the execution of the budget, and for this purpose it has a battery of administrative structures and arrangements to deal with such matters as the drawing up of tenders, the issuing of contracts, and the handling – either directly or indirectly – of payments.

An indication of the scale of the activities involved is provided by the fact that the Commission – and more particularly DGXX (Financial Control) – is responsible for over 360 000 financial transactions a year, including some 250 000 payment orders. These range from large CAP and Structural Fund transfer payments to employees' travel expenses (Commission Spokesman's Service, Press Release IP/96/993, 6 November 1996).

The second point is that the implementation of the budget has attracted considerable attention in recent years, not least from the media and the EP. This is partly, perhaps, because attention has been less focused on budgetary decision-making as that process has become much less fraught. It is mainly, however, because the Court of Auditors in a series of reports has exposed mismanagement and fraud in the implementation of EU policies (see Chapter 11 for examples of problems identified by the Court). The Commission is not slow to point out that many of the problems identified by the Court must be laid at the doors of the national agencies that are responsible for around 80 per cent of direct payments, but the fact is that the Court has also exposed inadequacies in the Commission's financial control systems. As was shown in Chapters 9 and 11, it was the exposure of such inadequacies that initiated the events that led to the resignation of the College of Commissioners in March 1999.

Characteristic features of the budgetary process

Some features of the budgetary process merit particular comment.

First, the budget, like the annual agriculture price review, is unusual in the EU decision-making context in the sense that it is supposed to operate according to a clear timetable. Legislative proposals can be pushed along if they are strongly supported, and the greater use of majority voting in the Council has greatly quickened the pace of much legislative decision-making, but it is only in the later stages of the cooperation and co-decision procedures that a timetable applies. It is still the case that legislative proposals can drag on in the Council until some sort of agreement is reached, and if this proves not to be possible they may be indefinitely postponed or even dropped altogether. With the budget such a relaxed and open-ended approach is not possible, since expenditure and resource decisions have to be made each year. The existence and exigencies of the timetable thus introduce an urgency into budgetary decision-making that is not always found in other spheres of EU decision-making.

Second, the power balance between the institutions is based on the Council and the EP jointly constituting the budgetary authority as co-decision-makers. The Commission remains important, but after the presentation of the PDB it is cast in an essentially servicing capacity: responding to what happens in the Council and the EP and doing what it can to bring the two sides together. As for the particular nature of the balance between the Council and the EP, the former is the stronger, but changes that have been made since 1988 have improved the position of the EP. They have done so in three ways: by binding the institutions into a financial framework that can only be revised by common agreement; by significantly increasing the proportion of the budget over which the EP has most control – non-compulsory expenditure; and by giving the EP a glimpse of shared control over compulsory expenditure – a condition of the EP's agreeing to the 1993–9 financial perspective was that it would have the right to scrutinise the compulsory expenditure part of the budget, with a view to forcing the Commission to justify the legal base of compulsory budget lines.

Third, many of the arguments and confrontations that have occurred during the budgetary process have been occasioned not so much by the financial sums involved – which have usually been relatively small – but more by a broader institutional struggle, especially between the Council and the EP. With the EP dissatisfied with its overall position in the EU system, it is only natural that it should have sought to use the budget to maximum advantage. There are a number of ways in which it has gone about this. One was a willingness in the 1980s to reject the budget. Another has been interpreting the treaties, along with inter-institutional agreements and understandings about budgetary decision-making, in ways that are advantageous to itself – as on matters such as the bases for budgetary calculations and the classification of expenditure in terms of compulsory and non-compulsory. And yet another way has been by attempting to exploit differences within the Council, for example, by seeking to exert pressure in a particular direction through the indication of preferences in plenary votes or, less formally, in inter-institutional exchanges such as conciliation meetings.

Fourth, certain fundamental budgetary decisions are not taken via the annual budgetary process. Most importantly, the multi-annual financial frameworks are essentially the outcome of exhaustive intergovernmental negotiations that culminate in European Council decisions. The Commission does, of course, structure these negotiations in that they are conducted from the starting point of Commission proposals, and the EP has a role to play too in that the frameworks require its approval, but the national governments are the key decision-makers – or, at least, key decision takers.

Fifth, and finally, the use of financial perspectives since 1988 has allowed for some use of the budget to guide incremental policy development. The perspectives have perhaps not established 'cohesive' or 'objective' budgetary planning, but they have at least enabled the budget to become the instrument for important, if perhaps rather modest, policy reform.

Concluding remarks

As Brigid Laffan (1997, p. 245) has observed, one of the most striking features of the institutional and policy dynamics of the EU since the late 1980s has been the achievement of relative budgetary peace.

At the organisational level, this relative peace has reflected the success of financial perspectives in providing an ordered framework for annual budgetary decision-making. The margins for manoeuvre within financial perspectives have been relatively narrow and so have not provided much opportunity for heated disputes over income or expenditure. Insofar as there have been problems within the annual budgetary process, they have tended to be focused as much on institutional/procedural issues (for example the disagreement in 1998 between the Council and the EP about extending flexibility in the reserves) as on resource generation and distribution issues.

At a more ideological level, the relative peace has reflected a growing consensus amongst policy actors that the EU's overall expenditure patterns are about right, or at least are acceptable. Certainly there was no great push from decision-making actors in the debates on the 2000–6 financial perspective either to dismantle existing budgetary commitments or to expand them significantly.

There was, however, a push in two directions, and it is by no means clear that they have been satisfactorily resolved. First, those states that are net contributors to the budget – especially Germany – wanted changes to the size of national budgetary contributions and receipts. At the March 1999 Berlin summit, where Heads of Government reached agreement on the 2000–6 financial perspective, not much was done to accommodate these national concerns. Second, some policy actors felt that bold initiatives were necessary to meet the challenge of enlargement. The response of the Commission and most member state governments was to recognise that the character of some policies – notably the CAP and the structural policies – would have to be further changed, but this was not seen as requiring major revisions to budgetary allocations. It remains to be seen whether this proves to be the case in practice, and whether the decisions taken at Berlin will be sufficient to avoid future budgetary problems whilst at the same time being of enough help to enable CEECs to make the transitions necessary for EU membership.

Chapter 15

Agricultural Policy and Policy Processes

What is special about agriculture?
How the Common Agricultural Policy works
The impact and effects of the Common Agricultural Policy
Policy processes
The annual price review
Concluding remarks

Despite the fact that it accounts for only 2.5 per cent of EU GDP and 5.5 per cent of EU employment, agriculture looms large in the life of the EU. It does so in three main ways. First, the EU has, via the Common Agricultural Policy (CAP), major policy-making and decision-making responsibilities for agriculture. Indeed, agriculture is the most integrated of the EU's sectoral policies. Second, as the major recipient of EU funds – accounting for almost half of total annual expenditure – agriculture is central to EU budgetary deliberations. Third, there is a greater institutional presence and activity in the agricultural field than in any other: the Agriculture Ministers normally meet more frequently than the ministers all other Councils except for the Foreign Ministers; uniquely, Agriculture Council meetings are prepared not by COREPER but by a special body, the Special Committee on Agriculture (SCA); DGVI (Agriculture) is the second largest of the Commission's Directorates General (only DGIX is larger and that deals not with a policy sector but with Personnel and Administration); and there are far more Council working parties and Commission management and advisory groups in the sphere of agriculture than in any other single policy area.

For its supporters, the CAP is important both in itself – the benefits accruing from joint policy-making and common management are seen as far outweighing the disadvantages – and important, too, as a symbol and indicator that real policy integration is possible at EU level. Those who criticise the CAP are thus liable to be attacked both on technical and efficiency grounds (with the claim that national solutions would be much less satisfactory) and more broadly for being *non communautaire* (with the assertion that this most integrated of EU policies should not be undermined). For opponents of the CAP, economic efficiency is the key issue. Subsidisation of wealthy farmers, high prices for consumers, and production of farm surpluses that nobody wants are the most frequently voiced criticisms.

Yet even amongst those who are most critical of the CAP, few seriously challenge the view that there should be an EU agriculture policy of some kind. Certainly no member state believes that the agricultural edifice should be uprooted and policy returned to national capitals. The view that there is something special about agriculture, something that distinguishes it from other sectoral activities and merits it receiving advantageous treatment, whilst not commanding such strong support as in the early days of the EC, still strikes a chord with EU decision-makers.

What is special about agriculture?

The attention given to agriculture in the EEC Treaty, and the subsequent creation of the CAP after long and often tortuous negotiations, is often seen as being part of a trade-off between France and Germany. There is some truth to this view. In exchange for the creation of a common market in industrial goods, which the French feared would be greatly to Germany's advantage, France – with its large but uneconomic agricultural sector – would benefit from an agricultural system that, though also in the form of a common market, would be based not on free and open market principles, but on foundations that would protect farmers from too much competition.

Important though it was, however, the Franco-German 'deal' is only part of the explanation of why agriculture, from the earliest days of the Community, was given an elevated policy status. For the fact is that when the CAP was being created in the late 1950s and early 1960s, none of the then six member states seriously objected to it in principle – the Netherlands, for example, was a strong supporter – though there were differences on the pace of its construction and the precise nature of its policy instruments. This consensus on the general principle was a result of a shared recognition that agriculture required special treatment.

Today, despite the original EC having greatly increased in size, despite the circumstances and conditions of agriculture having dramatically changed, and despite the CAP having caused major difficulties and disruptions to the whole EU system, agriculture is still generally regarded by the national governments as requiring special treatment. Many of the reasons for this are much the same as they were in the EC's early days. Others are more recent. The reasons can be grouped under two general headings: the distinctive nature of agriculture, and political factors.

The distinctive nature of agriculture

For many years, but especially since the Second World War, most governments of the industrialised world have taken the view that agriculture is not like other areas of economic activity. It is special and merits special treatment to encourage, assist and protect it. In the EU four main arguments have been, and in varying degrees still are, advanced in support of this view.

(1) If they are not controlled by governmental authorities agricultural prices are more subject to fluctuation than the prices of most other goods. Agricultural price instability is undesirable for two reasons. First, if prices suddenly go up, inflation is immediately fuelled (given that food constitutes around 20 per cent of the budget of the average EU citizen). Second, if prices fall too low, farmers may not be able to make an adequate living and may be forced off the land; even those who are able to stay in farming may experience severe difficulties as a result of high debt loads on land and capital purchases.

(2) Reliance on imports for vital foodstuffs creates a potential vulnerability to outside pressures. This is a particular source of weakness during periods of strained international relations, but in the relatively calm international trading climate that now prevails, and with many of the foodstuffs produced in the EU being in surplus – including cereals, dairy produce and meat – this argument is less weighty than it used to be. However, in the early years of the EC, when memories were still fresh of wartime shortages and the vulnerability and misery this occasioned, it played an important part in encouraging a drive for greater self-sufficiency.

(3) Because people must have food, insufficient domestic production means that the gap between output and demand has to be met by imports, with potentially damaging consequences for the balance of payments. Moreover, since the demand for food is fairly inelastic up to necessity levels (as long as income allows it, food will still be bought even if prices go up) the economic vulnerability of an importing state is high. This balance of payments argument used to be important in helping to underpin the CAP, but it has not been so forceful since the early to mid 1970s, when Community prices became significantly higher than world prices and Community production began to move significantly into surplus. High domestic prices mean that EU processors cannot maximise their value added exports by buying at the cheapest possible prices, and surpluses mean that national treasuries have to pay – via the EU budget – for their disposal.

(4) Social and environmental reasons for keeping farmers on the land have been increasingly voiced in recent years. Sometimes these have an

idealistic tone to them, with pleas that a populated countryside is part of the natural fabric, or the suggestion that management of the land is a desirable end in itself. Rather more hard-headed perhaps is the argument that, with relatively high levels of unemployment in most EU states, it is both undesirable and potentially dangerous to allow farm incomes to deteriorate to the point that poor farmers and agricultural workers are forced to move to the towns in search of employment that often does not exist.

Political factors

Farmers enjoy political assets that they have been able to translate into influence on EU policy. Three of these assets are especially important.

(1) At the national decision-making level, Ministries of Agriculture have traditionally tended to be slightly apart from mainstream policy processes, and since 1958 this has been reproduced at the EU level with the position of DGVI in the Commission. All policy-makers in all areas of policy, do, of course, attempt to use their own expertise, knowledge and information to provide themselves with some insulation from the rest of the decision-making system, but agriculture is particularly well placed to do this. Its supposedly distinctive nature, the complexity of much of its subject matter, and the customary close relations between agricultural decision-makers and producers, all combine to make it difficult for 'outside' decision-makers to offer an effective challenge or alternative to what is presented to them.

(2) Farmers enjoy considerable electoral weight. Even though their relative numerical importance has declined sharply over the years – in 1958 around 25 per cent of total EC employment was in agriculture, by 1999 it was just over 5 per cent – the agricultural vote is still very significant. The significance varies from state to state. The size of the domestic population engaged in agriculture is one important factor in determining this significance: proportions range from around 22 per cent in Greece and 15 per cent in Portugal to 2.6 per cent in Belgium and 2.2 per cent in the United Kingdom. Another consideration is the direction of the agricultural vote. On the whole, farmers, especially richer farmers, incline towards Centre-Right and Right parties, with the consequence that it is they, rather than parties of the Left, that are usually the strongest defenders of agricultural interests in EU forums. But this inclination to the Right does not, in most countries, amount to an exclusive loyalty, so few parties can afford to ignore the farmers: at a minimum, all parties must give the impression of being concerned and solicitous.

(3) In most EU countries farmers have long had very strong domestic organisations to represent and articulate their interests. When it became clear in the late 1950s and early 1960s that much agricultural policy and decision-making was to be transferred to Brussels, similar organisations were quickly established at Community level. As early as 1963, approaching 100 Community-wide agriculture groups had been formed. By the late 1990s the number was around 130. The most important of these groups is the Committee of Agricultural Organisations in the European Union (COPA), which is an umbrella or peak organisation representing all types of farmers on the basis of affiliation through national farming groups. Beyond COPA and a few other overarching organisations, specialist bodies exist to represent virtually every product that is produced and consumed in the EU, and every participant in the agricultural process – farmers most obviously, but also processors, traders, retailers and so on.

There can be no doubt that this agricultural lobby has been, and – though its influence has declined over the years – remains, a powerful force in the EU. It is worth setting out the reasons why this is so.

The sheer size of the lobby is formidable. It operates at two levels, the national and the EU.

At the national level there are considerable variations in the pattern and strength of agricultural representation. But in all member states there are groups of some kind that have as part of their purpose the utilisation of whatever devices and channels are available to them to influence both national agricultural policy (within the general principles of the CAP, states still enjoy a considerable policy discretion) and EU agricultural policy. Thus, the National Farmers' Union for England and Wales employs a full-time professional staff of around 240 at its London headquarters and 600 or so in the regions. In addition, it funds – in conjunction with the NFU of Scotland and the Ulster Farmers' Union – a Brussels office, known as the British Office of Agriculture, which has a regular staff of between five and ten who are topped up as required.

At the EU level the large number of Euro-agric groups means that lobbying activities across the agricultural sector are almost continuous. COPA moves on the broadest front, and with some 50 full-time officials it is by far the best resourced and staffed organisation (for further information on COPA see Chapter 11; Grant, 1997; Greenwood, 1997). The more specialised groups – for example the mustard makers (CIMCEE) and the butchers (COBCCEE) – are much more modestly provided for and at best may have just one full-time member of staff working in an office made available by a national affiliate. But since the interests of these small groups are usually narrowly drawn this may be enough to allow basic lobbying requirements to be fulfilled – meetings and consultations with decision-makers, feeding information through to the EU institutions, preparing policy and briefing documents. If necessary, reinforcements are usually available from national and Euro-umbrella associations.

Agricultural interests generally enjoy good contact with, and access to, decision-makers. Again, this factor operates at both national and EU levels. At the national level, influence with governments is vital, not only because of their control over nationally determined policies but also because they are the route to the Council of Ministers. Most governments are at least prepared to listen to representations from national agricultural interests, and some engage in a virtually automatic consultation on important issues. There are a number of reasons why governments are generally approachable in this way: there may be a pre-existing sympathy for the interests' views; a fuller picture of what is going on in the agricultural world is made possible; policy implementation may be made easier; and political support may be generated by being supportive, or at least by giving the impression that the government and the interest are as one. If, despite being sympathetically listened to by its government, a national agricultural interest is dissatisfied with what is agreed in the Council of Ministers, the government can always try to blame 'the awkward Italians', 'the impossible Greeks' or 'the immovable Germans'.

At the EU level, the Commission is the prime target for agricultural interests. For the most part it is very willing to listen. Indeed, it has encouraged the establishment of Euro-agric groups and readily makes itself available to them. Close Commission–group relations are viewed by the Commission as being as useful to it as to the groups: the groups can contribute their knowledge and experience, which may improve policy; the Commission can explain to the groups why it is engaging in certain actions and thus seek to sensitise them to Commission concerns and aims; face-to-face meetings can help break down barriers and resistance arising from suspicions that 'the Eurocrats' do not really understand farming practicalities; and if Eurogroups can do something to aggregate the conflicting national interests and demands that arise in relation to most proposals, they can considerably simplify the Commission's task of developing policies that are acceptable and can help to legitimise the Commission as a decision-maker in the eyes of the Council and the EP. All that said, however, it does appear that since about the mid 1980s the Commission, though maintaining close links with the agricultural lobby, has been less influenced by it. A major reason for this is that the Commission has been obliged to try to reform the agricultural sector, whilst organisations such as COPA have been, in Grant's words, 'seeking to defend the ancient regime' (Grant, 1997, p. 170; on the declining influence of COPA, see also Clark and Jones, 1999)).

The agricultural organisations are not counterbalanced by strong and vigorous groups advancing contrary attitudes and claims. 'Natural opponents' do exist – consumers and environmentalists most notably – but they are relatively weak in comparison. A major reason for their weakness is that whereas farmers constitute a clear section of the population with a readily identifiable common sectoral interest, consumers and environmentalists do not have such a group consciousness, are more widely dispersed and, in consequence, are just not so easy to mobilise or organise. So although there are many more consumers than there are farmers in the EU, the largest of the Euro-consumer groups – the European Bureau of Consumers' Associations (BEUC) – has a staff of only fifteen or so. This is sizeable enough when compared with most Eurogroups, but it pales in comparison with the massed ranks of the agricultural associations. Moreover, the BEUC has to cover the whole spectrum of relevant EU policies; agriculture takes up only part of its time.

In terms of access to decision-makers, the farmers' 'rivals' do not as a rule enjoy the 'insider status' granted to much of the agriculture lobby. They rarely have a 'sponsoring' ministry in the way that agricultural interests do. Nor are they necessarily consulted by the Commission on agricultural matters as a matter of routine, nor automatically called in for discussions when something of importance or potential interest arises. The fact is, they do not have the political and economic power of farmers, they cannot offer trade-offs in the way of cooperation on policy implementation, they are – in some instances – relative latecomers, and a few – notably the more radical greens – are seen as not quite conforming to established values and the rules of the game. Some of the more respectable of these 'oppositional' agriculture groups have their foot in the EU door, but none has quite entered the room in the manner of the agricultural lobby.

Agriculture has powerful friends. While farmers and those directly engaged in the agricultural industries have been the most obvious beneficiaries of the CAP, others have gained too, notably the owners of land. Huge profits have been made by investment institutions, financiers, banks, industrial corporations and private landlords from the rising value of land that has been associated with the CAP. Many of these interests have direct access to decision-makers, indeed are themselves amongst the decision-makers in some governments, and have sought to use their influence accordingly.

Unity has been a source of strength. Despite the great range of interests represented, the agriculture lobby was, until the early 1980s, more or less united in its aims: it pressed for comprehensive market regimes for as much produce as possible, and it sought the largest price increases it could get.

Since that time, however, as significant steps to bring spending on agriculture under proper control have been taken and as EC/EU enlargements have made the interests of the agricultural sector more divergent, the unity of the lobby has been subject to increasing strains and its effectiveness has accordingly been weakened. Sectors have vied with one another as careful attention has had to be paid not only to the size of the cake, but also to the way in which it is cut.

Farmers sometimes resort to direct action. In some EU countries, most notably France, farmers sometimes take matters into their own hands if they are dissatisfied with policies and decisions affecting their sector. Whilst decision-makers never care to admit that they have been swayed by direct action, there is no doubt that farmers' militancy has affected at least some of those who are responsible for running EU agriculture. Certainly, for example, the tough stance adopted by the French Government in the Council of Ministers in respect of the reform of the CAP in 1991–2 and in respect of the agricultural aspects of the GATT Uruguay Round in 1992–3, was at least partially influenced by the knowledge that angry farmers had already demonstrated their fear of a possible 'sell-out' by holding large demonstrations and causing widespread disruption of the French transport network.

How the Common Agricultural Policy works

Title II of the TEC (Articles 32–8, ex 38–46) – which, post the Amsterdam Treaty, is still as written in 1957 in the EEC Treaty, save for the removal of redundant transition measures – sets out the general rationale and framework of the Common Agricultural Policy. The objectives are laid down in Article 33 (ex 39):

(a) to increase agricultural productivity by promoting technical progress and by ensuring the rational development of agricultural production and the optimum utilisation of the factors of production, in particular labour;
(b) thus to ensure a fair standard of living for the agricultural community, in particular by increasing the individual earnings of persons engaged in agriculture;
(c) to stabilise markets;
(d) to assure the availability of supplies;
(e) to ensure that supplies reach consumers at reasonable prices.

Many matters are barely touched on in Title II because, in 1957, they were deliberately left aside for later consideration by representatives of the states. Amongst the first fruits of these deliberations was the adoption by the Council of Ministers in December 1960 of the three major operating principles of the CAP. These still apply today.

A single internal market with common prices

Agricultural goods are supposed to be able to flow freely across internal EU borders, unhindered by barriers to trade and unhampered by devices such as subsidies or administrative regulations that might distort or limit competition. However, it is not a free trade system based on pure market principles because common prices are set by the Council for most important agricultural products. These prices include: a target price, which is the price it is hoped farmers will be able to obtain on the open market; a threshold price, which is the price to which imports are raised when world prices are lower than EU prices; and a guaranteed or intervention price, which is the price at which the Commission will take produce off the market by stepping in and buying it up (see Figure 15.1). The amount of support a product is given is a consequence of how high these prices are set, the size of the gap between the prices, and the ways in which intervention mechanisms and practices function.

The price support system dominates the CAP. It does so mainly because it is so costly to finance. There are three principal reasons why it is so expensive. First, many products are produced in amounts that are surplus to EU requirements. High guaranteed prices are the main reason for these surpluses, but improved farming techniques and the concentrated use of fertilisers and additives have also played a part. Second, the range of products protected by a market regime has been extended over the years so that now 90 per cent of all EU produce is covered in some way. Different regimes provide different forms of protection – so that in practice there are several agricultural policies rather than just one – but most products (around 70 per cent) are the beneficiaries of support prices. For some products the support prices are available on an unconditional and open-ended basis, but more commonly, following a series of Council decisions since the mid 1980s designed to tackle the problem of surpluses and reduce CAP expenditure, they are subject to restrictions. The precise nature of the restrictions varies from product to product, but they usually take one, or some combination, of three main forms: quotas, co-responsibility levies, and stabilisers – the latter consisting of a mechanism in which production thresholds (maximum guaranteed quantities) are set, and if these are exceeded the guaranteed payments are automatically reduced. Third, apart from a brief interlude in 1974–5, EU agricultural prices have consistently

Figure 15.1   *Outline of the different price levels and the levy and refund system for a full market regime product*

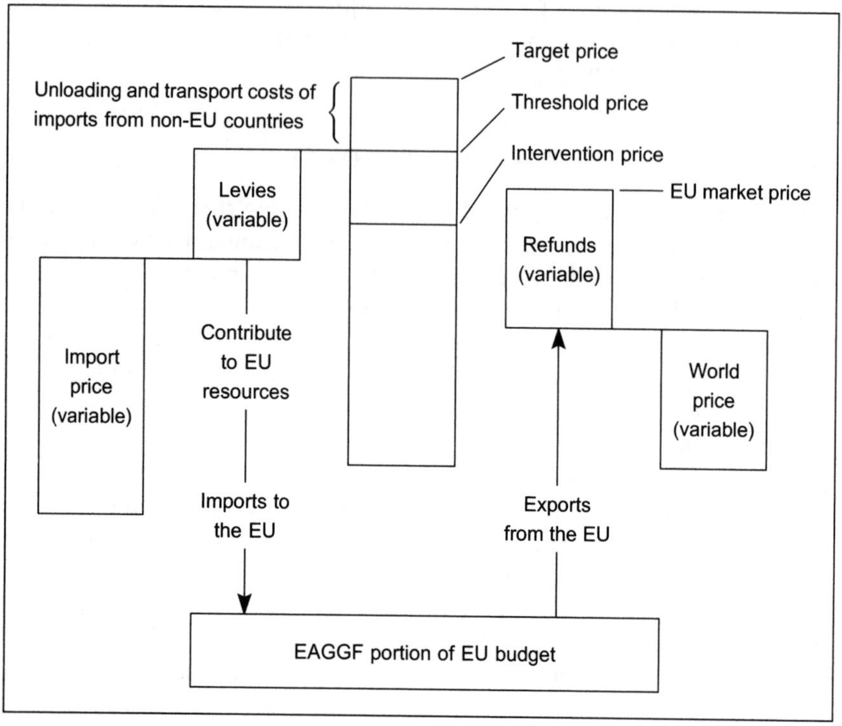

been above world prices, which has meant that it has not been possible to export surpluses without suffering a financial loss. Several devices are used to deal with the surpluses: exporting them and providing a refund (a 'restitution' in EU jargon) to exporters to ensure that no loss is incurred on transactions; storing them until EU prices rise; donating them as food aid; or converting them to animal foodstuffs. All these devices have to be financed from the EU budget, and together they constitute the bulk of CAP expenditure (see Table 15.1).

To try and deal with the problem of surpluses, and therefore also with the problem of heavy demands on the budget, a series of measures have been adopted since the mid 1980s. These have taken three main forms. First, devices have been set in place to stop the system of open-ended price guarantees. These devices include the above-mentioned quotas, co-responsibility levies, and stabilisers. Second, there has been a direct bearing down on prices, through tight annual price reviews. Third, farmers have been encouraged to take agricultural land out of production, through set-aside

Table 15.1 *Common Agricultural Policy: expenditure 1998*
(thousand million ecu)

Guarantee section	
Arable crops	17.102
Sugar	1.650
Olive oil	2.256
Fruit, vegetables and other plants	3.155
Wine	0.806
Tobacco	0.995
Others	0.352
Dairy products	2.976
Beef	5.786
Sheep and goatmeat	1.413
Pigmeat	0.329
Eggs and poultry	0.086
Fisheries	0.039
Others	0.654
Food aid	0.429
Anti-fraud measures	0.045
Product promotion	0.095
Other measures	0.505
Income aid	0.003
Environmental measures	2.280
Total (before clearance of accounts)	40.947
Guidance section	4.183

Source: European Voice, 14–22 July 1998 and Commission (1998).

schemes, schemes for the alternative use of farmland, and incentives for early retirement.

These various measures have had considerable success in that surpluses have been greatly reduced. However, by the mid to late 1990s pressures for further fundamental reform were again building. The pressures came from three directions. First, with the CAP still accounting for around half of the EU budget, several of the net contributor countries were either pressing for, or were inclining towards, further CAP reform. Second, as enlargement to Central and Eastern European countries (CEECs) loomed, it became clear that the CAP just could not continue in its existing form, or at least not without a very large increase in the EU budget – which would not be politically possible. The large increase would be necessary because all of the CEECs have large and underdeveloped agricultural sectors, which would be major beneficiaries of an unreformed CAP. Third, international pressures, especially from the United States, to open up the EU agricultural market were building. The EU was already required, as a result of the GATT Uruguay Round, to partially dismantle its protectionist system, and a further liberalising round was scheduled.

Proposals for responding to these pressures and for further reforming the CAP were set out by the Commission in its July 1997 *Agenda 2000* document (Commission, 1997a), which was followed up in March 1998 with more detailed proposals. The main features of the proposals were, on the one hand, further significant cuts in support prices – especially for beef, milk, and cereals – and on the other hand a strengthening of direct compensatory aid to farmers and of incentives for diversification. Following extensive negotiations between the member states, the Agriculture Ministers agreed in March 1999 on a package of reforms based on the Commission's proposals. A fortnight later, however, some of the key components of the package were diluted when the Heads of Government met in Berlin to decide upon the whole *Agenda 2000* reform programme. The softening was mainly at the insistence of President Chirac, who – looking to the interests of French farmers and the French exchequer – was not prepared to accept the Agriculture Ministers' agreement as it stood. After further negotiations at the Berlin summit, a final agriculture reform package was eventually agreed. The main differences between the Berlin agreement and the Agriculture Ministers' agreement were a reduction in planned cuts for cereals (from 20 per cent to 15 per cent) and a delay in planned cuts in dairy produce prices (from 2003–4 to 2005–6). Overall, the Berlin agreement involved a slight increase in total CAP expenditure over the period of the EU's 2000–6 financial perspective (see Table 14.1). It will allow EU agriculture prices to move closer to world prices, which will benefit consumers and should help the EU to fall more in line with WTO rules by reducing export subsidies.

In addition to the issue of its cost, another aspect of the agricultural price system requiring explanation is agrimonetary arrangements. Prior to the establishment of the euro in January 1999, agricultural prices were set in European currency units (ecu) and then converted into national currencies on the basis of special agricultural conversion rates – 'green' rates. The reason for the existence of green rates was to ensure that the functioning of the agricultural market was not distorted by, and farmers' incomes were not reduced by, currency fluctuations – green rates being fixed after they were (periodically) set by Agriculture Ministers.

Since January 1999, CAP prices and other CAP amounts have been fixed in euros, at a rate of one euro to one ecu. Conversions into national currencies are, of course, no longer required for euro members, but they are for non members. As part of the movement over to the euro system, it was decided not only to abolish green rates for euro member states but also for non euro states. At the same time, however, a compensation system applying to non euro states was established with the purpose of providing (on specified terms and within limits) protection to farmers suffering income loss from currency movements in market rates.

Community preference

A necessary consequence of the guaranteed price system is that the EU market should be protected from the international market. Since world prices are normally lower than EU prices, free access onto the EU market would clearly destroy the whole CAP system. Community preference (the term 'EU preference' is not used) is, therefore, required. Whether, however, it is required at quite such preferential levels as in practice apply is a matter of dispute.

The mechanics of the preference system vary according to the market regime for the product concerned. For the 20 per cent of produce that has a market regime but not one based on guaranteed prices (wines other than table wines, some fruit and vegetables, some cereals, eggs and poultry), external protection takes the form of levies, customs duties, and a combination of the two. For the 70 per cent of produce that does enjoy guaranteed prices (most cereals, dairy produce, beef, lamb) the system is such as to prevent imports entering the EU at prices below the agreed target prices. This exclusion is, as is shown in Figure 15.1, achieved by the threshold price which is calculated at a level to bring the world price up to the EU target price, minus an allowance for unloading and transport costs. The gap between world prices and the threshold price is bridged by the imposition of a levy, which is adjusted according to variations in EU and world prices. The levies become part of the EU's own resources.

The exclusion procedures just described do not apply to all the imports into the EU from all states. As will be explained in Chapter 16, the EU has negotiated arrangements whereby a large number of countries are given special access to EU markets for at least some of their products, including agricultural products. So, the EU grants 'generalised preferences' to more than 120 developing countries and one effect of this has been the abolition or reduction of levies on about 300 agricultural products intended for processing. Under the Lomé Convention, virtually all of the exports of the 71 ACP countries are allowed free access to the EU market. (It should perhaps be pointed out that these 'concessions' do not stem simply from generosity and goodwill. Much of the produce falling under the generalised preferences and Lomé agreements is tropical in nature and not in competition with EU produce.)

Joint financing

The CAP is financed jointly by the member states through the European Agricultural Guidance and Guarantee Fund (EAGGF) of the EU budget. This is divided into two sections: the Guarantee section which finances markets and prices, and the Guidance section which finances structural policy. The early intention was for the Guarantee section to be larger than the Guidance section by a ratio of two or three to one, but in practice this has never been even remotely approached and the Guidance section hovers at just under 10 per cent of total EAGGF expenditure. The demands on the Guarantee section occasioned by high EU prices is the main reason for this imbalance. A second reason is that, unlike expenditure on price support, expenditure on structural measures is not wholly financed by the EAGGF but is co-financed – usually by the EU in partnership with either member states or regions. A third reason is that member states have not always been enthusiastic supporters of EU agricultural structural policy – mainly because it usually involves contraction of the sector and/or changes to which agricultural interests are opposed.

But notwithstanding the limited size of the EAGGF Guidance section, there is still a very considerable amount of non-price-related agricultural expenditure in the EU. Some of this comes from other EU sources – in particular the Regional Fund and the European Investment Bank (EIB). By far the most of it, however, comes from national exchequers: member states are allowed to assist their farmers in almost any way they like as long as they do not – in the judgement of the Commission – distort competition or infringe the principles of the market. In some states national subsidies to agriculture far outstrip those provided by the EU.

It is possible that in the future there may be some increase in the funding of agriculture from national budgets. Certainly, as the Commission has pointed out, this would be one way of dealing with the problem of the distorting effect the CAP has on the EU budget and the closely related problem of some countries being large net budgetary contributors and others being large net beneficiaries. However, to start 'renationalising' so central an EU policy would cause major political difficulties.

The impact and effects of the Common Agricultural Policy

Whether the CAP is to be regarded as a success or not obviously depends on the priorities and interests of those making the judgement. Since, however, the issue has caused so much controversy it is worth examining some of the major developments under the CAP system. This will be done initially via the five aims set out in Article 33 of the TEC, which were listed above.

- *Agricultural efficiency has increased enormously as a result of modernisation and rationalisation.* That said, it might be asked whether the overproduction of certain products at great cost, and the encouragement that high prices have given to many who would otherwise have left the land to stay on their farms, is wholly consistent with 'ensuring the rational development of agricultural production'.
- Under the CAP, *agricultural incomes have grown roughly in parallel with incomes in other sectors.* However, this overall average masks enormous variations, both between large farmers (who have done very well for the most part) and small farmers, and between producers of northern temperate products (notably dairy produce, cereals, and beef, which are the main product beneficiaries of the price support system) and producers of other (mainly Mediterranean) products.
- *Markets have been stabilised*, in the sense that there have been no major food shortages and EU prices have escaped the price fluctuations that have occurred in the world market on some products.
- The EU *is now self-sufficient in virtually all of those foodstuffs its climate allows it to raise and grow.* In 1958 the six member states produced about 85 per cent of their food requirements; in 1998 the fifteen produced about 120 per cent. This movement beyond self-sufficiency to the production of surpluses has been expensive in that it has only been possible to dispose of the surpluses at considerable cost.
- The exclusion of cheaper (often much cheaper) produce from outside the EU means that the *aim of 'reasonable prices' to the consumer has had a low priority*. The undeniable fact is that, within the EU, the principal beneficiaries of the CAP's pricing system have been rich farmers (20 per cent of farmers receive 80 per cent of CAP subsidies), whilst the main losers have been poor consumers.

Beyond an assessment of the CAP through its five Treaty aims, three other significant consequences of the policy are also worth noting. First, the CAP's dominance of the budget has unquestionably made it more difficult for other policies to be developed. The financial perspectives that have been in operation since 1988 (see Chapter 14), coupled with the series of reforms to the CAP since the mid 1980s, have brought agriculture under greater financial control, but it still accounts for almost half of the total budget. Second, the CAP has been the source of many disagreements and tensions both within the EU and between the EU and non-EU states. For example, within the EU, France's generally protectionist attitude towards the CAP – which is explained by France accounting for almost a quarter of the EU's food production – has frequently caused it to be at loggerheads with other member states over aspects of agricultural policy. As for its effect on relations between the EU and non-EU states, the CAP has fuelled many trading disputes, and was the principal reason for the prolongation of the Uruguay Round negotiations. Third, protecting the EU market from cheaper world produce, and the release onto the world market of heavily subsidised EU produce, has distorted the international division of labour and the rational utilisation of resources.

Policy processes

In many respects, policy and decision-making processes for agriculture are much the same as in other policy sectors. However, the importance, range, and complexity of the CAP, plus the ever-changing nature of the world's agricultural markets, means that there are significant variations from the 'standard' EU model. The principal variations are as follows.

Commission initiation and formulation

Whereas the policy initiation and formulation responsibilities of the Commission in most sectors are much concerned with creating a policy framework, in agriculture they are inevitably directed more towards improving the efficiency of one that already exists.

But, as has been shown, there are formidable obstacles in the way of the Commission forwarding proposals that both go to the heart of the agricultural problem and are acceptable to the Council. As long ago as 1968, the then Commissioner for Agriculture, Sicco Mansholt, launched a major plan to reduce the size of the agricultural sector and improve the efficiency of what remained, but his proposals had little effect and were not followed up with sufficient Council legislation. As a result, in the 1970s the Commission approached its policy initiation and formulation responsibilities in a very cautious way. It became reluctant to advance wide-ranging schemes aimed at fundamental reform and concentrated more on short-term measures of an essentially reactive nature: reacting, that is, to specific problems in particular market sectors.

In the 1980s circumstances changed in such a way as to enable, even oblige, the Commission to bring a longer-term view back onto the agenda and force real and properly integrated reform to be seriously discussed. The most important of these circumstances were deteriorating market conditions and increasing surpluses, recurring budgetary problems, international pressures against the EC's high levels of protectionism and subsidisation, and the enlargement of the Community to states that would not do especially well out of the CAP as constituted. It was against this background that in 1985 the Commission launched a consultative Green Paper – *Perspectives for the Common Agricultural Policy* – which outlined policy options for the future of agriculture until the end of the century. After wide-ranging discussions with interested parties the Green Paper was followed up with more detailed guidelines in the form of a communication to the Council and the EP entitled *A Future for European Agriculture*. At the heart of the Commission's proposals lay an ambitious long-term strategy for a move towards a more market-based and restrictive pricing policy, greater flexibility in guarantees and intervention mechanisms, and a much greater degree of producer co-responsibility for surpluses. These objectives were restated in the Commission's influential 1987 document *The Single Act: A New Frontier for Europe,* and constituted the basis for important agricultural reforms that the Agriculture Ministers agreed to in December 1986 and the Heads of Government agreed to at their special summit at Brussels in February 1988.

Some of the pressures that obliged the Commission to propose measures for reform in the 1980s – notably surpluses and the hostile views of trading partners – were behind the even more radical reforms that the Commission proposed in 1991. As in 1985 the reforms were launched in two stages, starting with a consultation document – entitled *Communication. . . . The Development and Future of the CAP. Reflections Paper of the Commission* – followed six months later by specific proposals under the title *Communications . . . The Development and Future of the Common Agricultural Policy. Follow-up to the Reflections Paper. Proposals of the Commission.* Although subsequently watered down, these proposals provided the general framework for the still significant reforms of the CAP to which Agriculture Ministers agreed in May 1992 (see the third edition of this book for details of these reforms).

As was explained above, the latest round of agricultural reforms, which were agreed at the March 1999 Berlin summit, were again based on Commission proposals, with the key document this time being *Agenda 2000*. Significantly, the main thrust of the *Agenda 2000* proposals – moving towards a more market-based system – were very much in the tradition of all the proposals the Commission has made for fundamental agricultural reform since Mansholt issued his plan over thirty years ago.

Council decision-making

Of all the Councils, the Agriculture Council is perhaps the most reliant on issue linkages and package deals for the conduct of its business (see Exhibit 7.1 for an indication of the range of business covered by Agriculture Ministers).

One reason for the extent of this reliance is that whereas in some sectors issues can be allowed to drift, in agriculture certain decisions, most obviously those taken as part of the annual price review, cannot be continually postponed. They must be resolved, but a resolution is normally possible only if it is based on a recognition of the different interests and priorities of the states: most states, for example, are net exporters of agricultural produce, but a minority are net importers; some have temperate climates, some Mediterranean; some have mainly large and efficient farms, others still have many small and inefficient family-based units; and some have vast tracts of 'less favoured' land, whilst others have very little.

A major reason why the Council is able to make use of linkages and packages is that it has available to it a variety of possible policy instruments. By bringing these together in carefully weighted combinations the way can often be opened to agreements in which there is something for everyone.

An example of extensive political wheeling and dealing in the Council of Ministers being necessary before an agreement on agricultural matters could be reached occurred in the autumn of 1990. This was in connection with the negotiating mandate to be given to the Commission in the Uruguay Round of the GATT negotiations. Agriculture had proved to be the major problem in the Uruguay Round because of an insistence by most of the Community's major trading partners, notably the United States and the Cairns group of fourteen farm exporting countries, that the Community's system of subsidising agriculture should be virtually dismantled: the United States wanted the internal farm subsidies to be cut by 75 per cent and the export subsidies by 90 per cent over a ten-year period. The Council of Ministers was unable to accept this, but France and Germany, with some support from Ireland, were instrumental in temporarily blocking the Council from even agreeing to a compromise negotiating formula put forward by the Commission whereby Community farm subsidies as a whole would be cut by 30 per cent over a ten-year period backdated to 1986, which – since the post-1986 reforms had already had some effect in cutting subsidies – meant a real cut of only about 15 per cent between 1990 and 1995. As a result, the Community was unable to meet the mid October 1990 deadline, by which time it had been agreed that all the participating parties in GATT should formally table their negotiating positions. It was not until early November – after extensive negotiations on the matter in seven different Council of Ministers meetings involving the Agriculture, Foreign and Trade Ministers – that a marathon joint session of Agriculture and Trade Ministers was eventually able to agree a negotiating brief for the Commission. Almost inevitably the agreement bore all the hallmarks of both fudge and compromise, combining a commitment to cut subsidies by 30 per cent with other commitments to cushion farmers from loss of income, to protect them against any sudden increase in cheap food imports, and to introduce import levies on some products hitherto allowed free access to the Community.

In the event, the Community's stance on agriculture within GATT was still seen as too protectionist by the agricultural exporting nations, with the consequence that the negotiations became extremely protracted. A breakthrough was eventually achieved with the so-called Blair House agreement in November 1992, when the Commission, in its capacity as EC external trade representative, agreed in bilateral negotiations with the United States to reduce EC agricultural exports by 36 per cent and subsidies by 21 per cent. Further delays, however, then followed when the French government claimed that the Commission had exceeded its powers and offered the United States terms that would require greater cuts in subsidies than were implied by the May 1992 reforms. As a result, disputes rumbled on in the Council of Ministers during 1993 over the agricultural aspects of the Uruguay Round, the Commission was obliged to expend much time and energy attempting to demonstrate that the Blair House agreement was in conformity with the May 1992 agreement and, as the December 1993 deadline for the completion of the Uruguay Round loomed, the Foreign Ministers – who as well as nominally being the most senior Council also look after external trade – became increasingly involved in agriculture matters. It was they (the Foreign Ministers) who, on the very day before the negotiating deadline was due to expire, gave final approval to all parts – including the agricultural parts – of the Uruguay Round settlement.

The involvement of Foreign Ministers in the agricultural sphere of the GATT talks illustrates how agriculture cannot always be insulated from other policy areas in the way that it used to be. As Grant (1997, p. 148) has noted, '(i)n recent years, the circle of actors involved in agricultural policy formation in the EU has widened'. This widening has occurred partly because agriculture has become an important issue in international trade negotiations and partly because it has become more enmeshed with other policy areas, such as the environment, transport and consumer protection. The most obvious impact of this widening at Council level is that non-Agricultural Councils sometimes express views and make decisions that have direct implications for agriculture. Given the segmented nature of

Council structures, this can create problems in terms of developing rounded and properly integrated policy.

Retaining complete control over policy can also be difficult for the Agriculture Council (as indeed it can for most sectoral Councils) when policy issues assume a high political profile. Two examples may be taken to illustrate this. The first is the crisis that arose in the beef industry in 1996 as a result of BSE in British cattle and its suspected link to CJD in humans (on the crisis, see Westlake, 1997). Foreign Ministers in the General Affairs Council and Heads of Government in the European Council quickly became directly involved in the policy process when there was perceived to be an urgent need for action and a requirement that agricultural policy should be linked more closely to consumer protection policy. The second example is the agricultural reforms that were part of the Commission's *Agenda 2000* proposals. With the reforms being vital to agreement on the overall *Agenda 2000* package, Agriculture Ministers were left in no doubt by the General Affairs and Ecofin Councils (both of which discussed the agricultural component of *Agenda 2000* on several occasions) that their room for manoeuvre was limited. As the scheduled date for final agreement on *Agenda 2000* drew close in the first half of 1999, the German Presidency made it quite clear to the Agriculture Ministers – not least in statements by Chancellor Schröder himself – that they must recognise the need to be flexible and make concessions so as to open the way to a deal on the package as a whole (*European Voice*, 14–20 January 1999). As was noted above, the Agriculture Ministers eventually reached agreement on a range of reforms in March 1999, but parts of their agreement were changed later that month by Heads of Government at the Berlin European Council meeting.

Management and implementation of the Common Agricultural Policy

Because of the nature of the CAP, the EU is much more involved in the management and implementation of agricultural policy than it is in other policy spheres. The Commission, and particularly DGVI, are central in this regard. They oversee the general operation of the whole system, adjust it as necessary and, as far as possible, try to ensure that the national agencies that undertake the front-line implementation of policy – national Ministries of Agriculture, intervention agencies, customs and excise authorities and so on – fulfil their obligations in a proper manner.

In exercising these duties the Commission must operate within EU law and Council guidelines. This means that much of what it does in managing the CAP is of an essentially technical nature: making adjustments to match ever-changing market conditions. But in some spheres it can do this in ways that amount to rather more than the simple application of tightly drawn rules. Many of its decisions – for example on the operation of the intervention and support systems, on refunds, and on storage – are taken within margins of manoeuvre that give it at least some flexibility. This flexibility can result in the Commission's choices having important financial implications for producers, traders, processors, and the EU budget.

When payments and charges have to be adjusted almost daily, and in other instances when quick management decisions have to be taken, the Commission is authorised to act without reference to any other body. However, as explained in Chapter 6, the Commission's agricultural management responsibilities are not undertaken by Commission officials alone but via management committees made up of civil servants from the member states. There are around twenty such committees, including one for each category of products, and implementing measures that the Commission intends to enact are submitted to the appropriate committees for their opinion. There are usually between 300 and 400 meetings of CAP management committees each year. The Commission determines the direction and sets the pace in the committees, but the existence of the committees does mean that the member states have a direct input into, and ultimately a degree of control over, all but the fine details of agricultural policy and the management of that policy.

The annual price review

A distinguishing feature of decision-making in agriculture is that many of the key decisions are made as part of a regular annual process: the price review. Contrary to what the name suggests, prices are not the only element of the review. Many non-price elements are swept up and become components of what is usually a highly complex and interconnected package by the time the final agreement is made. The core of the package usually consists of a range of different price increases, adjustments to product regimes, and statements of intent about future action.

The date of the beginning of the marketing year varies between products, but as some begin on 1 April the intention of the Commission is to have a settlement before this date. To achieve this a timetable exists that is supposed to culminate with the Agriculture Council – which makes the final decisions – agreeing on the contents of the review in March. In practice the later parts of the timetable are never met and agreements are invariably delayed until May or June. This obliges the Council to extend the previous year's allocations in order to permit payments to be made.

There is an important sense in which price reviews are a constant part of the work of DGVI, since market situations are subject to constant monitoring, whilst medium to long term schemes for agricultural reform have to be implemented, to some extent at least, via reviews. The systematic work on particular reviews, however, is concentrated into the six to seven month period before they are due to come into effect. The main stages are as follows:

(1) In September the directorates and divisions of DGVI, working with the management committees, begin to analyse and draw up reports on such matters as quantities, the state of stocks, prices, and exports in their market sectors. This is essentially a technical exercise.

(2) During October and November consultations take place between the Commission and interested parties. Some of these are in the structured settings of management and advisory committees and working groups of national experts, while others are more informal exchanges between DGVI officials and representatives of governments and sectional interests. Amongst the sectional interests that feed their views to the Commission are farmers' organisations (notably COPA), consumers' organisations (notably BEUC), trade organisations (such as COCERAL, which represents the grain trade), and food industry organisations (such as ASSILEC, which represents the dairy industry).

(3) The first drafts from the various sectors should be ready by mid November. The process of integrating them necessitates several rounds of meetings involving the Commissioner for Agriculture, members of his *cabinet*, the director general, assistant directors general, directors, and senior officials representing the three main product areas of the review: livestock, crops, and wine. In attempting to bring everything together the Commissioner and his or her advisers have to bear in mind a number of considerations, of which the most important are the following:

• The limitations imposed by the agricultural reference framework. Since 1988 the EU annual budget has been framed within multi-annual financial perspectives, which have contained reference frameworks for agricultural expenditure. The 1993–9 reference framework planned total spending on agriculture to be capped at 35.2 billion ecu in 1993 rising to 38.4 billion ecu in 1999, at 1992 prices (in the event spending was below the capped totals). The 2000–6 financial perspective specifies corresponding figures of 40.9 billion euro in 2000 and 41.7 billion euro in 2006, at 1999 prices. (See Chapter 14 for more on the significance and nature of the EU financial perspectives and Table 14.1 for details of the 2000–6 financial perspective.)

- Commission and Council preferences drawn from both rolling programmes and continuing commitments. Several such programmes and commitments were, for example, contained in the reform measures agreed by the Council in May 1992.
- Political factors and the implications proposals may have for those who are affected by them. The Commission has no interest in making enemies in the Council, or indeed amongst sectional interests, so it may wish to soften the effect of proposals that are likely to arouse opposition.

(4) On being agreed in DGVI and by the Commissioner for Agriculture, a draft is submitted to the College of Commissioners for its approval. Ideally this submission is made by mid December, although usually the timetable slips and the actual submission date is later.

The Commissioners' deliberations are preceded by meetings of the relevant members of their *cabinets*, including *chefs de cabinet*, assisted by senior officials from DGVI. An important function of these inter-*cabinet* meetings is to ensure that the interests of the Commissioners dealing with the likes of external trade, the environment, and development cooperation are considered. If all goes well a general agreement on most key points can be reached at this stage. The Commissioners themselves, however, have to approve the final proposals. Whether this is largely a formality or involves difficult negotiations depends on what has happened at the pre-meetings.

(5) As soon as they are agreed – which should be by mid January – the Commission's proposals are sent to the Council, and also to the ESC and the EP for their opinions.

The influence of the ESC is very marginal. This reflects its limited role in the EU as a whole, though such potential for exerting influence on the review as it does have is not helped by its customary inability to take a united view on agricultural questions. Its opinion – which is usually issued at its March or April plenary session – frequently incorporates a mixture of agreements, disagreements, and agreements subject to conditions, and is sometimes adopted on the basis of a vote in which little more than a half of the ESC's members support the opinion.

The EP, by virtue of its greater power and authority, is listened to rather more seriously – or at least the Commission and the Council strive harder to give the impression they are listening. Most MEPs, however, fully realise that they are hardly central actors in the price review exercise. Indeed, largely because of this the EP has long since abandoned its former practice of holding a special session on the review and now incorporates its debate and the delivery of its opinion into the earliest practicable plenary session, which should be March if the timetable is on schedule, but because of slippages almost invariably means later (it was June in 1998). The proceedings are conducted on the basis of reports drawn up by the Committee on Agriculture in consultation with other interested committees – most notably the Committee on Budgets, the Committee on External Economic Relations, and the Committee on the Environment. In the plenary as many as 300–400 amendments to the Commission's proposals may be voted upon, with MEPs usually following the recommendations made to them by the Agriculture Committee's *rapporteur*.

In the Council, ministers are likely to have an early meeting, probably in February, to give their first reactions to the Commission proposals. All arrive well armed with briefs and analyses as to how the proposals would, if agreed, affect their farmers, their consumers, their budgetary contributions, their balance of payments and so on. Most usually say that the proposals are too restrictive in some respects, and all fifteen usually put down markers for future meetings by identifying particular points that are unacceptable as they stand. Subsequent ministerial meetings are arranged as necessary, by which time new points may have arisen and others may have been resolved as a result of meetings at lower Council levels: most of the agricultural working parties – of which there are around 25, including one for each of the principal commodity regimes – meet at least twice to consider the Commission's proposals as they affect their areas; the Agrifin working group deals with many of the financial aspects of the proposals; and the SCA (see Chapter 7) tries to pull the working parties' reports together and give them overall coherence.

(6) In the light of views expressed – and quite apart from formal pronouncements by the ESC, the EP and the Council, intense lobbying campaigns are conducted by national and sectional interests – the Commission makes adjustments to its proposals. These are designed to improve the prospects of a settlement in the Council, whilst clinging to as much of the original proposals as possible.

(7) It is normally May or June when the Agriculture Council meets to try to agree a settlement. Marathon sessions are common, and meetings may have to be reconvened if solutions cannot be found at the first time of asking.

Each minister naturally tries to get the best terms he or she can and also wishes to be seen to be putting up a vigorous defence of national interests. This can make for extremely difficult negotiations, with much posturing and striking of attitudes taking place alongside genuine differences on such matters as price preferences, EU budgetary implications, the elimination of surpluses, and commitments to farmers and consumers. Complicated package deals, with many non-price factors being dragged in to increase flexibility, are usually the only means by which a solution can be found. Voting is common, and ministers may well make their vote of approval on one issue dependent on guarantees of support on another. Frequently those who are dissatisfied with the proposed settlement on a matter – say rice prices, or the premium for producers of potato starch – seek 'compensation' elsewhere, perhaps in the form of permission to offer national subsidies of some kind. Wheeling and dealing and the trading of points can thus usually give all participants something to present in the way of national benefits when they leave the negotiating table.

After the negotiations, votes are held on the Council regulations that give the political deal legal effect. This often involves member states not giving their approval to the deal, or at least to parts of it. So, in respect of the 1998–9 review: the Netherlands voted against the whole package; France and Denmark voted against the rate of set-aside for 1999–2000 (the rate has to be agreed one year in advance); Denmark voted against the reform of the banana sector; and Greece voted against the reform of the tobacco sector (Council Press Release, 10395/98).

Looking at the overall nature of the annual agricultural price review, it is worth emphasising that it has been considerably affected by the use of financial perspectives since 1988, by the incorporation into the perspectives of agricultural guidelines, and by the adoption of measures to reduce surpluses and restructure agriculture. One effect has been to enhance a development that began to get under way in the mid 1980s, namely for price settlements to be restrictive and tight. Another, and closely related, effect has been to ensure that there are close alignments between the original Commission proposals and the final settlement. A third effect has been to make the deliberations in the Council just a little less acrimonious – because there are now tighter limits on what it can do.

Concluding remarks

Despite all the obstacles and hurdles that litter its decision-making processes, the CAP has been the subject of considerable reform in recent years. Much more reform is yet to come as the EU gradually moves towards a system in which its prices are more closely matched to world prices and in which its support measures focus less on price levels and more on farmers' incomes.

The reforms that have been and are being made have not, however, solved all of the CAP's problems. Outside the EU, many countries continue to be dissatisfied with what they regard as a still over-protected EU market and still over-subsidised EU produce on world markets. Inside the EU, sharp differences still exist over many aspects of agricultural policy. Where

Chapter 16

External Relations

External trade
Foreign and defence policy
Development cooperation
The external dimension of internal policies
External relations: the consistency problem
Concluding remarks

The EU is an extremely important, and increasingly important, actor on the world stage. It is so partly because of its size and resources and partly because of its ability to act in a united, or at least coordinated, manner in a range of external policy contexts and settings.

There are four main aspects to the EU's external relations: trade, foreign and security policy, development cooperation, and the external dimension of internal policies. Each of these will be examined in this chapter.

External trade

The EU in the world trading system

The member states of the EU present a united front to the world in respect of international trade, and they act as one in contracting the terms of trade agreements. If they did not do so the unified internal market would not be possible.

The main foundations of the united front are the Common External Tariff (CET) – or Common Customs Tariff (CCT) as it is also known – and the Common Commercial Policy (CCP). Together, the CET and the CCP enable, indeed oblige, the member states to act in common on matters such as the fixing and adjusting of external customs tariffs, the negotiation of customs and trade agreements with non-member countries, and the taking of action to impede imports – this being most likely where unfair trading practices, such as dumping and subsidies, are suspected.

The EU conducts trade negotiations in many forums: with single states; with other regional groupings, such as the European Free Trade Association (EFTA) and the Association of South-East Asian Nations (ASEAN); and in international frameworks, such as the World Trade Organisation

(WTO) and the United Nations Conference on Trade and Development (UNCTAD). In these forums the EU is able to bring very considerable economic and trading strength to bear:

- The combined Gross Domestic Product (GDP) of the EU countries accounts for around 26 per cent of world GDP. This places it a little ahead of the United States, which accounts for around 24 per cent, and well ahead of Japan, which accounts for around 16 per cent.
- EU exports to the rest of the world account for just over 19 per cent of world exports, whilst imports account for just under 19 per cent of world imports. The comparable figures for the United States are 15 per cent and 19 per cent respectively, and for Japan 12 per cent and 8 per cent. The EU is thus the world's largest external trading bloc.
- In terms of population, the EU market, with over 370 million people, is much larger than both the US market, which numbers just over 250 million people, and the Japanese market, which numbers around 125 million.
- Many of the countries and groupings with which the EU negotiates on trade matters are heavily reliant on the EU market for their exports – either for reasons of geography (most obviously non-EU European countries, including those of Eastern and Central Europe) or for reasons of historical linkage (most notably former French and UK colonies).

The combination of these economic and trading strengths, and the fact that in trading forums it acts as a single bloc, means that the EU is an extremely powerful world trading force.

Trade agreements and trade policies

The EU – or strictly speaking the EC in the context of external trade – has trade agreements, or agreements in which a substantial part of the content is concerned with trade, with just about every country in the world. These agreements take three main forms.

Trade agreements

These are based on Article 133 (ex 113) of the TEC, which obliges the EU to operate a common commercial policy: 'The common commercial policy shall be based on uniform principles, particularly in regard to changes in tariff rates, the conclusion of tariff and trade agreements, the achievement of uniformity in measures of liberalisation, export policy and measures to protect trade such as those to be taken in the event of dumping or subsidies.' Article 133 agreements may be preferential or non-preferential in kind, but they are all subject to the general framework of international trading rules established within the framework of the WTO.

The Commission has long pressed the other EU institutions to adopt an expansive approach towards what may be included in Article 133 agreements, arguing that this is necessary to reflect the fact that EU economic activity and trade has changed considerably since the EEC Treaty was negotiated in the 1950s. In particular, the Commission has called for services and intellectual property to be located within the remit of Article 133. This call has not been met, with the ECJ ruling (in Opinion 1/94) that the responsibility for negotiating services and intellectual property agreements is shared between the EU and its member states, and the member states deciding (in the 1996–7 IGC) not to include services and intellectual property in Article 133. (However, provision was made in the Amsterdam Treaty for Article 133 to be extended to services and intellectual property if at some point in the future the Council, acting unanimously, so decides.) In consequence, trade agreements are essentially confined to trade in goods.

Trade and economic cooperation agreements

The Treaty base of these agreements depends on their precise nature, but there is usually some combination of Article 133 and at least one other article. So, Article 300 of the TEC (ex 228), which sets out procedures for the contracting of external agreements, is almost invariably used, whilst Article 181 (ex 130y) applies when there is a development cooperation dimension to agreements. The number of trade and cooperation agreements has increased enormously over the years and their scope has steadily expanded. At their core are generally trade preferences of various kinds and assistance of some sort from the EU to the other signatory(ies). In some cases, as with partnership agreements that have been/are being negotiated with countries of the former Soviet Union, free trade is an eventual objective. Since the 1980s, political conditions – usually concerning human rights and democratic processes – have routinely been part of cooperation agreements.

Association agreements

These are based on Article 310 (ex 238) of the TEC, which states that 'The Community may conclude with one or more states or international organisations agreements establishing an association involving reciprocal rights and obligations, common action and reciprocal procedure'. Typically, association agreements include highly preferential access to EU markets, the prospect of a free trade area eventually being formed between the signatories, economic and technical cooperation of various sorts, financial aid from the EU, political dialogue, and – in some cases – the prospect of the associated countries eventually becoming members of the EU. There are currently four broad categories of countries that have association agreements with the EU. First, there are the ten Central and Eastern European countries (CEECs) that have applied for EU membership. Developed out of earlier cooperation agreements, these association agreements – called Europe Agreements – are very much part of the CEECs pre-accession strategy. They are seen by both sides as a means of assisting economic liberalisation, market adjustment, and political democratisation in the CEECs. Second, there are three Mediterranean countries that may become members of the EU: Cyprus (accession negotiations are currently underway), Malta (which reactivated its membership application in 1998), and Turkey (which wishes to become an EU member, but the EU sees this as only a long-term possibility). Third, there are several other Mediterranean states – including the Mashreq and Maghreb countries – that constitute part of the EU's Mediterranean policy. Fourth, there are the non-EU members of the European Economic Area (EEA) – Iceland, Norway and Liechtenstein. The EEA is the deepest of the EU's trading agreements in that it involves not only free trade in goods but also extends the EU's other so-called freedoms (of services, capital, and people) to the three EEA states.

With each of these three main types of agreement containing variations in both scope and depth, the EU is thus involved in a wide and complicated range of agreements with trading partners. The agreements can be thought of as constituting a hierarchy of preferences in which the EU and the other signatory(ies) of agreements are, moving from the bottom to the top of the hierarchy, bound together in increasingly complex and, for the most part, increasingly open market access and other arrangements.

The EU presents itself as being committed to a liberal trade policy, and as having as its main priority in external trade negotiations the opening up of markets. The most important international trade negotiations of recent years – the 1986–93 multilateral General Agreement on Tariffs and Trade (GATT) Uruguay Round – are seen as providing evidence in support of this view of the nature of the EU's trading stance. Priorities for the EU during the negotiations included: the lowering of international customs duties (as a result of the Uruguay Round average EU duties are falling from around 5 per cent to 2.5 per cent); the removal of non-tariff barriers to trade; and the opening up of hitherto restricted spheres of trading activity, especially those, such as financial services, in which the EU, or at least some of its member states, are strong.

It is a liberal trading policy, however, which is not always pursued with complete consistency or uniformity. The governments of the member states frequently seek to cope with 'special' national economic circumstances and accompanying political pressures by pressing for protectionist measures. EU trade policy is thus concerned not only with promoting the general liberalisation of trade, but also with ensuring that the consequences of this are not damaging. This results in trade policy also being much taken up with matters such as the seeking of special exemptions from general trade agreements, the negotiation of 'orderly marketing' agreements with more competitive countries, and the imposition of anti-dumping duties.

The most obvious sectoral sphere of EU protectionism is agriculture, which has long been sheltered from the full rigours of external competition by high tariffs on imports. EU negotiators in the Uruguay Round ensured that shelter would continue to be provided when agreements concluded under the Round gradually entered into force, though there was to be a progressive reduction in the extent of protection provided to EU farmers. Other sectors that attract EU special protection include the motor vehicle industry, which is assisted by export restraint agreements with Japan; steel, which is given protection under the terms of the association agreements with CEECs; and textiles, where there have long been restrictions of various sorts on imports from the Far East.

Policy processes

Trade agreements made on the basis of Article 133 and in the context of the CCP are essentially the responsibility of the Commission and the Council. The normal procedure for contracting agreements is as follows.

- The Commission makes a recommendation to the Council (General Affairs) that the EU should seek to conclude a trade agreement with a third country or organisation. (There is no separate Trade Council, although Trade Ministers sometimes accompany Foreign Ministers to the General Affairs Council when important trade matters are on the agenda.)
- The Committee of Permanent Representatives (COREPER) discusses the recommendation and places it on the agenda of the Council. The Council takes a decision as to whether negotiations should proceed. In making its decision the Council may, on the basis of proposals drawn up by the Commission and subsequently discussed, and perhaps modified, by COREPER, give to the Commission negotiating directives,

guidelines or – to use the most commonly used, but not most accurate term – mandates. If necessary the Council may act, as it may act on any decisions taken in connection with Article 133 agreements, by qualified majority vote.

- Working within the framework of mandates it has been given by the Council, the Commission negotiates on behalf of all fifteen EU states. The relevant External Relations (RELEX) DG normally takes the lead role on behalf of the Commission (DGI, DGIA, or DGIB – see Table 6.1), but other DGs, such as DGIV (Competition) and DGVI (Agriculture), are also involved if they have a direct interest. How much room for manoeuvre the Commission has when conducting negotiations varies according to the circumstances. Usually, differences of both principle and special interest between the member states result in negotiating mandates being fairly tightly drawn, often reflecting a compromise between those countries which tend towards protectionism and those which favour free trade. While Commission officials acknowledge privately that Council mandates are usually less of a dead weight than is often supposed, there is no doubt that the Commission's flexibility in negotiations can be constrained by the necessity of not disturbing compromises that have been agreed only with difficulty in the Council. (Although it should also be said that it is not unknown for the Commission to use Council reins to the EU's advantage: during negotiations it can be helpful to say in response to an unwanted proposal, 'the Council would never agree to that'.)

- Throughout the period of the negotiations, the Commission is in touch with the Article 133 Committee. This is a Council committee that normally meets weekly to review, discuss, and make decisions on trade agreements that come within the scope of Article 133. The Committee meets at two levels: full members, who are normally senior officials from the national ministries responsible for trade, gather once a month to consider general policy issues; deputies, who may be from either national ministries or the Permanent Representations in Brussels, usually meet three times a month to deal with detailed policy matters.

- During particularly difficult or important negotiations the Commission may return to the Council for clarification of the negotiating mandate, or for an amended mandate that might break a deadlock. The Article 133 Committee can adjust negotiating mandates, but anything that is especially sensitive or political is normally referred to COREPER and, if necessary, the General Affairs Council. (In the closing stages of the Uruguay Round negotiations in November and December 1993, the chief Commission negotiator, Sir Leon Brittan, presented written and verbal reports and made requests to several General Affairs Council meetings.)

- At the (apparent) conclusion of the negotiations the Commission may initial the negotiated settlements, but Council approval is necessary for agreements to be formally authorised and signed.

The powers of and relations between and within the EU institutions in connection with the CCP are such that tensions of various sorts are by no means uncommon. Four areas cause particular difficulties.

First, the power balance between the Council and the Commission can be very delicate, with the Council trying to ensure that the Commission remains under its control, and the Commission wanting and needing enough manoeuvrability to enable it to be an effective negotiator.

Second, the different national interests and preferences of the member states can create difficulties in the Council. Apart from specific differences that arise on specific issues, there is a broad underlying difference, with some countries – including France, Italy, Spain and Greece – tending to favour a measure of protectionism and other countries – led by Germany and the UK – tending more towards trade liberalisation.

Third, problems can arise within the Commission with disputes between Commissioners and between DGs about where policy responsibility lies and who has a legitimate interest in particular external trade policies and agreements. Thus in June 1990 the Farm Commissioner – Raymond MacSharry – stressing that he was determined to defend the Community's position on farm reform in the GATT Uruguay Round talks, felt obliged to state publicly that he, not the Trade Commissioner – Frans Andriessen – was 'in charge of agricultural negotiations'. In November 1992, when the much troubled bilateral negotiations with the United States on the agricultural aspects of the Uruguay Round were at their most difficult, MacSharry temporarily resigned from his position in the Commission negotiating team because of alleged excessive interference by the Commission President, Jacques Delors.

Fourth, MEPs are dissatisfied that the EP has no automatic right to be consulted, let alone to insist that its views be considered, in connection with Article 133 agreements. In practice, the EP is notified about agreements, and the Commission, and to a lesser extent the Council, do discuss external trade matters with the EP – primarily in the forum of the Parliament's External Economic Relations Committee – but it is clear that Parliament's influence is usually limited. However, there are signs that it is increasing. One reason for this is that the EP has constantly voiced its dissatisfaction and has done what it can to maximise its influence, not least by incorporating into its Rules of Procedure a range of measures aimed at persuading the Council to take note of the EP as regards the opening, negotiating, and concluding of trade agreements.

* * *

Turning to procedures in respect of cooperation and association agreements, the rules are set out in Article 300. In essence, these require the powers of, and the relationships between, the Council and the Commission to be similar to those which apply in respect of Article 133 agreements, with two exceptions. First, unanimity, rather than a qualified majority, is required for Council decisions when the agreement covers a field for which unanimity is required for the adoption of internal rules and when association agreements are being contracted. (Unanimity tends to weaken the negotiating position of the Commission, since it cannot afford to sideline the wishes of any member state.) Second, the powers of the EP are much greater with regard to cooperation and association agreements than they are with regard to Article 133 trade agreements, for it must at least be consulted on cooperation agreements and its assent is required for some types of cooperation agreement and for all association agreements. The power of assent gives the EP a useful lever to try to influence the course of negotiations, for it can block the outcome of negotiations if it finds them to be unsatisfactory. Such a block has sometimes been threatened, and occasionally imposed, usually as a protest against lack of democracy or abuse of human rights in the state with which the agreement is being contracted.

Foreign and defence policy

Evolution

There are many obstacles in the way of a developed, let alone a common, EU foreign policy. They include the following.

- The EU is not a state and therefore does not have the (usually) long established 'givens' that help to focus national foreign policy. Most notably, there is no national territory to protect and no national political, economic, social and cultural interests to promote. The EU's territory does not 'belong' to it in the way national territory 'belongs' to member states, and the EU's political, economic, social and cultural interests are by no means clearly defined.
- Following on from the point just made, many member states, especially the larger ones with long histories of being influential on the world stage in their own right, are reluctant to lose control of a policy area that is so associated with national influence, sovereignty, and identity.
- Some member states have traditional and special relationships with particular parts of the world that they are anxious to maintain.
- There are sometimes differences between EU states on foreign policy questions arising from conflicting ideological orientations.

- Defence, which of course is inextricably linked to foreign policy, is extremely problematical. It is so for a number of reasons, not least: (1) its close association with national sovereignty; (2) the varying defence capabilities of the member states; (3) differences between the member states in terms of their degree of commitment to the various defence/ security organisations that exist in the modern world – with the nature and importance of the transatlantic defence relationship being a particularly thorny issue; and (4) the differing degrees of willingness of member states to use armed force when pressed.

Notwithstanding these difficulties and obstacles, however, important developments have occurred since foreign policy cooperation was first launched under the name European Political Cooperation (EPC) in 1970. Initially on a tentative basis, and quite outside the framework of the Community Treaties, in the 1970s and 1980s the member states increasingly cooperated with one another on foreign policy matters – to such an extent that by the mid 1980s there were few major international issues upon which the EC did not pronounce. The developing importance of foreign policy cooperation was recognised when EPC was accorded its own section – Title III – in the SEA. Amongst other things, Title III stated 'The High Contracting Parties [the member states], being members of the European Communities, shall endeavour jointly to formulate and implement a European foreign policy'. However, unlike certain other policy areas that were also recognised in the SEA, Title III was not incorporated into the Treaties. This was mainly because the member states were unwilling to allow the normal Community decision-making processes to apply to foreign policy. As a result, EPC continued to be much looser and voluntaristic in nature than most other policy areas with which the Community concerned itself. No laws were made within EPC, most decisions were arrived at by consensus, and no state could be prevented from engaging in independent action if it so chose.

But although the SEA signalled the increasing importance of EU foreign policy and facilitated its further development, until the early 1990s the EU's international standing continued to be very much that of an economic giant on the one hand and a political pygmy on the other. That is to say, it exercised considerable international influence in respect of economic and, more particularly, trade matters, but its voice did not count for a great deal in respect of political and, more particularly, defence and security matters. Since the early 1990s, however, this situation has been slowly changing as it has come to be increasingly accepted by the member states that the EU ought to be doing rather more than issuing general, and often anodyne, declarations, or, very occasionally, imposing mild economic sanctions. Five factors have been especially important in stimulating change.

First, the ending of the Cold War and the collapse of Communism in the Soviet bloc and the Soviet Union have transformed the nature of international power relationships. In particular: the international political context in which Europe finds itself has changed dramatically, with a shift of focus from the global East–West dimension to regional issues and conflicts; strategically, Western Europe is no longer squeezed between two superpowers, with little choice but to ally itself to one – the United States – in a more-or-less subservient manner; and the bases of power relationships have altered, with nuclear and military capacity becoming less important and economic strength and geographical position (especially in relation to the rapidly changing Central and Eastern Europe and the troubled Middle East) becoming more important. In this 'new' world, in which international relations are much more fluid and the nature and future development of the European continent is far from clear, the EU countries naturally wish to play a leading part in guiding and managing events. In so doing they are being given encouragement by the United States, which is anxious to lighten some of its international and, more especially, some of its European commitments.

Second, German reunification has increased the pressure on the foreign and security policy front, as it has too on the economic and monetary union front, to create an EU framework within which Germany is firmly located and to which it is firmly attached. The much quoted determination of EU leaders, not least German leaders themselves, to ensure there is a European Germany rather than a German Europe, has been seen by many as needing to apply particularly to foreign and security policy given the sensitivities associated with Germany's past and the actual and potential political turbulence to Germany's east and south. That Germany must be 'tied in' more tightly was confirmed for many by the way in which, in late 1991, Germany successfully pressed other EU states to grant diplomatic recognition to Croatia and Slovenia much earlier than most would have preferred.

Third, the 1990–1 Gulf War and the events leading up to it demonstrated that EPC would always be restricted in its effectiveness if defence and security policy continued to be kept apart from foreign policy. The Community's response to Iraq's invasion of Kuwait was to coordinate diplomatic action and jointly impose economic sanctions, but on the key issues of the appropriate military response and national contributions to that response, the member states reacted in a piecemeal and uncoordinated fashion.

Fourth, the EU's response to the post-1991 break-up of Yugoslavia and the subsequent hostilities in the Balkans has been seen as being, in several respects, inadequately prepared, developed and mobilised. EU states have contributed in various ways and through various forums to policy formulation and the setting up of peacekeeping and humanitarian operations, but there has been no clear, consistent or coordinated EU response to the situation. What little leadership has been provided to deal with the turbulence in the Balkans has been mostly provided by the United States.

Fifth, and in response to the factors just identified, the Maastricht and Amsterdam Treaties have provided for significant advances in foreign and security policy cooperation, albeit on a basis that maintains their essentially intergovernmental nature and non-EC status. The relevant contents of these treaties were set out in Chapter 5, so only a brief reminder of the most salient points will be given here. The Maastricht Treaty provided for a Common Foreign and Security Policy (CFSP) to constitute the EU's second pillar. The key elements of the pillar were: (1) the general objectives of the CFSP were identified; (2) systematic cooperation was to be established between the EU states on any matter of foreign and security policy that was of general interest; (3) where it was deemed to be necessary the Council of Ministers should, on the basis of unanimity, define common positions to which the member states should conform; (4) on the basis of general guidelines from the European Council, the Council of Ministers could decide that a matter should be the subject of a joint action; (5) the CFSP was to include security issues, 'including the eventual framing of a common defence policy, which might in time lead to a common defence'; and (6) the WEU was to be 'an integral part of the development of the Union'. The Amsterdam Treaty strengthened the Maastricht provisions in a number of ways: policy instruments were streamlined and extended; there was an extension of qualified majority voting provisions; a 'constructive abstention' device was introduced, allowing a state not to apply a decision that otherwise bound the EU; security policy was advanced a little, with the Petersberg humanitarian tasks incorporated in the Treaty and with the reference to 'the eventual framing of a common defence policy' being replaced by 'the progressive framing of a common defence policy'; and support mechanisms were strengthened with the creation of a CFSP High Representative and the establishment of a policy planning and early warning unit.

Policy content and policy action

Two main criticisms were traditionally made of EPC. First, it was essentially reactive. Apart from a very small number of initiatives – such as pressing, from 1980, for the Palestine Liberation Organisation (PLO) to be included in Middle East peace talks – the EC was seen as following events rather than making and shaping them. Second, it was too declaratory: policy positions were not followed up with the use of effective policy instruments; at best, as in its protest against the then apartheid regime in South Africa, weak and essentially symbolic economic sanctions were employed against states engaging in activities of which the EC disapproved.

The CFSP pillar of the EU is designed, in large part, to enable the EU to tackle these weaknesses. The principal means being used to do this are the more conscious pursuit of common policies, and the development of properly coordinated policy actions and policy instruments.

Regarding common policies, Article 11 of the TEU (ex J.1) states the following:

The Union and its Member States shall define and implement a common foreign and security policy covering all areas of foreign and security policy, the objectives of which shall be:

— to safeguard the common values, fundamental interests, independence and integrity of the Union in conformity with the principles of the United Nations Charter;
— to strengthen the security of the Union in all ways;
— to preserve peace and strengthen international security, in accordance with the principles of the United Nations Charter, as well as the principles of the Helsinki Final Act and the objectives of the Paris Charter, including those on external borders;
— to promote international cooperation;
— to develop and consolidate democracy and the rule of law, and respect for human rights and fundamental freedoms.

Article 12 of the TEU states that the CFSP's objectives are to be achieved by:

— defining the principles of and general guidelines for the common foreign and security policy;
— deciding on common strategies;
— adopting joint actions;
— adopting common positions;
— strengthening systematic cooperation between Member States in the conduct of policy.

Joint actions and common positions were created by the Maastricht Treaty and common strategies were created by the Amsterdam Treaty.

The TEU does, of course, identify policy objectives and instruments only in general terms and it is left to policy actors — notably the European

Council and the General Affairs Council – to develop more specific objectives and to specify the precise nature of policy instruments and the circumstances in which they should be used. The June 1992 Lisbon summit was particularly important in setting out ground rules. It was agreed, for example, that when assessing whether important common interests are at stake and defining the issues and areas for joint action, account should be taken of the following factors: the geographical proximity of a given region or country to the EU; the existence of an important EU interest in the political and economic stability of a region or country; and the existence of threats to the security interests of the EU (European Council, 1992, p. 32).

The two new policy instruments created by the Maastricht Treaty – joint actions and common positions – have been used fairly sparingly. For example, in 1997, there were 16 joint actions (including four concerning the former Yugoslavia, two concerning the Middle East Peace Process, and two concerning Africa) and 13 common positions (including two concerning the former Yugoslavia, seven concerning Africa, and two concerning sanctions against Burma) (Commission, 1998, p. 249–51). Exhibit 16.1 provides an example of a joint action and Exhibit 16.2 of a common position.

Beyond the policy instruments set out in Article 12, the EU also has available, and makes use of, other instruments. These include diplomacy, political pressure (there are few significant foreign policy issues upon which an EU statement or declaration is not issued, often in harness with associated states), trade sanctions, economic and financial assistance, and technical, scientific, cultural and other forms of cooperation. The last three types of instrument involve the CFSP pillar 'using' the economic strength of the EU via its EC pillar. They have been applied in a number of contexts, including to put pressure on Turkey because of its human rights record and to interrupt relations with the Association of South-East Asian Nations (ASEAN) in protest at Burma's inclusion in that grouping.

But what of that most sensitive of all foreign policy instruments: military force? The Western European Union (WEU) – which, as was shown in Chapter 3, is a long-established defence organisation to which most EU member states belong – was identified at Maastricht as constituting an 'integral part of the development of the Union'. The Amsterdam Treaty confirmed the WEU's status and slightly strengthened its position in the TEU. Under the Treaty, the EU 'will avail itself of the WEU to elaborate and implement decisions and actions of the Union which have defence implications', and the possible future integration of the WEU into the EU is foreseen (Article 17, TEU).

To help give effect to the WEU's new role within the framework of the EU, various changes have been made since the Maastricht Treaty was agreed to bring the operation of the WEU more closely into line with that

---

Exhibit 16.1   A CFSP joint action

JOINT ACTION
of 30 April 1998
adopted by the Council of the basis of Article J.3 of the Treaty on European
Union in support of the Government of Montenegro
(98/301/CFSP)

THE COUNCIL OF THE EURO-
PEAN UNION

Having regard to the Treaty on
European Union and, in particular,
Articles J.3 and J.11 thereof,

Having regard to the general guidelines contained in the conclusions
adopted by the European Council in
Dublin on 13 and 14 December 1996,

Whereas a new President took office
in the Republic of Montenegro on 15
January 1998;

Whereas the European Union recog-
nises that the Government needs the
full support of the international
community to pursue political and
economic reform;

Whereas the Council on 27 April
1998 welcomed the continuing commitment shown by President Djuka-
novic to political and economic
reform in Montenegro, agreed that
the European Union should send a
clear and immediate signal of its
support for the formed process and
agreed to allocate an initial amount
of ECU 3 million in financial assistance to the Montenegrin Government to help it meet outstanding
social welfare payments;

Whereas the Council notes that the
Government of Montenegro intends
to disburse the relevant social welfare
payments as soon as possible and in
any case no later than 31 May 1998;

Whereas it is important to ensure
appropriate visibility for such Union
support; and

Whereas in order to ensure the
consistency of the Union's external
activities European Community additional measures in support of the
reform process, such as in the field of
independent media, should also be
assessed further in the near future to
go beyond this first step, notably on
the occasion of the Troika visit of 5
May 1998,

HAS ADOPTED THIS JOINT
ACTION:

Article 1

This joint action aims to provide, on
an exceptional basis, rapid, short-
term assistance to the new Government of Montenegro. The aim of the
Union's assistance is to help the
Government of Montenegro to continue its programme of economic and
political reform.

Article 2

1. To this end, an initial amount of
ECU 3 million shall be charged to the
general budget of the European
Communities for 1998.

→

2. The amount referred to in paragraph 1 shall be managed in accordance with the European Community procedures and rules applicable to the budget.

3. The amount referred to in paragraph 1 shall be made available immediately to the account specified by the Government of Montenegro.

Article 3

The Presidency shall report to the Council on the progress made by the Government of Montenegro in political and economic reform.

Article 4

The Council notes that the Commission in support of the objectives of this joint action intends to come forward where appropriate with proposals for project assistance in support of the Government of Montenegro.

Article 5

The European Union will encourage the international community to consider assistance in support of the objectives of this joint action.

Article 6

This joint action shall enter into force on the day of its adoption. It shall apply as from 1 March 1998.

Article 7

This joint action shall be published in the Official Journal.

Done at Luxembourg, 30 April 1998.

For the Council
The President
T. JOWELL

Source: *Official Journal of the European Communities*, vol. L138, 9 May 1998, pp. 1–2.

of the EU. These changes include the synchronisation of relevant WEU and EU meetings and moving the WEU Council and Secretariat from London to Brussels. The membership of the two organisations has also been more closely aligned, and those EU states that are not full members of the WEU (Austria, Denmark, Finland, Ireland, and Sweden) have been granted observer status.

This increasingly close relationship between the WEU and the EU does not of course mean that the EU can now be said to have a clear defence capability. Quite apart from the fact that the EU and the WEU are still very much separate organisations, the defence resources of the EU states essentially remain under national control – even if they do frequently operate within the framework of, or are 'lent out' to, international organisations such as the UN, NATO and the OSCE.

Exhibit 16.2   A CFSP common position

COMMON POSITION

of 8 June 1998

defined by the Council on the basis of Article J.2 of the Treaty on European Union
concerning the prohibition of new investment in Serbia

(98/374/CFSP)

THE COUNCIL OF THE EUROPEAN UNION,

Having regard to the Treaty on European Union, and in particular Article J.2
thereof,

Whereas on 7 May 1998 the Council adopted Common Position 98/326/CFSP ([1])
concerning the freezing of funds held abroad by the Federal Republic of
Yugoslavia (FRY) and Serbian Governments; whereas a further reduction of
economic and financial relations with the FRY and Serbia was foreseen in case the
conditions laid down in that common position for the FRY and Serbian
government were not met;

Whereas, as such conditions have not been fulfilled so far, further action to reduce
economic and financial relations with Serbia should be taken;

Whereas, the restrictive measures set out in Article 1 will be reconsidered
immediately if the FRY and Serbian Governments move to adopt a framework for
dialogue and a stabilisation package,

HAS DEFINED THE COMMON POSITION:

Article 1

New investments in Serbia are prohibited.

Article 2

The common position shall take effect from the date of its adoption.

Article 3

This common position shall be reviewed not later than six months after its
adoption.

Article 4

This common position shall be published in the Official Journal.

Done at Luxembourg, 8 June 1998.

For the Council
The President
R. COOK

([1])OJ L 143, 14.5.98, p.1.

Source: Official Journal of the European Communities, vol. 41, L 165, 10 June 1998,
p. 1.

In all probability an EU defence capability will not be established until there has been significant progress towards the establishment of an EU defence policy, and there are at least four obstacles in the way of this. First, a number of member states, especially those with a tradition of neutrality, are reluctant to develop a defence policy for ideological/historical reasons (on the position of the 'neutrals' see Laursen, 1998). Second, defence policy raises sovereignty concerns for some member states, most particularly the UK. Third, defence issues still sometimes divide member states in terms of both ends and means. This was demonstrated, for example, in 1995 when the French conducted nuclear tests in the South Pacific despite the disapproval of most EU governments, and again in 1999 when the UK joined with the United States to bomb Iraq despite clear disquiet in most EU member state capitals. Fourth, several member states see no pressing reason to change the existing inter-state defence arrangements.

These existing arrangements are essentially of two kinds. On the one hand, there are a number of security organisations and groupings, of which the most prominent are NATO, the OSCE and the WEU. These organisations and groupings bring states together in different combinations, in different structural arrangements, and for different purposes. In some situations more than one of these organisations may become involved in dealing with an issue or problem, as illustrated by the efforts from 1997 to stop repression and fighting in the Albanian enclave of Kosovo in Serbia. By mid March 1999, ground operations in Kosovo were primarily the responsibility of the OSCE – though it had only a modest and unarmed personnel deployment, composed mainly of civilians and retired military; there was no NATO ground deployment (although there was in neighbouring Macedonia and Bosnia), but it was threatening the Serbs with air strikes and promising to extricate OSCE personnel if necessary; and efforts to broker/pressurise a peace settlement were being undertaken by the UN, NATO, and the six-member Contact Group (France, Germany, Italy, Russia, the UK, and the US). When peace talks failed, NATO launched a sustained bombing operation from late March in which most of its members actively participated. On the other hand, states are able to come together when they judge it to be necessary in *ad hoc* coalitions of 'the able and the willing'. An example of such a coalition is the military intervention force that was put together by Italy in 1997 in response to a major outbreak of violence in Albania. Numbering 6000 personnel, the force involved Italian, French, Spanish, Greek, Austrian and Danish participation from within the EU, and Turkish and Romanian participation from outside (Allen and Smith, 1998, p. 71).

The obstacles to the development of an EU defence policy and capability are thus fomidable, but there are grounds for thinking that progress will be made at some point in the not too distant future. Amongst these grounds are: the progressive strengthening of treaty language and provisions on defence; the Amsterdam constructive abstention provision, which could be used to enable member states with concerns about defence actions not to participate; the steady enhancement of the WEU's position; developments of an integrating nature on a (to date) partial membership basis – such as the Eurocorps in which France, Germany, Spain, and Belgium are participating; and signs that countries that have traditionally opposed the idea of the EU having a defence dimension are softening their positions – for example, the UK Defence Minister, George Robertson, announced after a meeting of the EU Defence Ministers in November 1998 that a 'more effective European military capability' was needed to support the CFSP (*Financial Times*, 5 November 1998, p. 2).

The development of a defence policy and capability would, of course, do much to inject a dynamism into what many observers have seen as a somewhat listless and ineffective CFSP. There may be no shortage of CFSP activity, but how much of it, critics ask, really has much bite or impact? Is it not the case, it is argued, that the CFSP will inevitably be somewhat limp as long as the EU is unable to respond in a collective and effective manner even to security crises close to home? This is, for instance, the view of the EU's former High Representative in Bosnia, Carl Bildt, who has argued that the EU's lack of political and military commitment and of effective implementing instruments means that its influence is inevitably weak in high-tension and crisis situations. Writing about his experience as High Representative, he notes that 'The EU's involvement in the Bosnian crisis as luckless mediator, then ineffective peace-keeper and finally as America's junior partner as peace-maker was a grim experience' (Bildt, 1997, p. 24).

Policy processes

The functioning of the CFSP is centred on a network of cooperative and consultative activities between representatives of the member states, with regular rounds of meetings at political and official level at their heart. The aim of all this activity is to try to ensure a maximum information flow and cooperative effort between the member states, to enable the EU to issue joint statements on important foreign policy issues wherever possible, and to enable the EU to develop and use its post-Maastricht policy instruments when it is deemed necessary and appropriate.

The CFSP is based primarily on intergovernmental – predominantly inter-Foreign Ministry – arrangements. There are a number of interlinking and overlapping reasons for this, but they basically boil down to the fact that because of the politically sensitive nature of much of the content of foreign and security policy, the CFSP has been kept outside the framework of the TEC and the Community system.

Notwithstanding, however, this exclusion from the 'mainstream' EC system, over the years foreign policy has come to assume at least some of the characteristics of 'normal' Community policy-making, with all of the main EU institutions having at least some policy role to play. The policy-making processes of the CFSP, and the powers of the EU institutions within these processes, will now be described.

The European Council

Article 13 of the TEU – which is set out on p. 180 – assigns to the European Council responsibility for defining the principles and general guidelines of the CFSP and deciding on common strategies. Working through and with the General Affairs Council, the European Council is thus responsible for the overall direction of the CFSP.

As was noted above, the 1992 Lisbon summit provided an early example of the European Council giving such direction. Since then, numerous policy directional decisions have been channelled through the European Council, on matters such as the CEECs, the former Soviet states, Turkey, former Yugoslavia, the Middle East Peace Process, and the Euro-Mediterranean process.

In addition to laying down guiding principles, the European Council also commonly pronounces on foreign policy issues of current concern. To cite, by way of example, just one European Council meeting, the June 1998 Cardiff summit included statements on South Africa, Russia, India/Pakistan nuclear tests, Indonesia's activities in East Timor, the Ethiopia–Eritrea dispute, and the establishment of an International Criminal Court (European Council, 1998, pp. 26–33).

The Council of Ministers

The Council is at the very heart of the CFSP processes. It functions at several levels.

- *The General Affairs Council.* The Foreign Ministers of the member states, with the Commission in attendance, normally meet about once a month, but additional special meetings are convened when necessary. In addition to General Affairs Council meetings, Foreign Ministers also meet in other forums, notably at European Councils and at twice-yearly informal weekend gatherings.

  The General Affairs Council is the main decision-making body of the CFSP. Operating within the context of such general policy guidelines as have been issued by the European Council, it makes, or for routine matters formalises, most CFSP decisions – including those on defining common positions and adopting joint actions. As was explained in Chapter 5, the Amsterdam Treaty established qualified majority voting as the norm for adopting and implementing common positions and joint actions, though with the proviso that no vote can be taken if a member state 'for important and stated reasons of national policy' declares its opposition to the adoption of a decision by qualified majority.

Within the Council, the Presidency has a particular responsibility to 'represent the Union in matters coming within the common foreign and security policy' and to be 'responsible for the implementation of decisions taken under [the CFSP]' (Article 18, TEU).

The Presidency works closely with the previous and succeeding Presidencies in the so-called 'troika'. The purpose of the troika is to ensure a smooth transition between Presidencies, to help promote policy consistency and stability, and to facilitate some work sharing (which is of particular value to small countries). Since the Amsterdam Treaty, there has been speculation that this troika may be downgraded, if not replaced, by a new troika composed of the Council President and two new positions that are to be created as a result of Amsterdam provisions: a High Representative for the CFSP and a Commission external relations 'supremo'.

- *The Committee of Permanent Representatives* (COREPER). As was explained in Chapter 7, COREPER is composed of the Permanent Representatives of the member states to the EU. The Commission is always present and is usually represented by its Deputy Secretary General.

    Meeting weekly, COREPER acts on CFSP matters primarily as a filtering agency between the Political Committee (whose decisions it can discuss, but not change) and the General Affairs Council.

- *The Political Committee.* This is made up of the Political Directors of the member states (who are very senior civil servants from Foreign Ministries) plus normally two or three other senior national officials from each state. The Commission's representation is headed by its Political Director, who is the Director General for External Political relations.

    The Political Committee – which is generally known as PoCo – meets at least once a month (usually before Foreign Minister meetings), and about twenty times a year in all. It serves very much as the lynchpin of the CFSP in that it prepares all CFSP work for COREPER and the Foreign Ministers, and deals itself with routine matters such as non-controversial foreign policy declarations and the direction of the working groups. Compared with how it functioned under EPC, the Political

Committee has of, necessity, become more operational in focus under the CFSP.

In addition to their regular PoCo meetings, the Political Directors are in constant contact with each other by telephone.

- *The Correspondents' Group.* Composed of those officials who are responsible for the coordination of CFSP inside Foreign Ministries, and with the Commission in attendance, the Correspondents' Group meets at least once a month. As well as acting as a key liaising mechanism between Foreign Ministries, it regularly deals with business coming up from the working groups with which the Political Committee does not have the time or the inclination to deal. Correspondents are responsible for most of the day-to-day liaison between the Foreign Ministers of the member states: a liaison that involves, amongst other things, the transmission of thousands of messages each year via a special telex system.

- *Working groups.* There are usually around thirty or so working groups in existence, most of which are permanent but a few of which are *ad hoc*. A total of about 150 working group meetings are held each year, with permanent working groups meeting at least once during each Presidency. The groups are composed of senior diplomats – often departmental heads – from the member states, plus a Commission representative. Some working groups deal with regions, for example the Middle East, Central and South America, and Africa; some deal with themes, for example the OSCE, disarmament, and human rights; and some deal with operational matters, for example EU representation in third countries, the CFSP telecommunication system, and joint actions.

- *The General Secretariat.* Following the transmutation of EPC into the CFSP, the previously separate EPC Secretariat became a part of the Council's General Secretariat. The main responsibility of the 50 or so officials who deal with the CFSP aspects of the Council's work is to provide administrative support. About half of the officials are permanent and about half are on secondment from member states.

The 1996–7 IGC decided to strengthen the CFSP's permanent apparatus with the creation of a new position and a new unit.

The new position, which is to be held by the Secretary General of the Council, is High Representative for the CFSP. (A new post of Deputy Secretary General is to be created for the day-to-day running of the General Secretariat.) The remit of the position is to 'assist the Council in matters coming within the scope of the common foreign and security policy in particular through contributing to the formulation, preparation and implementation of policy decisions, and, when appropriate and acting on behalf of the Council at the request of the Presidency, through conducting political dialogue with third countries' (Article 26, TEU).

The new unit is a policy-planning and early-warning unit. Based within the Council's General Secretariat and under the responsibility of the High Representative for the CFSP, the tasks of the unit are to include the following: monitoring and analysing developments in areas relevant to the CFSP; providing assessments of the EU foreign and security policy interests and identifying areas for CFSP focus; providing assessments and early warnings of events or situations that may have significant repercussions for EU foreign and security policy; and producing policy option papers (Declaration 6 of the 1996–7 Inter-governmental Conference). The unit is to be staffed by 20 'A' grade officials, drawn not just from the General Secretariat, but also from the member states, the Commission, and the WEU.

The Commission

Since the 1981 London Report the Commission has been 'fully associated' with the work carried out in the foreign policy field. However, the intergovernmental and extra-Community nature of foreign and security policy has meant that the Commission's position has always been much weaker in the foreign policy context than it has in the EC context. This is no more clearly illustrated than by the fact that it was not until the Maastricht Treaty that the Commission gained the right, and then it was a non exclusive right, to refer foreign policy matters and proposals to the Council.

How much influence the Commission actually exercises over particular policy matters depends very much on individual circumstances. It is, for example, in a strong position when CFSP actions involve the use of EC policy instruments, such as the use of economic sanctions, for then the Council can only act on the basis of Commission proposals. Similarly, its position can be strong when the Council is reliant on it for specialised information and advice. The Commission is, however, less favourably placed in terms of 'purely political' matters, especially if the incumbent Presidency is a large member state with a big and effective Foreign Ministry and/or is a member state with a preference for key foreign policy matters to be conducted mainly on an intergovernmental basis.

Concerns within the Commission that the institution should take full advantage of the policy openings provided by the creation of the CFSP pillar have played an important part in stimulating a number of internal structural changes – at both College and DG levels – since 1993 in the external relations area. There is still, however, a feeling that the Commission's CFSP potential is not being fully realised. Commission insiders hope that the projected appointment (which was noted in Declaration 32 of the

1996–7 IGC) of a Commission Vice-President with overall responsibility for external relations will have a positive effect.

The European Parliament

Under Article 21 of the TEU

> The Presidency shall consult the European Parliament on the main aspects and the basic choices of the common foreign and security policy and shall ensure that the views of the European Parliament are duly taken into consideration. The European Parliament shall be kept regularly informed by the Presidency and the Commission of the development of the Union's foreign and security policy.
>
> The European Parliament may ask questions of the Council or make recommendations to it. It shall hold an annual debate on progress in implementing the common foreign and security policy.

What these provisions tend to mean in practice is that unless special circumstances apply – as, for example, when a foreign policy issue is linked to an association agreement and the assent procedure thus needs to be used – the EP is largely confined to an advisory role on foreign policy under the TEU.

All the EP can thus do is make maximum use of such mechanisms as it has at its disposal to try to ensure that the Commission and, more importantly, the Council really do consult and really do listen. Prior to the Amsterdam Treaty the main mechanisms were: exchanging views with the Council Presidency in the Committee on Foreign Affairs and Security; asking questions – written and oral – of the Council; holding debates in plenary sessions; and making recommendations, passing resolutions and tendering opinions. The Amsterdam Treaty created another mechanism that will doubtless be very useful to the EP: it formalised the already common practice of charging most administrative and operational CFSP expenditure to the EU budget. This gives the EP the opportunity to raise foreign policy issues during the budgetary procedure.

Embassies, delegations and missions

The development since the Second World War of rapid international travel and instantaneous electronic communications has undermined much of the role and value of diplomatic representations as a means for countries to communicate with one another. Nonetheless, embassies, delegations and missions are still used to promote and defend interests abroad.

Because it is not a state the EU is not able to maintain overseas embassies, but it does have an extensive network of external delegations

– technically, delegations of the Commission. There are over 120 such delegations in third countries, and five delegations to international organisations. (It might also be added – and this exemplifies the importance of the EU to the outside world – that over 160 countries have diplomatic missions officially accredited to the EU.)

Overseas representations are, of course, concerned with many issues other than foreign policy – most notably, the promotion of trade and, in the case of national representations, the safeguarding of citizens' interests. The CFSP is, however, a matter that embassies of the member states and Commission delegations need to be aware of and to promote. In this context Article 20 of the TEU states that 'The diplomatic and consular missions of the Member States and the Commission Delegations in third countries and international conferences, and their representations to international organizations, shall cooperate in ensuring that the common positions and joint actions adopted by the Council are complied with and implemented'.

Article 20 is assisting the continued development of processes that have been under way for some time, whereby embassies of EU member states in third countries and delegations attached to international organisations exchange information and coordinate activities. For example member state ambassadors to the UN meet weekly to coordinate policy, and vote together on about 75 per cent of Security Council votes (McCormick, 1999a).

Development cooperation

Policies

The EU is actively engaged in promoting development in the Third World. The general principles of the policy are laid down in Title XX – Development Cooperation – of the TEC. Article 177 (ex 130u) of Title XX states:

1. Community policy in the sphere of development cooperation, which shall be complementary to the policies pursued by the Member States, shall foster:

– the sustainable economic and social development of the developing countries, and more particularly the most disadvantaged among them;
– the smooth and gradual integration of the developing countries into the world economy;
– the campaign against poverty in the developing countries.

2. Community policy in this area shall contribute to the general objective of developing and consolidating democracy and the rule of law, and to that of respecting human rights and fundamental freedoms. 3. The Community and the Member States shall comply with the commitments and take account of the objectives they have approved in the context of the United Nations and other competent international organizations.

The reasons for the EU's active engagement in development policy are a mixture of the historical, the moral, and the economic: historical in that some EU countries, notably France and the UK, have long-established ties with parts of the developing world as a result of their colonial past; moral in that EU governments believe, although with different degrees of enthusiasm, that something should be done about world poverty and hunger; and economic in that developing countries account for around 30 per cent of EU exports, and the EU is highly dependent on the developing world for products such as rubber, copper and uranium.

Some of the forms of assistance made available by the EU apply to the whole of the developing world. Amongst these are:

(1) *Generalised preferences.* All developing countries can export their industrial products to the EU without paying tariffs (subject to volume limits for some products). Also, many agricultural products can also be exported free of duty.
(2) *Food aid.* Foodstuffs are sent to countries with serious food shortages.
(3) *Emergency aid.* Aid of an appropriate sort is made available to countries stricken by natural disasters and other crises.
(4) *Aid to non-governmental organisations.* The EU makes available aid to projects sponsored by non-governmental organisations in a number of developing world countries.

In addition to these general forms of assistance, the EU provides additional assistance and aid to countries with which it has special relationships. Most of these special relationships take the form of economic, trade, industrial, technical and financial cooperation agreements. The most important and most wide-ranging agreement is the Lomé Convention, which links the EU with 71 African, Caribbean and Pacific countries (the ACP countries) with which some member states have historical links. Lomé IV (covering the years 1990–2000) was signed in 1989 and contains amongst its main features: duty-free access to the EU market for virtually all ACP exports; schemes to stabilise export earnings (Stabex and Sysmin); and the European Development Fund (EDF), whose main purpose, using resources of 14 625 million ecu for the period 1995–2000, is to assist financially, on the basis of long-term concerted programmes, the development of ACP countries, especially with regard to rural development, industrialisation, and economic infrastructure. Negotiations on a successor agreement to Lomé IV opened in September 1998. It seems likely that whilst some of the features of the evolved Lomé scheme will remain in place, there will be significant changes to the system. In particular, there may well be a phased move towards reciprocal free trade agreements with groups of ACP countries (partly because the WTO is likely to rule at some point that the existing non-reciprocal preferential regime breaches its rules), and greater emphasis will probably be given to stimulating enterprise in the ACP states so as to enable them to integrate more into the global economy.

Development aid is financed in two ways. First, non-EDF aid is funded by the EU budget. Accounting for around four per cent of the budget, about half of this aid is used to provide financial assistance to non-ACP countries and about half is used for food aid purposes. Second, EDF aid is funded by special contributions from the member states. Taking EDF and non-EDF aid together, the principal beneficiaries are sub-Saharan Africa (which receives almost 60 per cent), southern Asia (about 10 per cent), and Latin America and the Caribbean (also about 10 per cent).

It should be stressed that these EU policies do not constitute the sum total of the EU's overall contribution to development aid. This is because, unlike with trade policy where there is exclusive EU competence, in the development policy field EU policy is conducted alongside the policies of the member states. In some aspects of development policy the EU takes the leading role, whilst in others the member states are the main players and the EU is confined to, at most, supplementing, complementing and coordinating national development policies. So, the trade aspects of development policy are necessarily the EU's responsibility, but the states are much more prominent in respect of financial assistance, as evidenced by the fact that EU financial aid only amounts to about 15 per cent of the combined sum provided by the member states.

Strains have sometimes arisen between member states and between member states and EU institutions (especially the Commission) regarding development policies. Particular problems have arisen when states have used aid for the purpose of promoting national political and economic interests. In an attempt to ensure that there is consistency and convergence in the policies and activities of the EU and its member states, the Council of Ministers has issued guidelines aimed at promoting maximum coordination in respect of policy content, policy operations and policy positions in international forums.

Policy processes

The EU makes all sorts of decisions in connection with its development policy. Just as in other policy areas, the actors involved and the procedures that apply vary enormously.

With regard to the actors, the most important players are: the Council of Ministers (Development Cooperation); the Commissioner for Cooperation and Development; DGVIII – Development; the EP Committee on Development and Cooperation; and the numerous diplomatic missions of developing countries in Brussels that are accredited to the EU.

With regard to the procedures, these are dependent on the type of decision envisaged. For example, if the Council is simply intending to issue a declaration or a resolution on a matter, it is not obliged to consult the EP and can move at its own pace – which may mean proceeding very cautiously and only after the receipt of proposals from the Commission and/or from a specially convened Council *ad hoc* working party. If a trade only agreement is envisaged, Article 133 applies – which, as noted above, means that the Commission and the Council are the key actors, qualified majority rules apply in the Council, and the EP has no formal role. If cooperation or association agreements are proposed, Article 300 applies – which means qualified majority voting rules for cooperation agreements and unanimity for association agreements, and the power of assent for the EP on all association agreements and some cooperation agreements.

As was shown above, the Lomé Convention is the most important of the numerous agreements to which the EU is party in connection with its policy on development cooperation. It is therefore worth saying a little about how it functions, for the Convention has its own institutional structure. This structure is made up of three principal bodies. The first is the ACP–EC Council of Ministers, which is composed of the members of the EU Council of Ministers, a member of the Commission, and a member of the government of each ACP country. The Council meets at least once a year and takes the major political and policy decisions that are necessary during the life of a Convention. The second body is the Committee of Ambassadors, which is composed of a representative of each EU state, a representative of the Commission, and a representative of each ACP state. The Committee meets at least twice a year and is charged with assisting and advising the Council of Ministers, monitoring the implementation of the Convention and the progress towards its objectives, and generally supervising and coordinating the work of the many committees and subsidiary bodies that exist under the general umbrella of the Convention. Finally, there is the Joint Assembly, which is made up of equal numbers of MEPs and ACP members of parliament or national representatives. It meets once a year and acts as a general advisory and deliberating body.

The external dimension of internal policies

Many of the EU's internal policies have significant external dimensions. For example, transport policy involves dealing with neighbouring countries on road transit arrangements and with countries throughout the world on numerous air and maritime transport issues. Energy policy includes dealing with countries that are energy suppliers about rights, guarantees, and terms of access. And environmental policy includes dealing with countries near and far on many aspects of air, land, and water damage and pollution.

The EU does not have explicit treaty powers to act as the external representative of the member states in such policy areas. However, the Court of Justice has established that the EU (more precisely the Community) does have implied external powers in respect of policy areas that fall within its internal jurisdiction. Just how extensive these implied powers are, and in what circumstances they apply, has been frequently contested over the years, but the key principle of 'parallelism' has been firmly established, by which the exercise of internal law-making powers by the EU in a particular policy area is taken to imply that it also has the power to negotiate and conclude international agreements in that area. (On the concept of implied powers see Hartley, 1994, pp. 67–76.)

The procedural arrangements by which the EU contracts external agreements on internal policy issues are set out in Article 300 of the TEC. Different procedures apply depending on the nature of the agreement concerned. A relatively straightforward agreement with no major institutional or budgetary implications is subject to much the same procedure as applies under Article 133, though with the difference that the EP must be consulted. In contrast, agreements that are constituent elements of more wide-ranging cooperation or association agreements are subject to the 'more difficult' procedures that apply to these latter agreements – that is, unanimity in the Council for association agreements and EP assent for some cooperation agreements and all association agreements.

To these perhaps already rather complicated arrangements, another complication is added by virtue of the fact that the EU does not necessarily have the exclusive right to negotiate external agreements on internal policies. Rather, there are many mixed competences where policy responsibilities are shared between the EU and the member states. This results in there being two main ways, with variations within each, as to how the EU is represented and conducts itself in international negotiations in such policy areas. On the one hand, where there is exclusive EU competence, as with fisheries, the Commission is the sole EU representative and negotiator. On the other hand, where there is a mixed competence, as with transport policy, the Commission acts on behalf of the EU and national representatives act on behalf of the member states.

The distribution of competences is highly complex in some policy areas. Bretherton and Vogler (1999, p. 89) provide a good example of such complexity, with the Basel Convention on hazardous waste: 'It has trade aspects where there is full Community competence, science and development assistance aspects (where there is Member State competence), and environmental aspects – where mixed competence prevails'. Such complexity and overlapping competences can naturally make it difficult for the EU fully to coordinate its inputs in international forums and negotiations. In turn, this can weaken its influence, but the extent of the weakening should not be overstated. In the environmental policy sphere, for example, the EU is a major global player as Bretherton and Vogler (ibid.) show. It is, for instance, party to, and an influential voice within, more than 30 different multilateral environmental agreements – including agreements on the protection of the ozone layer, the transboundary movement of hazardous wastes and their disposal, desertification, and the protection of the marine environment (there are several marine environment agreements covering different sea areas). Moreover in a few environmental policy areas – including climate change and biological diversity – it is not going too far to describe the EU as virtually a policy leader.

A key reason why the EU is often able to exert a significant policy influence even when there are problems with its 'actorness' is that it is usually well prepared for negotiations with third parties. Even when there have been internal disputes, accommodations – on competences, policy goals, and who is to take the negotiating 'lead' – are usually agreed before external negotiations begin. Furthermore, during the course of external negotiations EU 'coordination' meetings are normally held as and when they are deemed necessary.

An example of an accommodation being worked out occurred in the months preceding the first WTO Ministerial Conference, which was held in Singapore in December 1996. Since some of the subject matter at the Conference was of a mixed character – including, as the Court of Justice had ruled in Opinion 1/94, services and intellectual property rights – both the Commission and the Council spent much time and effort examining and establishing 'the overall aims to be pursued by the Community and its Member States' (Council Press Release 8913/96, 15–16 July 1996). As part of these preparations, there were several meetings of Foreign Ministers and one informal meeting of Trade Ministers, at which much of the work focused on reports, communications, and proposals produced by the

Commission on topics such as trade and the environment, the negotiation of an information technology agreement, and negotiations on basic telecommunications.

Such preparations do not always succeed in establishing agreed EU positions and a shared discipline, but for the most part they do.

External relations: the consistency problem

Article 3 of the Common Provisions of the TEU states that 'The Union shall in particular ensure the consistency of its external activities as a whole in the context of its external relations, security, economic and development policies. The Council and the Commission shall be responsible for ensuring such consistency and shall cooperate to this end.'

Consistency is a key factor in determining the extent to which would-be global actors can establish themselves on the world stage and be effective. Yet ensuring policy consistency is a major problem for the EU in the conduct of its external relations. There are many examples – including policies towards the former Soviet states, the Middle East Peace Process, Somalia, and Rwanda – of either the EU itself not being consistent over time or member states clearly not being in line with one another (see Regelsberger *et al.*, 1997 for case studies of policy inconsistencies). There are several overlapping and interrelating reasons why EU policy consistency is often difficult to achieve:

- The great spread of EU external relations interests and activities.
- The diversity of actors and processes that are involved in EU exernal relations policy processes.
- The differing powers of the EU in different policy contexts, with particular problems arising when competence is shared between the EU and the member states – as it is for most of the internal policies that have an external dimension.
- The differing powers of EU actors in differing spheres of external relations.
- The conflicting orientations and preferences of the member states on many policy issues.
- The varying levels of EU policy development – from the *common* commercial policy to the not yet born defence policy.

The consistency problem is being addressed in a number of ways: through attempts to strengthen the institutional apparatus, with the most obvious examples being the creation of the CFSP High Representative in the Council and the Vice President with overall responsibility for external relations in the Commission; through the convening, at different levels of seniority, of more intra- and inter-institutional meetings that have as their purpose the coordination of policy activity; through the extension and stiffening of CFSP policy instruments; and by basing policy-making procedures on a more holistic approach. It is still very much the case that the various possible dimensions of external policy are not always brought together, and indeed are not necessarily available – especially if security issues are involved. Nonetheless, there is evidence of growing coordination between different external policy areas, as for example in the increasing incorporation in EU development programmes of requirements on developing countries to respect human rights and promote democratic principles, and in the increasing appearance in cooperation and association agreements of political programmes and dialogues.

But although progress is being made to improve consistency, much remains to be done. This is no more clearly demonstrated than in the fact that the answer to the question first raised by the US Secretary of State, Henry Kissinger, in the early 1970s – who speaks for Europe? – is still not always clear.

Concluding remarks

This chapter has demonstrated that the EU is a major world player in important policy spheres. It is a very powerful voice and influence in respect of trade policy, a significant actor in respect of development policy, and can be expected to assume a key role in respect of monetary policy if the euro proves to be a successful currency.

A central question that is likely to loom large in the years to come is whether the EU will become a major player in the foreign policy field. Mechanisms to enable it to become so have been strengthened over the years, but capacity in itself is not enough. As Fraser Cameron, a Commission official working on external relations, has pointed out:

> Past experience suggests that appropriate structures alone will not suffice to ensure a coherent and effective foreign and security policy. The political will to exploit them must exist if a real CFSP is to emerge. This will require deeper awareness among members states of the interests they share as EU members as well as recognition that many of their own national interests might be better served when pursued jointly (Cameron, 1998, p. 41).

It should not, however, be assumed, as it often is, that the EU will never become an important global foreign policy player. There may be major obstacles in the way, not least with respect to how – if at all – defence policy is to be handled, but it should not be forgotten that what used to be seen as almost insurmountable barriers to the development of the CFSP have been removed in recent years. For example: the special relationships that some EU countries have with particular parts of the world have become less problematical as historical ties have been loosened; the difficulties created by the quasi-neutrality of some member states have largely been overcome since the end of the Cold War; and, for a host of reasons, EU member states – including those which are most concerned with the preservation of national sovereignty – have increasingly come to regard both foreign and security issues as wholly proper and legitimate matters for the EU agenda.

By their very nature external policies are guaranteed to continue to loom large on the EU policy agenda. However, the turbulence of the international system combined with the fluidity of internal EU dynamics means that extreme caution is required when looking to just how they will evolve.

Chapter 17

National Influences and Controls on European Union Processes

Governments
Parliaments
Courts
Subnational levels of government
Public opinion
Political parties
Interests
Concluding remarks

The most obvious price states pay for membership of the EU is a substantial loss of national decision-making powers. In some policy spheres – such as agriculture and external trade – most decisions are now taken at the EU level, whilst in many other spheres – such as environmental policy and competition policy – decision-making responsibilities are shared between the EU and the member states.

The reason why member states have been prepared to countenance this loss – or pooling – of sovereignty and have been willing to participate in collective decision-making in important policy areas is that their national decision-makers, supported by, or at least with the acquiescence of, large sections of their populations have believed it to be in their national interests to do so. The particular balance of perceived advantages and disadvantages arising from EU membership has varied from state to state, but each has judged that there is more to be gained from being inside the EU than from being outside.

But being inside means, given the nature of EU policy and decision-making processes, that great care and vigilance are required to ensure that national interests are fully articulated and properly defended. Since, however, there are competing views within member states about what these interests are, and since too there are a variety of domestic institutions, agencies, movements and parties that wish to be heard, there are many inputs from each of the states into EU policy-making and decision-making processes.

The precise nature of these inputs varies between states, reflecting such factors as different national political systems, traditions, and cultures. In broad terms, however, they can be seen as being directed through seven principal channels: governments, parliaments, courts, subnational levels of government, public opinion, political parties, and interests.

Governments

Governments are naturally in the strongest position to control or influence EU processes. This is most obviously seen in their relationships with the Commission and the Council of Ministers.

Influencing the Commission

The system of appointment to the Commission ensures that all member states are well represented within it. At College level, all member states are entitled to at least one Commissioner. At services levels, an informal national quota system exists for senior grades.

This, however, does not mean that Commissioners or Commission officials act as governmental representatives. As was shown in Chapter 6, they do, for the most part, look to the EU-wide interest and are not open to instructions from national capitals. But they may, quite naturally, be inclined to take a particular interest in the impact of proposals on their own country. And governments looking for sympathetic ears in the Commission may well make fellow nationals their first port of call (though not necessarily: competent government officials, especially from the Permanent Representations, cultivate a broad range of contacts in the Commission).

As well as the use of national contacts, there are many other ways in which governments can try to persuade, influence or bring pressure to bear on the Commission. Use can be made of formal channels such as the groups of experts who advise the Commission on all sorts of matters, the management and regulatory committees through which the Commission exercises many of its executive functions, and the numerous decision-making meetings that take place within the Council system from working party level upwards – meetings which the Commission always attends. Informal methods range from a minister ringing up a Commissioner, to a working party representative meeting a Commission official for lunch.

It should emphasised that government influence on Commission thinking is not necessarily a bad thing. On the contrary, it can be positively helpful by, for example, improving the prospect of legislative proposals being adopted. However, it can become unhealthy if governments try to lean too heavily on their fellow nationals in the Commission, or if clusters of nationals have a disproportionate influence on policy development in a key sector (as, for example, is frequently alleged of the French in respect of agriculture).

Influencing the Council

The potential for any government to influence what happens in the Council depends on a number of factors.

The size of the state it represents

No matter what is being discussed, the larger countries, especially France and Germany, are always likely to carry more weight than smaller countries such as Portugal and Luxembourg.

The importance of the state to particular negotiations

When an issue is important to a state it will be actively involved in Council processes and is likely to ensure that it is represented by senior figures in Council meetings. When, however, a state is not much affected by an issue it may not engage actively in Council deliberations and may send junior people to represent it. For example, in Common Fisheries Policy (CFP) deliberations the Spanish government is likely to be a much more central actor than the Belgian government.

The desire of the government to play an active role

The importance of this factor is illustrated by the fact that German governments, until the late 1960s, acted very much as political lightweights even though their country was clearly an economic heavyweight. This was partly because of Germany's historical legacy and partly because of the delicacies involved in the 'normalisation' of its relations with Eastern Europe and especially the German Democratic Republic (GDR). In more recent years, as Germany's position has come to be seen as not so unique or so special, its governments have increasingly asserted themselves across the EU's policy spectrum and have not been unwilling to adopt 'awkward' and even isolated positions.

The capacity of the government to play an active role

A government may have clear views on an EU initiative and may wish to play an active role in supporting or opposing it, but be restrained by domestic political considerations such as a finely balanced coalition government, opposition from key interest groups, or possible electoral damage.

Relations with other governments

Cohesive and fixed alliances within the EU between particular governments do not exist. Rather, governments tend to come together in different combinations on different issues. However, some governments make more of a conscious effort than others to seek general understandings and cooperation with one or more of their EU partners, and when this is successful they often appear to increase their influence as a consequence. The best example of this is the close relationship that has been consciously fostered between most French and German governments since the early 1960s. The so-called Franco-German axis is no longer as commanding as it was when there were only six member states, or when Chancellor Schmidt and President Giscard d'Estaing worked closely together in the 1970s, but it still plays an important part in helping to shape and set the pace of EU developments.

The procedures applying

Of particular importance is whether qualified majority voting is permissable under the relevant treaty article(s) and is politically acceptable in the circumstances applying. If it is, concessions and compromises might be preferable to being outvoted. If it is not, any government can cause indefinite delay, though by so doing it may weaken goodwill towards it and thus damage its long-term interests.

The competence of governmental negotiators

Given the extensive tactical manoeuvrings involved in EU processes, and given that many negotiations are not about the broad sweep of policy but are about highly technical matters, the competence of individual negotiators can be crucial. Are they well briefed and able to master details? Can they judge how far their negotiating partners can be pushed? Can they avoid being isolated? Can they build coalitions? Can they time their interventions so as to clinch points? The evidence suggests that variations in such competencies are not so much between states as between individual negotiators.

The arrangements for linking representatives in the Council with national capitals

This point is worth developing in a little detail because there are significant variations in the ways in which governments attempt to control, and do control, their input into the Council via their representatives. Two aspects of this are particularly worth mentioning.

First, some countries – including Belgium, Italy, and the Netherlands – generally allow their representatives to work within a relatively flexible framework. This is demonstrated by the way in which representatives are often able to negotiate on important policy matters not just at the ministerial level but also at lower levels. As well as assisting the functioning of the Council as a whole – by reducing the need for awkward issues to be referred upwards – manoeuvrability of this kind can be used to the national advantage by competent negotiators. At the same time, however, too much independence on the part of representatives can lead to the need for awkward backtracking at a later negotiating stage if a misjudgement is made. In contrast, the representatives of some other states – including France, Ireland and the United Kingdom – are generally reluctant to negotiate on policy issues below ministerial level. Whether, as is sometimes claimed, this greater rigidity improves the consistency and effectiveness of a country's negotiating position is doubtful. Undoubtedly, the more that countries lean in this direction, and all do at times, the more that negotiations at the lower Council levels are limited to technical matters and the more the overall Council process is protracted.

At the most senior Council level – ministerial meetings – there is, of course, not such a problem of control from national capitals. It is important to ensure that the minister is fully briefed on the national implications of proposals and is accompanied by national officials who fully understand all aspects of agenda items, but the political weight of the participants usually means that, if the will is there, commitments can be entered into without having to refer back for clearance. This is not to say that those in attendance at ministerial meetings can do as they like. At a minimum they are obliged to operate within the general guidelines of their government's policies. They may also be subject to special national constraints: perhaps occasioned by an inability of the minister him or herself to attend; perhaps linked to domestic political difficulties caused by the existence of a coalition government; perhaps caused by a national parliamentary committee having indicated concerns; or perhaps a consequence of a particular national interest having resulted in the establishment of a rigid governmental position in advance.

Second, all member states have established domestic arrangements to coordinate their policy towards and their participation in the EU.

According to Wright (1996, p. 154) four general observations can be made about these arrangements: major political and constitutional EU issues are handled by the Heads of Government, assisted by their Foreign and Finance Ministers; the formal link between the domestic capital and Brussels is generally coordinated through the Foreign Ministry, the Finance/Economics Ministry, or both; most ministries in all member states have adjusted their internal structures to meet EU requirements; and despite some convergence, the nature of the coordination arrangements varies considerably between the member states.

Some flesh can be put on these general observations by comparing the arrangements made by two member states: the UK, which has a centralised coordinating system, and Germany, which has a more fragmented system.

In the UK, the centralised governmental system and the majority party political system provide a favourable base for effective coordinating mechanisms. The mechanisms themselves are formalised, structured, and seemingly well integrated. At the general policy level, the Foreign and Commonwealth Office (FCO), the Cabinet Office, and the UK Permanent Representation to the European Union (UKREP) are the key bodies: the FCO has two European Union Departments – Internal and External; the Cabinet Office contains a European Secretariat which, amongst other things, convenes each year around 200 interdepartmental meetings of civil servants attended by representatives from appropriate ministries, including one regular weekly meeting which is attended by the Permanent Representative; and UKREP – which is formally an FCO overseas post – acts as the eyes and ears of the United Kingdom in Brussels. Working together, these three bodies attempt to monitor, coordinate and control overall EU developments: by giving general consideration to important matters due to come up at forthcoming meetings; by looking at whether a broadly consistent line is being pursued across different policy areas; by trying to ensure that ministries have issued sufficiently clear guidelines for representatives in Council meetings; and, in the cases of the FCO and UKREP, giving briefings to representatives when appropriate. 'Above' these three bodies, but not involved in such a continual manner, there is a Cabinet Committee on European Issues, the Cabinet itself, and the Prime Minister. 'Below' them, each ministry has its own arrangements for examining proposals that fall within its competence and for ensuring that specialist negotiators are well briefed and fully aware of departmental thinking. When EU matters loom large in a ministry's work, special divisions or units exist for coordination purposes. (For a more detailed account of the UK government's coordinating arrangements see Bulmer and Burch, 1998.)

Some of Germany's coordinating arrangements are not dissimilar from those of the UK. There is, for example, a European Division in the Foreign

Office and regular meetings are held of representatives from relevant ministries at (normally junior) ministerial and senior official levels. However, in Germany a number of factors combine to make coordination more difficult than it is in the UK: the existence of a coalition government and the need to satisfy (though not on a consistent basis across policy areas) the different elements of the coalition; the relative autonomy of ministers and ministries within the federal government (seen, most notably, in the long-running disagreement between the Finance Ministry and the Agriculture Ministry over the cost of the CAP); the lack of an authoritative coordinating centre – the Chancellor's Office and the Foreign Ministry both have a responsibility for major EU issues, whilst the Finance Ministry has a responsibility for routine matters; the relative independence from government of the Bundesbank (not so important since the establishment of the euro); the strong powers of the federal states (the Länder) in certain policy areas; and strong sectoral specialisation, allied with loyalties to different federal ministries, amongst the staff of the German Permanent Representation in Brussels. As a result, Germany's European policies are sometimes less than consistent. Fortunately for Germany, its position as the strongest single EU state seemingly enables it to avoid being too seriously damaged by this internal weakness. (For more information on Germany's coordinating arrangements, see Rometsch, 1996.)

But whatever the particulars of their arrangements for controlling and influencing their EU policy activities, all governments have found the task increasingly difficult in recent years. Three factors are especially important in accounting for this:

- Many more decisions are now being taken by the EU. This applies both to major and long term decisions – on EMU, institutional reform, enlargement and so on – and to more specific and technical decisions, such as much of the SEM-related legislation.
- Not only are more decisions being made, but many are being made much more quickly. The greater use of qualified majority voting means that governments can no longer always delay progress on a proposal until they are ready and satisfied.
- The increased scope of EU policy interests means that there are no longer just a few domestic ministries – agriculture, trade, finance and so forth – which are directly involved with the EU. The 'Europeanisation' of domestic politics and administration has resulted in most ministries in most states being affected by, and becoming actively involved in, EU affairs.

Parliaments

Parliaments have much less influence than governments over EU developments. Of course, governments normally reflect the political composition of their national legislatures and must retain their confidence, so – in an indirect sense – government activity in relation to the EU could be said to reflect the parliamentary will. But that is a quite different matter from direct parliamentary control.

One of the main reasons for the comparative lack of direct parliamentary control is that national parliaments have no formal EU treaty powers, so governments can choose what to consult their parliaments about. All governments consult their parliaments on fundamental matters when the treaties refer to ratification in accordance with 'respective constitutional requirements' (enlargements, treaty amendments, and the EU's budgetary base carry this provision), but otherwise there are variations between the states. Another reason for the weakness is the particular difficulties that arise in relation to what might be expected to be the major sphere of influence of national parliaments: advising on EU legislation. The difficulties here are legion: a high proportion of EU legislation is, or is regarded by governments as being, 'administrative' legislation and is therefore not within parliamentary competences; much EU legislation is so technical that it is almost incomprehensible to the average legislator; there is little opportunity to consider even the most important legislation at the formative and crucial pre-proposal stage; proposed legislation that is considered is often well advanced in, and may even be through, the Council system before it is examined by parliaments; and qualified majority voting in the Council means that a parliament whose government has been outvoted has no way at all of calling the real decision-makers to account.

But notwithstanding these problems and difficulties, all national parliaments have established some sort of specialised arrangements for attempting to deal with EU affairs. In different ways and with different degrees of effectiveness, these arrangements focus on examining proposed EU legislation, scrutinising ministerial positions and performances, producing reports on EU-related matters, and generally monitoring EU developments. Amongst the many differences that exist between the national arrangements three are particularly worth noting:

- All parliaments have established an EU committee of some sort. In some cases these serve as the main forum for dealing with EU matters, in others they serve more as coordinating committees and the detailed work is undertaken by appropriate 'domestic' committees.

- The regularity and circumstances in which ministers with EU policy responsibilities appear before appropriate parliamentary bodies to explain and be questioned about these policies varies considerably.
- Some parliaments have established close working relationships with their national MEPs, whilst others have not. In a few parliaments – including the Belgian, German, and Greek – the specialised EU committees include MEPs, whilst in a growing number of parliaments MEPs are used as experts when appropriate.

Despite the changes and adjustments made by parliaments in recognition of the importance of the EU, it is still the case, however, that parliaments are mostly confined to a relatively minor role.

The position of the Irish Parliament is fairly typical. Following Irish accession to the Community in 1973, arrangements were made that were supposed to give Parliament monitoring, advisory, and deliberating responsibilities in respect of Irish participation in the Community. In particular, these arrangements consisted of an obligation on the part of the government to present a six-monthly report to Parliament on developments in the Community, and the creation of a new committee – the Joint Committee on Secondary Legislation, comprising 25 Dail Deputies and Senators – to examine Community proposals and advise the government on their implications and suitability for Ireland. The arrangements had but a marginal effect on Irish policy in Europe and in 1993 the Committee was subsumed within a new Joint Committee on Foreign Affairs. The fact is that in Ireland, as in several member states, EU policy tends to be in the hands of a small, government-dominated, network of politicians and officials who listen to Parliament only when they deem it appropriate. In the case of agriculture, for example, the Minister of Agriculture, senior officials in the Department of Agriculture, and leaders of relevant organisations – particularly the Irish Farmers' Association – hold the key to decision-making and decision implementation, and they are not unduly inconvenienced by parliamentary probing.

The three Scandinavian EU member states – Denmark, Finland, and Sweden – have similar arrangements to each other and are the major exceptions to the general pattern of legislative weakness. Of the three, the Danish parliament – the Folketing – is probably the strongest. There are two main sources of its strength. First, there has been a powerful anti-integration sentiment among the people of Denmark since accession in 1973. No Danish government has been able to ignore the articulation of this in the Folketing, especially since Danish governments are invariably coalitions or minorities. Second, the Folketing has a very influential European Committee, composed mostly of senior politicians. The Committee and the ministers who are to attend Council meetings meet every

Friday to review the next week's Council business and to hear reports from the ministers on their proposed negotiating positions. The Committee does not vote or formally grant negotiating mandates, but it does tender advice, and it is necessary that a 'negative' clearance is given to the minister's position in the sense that there is no majority against it. The principal advantage of the European Committee procedure is that it helps to ensure that agreements reached by Danish ministers in the Council are not subsequently queried or endangered at home. The principal disadvantage is that it can make it difficult for Danish representatives to be flexible in the Council and can result in their being isolated if new solutions to problems are advanced during the course of negotiations. (For more information on the influence of the Folketing, and indeed on Denmark's other EU institutional arrangements, see Dosenrode, 1998.)

Courts

National courts might be thought to have a significant role to play as the guarantors and defenders of national rights against EU encroachment, but in practice they do not.

The reason for this, as explained in Chapter 10, is that the principle of primacy of EU law is accepted by national courts. There were some initial teething problems in this regard, but it is now extremely rare for national courts to question the legality of EU proceedings and decisions. The treaties, EU legislation and the case law of the Court of Justice are seen as taking precedence when they clash with national law. The frequent practice of national courts to seek preliminary rulings from the Court of Justice in cases where there is uncertainty over an aspect of EU law is testimony to the general desire of national courts not to be out of step with EU law.

That said, national courts have occasionally sought to assert national rights and interests against the EU. For example, in a few instances national courts have refused to acknowledge the legality of directives that have not been incorporated into national law by the due date, even though the Court of Justice has ruled that in such circumstances they may be deemed as having direct effect. Constitutional law, especially as applied to individual rights, has been another area where some assertion of national independence has been attempted by national courts, though less often since the principle of EU law having precedence over national constitutional law was confirmed by Court of Justice rulings in the early 1970s.

In recent years the most important instances of national court intervention have been in connection with Irish ratification of the SEA and German ratification of the Maastricht Treaty. The Irish intervention occurred in December 1986 when the Irish Supreme Court, by a margin of three to two, found in favour of a Raymond Crotty, who had challenged the constitutional validity of the SEA. The judges ruled that Title III of the Act, which put foreign policy cooperation on a legal basis, could restrict Ireland's sovereignty and might inhibit it from pursuing its traditionally neutral foreign policy. The SEA must therefore, they indicated, be endorsed by a referendum. As a result, the SEA was unable to come into effect in any of the twelve Community states on 1 January 1987, as had been intended, and was delayed until the Irish gave their approval in the duly held referendum. The SEA eventually entered into force on 1 July 1987. The German intervention occurred when several people – including four Green Party MEPs – appealed to the country's Constitutional Court to declare that the Maastricht Treaty was in breach of the German constitution, the Basic Law. The appeal was made shortly after the Bundestag and the Bundesrat had ratified the Treaty by huge majorities in December 1992, with the consequence that, instead of being one of the first countries to ratify the Treaty, Germany became the very last as the Constitutional Court did not issue its judgement until October 1993. In its judgement the Court declared that the TEU did not infringe Germany's constitution, but made it clear that certain conditions would have to be satisfied in respect of further integration – most notably, it would need to be accompanied by a parallel increase in democratic control of the EU.

Subnational levels of government

The parts played and the influence exercised by subnational levels of government in the EU were considered in Chapter 11 in the sections on the Committee of the Regions and on interests. Here, therefore, only a few observations will be made on key points.

Subnational levels of government have grown in importance within the EU system in recent years, with the consequence that national authorities, especially governments, have lost some of their power to articulate and advance 'the national position' in EU decision-making forums. The extent to which national authorities' gatekeeping roles have been undermined naturally varies according to a number of factors, not least the national constitutional status of subnational levels of government, but even in countries where central powers remain strong – for example Ireland and Denmark – by no means all EU-national official communications are channelled through the central authorities.

Channels of communication between the EU and subnational levels of government include the following:

- Most EU states have subnational levels of government of some kind that have offices or representations in Brussels. For example, all of Germany's Länder have offices, as do most of the regions of France and Spain. The tasks of these offices include lobbying, information gathering, generally establishing contacts and 'keeping in touch' with appropriate officials and decision-makers, and acting as intermediaries between the EU and the regions/localities.
- Many of the subnational levels of government that do not have their own offices in Brussels make use of Brussels based consultancies and/or have domestically based EU offices and officers.
- The Committee of the Regions exists for the precise purpose of enabling EU decision-makers to seek the views of regional representatives on regional issues.
- Two governments – the Belgian and the German – are sometimes represented in the Council of Ministers by regional ministers when agenda items are the responsibility of regional governments.

The EU may be a long way from the Europe of the Regions that some advocate and others claim to detect, but clearly the national dimension of EU affairs has an increasingly powerful subnational element attached to it.

Public opinion

National public opinion has both a direct and an indirect influence on EU decision-making.

The most direct means by which the populace can have their say is in referendums. A number of these have been held over the years on EC/EU-related matters. However, it can hardly be said that they have done much to deal with the problem of the so-called 'democratic deficit', for there have not been many of them and – apart from the special case of accession referendums – they are virtually never held on the big issues that are likely to have a major impact of the lives of EU citizens. On this last point, not one referendum was held in the eleven member states that joined the euro in January 1999, even though (or perhaps precisely because!) there was evidence of substantial opposition in some states.

The referendums that have been held are as follows.

- In 1972 France held a referendum to ratify the enlargement of the Community. In reality it was designed to boost the legitimacy and status of President Pompidou and produce a public split in the Socialist–Communist opposition. The enlargement was approved.

- In 1972 Denmark, Ireland and Norway held referendums on Community membership after their governments signed Treaties of Accession. The Danes and Irish gave their approval but a majority of Norwegians voted against membership and Norway withdrew its application.
- In 1975 a referendum was held in the United Kingdom on continued Community membership following the renegotiation of UK membership terms at the Heads of Government meeting in Dublin. The real purpose of the referendum was to settle a split in the Labour Cabinet on the principle of EC membership. Continued membership was approved.
- In 1986 Denmark held a referendum on the ratification of the SEA. This was brought about after the Folketing had rejected the Act, nominally on the ground that it undermined national sovereignty, but partly because those on the Left thought rejection would force an election that they might win. The Conservative Prime Minister, Poul Schlüter, outmanoeuvred them by calling a referendum rather than an election. The SEA was ratified.
- In 1987, in circumstances described above, Ireland held, and approved, a referendum on the ratification of the SEA.
- In 1989, on the same day as the EP elections, a referendum was held in Italy on whether the European Community 'should be transformed into an effective Union'. The referendum, which resulted in a large 'yes' vote, was initiated by senators and deputies in the European Federalist Movement and was designed to reinforce the authority of Italian ministers and MEPs in giving the process of European integration a push.
- In 1992–3 there were four referendums on the ratification of the Maastricht Treaty: in June 1992 the Danes narrowly voted, by 50.7 per cent to 49.3 per cent, to reject the Treaty; also in June 1992 the Irish voted by a large majority, 69 per cent to 31 per cent, to endorse the Treaty; in September 1992 – in a referendum that had been called by President Mitterrand in the immediate aftermath of the Danish vote and which he had anticipated would boost his authority by giving a ringing endorsement to the TEU – the Treaty was only just approved, by 51 per cent to 49 per cent; and in a second Danish referendum, in May 1993, the Danes voted to approve the Treaty by 57 per cent to 43 per cent.
- In 1994 referendums were held in the four EFTA countries whose governments had negotiated accession terms with the EU: in June the Austrians voted by 66 per cent to 34 per cent in favour; in October the Finns voted by 57 per cent to 43 per cent in favour; in November the Swedes voted by 52 per cent to 47 per cent in favour; and, also in November, the Norwegians – repeating what they had done in 1972 – voted by 52 per cent to 48 per cent to reject membership.

- In 1998 there were two referendums on the ratification of the Amsterdam Treaty. In May the Irish supported ratification by 62 per cent to 38 per cent (the lowest 'yes' vote for an EU referendum in Ireland), and in June the Danes gave their approval by 55 per cent to 45 per cent.

Apart from the membership referendums, the referendums that have had the most impact on the European integration process were those held in Denmark and France in 1992 on the Maastricht Treaty. At a general level they drew attention to how European integration is essentially an elite-driven process and emphasised that it is important for decision-makers not to get too out of step with public opinion. In recognition of this, the rhetoric of supporters of European integration tended to be more tempered from mid 1992, decision-makers moved more cautiously for a while, and much came to be made by all concerned of the merits of subsidiarity, transparency, and decentralisation. At a more specific level, at the 1992 Edinburgh summit Denmark was given, as an inducement to approve the Maastricht Treaty, opt-outs from EMU and from the projected common defence policy.

In contrast with the only occasional and localised opportunities for participation offered by referendums, the elections to the EP are regular and Europe-wide (see Chapter 9 for details). Some observers see these elections as providing the EU with a democratic base and, through the involvement of political parties and the election of MEPs, serving to link the peoples of the EU with EU processes. This view, however, must be counterbalanced by recognition of the fact that, since the elections are not in practice contested by European parties standing on European issues, but are more like second-order national elections, they can hardly be regarded as occasions when the populace indicate their European policy preferences. The fact that voter turnout is, in most cases, low by national standards, raises further doubts about the participatory and democratic impact of the elections.

Another way in which public opinion can exert an influence on EU affairs is via national elections, since most important EU decisions are taken by the elected representatives of the member states in the Council of Ministers. This influence, however, is indirect in the sense that it is two or three stages removed, with voters in national elections electing legislatures, from which governments are formed, which send representatives to Council meetings. It is also somewhat tangential, in the sense that in national elections voters are not overly concerned with 'European issues' or with the candidates' competence in dealing with European matters:

beyond some limited attention by far right and nationalist parties because of their generally 'anti-Europe' stance, there is not much evidence of 'Europe' as such being an issue, or of it swaying many votes.

Public opinion towards the EU and its policies is closely and extensively monitored, both at the EU level through regular Commission-sponsored *Eurobarometer* polls and at national levels through countless polls conducted on behalf of governments, research agencies, and the media. In broad terms it can be said that this ongoing trawling of public opinion reveals three main sets of findings. First, across the EU as a whole around one-third of citizens strongly support European integration, just over one half are ranged between ambivalence and cautious support, and under ten per cent are strongly opposed. Second, there are variations between countries, with Denmark, Sweden and the UK tending to show the lowest levels of support on most indicators, and Italy, Ireland and Spain being amongst the highest. Third, support usually dips when citizens are asked whether they would like further integration in particular issue areas, such as taxation or defence. As McCormick (1999a) argues, there are probably a number of reasons why there is less enthusiasm about the EU becoming more involved in such policies: the issues are complex, the implications often seem to be threatening, parts of the media are frequently hostile, and it can look like (and indeed can be) another example of political elites trying to force unwanted integration.

The extent to which governments respond to public opinion depends very much on their own ideological and policy preferences, their perception of the importance and durability of issues, and the time remaining until the next election. The existence of, for example, less than enthusiastic support for European integration amongst a sizeable proportion of national electorates may both restrain and encourage politicians depending on their viewpoint, but there certainly is no automatic relationship between what the people think about EU matters and what governments do. The UK Conservative government, for example, made no move to withdraw from the Community in the early 1980s even though a majority of the British population thought it should, and it did not weaken its opposition in the 1990s to the Social Charter even though polls suggested that the Charter was supported by about two-thirds of the British people. Similarly, in the late 1990s the German government did not weaken in its resolve to take Germany into the single currency even though polls showed that a majority of Germans were opposed to the deutschmark being subsumed within the euro.

That said, if an issue is generally accepted as constituting a national interest, or at least commands strong domestic support, then governments of whatever political persuasion are likely to pursue it in the Council. Even if they themselves do not wish to be too rigid, they may well be forced, by electoral considerations and domestic pressures, to strike postures and make a public display of not being pushed around. For example, Irish and French governments invariably favour generous settlements for farmers, Danish and German governments press for strict environmental controls, and Greek and Spanish governments argue for increased structural operations to enable them to modernise their economies.

Political parties

Political parties normally wish to exercise power, which in liberal democratic states means they must be able to command popular support. This in turn means they must be able to articulate and aggregate national opinions and interests. At the same time, parties are not normally content simply to act as mirror images of the popular will. Drawing on their traditions, and guided by leaders and activists, they also seek to direct society by mobilising support behind preferred ideological/policy positions. Judgements thus have to be made about the balance to be struck between 'reflecting' society and 'leading' it. Those parties which lean too much towards the latter have little chance of winning elections, although in multi-party systems they may well still find themselves with strong negotiating hands.

Of course, the precise extent to which parties are, on the one hand, reflecting and channelling opinions on particular issues and, on the other, are shaping and determining them is very difficult to judge since, in most instances, the processes are two-way and interrelated. But whatever the exact balance may be between the processes, both are very much in operation in relation to the EU. The experiences of Denmark, Greece and the United Kingdom in the 1980s and early 1990s illustrate this. In each of these countries there was widespread popular scepticism in the early to mid 1980s about Community membership and this found both expression and encouragement at the party political level, with some parties advocating a complete withdrawal from Community membership and others expressing considerable concern about aspects of the implications of membership – especially in relation to sovereignty. As the 'realities' of membership began to seep through, however, both public opinion and party attitudes began to change. So much so that by the early 1990s Greece had become one of the more enthusiastic Community states in terms of public opinion and a 'typical' one in terms of the attitudes of its political parties, whilst Denmark and the United Kingdom were not lagging too far behind the Community average on either count.

Apart from their interactive relationship with the attitudinal climate in which EU processes work, political parties also feed directly into EU decision-making. First, by providing much of the ideological base of the ideas of governments and most, if not all, of the leading personnel of governments, they do much to determine and shape the attitudes, priorities and stances of the member states in the Council. While it is true that many policy positions are barely altered by changes of government, shifts of emphasis do occur and these can be significant, as was clearly demonstrated in 1997 when the replacement of the Conservatives by Labour in Britain resulted in very important changes in both policy and style. Second, even when in domestic opposition political parties can influence government behaviour in the Council because governments do not wish to be accused of being weak or not strongly defending national interests. Third, national political parties are the main contestants in the European elections and their successful candidates become the national representatives in the EP.

Interests

Acting either by themselves or through an appropriate Eurogroup, national sectional and promotional interests have a number of possible avenues available to them to try to influence EU policies and decisions. Some avenues are at the domestic level, such as approaches through fellow national MEPs, government officials, and ministers. Others are at the EU level, such as contacts in the Commission and the EP, or taking a case to the Court of Justice. These avenues were discussed in some detail in Chapter 11.

In very general terms, the most successful national interests tend to fulfil at least one of two conditions. Either they are able to persuade their government that there is little distinction between the interests' aims and national aims. Or they have sufficient power and information resources to persuade at least some EU decision-makers that they ought to be listened to. A major reason why farmers have been so influential is that both of these conditions have applied to them in some countries. In France, Germany, Ireland, and elsewhere this has resulted in Ministries of Agriculture perceiving that a major part of their responsibility in the Council is to act virtually as a spokesman for the farmers.

Concluding remarks

The existence of different and frequently conflicting inputs from member states is the major obstacle in the way of the realisation of a smooth, efficient and decisive EU policy- and decision-making machinery. But it is vital that national views and requirements should be able to be articulated and incorporated into decisions if the EU is to work at all. For ultimately the EU exists to further the interests of those who live in the member states. If the citizens of the states and, more particularly, the political elites in governments and parliaments were to feel that the EU was no longer serving that purpose, then there would be no reason for continued membership. The EU must therefore be responsive to its constituent parts.

However, an interesting question for the future is whether these constituent parts will become increasingly similar with regard to the nature of their inputs into the EU and the way they handle EU business. As has been shown in this and earlier chapters, at present there are significant differences between the member states on both these counts, but convergences are nonetheless apparent. This is particularly the case in respect of policy inputs, but there are also signs of some 'institutional fusion' (Rometsch and Wessels, 1996). Such convergences can be expected to increase as the EU and national levels become increasingly enmeshed.

Stepping Back and Looking Forward

Introduction

Part 4 steps back from the detailed study of European integration and the European Union to consider a number of general issues and matters. It also looks forward to how the integration process and the EU might develop.

Chapter 18 is quite different in character from the previous chapters of the book. It examines conceptual and theoretical tools that have been used to capture and analyse the key features of the integration process, the main organisational characteristics of the EU, and particular aspects of the functioning of the EU.

Chapter 19 provides a conclusion for the book. It does so by placing the EU in its global context, by looking at factors that are likely to affect the EU's future development, and by examining the main challenges facing the EU.

Chapter 18

Conceptualising and Theorising

Conceptualising the European Union
Three key concepts: sovereignty, intergovernmentalism
and supranationalism
Theorising European integration: grand theory
Theorising the functioning of the EU: middle-range theory
Concluding remarks

The previous chapters of this book have been concerned with identifying and analysing the principal features of the evolution and nature of European integration and the European Union. This chapter has much the same focus, but takes a different approach. It does so by moving away from logging and analysing 'the facts' to examining the insights that are provided by conceptual and theoretical perspectives.

Conceptualising, which essentially means thinking about phenomena in abstract terms, and theorising, which means positing general explanations of phenomena, have constituted the base of much academic writing on European integration. There are, it should be said, some who question the value of much of this conceptualising and theorising, with doubts and reservations usually focusing on what are seen to be poor, and potentially misleading, 'matches' between over-simplistic models on the one hand and complex realities on the other. This is, however, a minority view and most EU academic commentators take the general social science position that the development and use of concepts and theories enhances the under-standing of political, economic, and social phenomena.

There are three broad types of conceptual and theoretical work on European integration and the EU.

- There are attempts to conceptualise the organisational nature of the EU. Such conceptualisations, which can be thought of as attempts to determine 'the nature of the beast', are explored in the first two sections of this chapter. The first of these sections examines conceptualisations of the EU as a political system and the second examines three key concepts that are habitually employed when assessing the political character of the EU.
- There are attempts to theorise the general nature of the integration process. Such theorising is not as fashionable today as it once was, but it

is still seen by many scholars as worthwhile, and it certainly marks the point of departure for a great deal of other conceptual and theoretical work. Grand theory, as general integration theory is commonly known, is studied in the third section of the chapter.

- There are attempts to develop conceptual and theoretical approaches to particular aspects of the functioning of the EU, especially policy and decision-making. Operating in the middle range, or as it is sometimes called the meso level, rather than at the general level, this has been a major growth area in scholarly work on the EU in recent years. It is the subject of the fourth section of the chapter.

As will be shown, within each of these three broad types of conceptual and theoretical work there is a wide range of different approaches. An underlying theme of the chapter is that the existence of many approaches is inevitable given the multi-dimensional nature of European integration as a process and the EU as an organisation. The complexities of the process and the organisation are such that different sets of conceptual and theoretical tools are necessary to examine and interpret them.

Before proceeding, two points of caution need to be raised. First, there is considerable overlap and intertwining between the many different dimensions of the conceptual and theoretical ideas that are to be described and analysed below. Although, for ease of presentation, the dimensions are sectionalised in the account that follows, it should be recognised that in practice there is considerable overlap between the sections. Most obviously, most broad theoretical work usually draws heavily on a wide range of more narrowly focused conceptual work. Second, the range of conceptual and theoretical approaches to the study of European integration and the EU is so great that only some of them can be considered here. Attention is necessarily restricted to examining some of the more important approaches and giving a flavour of their varying characters.

Conceptualising the European Union

What type of political organisation/system is the EU? This is a difficult question to answer. It is so for at least four reasons.

First, the EU itself has never sought to describe or define its political character in any clear manner. The closest it has come is in the Common Provisions of the TEU, especially as revised by the Amsterdam Treaty. Article 1 (ex Article A) of the TEU states that 'This Treaty marks a new state in the process of creating an ever closer union among the peoples of Europe, in which decisions are taken as openly as possible and as closely as possible to the citizen'. According to Article 6 (ex Article F), 'The Union is founded on the principles of liberty, democracy, respect for human rights and fundamental freedoms, and the rule of law, principles which are common to the Member States.' The TEU thus tells us something about the political character of the EU, but not much.

Second, as the above quotation from Article 1 of the TEU suggests, the EU is, and always has been, in constant transition. Its character has changed considerably over the years as the integration process has deepened and widened. Its nature has never been settled. For example, its decision-making processes have become progressively more supranational since the mid 1980s, as evidenced by the much greater use of qualified majority voting (qmv) in the Council of Ministers and the growing power of the EP.

Third, the EU is a highly complex, multi-faceted system. This means that there are abundant opportunities for different characteristics of the system to be generated by different focuses of analysis. Is, for example, the focus to be on the EU as an actor or as an arena? If the latter, is the focus to be on its territorial or its sectoral character?

Fourth, in important respects the EU is unique. It is so, for example, in the way it embodies both supranational and intergovernmental features in its system of governance, and in the extent to which it embodies shared policy responsibilities between different levels of government and different nation states. A perfectly reasonable answer to the question 'what type of political organisation/system is the EU?, is thus that it is not of any type – or, at least, of any established type – at all. Rather it is *sui generis* – the only one of its kind.

But recognition of the fact that the EU is in important respects unique, does not mean that attempts should not be made to conceptualise it. The reason for this is that conceptualisation can help to highlight the EU's essential features, and in so doing can draw attention to those features that are distinctive and those that are found elsewhere.

States and intergovernmental organisations

A useful starting point in attempting to conceptualise the EU is to compare it with the most important political unit of the international system, the state, and with the customary way in which states interrelate with one another on a structured basis, the intergovernmental organisation (IGO).

Definitions of the state are many and various. Generally speaking, however, the key characteristics of the state are: *territoriality* – the state is geographically based and bound; *sovereignty* – the state stands above all other associations and groups within its geographical area and its jurisdiction extends to the whole population of the area; *legitimacy* –

the authority of the state is widely recognised, both internally and externally; *monopoly of governance* – the institutions of the state monopolise public decision-making and enforcement.

These four features do not all need to be present in a pure, undiluted and uncontested form for a state to exist. They do, however, need to feature prominently and to constitute the essential bedrock of the system. With the EU there is no doubt that all four features are present, but with the exception of *territoriality* they are so only in a partial and limited way. So, the EU does enjoy some *sovereignty* – as witnessed by the primacy of EU law and the fact that EU jurisdiction applies to the whole EU population – but the reach of that sovereignty is confined to the policy areas where the EU's remit is established. Likewise the EU does command *legitimacy*, but opinion surveys show that its internal authority is somewhat thinly based, whilst its external authority is generally weak beyond the Common Commercial Policy. And as for *monopoly of governance*, far from being in such a position of dominance the EU monopolises governance in only a very few policy areas, and even then it is highly dependent on the member states for policy enforcement. To these 'weaknesses' might be added the very limited development of EU citizenship and the EU's comparatively limited financial resources.

The EU thus falls a long way short of being a state, as statehood is traditionally understood. However, the concept of the state is still of some use in helping to promote an understanding of the nature of the EU. It is so for two reasons. First, as has just been shown, the EU does display some of the traditional characteristics of a state, and the continuing development of the integration process inevitably means that these characteristics will strengthen. Second, the realities of traditional statehood are breaking down in the modern world, most particularly under the pressures of international interdependence. So, for example, no modern state can now be regarded as being fully sovereign in a *de facto* sense, and the EU member states cannot even claim that they are fully sovereign in a *de jure* sense. These changes in the realities of statehood mean there must also be changes in how the state is conceptualised. And in such new conceptualisations – involving, for instance, notions of the regulatory state and the postmodern state – the EU displays, as James Caporaso (1996) has argued, many state-like features.

Turning to IGOs, these are organisations in which representatives of national governments come together to cooperate on a voluntary basis for reasons of mutual benefit. IGOs have very little if any decision-making autonomy and cannot enforce their will on reluctant member states. Amongst the best known examples of IGOs are the UN, the OECD, NATO, the OSCE and the Council of Europe.

The differences between the EU and IGOs are striking:

- The EU has a much more developed and complex institutional structure than is found in IGOs. The standard pattern of advanced IGOs – permanent secretariats and attached delegations – is perhaps, in a much grander and more elaborated form, replicated in the EU with the Commission and the Permanent Representations, but to these are added many other features. Among the more obvious of such features are the regular and frequent meetings at the very highest political levels between representatives of the governments of the member states; the constant and many varied forms of contact between national officials; the Court of Justice; and the EP – the only directly elected multi-state assembly in the world.
- No IGO has anything like the policy responsibilities of the EU. In terms of breadth, few significant policy areas have completely escaped the EU's attention. In terms of depth, the pattern varies, but in many important areas, such as external trade, agriculture, and competition policy, key initiating and decision-making powers have been transferred from the member states to the EU authorities.
- The EU has progressed far beyond the intergovernmental nature of IGOs to incorporate many supranational characteristics into its structure and operation. The nature of the balance within the EU between intergovernmentalism and supranationalism will be examined later in the chapter.

The EU may thus be thought of as being, in important respects, less than a state but much more than an IGO. Are there, therefore, other conceptualisations that come closer to capturing the essence of the EU?

Three of the more commonly used conceptualisations of the EU are now explored.

Federalism

Interpretations of the nature of federalism vary. Not surprisingly, perhaps, when systems as diverse as Germany, India, Switzerland and the United States all describe themselves as federal.

Different interpretations within the EU of the nature of federalism were no more clearly demonstrated than in the run-up to the 1991 Maastricht summit, when the UK government became embroiled in a sharp clash with the governments of the other member states over whether there should be a reference in the TEU to the EU 'evolving in a federal direction'. The clash centred in large part on different understandings of what 'federal' entails and implies, with the UK government giving the word a much more centralist spin than other governments. Indeed, the solution that was eventually agreed upon – to remove the offending phrase and replace it with a statement that the Treaty 'marks a new stage in the process of creating an ever closer union among the peoples of Europe' – seemed to many EU governments far more centralist in tone than did the original formulation.

Academic commentators too have not been in complete accord on the precise nature of federal systems. In broad terms, however, most would regard the key characteristics of such systems as being as follows:

- Power is divided between central decision-making institutions on the one hand and regional decision-making institutions on the other.
- The nature of this division of power is specified in and is protected by constitutional documents. Disputes over the division are settled by a supreme judicial authority.
- The division of power between the central and regional levels is balanced in the sense that both have responsibilities – although not necessarily wholly exclusive responsibilities – for important spheres of public policy.
- Whilst the policy content of the division of power can vary, some policy areas are primarily the responsibility of the central level because they are concerned with the identity, coherence, and protection of the system as a whole. Such policy areas normally include foreign affairs, security and defence, management of the (single) currency, and specification and protection of citizens' rights – or at least the more important of these rights.

In applying the federal model to the EU it is readily apparent that the EU does display some federal traits:

- Power *is* divided between central decision-making institutions (the Commission, the Council, the EP and so on), and regional decision-making institutions (the governing authorities in the member states).
- The nature of the division *is* specified in constitutional documents (the treaties) and there *is* a supreme judicial authority (the ECJ) with the authority to adjudicate in the event of disputes over the division.
- Both levels *do* have important powers and responsibilities for public policy – with those of the central level appertaining particularly, but by no means exclusively, to the economic sphere.

At the same time, however, it is also clear that in some respects the EU falls short of the federal model:

- Although power is divided between the central level and the regional level, some of the responsibilities that lie at the centre are heavily dependent on regional acquiescence if they are to be exercised. This is most obviously the case where the unanimity rule applies in the Council, for example for decisions on constitutional reform, enlargement, and fiscal measures.
- The policy balance is still tilted towards the member states. The degree of this is much less than it was before the 'relaunch' of the Community in the mid 1980s, but for all but market-related policies the member states are still mostly in control of public decision-making. This is reflected in the fact that policy areas that involve heavy public expenditure – such as education, health, social welfare, and defence – are still essentially national policies, and the control of financial resources still lies overwhelmingly with the member states.
- Those policy spheres which in federal systems are normally thought of as being the responsibility of the central authorities, in the EU are primarily national responsibilities. Foreign affairs, security and defence, and citizenship rights are being developed at the EU level, but so far only to a limited degree and on a largely intergovernmental basis. Currency control is the most obvious exception to this, though of course not all member states are members of the single currency system.

These EU characteristics combine to suggest a system that may not fully embrace all the traits of the classical federal system, but is not as far removed from the federal model as is usually supposed (see Sbragia, 1992, for a supporting argument along these lines). This might lead one to agree with Warleigh (1998), who suggests that the most appropriate way of labelling the EU at present is as a confederation. That is, it is a union of previously sovereign states created by treaty in which supranational institutions exist but whose range of powers fall short of the powers exercised by their counterparts in federal systems.

State-centrism and consociationalism

State-centric models of the EU are advanced by those who take an intergovernmental view of the integration process. As such, they portray the EU as having the following features at its core:

- The system rests primarily on nation states that have come together to cooperate for certain specified purposes.
- The main channels of communication between EU member states are the national governments.

- The national governments control the overall direction and pace of EU decision-making.
- No governments, and therefore no states, are obliged to accept decisions on major issues to which they are opposed.
- Supranational actors such as the Commission and the ECJ do not have significant independent powers in their own right, but function essentially as agents and facilitators of the collective will of the national governments.

From this shared core, state-centric models branch out into a number of different forms, most of which involve some 'softening' of the core's hard edges. Variations occur in respect of such matters as the dynamics of inter-state relations, the nature of the policy role and impact of non-state actors, and the importance that is accorded to national domestic politics.

The last of these variations has produced a conceptualisation of EU policy dynamics as conducted on the basis of a two-level game, in which state-centrism is combined with a domestic politics approach. (See Bulmer, 1983, on this latter approach.) In the two-level game conceptualisation, most famously advanced by Putnam (1988), the governments of member states are involved in EU policy-making at two levels: at the domestic level, where political actors seek to influence the positions adopted by governments, and at the intergovernmental level, where governments negotiate with one another in EU forums.

A much employed variation of the core state-centric model is consociationalism. Originally developed – notably by Arend Lijphart (1969) – to throw light on how some democratic states which are sharply divided internally are able to function in a relatively smooth and stable manner, consociationalism has been championed as a model that can provide valuable insights into central features of the functioning of the EU.

Consociational states are normally portrayed as displaying the following main features:

- There is societal segmentation (which may or may not be geographically demarcated) and there are several politically significant lines of division.
- The various segments are represented in decision-making forums on a proportional basis, though with the possibility of minorities sometimes being over-represented.
- Political elites of the segments dominate decision-making processes. Interactions between these elites are intense and almost constant.
- Decisions are taken on the basis of compromise and consensus. The majoritarian principle, whereby a majority can proceed even if it is opposed by a minority, is not normally employed, especially when major or sensitive issues are involved. Decisional processes are

characterised by bargaining and exchanges, whilst decisional outcomes are marked by compromise and are frequently little more than the lowest common denominator.

- The interactions between the segments, and particularly between the elites of the segments, can be both positive and negative with regards to promoting solidarity: positive in that links are established and community-wide attitudes can be fostered between the segments; negative in that since the very rationale of consociationalism is the preservation of segmented autonomy within a cooperative system, segments may be tempted to over-emphasise their distinctiveness and moves towards over-centralisation may become occasions for resentment and unease within the segments.

Just as there are variations of the core state-centric model, so have the main features of the consociational model been developed and directed by analysts in various ways. In the EU context, the best known of these analysts is Paul Taylor (1991, 1996), who sees the model as extremely valuable in helping to explain the nature of the balance between fragmentation and cooperation/integration in the EU, the mutual dependence between the member states and the collectivity, and the ability – which does not imply inevitability – of the system as a whole both to advance and maintain stability.

At the heart of Taylor's analysis of the EU is the notion of there being a symbiosis – a mutual dependence – between the participating segments of the consociation (the member states) and the collectivity of the consociation (EU structures and frameworks). This symbiosis is seen as enabling many of the costs of fragmentation to be overcome, whilst at the same time preserving, and in some ways even strengthening, the power and authority of *both* the segments and the collectivity.

A particularly important aspect of this last point is the assertion that EU member states do not lose significant power or authority by virtue of their EU membership. Taylor is quite explicit about this:

> the system works not on the basis of what functionalists, or federalists, would call the Community interest, but much more on the basis of the low level consensus among segmented elites identified within consociationalism. There is a strong sense that the Community exists to serve the member states . . . there is no evidence to suggest that common arrangements could not be extended a very long way without necessarily posing any direct challenge to the sovereignty of states (Taylor, 1991, pp. 24–5).

Dimitris Chryssochoou (1994, 1995, 1998), another exponent of the consociational model, also emphasises this point about the resilience of states within the EU and their retention of fundamental sovereignty. For Chryssochoou (1994, p. 48), the EU is a confederal consociation, by which he means a system in which there is 'the merging of distinct politically organised states in some form of union to further common ends without losing either national identity or resigning individual sovereignty'. The internal mechanisms of the EU – which are seen as being largely under the control of state executive elites – are constituted, Chryssochoou suggests, so as to ensure that vital national interests are not 'mystically "subsumed" by the force of common interests in a neofunctionalist fashion' (ibid., p. 55).

The view of Taylor and Chryssochoou that EU membership does not of itself fundamentally undermine the sovereignty of member states is of course widely contested. Some of the contestants suggest that multi-level governance provides a more useful way of conceptualising and modelling the EU.

Multi-level governance

The conceptualisations considered so far are, broadly speaking, located within a comparative perspective. Their concern is whether and to what extent the EU 'matches' established models of governance. However, those who are firmly of the view that the EU is very much *sui generis* – or, as it is sometimes put, $n = 1$ – naturally wish to develop quite new conceptual ideas and models.

In this context, some EU scholars have drawn on the developing political science interest in what is commonly referred to as 'the new governance' and given it a particular emphasis and spin. At the general political science level, viewpoints included in the new governance are that government involves a wide variety of actors and processes beyond the state, the relationships between state and non-state actors have become less hierarchical and more interactive, and the essential 'business' of government is the regulation of public activities rather than the redistribution of resources. As applied to the EU, the new governance perspective 'is that the EU is transforming politics and government at the European and national levels into a system of multi-level, non hierarchical, deliberative and apolitical governance, via a complex web of public/private networks and quasi-autonomous executive agencies, which is primarily concerned with the deregulation and reregulation of the market' (Hix, 1998, p. 54).

Taking just one of these strands of the new governance, much has been heard since the early 1990s of the merits of conceptualising the EU as a system of multi-level governance. Advocates of this conceptualisation usually specifically set themselves against the state-centric model, suggesting that the latter model is too simple in its emphasis on the pre-eminence of state executives as actors and decision-makers. The great importance of national governments is not denied, but the claim that they dominate and control decision-making processes most certainly is.

Following the scheme advanced by Gary Marks, Liesbet Hooghe and Kermit Black (1996), three main characteristics can be seen as lying at the heart of the multi-level governance model of the EU:

- Decision-making competences are deemed to lie with, and be exercised by, not only national governments but also institutions and actors at other levels. The most important of these levels is the EU level, where supranational actors – of which the most important are the Commission, the EP, and the Court of Justice – are identified as exercising an *independent* influence on policy processes and policy outcomes. In many member states subnational levels are also seen as important, with regional and local authorities able to engage in policy activities that are not (wholly) controllable by national governments.
- Collective decision-making by states at the EU level is regarded as involving a significant loss of national sovereignty, and therefore a significant loss of control by national governments. The intergovernmental view that states retain the ultimate decision-making power is rejected, largely on the grounds that '(l)owest common denominator outcomes are available only on a subset of EU decisions, mainly those concerning the scope of integration' (Marks *et al.*, 1996, p. 346).
- Political arenas are viewed as interconnected rather than nested. So, rather than national political activity being confined to the national arena and national inputs into EU decision-making being channelled via state-level actors, a variety of channels and interconnections between different levels of government – supranational, national, and subnational – are seen as both existing and being important. 'The separation between domestic and international politics, which lies at the heart of the state-centric model, is rejected by the multi-level governance model. States are an integral and powerful part of the EU, but they no longer provide the sole interface between supranational and subnational arenas, and they share, rather than monopolize, control over many activities that take place in their respective territories' (ibid., p. 347).

Multi-level governance thus conceives of the EU as a polity, or at least polity in the making, in which power and influence are exercised at multiple levels of government. National state executives are seen as extremely important actors in the EU arena, but the almost semi-monopolistic position that is ascribed to them by many state-centrists is firmly rejected.

Critics of the multi-level governance conceptualisation naturally focus particularly on whether the supranational and subnational levels really do have the power and influence they are claimed to have. Supranational levels are seen by more state-centric observers as being largely subject to state-level controls (mainly through the various organs of the Council), while subnational levels are considered to have little room or potential to make a significant impact on policy outcomes. Is it not the case, multi-level governance critics argue, that in some member states there is no robust subnational level of government, and is it not also the case that there is little evidence of subnational actors exercising much of a policy role beyond the sphere of cohesion policy from which the advocates of multi-level governance draw most of their empirical evidence?

Three key concepts: sovereignty, intergovernmentalism, and supranationalism

As indicated in earlier parts of this book and throughout this chapter, much of the debate amongst practitioners and observers about the nature of the EU has centred on the related concepts of sovereignty, intergovernmentalism, and supranationalism. These concepts therefore merit special attention.

Defining the terms

Sovereignty is an emotive word, associated as it is with notions of power, authority, independence, and the exercise of will. Because of its emotiveness and its associations, it is a word to which several meanings are attached. The most common meaning, and the one which will be employed here, refers to the legal capacity of national decision-makers to take decisions without being subject to external restraints. This is usually called national, or sometimes state, sovereignty.

Intergovernmentalism refers to arrangements whereby nation states, in situations and conditions they can control, cooperate with one another on matters of common interest. The existence of control, which allows all participating states to decide the extent and nature of this cooperation, means that national sovereignty is not directly undermined.

Supranationalism involves states working with one another in a manner that does not allow them to retain complete control over developments. That is, states may be obliged to do things against their preferences and their will because they do not have the power to stop decisions. Supranationalism thus takes inter-state relations beyond cooperation into integration, and involves some loss of national sovereignty.

The intergovernmental/supranational balance in the EU

In the 1960s the governments of five of the Community's then six member states were willing to permit, even to encourage, some movement towards supranationalism. President de Gaulle, however, who wished to preserve 'the indivisible sovereignty of the nation state', was not. In order to emphasise this point, and more particularly to prevent certain supranational developments that were due to be introduced, in 1965 he withdrew France from most of the Community's key decision-making forums. The outcome of the crisis that this occasioned was the 1966 Luxembourg Compromise (see Chapter 7) which, though it had no legal force, had as its effect the general imposition of intergovernmentalism on Community decision-making processes: the powers of the Commission and the EP were contained, and decisions in the Council came customarily to be made – even where the treaties allowed for majority voting – by unanimous agreement.

The first enlargement of the Community in 1973 reinforced intergovernmentalism, bringing in as it did two countries – Denmark and the UK – where there was strong domestic opposition to membership and where supranationalism was viewed with suspicion. The Greek accession in 1981 had a similar effect. International economic uncertainties and recession also encouraged intergovernmentalism, since they forced states to look rather more critically at the distributive consequences of Community policies, produced a temptation to look for national solutions to pressing problems, and resulted in greater caution about the transfer of powers to Community institutions.

However, intergovernmental attachments and pressures were never able, and never have been able, completely to stop the development of supranationalism. The treaties, increasing interdependence, and the logic of the EU itself, have all ensured that national sovereignties have been progressively undermined. Indeed, not only has supranationalism become more embedded, but since the mid 1980s it has been given a considerable boost as most of the states have adopted a much more positive attitude towards its development. They have done so partly because the effects of the delays and the inaction that intergovernmentalism spawns have become more obvious and more damaging, and partly because it has been recognised that as the number of EU member states has grown, over-rigid intergovernmentalism is a greater recipe than ever for stagnation and sclerosis.

The EU thus displays both intergovernmental and supranational characteristics. The principal intergovernmental characteristics are as follows.

- In most of the major areas of public policy – including foreign affairs, defence, fiscal policy, education, health, and justice and home affairs – decisions are still mainly taken at the national level. Each state consults and coordinates with its EU partners on aspects of these policies, and is increasingly subject to constraints as a result of EU membership, but ultimately a state can usually decide for itself what is to be done.
- Virtually all major decisions on the general direction and policy priorities of the EU are taken by Heads of Government in the European Council: that is, in the forum containing the most senior national representatives. Only rarely does the European Council take decisions by majority vote. All of the important decisions on EU legislation need the approval of ministers in the Council of Ministers. Under the TEC some key Council decisions, including those of a constitutional or fiscal nature, must be unanimous. Where qualified majority voting is permissible, attempts are always made to reach a consensus if a state makes it clear that it believes it has important national interests at stake.
- The Commission and the EP, the two most obvious 'supranational political rivals' to the European Council and the Council of Ministers in that their responsibility is to look to the EU as a whole rather than to specific national interests, are restricted in their decision-making powers and cannot impose policies that the representatives of the member states do not want.

Of the supranational characteristics of the EU, the following are particularly important.

- The Commission does much to frame the EU policy agenda. Moreover, though it may have to defer to the European Council and the Council of Ministers where major decisions are involved, it is an extremely important decision-maker in its own right when it comes to secondary and regulatory decision-making. Indeed, in quantitative terms most EU legislation is issued in the name of the Commission.
- In the Council of Ministers, qualified majority voting is now common. This is partly a result of changing norms and expectations, and partly a result of the treaty reforms that have brought about extensions of the policy spheres in which majority voting is permissible.
- The EP may not enjoy the constitutional status and authority of national parliaments, but its influence over EU decision-making is now considerable. This influence has been greatly enhanced by the cooperation and assent procedures created by the SEA, by the co-decision

procedure created by the Maastricht Treaty and extended by the Amsterdam Treaty, and by a range of other powers it has acquired – including the right to confirm the appointment of new Commission Presidents and Colleges.

- The force and status of decision-making outcomes is crucial to EU supranationalism, for clearly the EU could hardly be described as supranational if its decisions had no binding force. Indeed, some do not and are merely advisory and exhortive. But many do, and these constitute EU law. It is a law that constitutes an increasingly prominent part of the legal systems of all member states, that takes precedence over national law should the two conflict, and that, in event of a dispute, finds its final authority not in national courts but in the interpretations of the EU's own Court of Justice.

Both intergovernmentalism and supranationalism are thus important features of the functioning and nature of the EU. This is no more clearly demonstrated than in the influence exercised by the Commission: on the one hand it is an important motor in the European integration process, but on the other it is constrained by the preferences of the governments of the member states. As Mark Pollack has put it in analysing the role of the Commission in terms of principal-agent relationships, 'Supranational autonomy and influence . . . is not a simple binary matter of "obedient servants" or "runaway Eurocracies", but rather varies along a continuum between the two points . . .' (Pollack, 1998, p. 218).

A pooling and sharing of sovereignty?

The EU is quite unique in the extent to which it involves states engaging in *joint* action to formulate *common* policies and make *binding* decisions. As the words 'joint', 'common' and 'binding' imply, the process of working together is resulting in the EU states becoming ever more intermeshed and interdependent. This is no more clearly seen than in the binding effect of many aspects of their relationships and shared activities: binding in the sense that it would not be possible for them to be reversed without creating major constitutional, legal, political and economic difficulties at both the EU and the national level.

Clearly a central aspect of the intermeshing and the interdependence, and one of the principal distinguishing characteristics of the EU, is the way in which the member states have voluntarily surrendered some of their national sovereignty and independence to collective institutions. However, viewed from a broader perspective, the EU is not only the cause of a decline in national powers, but is also a response to decline. This is because much of the rationale of the EU lies in the attempt – an attempt for which there is no international parallel – on the part of the member states to increase their control of, and their strength and influence in, a rapidly changing world. Although all of the states have reservations about, and some have fundamental criticisms of, certain aspects of the EU, each has judged that membership enhances its ability to achieve certain objectives. The precise nature of these objectives varies from state to state, but in virtually all cases the main priorities are the promotion of economic growth and prosperity, the control of economic and financial forces that are not confined to national boundaries, and the strengthening of political influence. Insofar as these objectives are being attained, it can be argued that the diminution in the role of the state and the loss of sovereignty that arises from supranationalism is counterbalanced by the collective strength of the EU as a whole.

Indeed, since international change and developing interdependence has resulted in all of the member states experiencing a considerable *de facto*, if not *de jure*, loss of national sovereignty quite irrespective of the loss that is attributable to EU membership, it can be argued that the discussion about national sovereignty, in the classical sense of the term at least, is no longer very meaningful. Rather should it be recognised that the only way in which medium-sized and small states, such as those which make up the membership of the EU, can retain control of their operating environments is by pooling and sharing their power and their sovereignty.

Theorising European integration: grand theory

Many scholars of European integration have explored ways in which the overall nature of the integration process might be theorised. The purpose of such exploration has been to develop a broad understanding of the factors underlying European integration, and in so doing to facilitate predictions of how integration is likely to proceed.

This search for what is commonly referred to as 'grand' theory – that is, theory which explains the main features of the integration process as a whole – began soon after the European Community was established in the 1950s, with US scholars leading the way. However, after about fifteen years of considerable activity and published output, interest in grand integration theory declined from the mid 1970s as disillusionment set in with what had been and could be achieved by such theory. Furthermore, the EC itself became less interesting, with its seeming retreat into retrenchment and even sclerosis. There followed a lull of ten years or so in which little was published in the sphere of grand integration theory. This lull ended in the mid to late 1980s, when interest was re-stimulated by the 'relaunch' of the integration process through the SEM and SEA in

1985–6, and with the appearance on the academic scene of new scholars who believed that though early grand theory may have had its limitations, the *raison d'être* of grand theory – to further understanding of the general character of European integration – was as valid as ever.

A notable feature of the reawakened interest in grand theory in recent years has been that much of it has centred on debating the respective merits of, and developing more sophisticated versions of, the two theories that dominated the early years of European integration theory: neofunctionalism and intergovernmentalism. Another prominent feature has been the extensive use that has been made of interdependency theory, which is not especially focused on European integration but is widely seen as being of much use in helping to explain the reasons for, and the course of, the European integration process.

This section of the chapter is thus primarily concerned with neofunctionalism, intergovernmentalism, and interdependency.

Neofunctionalism

The foundations of neofunctionalism were laid in the late 1950s and during the 1960s by a number of US academics, of whom the most prominent were Ernst Haas (1958) and Leon Lindberg (1963).

In its classic formulation, neofunctionalism revolves largely around the concept of spillover, which takes two main forms. The first form – functional spillover – arises from the interconnected nature of modern economies, which makes it difficult to confine integration to particular economic sectors. Rather, integration in one sector produces pressures for integration in adjoining and related sectors. The second form – political spillover – largely follows on from economic integration and has a number of dimensions: national elites increasingly turn their attention to supranational levels of activity and decision-making; these elites become favourably disposed towards the integration process and the upgrading of common interests; supranational institutions and non-governmental actors become more influential in the integration process, while nation states and governmental actors become less influential; and the increasing importance of integration generates pressures and demands for political control and accountability at the supranational level.

Early neofunctionalism thus suggested, though it certainly did not regard as inevitable, the progressive development of European integration. Drawing heavily on the experience of the ECSC, which had played such an important part in paving the way for the EEC, integration was seen as promoting further integration. The slowing down of the integration process following the 1965–6 crisis in the EC and the world economic recession of the early 1970s was thus something of a jolt for advocates of neofunctionalism. Far from policy integration proceeding apace and political behaviour and decision-making becoming increasingly supranational in character, policy integration became increasingly halting whilst political behaviour and decision-making remained essentially nationally based and conditioned. As a result, neofunctionalism lost much of its gloss and appeal, not least when its foremost figures – Haas and Lindberg – retreated from it and suggested that future integration theory would need to give greater recognition to, among other things, nationalism and the role of political leadership.

Since the late 1980s, however, as the pace of integration has again picked up, there has been a reassessment and a partial comeback of neofunctionalism. Jeppe Tranholm-Mikkelsen (1991), for example, has argued that much of the 'new dynamism' in Western Europe since the mid 1980s can be explained in neofunctionalist terms, though he also emphasises the importance of factors that were not part of the original neofunctionalist position – such as forceful political actors and changes in the external security environment. His main conclusion is that although neofunctionalism may be dealing only with 'some part of the elephant . . . it appears that those parts are amongst the ones that make the animal move' (ibid., p. 319).

Tranholm-Mikkelsen exemplifies those who argue that although original neofunctionalism may have had its limitations and faults – most notably, being overdeterministic and not giving due allowance to the continuing importance in the European integration process of the (often distinctive) interests of member states and their representatives – it still has, especially when updated and modified, considerable theoretical value. Evidence cited to support neofunctionalism's case relates both to functional and to political spillover. In respect of functional spillover, reference is most commonly made to the SEM, where the original 'requirements' for the completion of the internal market have steadily been expanded to include, amongst other things, the social dimension, the single currency, and a measure of fiscal harmonisation. In respect of political spillover, the great advances in supranational decision-making since the mid 1980s are commonly cited, with 'the motor role' of the Commission, the common use of qualified majority voting in the Council, and the Court's support for much integrationist activity all seen as falling within the neofunctionalist framework. Indeed, with regard to the role of the Court, Burley and Mattli (1993, p. 325) have explicitly argued that 'the legal integration of the Community corresponds remarkably closely to the original neofunctionalist model', and that the ECJ has not only had considerable scope to pursue its own agenda but has frequently done so in a manner that favours integration.

Intergovernmentalism

Intergovernmentalism has its origins in international relations theory, and more particularly the realist tradition within that theory. Put simply, realism is centred on the view that nation states are the key actors in international affairs and the key political relations between states are channelled primarily via national governments. Unlike neofunctionalism, realism does not accord much importance to the influence of supranational or transnational actors and only limited importance to non-governmental actors within states.

As applied to European integration, intergovernmentalism thus explains the direction and pace of the integration process mainly by reference to decisions and actions taken by the governments of European states. There is a recognition that other actors, both within and beyond states, can exercise some influence on developments, but not a crucial, and certainly not a controlling, influence. This focus on states – and the associated perception of states having their own distinctive national interests which they vigorously defend, especially in the spheres of high politics (foreign policy, security and defence) – has resulted in intergovernmentalists tending to emphasise, as Stanley Hoffmann (1966) put it over thirty years ago, 'the logic of diversity' rather than 'the logic of integration'.

For many years Hoffmann was the foremost proponent of this interpretation of European integration, but in recent years Andrew Moravcsik (1991, 1993, 1995, 1998) has established himself as its leading exponent. (Other exponents of forms of intergovernmentalism include Garrett, 1992, 1993, and Grieco, 1995.) Just as Tranholm-Mikkelsen and others have built on early neofunctionalism to develop a more sophisticated theoretical framework, so has Moravcsik performed a similar service for intergovernmentalism. He calls his framework liberal intergovernmentalism.

There are three main components of liberal intergovernmentalism. First, there is an assumption of rational state behaviour, which means that the actions of states are assumed to be based on utilising what are judged to be the most appropriate means of achieving their goals. Second, there is a liberal theory of national preference formation. This draws on a domestic politics approach to explain how state goals can be shaped by domestic pressures and interactions, which in turn are often conditioned by the constraints and opportunities that derive from economic interdependence. Third, there is an intergovernmentalist interpretation of inter-state relations, which emphasises the key role of governments in determining the relations between states and sees the outcome of negotiations between governments as essentially determined by their relative bargaining powers and the advantages that accrue to them by striking agreements.

Because liberal intergovernmentalism advances such a clear and, in important respects, almost uncompromising framework, and because it is seen by many as just not fitting the facts in an era of multiple international actors and complex interdependence between states, it has inevitably attracted criticism. Four criticisms are particularly worth noting.

First, it is suggested that Moravcsik is too selective with his empirical references when seeking to demonstrate the validity of his framework in the EU context. More particularly, he is considered to focus too much on 'historic' decisions and not enough on more commonplace and routine decisions. To over-focus on historic decisions is seen as distortional, since not only are such decisions untypical by their very nature, they also necessarily emphasise the role of national governments since they are channelled via the European Council.

Second, it is argued that liberal intergovernmentalism concentrates too much on the formal and final stages of decision-making and pays too little attention to informal integration and the constraints that such integration imposes on the formal decision-makers. For example, Wincott (1995) argues that the SEM programme and the SEA, which Moravcsik suggests were the outcome of negotiations between national actors, are in important respects better viewed as the formalisation by national governments of what had been happening in practice for some time.

Third, critics argue that insufficient attention is paid to the 'black box' of the state, and more especially to disaggregating the different parts of government. According to Forster (1998, p. 364), this means that liberal intergovernmentalism provides an inadequate account of how governments choose their policy options. 'The formation of objectives, the pursuit of strategies and the final positions adopted are every bit as disorderly and unpredictable as domestic policy-making. Politics is not always a rational process: ideology, belief and symbolism can play as important a role as substance.'

Fourth – and this is probably the most commonly voiced criticism of liberal intergovernmentalism, and indeed of any form of intergovernmentalism – it is said that it grossly understates the influence exercised in the European integration process by supranational actors such as the Commission and the ECJ, and transnational actors such as European firms and interest groups. For example, in a collection of essays edited by Wayne Sandholtz and Alec Stone Sweet (1998), several academic commentators provide evidence of EU supranational bodies seeking to enhance their autonomy and influence and having considerable success in so doing. Moravcsik's portrayal of the Commission as exercising the role of little more than a facilitator in respect of significant decision-making has attracted particular criticism, with numerous empirically-based studies claiming to show that the Commission does exercise an independent and influential decision-making role, be it as – the metaphors abound – an *animateur*, a policy entrepreneur, or a motor force. Such studies do not, it has to be said, convince Moravcsik that the Commission and other supranational actors are doing much more than responding to an agenda set by the governments of the member states. As he puts it '*intergovernmental demand* for policy ideas, not the *supranational supply* of these ideas, is the fundamental exogenous factor driving integration. To a very large extent, the demand for co-operative policies creates its own supply' (Moravcsik, 1995, p. 262, emphasis in original).

Forster (1998, p. 365) has suggested that liberal intergovernmentalism's weaknesses mean that it is 'perhaps best regarded less as a theory of intergovernmental bargaining, than as a pre-theory or analytical framework'. This may be so, but it should not be forgotten that although weaknesses in liberal intergovernmentalism can readily be identified, the approach has considerable strengths. In particular, it provides a reminder of the role of states in the EU and it does so in a much more nuanced and sophisticated manner than did early intergovernmentalism.

Interdependency

Whilst both neofunctionalism and intergovernmentalism recognise that external factors have at times triggered the pace and nature of European integration, both theories are concerned primarily with the internal dynamics of integration. Interdependency, in contrast, has been used by scholars of European integration to place integration in the wider context of growing international interdependence.

Interdependency theory was initially developed in the 1970s, most famously by Robert Keohane and Joseph Nye (1977). Its central thrust when applied to European integration is that the integration process should not be viewed in too narrow a context. Many of the factors that have influenced its development have applied to it alone, but many have not. This is most obviously in the ways in which post Second World War international modernisation in its various forms – including increased levels of wealth, vast increases in world trade, the technological revolution and the transformation of communications – has promoted many different forms of political and economic interdependency. These in turn have produced a transformation in the ways in which different parts of the world relate to and come into contact with one another. For example, there has been a steady increase in the number and variety of international actors – both above and below the level of the nation state – and a corresponding weakening of the dominance of states. An increasing range of methods and channels are used by international actors to pursue their goals, with relationships between governments, for instance, no longer being so controlled by Foreign Offices and Ministries of External Affairs. The range of issues on international agendas has grown, with, in particular, traditional 'high' policy issues (those concerned with security and the defence of the state) being joined by an array of 'low' policy issues (those concerned with the wealth and welfare of citizens). And paralleling the change in the policy content of international agendas there has been a decline, in the Western industrialised world at least, in the use of physical force as a policy instrument – conflicts over trade imbalances and currency exchange rates are not resolved by armed conflict but by bargaining, adjusting and compromising.

Interdependence theory is thus useful in helping to set European integration within the context of the rapid changes that are occurring throughout the international system. This system is becoming, like the EU system itself, increasingly multi-layered and interconnected. Whether the purpose is to regulate international trade, promote the efficient functioning of the international monetary system, set international standards on packaging for the transportation of hazardous material, or control the hunting and killing of whales, states now come together in many different ways, in many different combinations and for many different purposes.

Interdependency theory is distinctive from neofunctionalism and intergovernmentalism in that it emphasises that much of the European integration process is explained by factors that are global in nature, and it emphasises too that many of the systemic features of the EU are found elsewhere in the international system, albeit less intensively. Interdependency is also different from neofunctionalism and intergovernmentalism in that it has been less intensively applied to European integration and partly in consequence is less rigorous and systematic in the explanation it offers. Whilst most of those who have engaged in the theoretical debate on the nature of the integration process have recognised the importance of interdependency, they have tended to do so as part of the framing background rather than as front line causation. Indeed, it is not possible to point to any major scholar who has advanced interdependency as *the* central plank of his or her explanation of the European integration process. As Carole Webb wrote in the early 1980s, 'For most students the concept of interdependence has been used to explain the conditions under which governments and other economic actors have to contemplate some form of collaboration; but unlike the approach of integration theory, it does not necessarily help to define the outcome very precisely' (Webb, 1983, p. 33). Interdependency in the European integration context is thus perhaps best thought of as an approach and/or a perspective rather than as a theory.

The future of integration theory

Social science theories rarely satisfy everyone. Whatever phenomena they are seeking to explain and whatever forms they take, such theories almost invariably attract criticism for being deficient in important respects. Commonly identified deficiencies include focusing on only part of the phenomena under examination, being too general in scope and/or formulation, being excessively time-bound, and being insufficiently empirically grounded.

European integration grand theory has not been exempt from such criticisms. Indeed, it has been especially prone to them given that the European integration process is so complex, so constantly changing, and so capable of being viewed from different angles. But, as with other social science theories, grand integration theories do not lose all value because critics can show them to be less than complete and final in the explanations they offer. Rather, grand theories can be of considerable value in furthering understanding of the integration process by offering particular insights into it, providing partial explanations of it, and promoting further work and thought on it.

Of course, as long as existing theory is seen to be deficient in certain respects there will be attempts to improve upon it. In this context an increasingly important feature of the theoretical debate on European integration is the attempt by many theorists to move beyond what is now widely viewed as the over-narrow and restrictive nature of the jousting between classical intergovernmentalism and classical neofunctionalism.

One aspect of this new theorising is the development of theoretical explanations that, although emerging from one or other of these two schools of thought, are much more complex, sophisticated and nuanced than the theories in their original formulations. Moravcsik is by far the best known of those who are theorising in this way, but there are many others. Another aspect of the new theorising is the attempt to bring together key features of the traditional theories and link them, as appropriate, to relevant parts of other theories. Robert Keohane and Stanley Hoffmann (1991) adopt such an eclectic and synthesising approach in their analysis of the quickened pace of integration, particularly institutional integration, in the mid 1980s. Essentially they argue that neofunctionalism, interdependency, and intergovernmentalism all have something to contribute to the explanation of why the Community was 'relaunched'. Regarding neofunctionalism, '(s)pillover took place not as a functional expansion of tasks but rather in the form of the creation, as a result of enlargement, of incentives for institutional change' (ibid., p. 22).

Regarding interdependence, '(t)he 1992 program was . . . strongly affected by events in the world economy outside of Europe – especially by concern about international competitiveness' (ibid., p. 19). Regarding intergovernmentalism, they consider that the precise timing of the burst of integration was due 'not only to incentives for the world political economy and spillover but also to intergovernmental bargains made possible by convergence of preferences of major European states' (ibid., p. 25).

Janne Matlary (1993) is another who argues that the limitations of traditional models – especially, in her view, the limitations of intergovernmentalism, which she regards as failing to recognise the crucial interaction between EU institutions and member states and also between formal and informal integration processes – make a synthesing approach essential. There seems, she says, to be 'an emerging view that a comprehensive theory of integration must include not only realist assumptions of state behaviour, but also analysis of domestic politics and the role of the different EC institutions' (ibid., p. 376). Stephen George (1994) is less optimistic than Matlary that a comprehensive theory of integration can be developed, but he too is convinced of the need for a model that 'combines the insights' of the intergovernmentalist and neofunctionalist schools.

Searching for points of contact and overlap, perhaps even for a synthesis, between ever more sophisticated intergovernmentalist and neofunctionalist-inspired models is thus likely to be a feature of future integration theory. Whether, however, synthetic theory will ever be able to escape its basic problem, namely that attempts to develop it are almost inevitably drawn back into one of the dominant perspectives, must be doubted. For as Alexander Warleigh (1998, p. 9) has observed, '*rapprochement* of neo-functionalism and neo-realism would effectively deprive both theories of their respective *raison d'être* and guiding principles, a step which neither set of scholars [advocating the theories] can take without emasculating their theory'.

Another likely feature of the future course of integration theory is its placement within the context of wider interdependency and globalisation theory. As Ben Rosamond (1995) has pointed out, such theories should help to establish how integration is occurring in so many different ways in so many parts of the world: at the 'official' level between international, supranational, national, regional and even local institutions of government, but at the 'unofficial' level too as a result of changes in technology, communications, travel patterns and culture.

Michael O'Neill (1996, p. 81) has observed that European integration theory 'has been a constantly shifting dialectic between events as they have unfolded on the ground, and the efforts of scholars to track and accurately explain them . . . the paradigms and the intellectual tension generated by [the theoretical discourse on integration] have helped to map more accurately the actual developments in European integration, and to clarify our understanding of what the process means'. These observations on integration theory to date will doubtless also apply to future theory. In all likelihood, theorising will become more sophisticated and nuanced as new theory builds on previous theory and as the integration process itself continues to unfold. But the essential purpose of grand theory will remain unchanged: to assist understanding and explanation of the integration process.

Theorising the functioning of the EU: middle-range theory

Whereas grand theory looks at the nature of the integration process as a whole, middle-range theory looks at particular aspects of the process. More especially, it normally focuses on aspects of how the EU functions.

In recent years, much scholarly attention has shifted in the direction of middle-range theory. There are two main reasons for this. First, there has been an increasing feeling that grand theory is inherently limited in what it can achieve. It is prone, critics argue, to falling between two stools. On the one hand, if it restricts itself to identifying only major causational factors it inevitably misses, or at least does not adequately recognise, the many different dimensions of the integration process. On the other hand, if it attempts to encompass all the dimensions of integration it becomes too complicated and difficult to operationalise. Better, the argument runs, to be less ambitious and to focus on only parts of the beast, especially the more important parts. Second, as the European integration process has intensified, so has the EU attracted the attention of an increasing number and range of scholars. It used to be the case that most of the European integration scholars who were interested in theorising and conceptualising were steeped in and made extensive use of international relations theory. This has become much less the case in recent years. Many scholars today suggest that European integration should be studied not just through a traditional international relations approach but also, and arguably more so, through other subdisciplines of political science. If it is the case, as many scholars suggest, that the EU has many of the qualities of a state, then does it not follow that approaches that are deemed to be suitable for the study of states might also be suitable for the study of the EU? Those who answer this question in the affirmative have particularly advocated the merits of using comparative politics and policy studies approaches. As Hix (1994) states, they have used these approaches not to follow the international relations approach and examine European *integration*, but rather to examine EU *politics*.

To illustrate these approaches to EU politics, two of the more important will now be considered: new institutionalism and policy networks. Both approaches draw from the range of political science subdisciplines, but especially from comparative politics and policy studies.

New institutionalism

Much has been heard since the late 1980s about the merits of new institutionalism. In essence, new institutionalism has at its core the assertion that institutions matter in determining decisional outcomes. As such, new institutionalism is partly a reaction against behaviouralism, which was so influential in social and political science circles in the 1970s and 1980s, especially in the United States.

In what ways is 'new' institutionalism different from 'old' institutionalism? In general terms the main difference is that whereas old or traditional institutionalism did not go much beyond analysing the formal powers and structures of decision-making institutions, new institutionalism defines institutions in a very broad sense to incorporate a wide range of formal and informal procedures, practices, relationships, customs, and norms. As such, new institutionalism is much more all-embracing and expansive in its concerns and interests.

Beyond a core shared interest in institutions broadly defined, new institutionalism spreads out in different directions. As Hall and Taylor (1996) have noted, there are at least three analytical approaches within new institutionalism: historical institutionalism, rational choice institutionalism, and sociological institutionalism. Among the main concerns of historical institutionalism are the distributions of power that are produced by institutional arrangements, the ways in which these arrangements result in path dependence and unintended consequences, and the relationships between institutions and other factors that shape political activities and outcomes such as economic developments and ideological beliefs. Rational choice institutionalism is especially interested in the extent to which and the ways in which institutions shape, channel, and constrain the rational actions of political actors. And sociological institutionalism particularly focuses on how institutional forms and practices can often be culturally explained.

Most of the new institutionalist work undertaken on the EU has been within the historical institutionalist approach. For example, Bulmer (1994, 1998) and Pierson (1996) have both advanced the merits of this approach for analysing and, as Bulmer puts it, 'capturing', political and policy activity in the increasingly multi-layered system. More specifically, Bulmer has advocated and employed the framework of a 'governance regime' for analysing the EU at the policy-specific or sub-system level.

Policy networks

The policy networks approach can be thought of as an application of new institutionalism as that term is understood in its broadest sense. The approach is used to describe and analyse policy processes and policy outcomes.

Simply put, policy networks are arenas in which decision-makers and interests come together to mediate differences and search for solutions. Policy networks vary in character according to three key variables: the relative stability (or instability) of network memberships; the relative insularity (or permeability) of networks; and the relative strength (or weakness) of resource dependencies (Peterson, 1995, p. 77). From these variables a continuum emerges, 'At one end are tightly integrated policy *communities* in which membership is constant and often hierarchical, external pressures have minimal impact, and actors are highly dependent on each other for resources. At the other are loosely integrated *issue networks*, in which membership is fluid and non hierarchical, the network is easily permeated by external influences, and actors are highly self-reliant' (ibid.).

The EU is seen by those who champion the policy network approach as particularly lending itself to the emergence of such networks. Amongst factors identified as being conducive to policy networks are: the informal nature of much EU policy-making; the multiplicity of interests at EU level that are anxious to have access to policy-makers; the highly technical – almost non-political – nature of much EU policy content; the powerful policy positions held by senior officials, especially in the Commission and especially in the early stages of policy making; and the heavy reliance of officials on outside interests for information and advice about policy content and policy implementation. As Schneider *et al.* (1994, p. 112) state on this last point, 'The highly pluralist pattern exhibited by the EU policy networks is a consequence not only of numerous actors' efforts to influence the European policy process in an early stage of formulation, but also of a deliberate networking strategy employed by the European institutions, especially the Commission'.

The existence, the types, and the influence of networks varies considerably across the policy spectrum. Networks of a policy community type are often found in areas where EU policy is well established, where an organised 'clientele' exists, and where decision-makers benefit from the cooperation of interests. Examples of such policy areas include agriculture and research and development. In contrast, issue networks are more common where EU policy is not well developed, where the policy debate is fluid and shifting, and where such organised interests as do exist have few resources to 'exchange' with decision-makers. Consumer protection policy and much of environmental and social policy are examples of policy areas where issue networks are commonly found.

The usefulness of the policy networks approach is not, it should be said, accepted by all EU analysts. Amongst the reservations that have been expressed are that it cannot deal with the making of major directional decisions and it cannot capture the extreme fluidity and fragmented nature of EU policy processes (see Kassim, 1994, for a critique of the usefulness of policy networks in analysing EU policy processes). There is doubtless something in such criticisms, but they are arguably partly based on misplaced understandings of what advocates of the model claim on its behalf. As Rhodes *et al.* (1996, p. 381) suggest, when arguing that the approach is very helpful in the EU context, ' "Policy networks" is a useful tool for analysing the links between types of governmental units, between levels of government, and between governments and interest groups. It aids understanding of the policy process but it is only one variable in that process'.

Concluding remarks

A wide variety of conceptually and theoretically informed approaches to the understanding and study of European integration and the EU have been explored in this chapter. All have been shown to be subject to criticism and all have had reservations expressed about their usefulness. For example, of the three grand theories that were considered, amongst the central 'charges' laid against neofunctionalism and intergovernmentalism are that both press their side of the case too hard and both disappoint when applied empirically over time, whilst the central weakness of interdependence is seen to be its lack of a regional focus.

But all concepts and theories, and the methodological approaches based on them, should be judged not only on their deficiencies but also on their merits. As has been shown, there is extensive merit in much of the conceptual and theoretical work that has been undertaken on European integration and the EU. There may be no one body of work that has been able to capture and explain all aspects of European integration and the EU reality, but that is only to be expected. After all, as Hix (1998, p. 46) has observed, there is no general theory of American or German government, so why should there be one of the EU? Rather, we should admit, as Wayne

Sandholtz (1996, p. 426) puts it, 'that different kinds of theories are appropriate for different pieces of the EU puzzle'.

This chapter has examined some of these different kinds of theories, and also different kinds of conceptualisations and theoretically and conceptually based methodological approaches. They have been shown to further understanding of European integration and the EU by drawing attention to, and highlighting, key features of processes, structures, contexts, and outcomes.

Chapter 19

Conclusion: Present Realities and Future Prospects

The European Union and the changing nature of the
 international system
The uniqueness of the European Union
The future of the European Union
The EU and the reshaping of Europe

The European Union and the changing nature of the international system

The European Union should not be viewed in too narrow a context. Whilst many of the factors that have influenced its development apply to it alone, many do not. This is most clearly seen in the ways in which modernisation and interdependence, which have been crucial to the creation of many of the central features of the EU, have produced similar effects elsewhere in the international system – albeit usually to a more modest degree. There has, for example, been a steady increase in the number and variety of international actors, and some corresponding weakening in the dominance of states. A growing range of methods and channels are used by international actors to pursue their goals. Relationships between governments are no longer as controlled as they used to be by Foreign Offices and Ministries of External Affairs. The range of issues on international agendas has grown with, in particular, traditional 'high' policy issues – those concerned with security and the defence of the state – being joined by an array of 'low' policy issues – those concerned with the wealth and welfare of citizens. And there has been a decline, in the Western industrialised world at least, in the use of physical force as a policy instrument – conflicts over trade imbalances and currency exchange rates are not resolved by armed conflict but by bargaining, adjusting and compromising.

The EU must, therefore, be set within the context of the rapid changes that are occurring throughout the international system. It is a system that is becoming, like the EU system itself, increasingly multi-layered and interconnected. Whether the purpose is to regulate international trade, promote the efficient functioning of the international monetary system, set international standards on packaging for the transportation of hazardous material, or control the hunting and killing of whales, states now come together in many different ways, in many different combinations and for many different purposes.

The most obvious, and in many respects the most important, way in which states come together is via the creation of international organisations. Countless such organisations – each with different memberships, functions, powers, and structures – have been constituted since the Second World War. By way of illustration, the following are just a few of the more important international organisations that have been, and still are, used by Western European states: global organisations include the United Nations (UN), the International Monetary Fund (IMF), and the World Trade Organisation (WTO); Western-dominated organisations (although their memberships increasingly include non-Western countries) include the Organisation for Economic Cooperation and Development (OECD), the North Atlantic Treaty Organisation (NATO), and Group of Eight (G8) meetings (not perhaps quite officially an organisation, but increasingly structured and increasingly meeting not just at summit level but also at sub-summit levels); Europe-wide organisations include the Council of Europe and the Organisation for Security and Cooperation in Europe (OSCE); and Western European organisations include the Western European Union (WEU), the European Free Trade Association (EFTA), and more specialised organisations such as the European Space Agency and the European Patent Organisation.

Amongst this array of organisations with which Western European states have been and continue to be associated, the EU stands out as particularly important and distinct. Indeed, in many respects it is unique amongst international organisations.

The uniqueness of the European Union

The nature of the EU's uniqueness was explored at length in Chapter 18, but a few key points regarding its uniqueness as compared with other international organisations bear further stressing and development here.

First, the EU has more institutions, more decision-making arrangements, and more policy actors than are found in other international organisations. Regarding the institutions, there are five 'core' institutions – the Commission, the Council of Ministers, the European Council, the European Parliament, and the Court of Justice – and a battery of subsidiary institutions, including the Economic and Social Committee, the Committee of the Regions, and the European Central Bank. Regarding the decision-making arrangements, there are around 25 distinctive procedures laid down in the treaties, many with their own internal variations – no definitive number can be given since any estimate depends on the extent to which variations within main procedures, such as co-decision or CFSP procedures, are counted separately. Regarding the policy actors, in addition to those associated with the EU's own institutions, there are those associated with the member states, non member states, and sectional and promotional interests.

Second, other international organisations do not have so broad a range of policy responsibilities as the EU. Whereas the EU is involved, to at least some degree, in just about every sphere of public policy, other international organisations are normally fairly narrowly focused, being concerned, for example, with trade, monetary stability, or security issues. Where an international organisation's founding treaty allows for a potentially broad policy portfolio – as, for instance, with the UN or the Council of Europe – decision-making mechanisms make it extremely difficult for the potential to be realised.

Third, whereas other international organisations are essentially intergovernmental in their structures and internal processes, the EU is in many important respects supranational. This supranationalism is seen most particularly in the frequent usage of qualified majority voting in the Council of Ministers, in the Commission's wide-ranging executive powers, and in the EP's considerable post-Maastricht and post-Amsterdam legislative powers.

The future of the European Union

Factors affecting prospects

Integration in Europe has not evolved in quite the way, or as quickly, as was envisaged by many of the EC's founders. The expectation that policy interests and responsibilities would grow, with achievements in initially selected sectors leading to developments in other sectors, has been partly borne out, but only up to a point, and certainly not consistently – in the 1970s and early 1980s policy development was extremely sluggish. Similarly, the anticipation that national institutions and political and economic actors would become progressively entwined with one another has been partially realised, but it has also been partially frustrated – not least because of the continuing reluctance of governments to transfer particular responsibilities and powers to the EU institutions. The assumption that the focus of political activities and attentions would switch from national capitals to Europe has happened to an extent, but in many policy areas – particularly those involving heavy government expenditure such as education, health, and social welfare – the national level is still more important than the EU level. And finally, the belief that a

European spirit would emerge, based on shared perceptions of a common interest, has proved to be over-optimistic.

There has, in short, been no semi-automatic movement in an integrationist direction. But if integration has not inevitably and of itself led to greater integration, it has certainly stimulated pressure for greater integration. It has done so, for example, by creating 'client groups' – of which, in the EU context, Eurocrats are not the least prominent – that have strong vested interests in sustaining and extending integration. Integration has also provided an institutional framework into which integrationist pressures, of both an exogenous and an endogenous kind, have been channelled. Among such pressures on the EU today are: the international trade challenge presented by the United States, Japan, and the newly-industrialising countries; the transnational character of problem areas such as the environment and terrorism; and the need to respond to the integration that is occurring outside formal EU processes through developments as diverse as industrial mergers, closer cross-border banking and other financial arrangements, and population movements.

How the EU will respond to these and other pressures will depend on a number of factors, the most important of which are perceptions, support and opposition, and leadership.

The importance of *perceptions* is evidenced by the way in which the prospect of progress is considerably enhanced when all of the member states perceive an initiative to be broadly desirable, or at least regard the costs of not proceeding as being too high. Very frequently, of course, there is no such common perception, especially when new types of development are envisaged and/or initiatives have sovereignty or clear distributional implications.

The extent to which key actors are motivated to *support or oppose* an initiative depends on many things. Perception of merit is obviously central, but this can be offset by other considerations. For example, a government may fiercely resist a proposal in the Council of Ministers not because it regards it as innately unsound, but because acceptance could be electorally damaging or could lead to problems with an important domestic pressure group.

Leadership has long been a weakness of the EU in that there is no strong and central focus of decision-making authority. The Commission, the European Council, and the Council of Ministers are in many ways the key decision-making bodies, but their ability to get things done is subject to limitations. When attempts are made to provide forceful leadership – by, perhaps, an informal coalition of states, by an ambitious Council Presidency, or by a forceful Commission President – there is usually resistance from some quarter.

Perceptions, support, and leadership are of course not static, but are in constant transition. Since the early to mid 1980s they have undergone significant changes, in ways that have facilitated integrationist developments. The factors accounting for the changes are many and varied, and range from the specific, such as the appointment of the highly dynamic Jacques Delors to the Commission Presidency in 1985, to the general, such as the opening up of the Single European Market (SEM) and the related increasing interdependence of international economic and political life. These changes have helped to produce a climate wherein, for example, the European Council and the Commission are both offering bolder policy leadership than they formerly did, and in government circles there is now increased awareness of the need for further integration.

But although there has been a sense of dynamism about the integration process since the mid 1980s, there are still formidable obstacles to further integration. This is no more clearly seen than in the different public positions taken by the governments of the member states on the future shape of the EU. On the one hand, there are those who tend towards a 'maximalist' position, such as the Italians and the Belgians, who are generally enthusiastic about economic, monetary and political union and do not automatically recoil at the prospect of a federal Europe. On the other hand, there are those who are more cautious – most notably the Danes, the Swedes and the British – who tend to prefer cooperation rather than integration and still make much of the importance of preserving national independence and sovereignty.

Of course rhetoric is one thing and actual deeds are another. Statements by national politicians may reveal some of the many different ideas that exist about the future of the EU, but they sometimes also serve to mask them. So, for example, even in the pre-1997 'Eurosceptic years' UK governments did much to facilitate integration by approving the SEA and the Maastricht Treaty, accepting the 1988 Brussels and 1992 Edinburgh summit packages, and strongly supporting the SEM programme and the dismantling of barriers to the free movement of goods, services, capital and labour. At the same time, governments that are highly vocal in their support for integration processes are often quite prepared to drag their feet and create difficulties when specific proposals do not accord with their own preferences or national interests – as, for example, Germany did at the 1997 Amsterdam summit when Chancellor Kohl vetoed extensions to qualified majority voting that other governments were prepared to accept.

Challenges

Of critical importance in determining the future evolution of the EU will be how it handles the many challenges that are facing it. Five challenges are especially important.

Consolidating the euro

The launch of the euro in January 1999, with eleven of the EU's fifteen member states participating, clearly marked a major advance in the integration process. Not only do the participating states now share a single currency, but they have ceded independent control of basic levers of macro-economic and financial policy.

However it will be some time before the euro can be judged a success or otherwise. For there are many key questions about the euro that cannot be answered until troubled times have been faced. The most important of these questions are: will the balance that has been struck between politicians and bankers in respect of Euroland decision-making prove to be stable and acceptable?; will the 'one monetary policy for all' basis of Euroland prove to be too blunt?; what will happen if or when a member state breaks the terms of the Stability and Growth Pact?; and will the terms of the Pact come to be seen as too restrictive if high levels of unemployment persist and/or there is an economic downturn?

Preparing for enlargement

As was shown in Chapter 4, there are currently (early 1999) thirteen membership applications lodged with the European Union: ten from Central and Eastern European Countries (CEECs), plus Cyprus, Malta, and Turkey. Negotiations opened in 1998 on a five plus one basis – that is, with Estonia, Hungary, the Czech Republic, Poland, Slovenia, plus Cyprus. It is probable that other countries will be added to the five plus one group before the next enlargement round is completed, which is likely to be around 2005.

The preparations for enlargement are already well advanced both in the applicant countries and the EU. Much, however, remains to be done.

The particular preparations that are required in the applicant countries naturally vary from case to case. However, the scale of the challenge can be seen in the many 'deficiencies' that, in varying degrees, the CEECs share and must rectify if they are to compete in the internal market and meet the EU's *acquis*. Amongst the main deficiencies of the CEECs are the following: they have relatively low per capita incomes (overall, around 40 per cent of the EU average); most have large agricultural sectors; their industrial structures and plant require modernisation; they have inadequate transport, energy, and telecommunications networks; they are significant environmental polluters; and they have weak administrative structures. These and other problems are being addressed as part of an accession strategy drawn up and agreed in partnership with the EU. But it will take some years for the CEECs to become 'normal' European countries.

In the EU, it is recognised that enlargement requires fundamental reform of EU policies and institutions. This is partly because the next enlargement round will be the largest in EC/EU history, and partly because the nature of the acceding states is such that some policies would be taken beyond breaking point if they were to continue in their existing forms.

As is noted below, and as was shown at some length in Chapters 5, 12, 14 and 15, policy and institutional reforms have been made to meet the challenge of enlargement. However, by no means all of the necessary reforms have yet been made, especially in respect of institutional arrangements.

Policy reform

Policy reform in respect of enlargement has made progress, primarily through the *Agenda 2000* programme. In particular, changes are to be made to the CAP and the structural policies. However, many observers doubt whether the package of *Agenda 2000* measures that was agreed at the March 1999 Berlin summit is sufficiently bold to meet requirements. Aspects of the package – especially the CAP aspects (which were weaker than the Commission's original proposals) – may need to be re-visited.

Beyond policy reform that is being pressed by the requirements of enlargement, other factors are also likely to fuel debate on, and perhaps force the pace of, policy reform in the years to come. It is, for example, likely that internal market and single currency considerations will produce increased pressures for tighter coordination of national macroeconomic policies. The round of World Trade Organisation talks that are scheduled for the early 2000s will oblige – indeed are already obliging – the EU to think about the probable implications for its trade and development policies. And the tensions and upheavals in the Balkans, the war over Kosovo and more generally the security uncertainties on Europe's fringes, will doubtless result in a continuance of deliberations over whether, and if so how, the EU's foreign and security policies should be strengthened.

Institutional reform

Institutional reform of the EU has been extremely troublesome. A key task of the 1996–97 IGC was supposedly to prepare for enlargement by modernising structures that were, in their essentials, much as they had been since the EC was established with six member states in the 1950s. It was recognised that further enlargement meant that the EU would have to respond to the prospect of over twenty members by engaging in rather more root and branch reform than it had in the past. The size of the institutions could not be indefinitely expanded and changes to the working structure and practices of institutions could not be forever restricted to adjustment and trimming.

The IGC only partly met this challenge. There was agreement on a few changes – such as capping the size of the EP and modest extensions to qualified majority voting in the Council – but no agreement was reached on the two 'big' issues raised by the prospect of enlargement: the size of the College of Commissioners and voting strengths in the Council. The bases of an agreement were identified, however, with, as was shown in Chapter 5, provision made for, at the time of the next enlargement, the number of Commissioners to be restricted to one per member state 'in exchange' for the larger member states being given greater voting weight in the Council. Furthermore, provision was also made for 'a comprehensive review' of the composition and functioning of the institutions at least one year before EU membership exceeds twenty.

Since the IGC, debate on institutional reform has been further intensified by the events surrounding the resignation of the College of Commissioners in March 1999. Long-debated questions have been brought into sharper focus and given greater urgency. Amongst these questions are whether Commissioners should be directly accountable to the EP on an individual basis, whether the Commission President should be nominated by the EP rather than the European Council, and whether the relationships between the political and administrative arms of the Commission are sufficiently clear.

Institutional reform is thus very firmly on the EU agenda and from early 1999 preparations began to be made for another IGC to be convened in 2000. This IGC will be much concerned with Amsterdam 'leftovers' – that is to say, it will concentrate much of its attention on the size of the Commission, the weighting of votes in the Council, and further extensions of qmv (even after Amsterdam there are, according to UK Foreign Office estimates, still 72 treaty articles or sub articles where unanimity prevails). Other issues likely to be considered at the IGC include a further strengthening of CFSP structures, the full incorporation of the WEU into the EU, and the drawing up of a charter of citizen's rights.

Managing flexibility

In response to the different requirements and propensities of the member states, the EC/EU has long provided for limited flexibility and diversity in its structures and policies. When 'standard' methods have been judged as inappropriate or over-rigid, inter-state relations have taken other forms. For example, European Political Cooperation was developed from the early 1970s alongside but outside the formal Community structures. The European Monetary System was developed from the late 1970s on a partial membership basis, as was the Schengen System from the mid 1980s. And in the Maastricht Treaty flexibility was given formal treaty status with the creation of the three pillar structure and the identification of EMU and the social dimension as policy areas that could be developed without the participation of the full complement of member states.

Flexibility raises questions about the possible fragmentation of the EU. Such questions have intensified in recent times, particularly as a result of the flexibility provisions in the Amsterdam Treaty, the partial membership basis of the single currency, and the prospect of the EU becoming significantly more heterogeneous in its membership when the CEECs accede. On this last point, the EU will have a population of over 500 million people if all the CEECs eventually accede, and a population of nearly 600 million if they are joined by Turkey.

When thinking about how it is to manage flexibility, the EU may thus have to narrow the base of its *acquis* – that is, the common core that all member states must accept. But how far can it do this without undermining its very essence?

The EU and the reshaping of Europe

The identities and boundaries of Europe, which have always been somewhat imprecise, and indeed shifting, are being re-thought. The countries of Western Europe, which for almost half a century regarded themselves as virtually *being* Europe, have seen their assumptions about the nature of Europe, and about likely scenarios for the future, brought fundamentally into question by the end of the East–West division across the Continent.

As part of the re-thinking about the nature of Europe, a reshaping of Europe is under way. The most obvious aspect of this is the progressive incorporation of Eastern and Central European countries into what were previously Western and Western European settings and arrangements.

In its capacity as by far the most important of Europe's inter-state organisations, the EU clearly has an extremely important part to play in this re-shaping of Europe. It is approaching this task in a proactive manner, but it will need to be extremely careful given the many problems that the re-shaping raises. Most importantly, perhaps, the EU will need to strike a sensitive and appropriate balance between its own needs and requirements on the one hand and those of prospective member states on the other.

Appendix

The Amsterdam Treaty provided for the re-numbering of the contents of the Treaty on European Union and the Treaty Establishing the European Community. The following tables show the pre- and post-Amsterdam numberings.

Tables of Equivalences referred to in Article 12 of the Treaty of Amsterdam

Table A *Treaty on European Union*

Previous numbering	*New numbering*	*Previous numbering*	*New numbering*
TITLE I:	TITLE I	Article J.16	Article 26
Article A	Article 1	Article J.17	Article 27
Article B	Article 2	Article J.18	Article 28
Article C	Article 3	TITLE VI(***)	TITLE VI
Article D	Article 4	Article K.1	Article 29
Article E	Article 5	Article K.2	Article 30
Article F	Article 6	Article K.3	Article 31
Article F.1(*)	Article 7	Article K.4	Article 32
		Article K.5	Article 33
TITLE II	TITLE II	Article K.6	Article 34
Article G	Article 8	Article K.7	Article 35
		Article K.8	Article 36
TITLE III	TITLE III	Article K.9	Article 37
Article H	Article 9	Article K.10	Article 38
		Article K.11	Article 39
TITLE IV	TITLE IV	Article K.12	Article 40
Article I	Article 10	Article K.13	Article 41
		Article K.14	Article 42
TITLE V(***)	TITLE V		
Article J.1	Article 11	TITLE VIa(**)	TITLE VII
Article J.2	Article 12	Article K.15(*)	Article 43
Article J.3	Article 13	Article K.16(*)	Article 44
Article J.4	Article 14	Article K.17(*)	Article 45
Article J.5	Article 15		
Article J.6	Article 16	TITLE VII	TITLE VIII
Article J.7	Article 17	Article L	Article 46
Article J.8	Article 18	Article M	Article 47
Article J.9	Article 19	Article N	Article 48
Article J.10	Article 20	Article O	Article 49
Article J.11	Article 21	Article P	Article 50
Article J.12	Article 22	Article Q	Article 51
Article J.13	Article 23	Article R	Article 52
Article J.14	Article 24	Article S	Article 53
Article J.15	Article 25		

Notes:
(*)   New Article introduced by the Treaty of Amsterdam
(**) New Title introduced by the Treaty of Amsterdam.
(***) Title restructured by the Treaty of Amsterdam.

Table B   *Treaty Establishing the European Community*

Previous numbering	New numbering	Previous numbering	New numbering
PART ONE	PART ONE	Article 15	—
Article 1	Article 1	(repealed)	
Article 2	Article 2	Article 16	—
Article 3	Article 3	(repealed)	
Article 3a	Article 4	Article 17	—
Article 3b	Article 5	(repealed)	
Article 3c*	Article 6		
Article 4	Article 7	SECTION 2	—
Article 4a	Article 8	(deleted)	
Article 4b	Article 9	Article 18	—
Article 5	Article 10	(repealed)	
Article 5a*	Article 11	Article 19	—
Article 6	Article 12	(repealed)	
Article 6a*	Article 13	Article 20	—
Article 7	—	(repealed)	
(repealed)		Article 21	—
Article 7a	Article 14	(repealed)	
Article 7b	—	Article 22	—
(repealed)		(repealed)	
Article 7c	Article 15	Article 23	—
Article 7d*	Article 16	(repealed)	
		Article 24	—
PART TWO	PART TWO	(repealed)	
Article 8	Article 17	Article 25	—
Article 8a	Article 18	(repealed)	
Article 8b	Article 19	Article 26	—
Article 8c	Article 20	(repealed)	
Article 8d	Article 21	Article 27	—
Article 8e	Article 22	(repealed)	
		Article 28	Article 26
PART THREE	PART THREE	Article 29	Article 27
TITLE I	TITLE 1		
Article 9	Article 23	CHAPTER 2	CHAPTER 2
Article 10	Article 24	Article 30	Article 28
Article 11	—	Article 31	—
(repealed)		(repealed)	
		Article 32	—
CHAPTER 1	CHAPTER 1	(repealed)	
SECTION 1	—	Article 33	—
(deleted)		(repealed)	
Article 12	Article 25	Article 34	Article 29
Article 13	—	Article 35	—
(repealed)		(repealed)	
Article 14	—	Article 36	Article 30
(repealed)		Article 37	Article 31

* New Article introduced by the Treaty of Amsterdam

Table B *Treaty Establishing the European Community*

Previous numbering	New numbering	Previous numbering	New numbering
TITLE II	TITLE II	Article 68 (repealed)	—
Article 38	Article 32	Article 69 (repealed)	—
Article 39	Article 33	Article 70 (repealed)	—
Article 40	Article 34	Article 71 (repealed)	—
Article 41	Article 35	Article 72 (repealed)	—
Article 42	Article 36	Article 73 (repealed)	—
Article 43	Article 37	Article 73a (repealed)	—
Article 44 (repealed)	—	Article 73b	Article 56
Article 45 (repealed)	—	Article 73c	Article 57
Article 46	Article 38	Article 73d	Article 58
Article 47 (repealed)	—	Article 73e (repealed)	—
		Article 73f	Article 59
TITLE III	TITLE III	Article 73g	Article 60
CHAPTER 1	CHAPTER 1	Article 73h (repealed)	—
Article 48	Article 39		
Article 49	Article 40	TITLE IIIa(**)	TITLE IV
Article 50	Article 41	Article 73i(*)	Article 61
Article 51	Article 42	Article 73j(*)	Article 62
		Article 73k(*)	Article 63
CHAPTER 2	CHAPTER 2	Article 73l(*)	Article 64
Article 52	Article 43	Article 73m(*)	Article 65
Article 53 (repealed)	—	Article 73n(*)	Article 66
Article 54	Article 44	Article 73o(*)	Article 67
Article 55	Article 45	Article 73p(*)	Article 68
Article 56	Article 46	Article 73q(*)	Article 69
Article 57	Article 47		
Article 58	Article 48	TITLE IV	TITLE V
		Article 74	Article 70
CHAPTER 3	CHAPTER 3	Article 75	Article 71
Article 59	Article 49	Article 76	Article 72
Article 60	Article 50	Article 77	Article 73
Article 61	Article 51	Article 78	Article 74
Article 62 (repealed)	—	Article 79	Article 75
Article 63	Article 52	Article 80	Article 76
Article 64	Article 53	Article 81	Article 77
Article 65	Article 54	Article 82	Article 78
Article 66	Article 55	Article 83	Article 79
		Article 84	Article 80
CHAPTER 4	CHAPTER 4		
Article 67 (repealed)	—		

Notes: (*) New Article introduced by the Treaty of Amsterdam
      (**) New Title introduced by the Treaty of Amsterdam.

Table B   *Treaty Establishing the European Community*

Previous numbering	Previous numbering	Previous numbering	New numbering
TITLE V	TITLE VI	Article 104	Article 101
CHAPTER 1	CHAPTER 1	Article 104a	Article 102
SECTION 1	SECTION 1	Article 104b	Article 103
Article 85	Article 81	Article 104c	Article 104
Article 86	Article 82		
Article 87	Article 83	CHAPTER 2	CHAPTER 2
Article 88	Article 84	Article 105	Article 105
Article 89	Article 85	Article 105a	Article 106
Article 90	Article 86	Article 106	Article 107
		Article 107	Article 108
SECTION 2	—	Article 108	Article 109
(deleted)		Article 108a	Article 110
Article 91	—	Article 109	Article 111
(repealed)			
		CHAPTER 3	CHAPTER 3
SECTION 3	SECTION 2	Article 109a	Article 112
Article 92	Article 87	Article 109b	Article 113
Article 93	Article 88	Article 109c	Article 114
Article 94	Article 89	Article 109d	Article 115
CHAPTER 2	CHAPTER 2	CHAPTER 4	CHAPTER 4
Article 95	Article 90	Article 109e	Article 116
Article 96	Article 91	Article 109f	Article 117
Article 97	—	Article 109g	Article 118
(repealed)		Article 109h	Article 119
Article 98	Article 92	Article 109i	Article 120
Article 99	Article 93	Article 109j	Article 121
		Article 109k	Article 122
CHAPTER 3	CHAPTER 3	Article 109l	Article 123
Article 100	Article 94	Article 109m	Article 124
Article 100a	Article 95		
Article 100b	—	TITLE VIa(**)	TITLE VIII
(repealed)		Article 109n(*)	Article 125
Article 100c	—	Article 109o(*)	Article 126
(repealed)		Article 109p(*)	Article 127
Article 100d	—	Article 109q(*)	Article 128
(repealed)		Article 109r(*)	Article 129
Article 101	Article 96	Article 109s(*)	Article 130
Article 102	Article 97		
		TITLE VII	TITLE IX
TITLE VI	TITLE VII	Article 110	Article 131
CHAPTER 1	CHAPTER 1	Article 111	—
Article 102a	Article 98	(repealed)	
Article 103	Article 99	Article 112	Article 132
Article 103a	Article 100	Article 113	Article 133

Notes:
(*)   New Article introduced by the Treaty of Amsterdam.
(**)   New Title introduced by the Treaty of Amsterdam.

Table B   *Treaty Establishing the European Community*

Previous numbering	New numbering	Previous numbering	New numbering
Article 114 (repealed)	—	TITLE XIII	TITLE XVI
Article 115	Article 134	Article 130	Article 157
		TITLE XIV	TITLE XVII
TITLE VIIa(*)	TITLE X	Article 130a	Article 158
Article 116(**)	Article 135	Article 130b	Article 159
		Article 130c	Article 160
TITLE VIII	TITLE XI	Article 130d	Article 161
CHAPTER 1(***)	CHAPTER 1	Article 130e	Article 162
Article 117	Article 136	TITLE XV	TITLE XVIII
Article 118	Article 137	Article 130f	Article 163
Article 118a	Article 138	Article 130g	Article 164
Article 118b	Article 139	Article 130h	Article 165
Article 118c	Article 140	Article 130i	Article 166
Article 119	Article 141	Article 130j	Article 167
Article 119a	Article 142	Article 130k	Article 168
Article 120	Article 143	Article 130l	Article 169
Article 121	Article 144	Article 130m	Article 170
Article 122	Article 145	Article 130n	Article 171
		Article 130o	Article 172
CHAPTER 2	CHAPTER 2	Article 130p	Article 173
Article 123	Article 146	Article 130q (repealed)	—
Article 124	Article 147		
Article 125	Article 148	TITLE XVI	TITLE XIX
		Article 130r	Article 174
CHAPTER 3	CHAPTER 3	Article 130s	Article 175
Article 126	Article 149	Article 130t	Article 176
Article 127	Article 150		
		TITLE XVII	TITLE XX
TITLE IX	TITLE XII	Article 130u	Article 177
Article 128	Article 151	Article 130v	Article 178
		Article 130w	Article 179
TITLE X	TITLE XIII	Article 130x	Article 180
Article 129	Article 152	Article 130y	Article 181
TITLE XI	TITLE XIV	PART FOUR	PART FOUR
Article 129a	Article 153	Article 131	Article 182
		Article 132	Article 183
TITLE XII	TITLE XV	Article 133	Article 184
Article 129b	Article 154	Article 134	Article 185
Article 129c	Article 155	Article 135	Article 186
Article 129d	Article 156	Article 136	Article 187
		Article 136a	Article 188

Notes:
(*)   New Title introduced by the Treaty of Amsterdam.
(**)   New Article introduced by the Treaty of Amsterdam.
(***)   Chapter 1 restructured by the Treaty of Amsterdam.

Table B   *Treaty Establishing the European Community*

Previous numbering	New numbering	Previous numbering	New numbering
PART FIVE	PART FIVE	Article 166	Article 222
TITLE I	TITLE 1	Article 167	Article 223
CHAPTER 1	CHAPTER 1	Article 168	Article 224
SECTION 1	SECTION 1	Article 168a	Article 225
Article 137	Article 189	Article 169	Article 226
Article 138	Article 190	Article 170	Article 227
Article 138a	Article 191	Article 171	Article 228
Article 138b	Article 192	Article 172	Article 229
Article 138c	Article 193	Article 173	Article 230
Article 138d	Article 194	Article 174	Article 231
Article 138e	Article 195	Article 175	Article 232
Article 139	Article 196	Article 176	Article 233
Article 140	Article 197	Article 177	Article 234
Article 141	Article 198	Article 178	Article 235
Article 142	Article 199	Article 179	Article 236
Article 143	Article 200	Article 180	Article 237
Article 144	Article 201	Article 181	Article 238
		Article 182	Article 239
SECTION 2	SECTION 2	Article 183	Article 240
Article 145	Article 202	Article 184	Article 241
Article 146	Article 203	Article 185	Article 242
Article 147	Article 204	Article 186	Article 243
Article 148	Article 205	Article 187	Article 244
Article 149		Article 188	Article 245
(repealed)	—		
Article 150	Article 206	SECTION 5	SECTION 5
Article 151	Article 207	Article 188a	Article 246
Article 152	Article 208	Article 188b	Article 247
Article 153	Article 209	Article 188c	Article 248
Article 154	Article 210		
		CHAPTER 2	CHAPTER 2
SECTION 3	SECTION 3	Article 189	Article 249
Article 155	Article 211	Article 189a	Article 250
Article 156	Article 212	Article 189b	Article 251
Article 157	Article 213	Article 189c	Article 252
Article 158	Article 214	Article 190	Article 253
Article 159	Article 215	Article 191	Article 254
Article 160	Article 216	Article 191a(*)	Article 255
Article 161	Article 217	Article 192	Article 256
Article 162	Article 218		
Article 163	Article 219	CHAPTER 3	CHAPTER 3
		Article 193	Article 257
SECTION 4	SECTION 4	Article 194	Article 258
Article 164	Article 220	Article 195	Article 259
Article 165	Article 221	Article 196	Article 260
		Article 197	Article 261
		Article 198	Article 262

* New Article introduced by the Treaty of Amsterdam.

Table B *Treaty Establishing the European Community*

Previous numbering	New numbering	Previous numbering	New numbering
CHAPTER 4	CHAPTER 4	Article 220	Article 293
Article 198a	Article 263	Article 221	Article 294
Article 198b	Article 264	Article 222	Article 295
Article 198c	Article 265	Article 223	Article 296
		Article 224	Article 297
CHAPTER 5	CHAPTER 5	Article 225	Article 298
Article 198d	Article 266	Article 226	—
Article 198e	Article 267	(repealed)	
		Article 227	Article 299
TITLE II	TITLE II	Article 228	Article 300
Article 199	Article 268	Article 228a	Article 301
Article 200	—	Article 229	Article 302
(repealed)		Article 230	Article 303
Article 201	Article 269	Article 231	Article 304
Article 201a	Article 270	Article 232	Article 305
Article 202	Article 271	Article 233	Article 306
Article 203	Article 272	Article 234	Article 307
Article 204	Article 273	Article 235	Article 308
Article 205	Article 274	Article 236(*)	Article 309
Article 205a	Article 275	Article 237	—
Article 206	Article 276	(repealed)	
Article 206a	—	Article 238	Article 310
(repealed)		Article 239	Article 311
Article 207	Article 277	Article 240	Article 312
Article 208	Article 278	Article 241	—
Article 209	Article 279	(repealed)	
Article 209a	Article 280	Article 242	—
		(repealed)	
PART SIX	PART SIX	Article 243	—
Article 210	Article 281	(repealed)	
Article 211	Article 282	Article 244	—
Article 212(*)	Article 283	(repealed)	
Article 213	Article 284	Article 245	—
Article 213a(*)	Article 285	(repealed)	
Article 213b(*)	Article 286	Article 246	—
Article 214	Article 287	(repealed)	
Article 215	Article 288		
Article 216	Article 289	FINAL	FINAL
Article 217	Article 290	PROVISIONS	PROVISIONS
Article 218(*)	Article 291	Article 247	Article 313
Article 219	Article 292	Article 248	Article 314

* New Article introduced by the Treaty of Amsterdam.

Source: *Official Journal of the European Communities*, C340/85–91, 10 November 1997.

Chronology of Main Events in the European Integration Process

1947 March Belgium, Luxembourg and the Netherlands agree to establish a customs union. Subsequently an economic union is established in October 1947 and a common customs tariff is introduced in January 1948.

   March France and the United Kingdom sign a military alliance, the Treaty of Dunkirk.

   June General George Marshall, United States Secretary of State, offers US aid for the economic recovery of Europe.

   September Sixteen nations join the European Recovery Programme.

1948 March Brussels Treaty concluded between France, the UK and the Benelux states. The aim is to promote collective defence and improve cooperation in the economic, social and cultural fields.

   April Founding of the Organisation for European Economic Cooperation (OEEC) by sixteen states.

   May A Congress is held in the Hague, attended by many leading supporters of European cooperation and integration. It issues a resolution asserting 'that it is the urgent duty of the nations of Europe to create an economic and political union in order to assure security and social progress'.

1949 April Treaty establishing North Atlantic Treaty Organisation (NATO) signed in Washington by twelve states.

   May Statute of Council of Europe signed in Strasbourg by ten states.

1950 May Robert Schuman, the French Foreign Minister, puts forward his proposals to place French and German coal and steel under a common authority. He declares 'it is no longer the moment for vain words, but for a bold act – a constructive act'.

   October René Pleven, the French Prime Minister, proposes a European Defence Community (EDC).

1951 April European Coal and Steel Community (ECSC) Treaty signed in Paris by six states: Belgium, France, Germany, Italy, Luxembourg and the Netherlands.

| 1952 | May | EDC Treaty signed in Paris by the six ECSC states. |
| | July | ECSC comes into operation. |

| 1954 | August | French National Assembly rejects EDC Treaty. |
| | October | WEU Treaty signed by the six ECSC states plus the UK. |

| 1955 | June | Messina Conference of the Foreign Ministers of the six ECSC states to discuss further European integration. Spaak Committee established to study ways in which a fresh advance towards the building of Europe could be achieved. |

| 1956 | June | Negotiations formally open between the six with a view to creating an Economic Community and an Atomic Energy Community. |

| 1957 | March | The Treaties of Rome signed establishing the European Economic Community (EEC) and the European Atomic Energy Community (Euratom). |

| 1958 | January | EEC and Euratom come into operation. |

| 1959 | January | First EEC tariff cuts and increases in quotas. |

| 1960 | January | European Free Trade Association (EFTA) Convention signed in Stockholm by Austria, Denmark, Norway, Portugal, Sweden, Switzerland and United Kingdom. EFTA comes into force in May 1960. |
| | December | Organisation for Economic Cooperation and Development (OECD) Treaty signed in Paris. OECD replaces OEEC and includes Canada and the United States. |

| 1961 | July | Signing of Association Agreement between Greece and the EEC. Comes into effect November 1962. |
| | July–August | Ireland, Denmark and United Kingdom request membership negotiations with the Community. |

| 1962 | January | Basic features of Common Agricultural Policy (CAP) agreed. |
| | July | Norway requests negotiations on Community membership. |

1963	January	General de Gaulle announces his veto on UK membership.
	January	Signing of Franco-German Treaty of Friendship and Cooperation.
	July	A wide-ranging association agreement is signed between the Community and 18 underdeveloped countries in Africa – the Yaoundé Convention, which enters into force in June 1964.

1964	May	The GATT Kennedy Round of international tariff negotiations opens in Geneva. The Community states participate as a single delegation.
1965	April	Signing of Treaty Establishing a Single Council and a Single Commission of the European Communities (The Merger Treaty).
	July	France begins a boycott of Community institutions to register its opposition to various proposed supranational developments.
1966	January	Foreign Ministers agree to the Luxembourg Compromise. Normal Community processes are resumed.
1967	May	Denmark, Ireland and UK re-apply for Community membership.
	July	1965 Merger Treaty takes effect.
	July	Norway re-applies for Community membership.
	December	The Council of Ministers fails to reach agreement on the re-opening of membership negotiations with the applicant states because of continued French opposition to UK membership.
1968	July	The Customs Union is completed. All internal customs duties and quotas are removed and the common external tariff is established.
1969	July	President Pompidou (who succeeded de Gaulle after his resignation in April) announces he does not oppose UK membership in principle.
	July	Signing of the second Yaoundé Convention. Enters into force in January 1971.
	December	Hague summit agrees on a number of important matters: strengthening the Community institutions, enlargement, establishing an economic and monetary union by 1980, and developing political cooperation (i.e. foreign policy).
1970	April	The financial base of the Community is changed by the Decision of 21 April 1970 on the Replacement of Financial Contributions From Member States by the Communities' Own Resources. The Community's budgetary procedures are regularised and the European Parliament's budgetary powers are increased by the Treaty Amending Certain Budgetary Provisions of the Treaties.
	June	Preferential trade agreement signed between the Community and Spain. Comes into effect in October 1970.

	June	Community opens membership negotiations with Denmark, Ireland, Norway and United Kingdom.
	October	The six accept the Davignon report on political cooperation. This provides the basis for cooperation on foreign policy matters.
1972	January	Negotiations between the Community and the four applicant countries concluded. Signing of treaties of accession.
	May	Irish approve Community accession in a referendum.
	July	Conclusion of Special Relations Agreement between Community and EFTA countries.
	September	Majority vote against Community accession in a referendum in Norway.
	October	Danes approve Community accession in a referendum.
	October	Paris summit. Heads of Government set guidelines for the future, including reaffirmation of the goal of achieving economic and monetary union by 1980.
1973	January	Accession of Denmark, Ireland and United Kingdom to the Community.
	January	Preferential trade agreement between the Community and most EFTA countries comes into effect. Agreements with other EFTA countries come into force later.
1974	December	Paris summit agrees to the principle of direct elections to the EP and to the details of a European Regional Development Fund (ERDF) (the establishment of which had been agreed at the 1972 Paris and 1973 Copenhagen summits). It is also agreed to institutionalise summit meetings by establishing the European Council.
1975	February	Signing of the first Lomé Convention between the Community and 46 underdeveloped countries in Africa, the Caribbean and the Pacific (the ACP states). The Convention replaces and extends the Yaoundé Convention.
	March	First meeting of the European Council in Dublin.
	June	A majority vote in favour of continued Community membership in UK referendum.
	June	Greece applies for Community membership.
	July	Signing of the Treaty Amending Certain Financial Provisions of the Treaties. This strengthens the European Parliament's budgetary powers and also establishes the Court of Auditors.
1976	July	Opening of negotiations on Greek accession to the Community.

1977 March   Portugal applies for Community membership.
     July   Spain applies for Community membership.

1978 October   Community opens accession negotiations with Portugal.

1979 February   Community opens accession negotiations with Spain.
     March   European Monetary System (EMS) (which had been the subject of high-level negotiations for over a year) comes into operation.
     May   Signing of Accession Treaty between Community and Greece.
     June   First direct elections to the EP.
     October   Signing of the second Lomé Convention between the Community and 58 ACP states.
     December   For the first time the EP does not approve the Community budget. As a result the Community has to operate on the basis of 'one-twelfths' from 1 January 1980.

1981 January   Accession of Greece to Community.
     October   Community Foreign Ministers reach agreement on the London Report, which strengthens and extends European Political Cooperation (EPC).

1983 January   Common Fisheries Policy (CFP) agreed.
     June   At the Stuttgart European Council meeting approval is given to a 'Solemn Declaration on European Union'.

1984 January   Free trade area between Community and EFTA established.
     February   The EP approves The Draft Treaty Establishing the European Union.
     June   Second set of direct elections to the EP.
     June   Fontainebleau European Council meeting. Agreement to reduce UK budgetary contributions (which Margaret Thatcher had been demanding since 1979) and agreement to increase Community resources by raising the VAT ceiling from 1 per cent to 1.4 per cent.
     December   Signing of the third Lomé Convention between the Community and 66 ACP countries.
     December   Dublin European Council meeting agrees budgetary discipline measures.

1985 June   Signing of accession treaties between the Community and Spain and Portugal.
     June   The Commission publishes its White Paper Completing the Internal Market.

	June	Milan European Council meeting approves the Commission's White Paper. It also establishes an Intergovernmental Conference to examine various matters, including treaty reform. The decision to establish the Conference is the first time at a summit meeting that a decision is taken by a majority vote.
	December	Luxembourg European Council meeting agrees the principles of the Single European Act (SEA). Amongst other things the Act incorporates various treaty revisions and confirms the objective of completing the internal market by 1992.
1986	January	Accession of Spain and Portugal to Community.
1987	June	Turkey applies for Community membership.
	July	After several months delay caused by ratification problems in Ireland, the SEA comes into force.
1988	February	A special European Council meeting at Brussels agrees to increase and widen the Community's budgetary base. Measures are also agreed to significantly reduce expenditure on the CAP and to double expenditure on the regional and social funds.
	June	The Community and Comecon (the East European trading bloc) sign an agreement enabling the two organisations to recognise each other. As part of the agreement the Comecon states officially recognise, for the first time, the authority of the Community to negotiate on behalf of its member states.
	June	Hanover European Council meeting entrusts to a committee chaired by Jacques Delors the task of studying how the Community might progress to Economic and Monetary Union (EMU).
1989	April	The 'Delors Committee' presents its report (the Delors Report). It outlines a scheme for a three-stage progression to EMU.
	June	Third set of direct elections to the EP.
	June	Madrid European Council meeting agrees that Stage 1 of the programme to bring about EMU will begin on 1 July 1990.
	July	Austria applies for Community membership.
	September	The collapse of communist governments in Eastern Europe. The process 'begins' with the appointment of a non-communist Prime Minister in Poland in September and 'ends' with the overthrow of the Ceausescu regime in Romania in December.

1989 (cont'd)

December	Signing of the fourth Lomé Convention between the Community and 68 ACP countries.
December	Community and USSR sign a ten-year trade and economic cooperation agreement.
December	Commission advises Council of Ministers to reject Turkey's application for Community membership.
December	Strasbourg European Council meeting accepts Social Charter and agrees to establish an Intergovernmental Conference (IGC) on EMU at the end of 1990. Both decisions taken by eleven votes to one, with the United Kingdom dissenting in each case.

1990 April — Special Dublin European Council meeting confirms the Community's commitment to political union.

June — Dublin European Council meeting formally agrees that an IGC on Political Union will be convened.

July — Cyprus and Malta apply for Community membership.

October — Unification of Germany. Territory of former East Germany becomes part of the Community.

October — Special Rome European Council meeting agrees that Stage 2 of EMU will begin on 1 January 1994.

December — The two IGCs on EMU and on Political Union are opened at the Rome summit.

1991 July — Sweden applies for Community membership.

August–December — Break-up of the USSR

December — Maastricht European Council meeting agrees to The Treaty on European Union. The Treaty is based on three pillars: the European Communities, a Common Foreign and Security Policy (CFSP), and Cooperation in the Fields of Justice and Home Affairs (JHA). The European Communities pillar includes the strengthening of Community institutions, the extension of the Community's legal policy competence, and a timetable for the establishment of EMU and a single currency.

December — Association ('Europe') Agreements signed with Czechoslovakia, Hungary, and Poland.

1992 February — Treaty on European Union formally signed at Maastricht by Foreign and Finance Ministers.

March — Finland applies to join the EU.

May — After several months' delay caused by a Court of Justice ruling, the EEA agreement between the EC and EFTA is signed.

May — Switzerland applies to join the EC.

	June	In a referendum the Danish people reject the TEU by 50.7 per cent to 49.3 per cent.
	September	Crisis in the ERM. Sterling and the lira suspend their membership.
	September	In a referendum the French people endorse the TEU by 51 per cent to 49 per cent.
	November	Norway applies to join the EU.
	December	In a referendum the Swiss people vote not to ratify the EEA by 50.3 per cent to 49.7 per cent. Amongst other implications this means that Switzerland's application to join the EU is suspended.
	December	Edinburgh European Council meeting agrees on several key issues, notably: (1) Danish opt-outs from the TEU and any future common defence policy; (2) a financial perspective for 1993–9; and (3) the opening of accession negotiations in early 1993 with Austria, Finland, Sweden and Norway.
1993	February	Accession negotiations open with Austria, Finland, and Sweden.
	April	Accession negotiations open with Norway.
	May	In a second referendum the Danish people vote by 56.8 per cent to 43.2 per cent to ratify the TEU.
	August	Following great turbulence in the currency markets, the bands for all currencies in the ERM, apart from the deutschmark and the guilder, are increased to 15 per cent.
	October	German Constitutional Court ruling enables Germany to become the last member state to ratify the TEU.
	November	TEU enters into force.
	December	Settlement of the GATT Uruguay Round.
1994	January	Second stage of EMU comes into effect.
	January	EEA enters into force.
	March	Committee of the Regions meets for the first time.
	March	Austria, Finland, Sweden, and Norway agree accession terms with the EU.
	April	Hungary and Poland apply for membership of the EU.
	June	Fourth set of direct elections to the EP.
	June	In a referendum on accession to the EU, the Austrian people vote in favour by 66.4 per cent to 33.6 per cent.
	June	Corfu European Council. The UK vetoes Belgian Prime Minister, Jean-Luc Dehaene, as the new Commission President.
	July	Jacques Santer, the Luxembourg Prime Minister, nominated as the new Commission President at a special half-day European Council meeting in Brussels.
	October	Referendum in Finland on EU membership. The people vote in favour by 57 per cent to 43 per cent.

1994 (cont'd)

    November   Referendum in Sweden on EU membership. The people vote in favour by 52.2 per cent to 46.9 per cent.

    November   Referendum in Norway on EU membership. The people reject accession by 52.2 per cent to 47.8 per cent.

1995 January   Austria, Finland and Sweden become EU members.

        January   EP votes to confirm the Santer Commission: 418 votes in favour, 103 against, and 59 abstentions. The Commission is subsequently formally appointed by the representatives of the member states.

        March   Schengen Accord implemented by seven EU member states: Germany, France, Belgium, Luxembourg, the Netherlands, Spain, and Portugal.

        June   Romania and Slovakia apply to join the EU.

        October   Latvia applies to join the EU.

        November   Estonia applies to join the EU.

        December   Lithuania and Bulgaria apply to join the EU.

1996 January   The Czech Republic and Slovenia apply to join the EU.

        March   The IGC provided for in the Maastricht Treaty is formally opened at a special Heads of Government summit in Turin.

        May   The UK government announces a policy of non-cooperation with EU decision-making following a Council of Ministers decision not to agree to a timetable for the lifting of the export ban on UK beef products.

        June   A formula for ending the UK's non-cooperation policy agreed at the Florence European Council.

1997 June   Amsterdam European Council agrees to the Treaty of Amsterdam. The Treaty fails to provide for the institutional change that enlargement will require, but does contain some strengthening of EU institutions and policies.

        July   Commission issues its *Agenda 2000* programme, which contains recommendations on how enlargement to the CEECs should be handled and how EU policies – especially the CAP and the Structural Funds – should be reformed.

        October   Amsterdam Treaty formally signed by EU Foreign Ministers.

1998 March   Accession negotiations formally opened with Hungary, Poland, the Czech Republic, Slovenia, Estonia and Cyprus.

        May   At a special European Council meeting in Brussels it is agreed that eleven states will participate when the euro is launched in 1999: France, Germany, Italy, Belgium, Luxembourg, the Netherlands, Ireland, Spain, Portugal, Finland and Austria.

        May   Denmark and Ireland hold referenda in which the Treaty of Amsterdam is approved.

1999	January	Stage 3 of EMU and the euro come into operation.
	March	The College of Commissioners resigns following the publication of a highly critical report by the Committee of Independent Experts.
	March	At a special European Council meeting in Berlin, the Heads of Government reach agreement on *Agenda 2000* measures. The measures include a financial perspective for 2000–6, and CAP and Structural Fund reforms. It is also agreed to nominate Romano Prodi, the former Italian Prime Minister, to succeed Jacques Santer as Commission President.
	May	Treaty of Amsterdam enters into force.
	May	EP endorses Romano Prodi as Commission President-designate by 392 votes to 72, with 41 abstentions.

Guide to Further Reading

Official European Union sources
Other useful sources
Books

Official European Union sources

The EU issues a vast amount of material in paper and electronic forms. The material ranges in kind from brief information leaflets to weighty policy reports.

A good way of attaining a direct acquaintance of what is available is to browse at a European Documentation Centre (EDC). EDCs receive copies of most of the EU's published documents and are located throughout the member states. Usually they are attached to academic libraries. Another good way of 'getting started' is to access the EU's Europa web site at < http://europa.eu.int >. This web site contains links to a very large number of web pages covering EU institutions, policies and developments.

Clearly a detailed review of EU publications is not possible here. For that, readers should refer to the various guides and catalogues that can be found in all good libraries. What follows is an outline guide to major publications. Virtually all of the publications mentioned are available from the Office for Official Publications of the European Communities (EUR-OP), often in electronic as well as paper form, and/or directly from the appropriate EU institution.

The treaties should naturally be consulted by all those who wish to understand the nature and functioning of the EU. They have been published in several editions by, amongst others, EUR-OP and Sweet & Maxwell. The Treaty of Amsterdam and the consolidated versions of the Treaty on European Union and the Treaty Establishing the European Community can also be found in the *Official Journal of the European Communities*, C340, 10 November 1997.

The *Official Journal of the European Communities (OJ)* is issued on most weekdays and provides an authoritative record of decisions and activities of various kinds. It is divided into three series. The 'L' (Legislation) series is the vehicle for the publication of EU legislation. The 'C' (Information and Notices) series contains a range of information, including appointments to advisory committees, minutes of EP plenary proceedings and resolutions adopted by plenaries, ESC opinions, Court of Auditors reports, cases referred to the Court of Justice and Court judgements, Commission communications and notices, and Commission proposals for Council legislation. The 'S' (Supplement) series, which is only available in CD-ROM and Internet versions, is mainly concerned with public contract and tendering announcements. EP debates are published in *Annex. Debates of the European Parliament*. An index to the 'L' and 'C' series of the *OJ* is available in monthly and annual editions.

The monthly *Bulletin of the European Union* provides a general account of most significant developments. Some of the information contained amounts to a summary of material included in the *OJ* (with appropriate references). Much else is additional: there are, for example, reports – albeit rather brief ones – of Council of Ministers meetings, updates on policy developments, a monitoring of progress in the annual budgetary cycle, and information on initiatives, meetings and agreements in the sphere of external relations.

The General Report on the Activities of the European Union is published annually and provides an excellent summary of both institutional and policy developments. Where necessary it can be supplemented by the annual reports published by most of the institutions.

Information about the annual budget is available in the *Bulletin* and in the *General Report*. The full budget, which runs to about 1800 pages of text, is published in the *OJ* (L series) about one month after it has been approved by the EP. A useful publication is *The Community Budget: the Facts in Figures*, which usually appears on an annual basis.

The most detailed analysis of and information on EU policies is usually to be found in documents produced by the Commission. Leaving aside one-off publications, these appear in three main forms. First, serialised reports are issued on a regular basis and cover just about every aspect of EU affairs. As an indication of the sort of reports that are produced, four might be mentioned: *European Economy* covers economic trends and proposals and is issued quarterly, with monthly supplements; *Social Europe* provides information on the many facets of social and employment policy and is issued three times a year; *Eurobarometer* reports on public opinion in the EU and appears twice a year; and the *Agricultural Situation in the Community* is an annual report. Second, an enormous volume of information is issued by the Statistical Office, on matters ranging from energy consumption patterns to agricultural prices. *Europe in Figures*, which appears every couple of years or so, is a useful general publication. All Statistical Office publications carry the *Eurostat* logo imprint. Third, there are Commission documents (COMDOCS), which principally consist of monitoring reports, policy reviews and, most importantly, proposals for Council and EP and Council legislation.

Useful material stemming from other EU institutions on a regular basis includes: *Reports, Dossiers*, and *Research Documents* of the EP; the monthly *Bulletin of the ESC;* and *Reports of Cases Before the Court*.

Finally, it is worth mentioning that a number of EU publications are available free of charge. Most of these are rather slight and are primarily intended for those who know very little about the EU, but some do go beyond basics and can be used to build up a useful collection. All of the institutions, for example, produce pamphlets or booklets describing how they are organised and what they do.

Other useful sources

The governments of the member states produce a considerable volume of documentation on the EU. The precise nature of this material varies, but it mostly consists of a mixture of 'state of play' reports, reports from relevant parliamentary committees, and information pamphlets/booklets/packs. Because many of the latter are intended to stimulate a greater public awareness of the EU, or are designed to encourage business to take advantage of EU policies, they are often available free of charge.

Several sources contain detailed and regular updating and monitoring of information on the work of the EU. A daily bulletin of events is provided in *Europe* – commonly known as *Agence Europe* – which is published by Agence Internationale D'Information Pour La Presse. *European Report*, published by Europe Information Service, also provides a detailed monitoring of events, in its case on a twice-weekly basis.

European Voice, published by the Economist Group, is an excellent weekly newspaper on the EU.

In most member states the 'quality' press provides a reasonable review of EU affairs. In the United Kingdom the most comprehensive coverage is provided by the *Financial Times*.

Academic articles on the EU are to be found in a number of places. Particularly useful academic journals include the *Journal of Common Market Studies*, the *Journal of European Public Policy*, the *Journal of European Integration*, the *Common Market Law Review* and the *European Law Review*.

A very useful annual review of the EU is edited by G. Edwards and G. Wiessala – *The European Union. Annual Review of Activities* (Blackwell; this also appears as the fifth issue of the *Journal of Common Market Studies*).

Finally, an invaluable updating source of material issued by, and written about, the EU is *European Access,* which is published six times a year by Chadwyck Healey.

Books

The number of books published on the EU is now voluminous. Only a brief indication of what is available is attempted here, with references being confined to books in English and with preference being given to recent publications.

The titles listed are grouped into very broad sections. The boundaries between the sections are far from watertight.

General books on the government and politics of the EU

Dinan (1999), McCormick (1999a), George (1996), and Jones (1996) are all good introductory texts.

Cram, Dinan and Nugent (1999) focuses particularly on recent developments.

Richardson (1996) is valuable for those who are already familiar with 'the basics'.

The historical evolution

Stirk (1996) examines the integration process since 1914 and Urwin (1995) does so from 1945.

It is always helpful to consult primary sources and an easy way of doing this is through readers. The following are all useful: Giustino (1996), Harryvan and van der Harst (1997), Salmon and Nicoll (1997), and Stirk and Weigall (1999).

Memoirs of some of the Founding Fathers merit attention. See especially Monnet (1978) and Marjolin (1989).

Milward (1984, 1992) has written detailed and challenging analyses of the early years of European integration.

On the Maastricht Treaty see Church and Phinnemore (1994) and Duff *et al.* (1994). On the Amsterdam Treaty see Duff (1997).

The institutions and political actors

On the Commission see Edwards and Spence (1997), Cini (1996) and Nugent (1997a). On the Council see Westlake (1995) and Hayes-Renshaw and Wallace (1997). The most comprehensive books on the European Parliament are Corbett, Jacobs and Shackleton (1995), Corbett (1998b), and Westlake (1994). Hix and Lord (1997) examine political parties in the EU. For non-lawyers, amongst the best books on the Court of Justice and EU law are Kennedy (1998), Chalmers (1998), Dehousse (1998), Brown and Kennedy (1995), and Mathijsen (1995). Greenwood (1997) provides a comprehensive review and analysis of interests in the EU.

Policies and policy processes

Peterson and Bomberg (1999) and Wallace and Wallace (1996) both provide excellent overviews of EU policies and policy processes. Cram (1997) and Kassim and Menon (1996) are also very useful. Key journal articles are brought together in Nugent (1997d).

On particular policy areas see in particular: Armstrong and Bulmer (1998) on the Single European Market; Grant (1997) on agriculture; Cini and McGowan (1998) on competition policy; Peterson and Sharp (1998) on technology policy; and Peterson and Sjursen (1998) on external relations.

Laffan (1997) examines the finances of the EU.

Rometsch and Wessels (1996) and Mény, Muller and Quermonne (1996) examine the impact of the EU on member states.

Conceptualising and theorising

Most of the debate on integration theory has been conducted through articles in academic journals. Readers that bring together key writings include O'Neill (1996), Nelsen and Stubb (1998), and Nugent (1997c).

Hix (1999) examines the nature of the EU as a political system.

Recent books focusing on particular conceptualisations and theoretical approaches include Moravcsik (1998) on liberal intergovernmentalism, Chryssochoou (1998) on consociationalism, and Hooghe (1996) on multi-level governance.

Bibliography and References

Allen, D. and M. Smith (1998) 'External Policy Developments', in G. Edwards and G. Wiessala (eds), *The European Union 1997: Annual Review of Activities* (Oxford: Blackwell), pp. 69–91.

Alter, K. J. (1996) 'The European Court's Political Power', *West European Politics*, vol. 19, no. 3, pp. 458–87.

Andersen, S. S. and K. A. Eliassen (1993) *Making Policy in Europe* (London: Sage).

Archer, C. and F. Butler (1997) *The European Community: Structure and Process*, 2nd edn (London: Pinter).

Armstrong, K. and S. Bulmer (1998) *The Governance of the Single European Market* (Manchester: Manchester University Press).

Arter, D. (1993) *The Politics of European Integration in the Twentieth Century* (Aldershot: Dartmouth).

Baker, D. and D. Seawright (1998) *Britain For and Against Europe: British Politics and the Question of European Integration* (Oxford: Oxford University Press).

Bildt, C. (1997) 'The Global Lessons of Bosnia', in C. Bildt *et al.*, *What Global Role for the EU?* (Brussels: Philip Morris Institute for Public Policy Research).

Bretherton, C. and J. Vogler (1999) *The European Union as a Global Actor* (London: Routledge).

Brown, L. N. and T. Kennedy (1995) *Brown and Jacobs: The Court of Justice of the European Communities* (London: Sweet & Maxwell).

Bulmer, S. (1983) 'Domestic Politics and European Community Policy-Making', *Journal of Common Market Studies*, vol. XXI, pp. 349–63.

Bulmer, S. (1994) 'The Governance of the European Union: A New Institutionalist Approach', *Journal of Public Policy*, vol. 13, no. 4, pp. 351–80.

Bulmer, S. (1998) 'New Institutionalism and the Governance of the Single European Market', *Journal of European Public Policy*, vol. 5, no. 3, pp. 365–86.

Bulmer, S. and M. Burch (1998) 'Organising for Europe: Whitehall, the British State and European Union', *Public Administration*, vol. 76, no. 4, pp. 601–28.

Burley, A. M. and W. Mattli (1993) 'Beyond Intergovernmentalism: The Quest for a Comprehensive Framework for the Study of Integration', *Cooperation and Conflict*, vol. 28, pp. 181–208.

Cameron, F. (1998) 'The European Union as a Global Actor: Far From Pushing its Political Weight Around', in C. Rhodes (ed.), *The European Union in the World Community* (London: Lynne Rienner), pp. 19–43.

Caporaso, J. (1996) 'The European Union and Forms of State: Westphalian, Regulatory or Post-Modern?', *Journal of Common Market Studies*, vol. 34, no. 1, pp. 29–52.

Chalmers, D. (1998) *European Union Law. Vol. 1* (Aldershot: Ashgate).

Charlesworth, A. and C. Cullen (1994) *European Community Law* (London: Pitman).

550

Chryssochoou, D. N. (1994) 'Democracy and Symbiosis in the European Union: Towards a Confederal Consortium?', *West European Politics*, vol. 18, pp. 118–36.

Chryssochoou, D. N. (1995) 'European Union and Dynamics of Confederal Consociation: Problems and Prospects for a Democratic Future', *Journal of European Integration*, vol. XVIII, nos. 2–3, pp. 279–305.

Chryssochoou, D. N. (1998) *Democracy in the European Union* (London: Taurus Academic Studies).

Church, C. and D. Phinnemore (1994) *European Union and European Community: A Handbook and Commentary on the Post-Maastricht Treaties* (London: Harvester Wheatsheaf).

Cini, M. (1996) *The European Commission: Leadership, Organisation and Culture in the EU Administration* (Manchester: Manchester University Press).

Cini, M. and L. McGowan (1998) *Competition Policy in the European Union* (Basingstoke: Macmillan).

Clark, J. R. A. and Jones, A. (1999) 'From Policy Insider to Policy Outcast? Comité des Organisations Professionales Agricoles, EU Policymaking, and the EU's Agri-environment Regulation', *Environment and Planning C: Government and Policy*, vol. 17.

Commission (1985) *Completing the Internal Market: White Paper From the Commission to the European Council*, Com. (85) 310 final.

Commission (1992) *From the Single Act to Maastricht and Beyond: The Means to Match Our Ambitions*, Com (92) 2000 final.

Commission (1995) *White Paper: An Energy Policy for the European Union*, Com. (95) 682 final.

Commission (1997a) *Agenda 2000: For a Stronger and Wider Union*, Com. (97) 2000 final. Also available in *Bulletin of the European Union*, supplement 5/97 (Luxembourg: Office for Official Publications of the European Communities).

Commission (1997b) *Communication From the Commission. Towards a New Shipbuilding Policy*, Com. (97) 470 final.

Commission (1998) *General Report on the Activities of the European Union: 1997* (Luxembourg: Office for Official Publications of the European Communities).

Commission (1999) *General Report on the Activities of the European Union: 1998* (Luxembourg: Office for Official Publications of the European Union Communities).

Committee of Independent Experts (1999) *First Report on Allegations Regarding Fraud, Mismanagement and Nepotism in the European Commission* (Brussels: European Parliament), 15 March 1999.

Corbett, R. (1993) *The Treaty of Maastricht: From Conception to Ratification* (London: Longman).

Corbett, R. (1997) 'Governance and Institutional Developments', in N. Nugent (ed.), *The European Union 1996: Annual Review of Activities* (Oxford: Blackwell), pp. 37–51.

Corbett, R. (1998a) 'Governance and Institutions', in G. Edwards and G. Wiessala, *The European Union 1997: Annual Review of Activities* (Oxford: Blackwell), pp. 39–49.

Corbett, R. (1998b) *The European Parliament's Role in Closer EU Integration* (Basingstoke: Macmillan).

Corbett, R., F. Jacobs, and M. Shackleton (1995) *The European Parliament*, 3rd edn (London: Cartermill).

Cram, L. (1997) *Policy-Making in the European Union: Conceptual Lenses and the Integration Process* (London: Routledge).

Cram, L., D. Dinan, and N. Nugent, (eds) (1999) *Developments in the European Union* (Basingstoke: Macmillan).

Dehousse, R. (1998) *The European Court of Justice* (Basingstoke: Macmillan).

Devuyst (1997) 'The Treaty of Amsterdam: An Introductory Analysis', *ECSA Review*, vol. X, no. 3, pp. 6–14.

Dinan, D. (1998) *Encyclopedia of the European Union* (Boulder, CO: Lynne Rienner).

Dinan, D. (1999) *Ever Closer Union. An Introduction to the European Union*, 2nd edn (Basingstoke: Macmillan).

Dosenrode, S. Z. von (1998) 'Denmark: the Testing of a Hesitant Membership', in K. Hanf and B. Soetendorp (eds), *Adapting to European Integration: Small States and the European Union* (London: Longman).

Duff, A. (ed.) (1997) *The Treaty of Amsterdam: Text and Commentary* (London: Sweet & Maxwell).

Duff, A., J. Pinder, and R. Pryce (1994) *Maastricht and Beyond: Building the European Union* (London: Routledge).

Edwards, G. and D. Spence (1997) *The European Commission*, 2nd edn (London: Longman).

El-Agraa, A. M. (1990) *The Economics of the European Community*, 3rd edn (London: Philip Allan).

Ersbøll, N. (1997) 'The Amsterdam Treaty – II', *CFPS Review*, Autumn 1997, pp. 7–12.

European Central Bank (1999) *Organisation of the European System of Central Banks (ESCB)*, < http://www.ecb.int/about/absorg.htm >.

European Communities (1987) 'Interinstitutional Agreement on Budgetary Discipline', *Official Journal*, L185/33, 15 July.

European Council (1989) *Conclusions of the Presidency*, Strasbourg, 8–9 December (Brussels: General Secretariat of the Council).

European Council (1992) *Conclusions of the Presidency*, Lisbon, 26–7 June (Brussels: General Secretariat of the Council).

European Council (1995) *Presidency Conclusions*, Madrid, 15–16 December (Brussels: General Secretariat of the Council).

European Council (1997a) *Presidency Conclusions*, Amsterdam, 16–17 June (Brussels: General Secretariat of the Council).

European Council (1997b) *Presidency Conclusions*, Luxembourg, 12–13 December (Brussels: General Secretariat of the Council).

European Council (1998) *Presidency Conclusions*, Cardiff, 15–16 June (Brussels: General Secretariat of the Council).

European Council (1999) *Presidency Conclusions*, Berlin, 24–25 March (Brussels: General Secretariat of the Council).

European Parliament (1997) *The New Codecision Procedure Following the Treaty of Amsterdam* (Luxembourg: European Paliament Directorate for Research).

European Parliament (1998a) *Progress Report 1 August 1997 to 31 July 1998 on the Delegations to the Conciliation Committee*, Doc EN/PR/341/341981.

European Parliament (1998b) *Rules of Procedure*, 13th edn, (Luxembourg: Office for Official Publications of the European Communities).

Forster, A. (1998) 'Britain and the Negotitation of the Maastricht Treaty: A Critique of Liberal Intergovernmentalism', *Journal of Common Market Studies*, vol. 36, no. 3, pp. 347–68.

Garrett, G. (1992) 'International Cooperation and Institutional Choice: The European Community's Internal Market', *International Organization*, vol. 49, pp. 533–60.

Garrett, G. (1993) 'The Politics of Maastricht', *Economics and Politics*, vol. 5, no. 2, pp. 105–124.

George, S. (ed.) (1992) *Britain and the European Community: the Politics of Semi-Detachment* (Oxford: Clarendon Press).

George, S. (1994) 'Supranational Actors and Domestic Politics: Integration Theory Reconsidered in the Light of the Single European Act and Maastricht', *Sheffield Papers in International Studies*, no. 22 (Department of Politics, University of Sheffield). Also published in Nugent (1997c), pp. 387–408.

George, S. (1996) *Politics and Policy in the European Union,* 3rd edn (Oxford: Oxford University Press).

George, S. (1999) *An Awkward Partner: Britain in the European Union*, 3rd edn (Oxford: Oxford University Press).

Giustino, D. de (1996) *A Reader in European Integration* (London: Longman).

Grant, W. (1997) *The Common Agricultural Policy* (Basingstoke: Macmillan).

Greenwood, J. (1997) *Representing Interests in the European Union* (Basingstoke: Macmillan).

Greenwood, J. (1999) 'The Future of EU Level Interest Representation, *Journal of Communication Management*, vol. 3, no. 3.

Grieco, J. M. (1995) 'The Maastricht Treaty, Economic and Monetary Union and the Neo-realist Research Programme', *Review of International Studies*, vol. 2, pp. 21–40.

Grilli, E. (1993) *The European Community and the Developing Countries* (Cambridge: Cambridge University Press).

Guyomarch, A., H. Machin, and E. Ritchie (1998) *France in the European Union* (Basingstoke: Macmillan).

Haas, E. B. (1958) *The Uniting of Europe: Political, Social and Economic Forces 1950–57,* (Stanford, CA: Stanford University Press).

Hall, P. A. and R. C. R. Taylor (1996) 'Political Science and the Three New Institutionalisms', *Political Studies*, vol. 44, no. 5, pp. 936–57.

Hallstein, W. (1972) *Europe in the Making* (London: Allen & Unwin).

Hanlon, J. (1998) *European Community Law* (London: Sweet & Maxwell).

Harryvan, A. G. and J. van der Harst, (eds) (1997) *Documents on European Union* (Basingstoke, Macmillan).

Hartley, T. C. (1994) *The Foundations of European Community Law*, 3rd edn (Oxford: Clarendon Press).

Hayes-Renshaw, F. and H. Wallace (1995) 'Executive Power in the European Union: The Functions and Limits of the Council of Ministers', *Journal of European Public Policy*, vol. 2, no. 4, pp. 559–82.

Hayes-Renshaw, F. and H. Wallace (1997) *The Council of Ministers* (Basingstoke: Macmillan).

Hix, S. (1994) 'The Study of the European Community: The Challenge to Comparative Politics', *West European Politics*, vol. 17, no. 1, pp. 1–30.

Hix, S. (1996) 'CP, IR and the EU!. A Response to Hurrell and Menon', *West European Politics*, vol. 19, no. 4, pp. 802–4.

Hix, S. (1998) 'The Study of the European Union II: The "New Governance" Agenda and its Rival', *Journal of European Public Policy*, vol. 5, no. 1, pp. 38–65.

Hix, S. (1999) *The Political System of the European Union* (Basingstoke: Macmillan).

Hix, S. and C. Lord (1997) *Political Parties in the European Union* (Basingstoke: Macmillan).

Hoffmann, S. (1966) 'Obstinate or Obsolete: The Fate of the Nation State and the Case of Western Europe', *Daedelus*, vol. 95, pp. 862–915.

Hoffmann, S. (1982) 'Reflection on the Nation State in Western Europe Today', *Journal of Common Market Studies*, vol. 21, nos. 1–2, pp. 21–37.

Hooghe, L. (1996) *Cohesion Policy and European Integration: Building Multi-Level Governance* (Oxford: Oxford University Press).

Hurrell, A. and A. Menon (1996) 'Politics Like Any Other? Comparative Politics, International Relations and the Study of the EC', *Western European Politics*, vol. 19, no. 4, pp. 386–402.

Jenkins, R. (1981) *European Diary 1977–1981*, (London: Collins).

Joll, J. (1990) *Europe Since 1870*, 4th edn (London: Penguin).

Jones, R. A. (1996) *The Politics and Economics of the European Union: An Introductory Text* (Cheltenham: Edward Elgar).

Kassim, H. (1994) 'Policy Networks, Networks and European Union Policy Making: A Sceptical View', *West European Politics*, vol. 17, no. 4, pp. 15–27.

Kassim, H. and A. Menon (1996) *The European Union and National Industrial Policy* (London: Routledge).

Kennedy, T. (1998) *Learning European Law* (London: Sweet & Maxwell).

Keohane, R. O. and S. Hoffman (1991) *The New European Community* (Oxford: Westview Press).

Keohane, R. and J. Nye (1977) *Power and Interdependence: World Politics in Transition*, (Boston, MA.: Little Brown).

Kirchner, E. (1992) *Decision-Making in the European Community: The Council Presidency and European Integration* (Manchester: Manchester University Press).

Laffan, B. (1997) *The Finances of the European Union* (Basingstoke: Macmillan).

Lasok, D. and J. W. Bridge (1994) *Law and Institutions of the European Communities*, 6th edn (London: Butterworths).

Laursen, F. (1998) 'The EU "Neutrals", the CFSP and Defence Policy', TK1 Working Papers on European Integration and Regime Formation, no. 26 (Esberg: South Jutland University Press).

Lenaerts, K. (1991) 'Some Reflections on the Separation of Powers in the EU', *Common Market Law Review*, vol. 28, pp. 11–35.

Lijphart, A. (1969) 'Consociational Democracy', *World Politics*, vol. 21, no. 2, pp. 207–25.

Lindberg, L. N. (1963) *The Political Dynamics of European Economic Integration* (Oxford: Oxford University Press).

Lindberg, L. N. and S. A. Scheingold (1970) *Europe's Would-Be Polity: Patterns of Change in the European Community* (Englewood Cliffs, NJ: Prentice Hall).

Macleod, I., I. D. Hendry and S. Hyett (1996) *The External Relations of the European Communities* (Oxford: Clarendon Press).

Macmullen, A. (1997) 'European Commissioners 1952–1995: National Routes to a European Elite', in Nugent (1997a), pp. 27–48.

Marjolin, R. (1989) *Memoirs 1911–1986* (London: Weidenfeld and Nicolson).

Marks, G., L. Hooghe, and K. Black (1996) 'European Integration From the 1980s: State Centric v Multi-level Governance', *Journal of Common Market Studies*, vol. 34, no. 3, pp. 341–78.

Mathijsen, P. S. R. F. (1995) *A Guide to European Community Law*, 6th edn (London: Sweet & Maxwell).

Matlary, J. H. (1993) 'Beyond Intergovernmentalism: The Quest for a Comprehensive Framework for the Study of Integration', *Cooperation and Conflict*, vol. 28, no. 2, pp. 181–210.

Matlary, J. H. (1997) *Energy Policy in the European Union* (Basingstoke: Macmillan).

Mazey, S. and J. Richardson (1993) *Lobbying in the European Community* (Oxford: Oxford University Press).

McCormick, J. (1999a) *Understanding the European Union: A Concise Introduction* (Basingstoke: Macmillan).

McCormick, J. (1999b) 'Environmental Policy', in L. Cram, D. Dinan and N. Nugent (eds), *Developments in the European Union* (Basingstoke: Macmillan).

Mény, Y., P. Muller, and J–L. Quermonne (1996) *Adjusting to Europe: The Impact of the European Union on National Institutions and Policies* (London: Routledge).

Middlemas, K. (1995) *Orchestrating Europe: The Informal Politics of European Union 1973–1995* (London: Fontana).

Milward, A. S. (1984) *The Reconstruction of Western Europe 1945–51* (London: Methuen).

Milward, A. S. (1992) *The European Rescue of the Nation-State* (London: Routledge).

Monar, J. (1998) 'Justice and Home Affairs', in G. Edwards and G. Wiessela (eds), *The European Union 1997: Annual Review of Activities* (Oxford: Blackwell).

Monnet, J. (1978) *Memoirs* (London: Collins).

Moravcsik, A. (1991) 'Negotiating the Single European Act: National Interests and Conventional Statecraft in the European Community', *International Organization*, vol. 45, no. 1, pp. 19–56.

Moravcsik, A. (1993) 'Preferences and Power in the European Community: A Liberal Intergovernmentalist Approach', *Journal of Common Market Studies*, vol. 31, no. 4, pp. 473–524.

Moravcsik, A. (1995) 'Liberal Intergovernmentalism and Integration: A Rejoinder', *Journal of Common Market Studies*, vol. 33, no. 4, pp. 611–28.

Moravcsik, A. (1998) *The Choice for Europe: Social Purpose and State Power From Messina to Maastricht* (Ithaca, NY: Cornell University Press).

Nelsen, B. and A. C.-G. Stubb (1998) *The European Union: Readings on the Theory and Practice of European Integration*, 2nd edn (Basingstoke: Macmillan).

Neunreither, A. (1999) 'The European Parliament', in L. Cram, D. Dinan and N. Nugent (eds), *Developments in the European Union* (Basingstoke: Macmillan).

Newman, M. (1996) *Democracy, Sovereignty and the European Union* (London: Hurst).

Nicoll, W. and T. C. Salmon (1994) *Understanding the New European Community*, 2nd edn (London: Harvester Wheatsheaf).

Norton, P. (ed.) (1996) *National Parliaments and the European Union* (London: Frank Cass).

Nugent, N. (ed.) (1997a) *At the Heart of the Union: Studies of the European Commission* (Basingstoke: Macmillan).

Nugent, N. (ed.) (1997b) *The European Union 1996: Annual Review of Activities* (Oxford: Blackwell).

Nugent, N. (1997c) *The European Union. Volume I: Perspectives and Theoretical Interpretations* (Aldershot: Dartmouth).

Nugent, N. (1997d) *The European Union. Volume II: Policy Processes* (Aldershot: Dartmouth).

Nugent, N. (1999) 'Decision-Making', in L. Cram, D. Dinan and N. Nugent (eds), *Developments in the European Union* (Basingstoke: Macmillan).

Official Journal of the European Communities (various issues) (Luxembourg: Office for Official Publications of the European Communities, published most working days).

O'Keefe, D. and P. M. Twomey, (eds) (1994) *Legal Issues of the Maastricht Treaty* (London: Chancery).

O'Neill, M. (1996) *The Politics of European Integration: A Reader* (London: Routledge).

Page, E. C. (1997) *People Who Run Europe* (Oxford: Clarendon Press).

Peterson, J. (1995) 'Decision-Making in the EU: Towards a Framework for Analysis', *Journal of European Public Policy*, vol. 2, no. 1, pp. 69–93.

Peterson, J. and E. Bomberg (1999) *Decision-Making in the European Union* (Basingstoke: Macmillan).

Peterson, J. and M. Sharp (1998) *Technology Policy in the European Union* (Basingstoke: Macmillan).

Peterson, J. and H. Sjursen (1998) *A Common Foreign Policy for Europe?* (London: Routledge).

Petite, M. (1998) 'The Treaty of Amsterdam – Contents', Harvard Jean Monnet Working Paper, 2/98 (Faculty of Law, Harvard University).

Piening, C. (1997) *Global Europe: The European Union in World Affairs* (London: Lynne Rienner).

Pierson, P. (1996) 'The Path to European Integration: A Historical Institutionalist Analysis', *Comparative Political Studies*, vol. 29, no. 2, pp. 123–63.

Pollack, M. (1998) 'The Engines of Integration? Supranational Autonomy and Influence in the European Union', in W. Sandholtz and A. Stone Sweet (eds) *European Integration and Supranational Governance* (Oxford: Oxford University Press).

Pollard, S. (1981) *The Integration of the European Economy since 1815* (London: George Allen & Unwin).

Preston, C. (1997) *Enlargement and Integration in the European Union* (London: Routledge).

Putnam, R. D. (1988) 'Diplomacy and Domestic Politics: The Logic of Two-Level Games', *International Organization*, vol. 42, no. 3, pp. 427–60.

Reflection Group's Report (1995) (Brussels: General Secretariat of the Council).

Regelsberger, E., P. de Schoutheete de Tervarent, and W. Wessels, (eds) (1997) *Foreign Policy of the European Union: From EPC to CFSP and Beyond* (Boulder, CO: Lynne Rienner).

Rhodes, R. A. W., I. Bache, and S. George (1996) 'Policy Networks and Policy-Making in the European Union: A Critical Appraisal', in L. Hooghe (ed.), *Cohesion Policy and European Integration: Building Multi-Level Governance* (Oxford: Oxford University Press).

Richardson, J. (ed.) (1996) *European Union: Power and Policy-Making* (London: Routledge).

Robertson, A. H. (1961) *The Council of Europe: Its Structure, Functions and Achievements* (London: Stevens).

Rometsch, D. (1996) 'The Federal Republic of Germany' in D. Rometsch and W. Wessels (eds), *The European Union and Member States* (Manchester: Manchester University Press), pp. 61–104.

Rometsch, D. and W. Wessels (1996) *The European Union and Member States: Towards Institutional Fusion?* (Manchester: Manchester University Press).

Rosamond, B. (1995) 'Understanding European Unity: The Limits of Nation-State-Centric Integration Theory, *The European Legacy*, vol. 1, pp. 291–7.

Ross, G. (1995) *Jacques Delors and European Integration* (Cambridge: Polity Press).

Salmon, T. and W. Nicoll (1997) *Building European Union: A Documentary History and Analysis* (Manchester: Manchester University Press).

Sandholtz, W. (1996) 'Membership Matters: Limits of the Functional Approach to European Institutions', *Journal of Common Market Studies*, vol. 34, no. 3, pp. 403–29.

Sandholtz, W. and A. Stone Sweet, (eds) (1998) *European Integration and Supranational Governance* (Oxford: Oxford University Press).

Sbragia, A. (1992) 'Thinking About the European Future: The Uses of Comparison', in A. Sbragia (ed.), *Euro-Politics: Institutions and Policymaking in the 'New' European Community* (Washington, DC: Brookings Institution).

Schneider, V., G. Dang-Nguyen, and R. Werle (1994) 'Corporate Actor Networks in European Policy-Making: Harmonizing Telecommunications Policy', *Journal of Common Market Studies*, vol. 32, no. 4, pp. 473–98.

Shaw, J. (1996) *European Community Law*, 2nd edn (Basingstoke: Macmillan).

Smith, M. (1996) 'The EU as an International Actor', in J. Richardson (ed.), *European Union: Power and Policy-Making* (London: Routledge), pp. 247–62.

Spinelli, A. (1986) 'Foreword', in J. Lodge (ed), *European Union: The European Community In Search of A Future* (London: Macmillan), pp. xiii–xviii.

Stirk, P. M. R. (1996) *A History of European Integration Since 1914* (London: Pinter).

Stirk, P. and D. Weigall, (eds) (1999) *The Origins and Development of European Integration: A Reader and Commentary* (London: Pinter).

Swann, D. (1992) *The Economics of the Common Market*, 7th edn (London: Penguin).

Taylor, P. (1991) 'The European Community and the State: Assumptions, Theories and Propositions', *Review of International Studies*, vol. 17, pp. 109–25.

Taylor, P. (1996) *The European Union in the 1990s* (Oxford: Oxford University Press).

Teasdale, A. (1995) 'The Luxembourg Compromise', in M. Westlake, *The Council of the European Union* (London: Cartermill), pp. 104–10.

Tranholm-Mikkelsen, J. (1991) 'Neo-functionalism: Obstinate of Obsolete? A Reappraisal in the Light of the New Dynamism of the EC', *Millenium: Journal of International Studies,* vol. 20, pp. 1–22.

'Treaty of Amsterdam, Amending the Treaty on European Union, the Treaties Establishing the European Communities and Certain Related Acts' (1997) in *Official Journal of the European Communities*, C340, 10 November.

'Treaty on European Union, Together with the Complete Text of the Treaty Establishing the European Community' (1992) in *Official Journal of the European Communities,* C244, 31 August.

'Treaty on European Union: Consolidated Version' (1997) in *Official Journal of the European Communities,* C340, 10 November; also in *European Union Consolidated Treaties* (Luxembourg: Office for Official Publications of the European Communities, 1997).

'Treaty Establishing the European Community: Consolidated Version' (1997) in *Official Journal of the European Communities*, C340, 10 November; also in *European Union Consolidated Treaties* (Luxembourg: Office for Official Publications of the European Communities, 1997).

Tsoukalis, L. (1993) *The New European Economy: The Politics and Economics of Integration*, 2nd edn (Oxford: Oxford University Press).

Tugendhat, C. (1986) *Making Sense of Europe* (London: Viking).

Uçarer, E. (1999) 'Cooperation on Justice and Home Affairs Matters', in L. Cram, D. Dinan and N. Nugent (eds), *Developments in the European Union* (Basingstoke: Macmillan).

Urwin, D. W. (1989) *Western Europe Since 1945*, 4th edn (London: Longman).

Urwin, D. W. (1995) *The Community of Europe: A History of European Integration Since 1945*, 2nd edn (London: Longman).

Usher, J. A. (1998) *General Principles of EC Law* (London: Longman).

Vahl, R. (1997) *Leadership in Disguise: The Role of the European Commission in EC Decision-Making on Agriculture in the Uruguay Round* (Aldershot: Ashgate).

Van Schendelen, M. P. C. M. (1996) 'The Council Decides: Does the Council Decide?', *Journal of Common Market Studies*, vol. 34, no. 4, pp. 531–48.

Wallace, H. and W. Wallace (1996) *Policy-Making in the European Union* (Oxford: Oxford University Press).

Wallace, H. and A. R. Young (1997) *Participation and Policy-Making in the European Union* (Oxford: Clarendon Press).

Wallace, W. (1992) *The Dynamics of European Integration* (London: Pinter).

Warleigh, A. (1998) 'Better the Devil You Know? Synthetic and Confederal Understandings of European Integration', *West European Politics*, vol. 21, no. 3, pp. 1–18.

Weatherill, S. and P. Beaumont (1993) *EC Law: The Essential Guide to the Legal Workings of the European Community* (London: Penguin).

Webb, C. (1983) 'Theoretical Perspectives and Problems', in H. Wallace, W. Wallace and C. Webb (eds), *Policy Making in the European Community* (London: John Wiley), pp. 1–41.

Westlake, M. (1994) *A Modern Guide to the European Parliament* (London: Pinter).

Westlake, M. (1995) *The Council of the European Union* (London: Cartermill).

Westlake, M. (1997) 'Keynote Article: "Mad Cows and Englishmen". The Institutional Consequences of the BSE Crisis', in N. Nugent (ed.), *The European Union 1996: Annual Review of Activities* (Oxford: Blackwell).

Westlake, M. (1998) 'The European Parliament's Emerging Powers of Appointment', *Journal of Common Market Studies*, vol. 36, no. 3, pp. 431–44.

Westlake, M. (1999) *The European Union Beyond Amsterdam: New Concepts of European Integration* (London: Routledge).

Wincott, D. (1995) 'Institutional Interaction and European Integration: Towards an Everyday Critique of Liberal Intergovernmentalism', *Journal of Common Market Studies*, vol. 33, no. 4, pp. 597–609.

Wincott, D. (1999) 'The Court of Justice and the Legal System', in L. Cram, D. Dinan and N. Nugent (eds), *Developments in the European Union* (Basingstoke: Macmillan).

Wright, V. (1996) 'The National Co-ordination of European Policy-Making: Negotiating the Quagmire', in J. Richardson (ed.), *European Union: Power and Policy-Making* (London: Routledge), pp. 148–69.

Wyatt, D. and A. Dashwood (1993) *Wyatt and Dashwood's European Community Law* (London: Sweet & Maxwell).

Index